W9-BWM-868

Dictionary of Literary Biography® • Volume One Hundred Twenty-Two

Chicano Writers
Second Series

Dictionary of Literary Biography® • Volume One Hundred Twenty-Two

Chicano Writers
Second Series

Edited by
Francisco A. Lomelí
University of California, Santa Barbara

and

Carl R. Shirley
University of South Carolina

A Bruccoli Clark Layman Book
Gale Research Inc.
Detroit, London

Printed in the United States of America

Published simultaneously in the United Kingdom
by Gale Research International Limited
(An affiliated company of Gale Research Inc.)

The paper used in this publication meets the minimum requirements
of American National Standard for Information Sciences—Permanence
Paper for Printed Library Materials, ANSI Z39.48-1984. ∞™

Library of Congress Catalog Card Number 92-29057
ISBN 0-8103-7599-0

10 9 8 7 6 5 4 3 2

Contents

v

Contents

Plan of the Series

. . . Almost the most prodigious asset of a country, and perhaps its most precious possession, is its native literary product—when that product is fine and noble and enduring.

Mark Twain*

The advisory board, the editors, and the publisher of the *Dictionary of Literary Biography* are joined in endorsing Mark Twain's declaration. The literature of a nation provides an inexhaustible resource of permanent worth. We intend to make literature and its creators better understood and more accessible to students and the reading public, while satisfying the standards of teachers and scholars.

To meet these requirements, *literary biography* has been construed in terms of the author's achievement. The most important thing about a writer is his writing. Accordingly, the entries in *DLB* are career biographies, tracing the development of the author's canon and the evolution of his reputation.

The purpose of *DLB* is not only to provide reliable information in a convenient format but also to place the figures in the larger perspective of literary history and to offer appraisals of their accomplishments by qualified scholars.

The publication plan for *DLB* resulted from two years of preparation. The project was proposed to Bruccoli Clark by Frederick C. Ruffner, president of the Gale Research Company, in November 1975. After specimen entries were prepared and typeset, an advisory board was formed to refine the entry format and develop the series rationale. In meetings held during 1976, the publisher, series editors, and advisory board approved the scheme for a comprehensive biographical dictionary of persons who contributed to North American literature. Editorial work on the first volume began in January 1977, and it was published in 1978. In order to make *DLB* more than a reference tool and to compile volumes that individually have claim to status as literary history, it was decided to organize volumes by topic, period, or genre. Each of these freestanding volumes provides a biographical-bibliographical guide and overview for a particular area of literature. We are convinced that this organization—as opposed to a single alphabet method—constitutes a valuable innovation in the presentation of reference material. The volume plan necessarily requires many decisions for the placement and treatment of authors who might properly be included in two or three volumes. In some instances a major figure will be included in separate volumes, but with different entries emphasizing the aspect of his career appropriate to each volume. Ernest Hemingway, for example, is represented in *American Writers in Paris, 1920-1939* by an entry focusing on his expatriate apprenticeship; he is also in *American Novelists, 1910-1945* with an entry surveying his entire career. Each volume includes a cumulative index of the subject authors and articles. Comprehensive indexes to the entire series are planned.

With volume ten in 1982 it was decided to enlarge the scope of *DLB*. By the end of 1986 twenty-one volumes treating British literature had been published, and volumes for Commonwealth and Modern European literature were in progress. The series has been further augmented by the *DLB Yearbooks* (since 1981) which update published entries and add new entries to keep the *DLB* current with contemporary activity. There have also been *DLB Documentary Series* volumes which provide biographical and critical source materials for figures whose work is judged to have particular interest for students. One of these companion volumes is entirely devoted to Tennessee Williams.

We define literature as the *intellectual commerce of a nation:* not merely as belles lettres but as that ample and complex process by which ideas are generated, shaped, and transmitted. *DLB* entries are not limited to "creative writers" but extend to other figures who in their time and in their way influenced the mind of a people. Thus the series encompasses historians, journalists, publishers, and screenwriters. By this means

---

*From an unpublished section of Mark Twain's autobiography, copyright © by the Mark Twain Company

readers of *DLB* may be aided to perceive literature not as cult scripture in the keeping of intellectual high priests but firmly positioned at the center of a nation's life.

DLB includes the major writers appropriate to each volume and those standing in the ranks immediately behind them. Scholarly and critical counsel has been sought in deciding which minor figures to include and how full their entries should be. Wherever possible, useful references are made to figures who do not warrant separate entries.

Each *DLB* volume has a volume editor responsible for planning the volume, selecting the figures for inclusion, and assigning the entries. Volume editors are also responsible for preparing, where appropriate, appendices surveying the major periodicals and literary and intellectual movements for their volumes, as well as lists of further readings. Work on the series as a whole is coordinated at the Bruccoli Clark Layman editorial center in Columbia, South Carolina, where the editorial staff is responsible for accuracy of the published volumes.

One feature that distinguishes *DLB* is the illustration policy—its concern with the iconography of literature. Just as an author is influenced by his surroundings, so is the reader's understanding of the author enhanced by a knowledge of his environment. Therefore *DLB* volumes include not only drawings, paintings, and photographs of authors, often depicting them at various stages in their careers, but also illustrations of their families and places where they lived. Title pages are regularly reproduced in facsimile along with dust jackets for modern authors. The dust jackets are a special feature of *DLB* because they often document better than anything else the way in which an author's work was perceived in its own time. Specimens of the writers' manuscripts are included when feasible.

Samuel Johnson rightly decreed that "The chief glory of every people arises from its authors." The purpose of the *Dictionary of Literary Biography* is to compile literary history in the surest way available to us—by accurate and comprehensive treatment of the lives and work of those who contributed to it.

The *DLB* Advisory Board

Introduction

The antecedents of Chicano literature are as old as the Spanish presence in the New World, but the literature is a rather recent phenomenon in the so-called mainstream of American letters. Some Chicano families, or Mexican Americans as they are also called, have been in what is now the United States since the early seventeenth century, while others are newcomers. They all share, to a greater or lesser degree, language, culture, history, religion, traditions, and values that make them one people. Chicano literature is but one artistic manifestation of their increasingly significant place in modern North America.

A glance at a map of North America from around 1600 will reveal that Spain controlled the northern frontiers of what became Mexico, which today are the states of Texas, Arizona, New Mexico, California, Nevada, Utah, and Colorado. In addition to autochthonous peoples, the region was populated by Spaniards, Creoles (Spaniards born in the New World), and mestizos (a mixture of Spanish and Native American), all moving north from what is now Mexico. They established towns and built missions and roads; they brought with them the Spanish language, the Catholic church, Spanish laws, and new forms of agriculture, food, livestock, art, architecture, literature, and a literary tradition. As a result of the Anglo-Americans' westward expansion and Mexico's problem-plagued government and financial crisis, a conflict emerged when land interests, power bases, and worldviews clashed, resulting in the Mexican-American War of 1846-1848. Weakened by the strife and internal problems, Mexico reluctantly relinquished 50 percent of its territories after signing the Treaty of Guadalupe Hidalgo in 1848, thus setting the stage for a fundamental change in status for the people of Mexican descent in that area. After one year, all people who chose to remain in the region automatically became U.S. citizens. From that date to the present, Anglo-American culture, language, traditions, and values have been combined with or superimposed on the Hispanic ones to form Chicano culture.

Immigration, both legal and illegal, and the proximity to Mexico have continued to reinforce the Hispanic ways so that the majority of Chicanos have never been fully Americanized in quite the same way as most other ethnic groups. Rather, they are an adaptive and creative people who have assimilated elements from three cultures to form a separate, very distinct one. They are by no means a homogeneous group, but they do share a history, values, and traditions. Population estimates vary greatly, but most sources agree that there are at least 20 million Chicanos. While the majority live in the Southwest, there are large concentrations in other places, notably the midwestern states of Illinois, Indiana, Ohio, Minnesota, and Wisconsin. Chicanos presently live in every state in the Union. For a more extensive commentary on the history of Mexican American people, see "Chicano History," by Carl R. Shirley, *Dictionary of Literary Biography*, volume eighty-two: *Chicano Writers*, First Series.

There are several theories concerning the origin of the word *Chicano*, with the most prominent being that it is a derivative of *mexicano*, which is in turn derivative of *mexica* (pronounced "meschica"), which is the term Aztecs used to describe themselves. No matter what its origin, the term was in widespread use by the 1950s, supplanting the old designation of "Mexican" or the sociological sounding "Mexican-American." The older generation today sometimes resents the word *Chicano*, viewing it as pejorative, for its original application was to designate a recent arrival, but it has gained in use and popularity since the 1960s to the point that for many it symbolizes pride and cultural revival, especially among politically and socially active groups. Recent literary studies also use the term.

Many Chicanos are bilingual in standard Spanish and English (and the vernacular within each language), while some speak only English and others only Spanish. Most speak and understand a third variant, variously called "Caló," "Pocho," or "Pachuco." This is a mixture of English and Spanish vocabularies, grammars, and syntactical structures that is more than a hybrid in that it is greater than the sum of its parts. It is a new language that combines borrowings from each of its ancestors with additions of new words and structures. Contemporary Chicano literature is written in all three linguistic variants in varying combinations. While the blend may pose difficulties for the person who does not speak Spanish, it is a source of literary strength for a Chicano writer because it enables that writer to reflect three sometimes distinct realities: Anglo, Mexican, and Chicano. For a more extensive discussion of the topic, see "Chicano Language," by Erlinda Gonzales-Berry and Shaw N. Gynan, *Dictionary of Literary Biography*, volume eighty-two.

The Chicano literary heritage, like the cultural heritage, is tripartite: (1) The Indian past, embodied by the concept of *Aztlán*, after the name of the mythical home of the Aztecs (extant in the period prior to 1519, the date of the Hernán Cortés invasion into Mexico)—this term generally refers to the entire American Southwest (which before the Mexican-American War of 1848 was the northwestern borderlands of Mexico) but has also become a symbol for a homeland or a spiritual nation of Chicanos; (2) The Spanish and Mexican heritage, from 1519 to 1848, with reinforcement continuing to the present; (3) The Anglo overlay dating from the early and mid nineteenth century. The antecedents of Chicano literature can be said to extend as far back as 1542 with the Spanish explorer Alvar Núñez Cabeza de Vaca's *Relaciones*, and of course earlier if one takes into account Native American inspiration through legends, myths, and motifs. With the Spanish language brought by Spanish explorers, colonizers, and mestizos, a written literary tradition became implanted and began to develop in the region. Another example of early literature occurred in 1598 when Captain Farfán, a soldier among the troops of Spanish explorer Juan de Oñate, staged a play along the Rιio Grande near what is now El Paso, Texas. There is a rich history and tradition of folklore, poetry, prose, and theater from that time to the present. Most of this literature remained forgotten or ignored, accumulating dust. Much of it appeared in newspapers, from which we can potentially extract a large corpus of literary samples. However, other writings demonstrate a tradition that never died. See, for example, Miguel de Quintana (in this volume) or Eusebio Chacón in *DLB* volume eighty-two.

Following World War II, Chicano literature began to draw attention from outside its own circle, particularly during the so-called renaissance starting in 1965. Historically the themes and subjects are common to all literatures. In contemporary writing, however, there are some special ones that appear frequently in all genres. Among them are social protest and exploitation; the migratory experience; self-exploration or self-definition, which includes the exploration of myths and legends; and life in the barrio, the Chicano district of a city or town. There is also *La Raza* (The People), which, like Aztlán, has a spiritual connotation that joins all peoples of Spanish-speaking America. Beginning in the mid 1960s, much Chicano literature became a reflection of a social and political movement, with attitudes ranging from the advocation of complete separation from Anglo society to a stance calling for a Mexican-American cultural identification within the framework of the larger society. After 1975 the focus centered on technique and style while exploring personal issues more than social ones. The 1980s offered a great diversification of theme and content and more exploration of issues pertinent to families and women.

The history of prose written by Chicanos can be traced to the chronicles of the earliest explorers. These, combined with letters from government officials and clergy, provide not only valuable historical information but also entertaining reading. In the first half of the nineteenth century, there was a flourishing of histories, diaries, and memoirs; short narrative pieces were published in many newspapers, and novels began to appear toward the end of the century. Contemporary prose can be dated from 1947 with the short stories of Mario Suárez in the *Arizona Quarterly*. His characters live in Tucson in a barrio called "El Hoyo" (The Hole) and represent a variety of Mexican-American traits, customs, and values. Suárez's work is wryly humorous, and his figures are rather cynical, in marked contrast to most of the romanticized characters in Chicano prose prior to World War II. Although he is frequently dismissed as merely another local colorist, Suárez has been called the first truly Chicano writer because he used the term *Chicano* with the contemporary connotations and was not uncomfortable with the word as many were in his day. Moreover, his characters are not treated as comical, colorful, or eccentric members of a cultural minority, performing for the amusement of Anglos (see, for example, John Steinbeck's *Tortilla Flat*, 1935). They are proud, successful people, capable of coping and existing comfortably in either the majority culture or in their own world. They possess psychological depth and dimension that Mexican characters in American periodicals before 1947 generally lacked.

Contemporary Chicano drama also has an interesting history. There is ample evidence of a flourishing theater in the Southwest, consisting principally of religious or folk presentations, dating back to colonial times, oftentimes as a form of vaudeville. Most critics, however, give the year 1965 as the beginning of Chicano theater, marking also the explosion of a literary renaissance. This is the year of the founding of El Teatro Campesino, generally translated as "The Farmworkers' Theater." Luis Valdez, a drama student and son of migrant laborers, approached César Chávez, leader of the fledgling United Farm Workers' Union, and suggested the use of theater as a means of entertaining and educating strikers during the Delano grape strikes in California's San Joaquin Valley. Drawing on his experience with the San Francisco Mime Troupe, his knowledge of the Italian commedia dell'arte form and slapstick style, and the agitprop theater of Germany's Bertolt Brecht, Valdez developed the *acto*. As he defined it, the *acto* is short—ten to fifteen minutes—and improvised, with an intention of inspiring the viewers to social action or educating them about social problems. It is bilingual and always treats subjects and themes of the farmworkers and their world from their perspective. Frequently the early *actos* were collective efforts, with nightly revisions, thus reflecting their evolutionary and revolutionary nature. The scenery, costumes, and props were kept to a minimum, with the emphasis more on the message and immediate effect and less on theatrical trappings.

As El Teatro Campesino grew and moved to Del Rey and later San Juan Bautista, California, it also evolved and developed other forms, broadening its themes to include all aspects of contemporary Chicano existence, including mythic concerns. El Centro Campesino Cultural, or the Workers' Cultural Center, emerged in 1967 as an outgrowth of the theater. This complex, located in San Juan Bautista, became a significant center for dissemination not only of theater but also of music, art, and other artistic manifestations of Chicano culture.

While El Teatro Campesino was and still is the largest and best-known Chicano theater group, it by no means stands alone. There were many small groups in communities throughout the Southwest and Midwest in the 1960s, so many that El Teatro Campesino decided to hold a national theater festival in 1970. This led, in 1971, to the founding of TENAZ, an acronym for El Teatro Nacional de Aztlán, or the National Theatre of Aztlán. TENAZ was responsible for coordination and communication of theater activities; it also established a series of summer workshops for members and founded a journal (*TENAZ*). There have been summer festivals held most years since, and membership has grown to over fifty groups. Quite a few prominent Chicano playwrights have emerged from these groups.

A musical play, *Zoot Suit* (1978), by Luis Valdez, after a successful California run, was the first play by a Chicano to be performed on Broadway (Winter Garden Theatre, March 1979). Based on the incidents surrounding the Los Angeles Sleepy Lagoon Murder of 1942, it is the story of the pachucos, or zoot-suiters, who were tried and convicted of the crime and later exonerated. *Zoot Suit* is significant because it is a social and political play, founded in the *acto* form, which has been performed outside Chicano or academic circles, before all of America. It was also made into a commercial film, directed by Valdez in 1981.

Contemporary Chicano poetry also gained impetus in the 1960s. However, this poetry has deep roots. There is a large and significant body of verse dating from the Spanish colonial and Mexican periods prior to 1848. Virtually all these poems are in the Spanish language, drawing on the Spanish poetic traditions and forms. During the last half of the nineteenth century, works written in English began to appear, and after 1900 many Chicano poets wrote either completely or predominantly in English. The majority of Chicano verse prior to the 1960s appeared in newspapers or magazines and reflected themes following either the American or Spanish tradition, depending on the language in which it was written.

With the beginning of the Chicano social and political movement around 1960, many groups began to publish newspapers, in both languages, as a means of reporting their activities. Along with news and information, these periodicals included literature, chiefly poetry. So much poetry was written during the decade that it has been called the "Chicano Renaissance." It was a period marked not only by the quantity of material printed but also by a noticeable change in thematic concerns. In an effort to assert a new cultural and political identity, the renaissance Chicano poet looked not to Anglo America or European Spain; instead he turned to Aztec, pre-Columbian Mexico (Aztlán) or identified with modern Mexico, usually from the period following the revolution of 1910. Common subjects were at first political but also included cultural identity, Chicano life (either migratory or in the barrio), and *carnalismo*, or brotherhood.

A significant writer of this period was Rodolfo "Corky" Gonzales, the organizer of the Crusade for Justice. His major work is *Yo Soy Joaquín* (I Am Joaquín, 1967), an epic poem presenting a Chicano Everyman who resists assimilation and subjugation. Gonzales, an ex-boxer, writes in the introduction that his poem "was a journey back through history, a painful self-evaluation, a wandering search for my peoples and, most of all, for my own identity. The totality of all social inequities and injustice had to come to the surface. All the while, the truth about our own flaws—the villains and the heroes had to ride together—in order to draw an honest, clear conclusion of who we were, who we are, and where we are going." He concludes that there is "no inspiration without identifiable images, there is no conscience without the sharp knife of truthful exposure, and ultimately, there are no revolutions without poets." Some critics claim that poetry continues to be the most popular mode of artistic expression by the Chicanos, perhaps because of the relative ease with which a poem can be disseminated. Prose, however, has indulged more in experimental techniques and expanding themes in order to cover the full range of the Chicano experience.

Since the 1960s Chicanos have been reading their own literature or attending their own theater more than ever before. The great need for publishing outlets for writers has begun to be filled; among the outstanding firms are Arte Público in Houston, Tonatiuh-Quinto Sol in Berkeley, California, and Bilingual Press/Editorial Bilingüe in Tempe, Arizona. Major mainstream houses are beginning to publish works by Chicanos at an increasing rate. Greater academic recognition has led many colleges and universities to establish undergraduate majors as well as graduate programs in Chicano studies, all of which include literature courses. These developments have drawn much deserved attention from critics, not only in established literary journals but also in new ones (such as *MELUS* and *Explorations in Sights and Sounds*) whose focus is completely or partially on Chicano literature. In addition, full-length critical studies are being published by major university presses. Previously most aspects of Chicano culture were foreign or unknown to the majority of non-Chicanos. Like other ethnic American literatures, that of the Chicanos was relegated to second-class status. As the limits of American literature expand and as the vitality and excitement of Chicano literature are increasingly felt, it is taking its rightful place in the field of American letters.

Chicano literature, the aesthetic principles that define it, and the body of criticism that supports it resist comparison to mainstream American literature; indeed, Chicano writing is an assertive declaration of cultural identity that frequently assumes validity by its independence from Anglo traditions and standards. Throughout the 150-year history of Chicano literature, its writers have been motivated in large degree by their response to social oppression and by their attempts to define and embrace their cultural heritage. The result is a literature that is prepared expressly for the people about whom it is written and that is, as a result, often elusive to other readers.

The *DLB* volumes on Chicano writers are as valuable as social history as they are as literary history. The process by which literature is used by a people to declare their cultural identity is a complex one, involving not only writers and their works but also readers, the means by which works are made available to them, the critical responses of ethnic scholars, and the reactions of the literary establishment. Chicano writers have been criticized for their failure to adapt to mainstream standards. They answer by questioning the validity of a canon of national literature that excludes the Mexican experience in the United States and by rejecting the authority of an aesthetic standard that denies them their distinct voice. The debate about the validity of Chicano writing (as well as the criticism this writing stimulates) has frequently focused only on the social and political issues concerning the status of the Chicano people in American society and not on the literature itself. As the literature develops and changes, however, critics are shifting their viewpoints increasingly toward its literary merit. Precedent teaches that emerging ethnic literatures bear close scrutiny: they provide the energy and creative force that mold the future, offering vistas of the American social experience never before seen.

—Francisco A. Lomelí and Carl R. Shirley

Acknowledgments

This book was produced by Bruccoli Clark Layman, Inc. Karen L. Rood is senior editor for the *Dictionary of Literary Biography* series. Jack Turner and Henry Cuningham were the in-house editors.

Production coordinator is James W. Hipp. Projects manager is Charles D. Brower. Photography editors are Edward Scott and Timothy C. Lundy. Layout and graphics supervisor is Penney L. Haughton. Copyediting supervisor is Bill Adams. Typesetting supervisor is Kathleen M. Flanagan. Systems manager is George F. Dodge. The production staff includes Rowena Betts, Steve Borsanyi, Teresa Chaney, Patricia Coate, Rebecca Crawford, Henry Cuningham, Margaret McGinty Cureton, Mary Scott Dye, Denise Edwards, Sarah A. Estes, Robert Fowler, Mary Lee Goodwin, Bonita Graham, Avril E. Gregory, Ellen McCracken, Kathy Lawler Merlette, John Myrick, Pamela D. Norton, Thomas J. Pickett, Maxine K. Smalls, Deborah P. Stokes, and Jennifer C. J. Turley.

Walter W. Ross and Samuel Bruce did library research. They were assisted by the following librarians at the Thomas Cooper Library of the University of South Carolina: Jens Holley and the interlibrary-loan staff; reference librarians Gwen Baxter, Daniel Boice, Faye Chadwell, Cathy Eckman, Rhonda Felder, Gary Geer, Jackie Kinder, Laurie Preston, Jean Rhyne, Carol Tobin, Virginia Weathers, and Connie Widney; circulation-department head Thomas Marcil; and acquisitions-searching supervisor David Haggard.

Dictionary of Literary Biography® • Volume One Hundred Twenty-Two

Chicano Writers
Second Series

Dictionary of Literary Biography

Francisco X. Alarcón

(21 February 1954 -   )

Salvador Rodríguez del Pino
University of Colorado

BOOKS: *Tattoos* (Oakland: Nomad, 1985);
Ya vas, Carnal, by Alarcón, Rodrigo Reyes, and
Juan Pablo Gutiérrez (San Francisco: Huma-
nizarte, 1985);
Quake Poems (Santa Cruz: We Press, 1989);
Body in Flames / Cuerpo en llamas (San Francisco:
Chronicle, 1990);
De amor oscuro (Santa Cruz: Moving Parts, 1991);
Snake Poems (San Francisco: Chronicle Books,
1992).

OTHER: Otto René Castillo, *Tomorrow Trium-
phant*, bilingual edition, introduction by
Alarcón (San Francisco: Night Horn, 1984),
pp. vii-viii;
"Las repatriaciones de noviembre," in *Palabra
Nueva: Cuentos Chicanos*, edited by Ricardo
Aguilar, Armando Armengol, and Sergio
Elizondo (El Paso: Texas Western Press,
1984), pp. 14-24;
"Acoma: Léxico para desenterrar," in *Palabra
Nueva: Poesía Chicana*, edited by Aguilar,
Armengol, and Elizondo (El Paso: Univer-
sity of Texas Press, 1985), pp. 32-36;
"Oración / Prayer," "Raices / Roots," "Palabras
heridas / Wounded Words," and "Fugitive,"
in *Practicing Angels: Contemporary Anthology of
San Francisco Bay Area Poetry*, edited by Mi-
chael Mayo (San Francisco: Seismograph,
1986), pp. 1-4;
"A Small but Fateful Victory" and "Carta a
América / Letter to America," in *Lighthouse
Point: An Anthology of Santa Cruz Writers*,
edited by Patrice Vecchione and Steve

Wiesinger (Santa Cruz: M. Press Soquel,
1987), pp. 1-4.

SELECTED PERIODICAL PUBLICATION—
UNCOLLECTED: "Mi cama" and "El otro día
me encontré a García Lorca," *Poetry Flash:
The Bay Area's Poetry Review and Literary Calendar*, 174 (September 1987): 13.

Francisco X. Alarcón is one of the few
openly gay Chicano poets, yet his poetry is not centered only on his gay experience but takes in similarly important vital issues such as his ethnicity
and his views on femininity and equal rights. He
understands that his sexual preference is marginal both in the Anglo and Chicano worlds:

> I am
> a nomad
> in a country
> of settlers
> a drop
> of oil
> in a glass
> of water[.]

Francisco Xavier Alarcón was born in Wil-
mington, California, on 21 February, 1954, but
during his childhood he moved back and forth
to Mexico, getting his education in both countries
and in both languages. This bicultural education
is inherent in his work and ideology. Nevertheless, one of his earliest and most painful experiences was the double discrimination he suffered
as a child, being a "Pocho" (an Americanized Mexican) and a Chicano. Despite his bicultural education, Alarcón draws more on Mexican traditions.

Francisco X. Alarcón (photograph by Annie Valva)

Perhaps this emphasis is because of his paternal grandfather, a full-blooded Tarascan Indian from Michoacán, who first attracted Alarcón's childhood imagination with stories from the ancient and mythical world of Mexicans. From this grandfather (after whom he was named) he heard stories about the Mexican revolution, in which his grandfather fought with Pancho Villa. "Brought up in Mexico and nourished with these incredible stories, I wanted to write them down, but I didn't know how," he has said. "I decided to return to the United States and become a writer." He arrived in Los Angeles with five dollars in his pocket and took a series of jobs from dishwashing to grape picking: "This experience in my life was interesting for it made me realize that I could survive. It also made me respect the simple lives of millions of people that provide the labor in this country." Alarcón took his return to the United States as a personal quest, a need to find himself and his own voice.

Alarcón first enrolled at Cambria Adult School in Los Angeles to get his American high-school diploma, after which he spent a year at East Los Angeles College, then attended California State University, Long Beach, where he obtained his B.A. in Spanish and history in 1977. Losing no time, he obtained a graduate fellow-

ship and enrolled at Stanford University for an M.A. in contemporary Latin-American literature. While in college he began writing poetry, joined literary circles in the Bay Area, and did poetry readings anywhere he was invited. In 1981 Alarcón joined the coordinating staff of *El Tecolote*, a Bay Area monthly bilingual newspaper where he found a forum and an outlet for his writing. His poetry at that time reflected his mestizo roots and Latin-American solidarity. The Barrio Latino area in the Mission District of San Francisco was home to Chicano and Central American people with strong feelings of nationalism for their ancestors' countries. Alarcón's solidarity poems were recognized in 1981, when he won the "Rubén Darío" Latin-American Poetry Prize from Casa Nicaragua in San Francisco. This led to more regional recognition around the Bay Area and more poetry readings, which helped him to get a Fulbright Fellowship in Mexico City. He thus met the best-known current Mexican poets and took literary trips to Havana, where he was introduced not only to the Cuban mainstream literati but also to underground gay and intellectual life. In Mexico he met Elías Nandino, one of "Los Contemporaneos" (The Contemporaries), the literary and intellectual avant-garde group of the late 1920s, which also included

Octavio Paz, Carlos Pellicer, Celestino Gorostiza, and Salvador Novo. In his eighties Nandino was at last being recognized by the Mexican government, which awarded him the National Prize in Literature for his homoerotic book of poems *Erotismo al Rojo Blanco* (Red-Hot Eroticism, 1983). Alarcón was totally taken by Nandino's stand and ideology concerning his sexual preference, and Alarcón's discussions and conversations with Nandino had a profound influence on the former's subsequent poetry and ideological stance: he would be openly gay in his work and his life.

While in Mexico, Alarcón also became involved in theater and in promoting Chicano literature and experience. He was given an opportunity to get involved as a visiting researcher in El Colegio de Mexico, the Mexican "think tank" where he met more of the intellectual elite. He was invited to read his poetry in Mexico City and Guadalajara, followed by newspaper interviews and television guest appearances on the daily literary program *Noche a Noche* (Night to Night) on Channel 8 in Mexico City. Alarcón took advantage of the bustling and prestigious intellectual scene, coming back to California almost a celebrity. His Mexican and Cuban contacts enabled him to establish dialogues and artistic interchanges between Bay Area poets and writers and their Latin-American counterparts. His activities within literary circles and artistic centers in the Bay Area were influential in his being chosen a distinguished alumnus in the School of Humanities for 1984 by his alma mater, California State University, Long Beach.

By this time Alarcón was also writing in different genres, mainly essays and short stories. His short story "Las repatriaciones de noviembre" (The Repatriations of November) won second prize in the *Palabra Nueva* University of Texas, El Paso, literary contest in 1983, and he won a first prize in poetry from the Tenth Chicano Literary Contest at the Department of Spanish and Portuguese at the University of California, Irvine. These prizes established Alarcón as one of the most exciting young Chicano writers of the decade, known not only for his open and honest poetry but also for his energetic and "showmanlike" poetry readings. He was experimenting with his "tattoos," a sort of haiku. They won him another prize from the *Palabra Nueva* editors, who published his award-winning poems under the rubric "Acoma: Léxico para desenterrar" (Acoma: Words to Uncover) in 1985.

But just when he felt that his career and poetry were at their height, an incident occurred in San Francisco that was to bring a traumatic twist to his life. In 1984 a young boy was found sexually molested and murdered in Golden Gate Park.

According to Alarcón, because his car fit the description of a vehicle that had been near the scene of the crime, the San Francisco police began a media campaign against him, indicting him through newspaper and television news reports, although they had no evidence against him and had not even interrogated him. He had been at a poetry reading at the alleged time of the murder and had an entire audience as witnesses. He turned himself in to the police, secure in his alibi and witnesses, and was released on bond. But the persecution continued as the police were certain of his guilt. His whole barrio rallied behind him, holding fund-raisers and solidarity demonstrations; but his gayness and ethnicity were detriments. Alarcón says that he lived a Kafkaesque existence during this time and saw himself as both the protagonist and victim in a bizarre comedy of errors. He was experiencing discrimination that would leave a profound scar on his life. Eventually the real killer was caught in Oregon and confessed to the crime. In spite of this, Alarcón's life had been disrupted, and the police did not apologize or make reparations for their searches of his property and defamations of his character. Nevertheless, he could not stay in the past or become prisoner to an unjust incident. Thus Alarcón plunged into his work with more energy than ever, publishing his first volume, *Tattoos*, in 1985. In one of the poems, he writes:

> poems
> fillup
> pages
> tattoos
> puncture
> flesh[.]

With this pretext in mind, Alarcón created his tattoos to puncture complacencies and fossilized poetic concepts, and, most of all, to get into the reader's sensitivities. Having been burned by words in newspaper headlines and convicted by the flagrant lies implicit in those words, Alarcón sought to search for a type of language that could burn an image in the mind:

> words
> hurt me
> like open wounds

> no matter how much
> I clean & treat them
> never do they heal!

"Basically what I'm doing," he says, "is trying to retrieve the language that is being suppressed." And in so doing, Alarcón politizices his convictions, his roots, and his intimacy, for if he is going to be true to his convictions, he must involve and commit himself in action and creation. He does not live the recluse life of uncommitted poets but involves himself in the community, voicing their concerns and protests and casting his poetry in their voice: "I think maybe I'm sort of in the Latin tradition of the poet. There's no difference between the political and the personal, the social and the intimate.... It's very common in Latin America to have poets as the collective voice and the person who takes on a certain responsibility in the community." This involvement led him to become director of the Centro Chicano de Escritores (Chicano Writers' Center) and the president of the Board of Directors of the Mission District Cultural Center. Alarcón also teaches Chicano literature and Spanish at the University of California, Santa Cruz. Despite these demanding activities, his creativity is not hampered; he is an avid writer and always ready with fresh poems for any reading.

In *Tattoos* he does not yet involve himself with his sexuality, but rather with his community, his roots, and his political convictions. His ordeal with the police in San Francisco was still fresh in his mind, and he probably needed some distance to digest, explain, and accept the episode, for it had a profound impact on his vision of the world:

> the artist
> bled to death
> he had run out
> of real red
> for his canvas[.]

Later in 1985 Alarcón published another collection of poems, with Rodrigo Reyes and Juan Pablo Gutiérrez, titled *Ya vas, Carnal* (Right on, Brother), which is where he first alludes in poetry to his sexuality. He compares his life to a fugitive who does not know what he is running from: "Hiding behind / so many illusions / during / so many years / now / I don't / even recognize / the face of / my soul / nor remember / what brought me / to this fugitive's life...." His ability to cope

with his sexual reality is hampered by his ignorance of the immensity of his crime:

> my crime
> must have
> been
> as huge as
> the darkness
> found in
> my punishment[.]

Yet, he was able to cope with a fugitive life by learning to fake his emotions until something gave him away:

> I've learned
> to fake
> almost everything
> but
> still
> when next to you
> I'm given away
> by the empty
> pounding
> of my heart[.]

Alarcón contributed fifteen poems to the book and did not translate them all as he did in his previous collection, perhaps because *Ya vas, Carnal* was intended more for the bilingual community than for a wider audience. Some poems are written in Spanish, others in English, but "Fugitive," the main poem, was translated along with the ones that allude to his sexuality. His ability to write in both languages is one of his strongest assets, for his poetry is just as powerful and engaging in English as it is in Spanish. He has a mastery of both languages, and his metaphors do not diminish in either one. The Chicano poet, according to Alarcón, is one who is not only loyal to two languages and cultures but also to his personal and social convictions. By combining both premises, Alarcón creates a type of expression that is specific and particular to him.

The 1989 earthquake that hit the hardest in the Santa Cruz area in California was the motivation and impulse for his *Quake Poems* (1989), published only weeks after the disaster. He writes from the viewpoints of the victims, the homeless ones, the greedy opportunists, and the heros as he tries to encompass the tragedy of the people and their suffering:

> I was the looter
> and the fireman
> I was the preacher

and the hooker
the politician
the grabber of
headlines and
just another loner
I volunteered myself
I overcharged for water
and ice what the hell
I was rude I was generous[.]

Nandino's influence is evident in *Body in Flames / Cuerpo en llamas* (1990). Alarcón not only deals with his own sexuality and reality but also makes an inventory of his life. *Body in Flames / Cuerpo en llamas* takes its title from José Orozco's painting in the cupola of the Hospicio Cabañas in Guadalajara. This painting is the centerpiece of the book cover, and it is later complemented by Alarcón's poem "Body in Flames." The book is divided into five parts: (1) his childhood and family life; (2) his youth and confrontation with life and sexuality; (3) acceptance of his gayness; (4) his own angst and epitaph; and (5) his proclamation. The book seems to be a biography of his emotional life; feelings are central instead of actions and deeds. He leads readers through a life of constant confrontations, surrenders, and acceptances but not in a passive and meaningless way. It is a tour de force of survival, triumph, joy, and sorrow.

Alarcón was worried about the reception of the 1990 book, for it was the most intimate of all. In an interview with Gloria Wescott, Alarcón explained, "Western tradition divides man into body and soul. This division alienates our mind from our body. That is the reason we have to recuperate our entire being: to recuperate our body through poetry. . . . This collection tries to do that: . . . it celebrates my vision of the man who has to sacrifice his own body to become the light of humanity." Alarcón maintains that the body, long held as evil and corrupt in Western morality, is the ultimate mechanism for the spirit to manifest itself. It is the vehicle through which one's innermost feelings touch someone else. Alarcón writes in his title poem,

I want to abandon

words

go and awaken
the senses

I want
no memory

rather to embrace
every instant
to a frenzy

I want to think
with my feet

I want to cry
with my shoulders

I want to set
my body on fire[.]

Having syncretized opposing elements, Alarcón abandons the old myths, and he searches for a new god, since the old one betrays his new vision: "I want a god / as my accomplice / who spends nights / in houses / of ill repute / and gets up late / on Saturdays . . . a god / who whistles / through the streets / and trembles / before the lips / of his lover . . . I want a / more godlike / god."

Alarcón ends with a belated "Letter to America," reminding her who he and his people are and have been, and pleading for understanding:

America
understand
once and for all
we are
the insides
of your body[.]

Alarcón's poetry is neither conventional nor traditional, either in the English or Spanish tradition of versification and rhyming; rather, he experiments widely in the short form that gives him flexibility, expediency, and lyricism while denuding the structure of superfluous words. His intent is to fire his verses like arrows or darts into the reader's prejudices and sensibilities in order to shatter and dislocate conventions and complacencies. His poetry has been described as vibrant, and reviewer Nancy Scott said it "all but sizzles with the joy of living" (*San Francisco Examiner-Chronicle*, Spring 1990). Yet Alarcón tells of the dark side of living as a marginal person, a misfit who must live in fear and anger: "I've had / to bear / the days / anonymously / like a shadow / slip / through the city / without raising suspicions."

Interview:
Gloria Wescott, *Tiempo Latino*, 5 July 1989.

Gloria Anzaldúa

(26 September 1942 -   )

Héctor A. Torres
University of New Mexico

BOOK: *Borderlands / La Frontera: The New Mestiza* (San Francisco: Spinsters/Aunt Lute, 1987).

OTHER: *This Bridge Called My Back: Writings by Radical Women of Color*, edited by Anzaldúa and Cherríe Moraga (Watertown, Mass.: Persephone, 1981); translated by Moraga, Ana Castillo, and Norma Alarcón as *Esta puentí, mi espalda* (San Francisco: ISM, 1988);
Making Face, Making Soul / Haciendo Caras: Creative and Critical Perspectives by Women of Color, edited, with an essay, by Anzaldúa (San Francisco: Aunt Lute Foundation, 1990);
"El Paisano Is a Bird of Good Omen," in *Cuentos: Stories by Latinas*, edited by Moraga, Alma Gómez, and Mariana Romo-Carmona (New York: Kitchen Table/Women of Color, 1983).

Gloria Anzaldúa has come a long way from growing up in the town of Hargill, Texas, to her current status as university teacher, lecturer in Third World feminism, and accomplished author in the fields of Chicano and women's studies. Critics of Anzaldúa's work recognize the daring and innovative aspect of her mode of writing and they describe her as a writer who has the rare ability to write in a mixture of discursive styles and aims. In her major work to date—*Borderlands / La Frontera: The New Mestiza* (1987)—Anzaldúa writes with the clear, crisp prose of historiography as well as with the rhythms and images of poetry. The distinctive trait of the book is the decorum with which it stands in opposition to the traditional prohibition of mixing genres. In *Borderlands* Anzaldúa demonstrates the broad range of her talents as a poet and a philosopher. Through all her written work, Anzaldúa constantly articulates a deep commitment to the political issues that affect the lives of all Third World women of color.

Born a seventh-generation American on 26 September 1942 on the ranch settlement called

Gloria Anzaldúa

Jesus Maria of the Valley of South Texas, Gloria Anzaldúa is the daughter of Urbano and Amalia García Anzaldúa. Settlements such as Jesus Maria were plots of land where two, three, or four families would live together. Gloria's mother and father met because they lived on adjoining ranches, and they courted while quite young. They never made it to high school. Gloria was born when her mother was only sixteen. Until the age of eleven Gloria lived in a ranching environment, but then her family moved to Hargill, Texas, which she describes as one of those towns with "one signal light and 13 bars and 13 churches and maybe two mini-marts." Her father died when she was fifteen, and Anzaldúa talks about her family having to support itself from that time forward and having "to go back into the fields and work." That epoch of her life, says Anzaldúa, has instilled in her a deep "love and respect for campesinos just because it's really a hard life." As part of that experience, Anzaldúa also learned the hardships of being a migrant laborer as she and her family traveled from the South Valley of Texas to the fields of Arkansas. Exercising foresight, Anzaldúa's father had realized that if he attached his family to the migrant routes, his children would end up missing too much school and thus the Anzaldúa family only did this for a year. From then on the Anzaldúa family remained in the valley to work its fields, Gloria herself doing so until the time she earned her B.A. from Pan American University in 1969. Later on, after she received her M.A. in English and education from the University of Texas at Austin in 1972, she was selected by the state of Texas to work as a summer high-school teacher for the children of migrant families making the trek to the fields of Indiana. Hired by the state of Indiana because of the high quality of her work, she stayed on in that capacity for a year and a half.

For Anzaldúa, growing up in the South Valley of Texas meant, early on, having to rebel against the family traditions of her home life and of her Chicano culture. Anzaldúa talks with considerable candor about her early desire to step out of the oppressive confines of her home life and Chicano culture, saying, "I think Chicano families can be really hard on women and maybe they are hard on men, too. Very early on you start being taught how to be a man and being taught how to be a little woman and the divisions are pretty rigid." Of her relationship to her parents she says: "My father . . . and my mother had a very strong personality and I was very rebellious so they tried to mold me, especially my mother, into what a good Chicanita should be—which was that good Chicanitas don't go to school, they drop out in the 6th, 7th, and 8th grade . . . [and] cook, clean, and sew." Anzaldúa's parents knew about the value of education for their children—her father's decision to keep the family stationary was evidence of this—but her mother did not apply the idea to the girls of the family. Despite this disparity, the Anzaldúa girls both made it through high school, and her two brothers did not: "one almost graduated" she

says, "the other one dropped out as a sophomore and got drafted to go to Viet Nam." Only Gloria went on to pursue a higher education, recalling, "And then I went to college and I was the only woman, not just the only woman, but the only person from the area who ever went to college."

In the struggle to understand that her desire to read, study, and draw was not being lazy, as her mother thought and claimed, Anzaldúa credits reading as the chief activity that, as she describes it, gave her "an entry into a different way of being." From her early experiences with reading, Anzaldúa began to refine her instincts for personal freedom, to explore what was possible beyond the local Chicano culture of the South Valley. Anzaldúa's escape from the oppression of home and culture was not won without a toll; in many ways it was won at the expense of an oftentimes painful relationship with her mother and her sister. She recalls how in her mother's estimation, "it was all laziness—if you were reading in bed instead of washing the dishes or scrubbing the walls, it was not a useful activity."

In more recent times, as Anzaldúa's work was published more, she and her mother have had deep clashes over her Chicana-feminist-lesbian politics. Anzaldúa tells the story of how her mother and sister reacted to the publication of *This Bridge Called My Back* (1981) and to her essay "La Prieta" (The Dark One), an autobiographical piece in the book that speaks openly of matters concerning her lesbian sexuality, her near-encounters with death, and her vision of a political coalition of "Third World women, lesbians, feminists, and feminist-oriented men of all colors. . . ." "My mother," she recounts, "told me that if I told the people in my little town that I was a lesbian, she would take a gun and shoot herself. And she said that she felt very much ashamed, that, when she walked in the streets, she couldn't even raise her head because of this thing that I was, which was a filthy thing, and that she didn't want me to bring any gay friends to my house." Anzaldúa's response to her mother's reaction was just as extreme, and she vowed never to go home until she could bring whomever she wanted. "So she [Anzaldúa's mother] held out for three years," Anzaldúa says, and then adds, "I didn't go home for three years." Anzaldúa summarizes that episode with her mother by saying that when her mother relented, she "was realizing that I had not won, that both of us had lost."

The conditions that conspired to bring Anzaldúa to this realization were already at work in the essay "La Prieta," being expressed in these words: "But above all, I am terrified of making my mother the villain in my life rather than showing how she has been a victim. Will I be betraying her in this essay for her early disloyalty to me?" It seems that the three years of keeping each other at bay (they still talked occasionally on the telephone) served as a time for Anzaldúa to reflect more deeply on just how her mother had been a victim. She talks about her mother being a nurse's aide "who earned minimum wage, who did . . . backbreaking work for nothing . . . . And the only thing she had to be proud of was the fact that she knew how to give shots and take blood pressure. . . . And so that was her pride, and the fact that I had gone to college, even though she never wanted me to go to college." Anzaldúa's conclusion about her mother through that reflection shows her considerable ability to keep opposing forces in her life in dynamic tension.

From her sister, too, Anzaldúa's *This Bridge Called My Back* did not receive a warm welcome, although with her the iciness was not directly related to Anzaldúa's lesbianism. "What my sister was really upset about," explains Anzaldúa, "was the fact that I could talk about them [the family]. My sister is the kind of person who will not take a photograph." To her sister, by making such disclosures about herself and the Anzaldúa family, Gloria Anzaldúa committed a breach of family privacy.

Going against the oppressive aspects of her Chicano culture and home life has brought Anzaldúa her share of painful moments, but it also taught her to steel herself against the equally oppressive structures of white, Anglo-American society, especially in the domain of education. Throughout the pursuit of her education, the desire to read and learn beyond the traditional prescriptions of Anglo-American literature has often put her in tension with academic advisers unwilling to encourage her broad-based academic interests. At the University of Texas, Anzaldúa encountered considerable resistance to her diverse academic interests. After earning her M.A., Anzaldúa entered the comparative-literature department with the hopes of pursuing her interests in feminist studies, Chicano studies, and Spanish literature. From 1974 through 1977 Anzaldúa worked under the guidelines of this program but was not advanced to candidacy because she

wanted to write a dissertation that would focus on some topic in Chicano or feminist studies. Anzaldúa experienced a deep disappointment with the comparative literature program at the University of Texas. Her last year there (1976-1977) she spent as a lecturer at the Mexican American Studies Center, teaching in areas that, among others, have become her specialties: *la mujer Chicana* (the Chicana woman), Chicano culture, and Chicano literature.

Her long trek to educate herself—to fashion her own artistic and ideological face—brought her to the Ph.D. dissertation program at the University of California, Santa Cruz, where she focused on feminist theory and cultural studies. From 1979 to 1980 she was a lecturer at San Francisco State University, teaching feminist journal writing and Third World women's literature in the Women's Studies Program. From 1982 through 1986 she was an instructor in creative writing at Oakes College at the University of California, Santa Cruz. Intermittently from 1984 to 1986 she was a lecturer in the Adult Degree Program of Vermont College, Norwich University, where she taught creative writing, literature, and feminist studies. Anzaldúa says that it was in Vermont that the idea of *Borderlands* began to take hold. *Borderlands* first grew out of the sense of alienation she experienced while living in Vermont: "I started realizing how much of a foreigner I was there and how, when I walked in the street, people would sort of look at me and then sort of not look at me. And when I went into a store immediately everybody would take notice because there were so few people of color."

Anzaldúa returned to the University of California, Santa Cruz, in the spring quarter of 1988 as Distinguished Visiting Professor in Women's Studies. She taught a course in literature by women of color as well as a creative-writing seminar. The luster of that appointment soon began to wear off as she had to deal with the History of Consciousness Program to which she had applied for admission. Her admission was turned down because, as she puts it, "they felt I was too established. . . . I didn't know enough theory and was too far behind and wouldn't be able to catch up. The final blow was the fact that I was a creative writer and they already had too many creative writers."

In her teaching, as well, Anzaldúa has encountered resistance from students to her feminist pedagogical philosophy. In an interview with Elizabeth Baldwin for the May 1988 issue of *Ma-*

trix, a Santa Cruz County women's magazine, she spoke forthrightly about her teaching experience at UCSC that spring quarter. Referring to the white students in her Third World women-of-color class, she said: "Well, what happened was that—I'm very open, and I teach in a feminist style which gives them [the students] a lot of time to respond. And so they kept speaking out and abusing the dialogue—abusing in terms of taking over and wanting to talk about their thing: their anger, their view, just like . . . in regular school." About this issue of how to conduct her classroom Anzaldúa is adamant, because she strives to transform her classroom into a space in which women of color have the first priority to speak about their lives, a space in which they can discover and articulate their individual voices. It is in this type of context that Anzaldúa uses the metaphor of a bridge as a vehicle to communicate her pedagogical philosophy. Referring to that spring quarter class again, she talked to Baldwin about her effort to make clear what the agenda for that class would be: "I told them that what happened in class [the abuse of dialogue] . . . was a microcosm of what happens in the world and this was a course about women of color and that we had been silenced for a long, long time, and that women of color find it very, very hard to speak up because the context is always not theirs. And I wanted the context to be theirs and I wanted to hear from women of color first, men of color second. . . . And lastly, that I wanted to hear from white people. And that as a teacher I was a bridge, that I had chosen to mediate."

If her classroom agenda and philosophy are likely to be controversial with her students, it is because Anzaldúa is so keenly aware of the conditional status of the advancements that Third World women of color are making for themselves in the different domains of their experience. She speaks of this conditionality in her introduction to section 4 of *This Bridge Called My Back*, asserting: "The vision of our spirituality provides us with no trap door solution, no escape hatch tempting us to transcend our struggle. We must act in the everyday world. Words are not enough. We must perform visible and public acts that may make us more vulnerable to the very oppressions we are fighting against. But, our vulnerability can be the source of our power." Clearly, then, the standards she upholds—to articulate, listen to, and act on the voices of Third World women of color—is one that she applies to herself. By giving Third World women of color first priority in her classroom, Anzaldúa puts the flesh of her experience on the bone of her words.

The act of writing also comes to denote the substance of her political commitments, as one can see in her piece entitled "Speaking in Tongues: A Letter to 3rd World Women Writers" (in *This Bridge Called My Back*). Contemplating how to begin, she says: "It is not easy writing this letter. It began as a poem, a long poem. I tried to turn it into an essay but the result was wooden, cold. I have not yet unlearned the esoteric bullshit and pseudo-intellectualizing that school brainwashed into my writing." Anzaldúa shows her disdain not for theory and the model of the expository essay but for the way the academy teaches clientele to construct it. In an unpublished interview, Anzaldúa outlined one of the major differences separating mainstream from marginalized writers: "a minority writer . . . when he or she writes, a lot of times it is with the desire, the imperative, the urge, or the need to explain, interpret and present his or her culture against the silencing, the repression, the erasure by the dominant culture." This imperative leads to a very different type of theory construction in Anzaldúa's view. Under this imperative the minority writer produces a theory that is much more readable but not any less rigorous, precisely because the "fit" between fact and theory, description and explanation, life and text is more immediate in terms of the political context in which that theory/explanation is written. By contrast, continues Anzaldúa, the theory that proceeds from the academy, which she calls "high theory," is done in "abstract and convoluted language. . . . High theorists write from a very 'objective' perspective. They don't believe in putting autobiographical material into their theories." In this mode, a fledgling theorist must put his or her experience aside, master a canon of abstract ideas, and write in a fixed genre. The politics of such an approach are exactly what Anzaldúa's tenets for theory construction are intended to counteract. In her estimation, "Theory doesn't have to be written in an abstract and convoluted language. Writers like myself are considered low theorists, and writings like *Borderlands* are considered 'low theory' . . . because it's accessible. People can understand it. It's got narrative, it's got poetry and I do the unforgiveable—I mix genres."

Hence, for Anzaldúa, in the construction of a theoretical framework that would articulate the experience of the minority writer, anything is allowed. As she says, what characterizes this path for women of color is the continual struggle of "always having to fight, always, always having to go against the current with any idea. Never being able to be just ourselves because to be ourselves was never good enough." In taking this road herself, Anzaldúa recognizes the toll she has had to pay because of her commitment to write in a different mode, to speak in the voice of a woman of color.

Borderlands through its mix of genres, is work that does indeed open up a fresh space for inquiry and writing, exactly what educational institutions insist scholarly work should do. That *Borderlands* creates a new literary space as well as breaking new scholarly ground should come as no surprise since Anzaldúa has always had wide reading interests and has known how to create herself anew. When asked with what goals she had entered graduate school at UCSC, her response was unabashedly simple and direct: "My goal was to put this [future] book together on the mestiza and how she deals with space and identity. And it was to catch up on the reading—I wanted to continue reading [Jacques] Lacan whom I had started reading in Texas and to read some of the feminist psychoanalysts. I wanted to read some of the French feminists. I wanted to read the current important theoretical writing—things that were being done now. . . . And I also needed a refuge and the University has always been a refuge." That future book will be her dissertation, which she is calling "Llorona/The Woman Who Wails." Her latest publication, *Making Face, Making Soul / Haciendo Caras* (1990), can be seen as a preliminary step in the direction of that work.

A prolific writer, Anzaldúa places her work with regularity in myriad alternative presses, journals, and anthologies. It is in such alternative journals as *Trivia, Third Woman, IKON*, and *Sinister Wisdom* that one can find her work. Despite this low visibility in the mainstream publishing industry, her written work has been recognized as being of exceptional quality. For instance, *This Bridge Called My Back* won the 1986 Before Columbus Foundation American Book Award, and *Borderlands* was selected as one of the thirty-eight best books of 1987 by the *Library Journal*. Because her publications are so extensive and appear in so many diverse journals and anthologies, it is difficult to do an exhaustive analysis of all her work. However, by looking at some fiction pieces that have appeared in *Cuentos: Stories by Latinas* and *Third Woman*, it is possible to get a sense of her style and aims in this genre. As for the flavor of

her style in the expository essay, "La Prieta" in *This Bridge Called My Back* and her essay in *Making Face, Making Soul* provide excellent examples.

Cuentos: Stories by Latinas, edited by Alma Gómez, Cherríe Moraga, and Mariana Romo-Carmona, is an anthology intended, in the words of the editors, "to mention the unmentionable, to capture some essential expression—without censors—that could be called 'Latina' and 'Latina-identified.' " "El Paisano Is a Bird of Good Omen" is Anzaldúa's contribution toward that end. This short story forms a good complement to "La Historia de una Marimacho" (The History of a Masculinized Woman), which, written in Spanish, appears in *Third Woman*. While "El Paisano" may be read as a story of liberation, "Marimacho" may be read as a story of utopian vision. From the standpoint of narrative technique, "El Paisano" is interesting for its present-tense narration and the portrayal of the main character, Andrea. Through this combination, Anzaldúa achieves a powerful mood of foreboding that finally gets resolved when Andrea affirms her lesbian identity in the language of biblical discourse—"I am that I am." Thematically Andrea is confronted with the dilemma of either complying with an arranged marriage or affirming her *querer* (love). In the midst of this dilemma, Andrea has no guide but her grandmother who leads her to recognize that her *poder* (power) is her *querer*. The present-tense narration suggests that in the world Andrea is entering—unlike the world she is leaving behind, where self-identity is a matter of tradition—she must continually use her *poder* to affirm her *querer*.

Complementing the present-tense narration of "El Paisano," "Marimacho" is told in the past tense by a woman narrator, looking back on a time when same-sex marriages were not accepted. As such, it also forms a thematic complement to "El Paisano," by the way it projects a utopian society in which the initial act of revolution is no longer necessary. Of interest in this story is the way it assumes an interlocutor: "Para que le cuento, en aquel tiempo era mal visto que una mujer quisiera a otra" (What can I tell you, back in those days being in love with another woman was looked down upon). From this opening utterance, the story tells how the nameless narrator wins the heart of her beloved, who also remains nameless, and takes her away from her father to live far away in a society of their own making. As the story moves toward its climax and resolution, the father finally catches up with the lovers, pre-

Cover for the 1987 collection of Anzaldúa's essays and poems on her family history, lesbian feminism, the Aztec and Catholic religions, problems of migrant workers, and the pain involved in writing

sumably years later in narrative time, and there he and the narrator confront each other. In that confrontation, the narrator uses a machete to cut off the father's fingers and one of his ears. That trauma serves to tame the father, and in time he learns to work side by side with his daughter's love.

In their didactic aspects, both these stories may be read as calls to action and vision on the part of lesbian women. The physical violence the father suffers in "Marimacho" is matched by the psychological violence inflicted on Andrea in "El Paisano." In both stories one may read the violence, following what Anzaldúa says about the role of reading in her life, as a step in the direction of "a different way of being."

To date, Anzaldúa's *Borderlands* stands as her *obra maestra* (masterpiece). Full of passion, energy, and innovation, *Borderlands* is a far-reaching work, shifting in and out of the tradi-

tional literary and expository genres, blending poetry and prose, switching between English and Spanish, all in order to weave an autobiography resonating with the many voices of Anzaldúa's lived, imagined, and "read" experience. Anzaldúa shows herself conversant in several of the standard academic "codes"—such as critical theory, history, and sociolinguistics—but, not satisfied with any single one of them, she chooses to blend them into her own polyvalent voice. The result is an autobiographical work that, in suspending the traditional prohibition against mixing genres, functions both as literary and referential discourse. As a literary text *Borderlands* speaks in poetic, epic, and tragic voices. As referential text it designates the historical, sociolinguistic, and political realities that constitutes the U.S.-Mexican border area from Brownsville, Texas, to San Diego, California.

Borderlands is divided into two major sections, the first a long essay entitled "Atravesando Fronteras / Crossing Borders" and the second a collection of poems, "Un Agitado Viento / Ehécatl, the Wind." The essay is subdivided into seven constituent essays, each exploring the thematics of border crossing from distinct perspectives. The opening part, for example, sets the historical and political stage from which Anzaldúa will articulate what it means to live on the border, both literally and figuratively. Entitled "The Homeland, Aztlán / El Otro México," this short essay provides a sweeping view of the major historical events that have gone into producing the present-day border between the United States and Mexico. The first part of the title is derived from the available historical scholarship; the second part, "El Otro Mexico," she got from conversations with her family, who see the South Valley of Texas as becoming "un otro Mexico" (another Mexico) because, as an uncle of hers says, "it's full of wetbacks." Thus the slash in the title itself represents a border between scholarly writing and the everyday experience of people who live in the valley. As Anzaldúa says about this text: "I don't feel that I, Gloria, produced *Borderlands* all by myself. I just happen to be the mouthpiece . . . the channel. While I do feel that the images and words . . . the way that I speak . . . the structure and style are mine, I found the raw material out there in the world, in other people's experiences, and in books."

It is precisely this merger of scholarship and experience that makes Anzaldúa's "low" mode of theory construction so compelling. For instance, in the last subsection of the opening essay—"*El cruzar del mojado* / Illegal Crossing"—Anzaldúa, in a sense, replies to her uncle, agreeing that the valley is another Mexico—an *other* of Mexico: "We have a tradition of migration, a tradition of long walks. Today we are witnessing *la migración de los pueblos mexicanos*, the return odyssey to the historical/mythological Aztlán. This time the traffic is from south to north." This other Mexico is part of Aztlán, with a division (the U.S. border) running through it.

The historical outline she provides starts from the earliest migrations from north to south of the Cochise people circa 1000 B.C., through the conquest of Mexico in 1521, through the signing of the Treaty of Guadalupe-Hidalgo in 1848, and into the present. From personal experience Anzaldúa tells of her family's "ancestral lands": "A smart *gabacho* [Anglo-American] lawyer took the land away[;] *mamá* hadn't paid taxes. *No hablabla inglés* [She didn't speak English]." Out of such individual experience, the history of the American Southwest was formed.

In the metaphorical figure of the *mujer indocumentada* (undocumented woman) Anzaldúa exploits the full referential power of that history. She, as the undocumented woman, not only represents the dividing line but also *occupies* it as a matter of ongoing, personal history: "This is her home / this thin edge of / barbwire." As such, she is the perfect model for a theory of "the Borderlands," with a capital *B*. Anzaldúa explains it thus: "in the book, when I use the word Borderlands and it has a capital *B*, I use it in a symbolic way to mean that . . . it's more a psychological, cultural, sexual, spiritual borderlands. And this means that . . . where there's people of different cultures or different belief systems or different backgrounds or class backgrounds, that thin line between them is the Borderlands, is the boundaries."

Anzaldúa's language, linguistic codes, and ethnic identity also play key roles in her theory of the borderlands. "How to Tame a Wild Tongue" is one of the brief expository essays and deals with the negative social attitudes toward Chicano ways of speaking, and the effects of these negative attitudes on the linguistic and ethnic self. The description of Chicano Spanish that Anzaldúa offers is concise and informative, approaching the requirements of descriptive adequacy in linguistic theory. The analysis of language attitudes that she presents rigorously exposes the many ways in which language can be

used as an oppressive tool—in attitudes that prohibit Chicano school kids from speaking Spanish at recess, make the accent of Chicano English an impediment to economic advancement, and look down on Chicano Spanish as "mutilation of Spanish." Anzaldúa digs deep into the political roots of these attitudes with her radical equation between language and identity: "So if you really want to hurt me, talk badly about my language. Ethnic identity is twin to linguistic identity—I am my language."

The final short essay, "*La conciencia de la mestiza* / Towards a New Consciousness," is perhaps the most speculative and theoretically rich of the seven essays that make up "Atravesando Fronteras / Crossing Borders." The essay begins by boldly announcing that, like *la mujer indocumentada*, humanity is about to cross into an alien land: "From this radical, ideological, cultural and biological cross-pollinization, an 'alien' consciousness is presently in the making—a new *mestiza* consciousness, *una conciencia de mujer*. It is a consciousness of the Borderlands." The capital *B* indicates that Anzaldúa is talking about the symbolic borderlands, and, as a consequence, the dialectic that will be responsible for the formation of the mestiza consciousness, according to her, will be spiritual in nature. This does not mean, however, that the dialectic is ahistorical; on the contrary, like all her theories, the dialectic derives its power from the experience of daily life. Nor does the spiritual nature of the dialectic mean that it is moving, in Hegelian fashion, toward absolute synthesis and unity; on the contrary, the dialectic moves toward *mestizaje* (racial mixture). In the end the dialectic of the mestiza is spiritual in nature only because it works over, through, and on human consciousness, a phenomenon that cannot be reduced to anything like a stable empirical category. Consciousness cannot be just a subject, and neither can it be just an object. For Anzaldúa, it is both—the subject that studies, the object that is studied—and more, a third element: "That third element is a new consciousness—a mestiza consciousness—and though it is a source of intense pain, its energy comes from continual creative motion that keeps breaking down the unitary aspects of each new paradigm." The process of breaking down unities amounts to the daily work of resisting Anglo-American political hegemonies, while at the same time allowing for political alliances; resisting the oppressive elements of Chicano culture, while understanding their roots in oppression. Above all, mestiza consciousness designates what Anzaldúa calls "a tolerance for ambiguity," a concept that clearly links with her experience with language. Like the phenomenon of linguistic ambiguity, which requires that one strive to see through the surface structure of an utterance to understand how other potential meanings also reside in the deep structure, Anzaldúa points to the plurality of meaning with which one can invest reality. In this task it is once again the mestiza who is already in advance of others: "She has a plural personality, she operates in a pluralistic mode—nothing is thrust out, the good, the bad, and the ugly, nothing rejected, nothing abandoned."

The reviews of *Borderlands*, except for a dissenting voice here and there, have been overwhelmingly positive. One of these dissenting voices appeared in the April 1988 issue of *Choice*: I. Molina of Miami University at Oxford, Ohio, reads Anzaldúa's text as the expression of "a tortured soul, who, instead of pursuing her search for identity in the spirit of objective truth, indulges in both self-denigration and self-condemnation so prevalent in the writing of some Chicano intellectuals." How Molina arrived at such a reading is difficult to see in the light of the positive ideals Anzaldúa espouses in mestiza consciousness. As for the notion of objective truth, even a cursory reading of the text reveals that it is exactly this category of truth that Anzaldúa critiques and problematizes in the most radical of ways. More often, the dissenting voices tended to focus on Anzaldúa's elliptical style and her tendency to leave some of her points unstated. For instance, Cherríe Moraga, who for the most part gave *Borderlands* a good review, expresses some reservations toward Anzaldúa's elliptical style. Moraga held Anzaldúa to strong requirements of essay unity and coherence when she said that the prose in chapter 4—"La herencia de Coatlicue" (The Inheritance of Coatlicue)—"disorients, jumping around from anecdote to philosophy to history to *sueño* [dream], seldom developing a single topic" (*Third Woman*, 1989). Carolyn Woodward, reviewing *Borderlands* for the *National Women's Studies Association Journal* (Spring 1988), also seemed to address this point. After praising Anzaldúa's critique of Western society, Woodward ended her review by saying, "It is a book still with rough edges, so that we get Anzaldúa's intensity sometimes unmediated." Similarly, reviewing for the *Village Voice* (28 June 1988), Melanie Kaye-Kantrowitz wrote, "Sometimes . . . personal narrative follows historical anal-

ysis too abruptly, the juxtaposition of parts fragmenting the text. And sometimes the stretch towards absolute theory falls short." Whether these requirements of essay unity and coherence should be applied to "Atravesando Fronteras / Crossing Borders" will no doubt continue to be a pressing question. One wonders, however, if the textual spaces left open by Anzaldúa's elliptical style should not be evaluated in the light of her experiment with genre mixing, the concept of "the Borderlands" as an indeterminate space, and the dialectics of *mestizaje*, which project a consciousness that is becoming and is not yet solid. As Anzaldúa asserts, "So I am problematizing all these things that as a genre . . . we have been taught about autobiography. The first rule that I break is the rule that says that there is a cohesive, coherent, self-directed self."

Nevertheless, even the reviewers who had mildly negative reactions to *Borderlands* saw its innovative and energetic aspects as it cleared a space for women of color to articulate their voices. Kaye-Kantrowitz, for instances, recognized the borderlands for what they are, "as much a spiritual state as a geographical one. . . . In the borderlands new creatures come into being. Anzaldúa celebrates this 'new mestiza' in bold, experimental writing." And then, as if to take back her earlier criticism, she said: "Given the scope of the material and the boldness of Anzaldúa's reach, it seems churlish to ask for a smooth product." Similarly Woodward prefaced her mild critique by saying, "I hope I have conveyed my sense that this is an important book," and then gave a statement of the pedagogical value: "This is an accessible work, one that should provoke exciting discussion in introductory women's studies classes, in courses that focus on issues of concern to women of color, in seminars of feminist theory, and in groups meeting in women's centers. Much may develop from our interaction with Anzaldúa's consciousness." Moraga credited *Borderlands* for being a valuable articulation of "a kind of blueprint for *la nueva cultura* (the new culture) that Anzaldúa envisions. Oftentimes the symbols are so coded only the architect can interpret them and only to herself. But the best of the writing has wrought out a vision from a suffering which Anzaldúa does not objectify, but lives." Reviewing for *Belles Lettres* (May / June 1988), Elizabeth J. Bader pointed out the inclusive scope of Anzaldúa's work: "Not only does the author conjure a new person, a strong wo/ man in whom visions of justice and fairness prevail, but she seeks also to give voice to the silent, helping them exorcise the self-deprecation that has kept them down."

Other reviewers spoke of the breadth of the work, as for instance, the anonymous reviewer for the *Library Journal* (April 1988) did: "In a rich and moving personal account, Anzaldúa explains her roots and folk Catholicism, Indian religious symbolism, and lesbian feminism." In the same vein, Andrea Caron, reviewing for the same journal (1 September 1987), close to the publication date of *Borderlands*, also remarked on the scope: "Her essays and poems range over broad territory, moving from the plight of undocumented migrant workers to memories of her grandmother, from Aztec religion to the agony of writing." And in a review focusing closely on Anzaldúa's poetry, Margaret Randall, reviewing for the *Women's Review of Books* (December 1987), referred to her work as "major writing." Discussing certain specific poems, Randall stated that as she went back to reread these, "each time I find new doors challenging me to open them and walk through. I will walk through again and again, discovering with each passage further demands upon my own cultural myopia, racism, and conformity." What these reviewers attested to is the way in which Anzaldúa has succeeded in crafting a life that is truly her own. In the process, she has refused to hand it over to someone else to define it for her. By the same token, this stance has not meant an unwillingness to compromise. In the Baldwin interview, for instance, exploiting a certain ambiguity between the pair of Spanish and English words *compromiso* and *compromise*, she says: "In Spanish *compromiso* is a commitment, and I don't know how in my head *compromise* has the connotation of being a commitment. It's like I have a commitment to compromise so that I will yield, so that I won't be so inflexible, so that I won't be rigid, so set in my way. Because for me that is a movement toward death to have that rigidity." Throughout her life Anzaldúa has moved not toward rigidity but to a flexibility open to the differences.

One sees Anzaldúa's predisposition to be open, flexible, and conciliatory with the recent publication of *Making Face, Making Soul*. Her introduction to that anthology and her essay "En Rapport, in Opposition" issue a call for work that will promote greater solidarity among the different interests that make up the feminist movement of women of color. In the introductory essay she states, "*Necesitamos teorías* [we need theor-

ies] that will rewrite history using race, class, gender, and ethnicity as categories of analysis, theories that cross borders, that blur boundaries—new kinds of theories with new theorizing methods." And in the essay "En Rapport, in Opposition," when calling for solidarity, she says, "So if we won't forget past grievances, let us forgive. Carrying the ghosts of past grievances *no vale la pena*. It is not worth the grief."

Anzaldúa keeps busy, reading her work publicly, giving lectures, and being in workshops and on panels, not only at the local level but also at the national and international level. For instance, in 1990 Anzaldúa lectured at a literary-criticism conference held at Georgetown University, Washington, D.C. In the same month she participated in a panel at the National Women's Studies Association Conference in Akron, Ohio. March 1990 saw her lecturing and reading from her work at the University of Colorado. Later that month she delivered the keynote address at a conference at Stanford University on the occasion of Women's History Month. With such a busy schedule she still manages to maintain an equally busy correspondence. She responds to everyone who writes her, much of this mail being in the form of manuscripts that people want her to read and critique for them. This labor over the manuscripts of others has put her in close working association with the feminist press journal *Sinister Wisdom*, to which she has been a contributing editor since 1984. Whatever many activities will continue to fill her daily life, one thing is for certain with Gloria Anzaldúa, her writing will never be neglected. When asked how her writing fits into her life and relationships, she replied: "I definitely see myself connected with a community of writers and artists and activists and teachers, but I very early decided that I would not marry and I would not have children. This was even before I realized I was a lesbian. Because the art was going to take it. That was going to be my significant other. And that has not changed."

Interview:
Elizabeth Baldwin, *Matrix* (May 1988): 1-33.

References:
Melanie Kaye-Kantrowitz, "Crossover Dreams," *Village Voice*, 33 (28 June 1988): 60, 62;
Cherríe Moraga, "Algo secretamente amado," *Third Woman: The Sexuality of Latinas*, 4 (1989): 151-156;

Héctor A. Torres, "Experience, Writing, Theory: The Dialects of *Mestizaje* in Gloria Anzaldúa's *Borderlands/La Frontera: The New*

Mestiza," in *Cultural and Cross-Cultural Studies and the Teaching of Literature*, edited by J. Trimmer and T. Warnock (1991).

Juan Estevan Arellano
(17 September 1947 -   )

Reynaldo Ruiz
Eastern Michigan University

BOOKS: *Palabras de la vista / Retratos de la pluma* (Albuquerque: Academia, 1984);
Inocencio: Ni siembra, ni escarda y siempre se come el mejor elote (Mexico City: Grijalva, 1991).

OTHER: *Entre verde y seco*, edited by Arellano (Dixon, N.Mex.: Academia de la Nueva Raza, 1972);
"No es hablar de su vida, sino su muerte," in *Voces: An Anthology of Nuevo Mexicano Writers* (Albuquerque: University of New Mexico Press, 1987), pp. 208-221.

SELECTED PERIODICAL PUBLICATIONS— UNCOLLECTED: "No nos murimos este año," *Cuaderno* (1972): 28-35;
"A Las Tres de la Mañana," *Caracol* (1974): 22-26;
"Cuentos de Café y Tortilla: Las Grullas y Dios," *Cuaderno* (1976): 66-70;
"Cuentos de Café y Tortilla: Siempre es el mismo perro viejo nomás que con collar nuevo," *Cuaderno* (1976): 71-75;
"Cuentos de Café y Tortilla: Después de perdido volver a perder," *Cuaderno* (1976): 75-79.

The Academia de la Nueva Raza (the Academy of the New People) was founded in 1970 by several Nuevo Mexicanos (New Mexicans)—Tomás Atencio, E. A. Mares, Juan Estevan Arellano, and others—to study, analyze, understand, and appreciate the dimension and scope of the economy, society, culture, and psyche of the northern Nuevo Mexicano and to help the community appreciate the knowledge, wisdom, and culture of their environment and circumstances. Arellano, as one of the founders, stated: "hay que concientizar al pueblo . . . hay que regresarle al pueblo qué es de ellos. . . . Yo trato de documentar las cosas como están pasando y como pasaron" (one has to make the community aware . . . one should return to the community what is theirs. . . . I try to document the things as they exist and how they happened). The *academia* was founded during a time of social unrest in which Chicanos throughout the Southwest, and in particular in northern New Mexico, were not only going through a period of self-study and analysis but also questioning institutionalized bias at all levels of the social order. Within this context Arellano started to achieve success, not only as a news reporter and editor but also as a "commentator and thinker" who understood the Chicano's plight as lived and experienced in northern New Mexico.

Juan Estevan Arellano was born on 17 September 1947 to Adolfo and Celia Arellano, farmers in the tiny village of Embudo, which abuts the Sangre de Cristo mountain range. The young Arellano came to live and experience northern New Mexico's severe winters, beautiful springs, hot and dry summers, and mild falls. One of eleven children, he was raised by his aunt and uncle, Lucía and Carlos Arellano. The child's days were spent going to school and doing the daily chores most country boys do: planting, harvesting, picking fruit, chopping wood, and carrying water. In Embudo, Arellano gained a strong set of values. His family's pride and work ethic, along with their strong religious beliefs and their need to work and live off the land, instilled in him a sense of reverence and respect for nature, the land, the water rights, and the cultural traditions of his community. Arellano is a dedicated advocate for his people, and his writing, in part, reflects his concern for the abuse that northern Nuevo Mexicanos have experienced regarding their rights as landowners and citizens.

Arellano's interest in writing began when he was a young boy attending Dixon Elementary School. Together with friends he wrote about imaginary basketball teams and the games they played. His interest peaked when as a freshman in high school he was awarded an "Honorable Mention" certificate in a statewide writing competition in 1962. After receiving this award, he joined the newspaper staff at McCurdy Mission High School and received the praise of his teachers and members of the community for his writing.

In the mid 1960s, with the escalation of the Vietnam War and the need for manpower, Arellano felt the pressure of conscription. Having kept abreast of the particulars of the war and having lost two of his friends in it, Arellano did not support the war effort. He enrolled at New Mexico State University in Las Cruces in 1966, and he was instrumental in organizing a student group called "Los Chicanos" whose primary objectives were to underline the Chicano's presence and instill pride among themselves regarding their language and ethnicity. This was Arellano's first organized effort to address several political issues. While studying at the university, he wrote for the student newspaper, the *Round Up*, and also worked on a part-time basis for the *Las Cruces Sun News*.

In 1970, after graduation from New Mexico State University, he returned to Embudo, where he became one of the founders of the Academia de la Nueva Raza. His background in journalism and communications helped him obtain the position of editor of the journal *Cuaderno*. Through *Cuaderno* the *academia* not only pursued its goal of "looking for the gold in the pueblo" (community) but also shared with the outside world the ideologies, political and social views, knowledge, wisdom, and folklore of the local people. In 1971 Arellano was awarded a one-year fellowship at the Washington Journalism Center in Washington, D.C., and met leading newspaper reporters and high government officials who aided him in his professional development.

After his return to New Mexico in 1972, he married Elena Martínez. They have three children. Upon his return he resumed the responsibilities of editor of *Cuaderno* and continued his literary work. His short stories, in English and Spanish, are not only engaging, funny, and colorful but also contain many messages. Some messages deal with criticism of the social structure, while others deal with political games at all levels; injustices; criticism of local, state, and federal government; and the Chicanos' apathy and lack of pride in their language and culture.

In his 1972 short story (written in English and embellished with the Spanish dialect of northern New Mexico) "No nos murimos este año" (We Did Not Die This Year), he skillfully synthesizes a realistic picture of many maladies that the young Chicanos in northern New Mexico experience. His character Pacomio, an unemployed dropout and a Vietnam veteran, becomes disillusioned with life. The story begins when he is rejected at the "State Disemployment Office": "Sorry . . . the jobs we have available are at the Scientific Lab and the State Capitol. They require a college degree education. If you want—well, check back next week sometime, oh, you can register for the potato harvest in Colorado. At San Luis." To criticize the Chicanos' conscious effort to become anglicized, Arellano mentions Jane, one of the local girls: "She is cheerleader and a member of the Honor Society. In describing herself she says she is 'Spanish' and has no Indian blood, though her features don't substantiate her. She also maintains there is no discrimination against Chicanos." Further along in the story, in a dialogue between two other characters, Manuel and Arturo, one sees another glimpse of the Chicano psyche: "The matter with you, is you see everything like a gringo."

Arellano published two short stories in *Cuaderno* in 1973 and 1974 that became chapters in his 1991 novel, *Inocencio: Ni siembra, ni escarda y siempre se come el mejor elote* (Inocencio: Neither Plant nor Dig and You'll Always Eat the Best Corn). The two stories deal with the life of Inocencio, a picaro who always manages to survive without working. The first (title) chapter introduces him as he leaves school to become a sheepherder. In school, at the hands of nuns, in a hostile and indifferent environment, Inocencio faces a devastating experience: He is called "Inny" because his teacher can not pronounce his name. Inocencio is later pushed by scorn and indifference to survive as a bum, rogue, and a drunk who must depend on his astuteness and manipulations to exist. Years later Inocencio, a middle-aged drunk, finds himself alone. He lives in a shack, owns only a few articles of clothing, and has no money. Through the years he has learned to survive by cajoling, deceiving, and stealing, and by manipulating the welfare system, thereby working as little as possible.

The second story, first published in 1974, finds Inocencio a much older man who describes himself as a man with few teeth—not due to old age but because he has had to struggle with the world. The few remaining teeth that he has are "like isolated bells that alert everyone that he is close by. . . . " In this chapter Arellano elaborates scenes and monologues in which Inocencio comments on his experiences as a boy. As an adult, Inocencio laments the injustices of the system and the influx of the "gringos" who little by little are buying out the land from the Chicanos, thus disenfranchising them from having a voice in the political and economic process and structure.

The outstanding features in these two stories (and in the complete novel) are the use of authentic Spanish dialect as spoken in northern New Mexico; humor that ranges from the most basic to sophisticated plays on words; and the realistic depiction of the characters, showing Arellano's understanding of the northern Nuevo Mexicano psyche vis-à-vis the social circumstances.

The three 1976 short stories under the heading of "Cuentos de Café y Tortilla" (Tales of the Coffee and Tortilla) are essentially monologues Arellano uses to comment on several issues of importance. "Las Grullas y Dios" (The Cranes and God), which has a fablelike format, has several messages on performing good deeds and on the work of witchery. "Siempre es el mismo perro viejo nomás que con collar nuevo" (It Is Always the Same Old Dog Only with a New Collar) and "Después de perdido volver a perder" (After a Loss You Lose Again) are basically laments in which Arellano, in a storylike format, comments on the old days when people were hardworking, honest, and realistic with their dreams and aspirations. In "Siempre" he writes:

> Hoy en día nadie se ayuda si no es por dinero. Por eso nadie puede decir que es libre sin sufrimiento, siendo que la libertad no es tesoro que se compra con oro . . . y todavía oyemos a tontos hablar que el único modo que la raza se va a librar es por medio de la plata. ¡Qué triste, no hay peor soga que el dinero!

(Today, no one helps each other if there is no money involved. This is why no one can say that one is free without suffering, that is, liberty is not a "treasure" that can be bought with gold . . . and we continue to hear that the only way that Chicanos are to become free is by having money. "What a pity, there isn't a better hanging rope than money!")

In "Después de perdido volver a perder" he emphasizes the idea that the Chicano has not been able to break away from the shackles of the "welfare and food stamp" cycle and from Anglo-American domination because he suffers from an identity problem: "nosotros no nos ayudamos porque no sabemos quienes diablos somos . . . " (we don't help each other because we don't know who the devil we are . . .).

In "No es hablar de su vida, sino su muerte" (It Is Not a Question of His Life, but of His Death), published in *Voces* (1987), the principal character, a writer, accounts for and describes daily life in a village in northern New Mexico as it has evolved and developed during the twenty years before the story. Through the main character, Arellano presents, in a biting and critical manner, the people's apathy in being trapped and deceived by the values of Anglo-American society. He also shows the perceived need of the local people for instant gratification and their active interest in having the latest material symbols of success. He describes the Chicanos as "gente muy extraña . . . el Santo día trabaja y no se les hecha de ver nada" (very strange people . . . who work all day and have nothing to show for it).

Arellano's *Palabras de la vista / Retratos de la pluma* (Sight Words / Pen Portraits, 1984) is a collection of twenty-eight poems and twenty-two photographs, which have been arranged like frames in a film. Through this "fotoesía" (a word coined by Arellano), he combines the features of the poems with features of the photographs to tell a story, which deals with the life and people of northern New Mexico and with questions that humankind has been pondering for years. Arellano invites readers to join him and review some memories. He considers himself "un hombre individual y por eso universal, en este mundo colectivo" (an individual who, at the same time, is universal in a collective context). His story has different themes, hues, and messages. On the one hand, he presents life as innocent; on the other, he shows the selfishness, deceit, and hypocrisy in the development of society. To arouse the reader to react to the social predicament, he employs a garbage dump as a metaphor:

> animal maníaco que eres, hombre, aquí dejando
>   tu historia
> devorador de lengua y costumbres, todo tiras
>   hasta tu vida . . .

> (maniac animal that you are, man, leaving your his-
>   tory here
> devourer of language and customs, you throw away
>   everything
>   even your life . . .).

Another variant of the same theme that recurs throughout Arellano's writing is his perception of the role and importance of humankind:

> Yo soy nadie,
> sólo ese rayo frío
> que abraza el tuétano de tus huesos;
> caminante, sigue tu andanza que
> no es nadie, soy yo

> (I am nobody
> just that cold flash
> that embraces the marrow in your bones;
> traveler, continue on your journey that
> is no one, it is just me) [.]

A gradation on the same theme is seen in his "Gallo Blanco" (White Rooster): "me enseñaste que todos los pasos / son cortos, suspiros en el viento" (you taught me that all steps / in life are short, sighs in the wind).

Arellano's perception of his role as a writer, photographer, sculptor, news reporter, and human being is to give back everything he has received. The wisdom he has extracted from his people, which he regards as gold, is the knowledge gained from them, and the essence of being from northern New Mexico is returned in a different form—in poems, stories, riddles, maxims, photographs, criticism, insights, sculptures, and sayings. He describes his contribution in his poem "Para la Vecina del Casorio" (For the Hastily Married One):

> Pero más de todo, la ayuda más grande
> que hago a este mundo ingrato, es
> que por ser quien soy, los hago reír,
>   les doy plática, alegro su vida rutina,
> estoy tan viva que ni saben; los que saben
> con mi locura los curo, quiebrando el hielo tieso
>   telaraña sobre sus caras enmascaradas

> (But more than anything, my biggest contribution
> to this ungrateful world, is that
> because of who I am, I make people laugh,
>   I talk to people, I cheer their monotonous
>   life,
> I am so full of life that no one knows; and those
>   who do
> are cured by my madness, breaking down the hard
>   ice
>   cobwebs over their masked faces) [.]

Arellano continues to work at poetry and fiction, and he writes a weekly column, "El Crespúsculo" (The Twilight), for the *Taos News*; he is also the publisher and editor of *Resolana*, a monthly magazine whose primary audience is "el Nuevo Mexicano y los paisanos" (the New Mexican and the people). *Resolana* continues in the tradition of the former journal *Cuaderno*, to bring out in the open the issues and questions that affect the northern Nuevo Mexicano.

Arellano's journalistic skills have been acknowledged by both the Nuevo Mexicano and others who live outside the state. However, his literary contributions have not achieved the same level of recognition. A reason for this is that his literature has not been widely disseminated beyond his native New Mexico. Only recently have those exposed to his writing begun to appreciate and understand his contributions to Chicano literature. For many readers and critics, Arellano's style might be cumbersome and rustic, but he is particularly skillful at depicting the nuances of human beings as reflected in their speech. The content and style of his work reflect an authentic mode of expression. The expert use of local diction, expressions, and anglicisms distinguishes his work from other Chicano writing. Action in his narratives is well paced and engaging; his characters are developed with compassion and understanding. He attacks the materialistic ideology of the outsider who buys out the Chicano, and he also criticizes the Nuevo Mexicano who lets himself be exploited. In his writing, Arellano attempts to produce a realistic view of life, thereby inspiring the local people to examine their circumstances and look at themselves as they really are. Through his writing he returns to the people what is theirs by imitating their speech and ideology. On the other hand, he offers the outsider a peek into the psyche, beliefs, and socioeconomic conditions of the New Mexican Chicano.

Jimmy Santiago Baca

(2 January 1952 -)

A. Gabriel Meléndez
University of New Mexico

BOOKS: *Jimmy Santiago Baca* (Santa Barbara, Cal.: Rock Bottom, 1978);

Immigrants in Our Own Land (Baton Rouge: Louisiana State University Press, 1979); enlarged as *Immigrants in Our Own Land and Earlier Poems* (New York: New Directions, 1990);

Swords of Darkness, edited by Gary Soto (San Jose, Cal.: Mango, 1981);

What's Happening (Willimantic, Conn.: Curbstone, 1982);

Poems Taken from My Yard (Fulton, Mo.: Timberline, 1986);

Martín and Meditations on the South Valley (New York: New Directions, 1987);

Black Mesa Poems (New York: New Directions, 1989).

PLAY PRODUCTION: *Los tres hijos de Julia*, Los Angeles Theatre Center, Spring 1991.

OTHER: "Ancestor" and "So Mexicans Are Taking Jobs from Americans," in *New Worlds of Literature*, edited by Jerome Beaty and J. Paul Hunter (New York: Norton, 1989), pp. 176, 928;

"6:00 A.M. awake . . . , " in *The Pushcart Prize XIV*, edited by Bill Henderson (New York: Penguin, 1989), pp. 153-155;

"An Ear to the Ground," "Ese Chicano," "I Pass La Iglesia," and "Small Farmer," in *An Anthology of Contemporary American Poetry* (Athens: University of Georgia Press, 1989), pp. 25-27.

Poetry and personal circumstance, each inextricably linked to the other in a complete and unbroken cycle, are indispensable elements in coming to know and understand the poetic voice and the artistic development of Jimmy Santiago Baca, an award-winning poet who is the author of two chapbooks and five larger collections of poems. Baca's work has been widely anthologized and has appeared in such respected literary publications as *Ironwood, Bilingual Review, Harbor Review,*

Jimmy Santiago Baca

Confluencia, Las Américas, New Kauri, Quarterly West, Puerto del Sol, and several others. In 1987 he was awarded a National Endowment for the Arts grant for poetry, and in 1988 he was the recipient of the Before Columbus American Book Award in poetry for his book *Martín and Meditations on the South Valley* (1987). He has been a poet in residence at the University of California, Berkeley, and at Yale University, having received the Berkeley Regents' Fellowship in 1989 and the Wallace Stevens Fellowship from Yale University in 1990. Recently he was awarded a prestigious Ludwig Vogelstien award in poetry. Baca has served on the poetry selection committee for the

National Endowment for the Arts and has been invited to judge various poetry competitions, including the 1990 San Francisco State University Poetry Contest. With the publication of his 1987 book by New Directions, a press noted for having promoted the work of some of the most respected and enduring poets in world literature, including William Carlos Williams, Allen Ginsberg, Octavio Paz, and Denise Levertov, Baca has come to the forefront as one of the most widely read and recognized Chicano poets working today. Not the least of Baca's contribution to Chicano literature has been to widen the critical attention directed by mainstream critics and publishers toward his own work and that of other Chicano writers.

Baca first began to write poetry while incarcerated on drug charges in an Arizona prison. At the behest of publisher-friend Will Inman and with the encouragement of fellow inmates, Baca sent three poems to *Mother Jones* magazine. He was rewarded a couple of weeks later with a check for his efforts. The poems caught the attention of Levertov, the magazine's poetry editor, who began corresponding with Baca, eventually helping to locate a publisher for his first full-length book of poems, *Immigrants in Our Own Land* (1979). In her introduction to *Martín and Meditations on the South Valley*, Levertov describes Baca's poetry as work that "perceives the mythic and archetypal significance of life-events."

The biographical file on Jimmy Santiago Baca might well be read as the working sketch or preliminary study for much of the autobiographical elements that infuse his poetry and in particular the long narrative poem *Martín*. Baca was born on 2 January 1952 in Santa Fe, New Mexico, an event he records in his poem "Bells," from *Black Mesa Poems* (1989):

Bells. The word gongs my skull bone. . . .
Mamá carried me out, just born,
swaddled in hospital blanket,
from St. Vincent's in Santa Fe.
Into the evening, still drowsed
with uterine darkness,
my fingertips purple with new life,
cathedral bells splashed
into my blood, plunging iron hulls
into my pulse waves. Cathedral steeples,
amplified brooding, sonorous bells,
through narrow cobbled streets, bricked patios,
rose trellis'd windows,
red-tiled Spanish rooftops, bells
beat my name, "Santiago! Santiago!"

Despite the joyous tone of celebration in "Bells," Baca's early childhood was not easy. His parents, a Chicano mother and an Apache father, divorced when he was two. He was abandoned to a grandparent and later shuttled between relatives and orphanages. His mother died tragically at the hands of her second husband, and his father, with whom he had little contact, eventually died of alcoholism. When he was five, Baca was placed in St. Anthony's Home for Boys in Albuquerque, where he lived until he was eleven. During his teenage years Baca was in and out of detention centers and spent much of his time learning to survive on the streets of Albuquerque's urban barrios. After a couple of years on the road, wandering first to the southeastern states and then back west to Arizona, Baca at twenty was given a five-year federal sentence for possession of a controlled substance with intent to distribute. He refutes the charge made against him, explaining that his arrest was made on the basis of association, because he was present during a drug sale. Baca's sentence in Florence, Arizona, one of the toughest maximum security prisons in the state, was eventually extended to over six years.

Baca's experience in federal prison was marked by a succession of lockdowns, solitary confinements, electroshock therapy sessions, and beatings by prison guards, all of which would push him to the lowest ebb of his life. These experiences, he says, "reduced me, and whoever I thought I was, disintegrated and I fell into an incredible pit of humiliation where I began to disintegrate. . . . Nothing was being nourished to discover and create, and I finally destroyed myself in this huge cemetery called the prisons of America. When I went to prison I no longer existed. I was a non-entity." However, Baca began a prolonged process of self-discovery and education, which showed him that language could become a vehicle for bringing order to the chaos that surrounded him. In prison he eventually obtained his GED (General Equivalency [high-school] Diploma) and became fully literate, immersing himself in the world of books.

Initially drawn to poetry, Baca began to read the work of diverse poets. While teaching himself Spanish, he read the works of Pablo Neruda, Juan Ramón Jiménez, and Federico García Lorca; in English he read William Wordsworth, Mary Baker, Lawrence Ferlinghetti, Robert Frost, Ezra Pound, Walt Whitman, Levertov, and Ginsberg. Baca began to exercise a natural and gifted ability to arch his circumstance into metaphor and sling forth his poems as personal responses to the lived experience of his early years. His first real triumph in poetry came as a short, powerful stanza that would sound out in his mind with the force of a mantra:

> Did you tell them
> hell is not a dream
> and that you've been there?
> Did you tell them?

As Baca recalls, the emotions emerged from deep within a wellspring of harnessed feelings: "And that was some sort of voice in me talking to another voice in me, saying, you've lived this: Did you tell them? Did you tell them? . . . That was the most powerful five or six lines that got me going." Baca also became aware of a tremendous obligation, of a sense of responsibility and urgency that accompanied his newfound ability to write and to express his experience for others who could not do so.

Baca's poetry is to a large degree infused with elements drawn from his experiences, and the reader is struck by the recurrent themes of transformation, metamorphosis, and self-actualization that have accompanied the poet's own trajectory as an individual and a writer. The most significant turning point in Baca's life was his discovery of language and poetry as a means of expression. Prior to this revelation Baca describes himself as "an illiterate Chicano, who knew more of a plumber's wrench than a pencil, more of rebellion than submission, more of the inside of a cell than of a book."

Shortly after his release from prison in 1979 Baca went to visit his sister and was awestruck by a picture she had kept of him at sixteen. His reaction was one of disbelief as he viewed the photograph, and the moment caused him to reflect on how he had changed. Recalling that visit and the photograph he says, "I knew it was me, but my mind had taken such cosmic leaps through language, and consequently those leaps entailed a sort of immolation, a sort of ritual burning of the past . . . and language, the vowels, the consonants, the syllables all became a sort of pyre which the past was placed on, and burned in the flames of language."

Attuned to real-life circumstances, each of Baca's books represents a concrete step in the process of rebuilding his life from the point of nonexistence that he associates with the years spent in prison. Thus each book in turn marks a step in Baca's determination to move his personal and poetic endeavor toward full realization. His first published material is to be found in scattered anthologies, his chapbooks *Jimmy Santiago Baca* (1978) and *Swords of Darkness* (1981), and his two collections *Immigrants in Our Own Land* and *What's Happening* (1982). All contain poems centered on his experience in prison, which triggered Baca's often bitter and direct poetic introspection.

Baca's first chapbook, *Jimmy Santiago Baca*, consists of nine poems and a short essay on his thoughts on leaving prison. In a very telling way, these early poems became an essential scaffolding from which Baca began to address several key, recurring themes that he fully fleshed out in his subsequent works. His concerns are clear. He writes of the brutal harshness of prison, of regaining his own humanity, and of his personal and unbroken desire to reconnect to the world beyond the walls of his cell. The poetic style is terse but reveals the raw power of Baca's uncanny ability to create bold and forceful images, as in the poem "Just Before Dawn," which draws a clear bead on the desperation that inhabits the prison's world:

> And young prisoners hug their blankets
> like frozen carcasses strewn across
> timeless blizzard plains, and a few
> gnaw their hearts off
> caught in the steel jaws of prison.

Baca followed this slight and seminal collection of poems with the publication the next year of a major work entitled *Immigrants in Our Own Land*. This group of thirty-seven poems established Baca's potential as a serious and prolific new voice on the poetry scene. The publication of *Immigrants* coincided with Baca's release from prison, and its central focus is a series of reflections spanning the years of his incarceration. The title of the book and of a central poem in the collection alludes to the alienation of prison for newly arrived inmates, as they become divested of any human capacity to respond to the institution's vindictive nature. This underlying theme, along with Baca's chronological look at his years in prison, draws the poems in the book together and structures a unity of intent. In a review, the *Virginia Quarterly* stressed that the work is "a book rather than a collection of poems," an opinion shared by Joseph F. Vélez, who in *Revista Chicano-Riqueña* points out that in the work there is "a detectable progression, [a] development of character."

Baca's chief concern in *Immigrants* is regaining a sense of self, which is obscured by the prison system's ability to strip the individual of dignity and self-worth. While the collection is centered on lucid and sustained images and metaphors, the work is ultimately more strongly conditioned by visceral and passionate impulses than by poetry as formalistic craft or incidental pastime. The sense of urgency that emanates from Baca's struggle to release a passionate and desperate cry for recognition, above all else, lends a deeply moving and enduring quality to the collection.

Baca's efforts to reconstruct his own psyche and sense of identity immediately move him to reflect upon his connection to family and community. Present in *Immigrants* is Baca for the first time rekindling a connection to the collective meaning and past of his ancestors. His search for personal meaning emerges in *Immigrants* as an ever-widening series of concentric connections that lead him to an individual and collective examination of his incarceration. Each poem in the work to some degree answers the question "Who am I?" in the context of present and past circumstances.

Baca's second chapbook, *Swords of Darkness*, was edited by fellow Chicano poet Gary Soto. The poems were written during August and September 1977 and are about prison and about experiences—real or imagined—set in the outside world. Among these latter poems are vivid descriptions of a gaudy street atmosphere in which restless youths are caught in a surreal world of cruising, music, and weekend nightlife. The most inspired and intriguing poem of the collection is "Walking Down to Town and Back," in which the speaker walks along old and familiar rural roads that he remembers from his childhood. He recalls a visit he made with his father to the former home of an old widow. The incident, narrated in dreamlike fashion, includes the fantastic tale of how, after her husband's funeral, the old woman's small adobe house was beset by hoards of snakes and how she set fire to her adobe to rid herself of that plague, tossing gunpowder along with all her furniture and belongings into the fire. In the flames miraculously appeared an image of the Virgin Mary, which is held in reverence by all who come to know of it. The young man and his father visit the charred remains of the old woman's home, where they find people

kneeling and praying. As the speaker passes by, the people begin to cry out "miracle, miracle," for they have seen a light surrounding him. The impression left by the incident is indelible, and the poem concludes with the speaker years later revisiting the scene of the apparent miracle, only to find that it is now a hangout where people come to drink. Despite its open-ended conclusion, the poem is pivotal in Baca's poetic discourse in many ways. From a stylistic point of view, it signals his ability to create well-structured and engaging narrative poems that suspend the reader in narrative time. The poem also clearly places the protagonist in a kind of literal search for meaning among the ashes and debris of familial and communal identity, and it forges elements of oral tradition into the poet's world of visions and dreams. As evident in subsequent works, Baca uses each of these constructs to shape and give form to his wider poetic vision.

The title of Baca's second book, *What's Happening*, should be taken as a declarative statement to the reader that what lies ahead is a chronicle of the poet's most immediate experiences. The first five poems in the book return to Baca's continuing need to explore the psychological wounds left by his years in prison. The remainder of the collection centers on his experiences after having left prison.

The recovery of a sense of self, which Baca began with his first incursions into poetry, continues to infuse much of *What's Happening*. The collection in many ways figures as a bridge that explores Baca's transition back into society at large. Just as Baca, now several years after his release from prison, returns to the world he literally left as a juvenile, his poetry, too, begins to reestablish meaning with familiar places of his childhood and adolescence. Thus the second half of *What's Happening* begins to map out his search for identity and reintegration into a wider community. In the latter half of this collection Baca begins to inscribe several key concerns into his work, themes he will ultimately come to embrace fully in his life and in his poetry. Drawing upon his mestizo roots in New Mexico, he discovers his connection to the earth. He traces his search for love through unfulfilled relationships and the bitter pain of breakups. In other poems he evokes the sensuous and enticing spirit of the city at night that compels him to live vicariously. And, in one of Baca's purest lyrical poems, foreshadowing his own fatherhood, he evokes the magical world of children and registers his deep compassion and

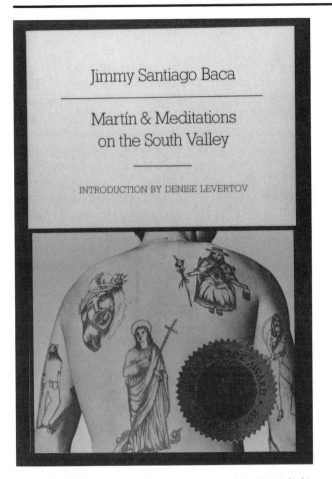

Jimmy Santiago Baca

Martín & Meditations
on the South Valley

INTRODUCTION BY DENISE LEVERTOV

Cover for Baca's 1987 collection of poems that chronicle his troubled early life, his subsequent happy marriage, and a fire that destroyed his home

tor, and laborer, and at other odd jobs, as he redirected his life through what was to be a sustained period of bittersweet events. During these years Baca fought and eventually overcame bouts of drug addiction and alcoholism. He would eventually view marriage and family as vital and central in providing meaning to his life. Indeed he attributes much of his success to the love and support of his wife, Beatrice, and his children.

After the birth of their first child, Jimmy and Beatrice moved to Albuquerque's South Valley, a rural, Chicano barrio where they decided to gut and rebuild a small adobe home that came to symbolize the aspirations of many long-held dreams and promises. Baca fully embraced his past and found a personal affinity with the predominantly Chicano community. *Poems Taken from My Yard*, published in 1986, chronicles in deeply moving poems the winter of the year that saw the birth of his first son and the rebuilding of his adobe home. These two acts of creation are paralleled by the poems in the collection, of which Baca writes, in "Poem XVII,"

> These are January poems—
> dollar down payments
> on an acre of sand dunes—
> . . . .
> What do they mean?
> a song of a man on the run,
> who uses each poem
> to break the shackles on his legs.

sensitivity toward them. In "I think of little people" he expresses his awe and inspiration as "This enchantment they tuck in twenty folds / like a special coin, laid in cloth."

The eight-year hiatus between the publication of *Immigrants* and that of *Martín and Meditations on the South Valley* in many ways reflects a long period of transition and uncertainty for Baca. These years were filled with restless, unresolved dilemmas and ongoing struggles in his personal life. Baca explains that, although he continued to publish minor works, he all but abandoned poetry and writing: "I was trying to figure out whether I was going to live in prison forever or whether I could live in this world. I wanted to go back to prison, 'cause I couldn't live in this world and I was bored and I couldn't deal with the world out here."

After having left prison, Baca spent some time in North Carolina before returning to New Mexico, where he then spent some years living in Albuquerque working as a night watchman, jani-

In the years that followed, Baca realized personal as well as artistic endeavors. His most critically acclaimed book, *Martín and Meditations on the South Valley*, was published in 1987, for example. But the late 1980s were also marred by a personal setback when the Baca family home was razed by fire. Consumed by the fire were ten years' worth of Baca's poems.

On the heels of the publication of *Poems Taken from My Yard*, Baca completed the manuscript for the long narrative poem *Martín*, decidedly his most autobiographical work. *Martín* was published along with a second grouping of poems titled *Meditations on the South Valley*. Together each half forms a complementary volume spanning several years of new work. Inspired by Baca's own experiences, the *Martín* narrative employs certain liberties in its recanting and recasting of Baca's own life story. He uses fictive names, adding or omitting events from his own life in an effort to distill the plot to those essential elements that reproduce a journey of one man's ascent from personal devastation and through the bitter searching that leads to an eventual triumph of the spirit.

The long narrative poem tells the story of the tribulations of Martín, a young Chicano. After his birth at Pinos Wells, a decaying ranching community, Martín is abandoned by his mother at a very early age. He lives first with his grandmother and then is placed in an orphanage, where he remains until he runs away at age ten. He is witness to the chaos and the hardening of the spirit that permeates the street life of the urban barrios of Sante Fe and Albuquerque. Through news relayed to him by relatives and friends, Martín learns of his mother's life and tragic death at the hands of her second husband and of his father's decay due to alcoholism. As Martín reaches manhood he leaves New Mexico to travel. Trauma and turmoil take their toll on his psyche: "I gave myself to the highway / Like a bellrope in the wind / searching for a hand."

Martín's disaffection leads to wandering through Arizona, the Texas Panhandle, the southeastern coast, the Midwest, and finally back to New Mexico. Fully three-quarters of the poem recreates and explains the cause of Martín's discontent and of his inner sense of reflection and desire to understand the shattered fragments of his broken life. The last part of the poem narrates Martín's final return to Albuquerque, the scene of earlier misfortunes and the obvious locus of his intense need to rebuild his life. The catalyst for change in Martín's life is Gabriela, the woman with whom he falls in love. Through Gabriela's love and the birth of their child, Martín salvages his humanity and finds purpose and a reason to live. The poem draws to a close enthusiastically as Martín works to refurbish an old adobe home on a half-acre lot in the South Valley that will house the dreams of his new family. Martín's search and quest for the validation of his spirit and its connectedness to "all living things" moves him, in the last verse of the poem, to vow never to abandon his son.

Although complementary to the *Martín* narrative, *Meditations on the South Valley* should also be viewed as a self-sustaining work framed by two events drawn from Baca's life: the destruction by fire of the family home and the raising of a second house, an act deeply imbued with a phoenixlike promise of rebirth from the ashes of past tragedies. Julián Olivares, in his article "Two Contemporary Chicano Verse Chronicles," views these events as having the metaphorical function

of marking the beginning of a new phase in Baca's poetry: "loosely structured around the loss of the family home and ten years of poetry, which is to be perceived as a mythic rite of passage or 'trial by fire.' "

The remaining poems in *Meditations* chronicle the time during which Martín's family is temporarily uprooted from the South Valley neighborhood and from the people they have come to know and love. Because of the fire, they are forced into the crowded and impersonal world of a suburban apartment complex for a while. The occasion is a time of reflection for Martín, who reaches back for the images of his neighbors and friends in the South Valley that will sustain his spirit in the sterile and anonymous surroundings: "To the South Valley / the white dove of my mind flies, / searching for news of life." Each poem in *Meditations* becomes a tribute and offering to the love and friendship that inspired Martín's return to the barrio. Present in the poems is the gallery of friends, neighbors, and acquaintances that populate the rich human landscape of Martín's South Valley. Baca paints with sharp and lucid details the *ancianos* (old folks), midwives, field hands, construction workers, "low riders," *cholos* (barrio men), longtime residents, village fools, and community activists, each of whom he weaves into a tapestry that reveals a people and a community living out the human saga of pain, joy, promise, and adversity.

With *Martín and Meditations on the South Valley*, Baca brings to closure that phase of his poetry that deals with loss, dejection, a searching for identity, and a sense of belonging. Baca deliberately chooses to omit any reference to a prison past for Martín and, in doing so, puts to rest the rage of some of his early poetry. Likewise absent are the self-destructive tendencies that typified Baca's earlier years of searching and wandering. In contrast, Martín's senses and aspirations are attuned to keeping the solemn pact he has made with life. The bond Martín has established with his community sustains itself through his period of alienation, and, as expected, *Meditations* ends with a return to the barrio, an act made easier since it includes the wisdom and inspiration Martín/Baca has found in his community.

Baca's 1989 book, *Black Mesa Poems*, can be seen as his ultimate and most complete recuperation and revindication of his barrio, of its Chicano, working-class ethos, and of the life that he has formed around his South Valley home. Baca has always acknowledged the tremendous signifi-

Jimmy Santiago Baca

Black Mesa Poems

Cover for Baca's 1989 book, which focuses on his family's second home and their involvement in the surrounding Chicano community

cance of his return to the South Valley: "the human being that I was found a total and wholesome and fulfilling relationship to the people of the barrio and now I had language. I was a language person and I listened to people and I looked at their lives and I saw how they suffered and how they loved, my gift to them was to use who I was, interpreting them on the page, and their gift to me was to love me and let me live next to them."

Black Mesa Poems is by far Baca's most ambitious work to date. It essentially becomes the final staging for a new phase of his poetry, as suggested by the theme of rededication to life and community with which *Martín and Meditations on the South Valley* ends. Viewed in the context of a poetic ascent toward self-definition that began with Baca's first chapbook, *Black Mesa Poems* represents the culmination of a long process of recovery and vindication through language and poetry.

Black Mesa Poems becomes in effect his manifesto of complete reintegration and strengthened sense of identity with the Chicano community and its geospiritual homeland that is the Southwest. As the work chronicles the acquisition of Baca's second home, a hundred-year-old adobe atop the ancient volcanic tablelands south of Albuquerque, it derives much of its mythic and archetypal significance from the ancestral presence of his mestizo forebears—Indian, Spanish, and Mexican—whose spirits still echo in the land and the traditions of New Mexico. Baca focuses on the vivid, detailed descriptions of people, geography, and events that surround his new home on Black Mesa. He explores such themes as reconciling his broken past, the sacredness of the earth (figured in Black Mesa), the courage and dignity he is witness to in the ordinary lives of his neighbors and friends, his abiding commitment to family and home, the birth of a second child, and an exploration of the historical confluence of cultures—Indian, Spanish, Mexican, and Anglo-American—that form the human landscape of the Southwest. The book is underpinned by Baca's vision of a man moving from violence to peace and from personal turmoil to spiritual harmony.

The collection encases Baca's most complex poetic vision of life, for he at once explodes the narrative and autobiographical elements of his other poetry. Thematically connected to the reconstruction of a second house, *Black Mesa* opens with a poem that describes how the poet and his family came upon and eventually were fortunate enough to acquire the adobe house atop Black Mesa. The significance of the poem conceptually is that Martín is no longer identified as the poetic speaker. This disappearance of the fictive persona Martín implicitly signals a dismantling of Baca's use of autobiographical narrative as poetic scaffolding upon which life is staged by example and depiction; what remains is a freestanding synthesis of his inner and outer realities. With *Black Mesa Poems*, poetic discourse and life merge, and poetry and personal circumstance in metaphorical relationship redeem not only the individual but his people and culture.

Baca's works have gained both acceptance and praise beginning with an early note by critic Juan Rodríguez (*Carta Abierta*, 1978): "The man's poetry is worth reading *más de una vez* [more than once]." Rodríguez's recommendation was followed by more generous estimations of Baca's talents in such noted journals as the *American Book Re-*

view, *Virginia Quarterly Review, Lamar Journal of the Humanities, Revista Chicano-Riqueña,* and others. Noted Chicano novelist Ron Arias, in a review of Baca's *Immigrants,* was one of the first to point out the powerful appeal of Baca's style and imagery by comparing it to the art of the jazz musician: "when he finds it [a melody] he takes it wherever it might lead": Arias observed that a mainstay in Baca's poetry is a dynamic quality that "continually surprises by squeezing meaning out of ordinary sights" (*American Book Review,* September-October 1981). The latter is most apparent in Baca's lyrical voice; Arias laments that the weakest parts of the book are the "essay pieces" in which Baca employs a literal style. Levertov's interest in Baca's early work rings prophetic in her afterword to *What's Happening*: "I look on Jimmy Santiago Baca as one of the most naturally gifted poets I've ever known. . . ." Most reviewers have been of one mind when considering his work as far beyond anything that might be labeled as jailhouse ranting and frustration; in the estimation of Joseph F. Vélez, Baca's work "is not poetry of prison, but poetry of life" (*Revista Chicano-Riqueña,* 1980).

Martín and Meditations on the South Valley represents a pinnacle in the progressive development of Baca's *ars poetica* and is to date the work that has drawn the greatest acclaim and review. The value of the book goes beyond the simple plot that tells the story of Martín/Baca's worst years and the realization of a personal quest; as with all inspired literature its value lies precisely in the manner in which the events are told—in the intensity of its language and in the transcendent, metaphorical significance of the events it depicts. Gary Soto, in a review for the *San Francisco Chronicle* (24 January 1988), wrote: "What makes the story succeed is its honesty, brutal honesty, as well as Baca's original imagery and the passion in his writing. Moreover, a history is being written, of a culture of poverty which except for a few poets like Phillip Levine, Thomas McGrath and the late James Wright, is absent in American poetry." As Levertov suggests in the book's introduction, Baca "writes with unconcealed passion: detachment is not a quality he cultivates." Critics and reviewers generally are in agreement regarding this aspect of Baca's work; their accolades resemble Liam Rector's. In the *Hudson Review* (Summer 1989) he noted that *Martín and Meditations on the South Valley* is "also a powerful orchestration and revision of narrative and lyrical admixture—both constructivist and expressionist in

its execution—with an utterly compelling dramatic form fueling the entire vivisection and the pilgrim's progress which makes it so much more than another 'collection' of poems. Baca's book is a page turner, almost a novel in verse. . . ."

The volume has also inspired debate and controversy. Olivares has suggested that the work is flawed by the facts that it is not the poem of epic stature that Baca seemingly intended to create, its publication reflects political opportunism on the part of a publisher intent on cashing in on a stereotyped, criminally prone minority experience, and Baca's writing depicts and promotes "a world of social misfits."

It is fair to say that by any measure *Martín* is not a poem of epic proportions that addresses an all-encompassing reality of the Southwest. What is clearly present is the story of a personal kind of redemption, but the redemptive act implies an interaction with the social forces that have shaped the individual. Any epic or definitive treatment of the Southwest as a geographical space that includes the confluence of many peoples and their histories may not be reducible to any one manuscript or any one voice. Taken as a new poetic agenda, Baca's suggestion "that the entire Southwest needed a long poem that could describe what has happened here in the last twenty years" makes ready sense if one considers that the evolution of his poetry in his last three collections does in fact begin the work of inscribing an epic, mythic, and archetypal significance to the confluence of the peoples and histories of the Southwest.

Those detractors who argue that Baca's work promotes the image of Chicano culture as a world of "social misfits" seem to have misread the work and to deny its intent by engaging in social typecasting that reduces the possibility of human potential to a predetermined and self-fulfilling prophecy of behavioral norms. As Baca registers the social world of his personal past, he is asking the reader, both Anglo-American and Chicano, to question his conditioned response, as Levertov suggests, by ascribing to the apparent social delinquency of Martín—the down-and-out wanderer—a complexity of impulse far beyond the surface reality that shapes his life: "Martín is a poet (and the reader—though not deliberately—is challenged: next time you see such a figure, remember that though his head may be filled only with quotidian banalities, and with crude and trivial wishes, it is also very possible that he is living an inner life at least as vivid as your own)."

At present Baca lives and writes at his Black Mesa farmhouse. He is at work on his first novel, "In the Way of the Sun," which he envisions as the first part of a trilogy on the peoples of the Southwest. His first play, *Los tres hijos de Julia*, was staged at the Los Angeles Theatre Center in 1991. Baca has recently completed a new collection of poems, titled "Healing Earthquake," which is forthcoming from New Directions Press, which has also published a retrospective of his poetry, *Immigrants in Our Own Land and Earlier Poems* (1990). He has been invited to write the screenplays for two upcoming movies and is producing a documentary about Hispanic culture that will be filmed in eight states. Between writing projects, Baca dedicates himself to sharing the responsibility of raising his two young sons, Antonio and Gabriel, and running the small family farm atop Black Mesa.

Interview:
John F. Crawford and Annie O. Eysturoy, "Jimmy Santiago Baca," in *This Is About Vision: Interviews with Southwestern Writers*, edited by Crawford, Eysturoy, and William Balassi (Albuquerque: University of New Mexico Press, 1990), pp. 180-193.

References:
Beth Ann Krier, "Baca: A Poet Emerges From Prison of His Past," *Los Angeles Times*, 15 February 1989, pp. V5-V7;

Denise Levertov, Afterword to Baca's *What's Happening* (Willimantic, Conn.: Curbstone, 1982);

Levertov, Introduction to Baca's *Martín and Meditations on the South Valley* (New York: New Directions, 1987), pp. xiii-xviii;

Julián Olivares, "Two Contemporary Chicano Verse Chronicles," *Americas Review*, 16 (Fall-Winter 1988): 214-231;

Liam Rector, "The Documentary of What Is," *Hudson Review*, 41 (Summer 1989): 393-400.

Gregg Barrios

(31 October 1945 -   )

Nuria Bustamante
Los Angeles Harbor College

BOOK: *Puro rollo (A colores)* (Los Angeles: Posada, 1982).

PLAY PRODUCTION: *Dale Gas Cristal*, Albuquerque, Floricanto IV Festival, 6 August 1977.

Gregg Barrios's many talents and wide range of interests have found expression in the novel, the short story, poetry, the critical essay, and journalism, this last constituting the bulk of his writing. However, it is as a poet that he assumes the most importance, by giving voice to the Chicano community spirit in simple, unrhymed, everyday language that captures the humor, mood, and tempo of life in the barrio. Characteristic of Barrios is the re-creation of situations with images and characters that move within a real-life, Chicano sociocultural context. Throughout Barrios's work the common person is given larger-than-life dimensions, and the poems are often an exaltation of life and of human values.

Born in Victoria, Texas, on Halloween 1945, Barrios is the son of a Mexican photographer, Gregorio Barrios, Sr., and Eva Falcón, a Texan. The young Gregg Barrios's interests in the movies and rock-and-roll music were awakened when he and his brother were allowed to attend, free of charge and as often as they wished, the movie house at which their father moonlighted by working as a projectionist. A voracious reader since his early years, Barrios recalls that he liked contemporary stories containing popular themes. At thirteen he started to write novels (unpublished) and some poetry, and also began to sharpen his critical ability by writing book reviews for the boys' school he attended. After he graduated from high school, at a time when discrimination against Chicanos in Texas was so bad that it was hard to get hired even as a janitor or store clerk, the editor of the *Victoria Advocate*, the local newspaper, told Barrios that they were looking for a book reviewer and said, "We think you can do it." He took the job.

Gregg Barrios in Crystal City, Texas, where he moved in 1970 (photograph by Isela Vega)

In the 1960s, while working as a medical corpsman in the U.S. Air Force for three years, Barrios entered the University of Texas at Austin, where he majored in English and received a B.A. in 1968. While still a student there he regularly contributed feature and literary articles to the local newspapers and magazines, such as *Sight & Sound*, *Village Boys*, and *Film Quarterly*. With this last one, and the experimental films called "underground movies," in 1966 he initiated his association with the New York circle of writers and the famed Andy Warhol factory.

The Chicano movement of the mid 1960s awakened Barrios's political conscience and deeply involved him from 1968 through 1976. In 1970 he accepted a teaching position and moved to Crystal City, Texas, the birthplace of the Chicano movement and, he declares, of his own spiritual birth. He became editor of the newspaper *La Verdad*; staged several politically oriented plays, including his *Dale Gas Cristal* (Give It Gas, Cristal, 1977); and wrote several poems with political content. His later disillusionment with the betrayal of Chicano hopes and ideals by the leaders of the movement prompted the writing of more poems and the publishing of *Puro rollo (A colores)* (Much Ado About Nothing [in Color]) in 1982.

Puro rollo is a collection of twenty-seven poems dedicated to *la plebe* (the people). The work is divided into three parts, each called a *rollo*, or reel (of movie film). Each *rollo* consists of nine poems and is introduced with an epigraph, respectively, by César Chávez, José Martí, and Rudy Martínez. In general the poems in the three *rollos* follow a progressive change of tone and mood that goes from optimism and hopefulness in "Rollo 1," moves through disillusion and even fatalism in "Rollo 2," and ends in a calm, reflective mood in "Rollo 3."

The first poem in "Rollo 1," titled "The Merry-Go-Round," sets the euphoric mood:

Flashing mirrors capture the world
in hi/speed and s-l-o-w m-o-t-i-o-n
a spherical view of the entire world
much like our poetry full of pride and joy
in the knowledge that this world is ours. . . .

It is in these mirrors that one sees reflected and united by that reflection the kaleidoscopic images of the Chicano community swirling around, alive in joy, sorrow, love, and hatred, always in pursuit of dreams and aspirations. The ups and downs are all part of living, and Barrios extends an invitation to *la plebe* to participate fully in life's feast:

as we go through the world riding on the horses
trying to catch that magic ring of fortune . . .
we raise our voice to sing and shout out loud
proud for having partaken and enjoyed
this carnival of life. Live it fully,
my people, live it!

Permeated with a different kind of optimism at a time when achieving common political goals seemed deceivingly simple, Barrios's "Advertisement for Chicano Unity" formulates a behavioral code:

Forget envy. We are nothing without each other.
Respect everyone. Even the least of us has need for
pride.
. . . .
Past injustices cannot be corrected retroactively. To
fail
to see this divides our goals permanently. Don't
look back.
Look forward.
. . . .
As long as our culture lives, we will continue to survive.

Even a poem injected with as heavy a dose of images of desolation and hopelessness as "La mirada mojada: SPRAY*PRAY*PAINT*-AINT (The Wet Look)," affirms in the end the prevailing strength of the people:

The faces are the same: chavos cafeses chamacas
chicanas
roaming this ancient Aztlán no longer the proud
owners
but fugitives from justice nowhere to run nowhere
to hide
the fact that there are thousands of you without a
chance
dropout fallout jumpout cryout against the slow genocide
that has been planned to make you completely obsolete.

(The faces are the same: brown boys Chicano
girls)[. . . .]

And then, in the midst of this dejection, a voice full of determination extols the endurance of "La raza" (the people), who keep an unfailing spirit in the struggle against cultural annihilation:

Yet still you persist: mujeres morenas machos mestizos
tratando de darle vida a la raza con colores no
dolores
gritar rezar llorar cantar contra la muerte de la
cultura
antigua que todavía nos dice que todo se puede
aguantar.

(Yet still you persist: brown women, mestizo men
trying to give life to the race with color not sorrows
to scream to pray to cry to sing against the death of
the ancient culture
that still tells us that everything is endurable.)

The images projected on the "mirrors" of the poems in "Rollo 2" are varied, but the predominant themes are those born of disillusionment experienced when hopes for the success of the Chicano movement were dashed. The poem that best represents this prevalent mood is "Don't it Make Your Brown Eyes Blue." The poem has eight subdivisions, each addressing a different problem that contributed to leadership corruption and the collapse of values for which the Chicano movement stood:

> "Ya se acabó" afirman los pesimistas
> "Fue de repente" confían los optimistas
> comenzaron unidos, acabaron divididos . . .
> hermanos comenzaron, enemigos acabaron.
>
> ("It's over," affirm the pessimists
> "It happened suddenly," remark the optimists
> They began united and ended divided . . .
> Started as brothers, ended as enemies.)

The indifference and neglect Chicano heroes and soldiers met on their return from Vietnam contributed to the general feeling of depression and pessimism. Barrios captures aptly the prevalent mood and synthesizes the tragedy of thousands in his poem "Chale Guerra":

> Chale Guerra de Corpus Christi came home
> with his body broken and crippled and hanging
>   from his neck
> he had an AirCom medal, a bronze star, a foreign
>   service
> medal, and a broken purple heart. What else?
> Oh, a broken back, a silver plated brace,
> a nervous tic, and a stainless wheel chair to race[.]

The content in the poems of "Rollo 3" is varied, but the inclination to reflect upon the multiple situations and predicaments of the human experience is apparent in most. In "Nocaut" (Knockout)—the longest poem, organized in nine sections significantly called "rounds" because it is dedicated to the Texan boxer Mike "Ciclón" (Cyclone) Ayala—the mood wavers between dreams of success and defeatism. Nevertheless, in the midst of all these turbulent emotions, which reflect the struggle to overcome drugs, a calm, resigned voice is heard in "Round 3": "And yet you must accept your FATE / that's the least any of us can do. . . ." At the end of "Round 9" the poem concludes by quoting Ayala's own words: "To be a great champion you have to accept things / the way they are."

However, the poem by Barrios that best expresses a reflective attitude is "I Am an Americano, Too," the last poem in the collection. He describes himself as the poet of *la plebe*, the people's spokesman, who, by giving voice to his own hopes and aspirations, expresses also the hopes and aspirations of the Chicano people striving toward self-fulfillment and unity:

> I am a poet of la plebe
> I reflect what I know I am
> aware of what I am not yet
> I find hope and pride in all
> that I know I can become
> I am an Americano, too.
> . . . .
> If no longer I hold rancor
> against the prejudiced past
> it doesn't mean I have forgotten
> rather strive toward that unity
> which signals a brave new world
> I am an Americano, too.

Barrios's love and appreciation for music started early in life, when he wrote record reviews for his high school, the Catholic Boys' School in Victoria, Texas, evaluated new songs and music, and made predictions as to which ones would be hits or win awards. This lifelong interest is obvious in the poems of this collection in that they contain frequent allusions and references to rock music and popular songs. While most of the content in the poems in *Puro rollo* deals with social protest related to Chicano issues, racial discrimination, social injustice, alienation, and cultural genocide, a strong underlying theme protests the lack of representation of Mexican-American music within the cultural mosaic in this country. Among Chicano writers, Barrios is practically alone in raising his voice against what he calls a "genocide of sound," and he strongly voices his protest in the poem entitled "Del mero corazón" (From the Bottom of My Heart):

> Our music is culture
> and our culture has made
> music, music, música
> for centuries yet as
> I watched thirty years
> of American Bandstand
> I somehow felt they had
> whitewashed us out of
> existence—we had been
> eliminated and exterminated
> a genocide of sound

I wanted to yell
one of those blood-curdling shouts
Jorge Negrete could deliver
in the movies I watched. . . .

There are references to popular songs or to music being played in the background in the poems. It is as if the tunes from the merry-go-round carousel kept blasting out throughout the three *rollos*, insistently reminding the reader that songs and music are part of the spiritual expression of a people, mark the tempo of barrio life, and cannot be dissociated from it:

Sentados en la cantina . . .
allí en San Anto
oyendo las rolas rancheras . . .

(Seated at the bar
there in San Anto[nio]
listening to the jukebox . . .)
. . . .
As we were cruising
in the '78 silver T-Bird, music was blaring out
    loud. . . .

Because Barrios considers music to be a valuable part of culture, the importance of safeguarding it from obliteration by the dominant culture cannot be overly stressed, and therefore he wants the reader to perceive the theme of certain poems against particular musical backgrounds, thus making music and songs part of the poetic structure. To achieve this he has set a few poems to music, so to speak, by alternating the poem's stanzas with verses of popular songs in such a way that through juxtaposition the themes of song and poem intertwine. In this manner, the song informs the poem, enriches its meaning, and adds a new dimension to it. Such is the case in "Salibacalifas" (Sally Was Going To California), "I Fought the Law," and "Nocaut," this last one being a poem in which most of the nine rounds are headed by quotations of popular song verses. In "I Fought the Law" the song verses that head the poem and alternate with the theme are set off by quotation marks and are written in italics.

Ever aware of changes and events in the world of art and in current affairs, Barrios makes his work reflect his wide range of interests, although most of the poems in *Puro rollo* deal with the theme of social protest as related to Chicano issues. In these poems the themes with political content predominate, and one poem, "Chicano Lament," crystallizes the main questions and preoccupations, as well as the concerns of *la plebe*. According to Barrios, during the early years of the Chicano movement, the verses of "Chicano Lament" were considered poetic and people fell in love with them, adopted their political contents, and, in Barrios's words, "revolutionaries were moved by great emotions of love":

If peace is now
And love is all around
When will discrimination end?

If hope is here
And full employment near
When will barrio poverty end?
. . . .
If white is right
And black is beautiful
When can brown begin?

This pervasive preoccupation with the Chicano plight expressed through diverse real-life situations, depicted in the language and imagery drawn from the Chicano experience, prompted favorable comments from two important critics. First, Tomás Rivera, in his introduction to *Puro rollo*, remarks that in this work Barrios achieves "the establishment of community" by conveying that, among Chicanos in general, there is a sense of unity of purpose, a strong bond created in the sharing of values and common aspirations. Rivera goes on to say that "in this collection . . . I find the Chicano community conversing in its own tongue. I find the Chicano community as judge-penitent, wrestling with the set of values that attempt to place the kindred group's set of values over those of the individual." He further calls *Puro rollo* a "spiritual history" of the Chicano community. Second, Luis Leal, in his review of *Puro rollo* points favorably at the human, social, and dramatic content of the poems, and remarks that, by re-creating daily, ordinary situations through language and particularly "by the use of images that can be considered typical of the literature of the border," Barrios achieves "the rescuing of the social life and culture of the Chicano community" (*La Opinión*, 12 December 1982).

Gregg Barrios's creative talents are still in the developmental stage. Some of his potential has been realized through the various genres, particularly the essay and poetry. He is currently working on several projects, such as a novel and plays, having completed "Birthmark," a second collection of poems written as a counterpart to *Puro rollo*. Although relatively unacknowledged by critics, his importance rests on the various mediums he uses to give voice to the aspirations of the Chicano community. Barrios forms part of a constellation of authors who have quietly but assertively contributed to putting Chicano literature on the American literary map.

Reference:
Tomás Rivera, Introduction to Barrios's *Puro rollo (A colores)* (Los Angeles: Posada, 1982).

Aristeo Brito
(20 October 1942 -   )

Dina Gutiérrez-Castillo
Santa Barbara City College

BOOKS: *Cuentos i poemas* (Washington, D.C.: Fomento Literario, 1974);
El diablo en Texas (Tucson, Ariz.: Editorial Peregrinos, 1976); republished as *The Devil in Texas / El diablo en Texas*, bilingual edition, translated by David William Foster (Tempe, Ariz.: Bilingual Review, 1990).

SELECTED PERIODICAL PUBLICATIONS—
UNCOLLECTED: "Sombra de cuerpo," *Mester*, 4 (November 1973): 6;
"El lenguaje tropológico en *Peregrinos de Aztlán*," *Luz*, 1 (May 1975): 42-43.

Aristeo Brito's work, written mostly in Spanish, exemplifies experimental innovation in the novel at the height of the Chicano Renaissance. As a committed writer his creativity goes beyond simply developing narrative plots to unveil the struggle toward consciousness. Brito's poetic and narrative style—baroque texture, linguistic detail, and sophisticated dialogue—are methods by which he communicates the various realities of a segmented society.

Brito's ancestors, originally from Chihuahua, Mexico, settled in the United States during the Mexican revolution of 1910. Years later the family sought refuge in Ojinaga, in the state of Chihuahua, when Brito's father defied the draft during World War II. On 20 October 1942 Aristeo Brito was born as the family was entering Mexican territory, near the Ojinaga train station. Nevertheless, he considers himself a native of Presidio, Texas, where he lived until he was eighteen

Aristeo Brito (photograph by D. Gutiérrez-Castillo)

years old and where his most influential childhood memories and recollections originated. In a personal interview with Salvador Rodríguez del

Pino, Brito has briefly described life in this border town: "It is a very small and poor community. . . . I was raised among farmworkers and my father was a sharecropper. Presidio is also known as one of the hottest spots in the nation. It is also like a hole . . . a Devil's hole."

Like his father before him, Brito knows farm work from firsthand experience. He labored in the fields while still in high school. After graduation he sought to break away from the repetitiveness of life in Presidio by attending Sul Ross State University in Alpine, Texas, where he received his B.A. in English in 1965. He continued his education by enrolling in the M.A. program at the University of Arizona in Tucson, and eventually obtained his Ph.D. in Spanish literature from the same institution in 1978. Since 1970 he has been teaching Spanish and Chicano literature at Pima Community College in Tucson. Brito, his wife Monica, and their four children have made Tucson their permanent home.

While a student, Brito claims to have been most impressed by the contemporary Latin-American novelists, especially the Guatemalan Miguel Angel Asturias; the Colombians José Eustacio Rivera and Gabriel García Márquez; the Venezuelan Rómulo Gallegos Freire; the Chilean Eduardo Barrios; and the Mexican writers Mariano Azuela, Juan Rulfo, and Carlos Fuentes.

Brito's own contribution to Chicano letters is significant. He has been credited by scholars as one of the first writers to make Chicano literature known in the United States, Mexico, and Europe. Brito and his close friend Miguel Méndez were also the first writers to identify openly their creations as "literatura chicana." In addition, during his tenure as a delegate to the Modern Language Association in 1971 he introduced Chicano literature to academia; consequently, Chicano literature received recognition and acceptance when it was made a permanent section of that renowned organization.

Recently he worked closely with David William Foster, who translated Brito's novel *El diablo en Texas* (1976) as *The Devil in Texas* (1990). This bilingual edition was awarded the Western States Arts Federation prize for fiction, giving this novel and its author recognition previously lacking due to the low distribution of the Spanish edition.

A friendly and unassuming individual, Brito is full of anecdotes about his past. But beyond his seemingly nonchalant attitude, he harbors a genuine preoccupation with the human psyche. This is clearly evident in his work. His characters are, most often, coping with identity problems caused by environments fraught with economic oppression, racism, and cultural alienation. Brito found this central theme to be appropriate for the type of experience he wished to present in his narrative, as well as in his poetry.

For example, the thematic concerns in his collection, titled *Cuentos i poemas* (Short Stories and Poems, 1974), range from poetics, religiosity, love, cultural identity, "Chicanismo," and death viewed from an existentialist perspective. Variety reigns in Brito's approach as well as in his themes. The collection comprises eight short stories written in both Spanish and English and seventeen poems in free verse, six of them reproduced solely in English. Brito himself admits that his first book is an "exercise in creative writing," which he began soon after reading the classic Mexican writers in the summer of 1970. Yet his creativity is not limited to Mexican or Chicano themes. He succeeds in going past national and racial distinctions by exposing human foibles in a hostile world. This is amply seen in three of the best-crafted stories in Brito's collection: "Pedro el tragaplumas" (Pedro the Feather Swallower), "Recuerdo" (Remembrance), and "La Víspera" (The Eve)—included also in English with a slightly altered title, "The Arrival." Critics have recognized Brito's obvious attempt to identify himself as a modern writer by employing in his short stories stream of consciousness, interior monologue, psychological analysis, fragmented narrations, vivid dialogue, language experimentation, and urban thematics. All are intertwined effectively to unveil the complexity of his characters.

In his poetry Brito again focuses on universal human concerns. "In Rain" demonstrates his preoccupation with the negative aspects of a mechanistic world. A compelling view of present and future human suffering resulting from acid rain, this poem depicts the effects of modern technology on humanity and the environment. Love is another constant in Brito's poetry. Though at times filled with overly crafted images in poems such as "Encuentro" (Encounter), these compositions vary in the treatment of the subject. They range from unattainable love ("Ideal") to descriptions of moments of blissful love ("Conjugating to Be" and "Consummation"). It is perhaps in "Verso romántico" (Romantic Verse) where the theme of eternal love is best handled. Reminiscent of the Spanish baroque *poetas conceptistas* (conceptual poets), Brito asserts that everlasting love will only be attained once all material matter is destroyed, leaving nothing of that which is ephemeral; love must transcend the physical and become spiritual.

While del Pino has recognized religiosity and the Chicano identity as the prevailing themes in Brito's poetry, it is obvious that other topics are equally important. Brito's concern with pressing social issues and internal turmoil gives rise to poems such as "Secreto" (Secret) and "Insomnio" (Insomnia). In them the poetic voice rejects a conforming, calm Christian God and the Judeo-Christian traditions as elements which keep Chicanos passive. Instead the poet embraces a mysticism rooted in Mexican Indian mythology. In "Insomnio," for instance, the poet invokes Tlaloc, the Toltec rain god, to ask for relief from the anguish his people are undergoing. His "social mysticism," as del Pino has termed Brito's vision of commitment, exposes the deprivation resulting from injustices perpetuated by the predominant society and the established mechanism of power.

Brito's reference to historical Mexican heroes and Indian legendary figures is also a point of departure for his definition of Chicanismo. The poet identifies himself with nonpassive entities which hold historical and cultural ties for all Mexicans in the United States. In "A Moctezuma" (To Montezuma), Brito rejects all that defines him as a child of a dehumanizing and alienating society. He asserts his origin proudly, almost in a romanticized manner, in an attempt to rescue Chicanos from anomie. He establishes the mestizo component of his culture as a positive quality. In effect the names evoked become symbols to guard against cultural loss and to regain human dignity.

Cuentos i poemas has received little critical attention due mainly to its limited availability. It soon went out of print, and Brito has no immediate plans to issue a second edition. Thus far the only review of the anthology is one by Jorge Febles. In general Febles finds Brito's short stories excessive in figurative speech and adjectives, which mar the stories' unity of impression and totality of effect. Nonetheless, the critic admires Brito's poetic ability, especially when he mixes images to produce the sudden tonal changes which give the poems their uniqueness and modernity.

In *El diablo en Texas*, Brito continues the thematic vein introduced in *Cuentos i poemas*. In it he traces the history of a small border town, Presidio-Ojinaga, from both sides of the Rio Grande.

Once a single entity, the community was divided in 1848 when the Rio Grande was declared the official political border between Mexico and the United States. Employing this historical event as the point of departure for the novel, Brito uncovers the backlash effects it had on the inhabitants. He makes use of two universal themes, man versus man and man versus nature, to fictionalize and chronicle the Anglos' systematic acquisition of Mexican-owned land and the population's constant struggle for survival in a threatening and inhospitable environment.

Very similar to the real Presidio—named for a Spanish fort built there in 1683—Brito's mythical town is often referred to as a living hell due to its high temperature all year around: "Yo vengo de un pueblito llamado Presidio. Allá en los más remotos confines de la tierra surge seco y baldío" (I come from a small town called Presidio. It rises up dry and barren there, in the farthest corner of the earth). This small town is nestled in the valley surrounded by cotton plantations: a harsh natural prison for the victimized and now landless population serving the new settlers. As time passes, each generation becomes more and more alienated. The prevailing pessimistic tone of the novel finally comes to an end when a young man—possibly an alter ego for the author—having left a few years earlier, returns to trace his origins and to write Presidio's history in an attempt to end the immutable state of despair of the town's inhabitants.

El diablo en Texas is divided into an introduction and three sections: "Presidio 1883," "Presidio 1942," and a brief third part, "Presidio 1970." The introduction as well as the last part, which functions as an epilogue, provides the novel with overall structural unity. In the introduction, Brito sets the narrative mood and touches upon the thematic concerns developed later, a technique Marvin A. Lewis recognizes as akin to that employed by the Latin-American experimentalists called the New Novelists.

The first part, "Presidio 1883," focuses on the beginning of the conflict between Anglos and the Mexican population. Through a series of fragmented narrations which defy unity of space and time, Brito depicts Presidio's social disintegration and the selfishness of an Anglo landowner, symbolically named Ben Lynch, who manipulated his way into gaining control of the town. Lynch marries the daughter of the Mexican lawyer-journalist Francisco Uranga, who outspokenly campaigns against his abuses. Mysteriously one of

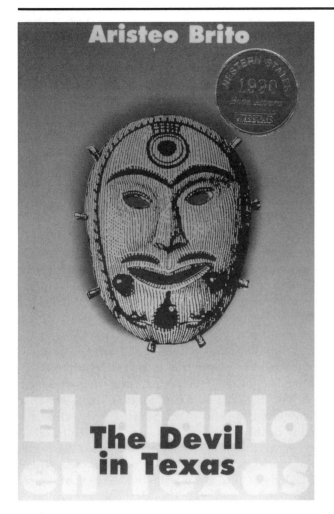

Cover for the bilingual edition of Brito's novel, which relates the disintegration of a border town

the lawyer's sons is shot and killed crossing the river, but another survives to become a social bandit.

In *Latin American Literary Review* (Spring-Summer 1977), Ernestina Eger correctly points out that "Presidio 1883" shows the years of conflict and wrongs that anticipate the twentieth century's stratified society. Indeed, the various points of view emitted by the juxtaposition of thoughts, dramatic dialogues, and straightforward narrations make it possible for Brito to show the characters' confused state of being and allude to Presidio's progressive degradation and loss of economic power. This is best exemplified when a man tricks his mother into signing over her land to Lynch in order to profit from the transaction, only to become one more of Lynch's workers.

Slowly, the people of Presidio succumb to a state of apathy and stagnation as they render

themselves helpless before a powerful man. Those brave enough to oppose him are killed in the old fort during a social gathering sponsored by Lynch. Their voices are often heard in the fort, however, recounting their losses and shouting ironic cheers to "Don Benito" (Ben Lynch). In essence, the fort becomes a metaphor for the prisonlike town while the wondering souls are mere extensions of the phantasmagoric beings that populate Presidio. Thus their anguish is emphasized with irony and pathos. They are suspended in time, trapped in an eternal and futile struggle. This section ends with the immigration of the Brito family—presumably the author's—into the United States shortly after the outbreak of the Mexican revolution in 1910.

"Presidio 1942" is peopled by a mixture of submissive, dispossessed agricultural laborers and young pachucos, or zoot-suiters, attempting to survive the effects of World War II and the constant abuses of the border patrol. Brito's ability as a writer is best demonstrated in this section as he goes behind the character types and examines the emotional frustrations and aggressions which motivate the deprived individual. Though the inhabitants now lack the proud defiance of their ancestors, they nevertheless reaffirm their existence through different ways ranging from their unique language to the manifestation of an intense and mocking black humor, a sign that their human dignity has not been totally suppressed.

Amid these conditions, a child is about to be born. The parents are José and Marcela Uranga, relatives of the rebellious lawyer-journalist Francisco Uranga. Uranga's sense of justice is passed on, as is evident by the fetus's awareness of a hundred years of indignant history. Brito presents this aspect of the story through original and imaginative means, steering away from realism and penetrating the realm of the fantastic, with echoes of Gabriel García Márquez's *Cien años de soledad* (1967; translated as *One Hundred Years of Solitude*, 1970). As the fetus addresses the host mother, he recognizes his affiliation with the past: "Apenas hoy me doy cuenta que yo me extiendo como un hilito muy fino hasta muy atrás, desde antes que tú nacieras" (I barely realized today that I've stretched myself out like a very fine thread that goes way back; I was with you in your veins since your childhood). This section comes to an end when Marcela dies giving birth while crossing the storm-lashed river to be with her husband in Ojinaga. Ironically, the child is born *a medio río* (at the middle of the river), which augurs a rootless existence and a future filled with uncertainty.

In the last section, "Presidio 1970," Brito shows astonishing insight and compassion in his portrayal of Presidio's old and new generation. A capacity for condensation is also made clear in this short confessional where the narrator (Marcela's son), who has returned to Presidio-Ojinaga to attend his father's funeral, avows his decision to remain and undertake his inherited mission. As Brito focuses on the history and antecedents of the child, he weaves poetically the memories and aspirations handed down from one generation to the next. Through a mixture of interior monologues, flashbacks, and dialogues, the reader learns that after the father was imprisoned for defying the draft, the son grew up without parents and eventually became disillusioned with the lack of progress in Presidio.

Like a messiah, and following the footsteps of Don Francisco, Marcela's son is determined to dispel the townspeople's passive abandonment to fate. He takes it upon himself to regenerate a collective consciousness so that individuals can liberate themselves. As the son concludes his monologue, he expresses a strong desire for action: "Sí, habrá que contar, pero no con sufrimiento y con perdón. Habrá que encender la llama, la que murió con el tiempo" (Yes, we'll have to tell them, but not with suffering and with pardon. A flame has got to be lighted, the one that died with time). The novel ends with a note of hope and potential for action. The narrator of Presidio's past then becomes the protagonist of the future. True to his ideas of Chicanismo, Brito implies that self-determination comes from collective awareness and ethnic consciousness.

As the title of the novel indicates, *El diablo en Texas* is the anatomy of the spiritual degradation of an entire collectivity instigated by the devil. Throughout the novel, recurring narrative techniques and leitmotivs establish the devil as the predominant force which turns the inhabitants of Presidio-Ojinaga into "souls of torment." His presence is made clear from the opening paragraph when he appears as a *víbora* (viper) wrapped around the cross at the top of the mountain, maintaining vigilance over the town and delighted by their suffering. Studies by critics have focused on the devil, noting his presence in practically every scene as he transforms himself into an array of objects which include natural and unnatural elements, animals and humans. According to Annie O. Eysturoy, the initial image of the viper

reveals the symbolic quality of and the mythical struggle between good and evil embodied in the novel; it also sets the stage on which the history of the oppressed will be played. Justo Alarcón observes also that in the symbol of the devil the narrative consciousness has fused all the forces of oppression and fear with an imaginative mixture of folk Catholicism and politically conscious fantasy. Eger concludes that through the devil, "the historical conflicts between many individuals merge into a single mythical struggle."

Critics Charles M. Tatum in *World Literature Today* (Autumn 1977) and Jorge Febles in *Revisto Chicano-Riqueña* (Autumn 1977) call attention to an apparent lack of structure and unity in *El diablo en Texas*. Nonetheless, Tatum concedes that Brito is a good storyteller who expertly synthesizes several generations of human suffering. Febles suggests, however, that Brito's narrative technique is not fully convincing at times. Febles insists that the fetus's narrative accounts are not believable, not because the author violates the rules of verisimilitude, but because the language employed fluctuates between infantile ingenuity and dialectical complexity. Febles recognizes a close affinity to the late Mexican writer Juan Rulfo in *El diablo en Texas*, especially in the narrative tone and the descriptions of the atmosphere. When asked about this, Brito admitted Rulfo's influence but points out that the desolate atmosphere brought about by descriptions of a barren and hot environment—coupled with detailed accounts of isolation and death, and death within life—are also stylistic resources he found in the works of the Spanish playwright Federico García Lorca.

Form and atmosphere are also the elements in Brito's work most strongly coincident with Rulfo's *Pedro Páramo* (1955; translated, 1959). Eger believes Brito's decision to follow Rulfo's techniques have made it possible for *El diablo en Texas* to incorporate the Mexican artistic traditions into Chicano literature. Moreover, Eger sees in *El diablo en Texas* artistic growth which successfully incorporates the multigenerational historical panorama, initiated by Richard Vásquez's *Chicano* (1970), and folk-based fantasy to transform history into myth. The achievement by Brito, she states, has been to combine these elements in a coherent whole, with delicate strength and but a fourth of the size of Vásquez's novel.

Marvin A. Lewis focuses on Brito's skillful portrayal of a collective experience. The characters, he affirms, are represented as mere blurbs of humanity. Individuals are not that important, but their collective contributions add to the novel's intent to show the spiritual and historical stasis of Chicanos. The use of popular language and the portrayal of the pachucos, Lewis concludes, are good examples of how Brito accomplishes accurate mental attitudes and believable characters. Del Pino agrees with Lewis. He further observes that Brito's manipulation of the language is on a level with that of Miguel Méndez and Alejandro Morales. *El diablo en Texas*, however, is the first Chicano novel to explore the use of different levels of Spanish and English: Mexican Spanish, Chicano Texan dialect, Texas English, and a mixture of all these. According to del Pino, Brito possesses "an expertise that reflects the experience of a Chicano *raconteur* thoroughly familiar with the Anglo and Chicano cultural systems."

In *El diablo en Texas* Brito succeeds in blending together his creativity and his social commitment, an accomplishment which also allows him to express a universal message. His commitment notwithstanding, in this novel he attains maturity and depth of style by incorporating expressive quality, thematic force, and a symbolic message. At the same time he has avidly inserted the Chicano experience within the Mexican, the Latin-American, and the Spanish literary traditions. Rightly so, *El diablo en Texas* has been cited as one of the significant works from the peak of the renaissance of Chicano letters during the 1970s.

When considering Brito's entire body of work, we find two constants: artistic exploration and social commitment. His is a labor which explores freely, yet consciously denounces unjust circumstances, especially in reference to Chicanos. A by-product of the militant 1960s and 1970s, Brito's work may now seem overly political; nevertheless, his treatment of common universal themes allows his work to transcend time and space. Though his writing productivity has decreased since 1974, judging from the lack of publications, his sole novel is gaining more and more critical recognition as time passes, especially after the English-Spanish edition was published, reassuring Aristeo Brito an important place in Chicano literature.

Interview:

Salvador Rodríguez del Pino, "Interview with Aristeo Brito," *Encuentro*, Videotape no. 4 (Santa Barbara: Center for Chicano Studies, University of California, 1977);

References:

Justo Alarcón, "La metamorfosis del diablo en *El diablo en Texas*," *Colores*, 5, nos. 1-2 (1980): 30-44;

Pepe Barrón, Introduction to Brito's *Cuentos i poemas* (Washington, D.C.: Fomento Literario, 1974), pp. iii-iv;

Annie O. Eysturoy, "*El diablo en Texas*: Una historia de arquetipos y símbolos," *Comunidad* (supplement to *La Opinión*), 12 July 1987: 6-7;

Marvin A. Lewis, "El diablo en Texas: Structure and Meaning," in *Contemporary Chicano Fiction: A Critical Survey*, edited by Vernon E. Lattin (Binghamton, N.Y.: Bilingual Press / Editorial Bilingüe, 1986);

Juan Rodríguez, Comments on *El diablo en Texas*, *Carta Abierta*, no. 5 (October 1976): iv;

Salvador Rodríguez del Pino, "Lo mexicano en la novela chicana; un ejemplo: *El diablo en Texas* de Aristeo Brito," in *The Identification and Analysis of Chicano Literature*, edited by Francisco Jiménez (New York: Bilingual Press/Editorial Bilingüe, 1979), pp. 365-373;

Rodríguez del Pino, *La novela chicana escrita en español: Cinco autores comprometidos* (Ypsilanti, Mich.: Bilingual Press/Editorial Bilingüe, 1982).

Manuel Cabeza de Baca
(1853 - 1915)

Ramón Sánchez
University of Washington, Bothell

BOOK: *Historia de Vicente Silva, sus cuarenta bandidos, sus crimenes y retribuciones* (Las Vegas, N.Mex.: Voz del Pueblo, 1896); corrected and augmented by Francisco L. López (Las Vegas, N.Mex.: Spanish-American Publishing, 190-?); translated by Lane Kauffmann as *Vicente Silva & His 40 Bandits* (Washington, D.C.: McLean, 1947).

Manuel Cabeza de Baca's regional, historical narrative, *Historia de Vicente Silva* (1896), came into existence in the context of late-nineteenth-century land grabbing in northern New Mexico (the loss of communal land holdings that were turned into private property by political bosses). This environment of struggle gave rise to the violence of the Gorras Blancas (White Caps), masked riders who cut fences, burned crops and buildings, tore up railroad tracks, and terrorized mainly wealthy Hispanics who were benefiting from the breakup of communal land. These masked raiders were supported by many townspeople, and local juries would not convict fence cutters. Cabeza de Baca, in his narrative, focuses on a single historical theme: that the Hispanic outlaws betrayed their community. He attempts to repair the social fabric that Silva and his men tore apart. In *Historia de Vicente Silva*, Cabeza de Baca tries to present the objective, narrative voice of the community through a narrator who is supposed to be a respected gentleman and an objective reporter. Cabeza de Baca means to narrate the Silva story as thoroughly and accurately as possible. What arises out of this attempt is a narrator who comes across as fulfilling a significant social function: he is the voice of morality, and he details the punishment of people who betray the Hispanic community.

Manuel Cabeza de Baca came from a prominent Las Vegas, New Mexico, family. His great-grandfather Luis Cabeza de Baca and his family were among the first settlers of the Las Vegas Land Grant in 1821. Manuel's parents were Tomás Cabeza de Baca and the former Estefanita

Manuel Cabeza de Baca

Delgado. Manuel became an active Republican politician in San Miguel County, in northern New Mexico. At the time of the writing of the Silva narrative, he was a staunch conservative, voicing the concerns of the elite. While a lawyer employed by the Atchison, Topeka and Santa Fe Railway, he edited the newspaper *El Sol de Mayo*, beginning in 1891, and later *El Independiente*, which in 1898 defended the U.S. seizure of Puerto Rico and the Philippines from Spain, justified the U.S. war against Filipino insurgents who sought independence, and advocated U.S. annexation of Puerto Rico and Canada, and, even more, of Mexico. Cabeza de Baca was probate judge of San Miguel County (1889-1890) and the superintendent of instruction in New Mexico by 1900. The Cabeza de Baca family's significance in New Mexico politics is proven by the fact that Manuel was the older brother of Ezequiel Cabeza de Baca, who was chosen lieutenant governor of New Mexico in 1911 and elected governor of the state in 1916.

Historia de Vicente Silva presents the story of a Hispanic who, through his criminal acts, which included murder, violently upset the Hispanic community. Silva is a real-life symbol not only for Hispanic criminals but also cultural renegades.

Silva and his associates were purported to have been White Caps and supporters of the Democrats through the Partido del Pueblo Unido (United People's Party). Some of the members of the Silva group belonged to the Caballeros de Labor (Knights of Labor) and probably rode with the White Caps. Following the arrival of the railroad in Las Vegas, New Mexico, in 1879, the lawlessness in the area increased. As the railroads expanded into the Southwest, hired guns were used to control the rights-of-way against other competing railroads. After the Atchison, Topeka and Sante Fe Company won the race through Raton Pass (between New Mexico and Colorado) and on to Las Vegas, New Mexico, the hired guns were dismissed, but many remained in the area. The Republican organization, which was a counterreaction to the lawlessness in the region, was called the Sociedad de Los Caballeros de Ley y Orden y Protección Mutua (Society of the Knights of Law and Order and Mutual Protection).

Historia de Vicente Silva concentrates on the title figure, who was born in what is now Bernalillo County, New Mexico, in 1845. Silva became a bar owner in Las Vegas, and under the banner of the Sociedad de Bandidos de Nuevo Mexico (Society of New Mexico Bandits) he led a group of landless men, which included three who were deputies of Sheriff Lorenzo López. The narrative follows Silva's rise to power and deepening criminal activity, which culminates with his own murder after he killed his wife, Telésfora, in 1893. A bounty of three thousand dollars had been offered for Silva (dead or alive) and five hundred dollars for each of his associates. The last section of the book describes the end of the remaining Silva gang members.

In *Historia de Vicente Silva* a conservative and elitist Hispanic voice is heard that contributes to the understanding of a given historical period. The book does not have an open-ended denouement; on the contrary, the closed ending is a moral condemnation of criminal Hispanics, seen as cultural traitors. The dominant voice of the narrative argues that the Silva-led criminal activities "deshonraron la comunidad" (dishonored the community), revealing a sense of community betrayal. The journalistic narrator illustrates a moral lesson by transforming documentary facts. He gives a sense of intensive reporting by conveying a great length and breadth of research on the Silva story, with which Cabeza de Baca was involved as both a gentleman with a noble obligation and as a journalist.

Cabeza de Baca wrote and published the narrative in Spanish. He added the poem "Duerme La Justicia" (Justice Sleeps)—first published in *El Sol de Mayo* in 1891—in an attempt to avoid being accused of giving an unfair assessment of the events. For as Doris L. Myers points out, this anonymous poem reflects a sense of the region's lawless situation. Researching for the book shortly after the body of Silva was found, Cabeza de Baca used as sources the district-court records and interviews of some of the accused associates of Silva. Cabeza de Baca took an active part in investigating Silva and his associates. It appears that for his assistance in uncovering and recovering the body, he received at least a five-hundred-dollar reward.

The different editions of Cabeza de Baca's book, including the one edited by Francisco L. López, have only been mentioned in relation to outlaw lore or historical data. They have not been examined as literary works. Lane Kauffmann's English translation of the narrative (1947) did not attract critical attention.

In his preface to the original edition, Cabeza de Baca indicates that his motive for writing the book is moralistic and is linked with pride in local history:

> no nos mueve por cierto el deseo de satisfacer los degenerados instintos de cierta clase de lectores que se gozan en contemplar la miseria humana en completa desnudez, ni tampoco es nuestro intento al lanzar á la publicidad estas páginas tintas en sangre, saciar la voracidad de un público hambriento de crónica escandalosas . . .[;] nuestro fin es altamente moral

> (we are not moved by certain desires to satisfy the degenerate instincts of a certain class of readers who rejoice at the naked human misery, nor is our intent to thrust into the public light these

pages marked by blood, to satisfy the voracity of a public hungry for scandalous tales . . .[;] our end is highly moral).

Cabeza de Baca attacks not only the criminals but also an audience that lacks morals, and publishers who cater to the morally degraded. Cabeza de Baca's *Historia de Vicente Silva* is graphically related by a "witness," in this case a narrator who purports to know all of Silva's inner motives and who serves to illustrate and give moral advice. Carlos C. de Baca (in his *Vicente Silva*, 1938) agrees that the point of the Silva narrative is to enlighten an audience morally, the lesson being that "crime never pays," but he adds, "Silva and his numerous cohorts . . . by no means tend to show the prevailing conditions of territorial days in New Mexico, but indeed a very isolated case." Kauffmann, in the introduction to his translation, also points out this moralizing tendency of the narrative, whereas Tom McGrath in *Vicente Silva and His Forty Thieves* (1960) stresses the historical basis of Manuel Cabeza de Baca's book, describing it as a factual account.

In reading the work, one gets the sense that Cabeza de Baca, as narrator, is ringing the bell of alarm and that his sense of history is colored by the perception of community betrayal, as in the following passage:

> pues queremos demostrar cómo y de que modo una cuadrilla numerosa de bandidos despues de haber burlado por años á la sociedad, ha venido desmoronándose y cayendo á pedazos uno á uno de sus miembros, ya heridos por el rayo vengador de la cólera divina, ya veniendo a recibir humillados su castigo, ante los altares del templo augusto de la justicia humana

> (for we want to demonstrate how and in what manner a gang of thieves, who after having laughed at society for years, have decayed and fallen apart one by one, wounded by the avenging light of divine wrath, and receive their punishment in humiliation before the altars of the highest temple of human justice).

Moralistic foreshadowing and dramatic presentations characterize the work. Cabeza de Baca clearly establishes a world in which the evil ones get punished, a world in which things are run by morality. What emerges is the desire to see and manifest the continuance of a Hispanic culture that is feeling the pressures of social change. Such changes, in their worst aspect, are represented by Silva.

HISTORIA DE

VICENTE SILVA,

SUS

Cuarenta ◦ Bandidos,

SUS

CRIMENES Y RETRIBUCIONES.

ESCRITA POR

MANUEL C. de BACA.

Copyrighted Junio de 1896,

Imprenta, LA VOZ DEL PUEBLO.
LAS VEGAS, N. M.
1896.

Title page for the first edition of Cabeza de Baca's book about a notorious New Mexican bandit

Cabeza de Baca attempts to give, through a moralistic and melodramatic style, the sense that the Hispanic community is losing its social order and to present the manners and customs that could fight against this loss. The narrator's work goes beyond just giving data, for Cabeza de Baca needs to explain how the Hispanic community of that region could produce a criminal such as Silva. The emotional experience of community betrayal is being communicated by a narrator who interprets and transforms documentary fact with the assistance of imaginative conjecture. This scenario supplies the narrative with melodramatic dialogues for which Cabeza de Baca, the chronicler/investigator, had no source but his own invention. For example, such reconstruction occurs when the narrator describes Silva's murder of his wife (no such information was available):

> Silva se quedó un instante contemplando a su víctima que se retorcía en un charco de sangre con las últimas convulsiones de la muerte. El rostro de aquella martir torno un color lívido; sus ojos se cerraron, sus labios se entreabrieron para dar paso al último suspiro, y un momento despues habia dejado de existir

> (For a moment, Silva contemplated his victim, who writhed in a puddle of blood with the last convulsions of death. The face of that martyr turned deathly pale; her eyes closed, her lips slightly parted to give way to her last breath, and a moment later she ceased to exist).

Scene construction becomes the primary element. Section after section develops the foreboding and sensationalism. The scenes do not connect smoothly, but they work as steps to the ultimate, unavoidable punishment of the criminals.

No full-length study of Cabeza de Baca's *Historia de Vicente Silva* has been done. The discussion of the work has most often been limited to Silva's place in a Western outlaw hierarchy (Billy the Kid always becomes the comparison). In discussing the Silva narrative, E. A. Mares, in "The Wrangle-Taggle Outlaws," notes the use of the theme of the "emergence of outlaws as a significant force in society" and the fact that the historical narrative is "heavily colored by the use of literary devices drawn from both fiction and poetry." Francisco A. Lomelí, in "Eusebio Chacón," identifies the narrative as a "historical novel or chronicle," adding that Cabeza de Baca's work "is history trying to assume literary trappings."

The narrator in Cabeza de Baca's book attempts to transform documentary fact into an immediate emotional experience with a moral message for quick consumption and less so for durable literary value. Two results of this approach are the creation of a journalistic narrator who injects himself into the work, and the use of literary devices on a nonfictional subject.

Many writers have attempted to describe the nineteenth-century lawlessness of the Las Vegas, New Mexico, region, but an examination of Cabeza de Baca's work not only presents an opportunity to recognize and understand the historical context but can also reveal an early literary attempt by a Hispanic to give meaning to a politically and culturally disrupting event. His use of scenes, of a narrator, of voices, and the symbolism of Silva make this more than a historical piece. In the process Manuel Cabeza de Baca buttressed what he considered to be Hispanic culture.

References:

Anselmo F. Arellano and Julián Josué Vigil, *Las Vegas Grandes on the Gallinas, 1835-1985* (Las Vegas, N.Mex.: Teleraña, 1985);

Carlos C. de Baca, *Vicente Silva: New Mexico's Vice King of the Nineties* (Las Vegas, N.Mex., 1938); republished as *Vicente Silva: The Terror of Las Vegas* (Española, N.Mex., 1968);

Francisco A. Lomelí, "Eusebio Chacón: An Early Pioneer of the New Mexican Novel," in *Pasó Por Aquí: Critical Essays on the New Mexican Literary Tradition, 1542-1988*, edited by Erlinda Gonzales-Berry (Albuquerque: University of New Mexico Press, 1989), pp. 149-166;

E. A. Mares, "The Wrangle-Taggle Outlaws: Vicente Silva and Billy the Kid as Seen in Two Nineteenth-Century Hispanic Documents," in *Pasó Por Aquí*, pp. 167-182;

Tom McGrath, *Vicente Silva and His Forty Thieves: The Vice Criminals of the 80's and 90's* (N.p., 1960);

Doris L. Myers, "Banditry and Poetry: Verse By Two Outlaws of Las Vegas," *New Mexico Historical Review*, 50 (October 1975): 227-290;

Lynn Perrigo, *Gateway to Glorieta: A History of Las Vegas, New Mexico* (Boulder, Colo.: Pruiett, 1982), pp. 82-84;

Robert J. Rosenbaum, "Mexicano versus Americano: A Study of Hispanic-American Resistance to Anglo-American Control in New Mexico, 1870-1900," Ph.D. dissertation, University of Texas, 1972.

Fabiola Cabeza de Baca Gilbert
(16 May 1898 -   )

Enrique R. Lamadrid
University of New Mexico

BOOKS: *Los Alimentos y su Preparación* (Las Cruces: New Mexico State University Extension Service, 1934; revised, 1937; revised again, 1942);

Boletín de Conservar (Las Cruces: New Mexico State University Extension Service, 1935; revised, 1937; revised again, 1941);

Historic Cookery, 2 volumes (Las Cruces: New Mexico State University Extension Service, 1939, 1956); 1 volume (Santa Fe: Museum of New Mexico Press, 1983);

The Good Life (Santa Fe: San Vicente Foundation, 1949);

We Fed Them Cactus (Albuquerque: University of New Mexico Press, 1954).

SELECTED PERIODICAL PUBLICATIONS— UNCOLLECTED: "New Mexico Diets," *Journal of Home Economics* (November 1942): 668-669;

"Foods for Easter in the Old Tradition," *New Mexico Magazine*, 35 (April 1957): 23, 47;

"Puerto de Luna," *New Mexico Magazine*, 36 (October 1958): 20, 42-43.

Fabiola Cabeza de Baca Gilbert is a beloved and almost legendary cultural heroine who roamed the mountains, valleys, and plains of her native New Mexico, collecting folklore, teaching in country schools, and working as an agricultural extension agent during the Great Depression and into the late 1950s. She wrote the first definitive description of the Indian-Hispanic cooking of the upper Rio Grande area, earning the title of "first lady" of New Mexican cuisine. Her biographical and fictionalized accounts of ranch life on the Llano Estacado, or Staked Plain, of eastern New Mexico are considered prime resource material for folklorists and historians.

Born on 16 May 1898 into a distinguished Hispanic ranching family of the *rico* (rich) class at La Liendre, headquarters of her family's large northeastern New Mexico ranch, Fabiola Cabeza de Baca was raised by her paternal grandmother. Fabiola was four years old when her mother died. Fabiola attended the Loretto school in nearby Las Vegas, New Mexico, and later graduated with a teaching degree from New Mexico Normal (later Highlands) University in 1921. One formative year of her college education was spent at the Centro de Estudios Históricos in Spain studying art, languages, and history. The next few years were occupied teaching in rural schools from Santa Rosa to as far north as El Rito. Of her students and their families, she wrote: "They were all simple, wholesome people living from the soil. They certainly were a hardy lot, for otherwise they could not have survived the cruelty of the wind, the droughts and the poverty which surrounded most of them. . . . My education was from books; theirs came the hard way. It was superior to mine" (*We Fed Them Cactus*, 1954).

After once being assigned to teach "Domestic Science," Cabeza de Baca began a lifelong career in that field. In 1929 she earned a second bachelor's degree, in home economics, from New Mexico State University in Las Cruces, and immediately thereafter entered the New Mexico Extension Service as a home demonstration agent. The next thirty years of work were spent in homes, ranches, Indian pueblos, and Hispanic villages all across New Mexico. From her work in the Taos and Española valleys, she gained an intimate knowledge of the indigenous Tiwa and Tewa cultures of northern New Mexico. As a community organizer, she founded many associations and clubs for women and children. In homes and community centers she taught new home industries such as food canning, while encouraging the more traditional methods such as food drying. Many people still comment that it was Cabeza de Baca who first taught them that beans and tortillas are not just "poor people's food" but the proud, ancient, and nutritional staples of the New World. She is probably the first American-trained nutritionist to combine progressive scientific principles with cultural values and traditions implicit in a regional ethnic cuisine.

Fabiola Cabeza de Baca Gilbert

In 1951 Cabeza de Baca's dynamic career attracted the attention of the United Nations Educational, Scientific, and Cultural Organization (UNESCO), which sent her to the Mexican state of Michoacán to establish a home-economics program among the Tarascan Indians and to instruct agents from other Latin-American countries in her techniques. The unavailability of pressure cookers and glass jars in Mexico did not discourage her. Some of the food-processing and fish-drying techniques she introduced in the Lake Pátzcuaro region are still in use today.

Cabeza de Baca won many awards for outstanding achievement in her field, including a National Home Demonstration Agents Association Distinguished Award for Meritorious Service and a U.S. Department of Agriculture Superior Service Award. She was also honored with the inclusion of her works in the New Mexico Bicentennial Exhibit (1976), which featured the role of women in New Mexico history. Cabeza de Baca's

strenuous career continued unabated even after an automobile accident claimed her right leg. For years she was married to insurance agent Carlos Gilbert, but they are currently separated.

Throughout her life Cabeza de Baca has participated in community organizations, including the New Mexico Museum Board, Red Cross, Girl Scouts, New Mexico Laboratory of Anthropology, Santa Fe Opera Guild, International Relations Women's Board, School of American Research, Delta Kappa Gamma, and La Sociedad Folklórica de Santa Fe. Cabeza de Baca now resides in a home for the elderly in Albuquerque. After her retirement in 1959 she was active on the lecture circuit and was a trainer and consultant for the Peace Corps. Her popular articles on folklore and food have appeared in several newspapers and magazines.

Cabeza de Baca's writing career stemmed from her work in home economics, beginning with New Mexico State University Extension Service pamphlets in Spanish on food preparation (*Los Alimentos y su Preparación*, 1934) and canning (*Boletín de Conservar*, 1935). Her article "New Mexico Diets" (November 1942) is a lesson in cross-cultural nutrition and an admonition to extension agents to respect and learn about the cultures of the people.

Her cookbook *Historic Cookery* (two volumes, 1939, 1956), first published and repeatedly reprinted in pamphlet form by the New Mexico State University Extension Service and later published as a book by the Museum of New Mexico Press (1983), has been a best-seller since its first appearance. From her field notes and observations in Hispanic, Indian, and Anglo-American kitchens across New Mexico, she developed the first definitive collection of authentic New Mexican recipes. Progressive and eclectic, she recommends a blend of old and new technologies—whatever is necessary to bring out the best qualities of each particular dish. Above all is her insistence on taking plenty of time to do things exactly right. Her definition of the verb *guisar* is a classic: "*Guisar*, which has no exact English equivalent, is the most popular word in the native homemaker's vocabulary. Roughly translated, it means to dress up food, perhaps only by adding a little onion or a pinch of oregano; good food always deserves a finishing touch. Food must never taste flat, but it will—if it is not *guisado*."

Cabeza de Baca's constant traveling and many contacts provided her with the appropriate human resources to pursue a major passion in her life, collecting folklore. In *The Good Life* (1949) she brings to life the folklore and folkways of a traditional, yet contemporary, northern New Mexico village by fictionalizing the biography of a local family. The cycles of seasons and feasts reveal the cultural wealth in a village that many outsiders would assume to be poverty-stricken. *The Good Life* is a kind of New Mexican version of the television series *The Waltons*. Cabeza de Baca portrays the communal qualities and strengths of village life without romanticizing rural living. Typically her heart remains in the kitchen, as she lavishes detail on the cultural context and folklore associated with the recipes included in the second half of the book.

Cabeza de Baca will probably be best remembered for her classic folk history of the Llano Estacado of eastern New Mexico, *We Fed Them Cactus*. To date, no other historical work has captured the folk spirit of life, work, and struggle on the plains as this one has. A participant and ob-

server, she blends her own memories with family history, interviews, and archival materials into a compelling synthesis of autobiography, folklore, and history. Her landscapes are often memorable: "It is a lonely land because of its immensity, but it lacks nothing for those who enjoy Nature in her full grandeur. The colors of the skies, of the hills, the rocks, the birds and the flowers, are soothing to the most troubled heart. It is loneliness without despair. The whole world seems to be there, full of promise and gladness."

Cabeza de Baca's ancestor Don Luis María Cabeza de Baca in 1823 received a land grant of a half-million acres in the Las Vegas, New Mexico, area of the llano. In the previous century the plains had been the natural barrier that separated the Spanish settlements along the valley and tributaries of the Rio Grande from the French settlements along the valley and tributaries of the Mississippi. Only the *ciboleros* (buffalo hunters) and *comancheros* (traders with the Comanche) ventured into the vast expanse before nineteenth-century Mexican and New Mexican cattlemen and sheep men began sending their flocks in search of new pastures.

To explore the early days, Fabiola Cabeza de Baca uses the voice and stories of El Cuate (the pal or twin), the ranch cook who could still recall the disappearance of the buffalo, the coming of the longhorns, and, most drastic of all, the coming of barbed wire. El Cuate is a repository of New Mexican folk culture and humor who taught her every song and story he could remember, as well as the more arcane bits of folk wisdom including *las cabañuelas*, a traditional system of weather prediction. True to her social class, Cabeza de Baca defends and idealizes the patron system, emphasizing the paternalistic responsibilities and philanthropy that were its benefits: "I can remember my paternal grandfather's sheep camps and the men who worked for him. They were loyal people, and as close to us as our own family. They were, every one of them, grandfather's *compadres*, for he and grandmother had stood as sponsors in baptism or marriage to many of their children." True to her times, she also tends to emphasize the Spanish heritage of New Mexico at the expense of the more historically accurate Mexican connection.

One of the strongest features of the book is the extended tribute paid to the valiant and resourceful women of the Hispanic frontier. Other chapters contain valuable accounts of the *Gorras Blancas* (White Caps), vigilante crusaders of the range wars, the infamous Vicente Silva bandit gang, and the coming of the American homesteaders. Within her personal experience was the great drought of 1918, when ranchers were forced to burn spines off cacti to feed their cattle after the grass was gone. The drastic dry-farming techniques brought by the homesteaders had broken the sod, and the ecological disaster that would culminate in the dust-bowl conditions of the 1930s had already begun. Since so little has been written about the Hispanos of the early-twentieth-century llano, her account is invaluable.

Due to her personal enthusiasm and the wide travels of her professional career, Cabeza de Baca has always been a well-known figure in New Mexico. A new wave of interest in her writings was generated by her inclusion in the Museum of New Mexico Bicentennial Exhibit, organized by the American Association of University Women. The 1985 book *New Mexico Women*, edited by Joan M. Jensen and Darlis A. Miller, contains a detailed appraisal of Cabeza de Baca's important contributions as the first agricultural extension agent to work in many areas of Depression-era New Mexico. Her literary career also continues to receive critical attention. *We Fed Them Cactus* attracted favorable newspaper reviews but received little critical treatment until Chicano literary historians such as Raymond A. Paredes started looking for precursors of the Chicano literary renaissance of the 1960s and 1970s. Although attracted by her colorful evocations of life on the llano, he expresses dismay for the patrician attitudes and lack of social concern in the writings of Cabeza de Baca and others of her generation. He accuses them of cultivating the New Mexican version of the Hispanic "fantasy heritage," complete with heroic conquistadores and noble Indians, and a romantic fascination with a largely fictional past. Tey Diana Rebolledo's treatment of Cabeza de Baca's work approaches the writing on its own terms, emphasizing the symbolic value of landscape in the midst of social change. In her reading of books by Cabeza de Baca and by another New Mexico writer, Cleofas Jaramillo, Rebolledo discovers a deep concern with the disturbing social and cultural changes brought by the Americanization of New Mexico: "The transformation from the stable society in which they had been born is recalled in their memories and shadowed by their perspective on the landscape. Both . . . use landscape to reflect changing cultural values."

Fabiola Cabeza de Baca Gilbert's imaginative and insightful depictions of life in the Hispanic Southwest are her major contributions to the literature of the area. Her pioneer documentation of the cuisine of the upper Rio Grande area and the cultural context of which it is a part have also played an important role in promoting cultural and intercultural awareness. Her first books on food and cooks initiate historical and cultural discussions that are more fully developed in her later works, which, like her life and career, embody the strength and resourcefulness of the Hispanic woman on the northern New Mexico frontier.

References:

Albuquerque Branch, American Association of University Women, *Women in New Mexico* (Albuquerque: Aiken, 1976);

Alice Bullock, "A Patrona of the Old Pattern," *Santa Fe New Mexican*, 19 May 1968;

Ralph Dohme, "Sante Fe Women to Talk on New Mexico Foods," *Santa Fe New Mexican*, 6 February 1966;

"Extension Service Agent to Retire after 30 Years," *Albuquerque Journal*, 24 June 1959;

Joan M. Jensen, " 'I've Worked, I'm Not Afraid of Work': Farm Women in New Mexico 1920-1940," in *New Mexico Women: Intercultural Perspectives*, edited by Jensen and Darlis A. Miller (Albuquerque: University of New Mexico Press, 1985), pp. 227-255;

Tey Diana Rebolledo, "Tradition and Mythology: Signatures of Landscape in Chicana Literature," in *The Desert Is No Lady*, edited by Vera Norwood and Janice Monk (New Haven: Yale University Press, 1987), pp. 96-256;

Marie T. Walsh, "New Mexico's Famous Home Economist," *California Farmer*, 201 (16 October 1954).

Reyes Cárdenas

(6 January 1948 -   )

Carmen Tafolla

BOOKS: *Chicano Territory* (Seguin, Tex: Rifan, 1975);

Get Your Tortillas Together, by Cárdenas, Cecilio García-Camarillo, and Carmen Tafolla (San Antonio: Cultural Distribution Center, 1976);

Anti-Bicicleta Haiku (San Antonio: Caracol, 1976);

Survivors of the Chicano Titanic (Austin: Place of Herons, 1981);

I Was Never a Militant Chicano (Austin: Relámpago, 1986).

SELECTED PERIODICAL PUBLICATIONS—
UNCOLLECTED: "La Autobiographia de Reyes Cárdenas," *Grito*, 7 (March-May 1974): 10-25;

"Los Pachucos y la Flying Saucer," *Caracol*, 1 (January 1975): 8-9; (February 1975): 6; (April 1975): 10-11;

"Anticarnalismo," *Caracol*, 3 (November 1976): 10;

"A Destruction and Reconstruction of Santos Rodríguez," *Caracol*, 3 (July 1977): 6-7.

Cover for the 1986 work in which Cárdenas explains, "I've always wanted / more than a revolution / can provide"

Reyes Cárdenas's creativity, mystically connected tragicomic images, and freedom from poetic tradition have set him apart from and often ahead of the avant-garde of Chicano literature, while at the same time revealing his inherent connections to the image, soul, and sociopolitical movements of the Chicano-Indian Southwest.

Born and raised in Seguin, Texas, Cárdenas is the eldest son of a Chicano family typified by financial poverty but also by an aesthetic-cultural wealth of philosophy and creativity, unique even within Chicano barrios. Because of frequent migrant work in the fields of West Texas, where he and his family picked cotton, Cárdenas did not enter school until age ten. His mother died in childbirth at the hands of a country doctor when Cárdenas was twelve, and his father retreated to a mechanic's job in the desert, an episode Cárdenas describes in *Chicano Territory* (1975):

"Whenever the desert breaks down, he fixes it / The Digger Indians pull out an old carburetor / To them / it looks like a delicious root . . . / My father drinks water / out of a wrench. / It's a spectacular blue water." Reyes, along with his two brothers and sister, went to live with his grandparents, whose strong Indian heritage provided a wealth of encouragement and inspiration for the four children, two of whom were subsequently to become writers, while the other two created sketches, welded sculptures, and other visual art.

At age sixteen Cárdenas, suffering from tuberculosis in both lungs, entered a hospital in San Antonio. He spent a year and three months there, undergoing surgery on his left lung and some experimental procedures, which took a further toll on his health. While in the hospital he began reading volumes of poetry lent him by another patient. His interest in poetry heightened, and he began to write extensively. Recuperating, Cárdenas returned to Seguin and to high school, where an English teacher provided further encouragement. Two weeks before graduation, however, Cárdenas was told that he lacked one unit and could not graduate with the class, so he "dropped out" in 1969, never again to return to formal education.

Cárdenas's upbringing in a small Texas town known historically for its prejudice against "Meskins" provided a stimulating contrast between the unconditional respect and acceptance for all things at his grandparents' house and the forced definition and limitation of all human beings in the sharply segregated schools. This contrast was subsequently to reveal itself in his "soft-hard" poetic themes and in his typical combination of gentleness and diamond-hard criticisms, exemplified by one of his poems published in *Chicano Territory*, "In Memory of My Mother":

Some name I try to remember softly,
was it Rebecca,
or a bare chinaberry tree slipping on ice?

Anyway, it doesn't get hurt yet
and my mother goes off to have her baby
at a country doctor's office.

Only because he's cheaper.
When she dies during childbirth
the baby dies, too.

Cárdenas's long bouts with tuberculosis, injustice, poverty, and the hardship of living in an eight-by-eight shack he had built himself behind his grandparents' house drained his health but solidified his commitment to writing. Poetry became his full-time job, and reams stacked up beside him. For him, money did not exist, and meals were forgotten or remembered only when offered by family or friends. He embraced a philosophy of acceptance of life without force, without push, except for his undeniable urge to write, and took violence on no one and nothing except the blankness of pages.

His early work resulted in "La Autobiografia de Reyes Cárdenas," which appeared in *El Grito* (1974), an instrumental journal that promoted Chicano literary work. He also published frequently in *Caracol*, a small magazine, and his first chapbook, *Chicano Territory*, followed in 1975. This collection provided autobiographical glimpses of a life characterized by standing out, but gently. In the title poem Cárdenas wrote:

My long black and white hair attracts too much attention.
Especially in a little redneck town like Seguin,
but even walking around inside a peach tree

I attract too much attention.
. . . .

Out of my life
have gone all the nagging doubts.
And with them even my vieja [woman].

But I keep on writing as if nothing has happened.
Sounds and colors drift into the poem
and go out of it.

This is what peace is all about.
And when this poem passes by
no one has to move out of the way.

By the time of the publication of *Get Your Tortillas Together* (1976), coauthored with Cecilio García-Camarillo and Carmen Tafolla, Cárdenas was known for his stream-of-consciousness technique and hard-hitting understatement. In an introduction to *Get Your Tortillas Together*, noted Chicano poet Alurista wrote that Cárdenas's work "explota en metáforas sutilmente cortantes y en haikus combativas" (explodes in metaphors that cut subtly and in haikus fit for combat). The book's cover bears the assessment of writer Max Martínez who calls it "poetry resplendent with primordial images." In "La Tracalada" (The Debt), Cárdenas seems to be pointing a direction by providing a clearer connection to essence and heritage as "La tracalada goes on / pero nada [but nothing] changes / . . . / the way that water / siempre sabe / como bajar . . . [always knows how to go down . . .]/ the roots / will always know / how deep to go / sin tener que preguntar [without having to ask] / without having / to think twice."

Cárdenas's involvement with the publishing of *Caracol* revealed another side of the writer— his hilarious and often sarcastic fantasies. "Los Pachucos y la Flying Saucer," "Anticarnalismo"

Cecilio García-Camarillo, Reyes Cárdenas, and Carmen Tafolla while they were writing Get Your Tortillas Together
(photograph by César Augusto Martínez)

(Antibrotherhood), "The Machismo Manifesto," and other frequently misunderstood pieces incited rage from other writers and, among some, a tendency to ignore his work. Undaunted, Cárdenas continued, experimenting with wilder shapes of poetry in *Anti-Bicicleta Haiku* (1976). In this chapbook Cárdenas explores side-by-side stanzas and ungrammatical word combinations. These more experimental poems made many critics reluctant to comment on him, and while many fellow writers praised his work in private, few did so in public. The few who did comment were other innovators such as Cecilio García-Camarillo, a poet-editor-journalist who also experimented with such forms as bottle poetry, sound poetry, and trilingual poetry. He contributed a blurb for the cover of Cárdenas's work: "Cárdenas assaults conventional logic in the most outrageous manner since the invention of lunacy . . . [with] flippant paroxysms, his now famous rubberization of time, his sexual calenturas [fevers], his surgically precise imagery and that notoriously Chicano gusto for language. . . ."

Cárdenas's sense of humor, like the person himself, is soft, quiet, and unmistakable. The back cover of *Anti-Bicicleta Haiku* carries not the usual photograph of the author but instead a photograph of three Chicanos who are each identified as "Reyes Cárdenas" in the manner of the television series *To Tell the Truth*.

A major operation in 1980 threatened Cárdenas's life and later forced him to take on a fifty-hour workweek in the freezer section of a chicken plant in order to repay medical bills. This turn of events, instead of detracting from the quality of his poems, seemed only to intensify it. With his subsequent work, *Survivors of the Chicano Titanic* (1981), his style matures, exhibiting an imagery that is concise and packed with protest and search for identity. In such poems as "Inherit the Pen," he reveals his purpose: "we try to comb / poverty out of / the pen by feeding / it more ink."

Cárdenas's acute awareness of the struggles for justice in Latin America is pronounced in his Spanish poems such as "El aeropuerto de Managua." In this poem he notes that in San Salvador, "la libertad es algo tan cara / las tiendas no la quieren vender" (liberty is such an expensive thing / the stores don't want to sell it). While most of his earlier works were either all English or in a combination of English and Spanish, the profound personal statement, the political intent, and the presentation of the entire Spanish-speaking world's contemporary political plight in "Poema Sandino" make Spanish the language of choice. Although a powerful indictment, this poem still shows Cárdenas's gentleness:

> estas cosas que nos arrastran por el piso
> tenemos que pararlas como un arbol seco de
>   navidad
> tenemos que echarle agua hasta que le salgan hojas
> hasta que podamos hablar otra vez
> hasta que podamos mover al siglo . . .
> . . . .
> pero nosotros, nosotros tenemos que resistir al
>   tiempo
> levantar la pluma aunque sea con huesos
> tenemos que ofender a los que cierran los ojos
> que hasta páginas vacías ahoguen sus sueños dulces
> que despiertan tosiendo buscando aire.
>
> (these things that drag us across the floor
> we have to stand them up like a dried-up Christmas
>   tree
> we have to sprinkle water on them until they sprout
>   leaves
> until we can speak again
> until we can move the century . . .
> . . . .
> but we, we have to resist time
> lift the pen, although it be with our bones
> we have to offend those who close their eyes
> so that even empty pages drown their sweet dreams
> and they wake up coughing searching for air.)

No matter how universal this poem is, the immediate context here is the Chicano barrio and its victims. Elsewhere in *Survivors of the Chicano Titanic*, Cárdenas reveals much of himself and of the world behind his tired eyes in a short poem entitled "In Kubla Khan":

> The phone rings
> like a campesina
> tired from a hard day
> in the fields.
> And again
> as in all my poems
> little Santos
> has his head blown off.

In "And Now, the Translation," Cárdenas openly admits the human hunger for blood and injustice: "What a comfort / injustice really / is . . . Imagine the / bullet's surprise / when the / corri-

dors alight! / And when / the terror of / being swallowed / dawns on the / trigger-set, too. / What a comfort." Cárdenas faces this hunger not as part of an external evil but as something within human nature. The last poem in *Survivors of the Chicano Titanic*, "Driving to the Future," gives an accurate picture of a writer being passed in speeding traffic that "doesn't give a damn / that earth's resources are / dwindling at a furious pace, / conspicuous consumption / becomes a steady diet, / that's why I'm so conscious / of how much I take. / A million years from now we'll / still be mining words together."

Although previously neglected because his writings were not "understood," in 1985 Cárdenas received the prestigious Austin Book Award for *I Was Never a Militant Chicano* (1986), an ironic title coming from a committed poet. In the title poem Cárdenas negates confinement in any of the mythological, literary, or historical stereotypes and states, "I was never / really a pachuco. . . . / I was never / the Che Guevara type. . . . / I was never / a militant / Chicano / but only because / I've always wanted / more than a revolution / can provide." In "The Poet's Birthday," Cárdenas confronts himself:

> Today I am thirty-eight
> my hair has become white,
> my politics
> have become non-political,
> the left and right
> oppose me,
> . . . .
> the path to wisdom
> is not followed,
> not even by the wise
> . . . .
> . . . I no longer
> use language
> to ask questions,
> my actions
> are shrouded in actions.
> I should be like a lyric
> in one of
> Víctor Jarra's songs.
> of protest,
> instead
> I am like
> the military
> and the guerillas
> always seeking the
> unattainable
> . . . .
> If somewhere on earth
> someone
> becomes more human today

then I celebrate,
And if it's me . . .
who becomes more human
then I celebrate
even more!

The work of Reyes Cárdenas, always provocative in imagery and global in concern, seems to be moving toward even greater connectedness with others and ultimately with the poet himself. His earlier abstraction and experimentation gave way to a bareness of line in a clearer, more human voice that passes up description in favor of direct action and tangible emotion. Cárdenas's words and images are still a primary facet of his work, but now they are leaner, more nakedly human, and, perhaps most important, clearly directed at the inner soul.

References:

José Flores Peregrino, "On the Mission and the Vision of Contemporary Chicano Literature with Some Notes on Its Development in Texas," *Threads of Texas Literature* (March 1980): 24-33;

Carmen Tafolla, "Chicano Literature: Beyond Beginnings," in *A Gift of Tongues: Critical Challenges in Contemporary American Poetry*, edited by Marie Harris and Kathleen Aguero (Atlanta: University of Georgia Press, 1987), pp. 206-225.

Adolfo Carrillo

(July 1855 - 24 August 1926)

Luis Leal
University of California, Santa Barbara

BOOKS: *Memorias inéditas del Lic. Don Sebastián Lerdo de Tejada*, by Carrillo [unnamed] and Lerdo de Tejada (Brownsville, Tex., 1889);
Memorias del Marqués de San Basilisco, anonymous (San Francisco: International, 1897);
Cuentos californianos (Los Angeles, 1922?).

SELECTED PERIODICAL PUBLICATIONS—
UNCOLLECTED: "Nubia," *Revista Azul* (Mexico City), 1 (1894): 411-412;
"Apreciaciones sobre el modo de ser de la sociedad norte-americana," *Dos Repúblicas* (Denver), 1 February 1896, p. 1.

When Benito Juárez, president of Mexico, died in 1872, he was succeeded by the chief justice of the Supreme Court, Sebastián Lerdo de Tejada, who acted as interim president until he was elected by popular vote that same year. He was reelected in 1876, but Gen. Porfirio Díaz revolted and forced Lerdo to abandon the presidency and the country. In New York, where Lerdo had established his residence, and where he later died in 1889, the deposed president gave daily receptions and was visited by his followers, as well as by those in exile who opposed Díaz. Among Lerdo's daily visitors was the newspaperman Adolfo Carrillo, one of the many Mexican writers and politicians who took refuge in the United States in order to escape persecution by the Díaz dictatorship. Carrillo's exile was due to his ceaseless fight for freedom of the press, especially the freedom to criticize the government.

Carrillo was born in July 1855 in the town of Sayula, in the central state of Jalisco, but spent his childhood and boyhood in the nearby village of Tapalpa. After completing his elementary education, he was sent to study at the Seminario de Guadalajara, in the state capital, where he developed an interest in journalism quite early. He published two newspapers—*La Picota* (The Gibbet), starting in 1877, and *La Unión Mercantil* (The Mercantile Union), beginning in 1878—in which he began to criticize the local government. As a conse-

quence he was persecuted and had to abandon Guadalajara and go to Mexico City, where he continued his newspaper activities and his opposition to the government. As the editor of *El Correo de los Lunes* (Monday's Mail), in 1885 he increased his criticism of Díaz, reproducing in the pages of his weekly newspaper the contents of a broadside titled "Al Pueblo, ¡Protesta!" (To the People, Protest!) and an editorial, "Desbarajuste" (Confusion). As the result of that criticism, later that same year Carrillo was detained, tried for crimes against the state, found guilty, and sentenced to four months in prison and a five-hundred-peso fine. From Belén, the federal prison in Mexico City, he was sent to the dreaded island-prison San Juan de Ulúa, outside the port of Veracruz in the Gulf of Mexico. After serving his time at San Juan de Ulúa, Carrillo was exiled to Cuba. From Havana he went to New York to be near Lerdo, who became his benefactor.

Making use of the extensive notes he took during his daily visits to Lerdo in New York and the political secrets that the former president had revealed to him, Carrillo was able to write *Memorias inéditas del Lic. Don Sebastián Lerdo de Tejada* (Unpublished Memoirs of Mr. Sebastián Lerdo de Tejada, Attorney at Law). He sent the manuscript to a printer in Brownsville, Texas, and there it was published, in 1889, without Carrillo's name. The book was very successful and was reprinted several times in Brownsville and San Antonio, and even in Mexico City. It became a powerful tool in the hands of those who wanted to attack Díaz, for it helped to mobilize the Mexican people, especially the exiles and those living along the border, against the Díaz dictatorship.

After Lerdo's death Carrillo went to Europe, living first in Spain and then in France. The Díaz government, knowing that Carrillo was in Madrid, brought pressure, via their ambassador Gen. Vicente Riva Palacio, on the Spanish government to have Carrillo deported. From Spain he went to France, where he studied law at the

Cover for the only book originally published under Carrillo's name. The collection of nineteen short stories chronicles life in early-twentieth-century California.

Sorbonne, but the Díaz government continued to persecute him, and therefore he had to abandon his studies and return to the United States.

Carrillo took up residence in San Francisco, and there, in 1897, he married and then established a printing shop. That same year, *Memorias del Marqués de San Basilisco* was anonymously published in the form of a novel, a work that critics have attributed to Carrillo. On 18 April 1906 Carrillo suffered the consequences of the great San Francisco earthquake, in which his only daughter died and his printing shop was destroyed.

When the revolution against Díaz broke out in November 1910, under the leadership of Francisco I. Madero, Carrillo joined the movement and became one of its press agents. After Madero's assassination in 1913, Carrillo joined the forces of Venustiano Carranza and Francisco (Pancho) Villa and began his press attacks against the government of Victoriano Huerta. In 1914 he was put in charge of economic affairs in the Los Angeles Mexican Consulate, and there he pub-

lished the newspaper *México Libre* (Free Mexico). Like the Mexican novelist Mariano Azuela, Carrillo was one of the first to attack in the press the wrongs attributed to the revolutionaries; as a consequence of the attack, he lost his position in the consulate. But this turned out to be a blessing, for he had more time to travel through California collecting materials for his book *Cuentos californianos* (Californian Tales, 1922?), published in Los Angeles, where he died on 24 August 1926. Four days after Carrillo's death the newspaper the *Tucsonense*, of Tucson, Arizona, published the following item:

> The funeral of the well-known newspaperman Adolfo Carrillo took place last Thursday in the Cementerio del Calvario in the city of Los Angeles, California. He had died there the previous Tuesday as the result of a long and painful illness. . . .
>
> He was a good man-of-letters. Three years ago [1923] he came to Tucson, where he remained a few days, hoping to recover his good health. He returned to Los Angeles, where his illness became worse. . . .
>
> He was irreproachably honest, and every time he was approached by the followers of Don Porfirio [Díaz] to join them he refused. . . .

Of the three books written by Carrillo, only one, *Cuentos californianos*, bears his name. In 1980, however, an edition of Lerdo's memoirs appeared under Carrillo's name. Having been persecuted in Mexico and Europe by the Díaz government, it is obvious why Carrillo did not want to publish Lerdo's memoirs under his own name. Even in the authoritative *The Life of Sebastián Lerdo de Tejada*, Frank A. Knapp, Jr., whenever he mentions *Memorias inéditas*, always refers to it as apocryphal.

Memorias del Marqués de San Basilisco has been attributed to Carrillo by several critics. This rare novel, of which there is a copy in the Rare Book Collection at Yale University, was almost unknown to literary critics until December 1928, when the Mexican poet and critic Bernardo Ortiz de Montellano published a review regarding the values of the work as a picaresque novel. He observes that there is a discrepancy in the title, which appears on the title page as *Memorias del Marqués de San Basilisco*, while on the cover it is *Memorias del Marqués de San Basilio*. Ortiz de Montellano assumes that *Basilisco* is a typographical error. Perhaps it was a conscious error, since the word *basilisco* (referring to a reptile like a small iguana) would attract the attention of the buyer, whereas *San Basilio* gives the idea that the book deals with the life of a saint. On the contrary, the subject of these memoirs, in picaresque form, is the life of Jorge Carmona (Camonina, as he is also called in the novel), born in a poor family in Sinaloa, Mexico. A true picaro, he goes from job to job, as a salesman, a gambler, a politician changing parties at will, and a soldier in the ranks of an invading army. In 1860 he lives in San Francisco, where he cannot adapt to a life of hard work, so he goes back to Mexico. There he joins Maximilian's French army and marries a rich woman who helps him buy in Paris the title of Marquis of San Basilio. Ortiz de Montellano, who belonged to the group of vanguard critics known as the "Contemporáneos," says in his article that he prefers this type of memoir because of its sincerity and purity, characteristics he does not find in the average romantic novel.

Cuentos californianos, a collection of nineteen short stories, was published without a date. The slender volume (ninety-six pages) was most likely published in the early 1920s, 1922 being the best estimate (based on his travels before that year). The plots of several of them unfold in San Francisco, while the rest take place in other California locations. Some of the tales are re-creations of legends found by Carrillo in old manuscripts preserved in the missions. The source of the last story in the collection, "La hija del contrabandista" (The Smuggler's Daughter), however, is not an old manuscript, but from the book *California Smugglers* (1902), by Douglas Grant. The tale, which takes place near Mission San Gabriel, explains the name of the Loveless Oak, a tree near where the cruel smuggler El Enano (The Midget) killed Fray Yorba for having denounced him to the authorities. The smuggler's own daughter had revealed her father's secrets to Yorba.

As a book of fiction, *Cuentos californianos* is typical of the narratives written by Mexican writers residing in the United States during the early decades of the century, among them Daniel Venegas and Jorge Ulica. In general, they wrote in Spanish, used few English words or phrases, and presented Chicanos in their stories from the perspective of the Mexican writer, who often considered them as persons who had lost part of their cultural heritage, or *pochos*, that is, as caricatures rather than well-developed characters. The style of these early short-story writers is characteristic of that of the newspaperman, since most of their narratives appeared first in the Sunday supplements of the Spanish newspapers published in the large urban centers of the Southwest and West, such as San Antonio, Los Angeles, and San Francisco. These authors are, however, the earliest to write short fiction, a genre that later became very popular among Chicano writers. *Cuentos californianos* is a worthy precursor of that trend.

References:

Colección de pedimentos . . . presentados en la causa seguida a algunos periodistas . . . responsables de conato de sedición cometido por medio de la prensa (Mexico City: Secretaría de Fomento, 1886);

Frank A. Knapp, Jr., *The Life of Sebastián Lerdo de Tejada, 1823-1889: A Study of Influence and Obscurity* (Austin: University of Texas Press, 1951);

Bernardo Ortiz de Montellano, "Librería de Viejo," *Contemporáneos*, 1 (December 1928): 412-415.

Olivia Castellano
(25 July 1944 -   )

Tiffany Ana López
University of California, Santa Barbara

BOOKS: *Blue Mandolin, Yellow Field* (Berkeley: Tonatiuh-Quinto Sol International, 1980);
Blue Horse of Madness (Sacramento: Crystal Clear, 1983);
Spaces That Time Missed (Sacramento: Crystal Clear, 1986).

OTHER: "Blue Horse for an Imaginary Death" and "A Singer's Song," in *Landing Signals*, edited by B. L. Kennedy, Anne Menebroker, and Kevin Dobbs (Sacramento: Sacramento Poetry Center, 1986), pp. 46-53;
"Writing," in *Beginnings in Literature*, edited by Alan Madsen, Sarah Durand Wood, and Phillip M. Connors (Glenview, Ill.: Scott, Foresman, 1987), p. 409.

SELECTED PERIODICAL PUBLICATIONS—
UNCOLLECTED: "Words," "Upon reading Dylan Thomas' Villanelle," and "Evenings in June," *Tejidos*, 2 (Fall 1975): 2-4;
"Coming of Spring," "Yes and No," "Words," "Evenings in June," and "A Surrealist Breakthrough," *Colores*, 4 (1978): 60-65;
"The Guest Who Never Came," *Hard-Pressed Magazine*, no. 4 (1978);
"Old Horse of Poetry," "Yellow Memory," and "Rider of the Plains: For José Montoya," *Montoya Poetry Review*, 1 (Spring 1980): 45-48;
"Bridges," "Yellow Memory," "Mama," "Seeing," "Las botas de las siete leguas," "Vivianne the Mandolin Girl," "Visitor," and "Manuel of the Ropes," *Grito del Sol*, 5 (1980): 35-43;
"How to Wear a Dead Girl's Shoes," "In The Plains of South Texas," "Estos Vatos With their Intellectual Conversations," and "The Price of Giving Up Dreams (or Inventing a New Landscape)," *Imagine*, 1 (Summer 1984): 45-51;
"Blue Horse for an Imaginary Death," *Literati Chicago*, 1 (Winter 1988): 89-91;
"Canto, Locura y Poesía: The Teacher as Agent-

Olivia Castellano

Provocateur," *Women's Review of Books*, 7 (February 1990): 18-20;
"Prologue for *The Comstock Journals* (or *Sotol City Blues*)," *Blue Mesa Review*, 3 (1991): 70-78;
"Breaking Ground, Making Space," *Women's Review of Books*, 5 (February 1992): 32-35.

Olivia Castellano was born into a life of subsistence in Del Rio, Texas, on 25 July 1944. She was the second of five children born to Secundino Peña Castellano, a Southern Pacific Railroad worker with a fifth-grade education, and Cruz Guerrero Castellano, who had left school in the second grade to help raise ten siblings. In "Canto, Locura y Poesía" (1990) Castellano recalls that in 1958 her father, "tired of seeing his days fade into each other without promise," moved his family to California where they became farmworkers. She then became serious about education, convinced that only through books and songs would she "be free to structure some kind of future" for herself.

The memories of her early Texas childhood are her source of creative energy; her work emerges from the Texas landscape. Her mythology is composed of horses, blue sky, yellow earth, and feelings of anger for her childhood artistic pursuits having been suppressed by her family and formal educators. The colors blue and yellow represent her strongest ties to south Texas: the vast blue sky above the landscape and *la tierra* (the land), vividly yellow due to its lack of mineral content. During her high school years in California, Castellano found encouragement to pursue her education, having discovered a love for French while learning it through songs and stories. This new language freed her to express herself artistically, eventually in English as well as French. Although Castellano felt her native Spanish connected her to her family and culture, she did not see it as a language of the learned. It was not until later in her writing career that she found artistic inspiration in being able to write from a cultural voice.

Castellano's artistic education was gained at home in the evenings where she voraciously read those authors whom she admired: the Marquis de Sade, Arthur Rimbaud, Honoré de Balzac, Comte de Lautréamont, and other French writers in translation, as well as Fyodor Mikhaylovich Dostoyevski, Walt Whitman, and Karl Marx. Despite her record as a straight-A student, Castellano felt anxiety in the classroom. At home she felt very isolated in her academic and artistic pursuits as a result of her family's insensitivity. In "Canto, Locura y Poesía," Castellano recalled family members saying, "Te vas a volver loca con esos libros. Esta nunca se va a casar" (You'll go nuts with those books. She'll never get married). In her junior year of high school she composed a poem in imitation of John Keats's "La Belle Dame Sans Merci" for her advanced composition course and was told by her teacher, "Stick to essay writing; never try to write a poem again because a poet you are not!" Reflecting on these painful comments, the poet wrote, "This was the tenor of my adolescent years. When nothing on either side of the two cultures, Mexican or Anglo-American, affirms your existence, that is how rage is shaped."

Beginning in 1962, Castellano's primary goal was to achieve a bachelor's degree in English at Sacramento State College (later called California State University, Sacramento) to further her skills as a writer, but, because of her strong feelings of alienation from traditional English departments, she settled on pursuing a degree in French with a minor in English. She graduated with a B.A. in June 1966, and after two years of teaching French and English in high school, she returned to the university in 1968 for a master's degree through a program called the Mexican-American Experienced Teachers' Fellowship. In "Canto, Locura y Poesía," Castellano described the program that changed her life and the course of her career: "I was allowed to express my rage and to examine it in the company of peers who had a similar anger. Most of the instructors, moreover, were Chicano or white professors sensitive to Chicanos. For the first time, at 25, I had found my role models. I vowed to do for other students what these people had done for me." Castellano's vast reading experience and her formal education have greatly shaped her poetic voice. Her master's thesis, devoted to the study of contemporary Mexican dramaturgy, concludes by offering these partial solutions:

> Become aware that drama has a history of being a mirror of society and that it can be used to reflect as well as to prefigure the course of events in a social movement . . . by doing this—and so much more—we Chicanos can create for ourselves a prouder self-image.

In *Blue Horse of Madness* (1983), her second book, she uses her poetry to deliver the same message. In the poem "If All Students Were This Good," the students have taken the advice given in her thesis: "weaving with their hands, eyes, hair / ad-libbing a brand new music / only they could have invented." Her university studies enabled Castellano to tap into her anger by first analyzing the issues of "Chicanismo" as a social scientist. Then, through her writing as a humanist, philosopher, and poet, she was able to explore the same themes on an emotional level outside of academic writing.

Soon after filing her thesis, she suffered a serious depression which led to a nervous breakdown. Though traumatic, the breakdown in terms of her writing was "the best thing that ever happened to me. It made me more sensitive to myself as a writer and how close the powers of creativity always are to the brink of insanity." In the fall of 1971 Castellano, fully recovered, went back to California State University, Sacramento—

this time to teach part-time. She accepted a full-time lecturer position in 1972. In the classroom Castellano uses Chicano literature to promote literary and racial awareness. She created her department's first course in the genre. By teaching Chicano literature, by bringing Chicano poets and writers to the university, and by sharing her works with students and fellow Chicano poets, Castellano provides what she did not have as a young writer: the nurturing atmosphere necessary for the creation of Chicano literature.

Throughout Castellano's poetry, she skillfully integrates English and Spanish, leaving a truly bilingual, Chicano mark on the language. However, the mainstay of her work as a poet is the remarkable use of imagery from her personal mythology that transcends language and includes archetypes from both English and Spanish cultures. Her first published poems appeared in *Grito del Sol* (1977). They are a sample of her larger body of poems published in 1980 under the title *Blue Mandolin, Yellow Field*. The prose poem "The Renaissance Men" is typical of Castellano's style, using everyday language to describe a field-worker's life of struggle:

> But even after the earth and the sun and fields (with hoes that were too small) had arched their backs completely . . . even after all that, they continued on their trek to clarity and compassion. Thus they remain suspended throughout time: two little men forever smiling, and walking perfectly straight.

This use of everyday language transforms the image of the laborer into a symbol representing all who suffer at the hands of others. The poet does not wish to invoke the reader's pity for these poor farmworkers who have become deformed as a result of their labors. Hence, she does not use words that would do so. The farmworkers are not broken by time; though their backs are curved, the two men walk "perfectly straight" in the poet's eyes. She sees beauty in their having labored to feed their families and, in a greater sense, feed the families of the world as well. Castellano's word choice is such that both students of poetry and *gente* (people) can discover the beauty of her poetic visions. The poem also reflects the Romantic poets' concern for nature and the people who live there.

The title of her first book, *Blue Mandolin, Yellow Field*, brings together the image of the earth and sky of her childhood memories. The book is broken into seven sections, but the many sections do not thematically connect. The themes seem to separate, rather than incorporate, in the tight form of textual structure that Castellano has chosen to shape her first book of poems. The first section is about the creative process. The book's beginning poem, "Old Horse of Poetry," illustrates the creation of a poem:

> A horse's skeleton
> lies disassembled
> on the beach.
> To revive it
> you must pick
> its bones clean
> and polish them
> until they glisten
> in blue moonlight.

Castellano uses the image of the horse as a metaphor for the imagination: the entire first section is Castellano's *ars poetica*. The following sections of the book cover a broad range of themes: family experiences, experiments in poetics, the sadness of love, imagistic observations, and tributes to four of Castellano's favorite poets. The book is a triumph of ambition over restraint. Castellano tries to cover all possible topics for poetry.

In choosing the title *Blue Mandolin, Yellow Field*, Castellano wanted to give the impression of a small child standing between a bright blue sky and a vibrant yellow, Texas earth. In the strongest section of the book, "La Familia," the narrator, an adult reflecting upon her childhood, describes the physical and personal landscape. Similarly, in the poem "Yellow Memory," about a young girl's discovery of her grandfather's poetry, the poet-persona uses her memories of family to examine the inspiration that causes her to create: "he kept his poems locked / in a box beneath his bed. / In small scraps of paper / he forgave those who hurt him." The most technically complex piece in this collection is "Words." The poem deals with the fear that all artists must face, the fear of failure. In this case, the poet fears words and the inability to bring them together into form. Words

> like Ophelia suicidal
> wander about and about
> listless and sluggish
> lost in a labyrinth
> of their own making.

AND WHEN SHE DIED, p. 7

shifting his weight from ... ... squinting at the sun

"Yes," the boy said, And at that very point, the boy, in *deep*

his blood, knew. And the old man felt he knew— *in that way that children can see things. The boy took a deep sigh. In his deepest heart he knew his mother was de*

"Well, son," he said, "when we get back, she won't be

home. She'll be at the hospital most likely." The old man

still couldn't quite say it. He let the tears simply spill dow

his cheeks freely.

I know, "Why because she's dead?" the boy *said* asked and sat down on

the ground next to the tree stump, *and began to draw circles on t*

"I don't know, son. But Aunt Susie is with her. Don't worry.

Susie will take care of everything."

"I/We should go, dad." "Let's go home, I want to see Mom," the boy said but he

didn't move. *There was no urgency in his voice; the boy ha already accepted the truth in his own little way.*

The old man wanted to make sure at least another hour

went by, just in case the ambulance had come late. For a while,

no one spoke.

Little "Hey, where is everybody?" Harry came over the ridge,

holding two *small* fish, his and Alberto's, on a piece of rope.

"Son, let's go see the fish. We'll go home in a minute,

okay?" *For a few seconds they stove silent, like two men.*

When they both stood up, the old man hugged the boy.

"Son, no matter what happens, you and I will always be

together, okay?" They were now partners forever, the

who shared the secret of death by a river on a bright summer

"Sure, Dad," the boy said, not quite mature to fully

understand but old enough to read the sorrow in his father's

eyes. *Later, when his rich aunt, his mother's sister, tried to adopt because the old man had become an alcoholic — the boy refused to lea his father. In desperation, his aunt had flown back to Chicago.* The old man managed to waste *spend* another hour with the boys.

He admired the two fish and helped the boys cast again, for the

umpteenth time! For a long time, the three fished in silence.

enough time Finally, making sure a full hour had elapsed, the old man

said, "Well, boys maybe we better head back."

Early draft for an unpublished short story (by permission of Olivia Castellano)

The poet-persona feels rejected and disillusioned by the words she loves most. Like "Words," the entire collection is highly concentrated in form. Castellano's personal concerns in the creation of *Blue Mandolin, Yellow Field* were to be a disciplined poet conscious of poetics and to experiment with how far she could linguistically push herself. The reader senses that Castellano is trying to see what kind of technical mastery she can achieve and how much she can impress her audience with her craft. The tight, one-page poems are an indication of Castellano's desire for structure. Though the poems in this work are technically sound, one has the feeling that the poet is emotionally holding back.

In *Blue Horse of Madness* the Texas child comes alive. The poet's central thrust is to tell the story of the Blue Horse of Madness, the muse that inspired the collection:

> Mandolin Girl is learning
> to sing again,
> and caress the blue hairs of her lyre;
> she did not drown:
> Pegasus was not for dying
> but for learning how to dream.

Blue Horse of Madness is a book of poetry that reads like a collection of *cuentos* (stories) in poetic prose told by a poet-persona more confident than the younger voice in *Blue Mandolin, Yellow Field*. The individual poems are much freer than the tight, compact, imagistic pieces of the earlier collection. Although divided into eight sections of various themes, *Blue Horse of Madness* is tied together by a single narrative voice. The narrator is fully immersed in the memories being written about, drawing the readers into the poet's world. Castellano paints a vivid portrait, creating an imaginary place rooted in childhood where all can visit. Written in an adolescent voice, as demonstrated by "Learning to Play," Castellano conveys the serenity of growing up in Comstock, Texas, dwelling on the many voices and images that reside there:

> All was cuentos [stories] and myths
> an exaggeration of time and river
> to make our lives seem important
> and real.
>
> I don't know what I learned
> from all this
> but a girl I know well
> sits alone in a yellow field

> playing a blue mandolin
> playing and playing
> weaving patterns through the power
> of her dreams[.]

Here, as in *Blue Mandolin, Yellow Field*, Castellano continues the use of first-person narration. Examining the mythology she constructs, we see Castellano as a girl, "alone" in a "yellow field" in south Texas, using words to give shape to her imagination, represented by the color blue. "Playing a blue mandolin" is her childhood practice of the art of poetry. Castellano believes that "Chicanos need to invent [their] own mythology." In *Blue Horse of Madness*, one begins to understand the experiences which are her source of mythology. Whenever the young Castellano looked up from playing, there seemed to be a horse looming above her as ranchers rode through Comstock. She always felt inches away from being trampled. The images of blue horses in her poetry come from Texas horses that once stood over her; but in her writing she has given them wings, symbolizing the flight of the imagination.

The image of the blue horse reappears in her next book, *Spaces That Time Missed* (1986), a work that reflects a sense of balance and a maturity of voice acquired through the writing experience. In "The Need for Horses in a Child's Dreams," the voice of the poet on her blue horse is that of a wise child-philosopher, soaring above a yellow country with the ghost of her ancestry:

> Soon Comstock was not enough.
> To escape I invented a winged horse,
> blue horse of madness,
> that could soar me high above South Texas
> and show me what else I could be.

Spaces That Time Missed is divided into four sections that examine childhood, poetry, perception, and current events. This was Castellano's last collection of poetry before she decided to concentrate fully on writing fiction. The poems are more meditative and mature than in her two previous books. They are written by an adult voice involved in the pure enjoyment of the writing process. The themes presented are thought-provoking and the characters interesting, and as a result, the reader yearns to learn more about the world of south Texas. In this way, *Spaces That Time Missed* serves as a springboard into fiction. The last poem in the book, "Poor Traveler," perhaps best describes Castellano's decision to move toward the genres of the novel and short story:

Years have passed.
All has sunk below the horizon
below my first angle of observation
and has become a blur,
a peaceful part of the space
I now inhabit; I have
come to see finally that
I am the places I visited,
and I have traveled
down deep inside myself,
have gathered dust in all corners
of my recollection.

Castellano published her last two books of poetry herself, a method she prefers over solicitation, for she finds that in this way she "creates art for art's sake" rather than for profit or fame. By being a self-published writer, she keeps the writing in her own hands. Because her books are not readily available through bookstores or published by large publishing houses, few articles have been written about them. Sandra Cisneros's review of *Blue Mandolin, Yellow Field* in *Third Woman* magazine (1984) is one of the few critical pieces available on Castellano's work. Cisneros writes, "Though her literary influences are diverse, Castellano assembles a voice that is intimately hers with a sparseness and depth. . . ." Tey Diana Rebolledo, in an article on the inspirations of Chicana poetry, says of Castellano, "the writing of poems, even in the face of despair[,] creates a sense of connectedness and functions as solace for the poet."

Castellano continues to explore new genres.

Her projects include "The Comstock Journals," a novel or collection of short stories about a young Chicana growing up in a Texas-Mexico border town; "The Jimmy Blues," a serious drama about destructive behaviors in a Chicano family; and "Fantasies in a Blue Garden," a musical comedy celebrating a Chicano barrio through music, dance, and song. She is also working on her fourth book of poetry, tentatively named "For Women: Thank God the Moon is Forgiving."

Castellano's recent work exudes the relaxed sense of an artist comfortable with the craft of writing, a more mature voice that is no longer trying to prove what metaphor and rhyme are. The stories and songs from her culturally rich childhood in south Texas are rooted to that land, and as a poet, storyteller, novelist, and playwright, she will continue to write of the spaces that time missed in her remembrances of things past.

References:

Roberto Cárdenas, ed., *The Life and Poetry of Olivia Castellano* [videotape] (Sacramento: California State University, Film Archives, Communication Studies Department, 1989);

Tey Diana Rebolledo, "Soothing Restless Serpents: The Dreaded Creation and Other Inspirations in Chicana Poetry," *Third Woman*, 2, no. 1 (1984): 83-102;

Marcienne Rocard, "The Remembering Voice in Chicana Literature," *Americas Review*, 14 (Fall-Winter 1986): 150-159.

Ana Castillo
(15 June 1953 -   )

Patricia De La Fuente
Pan American University

BOOKS: *Zero Makes Me Hungry* (Chicago: Scott-Foresman, 1976);

Otro Canto (Chicago: Alternative Publications, 1977);

The Invitation (Chicago, 1979; revised edition, San Francisco: La Raza, 1986);

Women Are Not Roses (Houston: Arte Público, 1984);

The Mixquiahuala Letters (Binghamton, N.Y.: Bilingual Press/Editorial Bilingüe, 1986);

My Father Was a Toltec (Albuquerque: West End, 1988);

Sapogonia (An Anti-Romance in 3/8 Meter) (Tempe, Ariz.: Bilingual Press/Editorial Bilingüe, 1990).

OTHER: "Napa, California," "1975," "A Christmas Carol: c.1976," and "Our Tongue Was Nahuatl," in *The Third Woman: Minority Women Writers of the United States*, edited by Dexter Fisher (New York: Houghton Mifflin, 1980), pp. 386-392;

"Ghost Talk," in *Cuentos Chicanos*, edited by Rudolfo Anaya and Antonio Márquez (Albuquerque: University of New Mexico Press, 1984), p. 48;

"Antihero," in *Nosotras: Latina Literature Today*, edited by María del Carmen Boza, Beverly Silva, and Carmen Valle (Binghamton, N.Y.: Bilingual Press/Editorial Bilingüe, 1986), pp. 71-72;

Victoria Miranda and Camilo Feñini, *On the Edge of a Countyless Weariness: Al filo de un cansancio apatrida*, translated by Castillo, Daniel Fogel, and Cathy Mahoney (San Francisco: Ism, 1986);

"The Dream," "This Hand," "Meeting No. 1," "One Fifteen," "Now I Know," and "Letters," in *The Renewal of Vision: Voices of Latin American Women Poets 1940-1980*, translated by Carol Maier (Newcastle, U.K.: Spectacular Diseases Imprint, 1987), pp. 21-25;

"Plática de fantasmas," in *Antología retrospectiva del*

Ana Castillo (photograph by Rubén Guzmán)

cuento chicano (Mexico City: Consejo Nacional de Población, 1988), p. 185;

Esta puente, mi espalda: Voces de mujeres tercermundistas en los Estados Unidos, translated by Castillo, Cherríe Moraga, and Norma Alarcón (San Francisco: ISM, 1988);

Third Woman Literary Magazine: Latina Sexuality, coedited by Castillo (December 1988);

"A Marriage of Mutes," in *An Ear to the Ground: An Anthology of Contemporary American Poetry*, edited by Marin Harris and Kathleen

Aguero (Athens: University of Georgia Press, 1989), p. 55;

"The Distortion of Desire: Roosters by Milcha Sánchez-Scott," in *The Sexuality of Latinas*, edited by Castillo, Alarcón, and Moraga (Berkeley, Cal.: Third Woman, 1989), p. 147;

"Christmas Story of the Golden Cockroach," in *A Gathering of Flowers: Stories About Being Young in America*, edited by Joyce Carol Thomas (New York: Harper & Row, 1990), p. 63;

"Conversations With An Absent Lover on a Beachless Afternoon," in *New Chicago Stories*, edited by Fred L. Gardaphé (Chicago: Chicago City Stoop, 1990), p. 119;

"La macha: Toward a Beautiful Whole Self " and "What Only Lovers," in *Chicana Lesbians: The Girls Our Mothers Warned Us About*, edited by Marta A. Navarro (Berkeley, Cal.: Third Woman, 1991), pp. 24, 60.

SELECTED PERIODICAL PUBLICATIONS— UNCOLLECTED: "Soy Mexicana" and "The New Declaration of Independence," *Revista Chicano-Riqueña*, 4 (Autumn 1976): 4-9, 38;

"Encuentros No. 1," "Cartas," *Revista Chicano-Riqueña*, 10 (Winter-Spring 1982): 42-46;

"I Don't Want to Know" and "Not Just Because My Husband Said," *Revista Chicano-Riqueña*, 11 (Fall-Winter 1983): 39-41.

Ana Castillo is a prominent and prolific Chicana poet, novelist, editor, and translator whose work has been widely anthologized in the United States, Mexico, and Europe. Beginning in 1977 with her first poetry chapbook, *Otro Canto* (Other Song), Castillo's literary credits include the Before Columbus Foundation American Book Award for her first novel, *The Mixquiahuala Letters* (1986), a nomination for the 1986 Pushcart Prize, and a 1988 nomination for the Western States Book Award for the manuscript of her novel *Sapogonia* (published in 1990).

Born on 15 June 1953 and raised in Chicago, where she lived with her parents, Raymond and Raquel Rocha Castillo, Ana Castillo attended public schools there and became involved with the Chicano movement in high school when she was seventeen. She credits her Mexican heritage with providing a rich background of storytelling and remembers writing her first poems at the age of nine after the death of her grandmother. Castillo received a B.A. in liberal arts in 1975 from Northern Illinois University and an M.A. in Latin-American and Caribbean studies from the

University of Chicago in 1979. In 1985 Castillo moved to California, then later relocated in Albuquerque in 1990 with her young son, Marcel Ramón Herrera, born on 21 September 1983.

In addition to creative writing, Castillo has taught a wide range of subjects—including U.S. and Mexican history, the history of pre-Columbian civilizations, Chicano literature, and women's studies—at various universities. She has been invited to lecture not only at U.S. universities but also at the Sorbonne in Paris and at schools in Germany, where she completed a university reading tour hosted by Germany's Association of Americanists in June 1987. In 1989 and 1990 Castillo was a dissertation fellow in the Department of Chicano Studies at the University of California, Santa Barbara.

Her awards include a National Endowment for the Arts Fellowship for poetry (1990) and a California Arts Council Fellowship for fiction (1989), and she was an honoree of the Women's Foundation of San Francisco annual celebration of women in the arts for "pioneering excellence in literature" (1988). She is the first Hispanic to be honored with a collection, the Archives of Ana Castillo, at the University of California, Santa Barbara. In Chicago she has served as writer in residence for the Illinois Arts Council and in San Francisco as a board member of Aztlán Cultural / Centro Chicano de Escritores.

Castillo's poetic voice speaks for all women who have at one time or another felt the unfairness of female existence in a world designed by men primarily for men. In *Otro Canto* this voice is raised in protest against "The heavy pressure of it all" in a poem that questions the way things are:

i see it all the way
god should and I'm
wonderin' why
he doesn't.

Her first collection of poems, *Women Are Not Roses* (1984), includes selections from *Otro Canto* and her second chapbook, *The Invitation* (1979), along with sixteen new poems in which Castillo continues to examine the themes of sadness and loneliness in the female experience.

The Mixquiahuala Letters, an epistolary novel based on forty letters written by the character Teresa to her friend Alicia, is a provocative examination of the relationship between the sexes. A far-ranging social and cultural exposé, the novel

Cover for Castillo's 1990 book, the story of a mestizo man's obsession with the one woman he cannot conquer

examines Hispanic forms of love and gender conflict. The conclusion of the novel leaves the reader with the distinct impression that the narrator's crusade for sexual freedom and self-determination is far from an unqualified success. In her 1989 study "The Sardonic Powers of the Erotic in the Work of Ana Castillo," Norma Alarcón suggests an interesting connection between Castillo's earlier poetry (in *Otro Canto* and *The Invitation*) and her epistolary novel in that "both reveal the intimate events in the life of the speaker, combined with the speaker's emotional response to them, thus exploring the personal states of mind at the moment of the event or with respect to it." Alarcón sees the epistolary novel as "Castillo's experimentations with shifting pronouns and appropriative techniques for the purpose of exploring the romantic/erotic" and suggests that the female narrator "is betrayed by a cultural fabric that presses its images of her upon

her, and her response is to give them back to us, albeit sardonically."

In *Sapogonia*, Castillo hits her full-fledged and sophisticated stride in an intricately woven tale of the destructive powers of male-female relationships. Told from the viewpoint of the male narrator, Máximo Madrigal, whom critic Rudolfo Anaya has described (on the book cover) as "an anti-hero who relishes his inheritance as Conquistador while he agonizes over his legacy as the Conquered," the novel traces the obsessive relationship between the narrator and the woman he is unable to conquer, Pastora Aké.

A make-believe country, Sapogonia is "a distinct place in the Americas where all mestizos reside, regardless of nationality, individual racial composition, or legal residential status—or, perhaps, because of all these." As such, it both attracts and repels Madrigal, who was raised by his Spanish father and a wise Indian grandmother, Mamá Grande, who told him, "not once but many times, the stories related to her people, their history, and her own ideas about their traditions." In this novel the survival of the native culture is entrusted to the women and is symbolically represented by the little clay statues Mamá Grande insists on placing "alongside and at the foot of the statue of the Virgin." These Indian statues reappear in Aké's Chicago room on her dresser, where she lights candles to them and calls them spirit guides. Their influence persists, as does that of Mamá Grande and Aké's own Yaqui grandmother, a reminder of a nurturing, mythological background in the turbulence of the meaningless present.

Critic Patricia Dubrava called Aké "a kind of Joan Baez, a singer and songwriter [while] Max is a kind of anti-Don Quixote on a quest for fortune and dominion" (*Bloomsbury Review*, March 1991). Aké's role of protest singer defines her as a woman of vision and courage, forging her personal place in a chaotic world but with her feet firmly grounded in the traditions of her heritage. Madrigal is caught between the vices of two cultures, and unlike Aké, who remains true to herself throughout, he is torn between his dual roles of conqueror and conquered. His obsession with her, the one woman in his life he cannot conquer, suggests a deeper psychological trauma that prevents him from finding satisfaction.

"The ways in which we perceive and misperceive each other is one of Castillo's most important themes," Alarcón has pointed out. This observation is particularly true of *Sapogonia*, which is a study of the infinite ways men and women have of misreading each other. This concern with relationships between the sexes is concisely and expertly treated in an earlier, anthologized short story about the same characters, "Antihero" (1986), in which Madrigal reviews his obsession with "*her*, that cancerous sore of [his] existence." This woman who provokes, in turn, the narrator's surprise, rage, murderous instincts, and obsessive desire, is never named in the story but is certainly the same enigmatic, emancipated Aké. "Why couldn't she be like Laura?" Madrigal asks himself. But that is exactly the point; Aké is not another Laura, a woman Madrigal has easily conquered and imprisoned in a marriage of convenience—for him. Aké is a woman a man may experience, "twisted like live wires in an explosion of passion," but whom he may never be sure of, never really possess, and never truly understand. Unable to conquer her and place her among his other "victims," Madrigal recognizes "her intensity, her power of destruction" and, in a sense, allows himself to be destroyed by his frustration that "such a woman exists." In *Sapogonia*, Castillo expands and elaborates this basic conflict, but the essence of the novel may be found in "Antihero."

Castillo has completed a manuscript on Chicana feminist theory, a series of essays titled "Massacre of the Dreamers: Reflections on Mestizas in the U.S. / 500 Years After the Conquest." She is working on a new collection of poems in English and Spanish from 1987 to the present, tentatively called "Guerillera Love Poems." Aside from this, she also has a new long work of fiction in progress, "Santos," and her novel *The Mixquiahuala Letters* was purchased by Doubleday for a 1992 reprint. Given the enthusiastic critical reception of her work to date, the addition of new contributions by Castillo to the increasingly prestigious canon of Chicana writers will be a welcome event indeed.

Interviews:

Wolfgang Binder, ed., *Contemporary Chicano Poetry II: Partial Autobiographies: Interviews with Twenty Chicano Poets* (Erlangen, Germany: Palm & Enke, 1985), pp. 28-38;

Marta A. Navarro, *Chicana Lesbians: The Girls Our Mothers Warned Us About* (Berkeley, Cal.: Third Woman, 1991), p. 113.

Reference:

Norma Alarcón, "The Sardonic Powers of the Erotic in the Work of Ana Castillo," in *Breaking Boundaries: Latina Writings and Critical Readings*, edited by Asunción Horno-Delgado, Eliana Ortega, Nina M. Scott, and Nancy Saporta-Sternbach (Amherst: University of Massachusetts Press, 1989), pp. 94-107.

Papers:

The Archives of Ana Castillo can be found at the University of California, Santa Barbara.

Rosemary Catacalos

(18 March 1944 -   )

Merrihelen Ponce
University of California, Santa Barbara

BOOKS: *As Long as It Takes* (Springfield, Mo.:
Iguana, 1984);
Again for the First Time (Santa Fe, N.Mex.: Tooth
of Time, 1984).

Rosemary Catacalos writes works that combine Greek mythology and Mexican-American folklore. Her poetry, a paean to her ancestry, is especially effective in *Again for the First Time* (1984), a collection she wrote over a ten-year span. (All the poems in *As Long as It Takes*, a chapbook also published in 1984, are included in *Again for the First Time*.) Catacalos incorporates themes, styles of language, and types of lyricism that bring to mind works by the Mexican writer Rosario Castellanos and the Argentine Alfonsina Storni. Catacalos has earned an international reputation, yet her poetry is not as well known as that of some other Chicana writers. Much of this lack of attention is due to Catacalos's resistance to being part of the "poetry scene" and her commitment to letting her work speak for itself. However, she has gradually begun to read her work in public more often and to become more involved in literary circles. Catacalos has received several prizes and awards, among these the 1985 Texas Institute of Letters poetry prize for the best collection of poetry published by a Texas-connected writer and, in 1986, the Dobie Paisano Fellowship, a writing grant awarded jointly by the University of Texas at Austin and the Texas Institute of Letters.

Born on 18 March 1944 to Greek-Mexican parents (Demetres and Beatrice Catacalos) in San Antonio, Texas, Catacalos attended local schools in the area. "Childhood was difficult," she says, but it was "complicated and gloriously rich in grounding." Because both her parents worked in their small commercial-sign shop, Catacalos was raised by both sets of grandparents, although for a time she lived only with her paternal grandparents. She spent a great deal of time with her paternal Greek grandfather and her maternal grandmother, who was from Mérida, Yucatán, in

Rosemary Catacalos (photograph by Carlos René Perez)

Mexico. Baptized in the Greek Orthodox church, Catacalos was as strongly grounded in the Greek community as in the Mexican: "I went to public schools and to Greek school afterward *every day* for what seemed like centuries," she recalls. Her extended family, which included both sets of grandparents and one sister, Linda, interacted on a daily basis. Most families in the San Antonio barrio were poor, Catacalos recalls, as was her family: "When I was small, all four of us lived in one room of my paternal grandparents' house." Her parents eventually built their sign business into a statewide endeavor. The young Catacalos worked in their shop, cleaning brushes and handing her father tools and paints. This sense of family and community is a recurring theme in her work, as is her rich bicultural heritage. Greek and Mexican myths, names, and cities are characteristics of Catacalos's work.

A bookish child and an excellent student, Catacalos spent a lot of time alone, talking to herself. From about the age of five, she "talked" on paper but believes she was about twelve when she consciously began to write poetry. None of her childhood poems exist; however, a love of words, images, and the stories told by her grandparents remained and later surfaced as poems. Catacalos cites the nightly family story sessions as a time of learning—and great happiness. Much of this feeling was based on the stimulation given her by her grandparents, the languages spoken at home, and the richness of the ethnically mixed barrio. The stories and songs that were part of her daily life were the stimuli that fed her imagination. Her bedtime stories were from Greek mythology: "I didn't know I'd been given 'the Classics' until I reached fourth and fifth grade," she says. "By then—and to this day—the characters of Greek myths were my friends, living *compañeros* (companions) who could never be relegated to the realm of learned abstraction."

Catacalos has worked as copywriter, arts publicist, and newspaper reporter. From 1974 to 1985 she conducted bilingual poetry workshops in Arizona, Arkansas, and Texas, at the elementary and secondary-school level, and edited over thirty student anthologies. As a producer of cable-television programs on the arts, Catacalos also worked with the San Antonio Arts Council. In 1985 she cochaired the City of San Antonio's first Fine Arts and Cultural Advisory Committee and helped to develop the city's arts-funding process. She has also cochaired the Texas and Arizona Arts Commissions and served as a National Endowment for the Arts Literature panelist. In 1986 she was elected to the Texas Institute of Letters and the year before was the recipient of a National Endowment of the Arts Creative Writing Fellowship.

From 1986 to 1989 Catacalos served as director for the Literature Program at the Guadalupe Cultural Arts Center, a multidisciplinary Latino arts group in San Antonio. In 1987 she initiated and organized the first San Antonio Inter-American Bookfair, which has attracted national and international attention due to a cultural exchange program that has included writers such as Isabel Allende, Alice Walker, and Carlos Fuentes. Catacalos has taught poetry in San Antonio schools, and in 1986 she held an appointment as Visiting Scholar at the University of Texas at Austin. She held the prestigious Wallace Stegner Fellowship at Stanford University from 1989 to 1991, and she is completing a new poetry collection. She is now the director of the Poetry Center at San Francisco State University.

As many Chicana poets do, Catacalos utilizes some Spanish in her work, embellishing verses with the lyricism inherent in the language. She also uses some Greek, but she remains essentially a writer of English, a language that serves her well. Her bilingual poems, unlike those written only in English, are infused with the sounds of the San Antonio barrio, as in "From Home" (in *Again for the First Time*):

> Desde tu tierra te dicen [News from home]
> The chicharras [cicadas] are beginning to die again
> and it is the end of summer fruit.
> . . . .
> The mornings become brittle and cool ·
> without their sound. Camarada [comrade]
> the moon is on the rise,
> dogs howl through the night,
> and it is September.

The cicadas, the summer insects that each summer invade sections of the Southwest, are a metaphor for Mexican migrants who each summer cross the U.S. border to work, and the cicadas also bring to mind the sparrows mentioned (as seasonal workers) in Gary Soto's book *Where Sparrows Work Hard* (1981). Indeed, Catacalos's poetics are based in the community and express the human condition of Mexicans and Chicanos living a marginal existence.

Catacalos feels she expresses herself best in English, and she uses Spanish sparingly and with care. Although she learned to speak Spanish and Greek at an early age, she learned to think in English, the dominant language at her school. She recalls, "I had some confusion about language, since there were three of them in my life. My Spanish has obviously stayed with me, but my Greek is quite rusty, since there have been fewer opportunities to use it."

Her paternal Greek grandfather, who fled the Turkish army and at sixteen landed on Ellis Island, lived for a time in Seattle, where he worked as a carpenter. He later earned a living selling popcorn and ice cream from a wagon on San Antonio's West Side. A strong man with a soft heart, he is immortalized in a poem in *Again for the First Time*, "Katacalos" (the old spelling of the name, no longer used by the family):

> The Old Man, we always called him.
> We said it with respect.
> Even when he embarrassed us
> by wearing his plaid flannel work shirt
> to church under the fine blue suit
> . . . .
> He had come off a hard island birthplace,
> a rock long ago deserted by the gods. . . .

In *Again for the First Time* Catacalos explores Greek-Mexican duality. The retelling of old stories throughout her early years familiarized Catacalos with Greek characters such as Penelope and Theseus, and also with Mexican folk legends, including that of La Llorona, the wailing woman who searches for the children she killed—a legend learned from her Mexican maternal grandparents, in particular her grandfather who taught her to speak Spanish and about Mexican folklore. In "A Vision of La Llorona," Catacalos departs from the usual portrayal:

> I see your mother every week
> now that you're gone.
> Sometimes she knows me
> and remembers to be polite. . . .

Catacalos's work is not an attempt at neoclassicism but the merging of classical myths and the present: the Chicano barrio of San Antonio and everyday people the writer has known, yet who may exist in any Southwest barrio. In "One Man's Family" she depicts Dog Man, a transient from the neighborhood who "carries his mother's wedding dress around in that filthy sack."

"Rosemary Catacalos is a poet who can see beyond the simple event," critic Dave Oliphant wrote in 1985. She "comes into her own as a spokeswoman for the 'daily returns' of a life that through her writing offers in itself mythic relations to worlds past, present, and future. Woven into the sixty-eight pages of *Again for the First Time* is a series of poems wherein Catacalos takes on the character of different women, from Penelope to La Llorona." Oliphant claims that whether writing of her Mexican or Greek side, she is concerned throughout her book with "old ties."

Indeed the ties between writer and community are most evident in the first part of the book, which reflects *chicanismo* (an orientation toward Chicano cultural values), the Mexican side

of Catacalos, while the second alludes to her Greek ancestry and Greek gods and goddesses. There are odes to Ariadne, the Greek princess who weaves and entangles her lovers. Catacalos explains her fascination for Ariadne and myths: "Ariadne is an obsession with me. It has to do with the idea of the labyrinth and her ability to master that tangle, albeit on behalf of someone else. The notion of her eventual triumph over her abandonment is a magnet for me." In "Ariadne to Dionysios," Catacalos melds myth to reality:

> We have hiked hours to get to this place.
> . . . .
> Nothing stands between us now. Now we know
> what it is to be on an island. Nothing stands
> between us and the *sea*, Dionysios.
> . . . .
> Even before, when you lay in all the red and purple
> beds of Asia, did you think about my breasts?
> That they are the fruit of the sacred wine?
> The way I would delight again in twining
> around your famous staff if you could only
> get me into the sun long enough?

Sexuality, in the work of Catacalos, while subtle and sensuous, is often related to unrequited love, to women who wait for a lover. Another recurring theme is that of the sea as sexual, pulsating with salty waters, spray, foam, and life. In this same poem she writes, "you ride me like a dolphin, half in, half out / of the water / Your teeth, ancient shells, imprinting my skin. . . ."

For most writers, personal space and the insulation it provides are crucial to their work. It is not surprising that much of Catacalos's work relates to loneliness and pain. Catacalos remembers that because she studied and worked most of the time, she was a "solitary child, with few playmates, who spent her free time in the company of adults." In "(There Has To Be) Something More Than Everything" the voice of the solitary muse is heard:

> But there are things that have been torn away.
> From all of us. And we need to collect the shadows,
> the pain as it ghosts along the soul in faded fragments.
> We need to put as many old pieces as we can together
> to make something else entirely.
>
> As many times as we have to and as long as it takes.

A politically astute Catacalos evokes the works of Carolyn Forché, author of *The Country Be-*

tween Us (1981), whose works remark on human suffering and are highly political. Catacalos's "Learning Endurance From Lupe at the A & J Icehouse" is about the plight of Salvadoran refugees such as Lupe, who, after witnessing the cold-blooded killing of his wife and family, has escaped to the United States. Lupe spends his days in a stupor, as he sweeps ice at a local icehouse in return for the free beer that will dull his pain.

In addition to being a fine poet, Catacalos is committed to working with the Chicano community of her hometown, particularly with literacy programs. She has served the San Antonio community both as an administrator and as a teacher of poetry. This love for community is evident in her writing; for example, the *chicharras* in some of her poems make sounds like the voices of the talkative women of the barrio—women Catacalos portrays with love and kindness.

A primary goal for Catacalos has been to bring poetry to the schools and Chicano communities of Texas. In 1985 in the aftermath of a large Mexican earthquake, she designed and produced mailers featuring student poetry and drawings as gifts for the children of that country, a work that later was exhibited at the United Nations offices in Mexico City and featured in the 1986 San Antonio Festival. At the international level, Catacalos took part in the Tercer Encuentro de Poetas del Mundo Latino (Third Conference of Poets of the Latin World), held in 1988 in Mexico City, and sponsored by the Mexican Secretariat of Foreign Relations, the National Fine Arts Institute, and the National Autonomous University of Mexico.

Rosemary Catacalos resides in the California Bay Area, where she is working on a new collection. "I'm still basking in my solitude," she claims. "The poems come slowly but steadily."

References:

Steven G. Kellman, "State Without Words as Writers Convene," *San Antonio Light*, 15 April 1985, p. 8;

Marise McDermott, "It took Houston to find Catacalos," *San Antonio Light*, 11 March 1988, p. 11;

Dave Oliphant, "Three San Antonio Poets," *Cedar Rock*, 5 (Winter 1985): 6-8;

James Whitaker, "Tangled Lines," *Texas Monthly*, 12 (September 1984): 184-188.

Denise Chávez

(15 August 1948 -   )

Rowena A. Rivera

BOOK: *The Last of the Menu Girls* (Houston: Arte Público, 1986).

PLAY PRODUCTIONS: *Novitiates*, Dallas Theatre Center, 1973;
The Mask of November, Espanola, N.Mex., Northern New Mexico Community College, 1975;
The Flying Tortilla Man, Espanola, N.Mex, Northern New Mexico Community College, 1975;
Elevators, Santa Fe, Theatre Arts Corporation, 1977;
The Adobe Rabbit, Taos, Taos Community Auditorium, 1980;
Nacimiento, Albuquerque, Nuestro Teatro, 1980;
Santa Fe Charm, Santa Fe Actors' Lab, 1980;
An Evening of Theatre, Santa Fe, New Mexico School for the Visually Handicapped, 1981;
How Junior Got Throwed in the Joint, Santa Fe, State Penitentiary of New Mexico, 1981;
Sí, Hay Posada, Albuquerque, Nuestro Teatro, 1981;
El Santero de Córdova, Albuquerque, Feria Artesana, 1981;
The Green Madonna, Santa Fe Council for the Arts, 1982;
Hecho en México, by Chávez and Nita Luna, Albuquerque, Kimo Theatre, 1983;
La Morenita, Las Cruces, N.Mex., Immaculate Heart of Mary Cathedral, 1983;
Francis!, Las Cruces, N.Mex., Immaculate Heart of Mary Cathedral, 1983;
Plaza, Albuquerque, Kimo Theatre, 1984; New York, Festival Latino de Nueva York, September 1984; Edinburgh, Scotland, Scotland Arts Festival, September 1984;
Plague-Time, Albuquerque, Kimo Theatre, 1985;
Novena Narrative, New Mexico Tour of 6 Cities, 1987;
The Step, Houston, Museum of Fine Arts, 1987;
Language of Vision, Albuquerque, Fiesta Artística, 1988;
Women in the State of Grace, Grinnell, Iowa, Grinnell College, 1989.

Denise Chávez (Las Cruces Sun News)

OTHER: *Life is a Two-Way Street*, edited by Chávez (Las Cruces: Rosetta Press, 1980);
"The Step: Monologue for a Woman," in *New America*, edited by Vera Norwood (Albuquerque: University of New Mexico Press, 1982), pp. 49-51;
"Our Lady of Guadalupe," in *New Mexico Magazine*, 64 (December 1986): 55-63;
"Lagaña of Lace," "Ya," "Mercado Day," "Purgatory is an Ocean of Flaming Hearts," "For My Sister in Paris," and "Birth of Me in My Room at Home," *Americas Review*, 15 (Spring 1987): 48-59;

"The Train Whistles," "The Space Between," "This River's Praying Place," "Our Linkage," "Progression from Water to the Absence," "Lagaña Lace," "Worm Child," "Sisters, Sisters, Sisters," "On Mamá Toña," and "Missss Rede," *Journal of Ethnic Studies*, 15 (Spring 1987): 48-67;

"Words of Wisdom," in *New Mexico Magazine*, 65 (December 1987): 73-78;

"La Comadre Braulia," *Sin Embargo/Nevertheless: A Woman's Journal*, edited by Rowena A. Rivera (Albuquerque: Southwest Hispanic Research Institute, University of New México, 1988), pp. 28-32;

"The King and Queen of Comezón," and "Love Poem," in *Las Mujeres Hablan*, edited by Tey Diana Rebolledo, Erlinda Gonzales-Berry, María Teresa Márquez (Albuquerque: El Norte Publications, 1988), pp. 114-118, 155-157;

"Novenas Narratives y Ofrendas Nuevomexicanas," in *The Americas Review*, edited by María Herrera-Sobek and Helena María Viramontes (Houston: Arte Público Press, 1988), pp. 85-100;

"Plaza" in *New Mexico Plays*, edited by David Richard Jones (Albuquerque: University of New Mexico Press, 1989), pp. 79-106;

Shattering the Myth: Plays by Hispanic Women, selected by Chávez, edited by Linda Marcías Feyder (Houston: Arte Público, 1992).

As a Chicana playwright whose dramatic productions began in the early 1970s, Denise Chávez continues in her early plays the tradition of Luis Valdez's 1960 Farmworkers' Theater, El Teatro Campesino: theater written by Chicanos and produced for the Chicano community. Like the experimental and improvisational *actos* performed by the El Teatro Campesino, Chávez's early dramatic productions frequently focus upon social and economic issues in society and bring to the stage bilingual speech, Chicano humor, and street theater techniques. Her more recent dramatic productions reveal, however, a further development of themes that are inherent in the Chicano experience, a deeper and more universal reflection upon the sense of self and society, and a wider experimentation with dramatic styles and settings.

Chávez also pursues the writing of poetry and fiction, bringing to these genres her extensive training and theater experience as an actress and dramatist; in 1986 she published a collection of interrelated short stories, *The Last of the Menu Girls*, frequently considered a novel. In its use of technical devices employed in drama and in its lyrical and poetic prose, this work unites all her previous work and serves as an important point of departure for all her future work.

Born on 15 August 1948 in Las Cruces, in southern New Mexico, to Epifanio E. Chávez, a lawyer, and Delfina Rede Chávez, a teacher, Chávez was drawn at a very early age to the artistic qualities of bilingualism. The Mexican-American border area and her home background afforded her the opportunity to appreciate the musicality of the spoken word in conversations, prayers, tales, and legends—a poetic speech that she soon identified as a potential means of literary recreation. At Madonna High School in Mesilla, New Mexico, she took a theater class and discovered that theater was the creative means by which she could integrate the different aspects of her artistic inclinations. The class, she told Jim Sagel, was a "revolution. Life had a new meaning. . . . I can extend myself, be more myself." Upon graduation she received a drama scholarship to New Mexico State University where she studied with Mark Medoff, author of the play *Children of a Lesser God* (premiere, 25 October 1979), and in 1971 she received a bachelor's degree in drama. She received a master of fine arts degree in drama in 1974 from Trinity University in San Antonio, Texas, and had the experience of working in the Dallas Theatre Center. She continued her studies in drama and writing and in 1984 received a master of arts degree in creative writing from the University of New Mexico.

She has taught play writing at the College of Santa Fe and English composition and literature as well as drama at Northern New Mexico Community College in Espanola, New Mexico. At the present time Chávez is assistant professor of drama at the University of Houston where she teaches acting and ethnic drama classes. She has been named writer in residence throughout New Mexico and has worked as a playwright and actress with La Compañía de Teatro de Albuquerque, a bilingual theater company, and with Theater-in-the-Red, in Santa Fe. Chávez offers in-service workshops at elementary and secondary schools and frequently does public readings from her works. Very active in community work, she has been involved with the Arts for Elders Program in New Mexico and has served as the director of the Senior Citizens' Art Project in Las Cruces. She has traveled throughout Europe and in 1977 spent nearly a year in France while teaching at the American School in Paris. In 1988 she spent two weeks in Moscow participating in a creative writing symposium in which artists from the United States and the then Soviet Union exchanged ideas on contemporary art. She and her husband Daniel Zolinsky, a sculptor and photographer, live in Houston and spend their summers in their home in Las Cruces.

A prolific playwright, Chávez has seen the production, throughout the Southwest and in New Mexico, of nineteen of her plays written from 1973 to 1987. Her plays range from one-act skits to full-length productions and deal with children's topics, religious observances, social issues, and existential concerns. She has received many national and state awards for her acting and play writing: her first play, *Novitiates* was selected to be presented in the Experimental One-Act Play Festival held at the Dallas Theatre Center in 1973, and in 1984 she received international recognition for *Plaza*, which premiered in Albuquerque in August of that year and was subsequently performed at the Joseph Papp Festival Latino de Nueva York and at the Scotland Arts Festival in Edinburgh.

Chávez is aware that drama, as a genre that is seen, heard, and felt simultaneously, has a direct and immediate effect upon audiences. The specific potential of drama for bringing about mental changes was deeply explored by Chávez in 1978 with the New Mexico Free Theater in Santa Fe. Employing techniques from mime and street theater (white-face, masks, bilingual dialogue, humor, and a minimum of props), she dramatized important themes like loneliness, estrangement, and alienation of family and society. Chávez also develops the themes of self-knowledge and personal growth in plays such as *The Flying Tortilla Man*, a children's play presented at the Northern New Mexico Community College in 1975, and *Sí, Hay posada* (Yes, There is Room), a play produced by the Compañía de Teatro de Albuquerque in 1981 in which the main character, a Vietnam veteran, has to come to terms with his past.

There are shifts of focus from individual to social responsibility in her 1983 production *Hecho en México* (Made in Mexico), the 1984 play *Plaza*, and *Plague-Time*, produced in 1985. *Hecho en México*, written in collaboration with New Mexican poet/playwright Nita Luna, presents the plight of undocumented workers in the United

States. In this play Chávez views Mexican-born workers not as intruders or peripheral beings in society but as persons whose presence and labor is central to daily life in the Southwest. The need for a more human relationship with others is also an important motif in *Plaza*, the play performed in Albuquerque, New York, and Scotland in 1984. The title of the play immediately suggests the traditional Hispanic meeting space in which characters move about reflecting upon their identity and their lost Hispanic values. The movement within the plaza symbolizes the constant changes in time and space that Chicanos have historically undergone: the confrontation of traditional and contemporary values and the inner transitions needed in order to attain a more authentic relationship with self and with others. This play emphasizes the importance of family and friendship bonds as means by which individuals can recover their personal and cultural heritage. In *Plague-Time*, Chávez creates allegorical figures representing debilitating and fatal diseases that taunt each other; they are, in essence, metaphors for the social illnesses that transcend national borders. This symbolic and poetic work, written with the help of a 1985 Rockefeller Foundation playwright-in-residence award, resembles classical Greek drama by integrating dance, dialogue, and poetry.

Nacimiento, produced in 1980 in Albuquerque for the Festival of New Mexican Playwrights, while not usually considered one of Chávez's most important dramatic works, is particularly interesting in that it reveals her ability to create symbolic theater design and well-defined characterization. For example, a stage direction tells the reader, "the main set piece is the Slab, a moving raked platform that alternately transforms into a cart, stone slab, couch, altar, possibly a fountain, the river, a nacimiento [manger scene], a confessional, a grotto, a picture frame, and altar piece. . . ." The set intimately relates to the life of each of the four women characters and showcases the psychological intensity of their reflections. *Nacimiento*, whose title is translated as "birth," is equally significant in that it reveals incipient themes—the passage of time, lack of communication, and the discovery of a new feminine self-identification—that Chávez later fully developed in her book, *The Last of the Menu Girls*. The play deals with the memories and contemplations of four women, all at different phases of their lives: Mida, the grandmother; her daughter, Cuca; the granddaughter, Lillie; and a middle-aged woman, Juanita, who takes care of the seventy-four-year-old grandmother. In a Christmas Eve gathering, each character recalls moments of happiness and despair she experienced as a young girl. These women recall the men in their lives and recognize the self-deceit and lack of openness with which they have lived. As the play comes to a close, the grandmother cries out to Lillie, "We are deceiving ourselves. I deceive myself, your mother, Lillie, she deceives herself. And you? Have you begun to lie to yourself, as we have, all these years? Lies, lies, and when will they stop?" *Nacimiento* is also important in revealing Chávez's exceptional skills in writing prose. The stage directions are frequently lyrical and poetic, as exemplified at the beginning of the play when she describes what the mood of the scene should be: "The Night is still cold. It is the in-between hour of the soul when, for some reason, the lateness of the hour, perhaps, the emerging tensions or desires or even Weariness Herself has entered in, releasing the daylight rigidities that make themselves to be. The Star of Truth hovers over this place. It is a night transcending any other, before or after. . . ."

The common element in most of Chávez's plays is the interrelation between the outer New Mexico landscapes of mountains and deserts and the inner worlds of her Hispanic characters. Since she believes that man's life is shaped by his social environment, she reveals a strong influence of older dramatists like Anton Pavlovich Chekhov and of contemporary playwrights like Luis Valdez. Yet she has also been deeply affected by expressionist writers like Edward Albee, Eugene O'Neill, and Federico García Lorca who have inspired her to reveal on stage the world as it appears to the imagination rather than to the senses. In being more intensified and more openly poetic, her latest dramatic work reveals the influence of O'Neill's presentation of man's self-discovery and García Lorca's surrealist explorations of the poetic quality of speech.

Since 1976 Chávez's poetry and short stories have appeared frequently in national and local publications and anthologies. And in 1986 seven of her short stories, written separately within the last few years, were published together under the title of *The Last of the Menu Girls*. While her play writing has more frequently focused upon a wider scope of social experience, her poetry and prose usually turn inward and explore the deeper dimensions of Chávez's past and personal life. Her family was the inspiration,

Cover for Chávez's 1986 collection of seven short stories about a young woman's coming of age

for the work reflects the world of women in which Chávez was raised, a world that included her sisters, Faride Conway and Margo Chávez; her divorced mother, Delfina Rede Chávez; and the memory of her absent father, Epifanio E. Chávez. The women in her life made a lasting impression upon her. According to Benita Budd, Chávez claimed that her mother, "a literary and cultured schoolteacher," was her "guiding light." Chávez recalled always having "a wonderful gallery of role models, strong beautiful women who taught me many wonderful things when I was growing up." These women included the many "helpers" from across the border who kept the house going and helped raise Chávez while her mother taught. Chávez also recalls in her writings the many other friends who grew into womanhood, married, and whose lives took a different path.

The primacy of the personal memory characterizes *The Last of the Menu Girls*, a work in which the main character, Rocío Esquibel, reflects on events in her childhood and young adulthood and on the family members and acquaintances connected to these past incidents. While each of the short stories brings into focus a different event, a different phase in Rocío's past, all stories are bound by the presence of the main character and secondary characters such as the mother, Nieves; the sister, Mercy; and el compadre Regino, the handyman. The absence of the father, Salvador, is another element shared by the stories. Rocío is the only character we get to know; all the others are seen through her memories. The stories are also connected to each other by their development of the major theme of the work, the passage of time and its corresponding changes. Disregarding chronology and using time in a fluid fashion, each story is a different moment of the past life of Rocío's family. In "The Closet," Rocío experiences the silence and "smell of her mother's loneliness" while going through her mother's closet, which contains the evidence of the mother's life as a young widow and eventually a divorced woman. Rocío reflects upon the portrait hidden in the closet, "For many years I wondered who the man in the wedding photograph was. It wasn't my father. My father still lived with us at that time, but he wasn't home much." It is a glimpse into her mother's silent and incommunicable past, a past "suffocated in cloth" and the sudden awareness of the present estrangement of her parents. In her home's shelves, she finds forgotten objects, "an ash tray filled with old cigarette butts" left by the father on his last visit, candles from another year's Christmas luminarias, half-empty containers of candy, and broken religious images and objects. The discovery of these dusty, discolored, and disfigured things recalls their previous role and function. Memories are represented in Rocío's home by these forgotten objects, these fragments of past lives.

In contrast, the past in "Shooting Stars" is not viewed as hidden and immutable; rather, it is a memory that constantly changes with time. This type of retrospection is related to the young girl's quest for identity. Rocío recalls thinking of her young friends as "shooting stars," for to her they were the embodiment of feminine beauty, self-assurance, and mystery—qualities that she aspired to. Comparing herself to admired girls like Eloisa, who reminded her of Venus; Diana, also a goddess figure; and the sensual and dark-haired Josie, Rocío felt incomplete and disillusioned. Time, however, changes her previous evaluations. As Rocío matures, she begins to see her friends as real women, not romantic figures, for their lives end up in unhappiness, tragedy, or desperate dullness. Most of them, however, do survive and attain, with age, profound wisdom and rich transcendent beauty. It is the significance of this sense of time and change that Rocío wishes to unravel, to understand: "Perhaps, some day when I grow older, I thought, maybe then I can recollect and recount the real significance of things in a past as elusive as clouds passing."

In this work Chávez brings to her prose skills learned from her play-writing experience, particularly the effective use of bilingual dialogue and monologue. Conversations and verbal reflections question, answer, repeat, and intuit the many mysteries that Rocío attempts to decipher. The constant flow of words also joins one story to another, fusing the past and present, the memory and the now, giving shape to the entire work. Most of the reviewers of *The Last of the Menu Girls* draw attention to Chávez's accurate ear for the speech of the Mexican American in the Southwest who sprinkles Spanish words and phrases into the flow of English. In Chávez's stories her characters speak with a special rhythm and a delicate interlocking of the two languages, a speech described by Mary Soete in *Library Journal* (July 1986) as possessing the "warmth, tones, and languages of the Southwest. . . ."

In the *Women's Studies Review* (September-October 1986), María C. González discusses Chávez's "Space is a Solid" and points out that the voice of the heroine Rocío is "at times disjointed" but that there is, however, "beauty in the prose with echoes of Virginia Woolf—the disembodied narration." In *Choice* (October 1986), I. Molina also calls attention to the work's most important novelistic devices: "Such techniques as stream of consciousness, flashbacks, and internal monologue are skillfully applied to keep the reader's attention and interest." Beverly Lyon Clark in *The New York Times Book Review* (12 October 1986) notes an autobiographical relationship between Rocío and Chávez and emphasizes this Chicana writer's rapidly developing skills in narration:

The interrelated stories in this first collection sketch the coming of age of Rocío Esquibel as the adolescent girl examines available models of

Notes for "Saints," a chapter in Chávez's forthcoming novel, Face of an Angel *(by permission of Denise Chávez)*

womanhood, tries out roles, comes to terms with the clutter of her past, and emerges as a writer.

María C. González also sees much of Chávez in Rocío and comments on the character's struggle:

> Throughout the novel, Chávez plays with the developing identity of her protagonist, Rocío, who explores and breaks the traditional bounds of identity for a seventeen-year-old Hispanic female in Southwestern New Mexico. This is not the story of a stereotyped Hispanic, but the fictional

creation of an individual who fights the traditional boundaries of identity that society has set up and expects her to follow.

The universality of womanhood expressed by this new Chicana writer is also indicated in *Vista* (6 July 1986) by Rudolfo A. Anaya, well-known Chicano novelist and poet:

> Woven delicately into the story are the language and customs of the Latina. But the story as told

through the eyes of women is universal in its appeal, touching on shared human strengths and frailties.

Eugenio García, in his review in the *Albuquerque Journal* (6 May 1986), also stresses the importance of Chávez's ability to render the new and universal feminine self-identity: "the universal appeal of her feminine voice is more important than her regional/ethnic interest."

Chávez's poetic re-creation of language and her experimentation with contemporary novelistic devices have been considered important in making this work a significant contribution to Chicano literature. *The Last of the Menu Girls* has been reprinted twice and has sold more than six thousand copies.

Chávez plans to continue writing dramas, short stories, and novels in which she can fully develop her recurrent themes—self-knowledge and growth, time and transitions, and the phases of womanhood. To accomplish this, she is studying ancient and contemporary drama, religious and meditative writings, other women writers, and modern authors like Mexican novelist Juan Rulfo, whose language perfectly reflects the dialect of his Jalisco characters. Chávez is now working on the dramatization of scenes from *The Last of the Menu Girls*. She is also drawing characters from her plays for use in short stories, and is preparing for publication her novel *Face of an Angel*. In order to develop further as a writer, Chávez listens carefully to the many nuances of people's everyday speech, remembering that her mother, who died 26 April 1983, advised her that "people are always narrating stories everywhere."

References:

Annie O. Eysturoy, "Denise Chávez," in *This is About Vision: Interviews with Southwestern Writers*, edited by William Balassi, John F. Crawford, and Eysturoy (Albuquerque: University of New Mexico Press, 1990), pp. 156-169;

Benita Budd, "Playwright Sees Through Eyes of Mexican Workers, *Performance* (8 April 1983): 6;

Jim Sagel, "Writer Wanders through Familiar Rooms," *Journal North* (14 August 1982): E4.

Sandra Cisneros

(20 December 1954 -   )

Eduardo F. Elías
University of Utah

BOOKS: *Bad Boys* (San Jose, Cal.: Mango, 1980);
The House on Mango Street (Houston: Arte Público, 1983);
My Wicked Wicked Ways (Bloomington, Ind.: Third Woman, 1987);
Woman Hollering Creek and Other Stories (New York: Random House, 1991).

SELECTED PERIODICAL PUBLICATIONS—
UNCOLLECTED: "Los Tejanos: Testimony to the Silenced," *Texas Humanist* (November-December 1984): 11-12;
"An Interview with Ana Castillo," *Tonantzin*, 1 (April-May 1984): 14-15;
"Bread, Dreams, and Poetry: Luis Omar Salinas, the Man," *Tonatzin*, 1 (June-July 1984): 14-15;
"Salvador Late or Early," *Humanizarte*, 7 (Summer 1986);
"Cactus Flowers: In Search of Tejana Feminist Poetry," *Third Woman*, 3, nos. 1-2 (1986): 73-80;
"Ghosts and Voices: Writing from Obsession," *Americas Review*, 15 (Spring 1987): 69-73;
"Notes to a Young(er) Writer," *Americas Review*, 15 (Spring 1987): 74-76;
"Do You Know Me?: I Wrote *The House on Mango Street*," *Americas Review*, 15 (Spring 1987): 77-79.

Sandra Cisneros, November 1985 (photograph by Rubén Guzmán)

Sandra Cisneros considers herself a poet and a short-story writer, although she has also authored articles, interviews, and book reviews concerning Chicano writers. She began writing at age ten, and she is one of the few Chicano authors trained in a formal creative-writing program. At the University of Iowa Writers' Workshop she earned a Master of Fine Arts degree in 1978. She has taught creative writing at all levels and has experience in educational and arts administration. Her creative work, though not copious, has already been the subject of scholarly papers in the areas of Chicano and women's studies. She has read her poetry at the Colegio de México in Mexico City; at a symposium on Chicano literature at the Amerikanistik Universität in Erlangen, Germany; and over Swedish Educational Radio. Some of her poetry is included in a collection of younger Chicano poets published in Calcutta, India. She has garnered several grants and awards in the United States and abroad, and her book *The House on Mango Street* (1983) was praised, winning the 1985 Before Columbus American Book Award.

Cisneros is a native of Chicago, where she grew up and attended Loyola University, graduating in 1976 with a B.A. in English. Her father was born in Mexico City to a family of means; his wanderlust and lack of interest in schooling led him to travel broadly and to venture into the United States. By chance he traveled through Chicago, met Sandra's mother, and decided to settle there for life. He and his family were influential in Sandra's maturation. Her mother came from a family whose men had worked on the railroad. Sandra grew up in a working-class family, as the only girl surrounded by six brothers. Money was always in short supply, and they moved from house to house, from one ghetto neighborhood to another. In 1966 her parents borrowed enough money for a down payment on a small, ugly, two-story bungalow in a Puerto Rican neighborhood on the north side of Chicago. This move placed her in a stable environment, providing her with plenty of friends and neighbors who served as inspirations for the eccentric characters in *The House on Mango Street*.

The constant moving during her childhood, the frequent forays to Mexico to see her father's family, the poor surroundings, and the frequent changing of schools made young Cisneros a shy, introverted child with few friends. Her love of books came from her mother, who saw to it that the young poet had her first library card before she even knew how to read. It took her years to realize that some people actually purchased their books instead of borrowing them from the library. As a child she escaped into her readings and even viewed her life as a story in which she was the main character manipulated by a romantic narrator.

"I don't remember reading poetry," Cisneros admits. "The bulk of my reading was fiction, and Lewis Carroll was one of my favorites." As she wrote her first poems, modeling them on the rhythmic texts in her primary readers, she had no notion of formal structure, but her ear guided her in matters of rhyme and rhythm. After the sixth grade, however, Cisneros stopped writing for a while. In her junior year in high school she was exposed to works by the finest of British and American writers and by Latin-American poets who impressed her deeply. Finally, in her junior year at Loyola University, she was introduced to writers such as Donald Justice, James Wright, and Mark Strand, poets who had influenced a whole generation of Spanish writers, thus bringing Cisneros into touch with her cultural roots. She was also introduced to the Chicago poetry scene, where there was great interest

in her work. She was encouraged to study in a creative-writing program and was admitted to the Iowa Writers' Workshop; she had hoped to study with Justice but discovered that he and Marvin Bell were on sabbatical leaves that academic year.

Cisneros looks back on those years and admits she did not know she was a Chicana writer at the time, and if someone had labeled her thus, she would have denied it. She did not see herself as different from the rest of the dominant culture. Her identity was Mexican, or perhaps Puerto Rican, because of the neighborhood she grew up in, but she mostly felt American—because all her reading was of mainstream literature, and she always wrote in English. Spanish was the private language of home, and she spoke it only with her father. Cisneros knew no Chicano writers in Chicago, and although she was the only Hispanic majoring in English at Loyola, she was unaware of being different—in spite of her appearance, which was considered exotic by her female classmates.

The two years at Iowa were influential on Cisneros's life and writing. She admits that the experience was terribly cruel to her as well as to many of the other first-year students, but it was also liberating. She had her share and fill of intimidating teachers and colleagues as well as some marvelous ones who helped and encouraged her. This was a time for Cisneros to mature emotionally, something she had neglected to do for some years—always having considered herself as somebody's daughter, lover, or friend. The poet struggled in these years with finding a voice for her writings. She imitated her teachers, her classmates, and what she calls the "terrible East-coast pretentiousness" that permeated the workshop, without finding satisfaction. An important friend at this time was Joy Harjo, a Native American from Oklahoma, who was well centered in her southwestern heritage and identity and who also felt lonely and displaced in the Iowa workshop. This friendship offered Cisneros the assurance that she had something to write about that would distinguish her from her classmates.

The bulk of Cisneros's early writing emerged in 1977 and 1978. She began writing a series of autobiographical sketches influenced by Vladimir Nabokov's memoirs. She purposely delighted in being iconoclastic, in adopting themes, styles, and verbal patterns directly opposed to those used by her classmates. *The House on Mango Street* was born this way, with a child's narrative voice that was to be Cisneros's poetic persona for several years.

The poem "Roosevelt Road," written in the summer of 1977, is most important to Cisneros because it forced her to confront the poverty and embarrassment she had lived with all her previous years and to admit the distinctiveness of this background as a positive resource that could nourish her writing. In this poem the language is completely straightforward and descriptive of the tenement housing where the poet lived as a child. Lines run into one another, so that the reader is compelled to follow the inherent rhythm, while working on the sense of the message:

> We lived on the third floor always
> because noise travelled down
> The milkman climbed up tired everyday
> with milk and eggs
> and sometimes sour cream.
> . . . .
> Mama said don't play in alleys
> because that's where dogs get rabies and
> bad girls babies
> Drunks carried knives
> but if you asked
> they'd give you money.
> . . . .
> How one time we found that dollar
> and a dead mouse in the stone wall
> where the morning glories climbed. . . .

Once the journals *Nuestro* and *Revista Chicano-Riqueña* accepted her first poems, Cisneros gained enough confidence to submit her work to other publications. These early texts were more concerned with sound and timing, more with the *how* than with the *what*, of what she was saying. A case in point is "South Sangamon," in *My Wicked Wicked Ways* (1987), a poem which, when read aloud, corroborates the fact:

> His drunk cussing,
> her name all over the hallway
> and my name mixed in.
> He yelling from the other side open
> and she yelling from this side no.
> A long time of this
> and we say nothing
> just hoping he'd get tired and go.

Cisneros's master's thesis, titled "My Wicked, Wicked Ways" (Iowa, 1978), is full of such poems on a diversity of topics—daily events, self-identity, amorous experiences, and encounters with friends. Her penchant for sound is obvious,

as is her representation of a world that is neither bourgeois nor mainstream. Revised and enlarged, the thesis was published as a book in 1987.

While Cisneros taught at Latino Youth Alternative High School in Chicago (July 1978 - December 1980), she spent time on writing but never finished projects fully as collections. Her involvement with many aspects of student life was too draining and consumed her creative energy. However, one poem she wrote was selected to be posted on the Chicago area public buses, thus giving her much-needed exposure and publicity. Cisneros was also seduced by the adulation and applause awarded to writers who read their material at public performances. After a period of "too much performing" (in her words) in coffeehouses and school auditoriums, she gave up the lecture circuit to spend more time on her writing.

Another Chicano poet, Gary Soto, was instrumental in helping publish Cisneros's chapbook *Bad Boys* in 1980. The seven poems depict childhood scenes and experiences in the Mexican ghetto of Chicago. One poem, "The Blue Dress," is Cisneros's effort to paint a scene full of visual imagery that depicts a pregnant woman seen through the eyes of the expectant father. The language of these poems has a musical ring, with short, run-on lines and compact statements.

By the time that *The House on Mango Street* was ready for publication, Cisneros had outgrown the voice of the child narrator who recounts the tales in the book, but this 1983 work gave Cisneros her broadest exposure. It is dedicated to "the women," and, in forty-four short narratives, it recounts the experiences of a maturing adolescent girl discovering life around her in a Hispanic urban ghetto. There are many touching scenes that Esperanza, the young narrator, recounts: her experiences with the death of relatives and neighbors, for example, and with girlfriends who tell her about life. In "Hips," young Esperanza explains: "The bones just one day open. One day you might decide to have kids, and then where are you going to put them?" Esperanza identifies herself to her readers: "In English my name means hope. In Spanish it means too many letters." As the stories of Esperanza in her Hispanic barrio evolve, the child breezes through more and more maturing experiences.

The reader sees many portraits of colorful neighbors—Puerto Rican youths, fat ladies who do not speak English, childhood playmates—until

Cover for Cisneros's 1987 book, which includes "The Rodrigo Poems," erotic monologues spoken by women who are romantically involved with the same man

finally Esperanza sees herself and her surrounding experiences with greater maturity. Thus the reader sees her at her first dance in the tale "Chanclas," where attention is first focused on the bulky, awkward saddle oxfords of a schoolgirl, then the vision is directed upward as Esperanza blossoms into a graceful and poised dancer, who draws everyone's glances. Esperanza retells humorous experiences about her first job and her eighth-grade girlfriend who marries; then Esperanza reveals more of her intimate self in the last two tales. In "A House of My Own" and "Mango Says Goodbye Sometimes," it is revealed that the adolescent has been nurturing a desire to flee the sordid, tragicomic environment where she has grown up. The image of the house is also useful to reveal the need for the narrator to find a self-identity.

An important contribution by Cisneros to Chicano letters is that this book about growing up offers a feminine view of the process, in contrast to that exemplified by leading works by men. As critics Erlinda Gonzales-Berry and Tey Diana Rebolledo have aptly pointed out, young Esperanza is a courageous character who must combat the socialization process imposed on females; the character breaks from the tradition of the usual protagonist of the female bildungsroman by consistently rejecting the models presented to her and seeking another way to be Chicana: "I have begun my own kind of war. Simple. Sure. I am one who leaves the table like a man, without putting back the chair or picking up the plate." Esperanza's experiences parallel those depicted by other Chicana writers.

In conversations about her life, Cisneros admits that up through her college years she had always felt that she was not her own person. Thus Esperanza yearns for "a house all my own. . . . Only a house quiet as snow, a space for myself to go, clean as paper before the poem." Cisneros's speaker feels the need to tell the world the stories about the girl who did not want to belong to that ugly house on Mango Street. Esperanza admits, at the conclusion of her stories, she is already too strong to be tied down by the house; she will leave and go far, only to come back some day for those stories and people that could not get away. The conclusion is that, in essence, Cisneros takes within her the memories from the house as she also carries her mementos from Mango Street, her bag of books and possessions. These are her roots, her inspirations, and the kernels of what Cisneros sensed, years ago in Iowa, that distinguished her from other American writers.

My Wicked Wicked Ways contains several texts that have been published singly. They show a different aspect of Cisneros's work. The speakers of several poems are adult women involved in relationships with a roguish male, Rodrigo. These poems are physically descriptive and sensuous—bordering on the erotic—and behind them lies a strong hand.

Woman Hollering Creek and Other Stories (1991) is a rare example of a work by a Chicana being published by a mainstream press. Writer Ann Beattie has said of this collection: "My prediction is that Sandra Cisneros will stride right into the spotlight—though an aura already surrounds her. These stories about how and why we mythologize love are revelations about the constant, small sadnesses that erode our facades, as well as those unpredictably epiphanic moments that lift our hearts from despair. A truly wonderful book."

Cisneros has been fortunate to earn several grants that have permitted her to devote herself full-time to her writing. In the spring of 1983 she was artist in residence at the Fondation Michael Karolyi in Vence, France. Earlier, in 1982, she received a National Endowment for the Arts grant, which she used to travel through Europe. During that time she began work on a series of poems she included in her 1987 book. Several of them are evidently based on fleeting encounters with men she met in her European travels. They are whimsical mementos of fleeting instances either enjoyed or lost. Still present are the familiar rhythm and musicality; the major change is in the themes and voice. Most definitely, she has outgrown the adolescent form of expression of her earlier writing.

In the late 1980s Cisneros completed a Paisano Dobie Fellowship in Austin, Texas, and then spent additional time in Texas. She also won first and third prizes for her short stories in the Segundo Concurso Nacional del Cuento Chicano, sponsored by the University of Arizona. Cisneros as a writer is growing rapidly. She feels that writers like herself, Soto, Lorna Dee Cervantes, and Alberto Ríos belong to a new school of technicians, new voices in Chicano poetry. Cisneros wants to maintain her distinctiveness and her dual inheritance and legacy, and not fuse into the American mainstream. She cannot tell in which direction her poetry will lead her; most recently she has expanded her writing to include essays. She hopes that years from now she will still be worthy of the title "poet" and that her peers will recognize her as such.

References:

Erlinda Gonzales-Berry and Tey Diana Rebolledo, "Growing Up Chicano: Tomás Rivera and Sandra Cisneros," *Revista Chicano-Riqueña*, 13, nos. 3-4 (1985): 109-119;

María Herrera-Sobek, "The Politics of Rape: Sexual Transgression in Chicano Fiction," in *Chicana Creativity and Criticism: Charting New Frontiers in American Literature*, edited by Herrera-Sobek and Helena M. Viramontes (Houston: Arte Público, 1988), pp. 171-188;

Julián Olivares, "Sandra Cisneros' *The House on Mango Street*, and the Poetics of Space," in *Chicana Creativity and Criticism: Charting New Frontiers in American Literature*, pp. 160-170;

Yvonne Yarbro-Bejarano, "Chicana Literature from a Chicana Feminist Perspective," in *Chicana Creativity and Criticism: Charting New Frontiers in American Literature*, pp. 139-145.

Margarita Cota-Cárdenas

(10 November 1941 -   )

Carmen Salazar
Los Angeles Valley College

BOOKS: *Noches despertando inConciencias* (Tucson, Ariz.: Scorpion, 1975);

Puppet (Austin, Tex.: Relámpago, 1985);

Marchitas de mayo (Austin, Tex.: Relámpago, 1989).

OTHER: *Siete poetas*, edited by Cota-Cárdenas and Eliana Rivero, includes poems by Cota-Cárdenas (Tucson, Ariz.: Scorpion, 1978);

"El velorio del Wimpy," in *Avanzando: gramática española y lectura, Cuaderno B*, edited by Sara Lequerica de la Vega and Carmen Salazar Parr (New York: Wiley, 1978), pp. 107-109;

The Third Woman: Minority Women Writers of the United States, edited by Dexter Fisher, includes poems by Cota-Cárdenas (Boston: Houghton Mifflin, 1980), pp. 398-400;

Chicanos: Antología histórica y literaria, edited by Tino Villanueva, includes poems by Cota-Cárdenas (Mexico City: Fondo de Cultura Económica, 1980), pp. 269-273;

Flor y Canto IV and V: An Anthology of Chicano Literature, includes poems by Cota-Cárdenas (Albuquerque: Flor y Canto, 1980).

SELECTED PERIODICAL PUBLICATIONS—
UNCOLLECTED: "Oda a una mosca," *Xalmán*, 1 (Fall 1977): 33;

"Principiante," and "Por nosotros," *Antología Canto al Pueblo*, 4 (1980): 31-32;

"A New Kind of Reader: The Chicana Feminist," *Reader*, 8 (1980): 23-28;

"The Chicana in the City as Seen in Her Literature," *Frontiers*, 6 (Spring-Summer 1981): 13-18;

"El hablante y el espacio en el 'Niágara' de Heredia: Un análisis estructural," *Explicación de textos literarios*, 12 (1983-1984): 19-28;

"Love, Hate, Love-Hate, Late," "To a Dark-Haired Lover," and "Aaay, Cucuy," *Imagine*, 1 (Summer 1984): 108-110;

"*Mi querido Rafa* and Irony: A Structural Study," *Revista Chicano-Riqueña*, 12 (Fall-Winter 1984): 158-169.

Margarita Cota-Cárdenas has made a notable contribution to Chicano letters as a poet and novelist. Although she dealt with personal concerns in her early work, she later focused on feminist themes and social issues, approaching these with bittersweet humor at times, but always with sensitivity and compassion.

Cota-Cárdenas was born on 10 November 1941 in Heber, California, in the Imperial Valley. Her father, Jesús Cota, from Sonora, Mexico, and her mother, Margarita Cárdenas de Cota, from New Mexico, had been migrant workers until they established permanent residence in California, where they worked as contractors. The oldest of eight children, Cota-Cárdenas spent her formative years in a bilingual, bicultural environment in the Imperial Valley, and it was this environment that provided the setting and stimulus for much of her work.

She became interested in writing at an early age and was always a good, conscientious student who derived pleasure from her schoolwork, particularly when writing assignments for her English classes. One such assignment, to write about an unforgettable experience, eventually developed into the poem "Nostalgia," published in 1978 (in *Siete Poetas* [Seven Poets]). The childhood memory Cota-Cárdenas drew on for the assignment and the poem was of seeing a particular film at the local Motor-Vu Drive-in Theatre. The film, which starred the beautiful María Félix, who as a nun rode off on horseback into the sunset, made an indelible impression on the young Margarita. Later that summer, her mother took Margarita on a casual visit to the Convent of the Good Shepherd near Mesilla, New Mexico. This visit convinced the young girl that she wanted to be a nun, and she begged to be enrolled in the establishment. Unable to dissuade her, Margarita's mother enrolled her in the convent for a few weeks. Soon Margarita was beginning to feel the pains of austere discipline and homesickness. Perhaps acting intuitively, her father came to visit her and took her home.

Margarita Cota-Cárdenas (photograph by Tom Parrish)

"Nostalgia" reveals her talent as a poet, particularly in the juxtaposition of images. With bittersweet irony, Cota-Cárdenas recalls the childhood fantasies of a girl:

creía entonces
que me gustaría ser monja de
velo largo blanco en el viento
montada a caballo como María Félix
cabalgaba cabalgaba hacia
un bello oriente cinematográfico

(I thought then
that I would like to be a nun with
a long white veil floating in the wind
mounted on horseback like María Felix
riding riding off into
a lovely cinema type sunset)[.]

Throughout her four years in Orestimba High School, from 1955 to 1959, Cota-Cárdenas wrote the column "Just Talking" in an informal, humorous style for the school newspaper. Her love for reading and writing had been nurtured by her teachers and, above all, by her father, who provided further encouragement when he bought her an old set of the complete works of Charles Dickens at a secondhand store. At the insistence of her English teacher, Cota-Cárdenas entered the American Legion Essay Contest and won third place in her district. She was later named the outstanding girl graduate and was presented with the American Legion Citizenship Award, an honor she had won earlier as an eighth grader.

While in high school, Cota-Cárdenas had many aspirations. At first she thought she wanted to go to medical school, but by the time she became a senior, she was convinced that she wanted to be an actress. When she graduated in 1959, she received a scholarship from the Department of Theatre Arts at the University of California, Los Angeles. Nevertheless, she turned it down and did not enroll in college until after the birth of her first child. By then, with the obligations of motherhood and with the birth of a second child, her options diminished. She attended Modesto Junior College and later California State College, Stanislaus, where she received her B.A. in 1966 with a major in Spanish and a minor in English. Her love for literature was rekindled, and she decided that she would definitely pursue a career in teaching. She enrolled in graduate school at the University of California, Davis, and received her M.A. in 1968. Although attending college in the turbulent 1960s, Cota-Cárdenas—a divorced mother with two children, struggling to put herself through school—found little time and energy to get involved in the activities of the Chicano movement. Nevertheless the influence of the Chicano movement and the women's movement became evident in her writing. Eventually, with the aid of scholarships and fellowships, Cota-Cárdenas earned a Ph.D. from the University of Arizona in 1980.

In 1975, following a break, Cota-Cárdenas had returned to her studies with renewed vigor. Significantly 1975 was International Women's Year. Although Cota-Cárdenas had started writing poetry in 1969, she flourished as a poet in the fall of 1975 and saw the publication of her collection *Noches despertando inConciencias* (Nights Awakening UnConsciences). She and Cuban poet Eliana Rivero had founded Scorpion Press, the publisher of *Noches*, for the express purpose of publishing works by bilingual, bicultural women. As a result, they edited and published several books, including *Siete poetas*, with the aid of a grant from the National Endowment for the Arts. Scorpion Press made accessible works by bilingual women that previously were dispersed in journals and magazines.

Noches was favorably received and was reprinted in 1976 and 1977. Reviewer Justo Alarcón observed that "dentro de la poesía femenina, y en el conjunto total de la obra chicana de los setenta, es un libro intrigante, consciente de su evolución, original y valioso en lo que abre de brecha y en lo que posee de valor cultural, humano y poético" (within feminist poetry, and within the total production of Chicano works of the seventies, it is an intriguing book, conscious of its evolution, original and worthwhile for its introduction of a new mode, and for its cultural, human, and poetic values). Since 1977 many of the poems have been reprinted in journals and anthologies, thus confirming the quality of the poetry.

Noches is written almost exclusively in Spanish, with an occasional word in English for special effect. Unlike other Chicano poets who mix English and Spanish or *caló*, the jargon of the barrio, Cota-Cárdenas relates better to Spanish, her first language, particularly in those poems that evoke childhood emotions. She has, however, translated many of her own poems and has begun to write poems in English, but she maintains that her lyric voice is still Spanish.

Noches is divided into two parts. The first section of part 1 comprises nine poems devoted to personal love, a search for everlasting love, and a response to an identity crisis. There is a conscious effort at "poetization," at precision in form, rhyme, and meter. The title of this section,

"Desveladas tempranas" (Early Wakefulness), is significant. On the one hand, it makes reference to the early efforts of Cota-Cárdenas in the task of writing; on the other, it refers to the thematic content. The section focuses on the anxieties and concerns of sleeplessness.

The second section of part 1, likewise, has a significant title: "Y de repente, en una nueva vena, poesiámbula" (And Suddenly, in a New Vein, Wandering Poetry). The created word "poesiámbula" reveals the new direction of her poetry, including free verse, a conversational tone, and social rather than personal concerns: the real awakening of the conscience. It is the flowering of her *ars poetica*. Cota-Cárdenas acknowledges the help and advice of her professor and friend Rivero, who encouraged her to experiment with free verse and new techniques.

The second part of *Noches* comprises thirty-five poems written in 1975, her most prolific period. The effects of International Women's Year are clearly in focus with her feminist perspective. She is aware of her role as a poet, a woman, and a Chicana. Reevaluating myths, legends, and archetypes, Cota-Cárdenas focuses on an examination of self and environment. Her lyric voice is that of an anguished woman who seeks fulfillment, yet it is not one of despair. It is a sensitive voice that offers hope and compassion.

Cota-Cárdenas expresses concern for sociopolitical problems, male-female relationships, and woman's role in society. To better understand the present, she returns to the past. Thus Cota-Cárdenas often evokes childhood memories to contrast the fantasy and illusion of growing up with the harsh realities of the adult world. She evokes the nostalgia of childhood, the time of make-believe in which all fantasies become real:

> como creía yo que se podía todo
> como en las películas de los '40
> del Motor-Vu
>
> (the way I thought one could do everything
> like in the movies of the 1940s
> at the Motor-Vu)[.]

Within the group of poems about children are those dedicated to a brother and sister, to her own children, and to other children who live in a hostile world. But the voice is always that of one who has an adult perspective regarding childhood fantasies and myths. The poems written as advice to her own children reveal her concern for their welfare. In "To a Young Son" she warns the child not to go to the park where ten- and twelve-year-olds are turned into junkies. In "A María Cristina" she offers compassion to a daughter who, as a woman, will have to struggle to surpass the limits set on her. Cota-Cárdenas recognizes the need for myths; nevertheless she tells her child that in the growing-up process she will eventually undo her own legends:

> pero por ahora
>   no te desesperes
> te dejé intactos al niño Jesús
>   a Cenicientas   a Santa Claus
>   y a tu padre
>   me controlé mucho
>   hija mía
> para que tú
>   desesperada y mujer
>   deshicieras tus leyendas
>
> (but for now
>   don't be so anxious
> I've left intact for you Baby Jesus
>   Cinderella   Santa Claus
>   and your father
>   I controlled myself much
> so that you
>   desperate and a woman
>   could undo your legends)[.]

There is a tinge of bittersweet humor reflected through a careful manipulation of irony. This humor is evident throughout the book but is especially effective in those poems that examine the stereotypical role of women. In "Creidísimas" (Gullible) Cota-Cárdenas pokes fun at the stereotype represented by Penelope, symbol of patience and utmost fidelity:

> te saciaba por egoística telepatía
>   o
>   tú tenías amante
>
> (he satisfied you through egotistical telepathy
>   or
>   you had a lover)[.]

In "Soliloquio travieso" (Mischievous Soliloquy) Cota-Cárdenas refers to the woman-as-object theme and humorously conveys the woman's refusal to be part of an identity that ultimately belittles her:

> mucho trabajo   ser flor
>   a veces
>   solitas
>   y en camino

> concentramos muy fuerte   así
>   arrugamos la frente
>   para marchitarnos antes
> y al llegar al mercado   ji ji
>   no nos pueden vender
>
> (it's very hard   being a flower
>   sometimes
>   when we're all alone
>   and on the way
> we concentrate real hard   like this
>   and wrinkle up our brow
>   so that we'll wither beforehand
> and when we get to the market   hee hee
>   they can't sell us)[.]

Cota-Cárdenas abandons the humorous tone when she alludes to the violent events that terrorize Chicanos living in an environment that is alien and hostile to them. In "Nocturno Chicano" she describes the frightening effects of the immigration patrol on Chicano children. In "Lápida para Puppet" (Tombstone for Puppet) she describes the death of a nineteen-year-old boy who was mistakenly killed by the police on 24 October 1975. "Lápida para Puppet" follows the form of the Mexican *corrido*, a type of ballad that is appropriate for its narrative qualities. The speaker praises the young man's kind nature, and laments his tragic and useless death and the fact that the poverty-stricken barrio could not give him a decent burial. The poem is a touching eulogy to the slain barrio boy (called Puppet), and is, ironically, an eternal marker, the "tombstone" that Puppet did not get.

"Lápida para Puppet" was the genesis for the novella *Puppet*, published in December 1985. Within the context of Chicano literature, *Puppet* is distinguished by the skillful handling of innovative techniques characteristic of the contemporary novel. The traditional linear development of plot gives way to a fragmented, seemingly chaotic structure that depends on juxtaposition as a principle of organization. As a result, the reader is forced to piece together the various references in order to derive meaning from the text.

Cota-Cárdenas has assembled literary influences and experimental techniques that test her talent as a writer. She has read the great masters and has been teaching contemporary Latin-American and Chicano literature at Arizona State University. Her doctoral dissertation focused on narrative technique in Mexican novelist Carlos Fuentes's *Terra Nostra* (1975). All of this experience had a significant effect on her writing. Yet

"Soliloquio"

mucho trabajo   ser flor

     a veces   ~~a solas~~   as solátes
concentramos muy fuente   en camino
~~nos~~ para ~~morimos~~ antes
      muchitamos
      asé
      ~~para~~
~~y~~ al llegar al mercado
~~que no~~
no ~~somos~~ vendidas
nos pueden vender

"Mí Bianca María"

no quiero dejarte

     italianita

    pero si es "por forza"

     que sea cuando ya
aunque   grandecita, ser
entonces   ~~será una~~ Mona Lisa ~~pequeña~~
que yo una   no te quiero dejar
~~aunque yo~~ Oqueví
     ~~necesito mucho~~
no ~~quisiera~~ ~~desampararte~~
~~mas~~ ~~de tí~~

Drafts for two poems published in Noches despertando inConciencias *(by permission of Margarita Cota-Cárdenas)*

Puppet has an extra dimension that enriches its structure: language. Cota-Cárdenas departs from the prevalent use of Spanish in her poetry to use Spanish/English code-switching. The oral form predominates, since the story is told almost exclusively through dialogues and interiorization.

Cota-Cárdenas states that it took her ten years to complete the novella. Some fragments were published earlier. *Puppet* is an intensely personal work, autobiographical in its inception, and based on an actual series of events. It is told from many different perspectives, but the story is about the social awakening of Petra Leyva, a professor of Spanish who is prompted to write a novel about the tragic life of a barrio boy. Puppet's senseless death unleashes in Leyva a social consciousness brought about by an effort to vindicate his death, and at the same time it thrusts her into an examination of her past. As a work of art, *Puppet* represents a solid contribution to Chicano letters.

Cota-Cárdenas continues to write while teaching at Arizona State. She is presently working on a book-length manuscript about Fuentes. She has completed another poetry collection, *Marchitas de mayo*, which was published in 1989.

References:

Francisco A. Lomelí, "Caja de pandora: mala conciencia, miedo y fantasía," *Tonantzin* (San Antonio), 3 (January 1986): 7;

Tey Diana Rebolledo, "The Bittersweet Nostalgia in the Poetry of Margarita Cota-Cárdenas," *Frontiers*, 5 (September 1980): 31-35;

Rebolledo, "Walking the Thin Line: Humor in Chicana Literature," in *Beyond Stereotypes*, edited by María Herrera-Sobek (Binghamton, N.Y.: Bilingual Press, 1985), pp. 91-107.

Sylvia Maida Domínguez

(28 November 1935 -   )

Patricia De La Fuente
University of Texas—Pan American

BOOK: *La Comadre María* (Austin, Tex.: American Universal Art Forms, 1973).

PLAY PRODUCTIONS: *Tesoro Español de Obras Originales*, Edinburg, Tex., Pan American University Ballroom, June 1971;

La Comadre María, San Juan, Tex., Saint John's School Auditorium, 19 March 1972;

Samuel la Carretilla, Edinburg, Tex., Pan American University Fine Arts Auditorium, 21 November 1974;

Tres Aguilas de la Revolución Mexicana, Reynosa, Mexico, Restaurante Elegante, 19 April 1990.

TELEVISION: *Tesoro Español de Obras Originales*, 3 parts, KRGV-TV, Weslaco, Tex., July-August 1971;

Christmas on the Rio Grande: A Blending of the Old and New, KRGV-TV, Weslaco, Tex., December 1973.

OTHER: "Curanderismo: A Dramatic Portrayal," in *Foreign Affairs Research Papers Available* (Washington, D.C.: Department of State, 1976).

Dramatist Sylvia Maida Domínguez was born and grew up in the Rio Grande valley of south Texas, the site of most of her later creative endeavors. Her parents, Jesús J. Vásquez and Adela de la Garza Vásquez, were also natives of this borderland region of Texas where the cultural heritage of neighboring Mexico informs the work of local writers, of whom Domínguez is among the most active.

As a child, the eldest of four girls, Sylvia spent many happy summers on a farm with her favorite aunts in nearby Peñitas, Texas, where her creative talent was encouraged. She recalls that she found an outlet for her dramatic energy in devising plots for *las comadritas*, a children's game involving the re-creation of everyday scenes. Be-

*Sylvia Maida Domínguez (photograph by
Gerald W. Whitaker)*

tween the fourth and eighth grades in her mission parochial school, she was often in charge of creating and producing the school pageants. Undoubtedly it was during this early period that her skill as a director and producer began to develop, a skill she later used to advantage in the direction and production of her own plays for the delight of local audiences. Domínguez herself feels that her early studies in music and ballet have provided her with invaluable background for writing her comedies.

Domínguez earned a B.A. and an M.Ed. in English and Spanish from Our Lady of the Lake University of San Antonio, and an M.A. and a Ph.D. in Spanish from the University of Arizona, with a minor in administration. Even as a doctoral candidate her interest in drama was evident in her selection of the Mexican romantic dramatist José Peón y Contreras as the subject of her dissertation. She married John F. Domínguez in 1959 and has one son who is a medical doctor. After obtaining her doctorate, Domínguez returned to the Rio Grande valley and joined the

Spanish faculty at the Pan American University in Edinburg.

Domínguez, who writes her plays in Spanish, draws on themes which reflect the rich Mexican-American cultural heritage of south Texas. Her main concerns, as evidenced in *La Comadre María* (Mary the Gossip, 1972) and *Samuel la Carretilla* (Samuel the Wheelbarrow, 1974), are social rather than political, and address the everyday conflicts of ordinary people. Her special strength is in her comic vision which wrings laughter out of simple situations and reveals, with charity and understanding, the human foibles of her simple characters. She feels that the Spanish poet and dramatist Federico García Lorca has had a distinct influence on her work.

Her television script *Tesoro Español de Obras Originales* (Spanish Treasury of Original Works, 1971) consists of sketches based on classical figures such as Socrates, Plato, Aristotle, Don Quixote, Dulcinea, and Don Juan Tenorio. *La Comadre María*, a typical example of the dramatist's intimate knowledge and understanding of her cultural heritage, is a three-act play about the practice of *curanderismo*, or faith healing. The main protagonist, Comadre María, is best described as a "Dear Abby" of the barrio who, with the help of her magical *charamusca*, or hard candy, assists various individuals with their personal problems and pairs them off with romantic partners in the third act.

Her third play, *Samuel la Carretilla*, which later became the subject of an M.A. thesis at New Mexico State University, Las Cruces, is a tragicomedy, and perhaps the most touching in its portrayal of Samuel, the village fool who turns out to be a hero. This play allows Domínguez to exploit her vast fund of folk wisdom and popular idiosyncrasies. In the first act the simple character Samuel reveals to the local barber and banker his ambition to be a policeman. The townsfolk, thinking to amuse themselves at the fool's expense, give him a fake badge and a wooden gun and persuade Samuel he is a real policeman. Laughter turns to tears, however, and the townsfolk learn an important truth about human nature, especially their own, when Samuel is gunned down by robbers while trying to protect the very ones who mock him with his wooden gun. The play ends with an impressive chorus in which the whole town makes a public confession and requests forgiveness.

The playwright's latest work, *Tres Aguilas de la Revolución Mexicana* (Three Eagles of the Mexican Revolution), was produced and directed by Domínguez on 19 April 1990 at a special one-evening presentation in Reynosa, Mexico, across the border from McAllen, Texas. It is a three-act play performed by a single actor who plays the roles of the three great personalities of the Mexican revolution—the three eagles of the title—Emiliano Zapata, Pancho Villa, and Francisco Madero. The play is historical in the sense that it explores the ideals and aspirations of the Mexican peasantry through the eyes and experiences of their three best-known leaders.

Although only one of Domínguez's plays, *La Comadre María*, has been published (1973), they have all been produced and directed with great success both by the author and by various local and national institutions that have found the themes and format adaptable to amateur theater groups and student productions.

Domínguez is also well known in her locality for her productions of the *Posadas* (reenactments of the journey of Joseph and Mary to Bethlehem) which she initiated at Pan American University in 1960 and continued through 1966. More recently, she produced and directed the *Posadas* in the public plaza of Edinburg, Texas.

According to the author, *La Comadre María* has been distributed in Spain, Mexico, Argentina, and other Latin American countries and throughout America, but no significant critical response to her plays is available. Local response has always been good, however, and in their written evaluations, visiting poets from Argentina, Uruguay, and Peru recently found her production of *Tres Aguilas de la Revolución Mexicana* to be an "excellent and thoroughly professional production."

Ernesto Galarza
(7 August 1905 - 22 June 1984)

Maria Montes de Oca Ricks
Washington State University

BOOKS: *The Roman Catholic Church as a Factor in the Political and Social History of Mexico* (Sacramento: Capital, 1928);

Thirty Poems (Jamaica Estates, N.Y.: Year-Long School, 1935);

La industria eléctrica en México (Mexico City: Fondo de Cultura Económica, 1941);

Rimas tontas para niños listos (New York: Committee on Art in American Education and Society, 1944; San Jose: Editorial Almadén, 1971);

The Case of Bolivia (Washington, D.C.: Pan American Union, 1949);

Strangers in Our Fields (Washington, D.C.: Joint United States-Mexico Trade Union Committee, 1956);

Report on the Farm Labor Transportation Accident at Chualar, California, September 17, 1963 (Washington, D.C.: U.S. Congress, House Committee on Education and Labor, 1963); republished as *Tragedy at Chualar: El crucero de las treinta y dos cruces* (Santa Barbara: McNally & Loftin, 1977);

Merchants of Labor: The Mexican Bracero Story: An Account of the Managed Migration of Mexican Farm Workers in California, 1942-1960 (Charlotte, N.C.: McNally, 1964); republished in Spanish as *Los braceros y mercaderes del trabajo* (Mexico: SEP, 1972);

Zoo-risa (Santa Barbara: McNally & Loftin, 1968);

Mexican-Americans in the Southwest, by Galarza, Herman Gallegos, and Julian Samora (Santa Barbara: McNally & Loftin, 1969);

Spiders in the House and Workers in the Field (Notre Dame, Ind.: University of Notre Dame Press, 1970);

Aquí y allá en California (San Jose: Editorial Almadén, 1971);

Historia verdadera de una gota de miel (San Francisco: Almadén, 1971);

Poemas párvulos (San Jose: Almadén, 1971);

Zoo-fun (San Jose: Almadén, 1971);

Ernesto Galarza

Barrio Boy (Notre Dame, Ind. & London: University of Notre Dame Press, 1971); republished in Spanish as *Traspasando fronteras* (Mexico: SEP, 1978);

La historia verdadera de una botella de leche (San Jose: Almadén, 1972);

Más poemas párvulos (San Jose: Almadén, 1972);

Poemas Pe-que Pe-que-ñitos (San Jose: Almadén, 1972);

Un poco de México (San Jose: Almadén, 1972);

Chogorrom (San Jose: Almadén, 1973);

Todo mundo lee (San Jose: Almadén, 1973);

Alviso: The Crisis of a Barrio (San Jose: Mexican American Community Service Agency, 1973);

Temas escolares (San Jose: Studio Laboratory, 1976);

Farm Workers and Agri-Business in California, 1947-1960 (Notre Dame, Ind.: University of Notre Dame Press, 1977);

Kodachromes in Rhyme: Poems (Notre Dame, Ind.: University of Notre Dame Press, 1982).

OTHER: Latin America for Young Readers Series, 10 volumes, edited by Galarza (Washington, D.C.: Pan American Union, 1942-1949);

"Mexicans in the Southwest: A Culture in Process," in *Plural Society in the Southwest*, edited by E. H. Spicer and R. H. Thompson (Albuquerque: University of New Mexico Press, 1972), pp. 261-297;

"Minorities: The Mirror of Society," in *Ghosts in the Barrio: Issues in Bilingual-Bicultural Education*, edited by R. Poblano (San Rafael, Cal.: Leswing Press, 1973), pp. 35-44;

"Humanization of Bilingual-Bicultural Schooling," in *Humanidad: Essays in Honor of George I. Sanchez*, edited by A. Paredes (Los Angeles: Chicano Studies Center Publications, 1977), pp. 58-74;

"Forecasting Future Cohorts of Mexicano Elders," in *Chicano Aging and Mental Health*, edited by M. Miranda and R. A. Ruiz (Rockville, Md.: National Institute of Mental Health, 1981), pp. 238-248.

SELECTED PERIODICAL PUBLICATIONS—
UNCOLLECTED: "Debts, Dictatorship, and Revolution in Bolivia and Peru," *Foreign Policy Reports*, 7 (13 May 1931): 101-108;

"The Latin American Universities in Step with History," *Pan-American Union Bulletin*, 73 (1939): 677-687;

"Study in Latin America," *Congressional Record*, 86 (25 November 1940): 6703-6705;

"Big Farm Strike," *Commonweal*, 48, (4 June 1948): 178-182;

"La mula no nació arisca," *Center Diary* (September-October 1966): 26-32.

In Ernesto Galarza there is a confluence of lyric poet, labor organizer, veteran educator, international economist, and renowned scholar. Although best known as "the loudest and, surely, most unusual of the voices that have been raised to demand economic and social justice for the farm worker," Galarza's fictional autobiography, *Barrio Boy* (1971), won him wide critical acclaim as a writer and a storyteller, and a special place in Chicano letters. A must in every anthology of Mexican-American writing, excerpts of this work have also appeared in increasing numbers of English language readers in public schools across the nation.

Galarza was born 7 August 1905 to Henriqueta and Ernesto Galarza, Sr. Henriqueta went to live among relatives in Jalcocotán, a village of western Mexico, just weeks before the author's birth. The village in which Galarza spent the first years of his life is brilliantly evoked in *Barrio Boy*: "Crosswise, it was about wide enough to park six automobiles hub to hub. Lengthwise, you could walk from one end to the other in eight minutes without hurrying." In view of Galarza's lifelong concerns, it is very suggestive that Jalcocotán is described as a *pueblo libre*, a free village in which people work for themselves and not for a *hacendado* (landowner). The village's history of proud independence goes back to the days of the Spanish conquest when surviving Huichol Indians avoided enslavement by fleeing to inaccessible areas of the Sierra Madre such as Jalcocotán.

As the Madero revolt swept over Mexico in 1910, Galarza, his mother, and two maternal uncles left Jalcocotán on a northward journey which took them to Sacramento, California. Along the way young Ernesto began his formal education at the Escuela Municipal Number 3 in Mazatlán, state of Sinaloa, during the year 1911. It would be 1919 before he finally completed his elementary education at Lincoln Elementary School in Sacramento.

For Galarza the road to English fluency would be paved with sad/funny episodes which, many years later, he would weave into stories filled with his special brand of humor. One anecdote he especially loved to tell had his mother enlisting the aid of the Italian huckster from whom they bought their beans and cabbage as an English tutor. As a result young Ernesto's vocabulary increased dramatically—albeit with an Italian accent—and he began reading more fluently. A sensitive teacher, moved by such initiative, lent a helping hand and, in the process, left her imprint on Galarza's future philosophy of education.

Although Galarza's mother died in an influenza epidemic in 1917, a surviving uncle and a string of part-time and summer jobs enabled the twelve-year-old to continue his education, avoiding the fate of many farm laborers' children. Galarza was always proud to state in his vita that by the time he graduated from Sacramento High School in 1923 he had been, "news boy, Western Union messenger, stock clerk, farm worker, cannery and packing shed laborer, camp counselor, Christmas card designer, social work aide, [and] court interpreter." Undoubtedly, he would draw

upon these early experiences in his prolific writing.

That fall Galarza went on to Occidental College in Los Angeles where he majored in Latin American history and quickly won the esteem of all his professors. Years later when Galarza earned a doctorate of humane letters *honoris causa*, the president of Occidental College, Richard C. Gilman, paid homage to the young man by describing him as "willing to do anything— scrub floors, mow lawns, wait on tables"—in order to get an education. The only student of Mexican descent in his graduating class, Galarza had compiled a distinguished academic record which, according to Gilman, included election to Phi Beta Kappa, writing for the school newspaper and becoming "one of the outstanding debaters of [his] college generation."

For his senior thesis at Occidental, Galarza did field work in Mexico, on a study-abroad program. This work, *The Roman Catholic Church as a Factor in the Political and Social History of Mexico*, would become his first publication in 1928. In this study Galarza used the writings of Mexican friars and other colonial documents to trace the role played by the Catholic church during the three hundred years of Spanish colonial rule in Mexico. Enriched with oral accounts gathered by Galarza himself, this work defends the reforms instituted by the Mexican revolutionary governments as a necessity of the times and a means of neutralizing the church's powerful political and economic influence in Mexican national affairs.

That same year Galarza was awarded a fellowship to work toward a master's degree in history and political science at Stanford University. Shortly after receiving his M.A. degree in 1929, Galarza and Mae Taylor, a Sacramento schoolteacher he met while at Stanford, were married. They moved to New York where Galarza entered the doctoral program in economics at Columbia University.

Galarza reaped dividends in areas other than economics since John Dewey did not retire from the School of Education until the year after Galarza enrolled at the university. Although it seems Galarza never studied directly under him, Dewey's philosophy of "learning by doing" would filter into Galarza's educational philosophy. To the end of his life, Galarza firmly believed in education as a means to an end, a tool which could improve his people's lives. While working on his economics degree at Columbia, Galarza and his wife were able to test their views on education at the

Gardner School, a progressive school, in Jamaica, Long Island, where they were coprincipals from 1932 through 1936. During this time they established the Year-Long School, an experimental elementary program where students spent summers working on a farm. Despite all of his activities, Galarza found time to write poetry, publishing his first collection of poems in 1935 under the unassuming title of *Thirty Poems*. He also conducted research on Latin America for the Foreign Policy Association.

For his dissertation Galarza wanted to "isolate and observe the capitalist process of production getting started in Mexico," so he traveled to Mexico to research the electric power industry there. The results of his study were published in 1941 by Mexico's highly respected publisher the Fondo de Cultura Económica as *La industria eléctrica en México* (The Electric Power Industry in Mexico). The dissertation, however, was not submitted until 1943. The doctoral degree was granted the following year.

From 1936 to 1947 Galarza worked with the Pan American Union—today the Organization of American States—first as a research associate in education, then as its first director of the Division of Labor and Social Information. During his eleven-year tenure at the PAU, Galarza traveled extensively throughout Latin America, getting involved in two labor crises which attracted a great deal of attention outside the organization: the 1942 U.S. intervention in the Bolivian tin miners' strike, and the Mexican contract labor, or bracero, program in the West and Southwest of the United States. Galarza supported Bolivian workers in many speeches and articles between 1943 and 1946 in U.S. publications such as the *Nation* and the *Inter-American Monthly* as well as in Latin-American publications such as *Acción Social*. For this he was awarded the Order of the Condor by the Bolivian government, the highest decoration bestowed on either civilian or military personnel in that country. In addition Galarza was made an honorary citizen of Bolivia's capital city, La Paz. A few years later Galarza resigned from the PAU, charging that the organization just sat by as a "coalition government composed of four parts tin barons, three parts corporation farmers, and two parts Communist Party" was installed in that country with the blessing of the U. S. government.

Galarza's interest in the bracero program—a program instituted on a wartime emergency basis in 1942, imbued with more prolonged life by Public Law 78 in 1951, and illegally used by growers until 1964 as a de facto strikebreaking force—stemmed from his desire to see neither the Mexican laborer nor the American farm worker hurt. In what was quickly becoming his trademark, Galarza put together an impressive report on the abuses he himself witnessed at more than twenty bracero camps and documented through detailed interviews with some two hundred braceros. Although this brilliant piece of research would have no more effect than his report on the Bolivian case, it would point the way for Galarza's efforts during the next two decades.

Before leaving the PAU, however, Galarza completed most of the Latin America for Young Readers Series—popularly known as the Young Readers Series (1942-1949). The series consisted of ten stories designed to introduce young people to the study of Latin America. The books were about figures such as Francisco Pizarro, Álvar Núñez Cabeza de Vaca, and José de San Martín; places such as the Panama Canal, the Guano Islands of Peru, and the Pan-American Highway; and peoples such as the Araucanians and the Incas.

In a position to pick his next appointment and with the goal of effecting some real change in mind, Galarza next accepted the position of director of research and education with the Southern Tenant Farmer's Union (STFU), which had just become the American Federation of Labor's (AFL) National Farm Labor Union (NFLU). This new job required Galarza, his wife, and two daughters to move to what would become their permanent home until his death—San Jose, California. For the best part of the next decade, Galarza would dedicate all of his energies to organizing farm workers and, apart from reports on these activities, he would not publish another major work until 1956. Between 1948 and 1959 Galarza and the union would be involved in some twenty strikes in the South and the West. Because of right-to-work laws in the South and Public Law 78 in the West and Southwest, these strikes were doomed. Facing, in addition, organized labor's indifference toward the farm workers' grievances, Galarza vowed that until Public Law 78 was struck down, he would not ask any farm worker to "stick his neck out where it could be chopped off by one stroke of the pen—a pen held in the hand of some bureaucrat in San Francisco or Washington, D.C.—certifying more *braceros*." Instead, he used his own pen to document thoroughly the program's abuses.

In this spirit Galarza accepted a grant in late 1955 from the Fund for the Republic to write a report on the bracero program which would become *Strangers in Our Fields* (1956). For four months the author traveled both sides of the border, inspecting over 150 bracero camps. He collected data on the transportation, housing, and feeding of braceros; their wages, health care, and worker representation; the system of "specials" which earmarked certain bracero consignments for special employers such as Lyndon B. Johnson; and the role of the labor contractor. Despite obstacles that would have overwhelmed a lesser man—he was denied access to records by employers, and potential witnesses were scuttled back across the border—Galarza succeeded in compiling a report several hundred pages in length and filled with eloquent photographs. This was condensed to the eighty-page booklet published by the Joint U.S.-Mexico Trade Union Committee.

Strangers in Our Fields ended all speculation as to the true purpose of the bracero program, and it fell like a bombshell in the midst of the bracero debate. Despite the attempts to discredit its accuracy, Galarza's report received wide critical acclaim, even in antilabor sources such as the *Los Angeles Times*. It went through two editions and ten thousand copies, and it was condensed for several important magazines. More satisfying to Galarza, however, was the fact that it succeeded in finally bringing the National Agricultural Workers Union to the attention of the top officials of the AFL-CIO (American Federation of Labor and Congress of Industrial Organizations).

Galarza continued to use his writing as a weapon, flooding the newspapers with open letters to Governor Goodwin J. Knight, coupled with press releases on the irregularities of the bracero program. He even wrote witty little essays, circulated mostly among his friends, in which he characterized the government's feeble attempts at regulating the program as "ten lashes laid on with a half-cooked noodle."

Bypassed by the national labor leadership in what the media termed "Big Labor's all-out drive in agriculture," Galarza nevertheless loyally stayed with the union as long as he could avoid compromising his principles, which he defined eloquently in his essay "Labor's Back Yard":

> If democracy, freedom of organization and collective bargaining are principles, they apply to all. The struggle to realize them must be pressed into every corner of the land, their enjoyment denied no worker, however destitute or ignorant he may be. Otherwise, labor's long, bitter and often tragic commitment to humanity becomes a game of odd-man-out.... Once the "right to work" men have laid the axe to the base ... no trade unionist need ask: "For whom does the axe fall?" It falls for him.

Officially outside organized labor as of January 1960, Galarza settled down to writing a history of the bracero program, which would become *Merchants of Labor* (1964). On 17 September 1963, however, the writing of the book was interrupted by the deaths of thirty-two braceros at Chualar, in the Salinas Valley, when a Southern Pacific freight train ran into a makeshift truck that was transporting the workers. Galarza was appointed chief counsel for labor to the Congressional Committee on Education and Labor, headed by Adam Clayton Powell. Galarza's brilliant 1963 report on the incident, reprinted in 1977 as *Tragedy at Chualar: El crucero de las treinta y dos cruces* (The Thirty-Two Cross Crossing), received little attention and the demise of the bracero program was delayed for one more year. The only immediate impact Galarza's report had was that, in documenting employer negligence, it gave the attorneys representing the relatives of the victims the means of obtaining more reasonable settlements.

Merchants of Labor was finally completed and published in 1964. First it traced the conditions in Mexico which paved the way for the bracero agreement; then it reported the collusion between U.S. governmental agencies and agribusiness to exploit Mexico's inability to employ all of its citizens. *Merchants of Labor* carefully documents the manipulation of labor and salaries through the practice of managed migration, which ensured the status quo in the region's agricultural production. Unable to find a publisher for his book, Galarza borrowed fifteen hundred dollars to have it published. The author himself had to do the publicity and distribution. Even though it received little critical notice, the first printing of *Merchants of Labor* quickly sold out, and it remains an invaluable contribution to the historiography of agribusiness in California. In December 1964, the same year Galarza's study was published, Public Law 78 was eliminated. In fulfillment of Galarza's prophecy, the demise of the law was quickly followed by the first successful strike, the now historic Delano strike.

The mid 1960s witnessed Galarza's growing involvement with urban Mexican-American is-

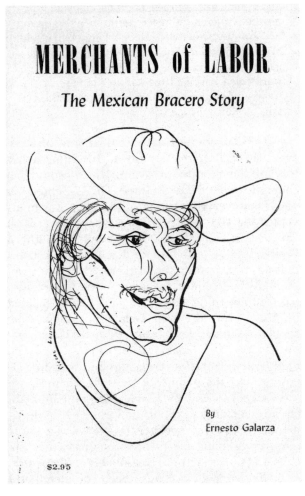

MERCHANTS of LABOR

The Mexican Bracero Story

By
Ernesto Galarza

$2.95

Cover for Galarza's history of the bracero program

sues, the Chicano movement, and the new militancy among Chicano students. Shuttling between teaching appointments at the University of Notre Dame, Harvard University, and the University of California, San Diego, Galarza made his contribution to the movement through extensive writing, lecturing, media appearances, and community work.

Toward 1965 Galarza began consulting for the Ford Foundation. As their expert in Mexican-American affairs, he had to review all grant proposals submitted by Chicano groups. In December 1966 he submitted to the foundation a report on a two-year study of many Mexican-American communities. Three years later he published a book largely based on this report, *Mexican-Americans in the Southwest* (1969). Written in cooperation with Herman Gallegos and Julian Samora, this work assesses the educational, political, economic, and demographic status of Mexican-Americans in California, Texas, Arizona, New Mexico, and Colo-

rado. In the process it examines the impact of farm mechanization and urban expansion upon these communities. Galarza's conclusions—the negative impact of urbanization upon Mexican-American communities—would soon receive dramatic validation. Alviso—a small, predominately Mexican-American community near San Jose—would be wooed by real estate developers from San Jose, Santa Clara, and Hayward into annexation with San Jose, not realizing that skyrocketing land values following their vote would quickly displace them. Galarza got involved in an unsuccessful attempt to contest the vote and wrote a forty-six-page pamphlet on the experience entitled, "Alviso: A Town Besieged by 'Progress' " which would be used in college courses throughout the Southwest.

The number of organizations requesting that Galarza serve on their boards was by now quite impressive. In 1967 he was elected chairman of La Raza Unida Unity Conference, a loose confederation of Hispanic civic, social, and cultural groups which by the following year would have chapters throughout the United States. For many years he would also serve on the Board of Directors of the Mexican-American Legal Defense and Educational Fund (MALDEF).

In 1970, a decade after retiring from active unionism, Galarza published *Spiders in the House and Workers in the Field*. With a foreword by noted chronicler and historian of the Southwest Carey McWilliams, this work painstakingly documents the stifling web spun around the farm labor union movement in California by agribusiness and its powerful friends in Congress—men such as Richard M. Nixon. *Spiders in the House* furnishes what is probably the most detailed account of the nine defamation suits brought by the DiGiorgio Fruit Corporation against the NFLU, the Agricultural Workers Organizing Committee, various labor publications, Galarza, and the Hollywood Film Council, an AFL affiliate. With the pretext that a twenty-minute documentary about the San Joaquin Valley entitled *Poverty in the Valley of Plenty* and broadcast over station KTLA-LA damaged the Kern County grower through innuendo, the latter succeeded in breaking the back of the strike that the NFLU had been leading in Arvin, California, against DiGiorgio. Furthermore, by embroiling the union in years of useless litigation, DiGiorgio in fact crippled the farm labor union movement in California for another decade. *Spiders in the House* received very favorable reviews, garnering praise not only as a well-researched document of labor history in America but also for its impeccable and, at times, inspired and elegant writing.

Barrio Boy (1971) was published by the University of Notre Dame Press the year after *Spiders* appeared. The epigraph that precedes the text intimates that readers are about to embark upon a "journey . . . remembered." And if "the actual journey may have been quite different," it is the author's contention that "The memory [is] all that matter[s]." The author's disclaimer as to the rigorous historicity of his account should, therefore, be kept in mind when approaching this "autobiography," for is he not in fact invoking the license of the fiction writer to sift reality through the sieve of his own responses to his story?

The way in which *Barrio Boy* came about is in itself a story worth retelling. It grew, the author states following the preface, out of a series of anecdotes about Galarza's early years in Jalcocotán, his northward journey, and eventual arrival in the Sacramento barrio. Told around the family hearth initially, these anecdotes were then shared with a group of "scholars and other boring people." The uniformly warm reception suggested to Galarza that not only would these sketches have a potential audience if published, but they might also be valuable to that audience for both historical and psychological reasons.

Barrio Boy is, as suggested by at least one critic, the epic of a Chicano family—from pueblo to barrio. As such it is a microcosm of the equally epic northbound migration of the Chicano people, emblematized in the book by the widening of the road stretching from Galarza's native village, Jalcocotán, to the next stop on the way north, Tepic. Consequently, *Barrio Boy* has a mythical-historical value well beyond that of a mere autobiography. Galarza indeed never made it a secret that he believed the loss-of-identity theme so harped on by psychologists and social scientists studying the Chicano community was definitely played out. Galarza, "for one Mexican, never had any doubts on this score," and he refused to believe he was the only one among six or seven million Mexican-Americans to feel this way.

Barrio Boy is a celebration of a people strongly rooted in an agricultural tradition who were able nonetheless to make the successful transition into both an urban Mexican setting and, across the border, a totally alien culture. The work is a tribute that was long overdue every Chicano—and, by extension, every member of a transplanted culture, and it bears witness to the blend of skillful writing and levelheaded analysis which always characterized Galarza's writing. *Barrio Boy* is, in a very real sense, the true culmination of Galarza's northward journey.

The closely knit family unit in the book is clearly offered as a paradigm of Chicano survival in the United States: the Galarza extended family, faced with seemingly insurmountable obstacles, tries to remain united at all costs and, as a result, triumphs where defeat would appear to be the only logical outcome. The narrative, then, effectively interweaves the family's tribulations and the leitmotiv of the Galarza desire to keep the family unit intact. Throughout his life Galarza would, in fact, credit the steadfastness of this family bond as peculiarly Mexican: "It was a Mexican family that I lived in. And we made no bones about it. . . . It was just natural, which is the way it should be." The critical reception of *Barrio Boy* was quite impressive, especially since Chicano works hardly ever get mentioned in mainstream American publications. *Best Sellers* in its 1 May 1972 issue praised the work as "illuminating, educating, well put down." The Honorable Dan McCorquondale in the *San Jose Sun* of 30 November 1977 listed it as one of the seven "Books that Shaped Lives," along with John F. Kennedy's *Profiles in Courage* (1956), John Steinbeck's *Grapes of Wrath* (1939), and the Bible. *Barrio Boy* has been praised equally for its "sensitive and evocative prose" and for its tribute to the "strength and compassion and resilience of working class people."

After six printings, with sales of some thirty thousand copies; a Spanish translation, *Traspasando fronteras* (Across Frontiers, 1978); and many excerpts in publications such as the MacMillan Literature Heritage Series, *Barrio Boy* is still considered a valuable piece of Chicano and Mexican historiography. Carlos B. Gil of the Department of History at the University of Washington described it as a "microscopic stud[y] persuasively written in human terms." Probably the most poignant tribute to Galarza's craft as a storyteller, however, has been the degree of his readers' emotional involvement with the characters and events in *Barrio Boy*. People from all walks of life invariably approached Galarza and anxiously inquired whether his mother had ever found her lost sewing machine, the Ajax, or why his aunt's family had not been permitted to stay in the United States.

By 1971 Galarza's involvement with the theories and strategies of bicultural education led

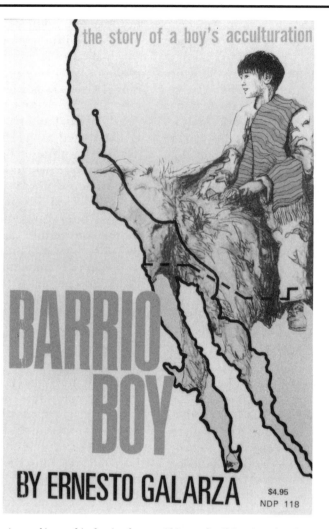

the story of a boy's acculturation

BARRIO BOY

BY ERNESTO GALARZA

$4.95
NDP 118

Cover for Galarza's autobiographical epic about a Chicano family's migration from pueblo to barrio

him to establish the Studio Laboratory for Bilingual Education. A resource center for students and teachers in the San Jose Unified School District, the Studio Lab, as it came to be known, stressed a hands-on approach to teaching cultural values, with particular emphasis on the creative arts, especially in the first and second grades. One of Galarza's favorite dicta would always be "If you give a child a creative environment, you can't stop him from learning." In Galarza's view the elementary curriculum could be made more responsive to children's needs only by shifting away from the then current emphasis on the three Rs—the six Rs as Mae Galarza was wont to call the three Rs and their remedial counterparts, which entrapped so many Chicano children in a vicious cycle.

Emphasizing the artistic and aesthetic aspects of Mexican culture, the Studio Lab began collecting art objects, costumes, toys, and other artifacts representative of the Latin-American countries from which they came. Funded from both private and local public sources, such as the John Hay Whitney Foundation, Model Cities, and, for a time, the San Jose School District, the Studio Lab soon came in conflict with the latter over how bilingual programs should be implemented and what curricula and materials should be used. The school district, favoring the three Rs approach, decided to form the San Jose Consortium for Bilingual Education with ten Santa Clara county school districts. When the consortium secured federal funding for a pilot bilingual program in 1974-1975, the Studio Lab was excluded and then forced out of existence in 1975. Galarza and others from the lab, however, still retained some input in bilingual education in the area through the Community Organization to

Monitor Education (COME), which they founded upon the demise of the Studio Lab. The following year, 1976, they published *Temas escolares* (About Schools), a white paper on the consortium containing fiscal data obtained by filing suit against the district.

Galarza's most enduring contribution to bilingual education, however, was a literary one, a bilingual collection of prose and poetry for children, the Mini-Libros (Mini-Books). Galarza had begun writing children's literature back in 1942 or 1943 when he wrote a series of Mother Goose-type rhymes in Spanish to teach his daughter the language. These poems would be published later in the series as *Poemas párvulos* (Short Poems for Youngsters, 1971). The first title in the Mini-Libros series, *Rimas tontas para niños listos* (Silly Rhymes for Smart Children), appeared in 1944 in a limited edition with illustrations by Art Schneider. At the time Galarza had no plans for further volumes, but his relocation to California in 1947 caused him to change his mind. In San Jose the veteran educator soon became convinced that there was an urgent need in the public schools for reading materials that were attractive to children, easy for teachers to use, and capable of rectifying the stereotypes of Chicano children which had been nurtured through years of Anglo-dominated language instruction. Galarza planned to follow *Rimas tontas para niños listos* with seventeen more books.

Of the eleven titles published between 1968 and 1973, five were poetry: *Zoo-risa* (Zoo-laughter, 1968), *Poemas párvulos* (1971), *Más poemas párvulos* (More Short Poems for Youngsters, 1972), *Poemas Pe-que Pe-que-ñitos* (Very, Very Short Poems, 1972), and *Chogorrom* (1973). The remaining titles are prose: *Aquí y allá en California* (Here and There in California, 1971), *Historia verdadera de una gota de miel* (The True Story of a Drop of Honey, 1971), *Zoo-fun* (1971), *La historia verdadera de una botella de leche* (The True Story of a Bottle of Milk, 1972), *Un poco de México* (A Bit of Mexico, 1972), and *Todo mundo lee* (Everybody Reads, 1973). With the exception of *Zoo-risa*, which was published by McNally and Loftin of Santa Barbara, all of the foregoing titles were published by Editorial Almadén; all eleven are short, ranging in length from forty-eight to sixty-four pages.

Years later Galarza recollected that his poems for children actually began as "rhythms" which he then set to words, the euphony enriched by the visual dimension given by an illustra-

tor "who sympathized with the style"—Vicent P. Rascon. Like a beneficent deity looking back on his creation, the man who came to be known as the Father Goose of Mexican children relished what was accomplished: "It worked out very well."

At the time Galarza embarked on the Mini-Libros series, few Chicanos indeed were writing children's literature. "They don't believe in writing things for children to have fun reading," Galarza would say. Neither could he go to the Mexican literary tradition and its rich poetic heritage for models because of the subsumption of children's poetry in rote learning of traditional poems or stories. Galarza not only encouraged the free flight of the child's imagination, he himself displayed the ability to fantasize as a child would. In "La gallina Clo-Clo" ("The Cluck-Cluck Hen"), a hen looks around for a place to lay an egg and is told by the child to lay it on its hand. Galarza felt that such a choice encompassed "something that children would like, I think . . . the idea of putting your hand out and having an egg in it." Many more of these poems, in fact, leave the lingering impression of having just peeked out at the world through the eyes of a child:

> Little shrimp, little pet
> don't come out
> and get caught
> in a fisherman's net.
>
> Camarón, camarón
> no te asomes a la playa.
> Que no vaya el pescador
> a meterte en la malla.

The above is from Galarza's *Poemas Pe-que Pe-que-ñitos*, a thoroughly bilingual collection of nature poems in which each poem first appears in English to be followed immediately by the Spanish version. The foregoing poem reveals the child's point of view—the "impracticality" of wanting the shrimp to escape its "fate" and the attendant disregard for the practicalities of earning a living. The child's flight of fancy, so often misunderstood by adults yet seemingly apprehended effortlessly by Galarza, finds a rich context thanks to Galarza's translingual and poetic gift.

Galarza's children's poems are not only filled with the fancy and delightful humor of childhood, they often include a moral or practical teaching. Consider, for example, the following poems:

> No es tan tonta
> la tortuga
> Sabe andar,
> sabe nadar
> y sabe comer lechuga
>
> (The turtle,
> she's no fool.
> She can walk,
> she can swim, and
> she even eats her lettuce).
>
> Juan, Juan
> el gran truhán
> al panadero
> le robó un pan.
> Se lo comió
> con mucha prisa
> y el panadero
> le dió una paliza.
>
> (John, John,
> the naughty lad
> He stole a loaf
> from the baker man.
> He gobbled it up
> fast, very fast,
> but the baker
> caught him at last.)
>
> A la luz colorada
> alto y parada.
> Anaranjado
> mucho cuidado.
> A la luz verde
> nadie se pierde.
> Las luces son tres,
> cuéntalas otra vez.
>
> (On a red light,
> cease all motion.
> On a yellow,
> exercise due caution.
> But on a green
> all can be seen.
> The street-lights three
> please count for me.)

In the first poem, from *Zoo-risa*, without an explicit admonition, the young child is made to appreciate the value of eating his greens; in the second poem, from *Poemas párvulos*, youngsters are left with an unequivocal moral lesson, since Juan's theft is not only detected but punished in the end. In the third poem, also from *Poemas*

parvulos, safety tips are adroitly combined with the application of math concepts.

An important aspect of Galarza's poetry for children is its capacity for cultural transmission. "Juan, Juan / el gran truhán," for example, paves the way for an effortless acceptance by the young reader of the door-to-door sale of bread in a big basket balanced on the baker's head, as an ingenious merchandising technique instead of an oddity. This eminently un-American practice, still found today in many small towns in Latin America, is, in fact, a very convenient system which provides the housewife with a great deal of choice while saving her a trip to the bakery. Galarza was convinced that the only effective way of transmitting culture was in the context of fun and games: "There is no way to appeal to a first grader by telling him that you are trying to save his culture, he could care less. He is interested in seeing himself by the hour in relation to these adults who surround him." When the Mini-Libros were awarded the Second AILIE (International Association for Children's Literature in Spanish) Annual Award in 1979, Galarza's letter of acceptance, read at the AILIE meeting in Mexico that summer, restated his credo: To aid in the retention of the Mexican culture, which "time and the hardships of migration were quickly erasing"; to celebrate authentic Mexican popular speech and counteract the dehumanization process of which the first casualty was invariably the migrant's speech; and to offer anchorage to those suffering from "incurable homesickness." Aware of the ambitiousness of this project, Galarza was the first to concede that his children's books were but "un hilillo de gusto emotivo que ofrece conducirnos hacia intuiciones sorprendentes" (an emotive if tenuous foretaste of things to be discovered). The impressionable age of the audience, and the emotive nature of the stimulus, Galarza hoped, would ensure far-reaching effects.

On the way to achieving his purpose, Galarza created some truly memorable characters. In *Más poemas párvulos*, for example, he introduced Requemorrocotudo, the redoubtable yet mild-mannered goose who proudly proclaims, "Yo soy de Jalcocotán" (I am from Jalcocotán). By making his character at home in his very own beloved pueblo, Galarza in fact offers his young reader a paradigm of the child's own journey toward English fluency from the safe harbor of his own community. If early reading materials were to be of any pedagogical value, Galarza would always maintain, they had to be anchored in the child's own culture and experiences. In one critic's opinion the uniqueness of these poems rests precisely in the coming together through language of the Mexican and Anglo cultures, closely paralleling Galarza's own ease on either side of the border as a result of his assimilating—rather than being assimilated by—the new culture.

Another interesting feature of Galarza's poetry for children, one that is particularly evident in the *Párvulo* collections, is the use he makes of the Mother Goose rhymes. Since the ultimate goal of these poems is to create reading material that would ease the Spanish-speaking child's transition into English, Galarza deliberately set out to phrase the Spanish text so as to simulate the rhythms of the English language. The result is a string of delightful poems rich with echoes of Mother Goose: "Gani, gani ganso" (Goosy, Goosy, Gander), "En la alacena / de dona Elena" (Old Mother Hubbard / went to the cupboard), "Chiste con chista" (Hey-Diddle-Diddle). Exposure to these strains, Galarza felt, would awaken in the child a desire to read the English version, or, at the very least, it would foster a more positive response to the English text when exposed to it in a classroom situation. In consequence Galarza was more interested in reproducing sound patterns and musicality—to the point of retaining versification patterns, such as the *aabccb* scheme in "Little Bo-Peep"—than he was in a faithful translation. His success with this technique would seem to support his claim that "the poetic ideal can be easily put in many languages. . . . *Poemas párvulos* is rhythmically English and genuinely bilingual."

Furthermore, in these poems Galarza exhibits an uncanny ability to insert his poems in the Mexican universe while retaining the rhythm of the English poem. Consider, for example, his version of "Little Miss Muffet":

Estaba la Chole
tomando atole
con azúcar de pilón
Zas!
la ventana
le salta una rana
y la pobre de Chole
con todo y atole
llorando de susto corrió.

(Chole was
drinking atole
sweetened with sugarloaf.
Suddenly,

through the window
in jumped a frog
and poor Chole,
with her atole,
ran crying in fear.)

Without a doubt, the affective bond between his young Chicano readership and this Galarza poem is cemented by the hominess of the new name as much as by the use of a popular Latin-American beverage.

In the same vein, Jack Sprat becomes Don Pedro Calabacitas, now of the town of Milpitas:

En el pueblo de Milpitas
Don Pedro Calabacitas
siempre tiene que comer.
El se come las pepitas
y las cáscaras refritas
se las come su mujer.

(In the town of Milpitas
Don Pedro Calabacitas
eats indeed very well.
He eats the seeds
and his wife gets to eat
the refried skins.)

In a 1 May 1979 letter addressed to Marianne Rafter of Harcourt, Brace, Jovanovich, Galarza made what is probably the most poignant statement of his poetics:

My intention was to try to express a certain degree of freedom from the limitations of language in expressing a possible range of subjective responses to the same stimulus. . . . I am afraid that a "more faithful" translation of the original text defeats my purpose by suggesting that there is only one way to smell a rose. . . . I would rather suggest that a poetic experience is open-ended in the direction of the surprising, the delightful, the unpredictable, the *personal*. The message that I wanted to send was that poetry is for anyone in any language. Perhaps this is also the message of "a rose is a rose is a rose."

And the message, that "poetry is for anyone in any language," was adopted by the publishers as their statement on the poetic ideal in their literature volume for second graders.

Most of Galarza's prose titles were intended for older children—grades four, five, and six. In *La historia verdadera de una botella de leche* (1972), for example, the engaging prose combines with excellent photography to follow the progress of a group of children through a dairy farm. Sparked by one child's question—"Where does milk come from?"—the journey carries the young reader through various aspects of dairy production and the daily routine of a dairy farm: how cows nurture their young, how and what they are fed as adults, how they are milked, and more.

Sales figures of the twelve Mini-Libros published reached sixty thousand copies, with sales recorded in the United States, Mexico, Spain, and the Soviet Union. In this country, interestingly enough, the reception of the Mini-Libros seems to have been as warm among Anglos as among Latino critics, teachers, and parents. In a testimonial which was included in the 1979 nomination of Galarza for the Nobel Prize in literature, Timothy Beard, an Anglo teacher, extolled the value of these little books for his classes since they communicated to the children a "sense of delight and validation of the cultural heritage of Mexico and the Southwest." Senator Ralph W. Yarborough, responsible for the introduction and passage of the first Bilingual Education Bill in 1968, wrote to Galarza that the Mini-Libros "would be an invaluable aid to the young bilingual student. I am very pleased to see you devoting your talents to this area." The experiences of Beard, as well as those of Elena López, a teacher at the Gardner School in San Jose, would seem to more than justify Yarborough's faith. For López the little poems not only opened up creative avenues for the children, they facilitated the acquisition of factual knowledge by making the children "eager to dramatize the action in the poem, and eager to speculate." In a letter to Galarza dated 29 October 1973, Lopez told how by approaching "Gani, gani ganso" through drama and music the children explored the way geese walk and talk. Praise for Mini-Libros also came from across the border, where Doris Heyden, of the Museo Nacional de Antropología (National Museum of Anthropology) in Mexico, compared the rhythm of the *Poemas párvulos* with that "of the ancient Nahuatl *Cantares*," a rhythm that was "so much a part of Mexico."

Probably the most touching testimonial came from an Evanston, Illinois, physician, Jorge Prieto, in a letter dated 9 April 1973, in which he thanked Galarza for making it possible for his younger children to get back in touch with the beauties of their ancestral language. According to Dr. Prieto, his nine-year-old daughter went from reading *Poemas párvulos* to the enjoyment of Rubén Darío, "gracias a la elegante sencillez de sus libros" (thanks to the elegant simplicity of your books).

In 1977 Galarza published his definitive work on agribusiness, *Farm Workers and Agri-Business in California, 1947-1960*, in which 405 pages give one of the best accounts of the development of agribusiness in the state of California. *Farm Workers* effectively examines the system's coordination of land, water, and labor supply with technology, mechanization, and mass-marketing techniques, as well as its need for bracero labor. It also analyzes the way in which powerful associations of producers, shippers, marketers, financiers, and government agencies combined to resist the demands of farm workers.

Galarza's last publication, two years before his death, was, appropriately enough, a collection of poems bearing witness to the heart of a poet that beat within the battle-worn frame of the septuagenarian. *Kodachromes in Rhyme*—published in 1982 by the publisher of *Barrio Boy*, the University of Notre Dame Press—represents, as Mae Galarza aptly put it in her foreword, "a digression from the extant injustices and . . . rational thought." Indeed in these poems the fierce warrior exchanges the weapons of denunciation and organization for the painter's brush and the bard's lute in a veritable explosion of lyricism. Consider, for example, the poem entitled "Copy from an Old Master:"

The Grand Dame looped her shawl around the sun
and in the sky a flaming dahlia spun
She drew a comb of colors down the hills
to make the rainbow tremble in the rills.
She blew upon the grain with all her might
—the stalks of wheat were strokes of ochre light.
Her crooked fingers, grappled to a tree,
she turned to look, breathless with ecstasy.
But it was gone. The sun was just a penny.
The hills were lumps. The hills? There weren't
   any.
There was no umber passion in the woods,
or barley stubble, bristling, as it should.
I said, "Old Grand Dame, you don't know the
   trick;
there's only one who's ever made it stick."
My Mother Nature sobbed, "I know, I know;
it's just that I've been looking at Van Gogh."

The sheer plasticity of the lyrical flight in this poem is breathtaking; the evocative qualities only glimpsed throughout *Barrio Boy* and the Mini-Libros poems are suddenly given full rein and explode in an apotheosis of sound and color.

In this collection of poems, the unabashedly lyric celebration of nature is rarely juxtaposed to harsh political realities. "Florin," however, is an exception: In it a boy's almost sensual delight in breathless runs through fields of wild poppies, "fall[ing] laughing on your belly, / arms cross-wise, / or hugging the earth" is brought up short by "the Southern Pacific Company / and the Bank of America / and Clayton-Anderson / and DiGiorgio" who destroy the boy's field but compensate for it by

> endow[ing] a million-dollar chair
> at the University of California
> for a botanical expedition
> to go and look for a poppy
> reported to have been seen
> about thirty miles east of Oroville
> by a boy.

The introduction to *Kodachromes* probably includes the most revealing statement of what poetry meant to Galarza himself, at a very personal level:

> How does one return from the javelins of barbarism, the jabs of barbarians, to an earthly equilibrium and a desire for life?. . . By thoughts such as contained herein to swath the realm of perception, a generous parcel for the soul. . . . By sturdy figures formed from inner speech, pillars without cracks.

The indomitable warrior's life came to a close on 22 June 1984. Behind remained his wife of fifty-five years, Mae; two daughters—Karla Pepe, of San Jose, and EliLu Neitsch, of Pasadena—and three grandchildren. News of his death was carried by major newspapers across the nation, including the *San Francisco Chronicle*, the *Los Angeles Times*, and the *New York Times*. Following his death, testimonials began flooding the media. Fernando Chávez, son of César Chávez, and a San Jose attorney, read about the deceased leader in a *San Jose Mercury News* article which appeared 23 June 1984. Quoted in the *Los Angeles Times*, Chávez praised Galarza for his pioneer work in organizing farm workers as much as for his books which offered "such a vivid description of the struggle and plight of the farm worker" that they had become "classics." José Villa, a San Jose State University professor, said of Galarza, "He would be the first person I would call teacher. I've used his books in many of my classes. . . . He was an inspiration. He was a hero to me." Frank del Olmo in "A Bequest to Chicanos From an Activist Scholar" in the 28 June 1984 *Los Angeles Times* called Galarza "The first Chicano Renaissance man." Del Olmo added that he had "hesitated to write that when he [Galarza] was alive, because he was modest and it would have embarrassed him." This modesty combined with mildness was also recalled by James Muray, Marin County lawyer and longtime friend: "He was very mild and very modest, but also iron-minded about social justice."

The gentleness was also remembered by two Stanford University students in the 25 July 1984 *Campus Report*: "Galarza spoke about a peach tree as one would talk about an old friend. The tree was now old and no longer bountiful, but the Galarzas decided to let it preside over their garden until it decided to wither away on its own."

Labor organizer, activist, educator, scholar, storyteller, and poet—Galarza's life and work continue to enrich the lives and the minds not only of Chicanos but of humanity everywhere.

Reymundo Gamboa

(2 February 1948 -   )

Salvador Güereña
University of California, Santa Barbara

BOOKS: *The Baby Chook and Other Remnants*, by Gamboa and Ernesto Padilla (Tempe, Ariz.: Other Voices, 1976);

Madrugada del '56 / Morning of '56 (La Jolla, Cal.: Lalo, 1978).

OTHER: "Every Child Has," in *New Voices in American Poetry*, edited by Norman Denison (New York: Vantage, 1972), p. 299;

"This Shears Is Not For Pruning," in *From Three Sides: Readings for Writers*, edited by Joseph Maiolo and Barbara Brentley (Englewood Cliffs, N.J.: Prentice-Hall, 1976), pp. 26-27;

"Dos palomas," in *Calafia: The California Poetry*, edited by Ishmael Reed (Berkeley, Cal.: Y'Bird, 1979), pp. 123-124;

"Your Disdain," in *Fourth Chicano Literary Prize* (Irvine: Department of Spanish and Portuguese, University of California, 1979), pp. 37-51;

"No quiero ser rico" and "Un pizcador," in *Chicanos: Antología histórica y literaria*, edited by Tino Villanueva (Mexico City: Fondo de Cultura Económica, 1980), pp. 181-183.

SELECTED PERIODICAL PUBLICATIONS—
UNCOLLECTED: "Anuncio cósmico," "Chairing a chingón," "For History," "Grooks," "His Holistic Regard," "Padres," and "La palabra," *Grito*, 3 (March-May 1974): 70-75;

"¡Qué chinga!," "Quiero creer en Dios," and "Tengo razón," *Café Solo*, 8 (Spring 1974): 7-9;

"Sense No Evil," *Out of Sight*, 1 (Summer 1974): 4;

"Cosmic Vagrants" and "Night and Day," *California State Poetry Quarterly*, 3 (Spring 1975): 8, 15;

"Your Eyes," *Luz*, 4 (May 1975): 26;

"Words," *Luz*, 4 (December 1975): 12;

"In My Freedom," *Caracol*, 4 (July 1978): 15-18, 22;

"Going Down," *Denver Quarterly*, 16 (Fall 1979): 107-112.

Reymundo Gamboa

Reymundo Gamboa is an ascending writer whose ethnographic poetry and prose reflect an intense, experiential, inward journey. Gamboa has been lauded for his linguistic style of writing which also evokes the universality of his life within the context of the Chicano cultural heritage. Born in Anthony, New Mexico, Gamboa is the son of José Leonardo Gamboa and María Concepción Gamboa. Both his parents were farm workers, his father being deeply involved in César Chávez's United Farm Workers Union. While Gamboa was not as active in the farm workers movement as were his parents and his brother, Jesse, he nevertheless supported their work and, on occasion, joined them on the picket line. Most of his support, however, was by the pen and voice at university sites.

Gamboa's family moved to California from New Mexico when he was not yet one year old. Gamboa's father, who was from Durango, Mexico, was a mine laborer in Mexico prior to working the railroads, first in New Mexico and then in California. Because of a company accident, his father was partially disabled and lost his job. Subsequently he toiled as a farm laborer almost until his death in 1986. Ironically it was Gamboa's father, who had very little formal schooling, who taught Gamboa the value of bilingualism and multiculturalism as well as a respect for formal education. Gamboa states that "tragically, his death was the inspiration for the short story 'José,'" one of four which are currently under editorial consideration.

Gamboa spent his growing-up years in the rural setting of La Mont, California, a town set in the San Joaquín Valley, one of the nation's richest agricultural valleys. It was here that Gamboa spent his early years, helping his family with a variety of farm work until the age of sixteen when he took a job as a stock boy in a local drugstore. He attended local schools until enrolling at Fresno State College in 1967. Gamboa thrived in school, scholastically and athletically. At the age of seventeen he was selected to represent Arvin High School at Governor Edmund Brown's Southern California Governor's Conference. Also during that year, he received the Bank of America's Achievement Award for his high marks in the humanities.

Gamboa earned his B.A. in Spanish and English at Fresno State College, graduating in 1970. While at the college, he took an active interest in Chicano theater, learning techniques and performing with Luis Valdez and his El Teatro Campesino, helping to put on political plays in the San Joaquín Valley, including the Delano area. Gamboa recalls writing a play titled "La sociedad cambia," a work that Valdez did not particularly like. In 1978 he earned his M.A. in multicultural education at Pepperdine University, and pursued graduate studies in English at California State Polytechnic University, San Luis Obispo, followed by two years of study toward the Ph.D. at the University of California, Santa Barbara.

Cover for Gamboa's 1978 collection, which includes poems that illustrate what he calls his "general intent to go from an 'ensimismado [withdrawn] I' to a 'comfortable us' and then to an 'ethnographic me'"

Gamboa currently is the director of bilingual-bicultural education for the Santa Maria Joint Union High School District. He previously taught in the graduate school of education at the California State Polytechnic University.

Gamboa classifies his writing as ethnographic fiction. He writes from a very personal frame of reference which reflects the cultural fluidity of the Chicano, Mexican, and Anglo experiences and influences upon his life. He explains, "I have tried nothing more than to restate such things as allegories and parables in such a way that my writing will reflect my life and the life of the Chicano, and sometimes the lives of people who have lived in my economic situation." Gamboa's interest in poetry was borne out of a challenge that went beyond what he calls "the barrio game of war by words" and which grew with his discovery that he need not be bound by traditional structures in order to write and publish poetry. Gamboa gained exposure and recognition through his contributions to various Chicano literary competitions. In 1976 he entered the Annual Chicano Literary Contest in Bakersfield, California, and took third place in the poetry category for his poem "The Baby Chook." A milestone in Gamboa's transition to prose writing occurred in 1979 when his short story "Your Disdain" won second place at the Annual Chicano Literary Prize competition sponsored by the Department of Spanish and Portuguese at the University of California, Irvine. The winning story is about the troubled relationship between a father and a son who are grappling with inner conflict in their inability to show affection to one another.

In 1984 Gamboa clearly identified the concept of his poetry as being from the perspective of "language writing—an avant-garde tendency that has nipped at the heels of American poetry's worn status quo." In an interview Gamboa said, "I have selected these words for their demonstration of disruptions of rational flow of thought, for their lack of absolute resolutions, being fragments and posing difficulties in and for themselves. Additionally, syntax is the internalized meter."

His first published collection of poetry appeared in *The Baby Chook and Other Remnants* (1976), a book which also featured selections by friend and colleague Ernesto Padilla. It was while Gamboa was teaching in San Luis Obispo that the idea was proposed for publishing an anthology of their selected poetry. Dennis Salas, owner/editor of Other Voices Publishing House and Gamboa's publisher, was at that time also teaching on the campus. Gamboa's association with Padilla remained close. Their complementary interests in Chicano literature resulted in a second book of Gamboa's selected poetry, *Madrugada del '56 / Morning of '56* (1978). Gamboa described Padilla as the wheel and energy behind Lalo Publications, which published the work.

In discussing his writing Gamboa states that "it has been my general intent to go from an 'ensimismado [withdrawn] I' to a 'comfortable us' and then to an 'ethnographic me.' " This development is seen most in *The Baby Chook, Madrugada del '56,* and his recent narrative writing. Autobiographical tendencies are reflected more in his short stories than in his poetry, although "The Baby Chook," one of his best-known poems, was

as much a statement about himself as it was about others at his age when it was written.

Published criticism on Gamboa's work is scant. The most in-depth commentary on Gamboa as a writer appears in the introductions to his published collections. Introducing the poems in *The Baby Chook and Other Remnants*, Frank Voci writes that with Gamboa "we clearly see what poetry and language can be. The poems that follow emit a clear light or image which is like a photograph of the simple process that is language or creative expression." Voci further observes, "Reymundo Gamboa is a sensitive spirit, a person alive and trying to attest to that simply and clearly. He is one of the few Chicano poets whose ear 'hears' poetry in English and Spanish . . . one of the few who doesn't manhandle the language. He is a man who celebrates the 'word' with a sensitive and intense deliberateness which subsequently becomes a celebration of humanity." Alternately, a much more reserved criticism of *The Baby Chook* appeared in *Chicano Perspectives in Literature: A Critical and Annotated Bibliography* (1976). The critic Francisco Lomelí remarks, "Reymundo Gamboa prefers the reflective flash technique which is rarely profound, but simply a segment of life. He often depends on flat wit with which to create a lyrical image."

In the introduction to *Madrugada del '56,* Ernesto Padilla writes that Gamboa's poetry "reveals a sensitivity to the desires and dreams of his existence as a thinking human being in a historical context. Through his images and contradictions he emerges as a highly self-conscious, brutally honest being who in the act of speaking for himself and defining himself—within Chicano culture and history—forces the reader toward a critical pinnacle of self understanding." Those perceptions were echoed somewhat, but also tempered, by Cecilio García-Camarillo, the editor of *Rayas,* in his review of *Madrugada.* Writing in *Rayas* (May-June 1978), he says, "The poems themselves are quiet: they are perceptions of the poet sensing, conversing, observing himself." The reviewer code switches as he states "Por el momento la poesía de Gamboa es de ensimismamiento [presently Gamboa's poetry is self-oriented]. At times it tends towards a metaphysical, philosophical anguish." García-Camarillo added that occasionally these same poetic elements were lacking in clarity and needed to be more strongly defined. While he liked Gamboa's unpretentious use of language, he voiced a need

suspensión parcial del vivir
dormant

There is no search for Aztlán, only

Tiempo Que Muere *for the self.*

~~VISIÓN~~ (Apuntes) del Tiempo Muerto

"Sobrino, tengo que contarle de lo que se compone la vida.
Si no le hubiera costado ~~la vida a su papá~~ y tanto dolor a nosotros no le quitara el tiempo. ¿Qué derecho tendría yo de pre-
tender que la vida es lógica y determinada. Lo que le cuento es
~~se~~ lo que han visto ~~por~~ estos ojos que han vivido y van a ~~vivir~~ seguir viviendo,
usted incluído, esta experencia ^de estar encarcelado^ tan común y semejante pero tan
diferente."

Yo lo escuchaba con respeto ^pero sin^ ~~sin~~ atención.

"Me disculpo con decir que esta es una advertencia paterna,
^con debida respeto a su padre^ en su sentido, basada en lo que siento, y si lo quieres, ~~creer lo~~
~~harás lógico.~~ Con el tiempo, usted también lo sentirá. ~~no~~ No es
invertir el ~~proceso~~ ^tiempo^ sino hacerse conciente. Si es cierto que todos
somos hermanos, ^carnalitos de Aztlán^ es porque ~~no damos cuenta~~ que hemos llegado a creer
igual."

^Pedro, mi^
~~Mi~~ buen padrino-tío, siempre se apuraba mucho por mi.

"Esto, entonces, no es un consejo porque no me siento dis-
tintamente superior a usted, ni es un cuento ~~s~~ de los que se
fabrican con tequilla. Es una advertencia de cosas ^de la vida^ con cuales se
enfrentará o se le enfrentarán. Lo digo porque lo he visto en
Michigan, California, Kansas, y en los lugares donde ~~anduve con~~ ^fui detenido."^
~~su papá."~~

"Ya dígame tío," le pedí.
~~Hácame el favor~~
de hacer algo conciente con su búsqueda en este país, ^que^
será su paraíso. Sí, lo ~~es~~', por eso andamos aquí y no nos quedamos
allá. Acuerdese que el espíritu con deseos de hacer bien sin
saber a quién no tiene limites."

"Siempre lo trataré."
^ya sabe bastante.^
"No lo insulto porque no pienso que ~~no sabe y puede~~. Lo que
deseo es que viva concientemente: El aventurero ya lo sabe y lo ha
subrayado con su sangre, el campesino con su sudor, el intelectual
^a un ideal,^
al comprometerse, el jóven con las ansias que lo acompañan; usted
lo hará ~~c~~ como ~~lo~~ llegue a sentir."

Así terminó la plática que me hizo ~~mi~~ padrino-tío. Se des-
ahogó. Mientras el buen ~~Pedro~~ manejaba el auto y mi suerte a su

1.- El empleo de Pensamientos filosofía...
2.- ...

Page from a draft for a short story (by permission of Reymundo Gamboa) for the poet to broaden his scope beyond introspective themes.

Robert Lint has probably written the most favorable criticism of Gamboa's poetry, albeit largely from the perspective of linguistic analysis. For example, in his article "Language As Original Sin" in *Café Solo* (Spring 1974), he provides an in-depth analysis of Gamboa's poem "Quiero creer en Dios" (I Wish to Believe in God). In this poem Gamboa fosters the idea that it is the influence of language that keeps people from God. Lint states that "one might have expected the contradictions and tensions of Gamboa's thesis to have produced a choppy statement. However, he skillfully employs the suave deceptions of language to hold the poem's movement under the smooth surface direction."

Gamboa's acceptance within the orbit of the more-established American literature can probably be seen best in the selections of his poetry which were published in the anthologies *New Voices in American Poetry* (1972) and *From Three Sides: Readings for Writers* (1976). It was Gamboa's view that "in the beginning I thought it was good to separate Chicano literature from other literatures because it was ethnically identifiable, but now it can be identified within the structures of American literature." The best example of this is seen in the anthology *From Three Sides*. Gamboa's poem "This Shears Is Not For Pruning" was chosen for inclusion in a section titled "Working," which deals with the various aspects of work. The several pieces in the section include an essay by Studs Terkel and a short story by John Galsworthy. In his preface to the book, Joseph Maiolo, one of the editors, remarks that he chose "all of the writers in this book because, at least, their writing equals what they write about. So I can promise selections written by those dedicated to the excellence of language."

As to Gamboa's future writing, his ethnographic fiction is bound to continue its intense introspective tendencies. Gamboa's creative comfort zone exists within the genre of poetry; thus, readers can expect to see him publish several more books of his collected poems. Not being overly ensconced in poetry, Gamboa has shown his flexibility and proven his adeptness in short stories as well, and more are certainly expected.

Juan Gómez-Quiñones

(28 February 1942 -   )

Enrique R. Lamadrid
University of New Mexico

BOOKS: *5th and Grande Vista: Poems, 1960-1973* (New York: Mensaje, 1973);
Piedras contra la luna, México en Aztlán y Aztlán en México (Los Angeles: University of California, 1973);
Sembradores: Ricardo Flores Magón y el Partido Liberal Mexicano: A Eulogy and Critique (Los Angeles: Aztlán, 1973); translated into Spanish by Roberto Gómez Ciriza as *Las ideas políticas de Ricardo Flores Magón* (Mexico City: Era, 1977);
Mexican Students por La Raza: The Chicano Student Movement in Southern California, 1967-1977 (Santa Barbara, Cal.: Causa, 1978);
Orígenes del movimiento obrero chicano, by Gómez-Quiñones and Luis Leobardo Arroyo (Mexico City: Era, 1978);
Porfirio Díaz, los intelectuales y la Revolución (Mexico City: Caballito, 1981);
Al norte del Río Bravo: Pasado lejano, 1600-1930, by Gómez-Quiñones and David Maciel (Mexico City: Siglo Veintiuno, 1981);
Development of the Mexican Working Class North of the Rio Bravo: Work and Culture Among Laborers and Artisans, 1600-1900 (Los Angeles: Chicano Studies Research Center, University of California, 1982);
Chicano Politics: Reality and Promise, 1940-1990 (Albuquerque: University of New Mexico Press, 1990).

OTHER: *Selected Bibliography for Chicano Studies,* edited by Gómez-Quiñones and Albert Camarillo (Los Angeles: Chicano Studies Center, 1974);
The Chicana: A Comprehensive Bibliographic Study, edited by Gómez-Quiñones, Roberto Cabello-Argandoña, and Patrick Herrera Durán (Los Angeles: Bibliographic Research and Collection Development Unit, Chicano Studies Center, University of California, 1976);
"Octubre, 1967, a Ché," "My Father's Land," "Canción," "Octubre," "Día Obrero," "Las viejas milpas," "México, 1971," "Barrio Sun-

day," "From Austin to Houston," "to D," "to R," in *Festival de Flor y Canto: an Anthology of Chicano Literature,* edited by Alurista and Gómez-Quiñones (Los Angeles: University of Southern California Press, 1976): 78-82;
"Walk Among the Seas," *California Bicentennial Poets Anthology,* edited by A. D. Winans (Los Angeles: Second Coming Press, 1976), p. 151;
"For a Young Comrade," in *Floricanto IV,* edited by José Armas (Albuquerque, N. Mex.: Pajarito, 1979): 19.

SELECTED PERIODICAL PUBLICATIONS—
UNCOLLECTED: "Stanzas de una épica," "barrio obrero," "octubre," "canción," "méxico, 1970," and "My Father's Land," *Despertador,* 3 (April 1973): 5;
"Ballad of Billy Rivera," *Tejidos,* 1 (November 1974): 12-18;
"To al.," "Yo nunca," "My Father's Land," "October 1967, a Pablo Neruda," "Mexico 1971," and "My Girl," *Tejidos,* 2 (May 1975): 11-13;
"A Che," *Poema Convidado,* no. 7 (June 1975): 3;
"A León Felipe," "If Hope Were. . . ," and "Guadalajara, 1962," *Revista Chicano-Riqueña,* 3 (Summer 1975): 15-17;
"For a Young Comrade," *Xalmán,* 1 (July 1975): 9;
"She gets her salt at the gypsy wagon," "Berkeley Woman," and "A León Felipe," *Forum Literario* 12 (Winter 1975-1976): 12;
"From Austin to Houston," "Barrio Sunday," *Revista Chicano-Riqueña,* 4 (Fall 1976): 25, 40;
"On Culture," *Revista Chicano-Riqueña,* 5 (Spring 1977): 29-47;
"Three Intellectuals: Justo Sierra, Trinidad Sánchez Santos, Ricardo Flores Magón," in *Humanidad: Essays in Honor of George I. Sánchez,* edited by Américo Paredes (Los Angeles: Chicano Studies Center Publications, University of California, 1977): 75-106;

Juan Gómez-Quiñones

"Walk Among the Seas," *Poema Convidado*, 49 (July 1978): 11.

Juan Gómez-Quiñones, to use social philosopher Antonio Gramsci's term, is one of the leading "organic intellectuals" of the Chicano movement, a cultural worker and ideological spokesman with roots in the struggle of his community. His efforts have been evident on various political, ideological, and cultural fronts, from the picket lines of Delano and East Los Angeles to the reorientation of major educational institutions. Best known as a Chicano historian, his major fields of research include Chicano labor history and the Mexican revolution of 1910. His well-articulated polemical essays on cultural resistance and his poetry are lesser known but, nonetheless, distinguish him as a creative writer as well. Since his sociological and historical works are well documented elsewhere, the focus of this article is his poetry and essays on culture.

Born to Juan Gómez Duarte and Dolores Quiñones in Parral, Chihuahua, Mexico, Gómez-Quiñones was raised in the "white fence barrio" of Los Angeles, as he terms it. He declares in a love poem, however, "Yo nunca he salido de mi tierra" (I have never left my homeland). He holds a B.A. in English (1964), an M.A. in Latin American studies (1966), and a Ph.D. in history (1970), all from the University of California, Los Angeles, where he has also been a professor since 1969. His community and political activities date back to his work with the United Farm Workers and the United Mexican American Students (now MECHA, Movimiento Estudiantil de Chicanos de Aztlán [Student Movement of Chicanos of Aztlán]), and include such positions as chairman of the East Los Angeles Poor People's March Contingent (1968), director of Chicano Legal Defense (1968-1969), co-organizer of the Chicano Council of Higher Education (1969-1970), member of the National Broadcasting Company Mexican American Advisory Committee (1969), member of the Board of Directors of the Los Angeles Urban Coalition (1970-1972), director of the UCLA Chicano Studies Center (1974-1987), and member of the Board of Trustees of the California State Universities and Colleges (1976-1984). He has done important editorial work on newspapers, research journals, and anthologies, and has written major works on Mexican and Chicano history. He has published numerous articles on Chicano sociology and labor history, several bibliographies, and has substantial media experience with radio, television, and film. His seminal essay on aesthetics, culture, and politics is entitled "On Culture" (1977) and has been reprinted several times.

Gómez-Quiñones defines culture from the perspective of a progressive historian and activist, and is one of the first Chicano thinkers to interpret for Chicanos the concept of "cultural resistance" first developed to apply to the case of African colonialism by Amilcar Cabral. In his essay "On Culture," Gómez-Quiñones is also one of the first to define the ideological and historical parameters of the Chicano cultural revival:

> Return to the source means not a recreating of the past but the building of the future: not to restore the past or to worship it as a false idol, but to build an authentic future, one which subsumes our past, not denies it.

Gómez-Quiñones warns that if culture is exalted with mystifying awe as something eternal, then the historical conditions and conflicts which created it are obscured.

The poetry of Gómez-Quiñones appears in many important Chicano literary journals in addition to several anthologies. His collection of poems, *5th and Grande Vista: Poems, 1960-1973* (1973) is named for a street corner in Los Angeles—the poet's address in sociological as well as spiritual terms. These poems provide penetrating insights into the person who has also produced a prodigious variety of historical and social-science writings. Many poems share the social concerns of his other writings, but once free from the rigorous methodology of objective historical analysis, they explore more subjective areas of the interface between historical forces and the individual consciousness. The prologue of the book is a homage to the poet's father entitled "Canto al trabajador" (Song of Working). Like Walt Whitman, Gómez-Quiñones enumerates his praise of the common worker and, as in the poet-

ry of Pablo Neruda, the human hand becomes the concrete icon of this reverence. Through his father's suffering, the poet first learns of the world:

> I remember my father's hand
>   etched in cries and sweat . . .
> What I know I learned
>   from my father's worker's hand
> who is we and who are they
>   of right and wrong
> who has built the cities
> and wherefrom came the riches.

Such knowledge rarely comes from books or institutions, and out of it grows the clarity and sympathy with which the future historian analyzes the exploitation and alienation of human labor.

"The Ballad of Billy Rivera," the most ambitious poem in *5th and Grande Vista*, evokes the tone and spirit of the traditional Mexican *corrido* (ballad) which interweaves history and legend to chart the dimensions of heroism and the human soul. The poem is a mosaic of fragments of personal impressions, episodes from the Mexican revolution and Chicano demonstrations interspersed with verses from popular songs. Historical, infrahistorical, and even mythical levels are juxtaposed and culminate abruptly in the announcement of the funeral of one Billy Rivera on 3 February 1958, dead from a drug overdose over a decade before many of the events described in the poem. Here Gómez-Quiñones joins several other Chicano poets in symbolically burying the admirable but anarchic nihilism of the pachuco era of the 1950s.

Two poems entitled "Those" and "Coming Home," both dedicated "To the familia LA," are the closest Gómez-Quiñones comes to political manifestos in poetic form. They evoke the unassuming but penetrating folk wisdom of Spanish *dichos* and *refranes* (proverbs), but are written in an English which borders the triviality of aphorisms:

> Those that don't believe
> that what is desirable is possible
> and with our help even inevitable,
> fear the better part of themselves.

A Chicano movement political slogan of the same era, "sí se puede" (yes, it can be done), expresses the same feeling in a less abstract and more popular vein.

Although historical and political themes are prominent in Gómez-Quiñones's poetry, the majority of his poems can be characterized as more personal and lyrical, an outlet, perhaps, for the subjective ideas and attitudes that would be inappropriate in his more scholarly writings. The most convincing love lyrics in the collection are in Spanish, the poetic register of his feelings of warmth and personal intimacy:

> Como palomas
> se escapan las palabras
> Y más que canción
> mi amor se vuelve
> vuelo
> No me dejes, compañera.
>
> (Words escape
> like pigeons
> And more than a song
> my love turns into
> flight
> Don't leave me, companion.)

Critic Inés H. Tovar, in an article written on Gómez-Quiñones's creative work, has noted that the poet uses Spanish when "documenting his subjective thoughts, his personal and mythic world, . . . the spirit of the people being reborn, speaking and taking form, and flowering." With the use of English, the otherworldly or ideal qualities vanish and the hard, cold realities of everyday life are starkly outlined.

Some of the best poems in the collection are minimalist and well within the imagistic Oriental tradition introduced to Mexican poetry by José Juan Tablada and continued by Octavio Paz. Gómez-Quiñones's haikus about the fall season are perhaps too directly derivative, but "From Austin to Houston" compresses into a concrete image his concept of time as part of the process of the relation of self to other:

> Aun en mi barrio
> añoro otro barrio,
> el tiempo pasa.
>
> (Even in my barrio
> I miss another barrio,
> time passes.)

The poetry of Gómez-Quiñones which follows the publication of *5th and Grande Vista* demonstrates a further mastery of the ironic possibilities of the terse English line that in earlier poems sometimes came through as rhetorical posturing.

In "For a Young Comrade" (1979), the poet's advice to his *compañero* uses rhetorical devices much more effectively:

> What is the sentence for the murder of the unborn hope of others
> What is fit punishment for he whose touch
> dooms the flower
> Listen, they talk of workers and set worker
> against worker
> call for ideas and live by slogans . . .
> If death it is, better
> the murder of the bright fervor of disbelief.

After the 1975 article by Inés H. Tovar, the poetry of Juan Gómez-Quiñones has attracted little critical attention, probably because his best known contributions are in the area of Chicano history. In 1976 Francisco A. Lomelí and Donaldo W. Urioste appraised Gómez-Quiñones's poems, noticing how they express the evolution of his political thought: their "end result is an ideological definition of himself." More recently the poems have attracted the attention of folklorist José Limón, who dedicates a chapter to them in his study on Mexican balladry (1992).

Juan Gómez-Quiñones is a poet who knows and can chart the impact of historical forces on the individual consciousness. Having achieved the old renaissance idea, the integration of *armas y letras* (arms and letters), of *poesis*, (poetry) and *praxis*, (practice) his words and images are confident and strong as they lead thought and feeling into action.

References:

José Limón, "Juan Gómez-Quiñones: The Historian, the Poet, and the Poetic Form of Androgeny," in *Mexican Ballads, Chicano Poems: History and Influence in Mexican-American Social Poetry* (Berkeley: University of California Press, 1992);

Francisco A. Lomelí and Donaldo W. Urioste, eds., *Chicano Perspectives in Literature: A Critical and Annotated Bibliography* (Albuquerque, N. Mex.: Pajarito, 1976), pp. 24-25;

Mary Helen Ponce, "Juan Gómez Quiñones: Escolar y Poeta," *Caminos*, 4 (June 1983);

Roberto Sifuentes, "Chicano Essay," in *A Decade of Chicano Literature 1970-1979*, edited by Luis Leal (Santa Barbara: Causa, 1982): 57-63;

Inés H. Tovar, " 'Roses are Rosas': Juan Gómez-Quiñones, A Chicano Poet," *Mester*, 5 (April 1975): 95-100.

Rodolfo "Corky" Gonzales

(18 June 1928 -   )

David Conde
Metropolitan State College

BOOK: *I Am Joaquín / Yo Soy Joaquín* (Denver: Crusade for Justice, 1967).

Rodolfo "Corky" Gonzales's most important contribution has been as a major leader of the Chicano movement. Critics, by and large, continue to regard his only published book, the epic poem *I Am Joaquín / Yo Soy Joaquín* (1967), more as a social statement than a literary work of art. To be sure, Gonzales sees his task as promoting Chicano nationalism and self-determination in everything he does. There is little doubt that *I Am Joaquín* was written as a social document that sought to instill Chicano pride and identity as well as encourage community activism in support of self-determination. The literary merit of the work comes from the manner in which the poem is constructed and how theme and structure come together to produce a superior artistic experience. Its epic quality comes from the depiction of a dual journey into the postclassic world of pre-Columbian meso-America as well as into the contradictions of the Chicano heritage. In doing so, the poem models the task of the modern hero who must not only resolve the sociopolitical struggle for self-determination but, more importantly, come to terms with the contradictions of the cultural and spiritual reality that is Chicano identity.

Gonzales was born on 18 June 1928 in Denver, Colorado, to a migrant-worker family. By the age of ten he was working in the sugar beet fields in the spring and summer. He attended public school in Denver during the fall and winter and graduated from high school at the age of sixteen. As a teenager, Gonzales acquired a love for boxing and became a Golden Gloves winner. He began his professional boxing career in 1947 and rose to become the third-rank contender in the World Feather Weight category of the National Boxing Association.

In 1955 he left boxing to become a successful business person and political figure. In 1957 he was elected the first Chicano district captain of the Denver Democratic party. He coordinated

Rodolfo "Corky" Gonzales (photograph by Bonnie Strote)

the Viva Kennedy presidential campaign in Colorado in 1960 and was appointed chairman of the Denver antipoverty program. In 1963 he organized "Los Voluntarios" (The Volunteers), a grassroots organization dedicated to community initiatives on behalf of Chicano youth. This organization became the forerunner of the Crusade for Justice founded by Gonzales in 1966. This was a pivotal year for Gonzales as he became the chairman of another organization, the War on Poverty, only to resign from all establishment positions to become a full-time activist in support of Chicano issues.

The Crusade for Justice took on the task of raising political awareness especially on the part of Chicano youth through political action and education. The Crusade headquarters became a gathering place for Chicano activists, the home of *El Gallo* (The Rooster), the newspaper published by Gonzales, a cultural center which featured the "Ballet Folklórico de Aztlán" and a school, "Escuela (School) Tlatelolco," which offered a formal education. The school was named after the city of Tlatelolco which shared the island on Lake Texcoco with Tenochtitlán, the Aztec capital. The school had classes from the kindergarten level to grade twelve as well as college-level programs which included sections on Chicano awareness and pride. Many of the youths educated here became the backbone of the Chicano movement in Denver, the state of Colorado, and the Southwest.

It is within this setting and context that *I Am Joaquín* was created. Reproduced for use by many elements of the Chicano movement, it was read as a poem, presented in the form of a drama and even made into a film produced by the Teatro Campesino. *I Am Joaquín*, along with "The Revolutionist," one of two unpublished plays written by Gonzales (the other being "A Cross for Maclovio" which appears to describe Gonzales's own career as a boxer) were used extensively to educate the public about the need for Chicano political awareness and self-determination.

Gonzales's Crusade for Justice participated in the 1968 Poor People's March where he presented the "Plan of the Barrio," a declaration of issues demanding improvement of housing and education that took into account the Chicano social and linguistic heritage, land reform, political rights, and the redistribution of wealth and resources. This was followed in 1969 by the First Annual Chicano Youth Conference in Denver, sponsored by the Crusade for Justice. The conference produced a manifesto, "El Plan Espiritual de Aztlán" (The Spiritual Plan of Aztlán), which established the concept of Aztlán, that is, the American Southwest, as a national homeland. Aztlán, said to be the mythical home of Aztec origins, tied Chicano identity to pre-Columbian roots.

I Am Joaquín begins with a description of the social and spiritual condition of Chicano contemporary reality. Then the protagonist, Joaquín, goes into the past to personify famous figures of the pre-Columbian Aztec world. He does the

same with the Spanish colonial period, the Mexican independence movement, the Benito Juárez era in nineteenth-century Mexico, and the Mexican revolution in 1910. The poem pauses to reflect on the role of women in the form of Our Lady of Guadalupe, the patron saint of Mexico, and Tonantzin, her pre-Columbian counterpart, before beginning the personification of important individuals in Chicano history. The poem returns to the present and recapitulates the negative condition of the Chicano in the contemporary world before ending on an optimistic note about the future.

In his introduction to the 1972 edition of *I Am Joaquín*, Gonzales describes the theme and structure of the work:

> Writing *I Am Joaquín* was a journey back through history, a painful self-evaluation, a wandering search for my peoples, and most of all, for my own identity. The totality of all social inequities and injustices had to come to the surface. All the while, the truth about our own flaws—the villains and the heroes had to ride together—in order to draw an honest, clear conclusion of who we were, who we are, and where we are going.

I Am Joaquín represents a search for identity in the form of a journey from the present into the past and back to the present again. The journey is both historical and spiritual. In the journey Joaquín plays a role similar to El Cid, the hero of *Poema del Cid*, and Roland of *Chanson de Roland*. The major difference is that while the Spanish and French heroes each struggle with a physical enemy on the field of battle, Joaquín battles an enemy within himself in the form of socio-historical contradictions which must be resolved if the Chicano is to come to terms with his identity. Heroic activity no longer occurs in the external world only, for wholeness of identity is the boon to be obtained.

The search takes the protagonist to roots long buried in the pre-Columbian indigenous past. The journey begins with the grandeur of the Aztec empire and its heroes such as Nezahualcóyotl, the great poet king of Texcoco, and Cuauhtémoc, the last emperor of the Aztec world. The poem then reflects on the Indian condition under Spanish colonial rule which eventually results in the independence movement under Father Miguel Hidalgo. It was Hidalgo's dream to reestablish the Indian world as a valued community. Benito Juárez, a full-blooded Zapotec and the most famous president of Mexico, personifies that aspiration. The Mexican revolution of 1910 serves to bring a renewed focus on Mexico's pre-Columbian past as essential to Mexican identity.

The entry of the Chicano into the historical panorama painted by *I Am Joaquín* occurs with the Treaty of Guadalupe Hidalgo, a document which in 1848 formalized the loss of one-half of Mexican territory to the United States. The resulting social and cultural clash between the former Mexican citizens and Americans in the Southwest led to acts of epic defiance by a number of social bandits including Joaquín Murrieta, the nineteenth-century historical figure from California who appears to have inspired the poem. Joaquín Murrieta is said to have been born in Sonora, Mexico, during the 1830s and came to the California gold fields in 1849. According to several accounts, his wife was raped and killed, and he was driven from his claim in 1851. Murrieta vowed revenge and became one of the most feared outlaws of the time.

In the poem Joaquín personifies the epic heroes of Mexican and Chicano history in order to bring about cultural pride and collective self-determination. These acts of personification occur in a series of key historical moments that emphasize Mexican-Chicano epic acts of sacrifice. They begin with Cuauhtémoc's last stand against the Spaniards in Tenochtitlán followed by the death of the "niños héroes" (young heroes), Mexican military cadets who chose to die rather than surrender to American forces invading Mexico City during the Mexican-American War (1846-1848). The protagonist goes on to World War II and finally to Vietnam.

Along his journey Joaquín confronts a series of contradictions which have historically threatened the spiritual and psychological well-being of the Chicano world. These contradictions are directly related to the fact that the Chicano is the product of two different cultures, and they are at the root of an inferiority complex and a fragmented identity which Joaquín must resolve. The role of the hero then is to struggle and triumph over these influences in order to regenerate the Chicano world.

The speaker reveals these contradictions beginning with the initial contact between the Spanish and the indigenous population of Mexico. The protagonist states toward the beginning of the poem that "I am Cuauhtémoc, proud and noble, leader of men, king of an empire civilized beyond the dreams of the gachupín Cortes, who

Cover for a 1972 edition of the long poem with which Gonzales hoped to inspire "the renewal of a fierce pride and tribal unity" among Chicanos

also is the blood, the image of myself." This personification of opposites sets the pattern throughout a large part of the work. When the protagonist discusses the relationship between the Spaniard and the Indian during the colonial period, he says, "I was both tyrant and slave." When Joaquín talks about Hidalgo and his independence movement, Joaquín appears both as Hidalgo and his executioner. When speaking about the Mexican revolution of 1910 he states, "I ride with revolutionists against myself."

The effort to resolve historical contradictions by personifying them in the hero Joaquín takes an important twist when dealing with the feminine deities Guadalupe and Tonantzin. "I am," states the protagonist, "the black-shawled women who die with me or live depending on the time and place. I am faithful humble Juan Diego, the Virgin of Guadalupe, Tonantzin, Aztec goddess, too." Both deities are associated with Mount Tepeyac in Mexico City; there Tonantzin was worshiped and Guadalupe later appeared in 1531. In a sense, they are not opposites. The Virgin of Guadalupe was a product of Spanish colonial Catholicism and Tonantzin of pre-Columbian Indian cultures. Both combine to reign over the mestizo, the European-Indian offspring of whom the Chicano forms a part.

Joaquín's journey, which takes him from the present to the past and back, establishes him as a collective hero who resolves the contradictions of history. He discovers the origins of Chicano identity in the maternal religious symbols of the Indian and Spanish past. On his return to the present, Joaquín finds the same contradictory elements which bar the self-realization of the Chicano. However, his experience has established the model for resolving them. His optimism is reflected in the last words of the poem: "I SHALL ENDURE! I WILL ENDURE!"

Critics have, for the most part, treated *I Am Joaquín* as a key work of Chicano literature, possessing both an important social statement and literary merit. Eliud Martínez wrote,

One may take issue with the historical accuracy or plausibility of the social vision that Corky Gonzales proposes for generations of Chicanos to come, but not with the fact that *I Am Joaquín* is a reliable reflection of Chicano nationalism and its ideology: the popular, folk-based, working-class oriented, "indigenista" [indigenist] historical perspective of at least the 1960's and early 1970's.

Gerald Head's comparative analysis of *I Am Joaquín* and José Hernández's *Martín Fierro* (2 volumes, 1872, 1879) puts them in the vanguard of the literature of social protest. The experience of both heroes reflects the social and spiritual condition of oppressed members of society. Juan D. Bruce-Novoa describes Joaquín's experience as a

voyage "gathering images from the centuries" to eventually arrive at unity.

However one views *I Am Joaquín*, it has become clear that this work is the classic epic poem of the Chicano movement. With more than one hundred thousand copies published, Gonzales's work is also one of the most popular Chicano works to date and the issues it raises continue to be among the most important to the Chicano community today.

References:

Juan D. Bruce-Novoa, "The Heroics of Sacrifice, *I Am Joaquín*," in *Chicano Poetry: A Response To Chaos* (Austin: University of Texas Press, 1982), pp. 48-68;

Bruce-Novoa, "The Space of Chicano Literature," *Colores*, 1, no. 4 (October 1975): 30-33;

Carlota Cárdenas de Dwyer, "Chicano Literature 1965-1975: The Flowering of the Southwest," Ph.D. dissertation, New York State University, Stony Brook, 1976;

Gerald Head, "El chicano ante *El gaucho Martín Fierro*: Un redescubrimiento," *Mester*, 4 (November 1973): 13-23;

Francisco A. Lomelí and Donald W. Urioste, *Chicano Perspectives in Literature: A Critical and Annotated Bibliography* (Albuquerque, N.Mex.: Pajarito, 1976);

Eliud Martínez, "*I Am Joaquín* as Poem and Film: Two Modes of Chicano Expression," *Journal of Popular Culture*, 13 (Spring 1980): 505-515;

Philip D. Ortego, "Backgrounds of Mexican American Literature," Ph.D. dissertation, University of New Mexico, 1971, pp. 229-230;

Miguel Pendas, "An Epic Poem by Corky Gonzales: I Am Joaquín / Yo soy Joaquín," *Militant*, 37 (January 1973): 16;

Carl Shirley, "*I Am Joaquín*," *Hispania*, 58 (September 1975): 593;

Stan Steiner, "The Poet in the Boxing Ring," in *La Raza: The Mexican Americans* (New York: Harper Colophon, 1969), p. 378.

Genaro González
(28 December 1949 -)

Manuel M. Martín-Rodríguez
Yale University

BOOKS: *Rainbow's End* (Houston: Arte Público, 1988);
Only Sons (Houston: Arte Público, 1991).

OTHER: "Un hijo del sol," in *The Chicano: From Caricature to Self-Portrait*, edited by Edward Simmen (New York: New American Library, 1971), pp. 308-317;
"A Bad Back," in *Quilt 1*, edited by Ishmael Reed and Al Young (Berkeley: Quilt, 1981), pp. 123-125;
"Home of the Brave," in *A Texas Christmas*, volume 2, edited by John Edward Weems (Dallas: Presswork, 1986), pp. 156-165.

SELECTED PERIODICAL PUBLICATIONS—
UNCOLLECTED: "Soil from the Homeland," *Nuestro*, 2, (July 1978): 40-42;
"A Simple Question of $200 a Month," *Riversedge*, 3 (Fall 1980): 3-17;
"The Heart of the Beast," *Riversedge*, 3 (Fall 1980): 84-97;
"Too Much His Father's Son," *Denver Quarterly: Journal of Modern Culture*, 16 (Fall 1981): 87-93;
"Real Life," *Riversedge*, 4 (1982): 25-37.

Genaro González

Born in McAllen, Texas, Genaro González is the son of migrant farmworkers of Texas Mexican descent. His father discovered he had been living as an undocumented alien only upon enlisting for World War II, while all of his mother's family were originally from Texas. From his childhood, González remembers the difficult relationship with his maternal grandfather with whom he and his mother lived after his parents divorced. When González was nine years old his mother remarried and the family moved again. Many problems arose in the new family and both young González and his mother were forced to work in packing sheds because of financial hardships. When she was diagnosed as tubercular and sent to a state hospital, González refused to move in with his father.

After a difficult beginning due to the serious family problems, González became a top student from the second grade on. Upon graduating from high school, he was awarded an honors scholarship to Pan American University. In his sophomore year, González published his first short story, "Un hijo del sol" (A child of the sun, 1971), winning an immediate reputation as a promising writer. In fact, Juan Rodríguez in "La búsqueda de identidad y sus motivos en la literatura chicana" (The quest for identity and its motifs in Chicano literature, 1979) considers this short story the best published by a Chicano author of the 1960s and early 1970s.

The plot focuses on the quest for identity of its protagonist, Adán. It is divided into five sections and proceeds chronologically. The story opens with a psychological portrait of the central character who is searching for his essence and his roots. After intense self-reflection, he decides to continue his quest in Mexico. In the final section, Adán is helped, almost accidentally, to transcend his personal isolation. Becoming involved in a barroom brawl between a group of Chicanos and Anglos, Adán kills an Anglo during the struggle. The killing is narrated in highly symbolic terms that suggest the reconciliation of Adán's roots, his inner life, and his new participation in social action: "An obsidian blade traces a quick arc of instinct—somewhere in time an angry comet flares, a sleeping mountain erupts, an Aztec sun explodes in birth."

This story, which marks the beginning of González's dedication to the writing of short fiction, establishes him as a new voice in expressing questions that were crucial at that time. Much in the line of Nick C. Vaca's "A Week in the Life of Manuel Hernández" (1969), "Un hijo del sol" delves in the existential angst felt by many young Chicanos at the time. Thus Adán's discovery of his identity conveys to the reader a message of hope. It reveals itself as a starting point for a new life that transcends the isolation of the individuals into a collective struggle.

Nevertheless, "Un hijo del sol" was criticized by several scholars who claimed the symbolic elements used in the story—such as Adán's own name, which reversed means "nothing" in Spanish, or the imagery presented in the quote—undermined its social message. Thus, in spite of Rodríguez's praise of "Un hijo del sol," Clara A. Lomas and Angie Chabram have found the representation of socio-historic reality limited within the work. They point out the lack of development of certain fundamental problems, the most important being the absence of a link between the individual and his ethnic group. Without such a relationship, Lomas and Chabram claim, Adán's stabbing of an Anglo is socially unproductive.

While at Pan American University, González became aware that the school was investigating his ties to Chicano organizations. He decided to transfer to Pomona College, in California, but he continued to be active in the Chicano movement and helped with the La Raza Unida (The United People's) party gubernatorial campaign in Texas, in 1972 (Ramsey Muñiz was the candidate). In 1973 he left the party because of political and personal conflicts.

González then undertook graduate work at the University of California, first at Riverside and then at Santa Cruz, earning a M.S. and Ph.D. in social psychology. In addition he took creative writing courses and continued writing short stories. He was encouraged to write a novel by the West Coast representative of Grove Press, who had read samples of his short fiction. González postponed this project until 1982 when he became unemployed after Pan American University denied him a permanent teaching position. While living on savings and benefits, he completed the first draft of a novel. In the interim he published several short stories, most of which revolved around isolation versus integration. From 1978 to 1981 came "Soil from the Homeland" (1978), "A Simple Question of $200 a Month" (1980), "A Bad Back" (1981), "The Heart of the Beast" (1980), and "Too Much His Father's Son" (1981). The first three were later incorporated into González's *Rainbow's End* (1988) with slight modifications. "Too Much His Father's Son" might likewise have been conceived as a part of a larger narrative. Depicting a difficult father-son relationship, it includes many autobiographical elements. Re-creating the confused state of mind of a youngster caught in the middle of his parents' arguments, González's psychological characterization is at its best. The son walks away hand-in-hand with his mother at the end of the story, the oppressive father figure having been defeated. The characters reappear in *Rainbow's End*, although the story itself is not included.

In "The Heart of the Beast," a child's anguished mind becomes the central point around which the elements of the story revolve. Even when bitten by a supposedly rabid dog, Arturo is afraid to tell his family because his grandfather teases him about his frequent illnesses. Because of his frail health, the boy must endure the teasing of the other children at school and is excluded from their games. Paradoxically, Arturo achieves self-affirmation in his seclusion and loneliness.

"Real Life" (1982) also presents a slightly isolated character and a psychological dilemma. Ernesto is orphaned and adopted by his aunt and uncle when he is one year old. At his aunt's deathbed, Ernesto is forced to reconsider his filial love for her. His uncle consults him about whether to prolong his aunt's life with hospital machines or allow her to die with dignity. Later Ernesto is unable to pick up the phone and hear his uncle's final decision. He wishes, probably self-

González in McAllen, Texas, where his parents did farm work during his early boyhood

ishly, that his uncle let her live, but at the close of the story it is clear that Ernesto cannot effectively externalize his feelings of love.

In 1982 González left for Mexico where he spent three years. From 1983 to 1985 he taught in Puebla, at the Universidad de las Américas (University of the Americas), where he conducted field research among victims of two earthquakes that occurred during his stay in the area. He continued his writing as well, condensing his novel by over half of its original length. The revised manuscript was accepted and subsequently published by Arte Público Press. *Rainbow's End*, which follows three generations of characters, is a fascinating look at life and death on the Texas-Mexico border. Structurally the novel revolves around a series of long flashbacks, all of them bound together by the motif of rainfall, which adds a mythical dimension. In essence the rain evokes both Tlaloc, the rain god of the Aztecs, and the rainstorms associated with death found in many contemporary Latin American novels. In addition, the rain is a subtle but constant reminder to the reader of the symbolism of the rainbow, as established in the first scene of the book.

When the protagonist, Heraclio Cavazos, is about to cross the Rio Grande for the first time, he contemplates the rainbow over the river, mistaking it for a bridge. Once on the other side, he does not find the proverbial pot of gold but instead a hard life in the fields as a stoop laborer. Thus, the pot at the end of the rainbow, although never mentioned explicitly, provides the basis for the pervasive irony of the work. González's novel is, in this way, connected to the satirical tradition of Chicano literature that demythologizes the popular belief of quick riches in the United States.

Heraclio's first crossing is not by any means the only one to occur in the story. In fact the constant going and coming is one of the key elements of the novel. By referring to this constant movement, González highlights the keen relationship between both sides of the border and the perception of the river as a central point, not as a divider. In that sense, *Rainbow's End* is a rich literary re-creation of the confluence found in border life and culture. The Chicano experience is portrayed in this novel in racial terms as well as in terms of class conflicts. Most of the first generation characters are farmworkers, while the subsequent generations move on to packing sheds or similar employment, still suffering from economic and social difficulties. In the hopes of improving their lot, the main characters migrate north at a certain point in the novel. As a result of their exposure to the abuses and harassment of farmers and police, they become disillusioned. While most of the characters return home impoverished, the only ones to profit from the trip, ironically, are those who turn to drug dealing. The cultural and ethnic problems throughout generations of Texan Chicanos is also explored. For many of the characters, acculturation is the key to survival, and Heraclio Cavazos's activism against it is not sufficient to stop irreversible changes in his own family. His death, the result of physically confronting a fumigating truck, demonstrates the quixotic nature of his struggle.

Heraclio's death, however, does not end the story, and the prolongation of the novel after this point is somewhat of an anticlimax. The continuation of the novel, which introduces new characters and events, leaves an impression of uncertainty about whether González is making a hero out of Heraclio or else going on with a generational saga. Given González's tendency to elaborate on previous material, this open ending provides him with an opportunity of extending the plot in a future work. This is even suggested in the final chapter, where Fela la Curandera (the Healer)—Heraclio's sister-in-law— decides to pass her knowledge on to a young apprentice.

As several reviews attest, *Rainbow's End* has been very well received. Phillip Parotti in the *Texas Review* (Spring-Summer 1988) stresses Genaro González's talent for characterization and his gift for humor. Writing in *Texas Books in Review* (Fall 1988), Rosario Torres Raines praised the novel's presentation of the full spectrum of daily events of working people in south Texas. The novel was designated a Critic's Choice selection by the *Los Angeles Times Book Review* (20 March 1988) and was also nominated for the American Book Award.

In a subsequently published short story— "Home of the Brave" (1986), which depicts the return of a Vietnam veteran—González returns to a historical episode treated in his novel. Rejecting the stereotyped codes of false patriotism and confronting family pressures to conform, the young protagonist decides to desert the army after realizing the futility of war. The only member of his family to show any support for his decision is his uncle, Plácido, an alcoholic veteran of the Korean War, who urges his nephew to go to Mexico. Addressing Chicano participation in twentieth-century wars, the story depicts army life as a false hope for eventual social integration.

González is currently a professor in cross-cultural psychology at Pan American University. Apart from his research in this field, he has compiled a collection of short stories, *Only Sons* (1991). He was awarded a 1990 National Endowment for the Arts Fellowship for creative writing and was also selected as a Dobie Paisano fellow by the Texas Institute of Letters and the University of Texas at Austin. Already an accomplished writer, González's mature style holds great promise for his future literary contributions to Chicano letters in general and the Texan Chicano narrative in particular.

References:

Clara A. Lomas and Angie Chabram, "La conciencia culturalista chicana: El caso del escritor Genaro González," *Palabra*, 1 (Fall 1979): 3-16;

Juan Rodríguez, "La búsqueda de identidad y sus motivos en la literatura chicana," in *The Identification and Analysis of Chicano Literature*, edited by Francisco Jiménez (New York: Bilingual Press, 1979), pp. 170-178.

Ray González

(20 September 1952 -   )

Cordelia Chávez Candelaria
Arizona State University

BOOKS: *Apprentice to Volcanos* (Fort Collins, Colo.: Leaping Mountain, 1986);

From the Restless Roots (Houston: Arte Público, 1986);

Twilights and Chants (Golden, Colo.: Andrews, 1987).

OTHER: *Travois: An Anthology of Texas Poetry*, includes poetry by González (Austin: Thorp Springs, 1974);

Karl and Jane Kopp, eds., *Southwest: A Contemporary Anthology*, includes poetry by González (Albuquerque: Red Earth, 1977);

Mestizo: An Anthology of Chicano Literature, includes poetry by González (Albuquerque: Pajarito, 1978);

Dave Oliphant and Luis Ramos-García, eds., *Washing the Cow's Skull: Texas Poetry in Translation*, includes poetry by González (Forth Worth, Tex.: Prickly Pear, 1981);

Voz, edited by González (Denver, 1981-1982);

Bloomsbury Review, edited by González (Denver, 1982-1989);

City Kite on a Wire: 38 Denver Poets, edited by González (Denver: Mesilla, 1986);

High Plains Literary Review, edited by González (Denver, 1987);

Crossing the River: Poets of the Western U.S., edited by González (Sag Harbor, N.Y.: Permanent Press, 1987);

The Midnight Lamp, edited by González (Denver: Mesilla, 1989);

Tracks in the Snow: Essays by Colorado Poets, edited by González (Denver: Mesilla, 1989);

"White Sands," in *Readings from the Red Earth* (Denver: Colorado Council on the Arts & Humanities, 1989);

After Aztlan: Latino Poets of the Nineties, edited by González (Boston: David Godine, 1992);

The Texas Poetry Anthology, edited by González (San Antonio, Tex.: Corona, 1992);

This Is Not Where We Began: Interviews with Chicano Writers (Tucson: University of Arizona Press, 1992).

Ray González circa 1986 (photograph by Peter Ashkenaz)

A true southwesterner, Ray González was born and grew up in El Paso, Texas, but has also spent long stretches of time in the Rocky Mountain front-range of Colorado, and he travels frequently in New Mexico, Arizona, and California. In 1989 he returned to his native state to head the literature programs of the Guadalupe Cultural Arts Center in San Antonio. This move followed over a decade of work in the Denver, Colorado, area as a writer, editor, and avid promoter of the arts and literature, especially poetry.

Having earned a B.A. in creative writing from the University of Texas at El Paso in 1975, González moved to Colorado and began work almost immediately in his chosen field. He taught writing to juvenile offenders at the Emerson House Detention Center in Denver and also participated in the poet-in-the-schools public school program. After a brief stint (1981-1982) as editor in chief of *La Voz*, Colorado's Latino newspaper and one of the longest running periodicals of its kind in the country, he moved to the *Bloomsbury Review* where he served as poetry editor from 1982 until his 1989 move back to Texas.

Bloomsbury, a literary review covering literature in general with emphasis on Colorado writers, led to González's most productive period to date as a poet and editor. His work there gave him the hands-on experience of journalism, from research and writing to the technical and promotional aspects. The experience also placed him in a literary environment which he eagerly translated into an opportunity for further development of his craft and his contacts with writers both locally and nationally. While at *Bloomsbury* he also founded his own press, Mesilla. Although Mesilla published some of the best-produced volumes of poetry released by any American little magazine, González's efforts received little notice from Chicano literati. Throughout this period, he supported the work of other poets and became a respected fixture in the Denver arts and humanities community.

Among his honors are the 1988 Four Corners Book Award for Poetry for *Twilights and Chants* (1987) and the prestigious Colorado Governor's Award for Excellence in the Arts in 1988. He has also received several writing and publishing grants from the Colorado Council on the Arts and Humanities. In 1987 he was selected by the Woodinville, Washington, public schools to serve as poet in residence.

The quiet power inherent in González's body of poetic work matches his personal and physical presence. A large soft-spoken man who sometimes appears to melt into his surroundings at readings and conferences, he nonetheless leaves a strong presence behind him. He is like the speaker in the title poem of his collection *From the Restless Roots* (1986) who states matter-of-factly, "I live like a follower, / a noise in the trees no one can claim." In the poem the speaker's power as an observer and seer comes from his very invisibility:

> I am the twig that sparrow overlooked
> in building its nest.
> . . . .
> a noise to startle you as
> I stare at you, mysteriously,
> through the trees.

Similarly, in "Then" from the same volume, González captures the haunting power of the desert's "silent mesquite" and "dryness of the sand," locating the sense of the lyric in his bold but

Cover for González's 1987 collection, which prompted reviewer John Bradley to call him "one of our most valuable explorers of the desert, as well as the heart"

quiet comparison of human consciousness with nature's timelessness: "My footprints remain. / There is a presence in that canyon." González's tenacity is like that of the poem's "deep arroyos."

Although some of the physical settings and place names in the poetry evoke a Chicano consciousness, it is at most a vague mood and buried sensibility. Too young to have actively participated in the Chicano movement of the 1960s and 1970s, González's work shows little or no interest in the explicit social protest described in Cordelia Candelaria's *Chicano Poetry, a Critical Introduction* (1989) as "phase I poetry." Nevertheless, he does not ignore the material reality of his Mexican roots. In "Blind House," also in *From the Restless Roots*, González etches a lyric portrait of a slice of that humble life: "footprints of a departing family. / They tremble in love / as they cross the border." Shifting from second-person voice to the personal I (eye) in the title poem of *Twilights and Chants* (1987), González effectively locates his speaker in the midst of material reality ("Below concrete bridges / ... a Mexican father ... searches / for his drowned son") even as the speaker teeters on a high wire of dreams "from childhood."

González has not received wide critical attention, but that will change. John Bradley, reviewing *Twilights and Chants*, describes the author "as one of our most valuable explorers of the desert, as well as the heart." Bradley also notes that González "is not afraid to work in the traditions of the emotive imagination seen in the poetry of [Pablo] Neruda and ... [Robert] Bly" (*Mid-American Review*, July 1988). In his essay "The Active Poet," included at the beginning of *Tracks in the Snow* (1989), González admits to being influenced by these writers and, indeed, traces his discovery of poetry to his classroom encounter with the landmark *Naked Poetry* anthology (1969). Writing in *Contact II* (Fall 1989), John Repp finds González "a bit too rehearsed" and "comfort-able," but he praises the poet's "undeniable talent" for "wrestl[ing] movingly with the past—his own, his family's, and his culture's." The measure of this poet's worth, although solid and forceful in its apprenticeship, ultimately awaits the flourish that clearly appears ahead. His unrelenting persistence in contributing to the vigor of public poetry through publishing and readings has already left his "tracks in the snow."

References:

Tom Auer, "Literary Arts," *Muse* (March-April 1990): 18;

Cordelia Candelaria, *Chicano Poetry, a Critical Introduction* (Westport, Conn.: Greenwood, 1986);

Samuel Maio, "Poetry as Shamanism," *Puerto del Sol* (Spring 1988): 210;

Monte Whaley, "Writer: Poetry Tool of Common Man," *Longmont Times-Call*, 14 November 1988, p. 12.

Jovita González de Mireles
(1899 - 1983)

Cida S. Chase
Oklahoma State University

BOOKS: *Mi Libro de Español*, 3 volumes: volumes 1 and 2 by González de Mireles, E. E. Mireles, and R. B. Fisher; volume 3 by González de Mireles and E. E. Mireles (Austin: Benson, 1941-1943);

El Español Elemental, 6 volumes, by González de Mireles and E. E. Mireles (Austin: Benson, 1949).

OTHER: "Folk-Lore of the Texas-Mexican Vaquero," in *Texas and Southwestern Lore*, edited by J. Frank Dobie (Austin: Texas Folk-Lore Society, 1927), pp. 7-22;

"Tales and Songs of the Texas-Mexicans," in *Man, Bird, and Beast*, edited by Dobie (Austin: Texas Folk-Lore Society, 1930), pp. 86-116;

"America Invades the Border Towns," *Southwest Review*, 15 (Summer 1930): 469-477;

"Among My People" (first series), *Southwest Review*, 17 (January 1932): 179-187;

"Among My People" (second series), in *Tone the Bell Easy*, edited by Dobie (Austin: Texas Folk-Lore Society, 1932), pp. 99-108;

"Historical Background of the Lower Río Grande Valley," in *LULAC News*, 2 (September 1932): 5;

"The Bullet-Swallower," in *Puro Mexicano*, edited by Dobie (Austin: Texas Folk-Lore Society, 1935; facsimile, Dallas: Southern Methodist University Press, 1965), pp. 107-114;

"Latin Americans," in *Our Racial and National Minorities*, edited by Francis J. Brown and Joseph Slabey Roucek (New York: Prentice-Hall, 1937), pp. 497-509;

"The Mescal-Drinking Horse," in *Mustang and Cow Horses*, edited by Dobie, Mody C. Boatwright, and Harry H. Ransom (Austin: Texas Folk-Lore Society, 1940), pp. 396-402;

"Stories of My People," in *Texas Folk and Folklore*, edited by Boatwright, Wilson M. Hudson, and Allen Maxwell (Dallas: Southern Methodist University Press, 1954), pp. 19-24.

Jovita González de Mireles is one of the significant female writers of the first half of the twentieth century. History and fiction converge in her essays as she describes the life, customs, and beliefs of her people along the Mexican border. Born in Roma, Texas, in 1899, Jovita González belonged to a prominent Spanish family descended from the original settlers of what became the American Southwest. She was raised on her grandfather's ranch in the Rio Grande valley. The ranch had come to her family when her great-great-grandfather, as one of the *agraciados* (grantees), received a land grant from the Spanish crown in the northern frontier of New Spain.

At a time when education was a precious commodity for minority group members, Jovita González obtained a B.A. with a teaching certificate in history and Spanish at Lady of the Lake College in San Antonio. After teaching at Saint Mary's Hall in San Antonio, she continued her education at the University of Texas at Austin and graduated with a master of arts on 19 August 1930. Her master's thesis, "Social Life in Cameron, Starr and Zapata Counties," is a well-documented study of the history and the inhabitants of those counties. While at the University of Texas in 1925, she became acquainted with J. Frank Dobie at the Texas Folk-Lore Society. With Dobie's encouragement she initiated her research work on the Mexican folklore of Texas and became a prominent member of the society. She was elected president of the Texas Folk-Lore Society in 1930. On 17 and 18 April 1931 and 22 April 1932, she presided over the annual meetings of the society held respectively in San Antonio and in Austin. González's essays and folkloric tableaux appeared periodically from 1927 through 1940 in various publications of the Texas Folk-Lore Society and in the *Southwest Review*. She was also associated with the League of United Latin American Citizens (LULAC), one of the earliest Chicana organizations that attempted to formulate a Chicano ideology in regard to the socioeconomic situation of the Chicano. She became vice-president and president of LULAC, and her essays appeared in the early 1930s in *LULAC News*, a publication of the organization. In her master's thesis she dedicates a section of chapter 5 to LULAC and discusses its creation, purpose, and constitution.

González married Edmundo E. Mireles, who also worked in the field of education. He was president of the Educational Committee of LULAC in 1937. In 1940 she and her husband were in Corpus Christi, Texas, where he was coordinator of the Spanish programs in the public school system. After W. B. Ray High School in Corpus Christi was founded in 1959, González taught Spanish and history there and sponsored the activities of the Pan American Club. She remained at Ray High School until her retirement in 1966.

Besides being one of the earliest Chicana folklorists, González had a keen interest in the pedagogical aspects of the Spanish language at the elementary level. She assisted her husband in the production of the three-volume series *Mi Libro de Español* (My Spanish Book, 1941-1943) and the six-volume reader *El Español Elemental* (Elementary Spanish, 1949).

Although González produced her essays and her picturesque folkloric tableaux using an upper-class point of view, she shows an awareness of the socioeconomic realities of the Chicano population of the Southwest. In her master's thesis and in some of her essays she points out that some of the conflicts that have arisen among the border inhabitants were produced by the Anglo-American colonization of that region. She states that Anglo-Americans, who consider the Texas-Mexicans of the border counties as interlopers and undesirable aliens, should reflect on the following facts: that the majority of those Mexicans were living in what is today Texas long before Texas was Texas; that Mexicans were in those territories long before many Americans crowded the decks of immigrant ships; that a great number of Mexicans along the border did not come as immigrants but were the descendants of people granted land by Charles V, the Spanish king.

González hoped that through her writings she would promote a better understanding between two culturally and ideologically opposed races, the Mexicans and the Anglo-Americans. Her folkloric sketches are humorous, lively, and colorful. They usually begin with a description of a character who is later the subject of an event or series of events. The resulting anecdotes are always odd and interesting. For example, González's "Folk-Lore of the Texas-Mexican Vaquero" (1927) discusses the frontier vaquero (cowboy), an extraordinary type of range man born and bred in Texas; yet he is either unknown to most people or considered an undesirable character. She says that this vaquero is the product of both the Native American and the Spanish conquistador. From his Indian ancestors, he inherited his love for the open prairie and for his freedom, as well as his melancholy and his fatalistic view of life. From the Spaniards he derived his courteous personality, a love for music and poetry, and religious devotion. The life of the vaquero revolves around myths through which he attempts to understand nature. He has, for example, the myth of "El Cenizo" (a silvery shrub which produces white, pink and lavender flowers), which tells the story of how this plant was a gift of the Virgin Mary to the vaqueros during a drought. Since this plant appeared on the prairie on Ash Wednesday, it was called El Cenizo (The Ashen One). "The Mocking Bird" is another vaquero story that relates how this bird became endowed with white feathers on its wings at a time when all creatures spoke a common language: Spanish. "El Cardo Santo" (The Thistle) was a gift to Antonio, a vaquero who disliked flowers with thorns and criticized nature for creating beauty that one could not gather without pricking one's hands. "The Guadalupana Vine" is a tale that centers on a South Texas vine which has medicinal properties. Legends of ghosts and treasures abound among the vaqueros, states González. The great majority of the legends deal with buried treasures in southern Texas which the Spaniards left behind during Indian raids. In the legend of the Chimeneas Ranch (Chimney Ranch), the ranch is haunted by the spirits of the former owners who frighten the vaqueros at nightfall. Along with all these tales, González includes several folk songs and epic compositions that come from the border vaqueros.

"Tales and Songs of the Texas-Mexicans" (1930) concentrates on the folklore among the pastoral people of the borderlands. In addition, the narrator laments that the goatherds and the old type vaqueros are becoming extinct and that their traditions are viewed with contempt by young Chicanos. The essay is divided into two parts, "Folk Tales" and "Songs." Vaquero tales, says the narrator, are humorous and somewhat realistic while goatherd stories are mystical and focus on nature. There are two goatherds that stand out in the narrator's mind, Tío Patricio and Chón. They are depicted in a picturesque manner in González's charming, straightforward style:

> Chón was little, black, and ugly; his wrinkled, withered face resembled a bat's, and his sharp eyes blinked with the regularity and solemnity of a toad's. He was a little heathen, a materialist who could see and understand nothing beyond his goats. On the other hand, Tío Patricio was a mystic, a visionary who saw in nature the handiwork of his Creator.

When these two characters visited the narrator's family ranch, all rejoiced, for their visit meant tales from Tío Patricio and songs from Chón. The latter produced extremely brief compositions; hence at the ranch emerged the following saying: "Es corta como la canción de Chón" (It is short like Chón's song). The narrator records and translates into English Chón's favorite song, "La Urraca" (The Magpie). In addition, this collection includes the following narratives: "Tío Patricio," "The Carpenter," "The Cicada," "The Cardinal," "The Dove," "Ambrosio the Indian," "The First Cactus Blossom," "The Gift of the Pitahaya," and "The Devil on the Border," which is made up of three tales about the Evil One. The section of the essay entitled "Songs" includes "Remigio Treviño," the earliest *tragedia o corrido* (Mexican ballad) on Texas soil that González found. The ballad relates the story of Remigio Treviño, a soldier stationed at Camargo who in the early 1860s decided to expel the Americans who were settling along the border. He succeeded in killing ten Americans, but in 1863 he was captured while raiding Rio Grande City and was later hanged. Other songs included are "The Tío Pancho Malo Song" (Mean Uncle Pancho Song), "El Sombrero Ancho" (The Broad-Brimmed Hat), "Coplas Del Payo" (The Rustic's Song), "El Rancho Grande" (The Big Ranch), "La Palomita" (The Little Dove), and "La Trigueñita" (The Pretty Brunette).

In "America Invades the Border Towns," which appeared in the *Southwest Review* (Summer 1930), González comments on the rude awakening experienced by the inhabitants along the Texas border at the beginning of the twentieth century. In those parts, Texas-Mexicans had lived quite happily, unaware that they could be considered foreigners and experience racial discrimination. With an insurgence of Anglo-Americans from the North and the Middle West, the border towns underwent serious economic changes.

Middle-class shopkeepers and grocers went out of business when the new commerce opened chain grocery stores and devised new methods of merchandising. Mexican people began to be banished from public places and social events. Such treatment caused extreme anger and resentment, but many Mexicans realized that they had to assimilate into the American way of life. Their children, who up to that time had gone to Mexican schools, began attending American schools where they were penalized for speaking Spanish. González states that the only Mexicans who benefited from the arrival of Americans were the *peones* (agricultural laborers and farmhands), for the new system meant higher wages for them and a simple change of masters. The border situation during the 1930s disturbed González and she hoped that the Americanization of young people might bring an understanding between the Texas-Mexicans and the Anglo-Americans.

In 1932 she published two series of short sketches under the title "Among My People." The first series appeared in the *Southwest Review* in January, and the second series was included in J. Frank Dobie's *Tone the Bell Easy*. The following narratives comprise the first series: "Juan, El Loco" (The Mad John), "Don José María," and "Don Tomás." These three tableaux are portrayals of picturesque border characters. The narrator reminisces about the old border communities, which were changed forever by the American way of life. One could still find areas, however, where the language and traditions remained untouched. From one of these areas emerged Juan, El Loco, a strange shepherd whose only worldly possessions were a comb and a broken mirror. He claimed that he had witches inside him ordering him about, a belief supported by the narrator: "It was said by the *vaqueros* and the *rancheros* that he became worse on Fridays and when the moon was full." In the second sketch, Don José María was one of the richest and most pretentious landowners of the lower Rio Grande Valley. He lived like a feudal lord and exercised his authority over his family and his land. However, Don José María would become a lamb when his wife, Doña Margarita, spoke to him. The third sketch, "Don Tomás," provides a glimpse of a man whose absolute patriarchal authority came to an end with the arrival of American law and order.

The second series is made up of "Shelling Corn by Moon Light," "Pedro the Hunter," "The Mail Carrier," "The Perennial Lover," and "Tío

Pancho Malo" (Bad Uncle Pancho). "Shelling Corn by Moon Light" recalls the late summer nights when the ranch help congregated at the Big House to shell corn and tell ghost stories. In the second sketch, Pedro the hunter was a famous man among border folk because he spoke English and had seen the world. He had worked on the plantations of the South, had seen the "Tren Volador" (The Swift Train), and had been in Houston. However, Pedro had returned home longing for the familiar sights and smells of the border countryside. "The Mail Carrier" focuses on the character of Tío Esteban (Uncle Esteban), who not only delivered mail, but knew and told "All the scandal of the two counties through which he passed." He was also the Cupid of the area, for he promoted love affairs and even delivered letters free of charge for lovers. "The Perennial Lover" is the story of Carlitos, a man who was in the habit of writing love letters every spring to all eligible ladies. One year, much to his astonishment, a lady accepted his advances and he had to marry her. Finally, the tale of Tío Pancho Malo portrays an old man whose nonconformity with the ways of the world earned him the nickname of "Malo" (Bad).

"The Bullet-Swallower" (1935) depicts a character whose partly paralyzed right arm ended in a clawlike hand with dirty fingers. This deformity and a partially closed eye were the result of numerous fights. Squatting on the floor, he told wild stories about border feuds, bandits, and smugglers while making vicious gestures in the air with an antique knife. According to the narrator, this man was born in the wrong time, for he would have made an excellent conquistador, or perhaps a knight in a chivalry novel. The anecdote, narrated in the first person, reveals that the character was called "Antonio Traga Balas" (Anthony the Bullet-Swallower) because he had been shot in the mouth by a Texas Ranger but had survived the ordeal. On another occasion he was almost frightened to death. This occurred when he helped a man to die in peace in a miserable shack and went to find some neighbors to come watch the corpse with him until the burial. Not finding anyone to help him, he returned to the shack, which was in flames. At this point of the story González's descriptive talent is made evident:

> I ran inside. The sight that met my eyes was one I shall ever see. I was nailed to the floor with terror. The corpse, its hair a flaming mass, was sitting up in the coffin where it had so peacefully

lain all day. Its glassy, opaque eyes stared into space with a look that saw nothing and its mouth was convulsed into a most horrible grin. I stood there paralyzed by the horror of the scene.

"Latin Americans" is an essay by González included in a 1937 Prentice-Hall publication on the United States minority population, *Our Racial and National Minorities*, edited by Francis J. Brown and Joseph Slabey Roucek. González's participation in this early study of American minority groups indicates the professional respect she had acquired in her time. Her entry is documented with interviews and, following an introduction, is divided into three sections: "Cultural Differentiation and Assimilation," "Organizations," and "Contribution to American Life." Utilizing a historical, upper-class perspective, González introduces the study by discussing the social class system that Spanish conquistadores implanted in the New World. The criollos, descendants of the early Spanish colonizers, were at the top of the socioeconomic structure. The mestizos, people of Indian and Spanish ancestry, were next. Their social position varied according to their percentage of Spanish blood, measured by the color of their skin. At the bottom of the social totem pole were the peones, who were direct descendants of the Indians. This hierarchy was applied to all Latin Americans regardless of their location in the New World.

González also includes a historical account of the presence of Spain in what later became United States territory. The explorations of Juan Ponce de León in Florida, the remarkable journey of Alvar Núñez Cabeza de Vaca from the Gulf of Mexico to the Gulf of California, and the great explorations of Francisco Vázquez de Coronado through the southwestern territories are emphasized. To González, all Latin Americans are similar in spirit, for they have been marked by the procedures of the Spanish explorations and conquest. She believes the motto of the National University of Mexico, "Through my race speaks my spirit," might as well be the motto for all Latin Americans in the United States. The annexation of the Spanish Southwest to the United States, which took place with the Treaty of Guadalupe Hidalgo in 1848, was an extremely painful experience for the Latin Americans, especially those of the gentry class who were proud of their Spanish heritage and aristocratic stock. Having lived isolated for centuries, exercising a patriarchal way of life, they considered Americans vandals who had deprived their mother country of a large territorial mass.

The first Anglo-Americans who ventured into what had been Spanish territories were the Southerners, fleeing from the carpetbaggers after the Civil War. These were congenial Anglos who lived in peace with the Mexican inhabitants. However, the gold rush of 1849 and the development of the Rio Grande valley brought Anglo-Americans of a different mind. They were shrewd, intolerant, and for the first time made the Mexicans feel like foreigners in their own land. Political power slipped from Mexican hands just as lost territories had slipped from them, and a sense of animosity and resentment developed toward Anglo-Americans.

González provides a review of the Mexican immigration that began with the Mexican revolution of 1910. Different from the old inhabitants of the Southwest, these immigrants belonged to the underprivileged class and were uneducated to the point of illiteracy; from them came the migrant workers, who face poverty on a daily basis. González testifies that these people maintain a fatalistic attitude toward life as a direct result of their Indian heritage.

According to González in the 1937 study, the Mexican middle class in the United States is made up of urban artisans and shopkeepers. They are descendants of landowners or middle-class Mexicans who have immigrated to the United States. They own homes and are able to send their children to school. Nevertheless, they live segregated by the Anglo-Americans, a condition that they view as abominable. This situation has contributed greatly to weaken the process of Americanization. LULAC was founded in order to promote Americanization by encouraging the political ambitions of the Latin Americans, promoting the learning of the English language, and instilling a sense of loyalty to the ideals and principles of the United States.

González emphasizes the multiple contributions of Latin Americans to American life and culture in regard to architecture, art, artisan products, film, music, and language. The greatest contribution, however, is the literary influence of Latin American legends, traditions, and ballads, which emerge in American literature. Concluding that Latin American influence in the United States has been constructive, González seriously questions why Anglo-Americans, who are enthusiastic about Spanish art and culture, have yet to accept the Latin Americans in their midst.

"The Mescal-Drinking Horse" (1940) is a refreshing sketch about a horse named "El Conejo" (The Rabbit)—a gentle, trembling animal only appropriate for a child's pet. However, his personality changes when a smuggler, Juan José, gives him daily doses of Pájaro Azul Mescal (Blue Bird Mescal). The animal then becomes famous for his smuggling adventures and, due to his fondness for Pájaro Azul Mescal, is renamed "Pájaro" (Bird). On one occasion he saves his master from the Texas Rangers and earns a reputation as a "Ranger Sniffer." The horse's life undergoes further change when Juan José decides to repent from his sinful life and become religious. He gives Pájaro to a man named Don Manuel, who, continuing to inebriate the horse, claims to be the only person who can ride him. One day, however, Father José María sees a drunk Don Manuel trying to ride the animal. Through a clever bet, the Father acquires Pájaro, changes his name to Stella Matutina (Morning Star), and, after curing the animal of his mescal-drinking habit, proclaims that the horse is an example of what religion can do.

Although they tend to stereotype Chicanos, Jovita González's essays and folkloric tableaux are invaluable in the study of the evolutionary process of Chicano literature. In an epoch when it was almost impossible for Chicanos to stand out in the American intellectual scene, González was singled out as a woman of talent. Probably one of the earliest folklorists in the field of Chicano studies, she will remain one of the most prominent Chicano figures in the first half of the twentieth century.

References:

Tatum, ed., *Mexican American Literature* (New York: Harcourt Brace Jovanovich, 1989);

Gloria Louise Velázquez-Treviño, "Cultural Ambivalence in Early Chicano Prose Fiction," Ph.D. dissertation, Stanford University, 1985;

Velázquez-Treviño, "Jovita González: una voz de resistencia cultural en la temprana narrativa chicana," in *Mujer y literatura mexicana y chicana: culturas en contacto: primer coloquio fronterizo 22, 23 y 24 de abril de 1987* (Tijuana, B.C.: El Colegio de la Frontera Norte, 1988), pp. 76-83.

Alfonso C. Hernández
(18 September 1938 -   )

Nuria Bustamante
Los Angeles Harbor College

BOOKS: *Arrullos de revelación: Manantiales, paradojas, anatemas / Lullabies of Revelation: Springs, Paradoxes, Anathemas* (Guadalajara: Summa, 1979);

The False Advent of Mary's Child, and Other Plays (Berkeley: Justa, 1979).

SELECTED PERIODICAL PUBLICATIONS—
UNCOLLECTED: *The Lemon Tree, The Potion,* and *The Wedding Dress, El Grito,* 7 (June-August 1974): 38-54;

"The Manfly," *Grito del Sol,* 1 (April-June 1976): 75-78.

Playwright, poet, novelist, and actor, Alfonso C. Hernández is perhaps one of the most versatile but least known of the Chicano writers. He is restlessly innovative in his drama and likewise always in search of new horizons in his poetry. Although his poetic output is important, his most significant contribution to Chicano letters is through drama. In this medium, his fertile imagination and scenographic talent are best employed, creating bizarre characters that move within an ambience that often partakes of the world of dreams, the subconscious, and the supernatural. His dramatic output is entirely in English, but even his published plays have heretofore not been staged, probably because of their graphic sexual elements.

He was born on 18 September 1938 in Atotonilco, Mexico, to Alfonso Hernández Velázquez, landowner, and Sabina Cázeres. The younger Alfonso's literary interests were awakened and nurtured early in childhood when his father read to him classic tales, history, and legends of Mexico from his well-stocked home library. His especial interest in drama was evident early when at home he acted out scenes from the classics and later in school when he was often called upon to recite dramatic poetry or to participate in plays on holidays and special occasions. At seventeen he felt compelled to express in writing his feelings and experiences: several

poems and an unpublished novel, "La muerte se llama azahar" (Death's Name is Orange Blossom), were the result.

Hernández completed elementary and high school in Mexico. In 1960 he came to the United States, obtained a B.A. in French from San José State University, and then earned an M.A. in French literature from Claremont McKenna College, California. Upon learning about the deplorable conditions of the Mexican and Chicano workers, he joined the Chicano Movement. When Luis Valdez began to write his political plays in the 1960s, Hernández was one of the first to stage them. He also wrote and staged, in collaboration with his students, several plays of denunciation and protest. He actively participated in the César Chávez-inspired grape boycott and in protest marches, and he delivered speeches at rallies to awaken political conscience in favor of the movement.

In the 1970s Hernández traveled extensively through Europe, attending courses at centers of learning in Paris, Strasbourg, Stuttgart, Salzburg, Regensburg, and elsewhere. He continued to write poetry and drama but modestly kept his writings to himself. Finally in 1974 A. Rivas Sáinz, editor of the Guadalajara periodical *Summa,* submitted three of Hernández's one-act plays to the Chicano periodical *El Grito,* where they were published immediately.

These three short one-act plays—*The Lemon Tree, The Wedding Dress,* and *The Potion*—form a trilogy bound by a common pessimistic theme. As the action develops, the women characters undergo physical and psychological transformations. In *The Lemon Tree* the innocent games of children, first communion, and simple flirtation culminate in highly erotic love games. Frustrated hopes, depicted in *The Wedding Dress,* form the continuing theme of *The Potion* (but now in a religious context) in the coupling of elaborate Christian with pagan rituals that effect metamorphoses in some of the participants. The ending of the tril-

Alfonso C. Hernández

ogy is apocalyptic, with a film projection of the mushroom cloud of an atomic explosion.

In this well-crafted, highly artistic trilogy there is little or no dialogue, and the action is conveyed by dance, pantomime, music, songs, and film. The motivation for the action is revealed through poems, prayers, short monologues, or recorded voices that express the characters' inner conflicts. Each play has detailed stage directions that include the use of strategically placed mirrors that create the effect of the merging of players and audience. Audience involvement is a prominent feature in all of Hernández's plays.

"The Manfly," published in 1976, is one of five short stories within a larger, unpublished work called "The Education of Inocencio," in which Inocencio is the connecting character. Each story presents him within a different world, receiving a lesson related to existence. In "The Manfly," a famous daredevil attempts to climb a church facade up to the steeple in order to find and extract the secret of the "Great Bell." His daring arrogance (a case of hubris) is first encouraged and then punished by the animated facade

that allows the Manfly to secure his ropes in all the right places except for the last stone, which bursts and hurls the Manfly to his death. Inocencio here is just an onlooker.

With descriptive passages Hernández creates situations with concision, clarity, and power, using strong imagery which at times reaches the grotesque:

> The Manfly starts climbing. The people become an abstraction, a whole breathing abstraction . . . cries of optimistic encouragement: Keep on! Go on! Good! The old women, wiser, put their black shawls into their mouths grasping between their teeth the Manfly's future. The men look, smiling sarcastically because it is an easy way to make a living. . . .
>
> The Manfly climbs half of the tower without a single incident . . . can feel the last stone with his hand. He grasps it strongly. Blood pours out from his fingers, his toes, his chest. The facade laughs. . . .
>
> The last stone bursts. . . . The Manfly loses his balance. He falls and blots the sidewalk with blood and brains. . . . One eye runs toward the gutter. Teeth fly around. Bones break. Lungs ex-

plode. Blood flows. . . . The priest throws holy water on the sidewalk. Nuns bring more holy water and begin cleaning. Impassible. Rigid. Their faces made of marble. Their whiteness lights the starched laced caps. When they lower their black dresses, their arms become wings, their noses beaks and they start devouring the Manfly's flesh. They pray and eat. They chant and they drink the blood. They lick the body and the stone with their tongues. They suck every morsel of brain from the sidewalk.

By using an effective combination of magic realism and surrealist techniques, Hernández creates a world in which inanimate things are endowed with feelings and powers, which are used to retaliate against the humans who inflicted abuses on them.

After composing the Inocencio group of stories, Hernández turned his attention again to the drama. More extensive storylines and better-developed characters are found in three plays published together in 1979: *The False Advent of Mary's Child, Every Family Has One*, and *The Imperfect Bachelor*. Fond of pastorals since childhood, Hernández wanted to write a modified version of one that would include witchcraft. He was inspired to write the first play one summer afternoon, when, while strolling under the Claremont McKenna College campus trees, he suddenly saw, as if projected on a screen, a vision of the complete play, and he felt challenged to duplicate in writing what he had seen. In *The False Advent of Mary's Child*, the action centers on the mysterious happenings visited upon an upper-middle-class Hispanic family. Lupe, the husband's mistress, resorts to witchcraft to induce a false pregnancy in the husband's wife in order to alienate and eventually destroy the marriage. The spell is checked through the help of a *curandero* (witch doctor or healer). Most of the characters have no names and are allegorical representations of different types of people with well-defined roles in society: The Father, The Mother, Curandero, Priest, Doctor, Nurse. All are one-dimensional except the daughter, Carmen, who strongly protests and rebels against her female destiny and the double standard invoked by men and sanctioned by society. By staging the play on platforms, Hernández facilitates the representation of simultaneous action, flashbacks, and scenes within scenes, the latter aided by slow-motion cameras. Again, effective use is made of audience participation and improvisation.

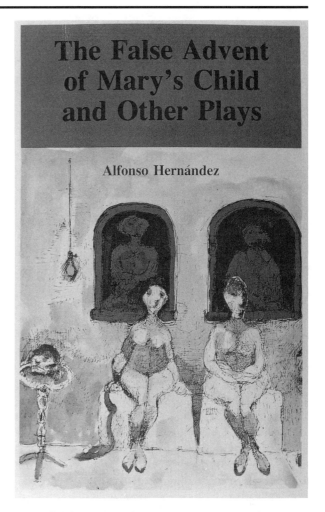

Cover for the 1979 collection of three plays by Hernández. The title work relates the story of a bewitched Hispanic family.

"Most of what I write," Hernández says, "is based on an incident, a personal experience, or an anecdote someone has told me." When he was in Germany in the 1970s, a friend told him about reading in a newspaper of a gay, rich, older man killing a poor, younger man. Impressed by the story, Hernández immediately started to write *Every Family Has One*, a play that deals with social classes and exploitation among a group of homosexuals. Hans, one of the older men in the German group, invites seven of his friends to a farewell party for Al, his summer visitor from the United States. There is very little action and plenty of dialogue as the characters openly discuss the joys, hopes, and frustrations they experience in their complicated relationships. The revelation of the emotional complexity binding the characters is gradual, structured like a musical crescendo; it begins unfolding with the first guest's arrival, increases in intensity with every newcomer, and reaches its climax when the last guest arrives. Unable to deal with the social pressure, depression, and feelings of rejection, this last visitor takes his own life. In *Every Family Has One*, Hernández best shows his skill at creating strong characters with well-defined personalities.

The Imperfect Bachelor, the third play in the collection, calls for a great deal of interaction between actors and audience. John, a bachelor in search of a wife, acts as a master of ceremonies throughout the play, introducing his three prospective brides. At John's request, the women undergo a series of tests to prove their suitability, from dancing stark naked and lovemaking to a close and often grotesque inspection of their teeth, legs, hips, and unmade-up faces. In this play the women are not developed as characters. They are rather caricatures of sensual, simple, and liberal American women. Angry and discontented, the three are transformed into Furies at the end of the play. While John prepares once more to address the audience, the women unite, march against him, kill him, and eat his heart. The chauvinism of the play is bound to offend at least some of the women in the audience in spite of the play's humorous undertones. *The Imperfect Bachelor* is challenging to the leading actor, who must extemporaneously adapt and modify his lines, responding to and improvising on suggestions he solicits from the audience. A feeling of expectant tension is created since no one can know how the audience is going to react or what is going to happen.

Aside from drama, Hernández has been writing poetry since his early teens, but at first he kept this mostly to himself. Many of his poems were lost, and only a few were published in a campus newspaper in San Jose, California. "Poetry," the author declared, "is such an intimate expression, that I just don't know why I permitted my poems to be printed." In spite of this attitude, *Arrullos de revelación* (*Lullabies of Revelation*, 1979), with a prologue by A. Rivas Sáinz, is a trilingual (Spanish, French, English) selection of Hernández's poems up to 1975. The collection is divided into three parts that correspond to three sources of Hernández's poetic inspiration: "Manantiales" (Springs), "Paradojas" (Paradoxes), and "Anatemas" (Anathemas). A thematic progression begins in "Manantiales" with impressions, memories, and reminiscences of childhood and early adolescence. The poems in this section were originally written in Spanish, using mostly impressionistic and associative imagery techniques:

Qué fascino
Qué fascino
cuando veo
el filo plateado
de un cuchillo
me reflejo
en su blancura
y la negrura
silenciosa
de la muerte
se asoma
en la ventana
plomeada
de la hoja
delgada

What fascination!
What fascination!
When I see
The sharp blade
Of a knife
I mirror
In its whiteness
And the silent
Blackness
Of death
Shows its skull
In the leaden
Window
Of the thin
Blade[.]

The second section, "Paradojas," which was originally written in French with Spanish translations by the author, deals with feelings of contradiction, alienation, and puzzlement at facing the ambiguity of the human condition. Heavily influenced by the French impressionist poets, Hernández experiments with phrase clusters and makes frequent use of associative and surrealist imagery to express the feeling of alienation in some of these poems.

"Anatemas," the third section, was originally written in English and is based on Hernández's American experience. The poems express a mixture of alienation, anger, heavy protest, and rebellion in which sexuality is expressed in bold, explicit, uninhibited, and sometimes tortured images. "Anatemas" includes some of Hernández's best poetic expression, with a more consistently succinct verse and a more sustained lyricism, rich in sensual, oneiric, and synesthetic imagery. Particularly noteworthy are "Poem to My Other Selves," the longest poem in the collection, and the one beginning, "I am here, but I don't know where, nor how I have come. . . ." The first piece expresses puzzlement about the many aspects integrating the self, the persona of the poem recognizing himself in a diversity of forms of being. He asks, "When did I being one become various? / And is it you the other or is he still lost?" Then, he remarks,

> I perceived you among the sculptures of millennial
>   museums
> With multiple hearts, several souls, divergent minds
> Wavering among degrees, forms, textures
> Polivalent keys to sing a melody of singularity
> Perplexing peaks, anarchic gardens
> Strangeness of strange pariahs.

In "I am here, but I don't know where," the last poem of the collection, the poet slowly probes and delves into the most recondite recesses of the self through a wide range of varied sensorial images, describing the awakening of consciousness. The description of this highly introspective journey within the inner realms of the psyche shows that the author has gained considerable technical control over his craft. This achievement heralds a new direction toward a more abstract form of poetic expression for Hernández's future writing.

The few comments critics have made on Hernández's literary work have been favorable. Herminio Ríos-C. places the plays *The Lemon Tree*, *The Potion*, and *The Wedding Dress* within the tradition of the theater of the absurd because of their high content of "dreams and fantasy in which the internal psychological realities of the characters are presented in poetic images on stage." Assessing Hernández's entire literary output, Charles Tatum remarks that the writer "represents a departure from the strong social current that characterizes most of contemporary Chicano theater," pointing out that Hernández "is perhaps the most artistically radical contemporary Chicano writer in terms of his techniques." Indeed, as clearly shown throughout his plays, stories, and poems, Hernández's restless artistic creativity is ever in search of new expression, perspectives, and images with which to portray the depth, breadth, and richness of the human experience.

Reference:

Herminio Ríos-C., Introduction to "Chicano Drama," *El Grito*, special issue, 7 (June-August 1974): 4-6;

Inés Hernández

(28 February 1947 -   )

Laura Gutiérrez Spencer
University of Nevada at Las Vegas

BOOK: *Con razón, corazón* (San Antonio: Caracol, 1977; enlarged edition, San Antonio: M&A, 1987).

PLAY PRODUCTION: *El día de Guadalupe*, California State University, Fresno, 12 December 1984.

OTHER: "Para José, en vez de introducción," in *Mesquitierra* (Albuquerque: Pajarito, 1977), pp. 9-10;
"Presente," "Y al baile," ". . . And Then There Are Other Realities," "Llegaste como relámpago," "Recreando," "La guerrillera," and "Reconozco esta tierra," in *Ta Cincho*, edited by David Cavazos (Austin: CASA, 1977);
"For the People of El Salvador," in *1984 Appointment Calendar* (Fresno, Cal: International League for Peace and Freedom, 1984);
"Cosmic Grito," "After the Name-giving," and "My Indi'n Woman's Silence," in *Winter's Nest: A Poetry Anthology of Midwestern Women Poets of Color*, edited by Angela Lobo-Cobb (Madison, Wis.: Blue Reed Arts, 1987), pp. 78-80;
"Cascadas de estrellas: La espiritualized de la chicana / mexicana / indígena," in *Esta puente, mi espalda*, edited by Cherríe Moraga, Ana Castillo (San Francisco: Ism, 1988), pp. 256-266.

SELECTED PERIODICAL PUBLICATIONS—
UNCOLLECTED: "Roses are *Rosas*: Juan Gómez-Quiñones—A Chicano Poet" *Mester*, 5 (April 1975): 95-100;
"So You Say to Yourself," "I See Risas When I Think of You," "Disciplina," and "Enfrentándome," and *Caracol*, 3 (May 1977): 23;
"Trenzas singulares," *Revista Chicano-Riqueña*, 6 (Summer 1978): 33-34;
". . . Paso la vida en silencio, anhelando libertad," *Caracol*, 5 (November 1978): 13;

"Trenzas singulares," "Para mi ánimo," "Llegaste como relámpago," "Verse en el espejo ajeno, otherwise known as feeling someone's distrust," "Anhelos," and "Sola," *Tejidos: Arcoiris*, 5 (1978): 48-53;
"Salgo a caminar," and "Cáscaras y sustancia," *Tejanos: Revista Chicano-Riqueña*, 8 (Summer 1980): 29;
"Cuernavaca—pensavientos," "Con ciencia," "Noche de mi noche," and "I'm Suffering from the Blues," *Chicanas in the National Landscape, Frontiers: A Journal of Women's Studies*, 5 (Summer 1980): 52-53;
"When We are All Ready I Will be There," *Así Es: Revista Literaria*, 1 (April 1981): 19;
"Guerrillera soy," *Huehuetitlan*, 1 (January 1982): 2;
"Now I Wear," "Reconozco esta tierra," "For my Father, Rodolfo," "For Tomás, Kushtimni," "Remembering—para mi primo William," *Revista Río Bravo*, 2 (Spring 1982): 6;
"Man-made Lakes," *Huehuetitlan*, 3 (February 1984): 2;
"Burned Some Coffee . . . ," "Reflexiones," and "Para un mentado tap . . . ado," *Third Woman*, 2 (1984): 19-22;
"Yollotl," and "Momentos," *Bearing Witness/ Sobreviviendo: An Anthology of Native American/ Latina Art and Literature, Calyx: A Journal of Art and Literature by Women*, 8 (1984): 9-10;
"Risas, felicidad cantando," *Tonantzin*, 2 (May 1985): 13;
"Cemanahuac," "With Due Respects to La Llorona," "Red," and "Small change," *ECOS*, 3 (1985): 31-34;
"For the Wild Blue's First Tuesday of November Poetry Reading, Election Night, 1984," and "Against the Wind," *Americas Review*, 14 (1986): 94-98.

Inés Hernández has enriched the general body of Chicano poetry with works that reflect not only her Chicana heritage but her Native American roots. She also delivers candid critiques

Inés Hernández

of the Chicano movement and its participants, especially of the role that sexism and sexual politics have played in limiting the contributions of Chicanas in the struggle. Her perspectives as activist, feminist, and woman of color have an impact on her political, cultural, and personal commentary. Hernández's poetry expresses the convictions of a woman entering maturity with the confidence of one who, having struggled against a sexist/racist society, has found her way by discovering her own voice.

Inés Hernández was born in Galveston, Texas, and is the daughter of Janice Tzilimamúh Andrews Hernández of Nespelem, Washington, and Rodolfo Hernández born in Eagle Pass, Texas. Hernández's mother is a Nimipu (Nez Percé) Indian and her father is of Mexican descent. Hernández declares herself to be Nimipu and Chicana. She is an enrolled member of the Colville Confederated Tribes of Nespelem, Washington, and has been an active participant in the Chicano movement. Hernández has worked with many community-based and politically oriented organizations, including the Mexican American Youth Organization, La Raza Unida (The United People's) party, Chicanos Artistas Sirviendo a Aztlán (Chicano Artists Serving Aztlán), and the Committee in Support of the People in El Salvador. Hernández received her B.A., M.A., and Ph.D. in English from the University of Houston in 1970, 1972, and 1984 respectively. From 1970 to 1971 she taught English at La Marque High School in La Marque, Texas. From 1971 to 1976 she was a recipient of the Ford Foundation Doctoral Fellowship for American Indians. While working toward completion of her doctoral degree, she moved to the West Coast, motivated by her interest in working with Native Americans. She is currently an assistant professor at the University of California, Davis, in Native American Studies and Chicano Studies and lives in Benicia, California.

Con razón, corazón (No Wonder, Heart, 1977), a compendium of Hernández's early works, is constructed as a poetic self-portrait in which the author traces her mestiza roots, recalls her family genealogy and history, and imparts her feminist values through examinations of her multiple roles as mother, daughter, activist, lover, and friend. Many of her poems are written in either English or Spanish but most employ code-switching, a mixture of the two languages. Hernández's imagery during this period derives in part from meso-American symbolism popularized during the Chicano poetry of the 1960s. Her creation of neologisms like "pensavientos" (pensive winds) adds interesting metaphoric effects to various poems, reminiscent of the Nahuatl (Aztec) preference for synecdoche.

Hernández begins *Con razón, corazón* with the poem "Presente" (Present) in which she introduces herself to the reader by tracing her family genealogy. She recounts the circumstances under which her parents met, and then switches into a declaration of solidarity with the pain and struggle of fellow activists in the Chicano movement. In the conclusion she explains that her heritage and sense of social responsibility provide the inspiration for her work.

In "Rezo" (Prayer) she uses the structure and rhythms of the "Hail Mary" in Spanish in an invocation of powerful pre-Columbian female deities, the predecessors of the Virgin of Guadalupe, the patron saint of Mexico. Hernández implores these benevolent and powerful spirits to intercede on behalf of the oppressed and silenced mestizas. She utilizes another form associated with the Hispanic oral tradition in her poem "Canción de madre" (A Mother's Song). This poem takes the form of an antilullaby in which the mother, instead of comforting her daughter, challenges her daughter to confront herself and to reject fear. In an article in *Esta puente, mi espalda*, "Cascadas de estrellas" (Cascades of Stars, 1988), Hernández explains that after she wrote both poems, she realized that "Canción de madre" was really an answer to "Rezo." Apparently the wise maternal voice in "Canción de madre" is the voice of what she calls "la madre más anciana, la madre de todo" (the most ancient

mother, the mother of everything). Hernández states, however, that this maternal voice also represents herself in her role as a mother and as a friend to women of color. The poems celebrating the heritage and teaching of women continue in "For Janice Tzilimamúh." Here she recounts the ways in which an Indian mother instilled values in her daughter that helped her survive the ravages of poverty and prejudice.

The most powerful poems in the collection are the ones directed to other women. In "A tí" (To You) the speaker warns her friend that her male lover is unfaithful to her, concluding with, "Igual como te lo hace / a tí / me lo hizo / a mí / hermana" (Just as he does it / to you / he did it / to me / sister). Of all Hernández's works, "Para Teresa" (For Theresa) has received the most critical and popular attention. In this poem a studious Chicana is cornered by a girl named Teresa and a group of pachucas who accuse her of being a traitor to their race, but the speaker defends her efforts to succeed in school. As Elizabeth J. Ordóñez states, Hernández displays sensitivity and restraint, "avoiding self-righteousness, the poet comes to acknowledge her own and Teresa's attitudes as two different, yet valid existential choices within Chicana/o culture."

Other important feminist poems include works like "To Other Women Who Were Ugly Once," an analysis of the controlling effects of the media in its ethnocentric/sexist representations of female beauty. "Do you remember / the panic you felt / when *Cosmo*, *Vogue*, / and *Mademoiselle* / ladies / would *Glamour*-us out / of existence." "Chiflazones" (Hard Whistles) features a dialogue between a couple in which the male states that he will believe that his partner is equal to him when she is able to beat him at a game of pool. The woman responds: "The day you choose / to wash the dishes / I'll know we are."

Con razón, corazón also includes a series of poems following the ars poetica theme: "Poema," "Cachito," and "Cachito II," as well as some love poems which number among the least innovative of her works. The collection ends with a prose epilogue entitled "Reconciliations" in which the poet explains her position on issues relevant to the Chicano movement and her writing. She bluntly responds to her critics:

I know what I want Inés to be, what I say she is, and I feel a responsibility to act upon that—es

Hernández singing at a November 1980 book fair

todo [that's all]. I am also painfully aware of my weaknesses, at the same time it occurs to me that some have called me arrogant. Our egos make us all vulnerable to presumption, I believe.

In her writings after 1977, a shift to a heavier reliance on English coincides with a more sophisticated poetic style. The comparative predominance of English and the shorter lines accompany a use of internal rhymes absent in *Con razón, corazón.* This more austere style generally increases the impact of the social criticism conveyed in her poems. One of the most striking features of her recent work is her ability to reveal culturally imbued prejudices through her incisive examinations of the English language. "Manmade Lakes" (1984) exemplifies this technique: "*Man*-made Lakes, my mother says, / *Man*-made words, I say."

Hernández also contributes to feminist revisions of Chicano myth in her poem "With Due Respects to La Llorona" (1985). Here the poet rewrites the traditional myth of the ghostly figure who haunts the night with her cries of longing for her lost children. In Hernández's version, the cry of "La Llorona" is represented as a war whoop intended "to scream us out of apathy" and spur her people on to activism. Hernández's commitment to issues of social justice is not limited to the struggles of her own people. Awareness of human rights abuses in the Third World is evident in poems like "For the People of El Salvador" (1984). Hernández's most recent (unpublished) works include "Testimonio de memoria" which focuses on the status of women within the movements which they help to promote.

Hernández's poetry in both Spanish and English is characterized by simple language and a natural, narrative style. Her most recent poems in English rely on the point and counterpoint effect of short lines to give a rhythmic effect to her free verse. Many of these poems resemble prayers as Hernández employs both a rhythmic lyricism and the repetition of important words or phrases, forming a chantlike refrain. In these and other characteristics of her poetic style, one can note the importance of Native American oral tradition. Mythological figures are the central metaphors of her poems, which often begin with invocations to spirits or natural forces for guidance in confronting the injustices and brutality of modern society. The importance of ritual to Hernández's work is evident in her preference for lighting candles and chanting as a prelude to her public poetry readings.

Throughout her work, Hernández presents even the most basic elements of life in a ritualistic form. Her spiritualism is reflected in her celebration of the female body as a source of strength, knowledge, and redemption. She fiercely asserts the need for women of color to realize the beauty and wisdom incarnate in their bodies and to reject—as oppressive—white, middleclass norms of beauty. Especially important to Hernández is the metaphor of the womb as a place of psychic and physical female power. She recalls Native American traditions that recognize this power as both positive and potentially negative.

The work of Inés Hernández at once reflects her commitment to the ideals of social and economic justice for women and men of all races. Although she often expresses anger or disillusionment in her social critique, she also displays restraint and wisdom, the result of years of struggle and experience. Just as she resists efforts by Anglo, Chicano, and Native American institutions to limit the multiple facets of her identity, Hernández also chooses to express herself in Spanish, English, and occasionally with Native American phrases.

Hernández has been recognized most notably by critics for her authentic indigenous perspective on Chicano literature especially in debunking simplistic images of Indian life. Miriam Bornstein recognizes in Hernández an ability to reevaluate traditional feminine archetypes and revise them in a way that reveals feminine power and complexity. Bornstein notes, for instance that the earth—usually represented as a warm, nurturing mother figure—is depicted as cold and indifferent in the poem "The Earth is Cold Sometimes When a Man Dies" (1978). Hernández is also credited with contributing a feminist perspective to certain aspects of Chicano myth. Elizabeth Ordóñez has praised the realistic and frank representation of pachuco values in Hernández's poem "Para Teresa" and commends the poet for providing a needed response to the traditional image of the pachuco that has been imbued with male bravado.

The poet has also received critical attention for her ability to manipulate language to enhance its poetic strength and expression. The influence of the Chicano poet Alurista has been noted in Hernández's use of pre-Columbian images, mythology, and language, and in the use of word blends such as "Chicanohermano" (Chicanobrother), and "casaztlán" (houseaztlán). Frances Sage comments on the importance of Hernández's consistent use of "Chicano language" in order that her poetry may be accessible to the people and serve as a social force and creative inspiration to them.

References:

Miriam Bornstein, "La poeta chicana: visión panorámica," *Palabra*, 2 (Autumn 1980): 43-66;

Clara Lomas, "Inés Hernandez," in *The Longman Anthology of International Women Writers 1895-1975*, edited by Marian Arkin and Barbara Shollar (White Plains, N.Y.: Longman, 1989): 1019-1020;

Elizabeth J. Ordóñez, "The Concept of Cultural Identity in Chicana Poetry," *Third Woman*, 2 (1984): 75-82;

Frances Sage, "Contemporary Women Poets of Texas," *Texas Quarterly*, 10 (Summer 1987): 85-108;

Juan Felipe Herrera

(27 December 1948 -   )

Lauro H. Flores
University of Washington

BOOKS: *Rebozos of love we have woven sudor de pue-
blos on our back* (San Diego, Cal.: Toltecas en
Aztlán, 1974);
Exiles of Desire (Fresno, Cal.: Lalo, 1983);
Night in Tunisia, by Herrera and Margarita Luna
Robles (Stanford, Cal.: Diseños Literarios,
1985);
Facegames (Berkeley, Cal.: As Is/So & So, 1987);
Zenjosé: Scenarios (San José, Cal.: Hot Colors,
1988);
Akrílica (Santa Cruz, Cal.: Alcatraz, 1989).

OTHER: "A Certain Man," in *From the Belly of the
Shark*, edited by Walter Lowenfels (New
York: Vintage, 1973), p. 101;
"In the Cannery the Porpoise Soul," "Mar 3," "At
the Moon Café," "Gallery of Time," and
"Let Me Talk of the Years," in *Calafia: The
California Poetry*, edited by Ishmael Reed
(Berkeley, Cal.: Y'Bird, 1979), pp. 144-148;
"Quetzalcóatl," "Muchacha guinda," and "Cielo
rojo," in *Chicanos: Antología histórica y lit-
eraria*, edited by Tino Villanueva (Mexico
City: Fondo de Cultura Económica, 1980),
pp. 296-299;
"Para siempre, Maga," in *Cuentos Chicanos: A
Short Story Anthology*, edited by Rudolfo A.
Anaya and Antonio Márquez (Albuquerque:
University of New Mexico Press, 1985), pp.
100-105;
"Mexican World Mural, 5x25," in *Conspire: To
Breathe Together*, edited by Merle Bachman
and others (San Francisco: Fire in the Lake,
1985);
"Foreign Inhabitant," "Story & King Blvd./Teen-
Age Totems," and "Velvet Baroque/Act," in
*An Ear to the Ground: An Anthology of Contempo-
rary American Poetry*, edited by Marie Harris
and Kathleen Agüro (Athens & London: Uni-
versity of Georgia Press, 1989), pp.
122-124;
"Memoir: Checker-Piece," in *Best New Chicano
Literature 1989*, edited by Julian Palley

*Juan Felipe Herrera in front of the photograph published on
the cover for his 1983 book,* Exiles of Desire *(photograph
by Yolanda M. Lopez)*

(Tempe, Ariz.: Bilingual Press/Editorial Bilingüe, 1989), pp. 83-87.

Juan Felipe Herrera is one of the finest,
most innovative, and most challenging contemporary Chicano poets. He has also participated in
theater as an actor. His unquestionable talent, his
sustained production, and the maturity and coherence of his poetic endeavors have earned him—
among other honors—National Endowment for

the Arts awards (1980, 1985), and several literary prizes (American Book Award, 1987; University of Texas at El Paso Chicano Poetry Prize, 1985; University of California, Irvine, Chicano Literary Prize, 1979 and 1985), and also guarantee him an outstanding place in the history of Chicano literature. Herrera's poetry has moved from a cultural revival of pre-Columbian themes and motifs—a tendency that characterized a large portion of Chicano poetry and other artistic genres in the late 1960s and early 1970s—into the realm of contemporary urban life. Firmly grounded in the imagery of the city and alienated inhabitants, Herrera's most recent writings can best be described as postmodern expressionism that incorporates elements from drama, music, and the visual arts. A free spirit committed to social change and justice, Herrera refuses to be branded as a particular kind of poet or to encase his works in a neatly defined genre. Likewise, his compositions stubbornly resist any traditional mode of poetic analysis and, at times, even a strict classification as poems.

Born in Fowler, California, on 27 December 1948, Herrera is the only child of a migrant worker couple. His father, Felipe Emelio Herrera (who died when the poet was sixteen years old), was from a small village in Chihuahua, Mexico. He had migrated northward to the United States at age fifteen and worked as a ranch hand, as a "Mexican cowboy," and later as a farm worker. María de la Luz (Lucha) Quintana de Herrera, the poet's mother, deceased since 1986, was from a family of nine from the Niño Perdido (Lost Child) district in Mexico City. Her brothers, according to Herrera's account, joined the U.S. Army in order to be able to travel north to America. They arrived at El Paso, Texas, in 1920, and one-and-a-half years later the whole family reassembled in that city. There, Lucha almost joined a Mexican theater troupe, "Los Pirrines." She did not, however, due to her family's traditional outlook.

Juan Felipe Herrera's parents met in El Paso and then moved to California, where they continuously followed the seasonal crops circuit. This sense of being constantly in transition, of continuous motion, always remained in the poet's psyche and eventually became a strong element in his artistic expression. Herrera's parents finally settled down in San Diego when he was eight years old. Thus, aside from the fact that he changed schools quite often, his life entered a new stage of apparent stability in 1956. Herrera's

San Diego years were divided into two stages. First he lived in Barrio Logan, an old Chicano community, until he was about to enter junior high school; then he moved near downtown: "All of a sudden I became a downtown boy," Herrera recalls.

This change is one of the most important experiences of his life and has a fundamental importance in the thematic content and imagery of his works. About those years he says: "I used to spend a lot of time alone downtown . . . in Market Street, in La Placita, in the movie houses, near the Cine Azteca, the Casino Theatre, the Savoy Theatre, the Moon Cafe. . . . I used to spend day after day in the Greyhound bus depot, looking for things in the lockers, playing the pinball machines, taking photos for twenty-five cents . . . there, in *güaino* [wino] land. . . . It was a strange scene. I was more used to the Logan atmosphere, which was more festive, more of a family neighborhood. But this was not a neighborhood, it was the phantasmagoria of downtown San Diego in the early 60's."

Herrera attended Roosevelt Junior High School in San Diego and graduated from San Diego High School in 1967. He went on to UCLA, and, despite his earlier interest in music and art, Herrera majored in sociology and obtained a B.A. in social anthropology in 1972. He admits that not following his natural inclination toward art or music was probably a mistake.

In 1968, in Dolores Park in San Francisco, Herrera saw El Teatro Campesino perform for the first time. He subsequently formed his own group (Teatro Tolteca) and, two years later, submitted a proposal to go to Mexico to study the indigenous theatrical expression. The proposal was funded by the Mexican-American Center at UCLA. Herrera says, "The teatro and the journey through Mexico changed my life entirely. . . . But I didn't get anything out of school. What I got out of it was the moment, the political moment, the cultural, artistic, theatrical moment; the moment of personal development, of artistic expression."

Herrera returned to San Diego to work with the Centro Cultural Toltecas en Aztlán (now the Centro Cultural de la Raza). Recalling those years, Herrera says: "I started out as a member of the photography department and ended up being the director of the Center; I went in as a friend and left an enemy. But that has been resolved since then." The salient feature of this period in Herrera's life was the writing and publica-

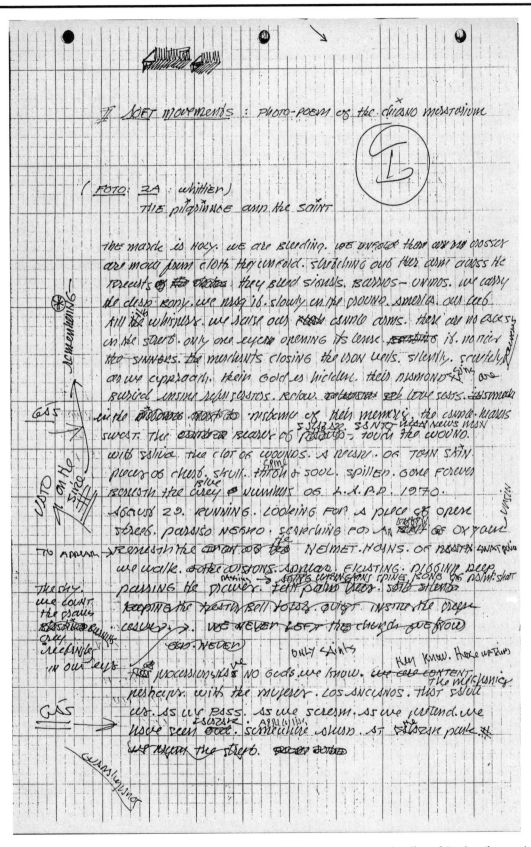

Draft for a section of "Photo-Poem of the Chicano Moratorium 1980/L.A.," chapter 3 of Exiles of Desire *(by permission of Juan Felipe Herrera)*

tion of his first book, *Rebozos of love we have woven sudor de pueblos on our back* (1974). After his experience with the Centro Cultural, Herrera worked for the Center for Cultural Pluralism in the School of Education at San Diego State University, and he subsequently left for the San Francisco Bay area.

In 1977 Herrera was admitted to graduate school in the anthropology department at Stanford University. In 1984 he began to write his doctoral dissertation but has since abandoned the program. He explains: "I became frustrated with the department. And, besides, this is the kind of life I have lived, one day I like to do this and the next day I like to do that. My interests change and it is almost as if I have to be excited all the time. If I cease to be excited, I get bored and if I get bored, I do not do things."

In 1988 Herrera joined the prestigious Iowa Writers Workshop to pursue an M.F.A. in creative writing. Two years later he completed the program and became a faculty member in the Department of Chicano and Latin-American Studies at Fresno State University.

Although Herrera began to write poetry in his first year of high school, "poems with themes of reincarnation, astrology, the obscure"—none of which he has kept—it was not until the late 1960s that his real moment of personal, political, and artistic self-discovery came about. Herrera's first published poem, "A Certain Man," initially appeared in *Inside Eastside*, a community newspaper from East Los Angeles, in 1968, and was later in Walter Lowenfels's anthology *From the Belly of the Shark* (1973). "A Certain Man" deals with a degraded human, "half-animal and half-man," and is of special relevance because it represents both the beginning and the ultimate points of his poetics. The poem unveils some concerns as constants of the way he views the world. For example it combines disparate symbols to demythologize and invert icons.

Herrera developed his first book, *Rebozos*, between 1971 and 1972. Conceived as experimental in a technical sense, *Rebozos* is a book intended to have neither a real beginning nor an end. It is a book without pagination, without titles, and without a conventional cover, because the poet decided to make a poem out of it:

> rebozos of love
> we have woven
> sudor de pueblos
> on our back

> (shawls of love
> we have woven
> sweat of peoples
> on our back)[.]

The opening line, with the first letter capitalized, has been adopted as the title of the book.

All poems in *Rebozos* intertwine in a tapestry of colors and movement. Herrera uses haiku to differentiate rhythms, "to change pace," he says. The structure of the book, therefore, is characterized by the alternation of long poems and haiku. The latter, however, do not constitute "separate poems." They only function as a canal through which one poem becomes linked with the next. Thus the overall movement of the book resembles a series of wavelengths. Paradoxically, however, despite Herrera's emphasis on the format and structural arrangement of the book, *Rebozos* is conceived within the context of the oral tradition. For example, the credits at the end of the book refer to the compositions as "chants" instead of poems. The sense of experimentation extends beyond its structural aspects and flows into the syntax and other linguistic elements of the poems. As Francisco A. Lomelí and Donaldo W. Urioste have observed in their *Chicano Perspectives in Literature* (1976), Herrera "goes beyond the limitations of conventional language (words and syntax) creating neologisms (for example, 'calaveralmas' [skeleton-souls]), . . . combinations of Spanish and English ('a celebrar woven brazos branches ramas' [to celebrate woven arms branches branches]), echoing constructions ('raza rise / RAZA-raiz' [people rise / PEOPLE-root]) and innovative calligrams."

On a more visceral level *Rebozos* contains a whirl of energy, and Herrera attempts to be prophetic of a new world. Through his chants he is invoking and designing at the same time the vision of a Chicano people, the vision of a flourishing human group. *Rebozos* is a multicolored rainbow, a world of many powers and revelations, a space where the ancient prophecies become fulfilled ("ancient vientre [womb] of dawns today") and where the mythical, endless continent of *Amerindia* (Indian-America) emerges, providing a sense of reassertion, unity, and totality:

> a m e r i n d i a
> one heart
> una tierra
> roja burning rain
> jewel rising

(Indian-America
one heart
one land
red burning rain
jewel rising)[.]

Rebozos is clearly a book inscribed within the social environment in which it was produced. The late 1960s and early 1970s were a period of cultural and political redefinition for Chicanos. Cultural-nationalist perspectives dominated the first stage of the movement. Accordingly, romanticized interpretations and motifs of the pre-Columbian past—myths, deities, and heroes—were introduced as a point of departure to explain contemporary reality and to make projections of a utopic future for the Chicano. These traits are well expressed and documented in the type of poetry of which Herrera's book is representative.

Between 1974 and 1976 he wrote two manuscripts, "Rayos de invierno" (Winter Rays) and "Thirteen Gods," which continued the thematic line he established in his first book. However, he has destroyed both of those works.

In 1977 Herrera left behind the world of *Rebozos* and began to focus on more quotidian elements. This new stage was similar to his earlier downtown San Diego days. "Walking Down 'F' Street" is the poem that marks the transition. However, "Niña de agua" (Water Child), written shortly thereafter, is the composition that launched his new manuscript, *Akrílica*. Written almost entirely in Spanish, the collection was basically complete by 1981 but remained dormant until 1989, when Alcatraz Editions published it in a bilingual edition.

In contrast to *Rebozos*, the world of *Akrílica* is dark (the first poem of the book, for example, is "Eklipse"); it is a nocturnal realm where colors and textures are different. The created world is much more static and quiet. The book was conceived as a verbal art gallery in which visual textures are of fundamental importance, and the objective was, according to Herrera, "to exhibit reality instead of writing about it." Significantly the table of contents listing the six chapters is headed by the word "Exhibiciones" (Exhibits), and the preface is titled "Nota sobre las exhibiciones" (Note about the Exhibits). The first chapter, "Galería" (Gallery), contains seven poems intended to be specific paintings, such as "Eklipse/Aquarela 41x80/San Francisco." This sec-

tion, therefore, presents the concept of literature as an exhibition.

The second chapter is called "Terciopelo" (Velvet) and is intended to enmesh the reader in certain textures. The third chapter, "Amarillo" (Yellow), takes readers into a world of intensity. The fourth one is "La América" and focuses on urban life, the Chicano exile, and the ghostlike aspects of street life. "Noche verde nuclear" (Green Nuclear Night) is probably the most extreme poem in this section, if not in the whole book, as it elaborates on the nightmarish aftermath of nuclear war. Pursuing his continuous interaction with other artistic genres (music, painting, and drama), or his refusal to abide by the limits of traditional poetry, Herrera subtitles this poem "Coro—poema en dos láminas" (Choir—Poem in Two Frames) and provides it with a theatrical structure—the two voices (characters) in the poem are listed, and an introduction to the setting is provided:

Escenario:
Todo toma lugar sobre las ruinas de una metrópolis destruida. La guerra nuclear acaba de terminar. Sólo permanecen Los Ultimos, dos hombres y una mujer que se reúnen después de haber caído debajo de los despojos. Cerca de ellos, entre los enredados metales de un edificio respire otra mujer. Todo relumbra verde.

(Setting:
Everything takes place on the ruins of a destroyed metropolis. Nuclear war has just ended. The only ones left are The Last Ones, two men and a woman who get together after falling under the rubble. Near them, among the twisted metal beams of a building, another woman breathes. Everything shines green.)

The fifth chapter of the book, "Eras" (You Were), is made up of three compositions ("Jazmin," "Arco," and "Saguaro") in which Herrera re-creates two lovers' intimate moments. Finally, in the last section, "Kosmetik," he develops larger frameworks, such as "Gráfika," which is neither a poem nor a short story but seems both a poem and a story at the same time. More accurately perhaps, suggests Herrera, one could talk about it as a collage, since it borrows and incorporates parts of poems written by other authors who are friends of his. In terms of experimentation, Herrera's fundamental trait, "Gráfika" is a salient example. *Akrílica* represents a peculiar type of Chicano expressionism and paints the dark colors of a surreal urban world, the anguish of the individual with no exit, and, Herrera has stated,

Draft for the first poem in "Mission Street Manifesto," the last part of Exiles of Desire *(by permission of Juan Felipe Herrera)* "the black holes of the Chicano mind."

In 1980, traveling between San Francisco and Seattle, Herrera began to write some sketches in English, which would eventually come to shape as *Exiles of Desire* (1983). Herrera claims that "*Exiles* is the same as *Akrílica* but at a colder and more condensed level. The dark and phantasmagoric world of *Akrílica* still preserves some warmth in it; in *Exiles*, I put on my surgeon gloves, I lock myself in a steel room, I place a sea rock on a table made of steel and I begin to carve it with a sharp instrument." The visionary dream transpires in *Rebozos*; the nightmare takes precedent in *Exiles*—in a sharper and more palpable manner than in *Akrílica*. In the final of four chapters the text emerges in some measure to a more public and social level; it acquires a certain amount of warmth. The rest of the book, however, is fundamentally a cold body made of "metallic poems."

The first chapter, whose title was chosen to name the whole collection, is the heart of the book and contains such poems as "Exiles," "Black Tenor on Powell Street," and "Children of Space." Everything is especially dense, heavily saturated, and offers no exit. For example, "Children of Space" rapidly introduces the setting and the various characters and elements of an apparently chaotic plot:

> On Valencia Street the playground aches. Children
>   float
> through parking lots
> riddled with the screams of distant throats.
>   Daughter-hands
> toss the toy
> over the clouds; invisible. The mother in
>   apartment G
> gazes, not inhaling.
> The father coils the fingers around transparent
>   shoulders in
> the air. Slowly,
> they undress. Only the stains of the assassinations
>   remain
> on their bodies.
> They do not speak now. They cannot speak.
>   Willingly, they
> have cut something
> inside. Vowels bleed across the sheets.

Pain, anguish, frustration, and a whirlpool of violent, cold images are the elements of this metropolitan, plastic, and alienating universe. Paradoxically, progress and technology have brought about a process of collective depersonalization, drowning the individual in a pool of chaos and ab-

solute loneliness. The deepest meaning of that strange and dialectical thing called civilization has been irremediably negated. Doom is imminent.

At first sight, the second chapter of the book, "Tripitas," constitutes a playful exercise. The title itself operates as a pun, as a play on words, insofar as *tripitas* ("little intestine," literally translated) refers to a popular Mexican dish, but it can also be interpreted—in the immediate context of the poems—as "little (L.S.D.) trips," popular among the youth of California in the 1960s and 1970s. These are not the only connotations that can be ascribed to the word (it can also be translated as "guts," for example). Thus it complies with an old postulate of Herrera's writings: to endow them with a polysemous quality, to give them what he calls "a multi-central amplitude."

The poems making up the section, all untitled, focus on various social types that Herrera transforms into cartoons: "Styly Stella," "Polyester Paul," "Hot Lefty," "Aspiring Arnold," and so forth. They inhabit the vertiginous urban dwelling; they all partake of the elements that attract, nurture, and disturb—all at the same time—the sensibility of the poet. The laughter these cartoons may produce—if they do so—is a peculiar, almost painful, type of laughter. These humorous commentaries are a poignant attack against the hypocrisy and superficiality that the urban milieu engenders, and ultimately they constitute an indictment of that society. The irony and satire of these sardonic sketches (all typed in boldface capital letters) are enhanced and softened by the low-key remarks closing the compositions, all in small regular letters.

"Photo-Poem of the Chicano Moratorium 1980/L.A." is the third chapter of the book and is made up of six "photo-poems" "taken" by Herrera during the tenth anniversary of the Chicano moratorium against the Vietnam War. Just as he juxtaposes painting and poetry in *Akrílica*, Herrera keeps exploring the possibilities of other visual arts, in this case photography. "What is a photograph?" he asks, and he provides his own answer: "A photo is a frame, it is a cold recording of a moment which offers no resolution. You see what the lens frames. So, what I try to do here is to experiment, to use the poem as a critical lens in order to talk about the Moratorium as a political Chicano Movement. And I purposely name people, because that's what the Moratorium was all about; there were people involved. I name people, not to slander them, but simply because they were there. The photo captured them."

The last section of the book, "Mission Street Manifesto," is the counterpart of the first chapter, like two sides of a coin or bookends that hold the rest together. The poems in the first chapter focus on the isolation and solitude of the urban being; those in the final one emphasize the social, collective experience.

Of the seven poems grouped in this closing chapter, "ARE YOU DOING THE NEW AMER-IKAN THING?" is the one that synthesizes the elements in the previous chapters: the nightmarish, condensed, familiar-yet-strange world of "Exiles"; the irony and sarcasm directed against social hypocrisy in "Tripitas"; and the theme of the Chicano moratorium. "Ode to the Industrial Village of the World," at the center of the last section, addresses and elaborates on the expansion of finance capital as the root of poverty and exploitation on a world scale and, by extension, as being responsible for making the nightmare a universal experience: "Empire of the World Bank / How long have we sailed and battled in this sinister ship? / How long have we been flayed over its corporate altars?" Bayer, Union Carbide, General Mining and Finance Corporation, and Kerr-McGee are all named as part of the monster engulfing the Third World. But there seems to be hope, and the poem ends with a call to the industrial village: "lift up your green phosphorescent voice . . . / And deliver the fatal strike into the billowing and bloodless global heart / Of the World Bank Master . . . / And our village shall sing in harmony of our sovereign independence."

The last poem in the book, the one giving its name to the whole chapter, finally makes an appeal for a regaining of consciousness, and reclaims a collective poetic voice that will speak for freedom and against social evil:

> the patrolling gods the corporate saints the
>   plutonium clouds
> strike the right the new Right to crucify the
>   right to decay
> the triple K the burning cross the territorial
>   rape game
> and stop the neutron man the nuclear dream the
>   assassination line
> the alienation master the well groomed empire the
>   death suit
> and rise and rise libre libre and rise and rise
>   and rise libre
> and rise sisters rise brothers and spill the song and
> sing the blood that calls[.]

Cover for Herrera's 1987 collection, which prompted reviewer Marvin Bell to say that "such poetry makes the argument between poetic formalists and informalists appear to be taking place in a closet"

The poems in the last section are "oral" compositions based on jazz and other rhythms. These are poems intended to be performed, not read privately. In this sense, the section is also indicative of the new directions and experiments that Herrera was undertaking: "I have this fantasy to get into digital synthesizing . . . into 'digital literature' . . . where you can play with the text in a synthetic manner, where you can synthesize your voice and you can further dismantle the text, further decentralize it—not only the text but the poet and his voice. . . . I'm constantly looking for the unnameable and the life-force, the centers of life-force that haven't been labelled or found yet. Because that's what makes poetry live or vibrate."

Perhaps because of this ambitious projection, Víctor Hernández Cruz, in his introduction to *Facegames* (1987), has said about Herrera: "He is as close as we come to a total expression machine." Marvin Bell, writing in October 1989 in the *Boston Review*, captured well the essential meaning of this totality: "Juan Felipe is a storyteller, a surrealist, and a polemicist all at once, and as a writer he goes beyond the sometimes brittle and insular thought model we are taught to recognize as poetry into an array of forms for play and politics. By its sinuosity and vibrancy, and by its octopus reach into sources, such poetry makes the argument between poetic formalists and informalists appear to be taking place in a closet."

Among many projects, Herrera continues to work on a manuscript he has tentatively titled "Sin chaqueta" (Without a Jacket), which stems from an experiment he initiated in 1980 and used to call "Covers." Preserving a large degree of autonomy, the various parts of this manuscript deal with the problem of representation as a cultural-political phenomenon. Writing, literature, and authorship are concepts Herrera questions in his work. What is literature? How is it represented, as a process or as a product? How does the mechanism of being an author function? These are questions he poses, challenging traditional notions and conducting a literary experiment at the same time. Herrera simultaneously utilizes or plays with various literary forms and other artistic expressions and cultural elements: humor, fables, memoirs, poetry, antipoetry, sketches, and photography.

Juan Felipe Herrera is one of the finest and more experimental contemporary Chicano poets. His continuous process of maturation and the coherence of his overall poetic project assure him a prominent place in Chicano literature. Unfortunately his works have remained almost unattended to by specialized Chicano critics. Al-though he has been widely anthologized and is well known in literary circles, his books have received only a few reviews and a couple of serious articles. Perhaps this relative disregard is partially due to the fact that Herrera, technically and thematically, has always been in the vanguard of Chicano poetry. A correct appraisal of his contribution is long delayed. In the meantime the reader can expect many more surprises from the constantly innovative Herrera.

Interview:

Sesshu Foster, "From Logan to the Mission: Riding North through Chicano Literary History with Juan Felipe Herrera," *Americas Review*, 17 (Fall-Winter 1989): 68-87.

Bibliography:

Francisco A. Lomelí and Donaldo W. Urioste, *Chicano Perspectives in Literature: A Critical and Annotated Bibliography* (Albuquerque: Pajarito, 1976), pp. 26-27.

References:

Marvin Bell, "A Poet's Sampler: Juan Felipe Herrera," *Boston Review*, 14 (October 1989): 6;

Héctor Mario Cavallari, "La muerte y el deseo: Notas sobre la poesía de Juan Felipe Herrera," *Palabra*, 4-5 (Spring-Fall 1983): 97-106;

Lauro H. Flores, "Auto-referencialidad y subversión: Observaciones (con) textuales en torno a la poesía de Juan Felipe Herrera," *Crítica*, 2 (Summer 1990);

Víctor Hernández Cruz, Introduction to Herrera's *Facegames* (Berkeley, Cal.: As Is/ So & So, 1987), pp. i-ii;

Stephen Kessler, "Poet with a Mission," *Santa Cruz Express* (February 1982).

Arturo Islas
(24 May 1938 - 15 February 1991)

Roberto Cantú
California State University, Los Angeles

BOOKS: *The Rain God: A Desert Tale* (Palo Alto, Cal.: Alexandrian Press, 1984);
Migrant Souls (New York: Morrow, 1990).

OTHER: "Mama Chona," in *Mirror and Mirage / Fiction by Nineteen*, edited by Albert Guerard (Stanford: Portable Stanford, 1980), pp. 83-86;
"Interview: Maxine Hong Kingston," in *Women Writers of the West Coast*, edited by Marilyn Yalom (Santa Barbara: Capra, 1983), pp. 11-19.

SELECTED PERIODICAL PUBLICATIONS—
UNCOLLECTED: "Writing from a Dual Perspective," *Miquiztli*, 2 (Winter 1974): 1-2;
"Can There Be Chicano Fiction?," *Miquiztli*, 3 (Winter-Spring 1975): 22-24;
"Hostility," "Motherfucker or the Exile," and "Drunk," *Poetry*, 131 (January 1978): 199-203;
"Chile," *Nuestro* (September 1984): 43-47;
"The Meeting of Saint Anthony and Saint Paul," *Sequoia*, 29 (Winter 1985): 1-3;
"Videosongs: Isabel, Emma, Anna & Albertine," *Sequoia*, 31 (Centennial Issue 1987): 90-94;
"Chakespeare Louie," *ZYZZYVA*, 4 (Spring 1988): 79-84.

After years of being ignored by New York publishers, Arturo Islas was encouraged by the 1990 publication of *Migrant Souls* by William Morrow, a major eastern firm. His literary success with *The Rain God: A Desert Tale* (1984), which reached its twelfth printing in 1990, undoubtedly influenced the publication of his second novel. This relative success, however, gave Islas mixed feelings, for he believed that Chicanos are judged by New York publishing firms as a people without a literature. "It's a shame"—Islas said in an interview with Frank Quaratiello—"because there are a lot of talented Chicano writers out there." Aside from its redefinition of an "ethnic" self in a postmodern world, Chicano literature also rescues a collective history from oblivion, and the work of Arturo Islas has become fundamental to the rethinking of the cultural history of the United States.

Arturo Islas was born in El Paso, Texas, on 24 May 1938, two months after Mexican oil was nationalized on 18 March 1938 by Lázaro Cárdenas, then president of Mexico. Cárdenas's action brought hostility from the United States, but by the time Islas enrolled in elementary school, World War II had brought the two countries together as allies against the Axis powers. As a result, one of the first lessons learned by Islas as a child was that Mexican-American relations were extremely vulnerable to sudden change, and that the first to know of such reversals in diplomatic relations were border Mexicans.

Islas's father was an officer in the El Paso Police Department and one of its first members to be recruited from the local Mexican community; Islas's mother was employed as a secretary. The family included three children: Arturo was the firstborn, followed by Mario, who grew up to be a priest, and the youngest, Luis, now a criminal lawyer in El Paso. During the years 1951 to 1956, Islas attended El Paso High School and received an Alfred P. Sloan Scholarship to study at Stanford University from 1956 to 1960. Islas earned a B.A. in 1960, graduated with distinction, and was elected the same year to Phi Beta Kappa. Similar academic accomplishments will serve as a background for Miguel Chico, a fictional counterpart for Islas, appearing prominently in both of the author's novels. In an interview with Laura Paull in the Stanford University *Campus Report* (7 March 1990), Islas commented,

> One of the reasons I invest Miguel Chico with many of my own accomplishments—being a university professor and a writer—is because I have noticed that no matter how much a human being accomplishes on what we call the ladder of success, the minute he or she says that he or she is

146

Arturo Islas (photograph by Margo Davis)

gay, it's like nothing else existed. All of a sudden, whammo, down to the bottom of the scale.

Islas's time at Stanford was decisive. While supported by a fellowship from 1960 to 1963, he completed all requirements for the Ph.D., except for the dissertation. After being a Woodrow Wilson Fellow from 1963 to 1964, Islas left Stanford to teach speech and literature courses at a local hospital and in an adult school in the San Francisco area. Islas returned to Stanford in 1967 and wrote a dissertation on Hortense Calisher under the direction of Wallace Stegner, earning a Ph.D. in English in 1971. He was a Howard Foundation Fellow from 1973 to 1974, and in 1976 he received the Lloyd W. Dinkelspiel Award for outstanding service to undergraduate education.

These awards and academic honors were granted during difficult times for Islas, who, by 1969, had gone through three major surgeries

for intestinal cancer that seriously threatened his life. Similar brushes with death became an essential part of *The Rain God*, adding to the narrative a tone of authenticity while providing occasions to reflect on the symbolic function of death and the afterlife in Mexican culture. After being appointed to a tenure-track position at Stanford in 1970, Islas's career was marked by a growing advocacy for Chicano-related issues, participation in numerous conferences on women and minority literatures, and a noticeable interest in autobiographical writing. These professional activities and achievements coincided with the writing of his novel, which he finished in 1976 under the title "Día de los Muertos / Day of the Dead." This manuscript was partly responsible for Islas receiving tenure the same year. Eight years passed before Islas's novel was published. After being reviewed and repeatedly rejected by New York firms, the novel was printed and released by Alex-andrian Press, founded by Patrick Suppes, professor of philosophy at Stanford, and his wife, Christine Johnson, a novelist. Islas's original manuscript was revised and the novel was published as *The Rain God* (1984). In January 1986 it won the Southwest Book Award for fiction given by the Border Regional Library Association.

The Rain God consists of six interrelated texts narrating the lives, internal conflicts, and deaths that take place in a Mexican family, the Angels, who settled in an American border town as a result of the Mexican revolution of 1910. The novel's subtitle, "A Desert Tale," situates itself in an antithetical relation to the main title, stressing the presence of binary opposites. The "tale's" desert covers a geographical area of the United States and Mexico—divided by water, the Rio Grande, and by what is frequently referred to as a political "imaginary line," due to the scope of U.S. influence in Mexico. Although never identified in *The Rain God*, the "twin" border cities are El Paso and Ciudad Juárez, as later insinuated in *Migrant Souls* through an anagram, in which El Paso becomes Del Sapo. At a different level of abstraction, the duality of the title symbolizes a frontier: geographical, historical, cultural, and sexual (Felix, Lola, and Miguel Grande, characters whose sexuality drives them out of "boundaries"). Islas's novel not only includes the traditional theme of the conflictive frontier between two countries but also touches on the historical limits of remembrance; in addition, it stresses the cultural bridges linking Chicanos to pre-Columbian Mexico (before 1521), and to postrevolutionary Mexico (after 1917); the former is done through Miguel Chico's spiritual identification with Indian Mexico, plus the overall presence of the rain god (Tláloc) and its implied ceremony of sacrifice; the latter, through the history of the family's migration to the United States.

The key to this thematic cluster is the symbolism of a matriarch's name: Encarnación Olmeca de Angel (Mama Chona). She is the "incarnation" of the pre-Columbian mother culture (the Olmecs) miscegenated with Christian Spain (the Angel family): the former symbolizes the earth, pagan Mexico, the "repressed" past; the latter, heaven, Christianity, and an invented family history. Mama Chona, therefore, is a mestiza, having the blood of two past enemies. One of the many family portraits in *The Rain God* gives expression to this condition:

family members were taught that only the Spanish side of their heritage was worth honoring and preserving; the Indian in them was pagan, servile, instinctive rather than intellectual, and was to be suppressed, its existence denied . . . Miguel Chico's father practiced this kind of bigotry when he referred to the Mexican women . . . as "wetbacks."

Remembering Mama Chona, Miguel Chico admits hating her because of her "Spanish conquistador snobbery . . . what, Miguel Chico asked himself, did she see when she looked in the mirror?"

The justification of the novel's title is found almost at the end of the narrative in a poem by Netzahualcoyotl (1431-1472), a pre-Columbian poet and Lord of Texcoco. This poem, originally transcribed by Mama Chona's firstborn son (also named Miguel), is sent years later to a dying Miguel Chico by his aunt Mema, wishing him a quick recovery from surgery. The poem arrives accompanied by a photograph taken many years ago of Mama Chona and Miguel Chico, a photograph which becomes a leitmotiv throughout the novel. Both photograph and poem function within the narrative as object of recollection and symbol of fate, respectively. The tone of Netzahualcoyotl's poem is mournful and of a quiet resignation to the ephemeral nature of existence, contributing to the elegiac mood of the novel. Commenting on "men who sat upon thrones, / decided cases, presided in council, / commanded armies," the last verse of the poem is the fulcrum of the entire narrative: "Nothing recalls them but the written page." This takes the reader's attention back to the novel's epigraph, with its six verses taken from a poem by Pablo Neruda ("*I come to speak through your dead mouths / . . . / Speak through my words and my blood*"), and to the function of the novel's narrator, who appears to be speaking through the mouths of dead family members while, simultaneously, allowing them to speak through his "words" and his "blood" (read both in its ancestral and sacrificial resonances).

If Netzahualcoyotl speaks almost prophetically about a civilization soon to vanish, Neruda's poem describes the narrator as a medium for a historical past in need of a voice. The past, therefore, still lives; the frontiers of history are, consequently, overcome by two American poets who represent past and present of Latin America. Seen in this light, the six parts that compose the novel, along with the "framing" done by Netzahualcoyotl's and Neruda's poems, orches-

Cover for Islas's second novel to feature Miguel Chico, Islas's fictional counterpart

trate a lofty requiem to an ancestral past which finds its "incarnation" in the act of storytelling. The writer thus becomes more than a symbolic cemetery: he is the code figure for a collective insurrection, a Day of Judgment, made possible by the narration of a desert tale.

In the development of these two novelistic motifs—death and *la familia* (the family)—Islas deploys what are considered two idiosyncratic features of Mexican culture. Although in time both became romanticized notions regarding the "Mexican view" on death and the family, it is undeniable that these motifs were part of the Chicano cultural expression of the 1960s. Hence, the original title of Islas's novel, "Día de los Muertos / Day of the Dead," is an index of a cultural, bilingual expression of the era. Yet Islas wrote at least three major drafts, with a different title for each (the second draft carried the working title of "American Dreams and Fantasies"), with such revisions trans-

forming both the structure and implied audience of the narrative. In addition, the novel became enriched with Islas's sustained theoretical interest in autobiography and in the study of Chicano and Latin-American writers.

One could well argue that the emotional center of *The Rain God* is found in the thematic elaborations of death and the moral decline of a family of "sinners." Nonetheless, if one's attention moves temporarily to Miguel Chico, the fundamental theme of the narrative appears to be the transfiguration of the writer's life through a "recaptured" past populated by dead family members and friends, such as María, Mama Chona, Felix—the maid, the grandmother, and an uncle, respectively. Although narrated in the omniscient mode, much of the employment of the novel is dramatized through Miguel Chico, who is portrayed on six occasions as sitting in front of his desk, remembering his past as he observes a photograph of himself and Mama Chona, rereading a letter written by María shortly before her accidental death, trying to imagine an uncle's death, or recording a dream. Presented intermittently as Miguel Chico's "double," Felix is also portrayed six times as sitting at a bar, pensive and unconsciously anticipating the nearness of his impending murder ("Felix felt the cold air of the desert winter as someone came into the bar"). Throughout the six "stories" that make up the novel, the reader views various portraits of the writer as a young man who is in turn watching a photograph of himself when he was approximately six years old, holding Mama Chona's hand.

The constant appearance of number six throughout the novel creates a numerological design that adds an intriguing dimension to the novel's framework. For example, biblical discourse affirms that God's creation took six days to reach completion, yet the same number repeated three times is associated with a "monster" (the beast), thus establishing a semantic configuration associated with "celestial relations" (heaven/hell). One must also recall that nocturnal sacrifices were dedicated to Tláloc in the sixth month of the Aztec calendar. At this crossing of numerical paths, where one distinguishes the presence of oppositions based on Judeo-Christian categories (God/devil, virtue/sin, beauty/ugliness), Islas outlines a complex dimension of Mexico's cultural history, rewritten in the form of an extended cryptogram. In his interview with Quaratiello, Islas stops to reflect on his mode of writing, and says, "I write in a circular way and an inner coherence develops and connects scenes." One could add that the "circularity" of Islas's writing turns, by sheer force of its hermetism, into a reader's strategic means of access to his narrative.

The narrative techniques used by Islas include the "observer being observed" (the narrator observing Miguel Chico, who in turn is observing himself in a photograph); interior monologues (such as Lola's on page 65); dechronology through multiple exposures, scene displacements, and flashbacks, revealing how much Islas has incorporated from cinematic praxis. One finds, furthermore, a leitmotiv technique (a photograph, the reference to an uncle's murder) and structuring metaphors in the novel such as the border, sunsets (always dusk or twilight), the moon, or homosexuality: all appearing as frontiers which bridge opposites—countries, time, cosmic rhythms, and gender differences. Through the technique of "doubling," Islas organizes a network of correspondences linking Miguel Chico (who dreams of "monsters") with other characters, such as JoEl (an imaginative storyteller who also dreams of "monsters") and Mama Chona (another weaver of tales who also, in solitude, "resurrects" the dead in her memory and who, just before her death, believes she is giving birth to a "monster"). The trope of the monster thus becomes a rhetorical technique that links notions of sin, aberration, and the unnatural to the narrative. Through this doubling technique, frequently employed in the novels of Carlos Fuentes and Gabriel García Márquez, *The Rain God* acquires dimensions of meaning which only the unhurried reader will fathom and appreciate.

The ideological framework of *The Rain God* includes an embedded critique of gender, patriarchy, and traditional views on homosexuality (a critique regiven in *Migrant Souls*), and key characters such as the brothers Miguel Grande and Felix are chosen as representative figures, with the former being the personification of a Mexican "macho" and the latter of a homosexual. While Miguel Grande submits to his circular, biological pursuit of women, Felix, on the other hand, gloats over the seduction of young men; one ends up utterly confused ("I love them both so much. I want them to be one person"), the other, murdered. As expected, the murder of Miguel Grande's homosexual brother will be the excuse used by the police department to deny him the position of chief. Discussing this with his godmother Nina, Miguel Grande's son, Miguel Chico, observes, "When he didn't get Chief of

the department, he lost a lot of faith in himself and what he's believed in all his life about this country." Pages before this, the omniscient narrator comments:

> When Miguel thought about his brother after all the facts were known, he felt ashamed and frustrated. He had never been able to understand Felix's obsession and did not want to.... his knowledge that Felix enjoyed doing such things had created a barrier between them that neither ever made the effort to overcome.... Felix's behavior embarrassed Miguel Grande, and he hoped that the stigma of being *jotos* [homosexual] would not reach past his brother.

In an area of the United States where everyone "treated the death of a Mexican in a routine, casual manner," the death of a Mexican homosexual makes headlines for the wrong reasons: namely, to embarrass Miguel Grande publicly, simultaneously producing an excuse to deny him the coveted position of chief of police. The crime is left unpunished ("the young soldier had acted in 'self-defense' "), but in the reader's judgment the soldier is guilty of what appears to be a planned murder. Every detail exposes the soldier's plan to cross into Mexico, search for the Mexican homosexual who has been seducing "white" youth from the army base, and, once found, kill him. The effacement of Felix's identity at the time of his murder ("It was unrecognizable. There was no face") along with the partial castration ("One of the testicles was missing") suggests the frequent, southern retribution against blacks for an interracial sexual transgression. Racism is further illustrated in *The Rain God* through the anecdote of the local mayor who, in spite of his political position, is denied membership in the town's country club because of his Mexican ancestry.

Although Islas elaborates in detail the racism felt toward Mexicans in the border city of the novel, he also points to the apathy, both in the Anglo-American and Mexican populations, toward crimes committed against homosexuals. The political concerns expressed in *The Rain God* are, therefore, illustrated through injustices perpetrated on Miguel Grande and Felix, but whereas the former's predicament may simply seem unfair, the murder of Felix compels the reader to rethink the nature of homophobic violence. The exact narration of the murder itself is coldly given in shocking detail; even though the reader knows beforehand what is about to happen (for much of the novel has been mounting to this narrative point), the anticipation of Felix's violent death—instead of weakening the reader's visceral response—seems to increase the effect. *The Rain God* gives us an example of a murder presented with calculated narrative artistry. At the end of the novel, just before the death of Mama Chona, it is her favorite son, Felix, who comes to her "out of the shadows," smelling "like the desert after a rainstorm," and—taking her in his arms—carries her with him as if she were a young bride: a dominating matriarch in the arms of a homosexual son, finally united in their own Day of Judgment.

In a paper on the novel read during a 28-30 May 1986 conference at Stanford University, Rosaura Sánchez wrote, "Felix's homosexual preferences . . . cannot be seen to negate patriarchal structures, for not only is he an authoritarian husband . . . but in his relations with men he also assumes the position of power and takes advantage of his subordinates." Although Felix exhibits at times signs of an authoritarian, Sánchez's judgment overlooks Felix's feelings of remorse ("He was unbearably ashamed of his remarks to the young laborer . . . he choked on his shame"). His "love" of youth is hardly one of being in a position of power or of taking advantage of innocent males ("gazing upon such beauty with the wonder and terror of a bride, his only desire was to touch it and hold it in his hands tenderly . . . the men submitted to Felix's expert and surprisingly gentle touch, thanked him, and left"). The portrayal of Felix as a "bride" torn between terror and wonder followed by episodes of authoritarian rigor within his family parallels the ambivalence of a matriarchal model which oscillates between poles of symbolic patriarchal authority (Mama Chona's power over the family) and conventional patterns of motherhood ("Mama Chona bore her children out of duty to her husband and the Church"). When read contextually, the poems Islas published in 1978 disclose to what extent Islas's narrative contributes to a critique of discursive structures (and practices) of domination. This critique forms the subversive narrative undercurrent in Islas's second novel.

In *Migrant Souls*, Islas concentrates his narrative hold on the development of two characters—Josie Salazar and Miguel Chico—with memorable character sketches made of Jesús María (the emerging matriarch after Mama Chona's death), Gabriel (a priest and Miguel Chico's brother), and Sancho Salazar (Josie's father). The novel is

divided into two books, "Flight into Egypt" and "Feliz Navidad." The first book narrates the early years of Josie and Miguel Chico (two cousins who become good friends and who develop existentially along parallel lines), and the second book is an account of the "annual ritual of hypocrisy" which gathers the Angel family. Both books are defined ironically by biblical metaphors originally associated with deliverance ("flight from Egypt") and the Nativity.

Reviews of *Migrant Souls* have been generally positive, yet some critics voice a preference for Islas's first novel. In a review in the *San Francisco Chronicle* (18 February 1990) Henry Mayer claimed *Migrant Souls* "is more conventional in both theme and structure than its predecessor." While it is probable that Islas's second novel will not dazzle or overwhelm its readers with the narrative experimentation one finds in *The Rain God*, a rereading of *Migrant Souls* will reveal its rhetorical complexity, specifically in the manner in which Islas reveals the internalized constructs which define Christian cultural symbolism through notions of good and evil, virtue and sin, grace and damnation. The result is a model of cultural criticism which takes place in the narrative itself, challenging the reader to reexamine and distinguish between cultural features which oppress and those which liberate. This meditation on cultural and religious constructs was proposed initially in *The Rain God*.

An ostensible critique of what could be called a neocolonial mentality is proposed in the first paragraph of *Migrant Souls* through a sibling differentiation: girls who act like "Indians" (inarticulate, unclean, immodest) contrasted with girls who behave like "Spanish ladies" (articulate, delicate, tactful). The opposition between Indians and Spaniards in members of the same family creates a hierarchy of power which, if left to stand as the natural order of society, identifies family members as either inferior or superior, depending mostly on skin color and manners. Islas, therefore, allows the reader to avoid returning to Mexicans/Anglo-Americans as *absolute* opposites (one as "conquered," the other as conqueror), and focuses instead on how language itself becomes the framework which both delimits and defines our daily conflicts, making it possible to question the "natural" order of a cultural world.

Mama Chona, for example, informs Josie and her sisters about the "heavenly relations" between gnomes and angels: the former act as guardians of "the treasures inside the earth" while the

Flight -- 27   From <u>Migrant Souls</u>   Islas

wide, and let it pour in until they drown. They ~~just~~
keel over all bloated. That's how stupid they are." He
bent his ~~own~~ head back and showed them as they ~~passed~~ *walked by*
an~~other~~ enclosure. *"Gobble, gobble," the guide called and* ~~and the one bird set the rest off again.~~
the turkeys answered hysterically.
~~When they stopped, the guide said, "Gobble, gobble," and~~
~~got them going while~~ Josie and Serena laughed ~~their heads~~ *all the way back to*
~~off.~~ *the pickup.* Ofelia had not been allowed to join them because
of the way their mother thought the guide was looking at
her. *She was dreaming away in the back seat of*
the Chevy while ~~————~~
~~When they returned to the pickup,~~ their father ~~was~~ *struggled*
~~trying~~ *newly bought and nervous* to get the ~~struggling and hysterical~~ turkey into a
slatted crate. ~~box~~ ~~they had found during a search of the~~
~~alleys in the warehouse district of Del Sapo. Josie felt~~
~~a rush of affection for Sancho as she watched his struggles~~
~~with the bird. Her mother, typically,~~ *Eduviges* was criticizing every
move he made. At last, the creature was in the box∧ *and eerily silent.*

    "Now remember, girls," Sancho said, wiping his face;
"I'll do all the talking at the bridge. You just say
'American' when ~~it's your turn.~~ *the time comes.* Not another word, you
~~understand,~~ *hear?* Think about Mrs. Moulton, Josie." He gave
her a wink.
    The turkey~~, now mysteriously subdued, seemed~~ *— remained —* frozen
inside the crate. Sancho lifted it onto the pickup, covered
it with a yellow plastic table cloth they used on picnics,
and told Serena to sit on top of it with her back against

ok?

Manuscript for "Flight into Egypt," the first section of Migrant Souls *(by permission of the Estate of Arturo Islas)* latter stand "watch over the treasures of heaven." Mama Chona says: "You see, children, our Father created the highest and the lowliest of creatures. Good men like your Grandfather . . . are very close to the angels." Although she encourages her mestiza granddaughters "to try to be like the angels," Mama Chona ends the lesson by saying, "It's more difficult for girls to be like angels because they are born wicked in a different way from boys."

Identifying with her father, Sancho, who loves to go hunting and claims that his Indian blood is invigorated in the Chihuahua mountains, Josie develops into an intelligent and independent woman ("I'm a woman . . . I'm not afraid of anything"). Told that the Indians will "drag her off to Ysleta" if she is recalcitrant in her Indian ways, Josie eventually marries an Anglo-Mexican husband, and yet her amorous passion will only be aroused by a French-Cherokee lover who "took her hunting and fishing in his lakes and mountains." Josie's knowledge that her family considered her to be more Indian than Spanish determines her future: an early attachment to her Indian father, her fate (to be dragged into adultery by an Indian), and her condition as "the only divorced woman in the Angel family." Mama Chona's concept of "heavenly relations" thus has disastrous effects on the family of "sinners."

Her distinction between angels and gnomes, with profound roots in tradition, receives its full power of meaning from an ideological discourse that uses the trope of heavenly relations to separate what is "above" (heaven, light, wisdom) from what is "below" (hell, darkness, ignorance). By the same reasoning, those who are "light" are wise and moral while those who are "dark" are close to the infrahuman. Mama Chona's notion of a spiritual hierarchy in humanity takes us back to a colonial mentality and to what is generally understood in Latin-American intellectual history as the eighteenth-century European "denigration" of Native America. It is in these disturbing "heavenly relations" that the title *Migrant Souls* becomes much more complex than suggested at first glance.

Other narrative dimensions that reveal a developing sensibility in Islas's writing are, for instance, the tender and at times humorous portrayal of children (particularly girls), the love between father and daughter (Sancho and Josie), the loneliness of widowhood, and the growing in-sularity of the aged. In addition, Islas allows for moments of extraliterary recognition to well-known Chicano writers or critics (Rolando Hinojosa, Luis Leal) when, for example, Sancho and his family go to "Don Luis Leal's Famous Tex-Mex Diner" or when Tano Hinojosa, who lost a leg in the Korean War, stands paralyzed with desire, almost out of his mind, before the gorgeous Portillo twins because he is unable to decide "which of the two he desired more." Communication in *Migrant Souls*, much like in *The Rain God*, occurs at various levels, and this in itself should be a challenge to readers and literary critics.

In *The Rain God*, Arturo Islas re-creates with acknowledged craftsmanship such motifs as death, the Mexican family in the United States, desire, and the uprootedness of the modern Chicano intellectual from his traditional community; in the process, Islas transcends the realism of past works of fiction by Chicano writers as well as the conventional modes of Chicano autobiography. Islas adds to the Chicano novel a more sophisticated handling of plot and point of view, incorporating a dimension frequently absent in Chicano literature—a critical reexamination of cultural discourses. In *Migrant Souls*, Islas advances other narrative dimensions to a higher aesthetic level, returning with a stronger force to a form of cultural criticism that touches on discursive practices that determine the way readers interpret their immediate social world.

Islas published only a few poems, the most recent in 1987. In his interview with Quaratiello, he said, "Poems are like gifts. Many of my poems sit in my drawer. They are too depressing to publish." Depressing they may have been to Islas; nonetheless the published poems reveal a rare sensibility (psychological, hermetic) not often found in Chicano poetry; one hopes, therefore, that Islas's poems will appear in a future volume. Chicano poetry will be enriched.

In his interview with Paull, Islas revealed that in his projected picaresque novel, "Miguel Chico will come more into his own, as divorced from the narrator and from the burdens of narration." What kind of reader response brought happiness to Islas? "Don't tell me my book is brilliant," he declared in the same interview. "To me, the highest compliment I as a writer can receive is when readers tell me they want to know more about my characters." At fifty-two, Islas died of AIDS on 15 February 1991.

Interviews:

Frank Quaratiello, "Second Novel Helps Establish Stanford Author in Spite of the Odds," *Stanford Daily*, 12 February 1990, p. 7.

References:

Cathy Bledsoe, "Prof. Islas Moves Into Publishing Traffic," *Stanford Daily*, 7 November 1984, pp. 8-9, 13;

Alex McSweyn, "Interview with Arturo Islas," *Onda* (Stanford), 1 (October-November 1975): 4-5;

Laura Paull, "New Islas Novel, *Migrant Souls*, Explores 'The Condition of Being on the Border,'" *Campus Report* (Stanford University), 7 March 1990.

Papers:

Islas's papers are held at Stanford University in the Special Collections Department of Green Library.

Cleofas M. Jaramillo

(1878 - 1956)

Ramón Sánchez
University of Washington, Bothell

BOOKS: *The Genuine New Mexico Tasty Recipes: Portajes Sabrosos* (N.p., 1939); enlarged as *The Genuine New Mexico Tasty Recipes; With Additional Materials on Traditional Hispano Food* (Santa Fe, N.Mex.: Ancient City, 1981);

Shadows of the Past (Sombras del Pasado) (Santa Fe, N.Mex.: Seton Village, 1941);

Romance of a Little Village Girl (San Antonio: Naylor, 1955).

OTHER: *Cuentos del hogar (Spanish Fairy Stories)*, compiled by Jaramillo (El Campo, Tex.: Citizen Press, 1939).

The fear of her culture rapidly vanishing was what motivated Cleofas M. Jaramillo to write and to establish La Sociedad Folklórica de Santa Fe (The Folkloric Society of Santa Fe) in 1935. All her books, starting with her cookbook and her collection of folktales, both published in 1939, were a reaction to the fear of seeing her culture disappear. "My humble effort in writing this book is with the sole desire of preserving in writing our rapidly vanishing New Mexico Spanish folklore," Jaramillo stated in a handwritten note in a copy of *Shadows of the Past* (1941). She is especially conscious in her writing of the loss of Spanish and the use of English as her means of communicating the culture's disappearance. Conse-

quently Jaramillo's work is nostalgic with romantic and religious overtones. What her books reflect are the concerns of an upper-class, Hispanic elite (the *ricos*) from a female perspective.

Cleofas Martínez Jaramillo was born in Arroyo Hondo, in northern New Mexico. The Martínez family Bible indicates her birthday as being in 1878. The family name was originally Martín but was later changed to Martínez. She was one of seven children (five sons and two daughters) born to Julián Antonio Martínez, a successful businessman in livestock, mining, and the mercantile trade, and Mariana Lucero de Martínez. Both parents were descendants of the original pioneer families of Arroyo Hondo. When she was nine, Cleofas attended the Loretto Convent School established in Taos, but she resented not being allowed to speak Spanish. After five years, she went to Loretto Academy in Santa Fe, where she was allowed to study Spanish formally.

While at the academy, she was courted by her cousin, Col. Venceslao Jaramillo of El Rito (a member of Territorial Governor Miguel A. Otero's staff). Cleofas married Jaramillo in 1898; Otero and many New Mexico politicians attended the Taos wedding. The couple honeymooned in California then returned to live in El Rito. Venceslao Jaramillo owned a store, farmland,

Cleofas M. Jaramillo

and a thirty-three-thousand-acre sheep ranch at Chama. He entered politics, serving as state senator from Río Arriba County, and was a member of the New Mexico Constitutional Convention that drafted the laws for the new state in 1912.

The Jaramillos' first two children died in infancy (a boy in 1908 and a girl in 1909). Their daughter, Angélica, was murdered in 1931. Cleofas Jaramillo wrote about her reaction to the murder: "some weeks after, when I took courage to go out for a walk, the sun seemed to have lost its bright rays and the whole world to be in an eclipse" (*Romance of a Little Village Girl*, 1955). This incident reinforced her cultural sense of loss and added to the yearning for an idealized past. Another element that affected her writing,

concerning the view of the rise and fall of the Hispanic people of New Mexico, was the deteriorating health and then death of her husband. Because of his declining health, the family moved to Denver; he was later treated with radium at Johns Hopkins in Baltimore; and on 27 May 1920 he died in Denver.

At forty-two years of age his widow became aware that the family's extravagant life-style could not be sustained. With the family's fortune lost or what was left heavily mortgaged, Cleofas Jaramillo became a businesswoman and struggled to make a life in Santa Fe with the help of family and friends.

Jaramillo's literary career began when a neighbor showed her a copy of *Holland's Magazine* (June 1935), which contained an article on the annual Natchez pilgrimage and an article on Spanish and Mexican cookery. Her reaction to the Natchez article was stated in a talk in the 1950s to La Sociedad Folklórica: "it occurred to me that if we would look in our mothers' trunks we would find old costumes and jewelry which could be displayed at our Fiesta. I thought we who know the customs and styles of our region are letting them die out." Later, in *Romance of a Little Village Girl*, she called the 1935 cookery article "deficient as to knowledge of our Spanish cooking." Her exposure to these articles motivated her to publish *Cuentos del hogar*, a book containing twenty-five of her mother's stories, which Jaramillo translated into English. The 1939 version of her cookbook, through the subject of food, preserves an aspect of the culture she saw disappearing; her brother Reyes Martínez, who was involved with the Federal Writers Project, encouraged her in this endeavor. As Tey Diana Rebolledo notes in "Tradition And Mythology" (1987), "The Federal Writers Project, active in New Mexico in the 1930s, awakened . . . a sense of the value of Hispanic folk histories and culture." The *cinco pintores* (five painters), also involved in the Federal Writers Project, influenced Jaramillo through the images they painted to document folklore.

The *Holland's* articles also led to the founding of La Sociedad Folklórica. The articles reminded Jaramillo of Hispanic celebrations and motivated her to continue them and not let them vanish. The folkloric society she founded (which consisted of thirty members then) established the rules: the members had to be of Hispanic descent, and meetings were to be in Spanish. Jaramillo insisted on these two requirements. In addition, she chose Saint Anne as the patron saint of the organization.

Shadows of the Past presents folklore material combined with personal experience. Domestic and school customs, foods, witchcraft, and superstition are discussed. Especially important in the book are religious customs that involve hymns, prayers, weddings, baptisms, wakes, feast days, processions, invocations to special saints, Holy Week, religious dramas, and the Penitentes (a Hispanic fraternity organized for pious observances involving the expiation of sin through prayer or, sometimes, corporal penance, and for mutual aid). In the process Jaramillo gives portrait after portrait of the women in her family. But Jaramillo's profound sense of her culture's disappearing is manifest. Reviewer Hester Jones echoed this concern, describing the work as "excellent material" by a member of an "old [family] of the region" and adding that Jaramillo's culture is a little island of "European culture" isolated from the modern world (*Palacio*, October 1941).

Under the banner of romance and religion, in *Shadows of the Past* she attempts to present traditionally derived and orally or imitatively transmitted customs, social conventions, and literature. She starts the book by describing nature, which supplies "all the simple wants of the people." She proceeds to link factors of Hispanic descent, language, and place of residence. In the introduction, however, the language conflict arises once more, and she provides her reason for the use of English: "to preserve some of the folklore of New Mexico, and in the interest of the rising generation—so few of whom now read the Spanish language—I started some years ago to write this book in English."

One important element in Jaramillo's writing is her choice of English as the language through which she would communicate in writing about the vanishing Hispanic culture. In *Romance of a Little Village Girl* she reveals how uneasy she felt with the English language and the social context that came with it: before English-speaking gatherings she was reserved and felt dissatisfied with herself. Jaramillo agonizes over her choice of language, for she feels she has no mastery over the language and because its use reflects the loss of the Spanish culture she is attempting to preserve: "I feel an appalling shortage of words, not being a writer, and writing in a language almost foreign to me."

Jaramillo's folkloric and autobiographical writings describe the transition from a tradition of communication based on oral narrative and a shared experience (characterized in her work by bursts of information) to one based on a standardized written narrative followed by fragmentation of experience.

Her autobiographical *Romance of a Little Village Girl* is considered by Rebolledo as her "most important contribution to documenting the past because in it she gives us the perspective of almost seventy years of her life" ("Las Escritoras," 1989). Rebolledo notes how the narrative starts with the land as an "Eden where humans and animals . . . lived in harmony with nature." Jaramillo then traces the gradual loss of the traditions of New Mexican Hispanic culture. She frames the narrative sections of the work with poetry, which attempts to convey the idea that Hispanics of New Mexico were integrated with nature. But she clearly denies that outsiders can understand her culture. She states that only a select few can comprehend it: "Under the apparent deadness of our New Mexico villages there runs a romantic current invisible to the stranger and understood only by their inhabitants." She notes how folklore forges her identity and character but denies access to most, even many young Hispanics.

Two writers who had an effect on Jaramillo were Willa Cather and Mary Austin. In Cather's case the influence was political. *Death Comes for the Archbishop* (1927), according to Jaramillo, gives "an authentic picture of his [Archbishop John Baptist Lamy's] noble, energetic life." Lamy attempted to reform the Catholic church and religious practices of New Mexico without understanding the local conditions, which included the effect of poverty on the population. Lamy was a Frenchman who, according to critic Carol Jensen, "reflected the same remnants of European colonialism that marked much nineteenth-century activity." Jaramillo supported Lamy's efforts to reform the New Mexican church, despite the fact that the reforms forced her and Venceslao Jaramillo to ask for the church's dispensation to marry, for they were second cousins. Yet she agreed with Lamy's assessment of the surface adherence to religion of the New Mexicans. As she writes in *Romance*, "The smart vicar saw at once how sadly neglected education had been and set to work to remedy it."

Jaramillo's view on the disappearance of Hispanic culture in New Mexico is essentially from the *rico* perspective, which leads to a simplistic explanation of why New Mexico's Hispanics lost their land and culture. Jensen writes about how,

Col. Venceslao Jaramillo and Cleofas M. Jaramillo on their honeymoon in Los Angeles, 1898 (Collection of Virginia Rogers)

for instance, when Jaramillo discusses the marriage ritual, "she tends to obscure the differences between marriage celebrations for the rich and marriages for the poor." Critic Raymond A. Paredes condemns this type of writing, calling it a "hacienda" mentality, which ignores social problems and differences. Yet Rebolledo points out that "to ignore the writing of the middle class is to ignore literary history as well as the origins of much women's literature." Rebolledo calls attention to the remarkable writing that came from Hispanic women who wrote "against the overwhelming dominance of Anglo-culture and language, against patriarchal norms," adding that these female narratives "document the customs a woman thought important to record" ("Las Escritoras").

But Jaramillo's writing was a response from a generally upper-class Hispanic perspective. To maintain a connection with the changing situation, she looks back at Hispanic traditions and makes them come across as symbolizing a harmonious time. She envisions a past that is morally, religiously, politically, and socially cohesive. Her work focuses in general on a reality that was not a given, for she holds onto a rigidly idealized New Mexican culture, which she saw as vanishing

in her lifetime. From her perspective, the natural order that derived from church, state, and class was no longer familiar.

After World War II Hispanic women writers of the Southwest, in general, were forgotten, with little of their work published or distributed. Not until the Chicano civil-rights movement in the 1960s were Hispanic women writers heard again. By this time the environment was one that recognized the mixture of Indian and Spanish elements, the mestizo, in Hispanic culture. Though republished, Jaramillo's works that rely on memories of a rural environment where people lived in harmony with nature do not present a dynamic and fruitful vision that fit the politically active period of the 1960s and early 1970s.

Still, Jaramillo collected folk information that can assist in the cultural study of the northern New Mexico area. Jaramillo's narratives display the reaction of a folklorist who gathers and distributes information about a culture perceived as vanishing, which in her case includes the Spanish language. Her work displays a sense of enthusiasm for Hispanic traditions, tenderness toward family relations, and sacrifice, as she writes to preserve Hispanic culture. She attempts to describe

*Cover for Jaramillo's first book, which she wrote because she
wanted to preserve the culture of her region,
including its cuisine*

the grandeur of Hispanic people in a northern
New Mexican landscape. In this setting, history occurs by patient accumulation of small acts.

A harmonious past with its idealized Hispanic framework dominates Jaramillo's work.
These elements are the basis of her writing. Repeatedly her works dramatize the sense of cultural loss and the conflict involved in change,
which includes her reluctant decision to write her
works in English. She does not create nor develop an identity that reflects autonomy and initiative. Instead, she presents one that depends on a
social structure, and she buttresses that community in reaction to perceived cultural assaults.

Although her approach engendered nostalgia, it also sharpened her vision of a homeland.

Her creative-writing process reveals a culture
steadily evolving and presents the gulf between
what she desired and the situation as it was. By
dealing with her inner and outer conflicts in a
changing Hispanic culture amid an Anglo-
American one, Jaramillo revealed her faith in the
power of writing, an act that can have more than
a personal effect.

She collected material and recorded and
worked with oral material, such as her mother's
stories. In the process, she touched upon different genres, such as fairy tales, proverbs, and
folktales, and reinforced a sense of ethnic identity. In part, identity was revealed by expressing
a group's inner cohesion through the attempt to
maintain shared traditions, such as language,
place of residence, and religion. Through her folkloric narratives, she revealed events that arose
not in isolation but from the interaction between
a person and her society. In this fashion, Jaramillo contributed to the understanding of Hispanic culture and folklore.

References:

Carol Jensen, "Cleofas M. Jaramillo on Marriage
    in Territorial Northern New Mexico," *New
    Mexico Historical Review*, 58 (April 1983):
    153-171;

Howard Roberts Lamar, *The Far Southwest, 1846-
    1912: A Territorial History* (New Haven: Yale
    University Press, 1966);

Raymond A. Paredes, "The Evolution of Chicano
    Literature," in *Three American Literatures*, ed-
    ited by Houston A. Baker, Jr. (New York:
    Modern Language Association, 1982), pp.
    33-79;

Tey Diana Rebolledo, "Las Escritoras: Romances
    and Realities," in *Pasó Por Aquí: Critical Es-
    says on the New Mexican Literary Tradition,
    1542-1988*, edited by Erlinda Gonzales-
    Berry (Albuquerque: University of New Mex-
    ico Press, 1989), pp. 199-214;

Rebolledo, "Tradition and Mythology: Signature
    of Landscape in Chicana Literature," in *The
    Desert Is No Lady*, edited by Vera Norwood
    and Janice Monk (New Haven: Yale Univer-
    sity Press, 1987), pp. 96-124;

Marta Weigle, "About Cleofas Martínez de Ja-
    ramillo," in Jaramillo's *The Genuine New Mex-
    ico Tasty Recipes; With Additional Materials on
    Traditional Hispano Food* (Santa Fe: Ancient
    City, 1981), pp. 19-20.

Yolanda Luera
(4 March 1953 -   )

César A. González-T.
San Diego Mesa College

BOOK: *Solitaria J* (La Jolla, Cal.: Lalo, 1986).

OTHER: "Aborto," "A mi muerte," "Cenizas,"
    "Clase del '76," "Época de maíz," "Piensan
    mis pensamientos," "Voz que llegó tarde,"
    and "Por ahí dicen," in *Second Chicano Liter-
    ary Prize: Irvine 1975-1976* (Irvine: Univer-
    sity of California, 1977), pp. 127-140;
"Sangra pluma," "Aborto," "Voz que llegó tarde,"
    "Cenizas," and "El obscuro corredor," in *Chi-
    canos: Antología histórica y literaria*, edited by
    Tino Villanueva (Mexico City: Fondo de
    Cultura Económica, 1980), pp. 312-316;
"De Domingo a Domingo," in *Irvine Chicano Liter-
    ary Prize, 1985-1987* (Irvine: University of
    California, 1988), pp. 101-105.

SELECTED PERIODICAL PUBLICATIONS—
UNCOLLECTED: "Metamórfosis!" and "Delirio,"
    Café Solo, 8 (Spring 1974): 2, back cover;
"Chile," *Sage: C.S.U.F.* [California State Univer-
    sity, Fresno] *Journal of the Arts*, 2 (10 Decem-
    ber 1982): 11;
"Martín" and "Las Comadres," *Saguaro*, 3, no. 1
    (1986): 16, 57-58;
"La Chirrionera," *Saguaro*, 4 (1987): 43-46.

Yolanda Luera, a talented, promising poet
and fiction writer of the United States-Mexico border, is a student, wife, and mother of three children. To date she has published exclusively in
Spanish. Although she is ambivalent about writing in English, there is some considerable promise in this regard. She has a keen sense of the
pain of the life of the poor, especially of women,
and of the language and wisdom of the common
people, as well as their will to endure. Her writing is artistically salted with a wry, picaresque
sense of humor.

In 1950 Luera's parents, Pedro Luera and
Amada Salas de Luera, moved from Sinaloa and
Durango in northern Mexico to Mexicali, where
she was born on 4 March 1953. The family
moved to Tijuana in 1958 and lived there until

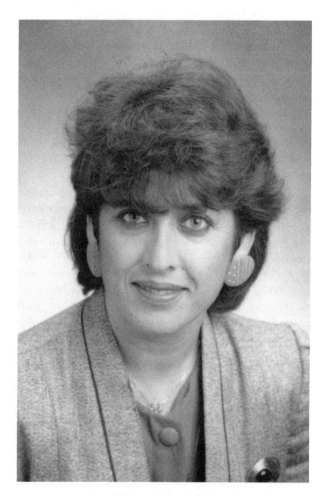

Yolanda Luera, 1987

1970. Her education in Mexico, after the sixth
grade, included secretarial school for six months,
after which she worked for a pittance from 1967
to 1968 at a lithography shop, and the following
year with one of Tijuana's leading paint manufac-
turing and wholesale companies. Later her family
settled in San Ysidro, California. Her cousins
who were attending the University of California,
San Diego (UCSD), introduced her to the High
School Equivalency Program. Before getting her
high-school degree, and while still struggling to
master the English language, she worked as a baby-

159

sitter and field hand. Encouraged by friends and family, she found her way to San Luis Obispo, California, in 1971. There she earned her High School General Education Diploma. One month after she began her studies at San Diego State University in 1972, they were interrupted by a serious auto accident that left her unable to walk for a year. On 26 August 1972 she married Ernesto Padilla in San Diego, and they moved back to San Luis Obispo, where she renewed her studies, this time at California Polytechnic. Yolanda decided to suspend her studies when she was pregnant with her first child, Mayela. Ernesto and Yolanda have two other children, Gabriela and Santiago. Her years in the United States as a working woman and her determination to write and to achieve academic excellence make her a paradigm of the Chicana who creates new personal and literary realities. She is now a naturalized citizen of the United States.

With the encouragement and support of her husband, she published her first book of poems, *Solitaria J*, in 1986. Written in Spanish, as are her other publications to date, these collected poems have been translated into English by James Hoggard. She is an unpretentious artist and takes her place among the new generation of poets who speak forthrightly to the world with compelling honesty and insight.

Like Sergio Elizondo, Lucha Corpi, and other Chicano writers who lived their formative years in Mexico, Luera demonstrates a command of Spanish and an attraction to the folklore and traditions of Mexico while writing within the context of her Chicana experience in America. Critic Gabriel Trujillo Muñoz includes her among notable women writers of the U.S.-Mexico border area who began to write in the late 1970s and continued through the 1980s. Their themes, according to Trujillo Muñoz, include dealing with "el ámbito familiar, las relaciones amorosas y la visión del entorno fronterizo que viven y experimentan en toda su compleja magnitud" (the family circle, love relationships, and their vision of the reality of the border which they live and experience in all of its complexity and magnitude). Prior to the 1970s the women of the borderlands were essentially limited to writing society columns, recipes, and advice to the lovelorn in newspapers.

Throughout her academic career, Luera has given expression to her talent as a poet and short-story writer, publishing as opportunities have presented themselves. She is a serious reader, and, aside from mainstream Latin Americans and other writers to whom she has been exposed in the course of her regular studies in literature, she has been greatly influenced by Lorna D. Cervantes, as well as by Carmen Tafolla, Xelina Rojas-Urista, Margarita Luna Robles, Emily López, and Ana Castillo, whom she admires greatly.

Some of her publications have been prompted by writer-friends who have given her feedback throughout the years, notably Tafolla, who has written a sensitive and poetic appreciation in English in her introduction to *Solitaria J*:

> That uncommon letter "J," once the proud Mexicano "X," then changed, so arbitrarily, so colonizingly, from the rhythmic sonete-sound of "sh" to the forced breath of a "J," punctuated like some upside-down exclamation mark, with no thought for its implications or consequences, even its name an obscenity [lesbian], is a reflection of our own personal history; we have had our Indian "X" conquered, we stand alone, without our heritage, without even our identity, trying to survive in the barrio of our forgotten and sacrificed x's, with nothing but a solitary "j" standing there watching us, blank faced.

Getting *de allá a aquí* (from there to here) is a dominant theme of Luera's writing. She and her readers are in the process—at once bridges and wayfarers, in evolution—of becoming, of struggling through the irrationality of society and social institutions, toward the discovery of a common humanity.

Trujillo Muñoz praises Luera for her portrayal of the family, and in particular of other women in families, as a means of self-definition. As an example, he quotes "Amada" from *Solitaria J*:

Quiero ser feliz, dice mi madre
. . . .
Sufre a mi padre que babea alcohol cada fin de semana. Sufre a mi hermana tristemente retardada que golosea dulce bajo la cama. Y sufre a la abuela en sus últimos años goteantes que dejó de ser matriarca y se convirtió sólo en abuela enferma.

(I want to be happy, says my mother
. . . .
She suffers my father who slobbers alcohol each weekend. Suffers my sadly retarded sister
enjoying her candies beneath the bed. And suffers my grandmother
in her last drop-by-drop years, who left off being the matriarch and became just a sick grandmother.)

Luera is also a poet of the community. Her social awakening began when she was a young girl experiencing some of the injustices of society against minorities. Her mother, a farm worker, introduced her to the marches of César Chávez when they came through the area in the early 1970s. As Luera listened to the people, she began to discover a sense of community. In 1974 she met Chilean exiles at UCSD after the assassination of Salvador Allende. "The pain of the expatriates," she says, "made me realize the false sense of security which we have in the United States." She writes of them:

> Existen entierros
> que llevan flores,
> llevan llanto,
> solo les falta un cuerpo.
>
> (There are burials
> which bear flowers,
> bear grief only,
> not a body.)

She speaks of social injustices, of being forced to the margins of a male-dominated society, of fears—the fear of nuclear annihilation and of the uncertainty of life.

In one of the first poems in her collection, "Vida para siempre" (Life without End), she speaks of Benjamina, who lives "encerrada / en una tarjeta postal / con sello extranjero (enclosed / in a postcard / with a foreign stamp):

> Notó que de sus ojos
> ya no salían colores,
> solo sombras
> en blanco y negro.
> Solo el latido de su corazón
> seguía palpitándole en el pecho
> con insistencia pordiosera.
>
> (She noted that her eyes
> no longer showed colors,
> just shadows
> black and white.
> Alone just the beating of her heart
> thudding in her breast
> insistent as a beggar woman.)

Commenting on her poem "El que entre locos anda" (He Who Walks among the Mad)—which is reminiscent of Ken Kesey's *One Flew Over the Cuckoo's Nest* (1962)—Salvador Reza, editor of *Voz Fronteriza* (the newspaper of UCSD), wrote:

Cover for Luera's 1986 book, a collection of poems that focus on Chicanas in families along the border between the United States and Mexico

Luera en su poesia nos muestra que es parte de un grupo de "consciencias sanas" consideradas locas por ciertos sectores de "Aquí" y hace un llamado a tantos y tantas "conciencias" solitarias para que se haga la unión entre ellas y abrir las puertas del manicomio social en el que existimos.

(In her poetry, Luera shows us that she belongs to that group of "healthy consciousnesses" considered mad by certain sectors of "Here," and she gives a rallying cry to all those men and women, solitary "consciences," to unite and open the doors of the insane asylum in which we live.)

In this poem there is a suppressed rage against the enforced conformity to which people submit in their hypocrisy and posing.

Luera refuses labored metaphors and contrived insights. "My context," she says, "is simple. This is my principal concern: to be brief, to be direct. It is essential that I communicate what is basic—with economy, with simplicity." She uses everyday images to make her point with un-spoiled originality, as in the poem from which the collection takes its name, "Una solitaria J":

Quisiera poder mentir
como el calendario alocado
que corre y grita nombres
de santos y santas sin ser bautizado.

(I wish I could lie
like the heathen calendar
which rushes about madly screaming the names
of all the unbaptized saints.)

Luera speaks with modesty and humor of her poems as "mis toothless y pelones hijos; but you have to love them porque te cuestan!" (My toothless and baldheaded children; but you have to love them because they have cost you dearly!). Her next book of poetry, she says, may be in English.

She is also a promising fiction writer and is presently working on a collection of short stories, "La mujer que esperó sentada" (The Woman Who Waited Sitting). She took third place in the Thirteenth Chicano Literary Contest with her 1987 story "De Domingo a Domingo" (Sunday after Sunday), published in 1988 in *Irvine Chicano Literary Prize, 1985-1987*. In this woman's narrative, Casimira de Díaz is preparing for her customary Sunday visit to her sick grandmother. Casimira stands naked before the mirror making a frank and humorous appraisal of her thirty-three-year-old body. She sees herself growing older, changing as are her children and her language while San Diego insinuates itself into her Mexican reality. She drives through the numbing monotony of traffic to her grandmother who is hooked to life-support systems that drip glucose. The grandmother is the focus of Casimira's tender remembrances of another reality they shared when Casimira was a child: "¡Abuela! ¡Abuelita! ¿Me oye? Soy yo. Soy yo, Casimira, abuelita. Hoy es domingo como aquel día en el que caí al canal en Mexicali y me salvó jalándome por las greñas" (Gra'ma! Granny! Do you hear me? It's I. It's I, Casimira, Granny. Today's Sunday like that day I fell into the canal in Mexicali, and you saved me dragging me out by my hair). Casimira goes to the hospital window, her watch strangling her left wrist, as time drags her into the image in the window. She sings a song her grandmother used to sing when "De domingo a domingo te vengo a verrrr ... cuándo será domingo cielito lindo para volveeeer" (Sunday after

Sunday I come to seeee you ... when will it be Sunday lovely sky again so that I'll retuuuurn).

In "La Chirrionera" (*Saguaro*, 1987) Luera presents an adaptation of a folktale from Mexican oral tradition, making it a part of literature. The story as told to her by her grandmother from Durango tells of La Chirrionera, a snake with a very long tail it uses to enchant children while it drinks the milk from their nursing mothers. Luera develops the story, using images of water and of a woman singing a siren song. This unusual story filled with symbols of life and death, along with traditional, stereotypical negative images of women, is not intended, she says, as a variant of the tale of La Llorona (The Weeping Woman) from Aztec and Mexican tradition. The story opens with the first-person narrative of the protagonist Toño—no one knows where he came from—left behind in a town abandoned by the people, who have given him an herb, *la dormilona* (the sleepyhead), which is making him swell up and break out in boils. At first, when children disappeared from town, people blamed La Chirrionera. But later they discovered that it was Toño who killed the children left in his care by the old Chona, the oldest woman in town, and that he fed them to La Chirrionera. He has been left behind so that La Chirrionera will have only him to devour when the snake enters the town. The story closes with Toño recalling the useless parting words of the priest, urging him to think good thoughts and think about something else, as a breathy smell of warm milk and monstrous swelling eyes engulf him.

Yolanda Luera's fiction and poetry present a common-sense and imaginative voice, which speaks for those on both sides of the border, with a strong sense of respect and love for traditions. She still aspires to obtaining a doctorate in literature and hopes some day to extend her travels beyond the little she has seen of Europe—including Madrid, Barcelona, Paris, and London—which she says she has seen "con ojos desilusionados y admirados" (with eyes filled with disillusion and wonder). If it were possible, she would live for a year in Brazil, away from the United States and Mexico, to learn Portuguese and to work on a novel in the land of Jorge Amado, one of her favorite writers. But wherever she travels, she is analyzing and contrasting what she discovers with what is on the border and in Mexico City. "I want to see with greater objectivity and precision," she says, "my world in transition, hacia acá ... desde allá" (over here ... from over there).

References:
Carmen Tafolla, Introduction to Luera's *Solitaria J* (La Jolla, Cal.: Lalo, 1986);

Gabriel Trujillo Muñoz, "La literatura contemporánea: El punto de vista femenino," *Ranura del Ojo*, 1 (Summer 1988): 6-14.

E. A. Mares
(17 May 1938 -)

Enrique R. Lamadrid
University of New Mexico

BOOKS: *The Unicorn Poem* (Cerrillos, N.Mex.: San Marcos, 1980);
Las Vegas, New Mexico: A Portrait, by Mares and Alex Traube (Albuquerque: University of New Mexico Press, 1983);
I Returned and Saw Under the Sun (Albuquerque: University of New Mexico Press, 1989).

PLAY PRODUCTIONS: *Lola's Last Dance*, Albuquerque, Compañía de Teatro de Albuquerque, 21 December 1979;
Padre Antonio José Martínez de Taos, Raton, N.Mex., New Mexico Endowment for the Humanities Chautauqua Program, 21 March 1983;
Vista del Puente, bilingual adaptation of Arthur Miller's *View from the Bridge*, by Mares and Cecilio García-Camarillo, Albuquerque, Compañía de Teatro de Albuquerque, 28 October 1983;
El Corrido de Joaquín Murieta, Albuquerque, Compañía de Teatro de Albuquerque, 25 May 1984;
Santa Fe Spirit [musical], book and lyrics by Mares, Santa Fe Spirit Company, 5 June 1989;
The Shepherd of Pan Duro, Albuquerque, Compañía de Teatro de Albuquerque, 14 December 1989.

TELEVISION: *New Mexico and the Multilingual Experience*, teleplay by Mares, KNME, Albuquerque, Fall 1981.

OTHER: "Selected Characteristics of New Mexico Culture," in *New Mexico Regional Medical Program Triennial Application, Part XII* (Albuquerque: UNM Medical School, 1971), pp. 30-39;
"The Fiesta of Life: Impressions of Paulo Freire," in *Parameters of Institutional Change: Chicano Experiences in Education* (Hayward, Cal.: World, 1974), pp. 167-177;
A Ceremony of Brotherhood: Commemorative Anthology of the Pueblo Revolt, edited by Mares, Rudolfo Anaya, and Simon Ortiz (Albuquerque: Academia, 1980);
Hispanic Humanities in the Schools, edited by Mares, J. C. Atkins, and M. J. Justiz (Albuquerque: Latin American Programs in Education, 1982);
"Florinto," in *And the Ground Spoke: Poems and Stories by Cecilio García Camarillo, Joy Harjo, E. A. Mares and Jim Sagel* (San Antonio, Tex.: Guadalupe Cultural Arts Center, 1986), pp. 26-35;
Un Ojo en el Muro / An Eye through the Wall: Mexican Poetry 1970-1985, edited by Enrique R. Lamadrid and Mario del Valle, includes translations by Mares (Santa Fe: Tooth of Time, 1986);
Padre Martínez: New Perspectives from Taos, edited by Mares (Taos, N.Mex.: Millicent Rogers Museum, 1988);
Flow of the River, epilogue by Mares (Albuquerque: Hispanic Culture Foundation, 1988);

En Breve: Minimalism in Mexican Poetry, edited by Lamadrid, includes translations by Mares (Santa Fe: Tooth of Time, 1988);

Lola's Last Dance, in *New Mexico Plays*, edited by David Richard Jones (Albuquerque: University of New Mexico Press, 1989), pp. 63-78;

"The Wrangle-Taggle Outlaws: Vicente Silva and Billy the Kid as Seen in Two Nineteenth Century Hispanic Documents," in *Pasó Por Aquí: Critical Essays on the New Mexican Literary Tradition*, edited by Erlinda Gonzales-Berry (Albuquerque: University of New Mexico Press, 1989), pp. 167-184.

SELECTED PERIODICAL PUBLICATIONS—
UNCOLLECTED: "El Lobo y El Coyote: Between Two Cultures," *Cuaderno*, 2, no. 1 (1972): 20-23;

"Myth and Reality: Observations on American Myths and the Myth of Aztlán," *Cuaderno*, 3 (Winter 1973): 35-50;

"The Center Is Everywhere: Hispanic Letters in New Mexico," *Century*, 2 (February 1982): 9-11;

"Los Alamos: From Where the Zig-Zag Lightning Strikes," *Impact*, supplement to the *Albuquerque Journal*, 6 August 1985.

E. A. Mares is a New Mexican poet who owes his considerable success as a playwright and essayist to his rare talent for entwining poetry and history without betraying either. In his own words, he is "a writer who is Indo-Hispanic in culture, global in perspective, and as much at home in the international community as in his own mixed ethnic communities."

Born near La Plaza Vieja de Albuquerque (The Old Plaza of Albuquerque) on 17 May 1938, to Ernesto Gustavo Mares and the former Rebecca Devine, Ernesto Antonio Mares was a product of the cultural contradictions he was later the first to define in terms of the popular New Mexican concept of the "coyote," or the mixed-breed Hispanic. By the 1920s Mares's father's family had been dispossessed of their ancestral lands near Raton, New Mexico, and migrated to Albuquerque; their fate was shared by many native New Mexicans of the era. The lure of employment with the railroad promised economic survival, but at the high price of social and cultural alienation. The draconian rumblings of the locomotives and clash of cold steel are images in Mares's later poetry.

On his mother's side Mares is a descendant of an Irish sergeant of Gen. George Custer's Seventh Cavalry. (The sergeant retired before the Battle of the Little Bighorn.) As with other early Irish immigrants, he and his descendants became Hispanicized. Through his father, Mares is related to the family of the controversial nineteenth-century New Mexican priest Antonio José Martínez, of Taos, who defined for later generations of New Mexicans the meaning of cultural resistance under American occupation. But Mares himself is his own best genealogist in this eloquent passage from the autobiographical short story "Florinto" (1986). A boy is awakened into a historical consciousness of himself by an intense, silent encounter with the neighborhood picaro junkman, the title character:

Cover for the 1983 book that includes Mares's "docu-drama" on the history of Las Vegas, New Mexico

We stood there in a moment of time that had no beginning and no end. His eyes held me and as I looked into them I had the sensation that the whole history of my family was unfolding in that gaze. I saw my father and my father's father before him, and an infinite regression of lives and passions and histories which had led to this moment. They were all there: the Mares brothers who drove cattle north from Guadalajara deep in Mexico across the Jornada del Muerto and then on to Santa Fe and Taos; the Martínez clan which settled in Abiquiú and pushed branches of the family into the valleys of the Chama and up into the high country of the Sangre de Cristos; the Gutiérrez and Garcías who helped found Old Albuquerque and built the San Felipe Church as a testament to their great need to span the distance from earth to heaven; the Devines, those restless Irishmen who were dreamers, adventurers, poets and musicians. . . . I knew what it was to be a *coyote*, a half-breed who was to live forever on the fringes of the swirling cultures to which I was heir. . . .

Mares attended the San Felipe de Neri School in Old Town Albuquerque, where he was impressed with the midwestern missionary zeal of the young Sisters of Charity, who were the first to initiate him into the ways of the dominant cul-

ture. Mares recalls that the stunning contradictions revealed in the process of his own indoctrination and anglicization remain the source of his curiosity as a historian, his perseverance as a political activist, and his inspiration as a poet.

After graduating from the parochial St. Mary's High School, he completed a bachelor's degree in Spanish in 1960 from the University of New Mexico, where he studied with the exiled Spanish novelist Ramón Sender and the New Mexican author Sabine Ulibarrí. In 1962 he obtained a master's degree in Spanish from Florida State University, with a thesis titled "The Philosophy of José Ortega y Gassett: Towards an Ultra-Utopian Society." Two years of teaching Spanish at North Texas State University in Denton dampened Mares's enthusiasm as a language teacher but awakened his professional interest in history and political activism. He returned to the University of New Mexico in 1965 as a doctoral student in history and helped organize the UNM chapter of Students for a Democratic Society. His 1974 dissertation at the same university is titled "Elements of Myth in Spanish Thought and in the Writings of the Generation of 1898." While at the University of Arkansas from 1967 through 1969, he spent more time in the poetry workshops conducted by

Jim Whitehead than he did in the history department, where he was officially employed. It was during these workshops with Whitehead, James Seay, James Dickey, Allen Ginsberg, and Miller Williams that Mares honed his poetic craft. Afterward he occupied himself with diverse pursuits: working as a rural health planner and child development specialist, and teaching in the social-work program at New Mexico Highlands University. After earning his Ph.D. and teaching in several other institutions, including Colorado College and the University of New Mexico, Mares was curator of education at the Albuquerque Museum until 1987. Recently he has dedicated his full-time efforts to writing projects, and he is a frequent contributor to the review pages of local newspapers and journals, such as the *Albuquerque Journal* and the *Santa Fe Reporter*. Currently, he holds a teaching position at North Texas State University. In 1987 Mares and Carolyn Meyer, writer and author of numerous works of fiction and nonfiction for adolescents, were married.

Mares's most significant early publications as a poet and essayist were with the Academia de la Nueva Raza (Academy of the New Chicano People) in Dixon, New Mexico, and its journal, the *Cuaderno*. After experiencing the frustrations of political organizing in the 1960s, his association with the cultural workers and community activists of the academia provided the forum and inspiration necessary for furthering his creative and analytical work. As the most active and progressive cultural organization of the Chicano movement in New Mexico, the academia developed culturally based models of political, cultural, and social work. Early ties were made with such Latin-American social philosophers as the Brazilian Paulo Freire, and his model of "concientización," or political and cultural consciousness-raising, was closely related to the academia philosophy. Mares documented this contact in his article "The Fiesta of Life: Impressions of Paulo Freire" (1974), which explores the ludic dimension of Freire's process of popular education, a necessary playfulness largely lacking in the political manifestos of the early 1970s.

When other Chicano groups across the Southwest were giving full and strident voice to a newly defined cultural nationalism modeled in part on the populist and indigenist ideology of the ruling PRI (Institutional Revolutionary Party) of Mexico, Mares was dealing with such unpopular issues as the acculturation of the Chicano, as in his article "El Lobo y El Coyote: Between Two Cultures" (1972). Aware of the necessary function of cultural nationalism, Mares points out the dangers of marginalizing those individuals who do not fit neatly within defined ethnic parameters. Since culture is not "in the blood," but rather learned behavior, the "coyote" becomes a metaphor for the Indo-Hispanic-Anglo cultural mix that currently prevails in New Mexico.

In 1972, when it was most stylish to speculate on the Aztec influences on Chicano culture, Mares proclaimed that "We are not Aztecs, and we are far from Aztlán." Yet his essay "Myth and Reality" (1973) reveals an awareness of how unifying and compelling the central concept of Aztlán was to the Chicano movement as a whole.

In subsequent essays Mares comments on the state of the Spanish language and Hispanic letters in New Mexico. Although Spanish has traditionally been largely relegated to family settings and rural contexts, Mares notes the growing presence of Mexican Spanish in the cities and the new accessibility of Spanish-language television. In "The Center Is Everywhere: Hispanic Letters in New Mexico" (1982), he documents the end of the colonial status of literary creation in the Southwest: "There are two basic attitudes that writers of a region may take towards their position in the larger society. One is to view themselves as peripheral to the mainstream of American letters and resigned forever to the imitative and derivative backwaters. The other is to view the region or, in this case, New Mexico, as a center from which creativity flows out to the nation and the world."

In 1983 Mares wrote a book-length essay, a "docu-drama" of words as he calls it, to "illustrate" and give intellectual resonance to a book of extraordinary photographs by Alex Traube, *Las Vegas, New Mexico: A Portrait*. The essay is an impressionist history of the town at the edge of the Great Plains that was once the most thriving economic center in New Mexico. Divided by the Gallinas River into Hispanic West Las Vegas and Anglo-American East Las Vegas, the town is a microcosm of the contradictions that still divide New Mexico. Mares weaves history with poetry in different levels of discourse. The following digression is based on an incident at a university construction site where students stole skulls from an unmarked cemetery that was mistakenly excavated:

There is something peculiarly appropriate about human skulls moving about above the earth in Las Vegas, New Mexico. Here, life and death

Poster advertising the premiere (1984) of Mares's play about a legendary California outlaw

have been as finely balanced as mountain and plain, Anglo and Hispano, merchant and rancher, lawman and gunslinger, here where Billy the Kid passed through, where Pat Garrett enforced the law and order, here where *Las Gorras Blancas* [The White Caps, a nineteenth-century Hispano vigilante group] tore up railroad tracks and turned them into Sherman neckties, here where a boomtown settled into its old ways like a grandfather into his rocking chair, here the skulls of the dead come back to share the incredible landscape, to walk about again before settling down one more time in the earth. Here the dead come back to share the past and the present with the living, to haunt the living who haunt the dead.

In his most recent essays, the topics of science and ethics loom large, due in great part to New Mexico's distinction of being the testing place of nuclear weaponry, the new-age equivalent of original sin for New Mexicans. He laments the fact that the genius and progressive ide-

alism of Robert Oppenheimer and the founders of Los Alamos could be so totally co-opted by the rapacious and devious bureaucracy of the U.S. military establishment. Mares's essay "Los Alamos: From Where the Zig-Zag Lightning Strikes" appeared on 6 August 1985 in *Impact*, a supplement to the most widely circulated newspaper in the state, the *Albuquerque Journal*. After decades of international debate on the topic, at last an authentically native New Mexican perspective of the dilemma is revealed.

As Mares often insists, poetry is the core of his creative visions and the source of all his work in theater, history, and the essay. Although he has published in many regional and national journals and magazines and has one chapbook, *The Unicorn Poem* (1980) to his credit, much of his poetry has yet to be collected under one cover. Epic in scope as it interweaves history and myth, *The Unicorn Poem* is a mural of words, maps, and photographs that is also a catalogue of Mares's poetry prior to 1980. The poem begins with a common theme in Chicano literature, telling an untold story and filling in the blank pages of history:

On seeing a Detailed Map
I noticed the empty space
where there is no map,
only theatre of man and myth,
the land of the unicorn
and less lovely beasts
trying to corral him.

Chicano critic Juan Bruce-Novoa notes that "Mares will work a series of overlayed metaphors: the map, the myth, the search, and the struggle for survival and freedom. His poem fills empty space with the silenced history of the Chicanos of New Mexico." Bruce-Novoa continues by noting that Mares's choice of the unicorn as a metaphor for *chicanismo* "links Chicanos with a universal myth not usually associated with Mexican culture." Thus, Mares emphasizes the fundamental unity of peoples. And at yet another level, its blatant artificiality precludes simplistic historicism or realistic interpretation, forcing a reading in the realm of the symbolic." Fragments and stanzas alternating between English and Spanish are taken from a series of individual poems and forged into what New Mexico poet Keith Wilson has termed (on the cover of the book) a truly New Mexican epic: "Caught up in the flash of incidents that make up New Mexico, past and present, this poem moves gracefully across our stark landscapes with the mystery and power of a *matachín* dancer, illuminating our darkness and joying in our light." Light in the poem is the illumination of the poet's own consciousness as he tries to understand the visions that swirl around him:

A star is a sharpshooter
aiming at my eyes
from across the universe.

Light is a pack of coyotes on fire
scattering in all directions
towards the future and the past.

Mares, the poet-hunter, stalks the histories and mythologies of Europe and Mesoamerica to define his illusive prey, the consciousness that includes them both:

Words of ancestors
spoke of fabulous islands and beasts,
fountains of youth,
cities of gold and heavenly utopias

where the saints would wait
for the second coming of Christ.

Words of ancestors
spoke of Hummingbird-on-the-Left,
eagles devouring the hearts of men,
the sun who did battle with darkness
and arose every morning
from the pool of night,
human blood and tears. . . .

History is a also a graveyard (*camposanto*, or holy ground) of words that Mares turns into song:

Camposanto of words
uncoupling from flesh
camposanto of words
seeking the lips of a lover
camposanto of words
unmoved by time[.]

Mares's career as a dramatist began in 1979 with the Compañía de Teatro de Albuquerque's production of the successful bilingual comedy *Lola's Last Dance*, one of a trilogy of one-act New Mexican plays, which also included works by Denise Chávez and Rudolfo Anaya. Lola is an aging prostitute from Old Town Albuquerque whose collection of rag dolls represents all her previous lovers, including a procession of Chicano politicians; Anglo-American merchants; a priest; and the true love of her life, Florinto, the Old Town junkman and the only "real man" of the lot. Lola's anarchist philosophy (close to Mares's own view of the human condition) and picaresque language delighted Albuquerque audiences. After this success Mares has become a regular collaborator with the Compañía de Teatro, assisting in Spanish-language adaptations of plays such as Arthur Miller's *View from the Bridge* (1955); the 1983 adaptation is set in the Barelas barrio of Albuquerque.

When asked to do a bilingual adaptation of Pablo Neruda's play *Fulgor y muerte de Joaquín Murieta* (Splendor and Death of Joaquín Murieta), Mares instead wrote an original script entitled *El Corrido de Joaquín Murieta* (The Ballad of Joaquín Murieta, 1984). In his search for historical information on the legendary California social bandit, Mares found a source that said Murieta was a *mesteñero*, or "mustanger," before trying his hand at digging for gold. In the 1840s there was a lively mustang trade based in New Mexico that extended as far as California. In Mares's version, therefore, Murieta in logical fashion is a New Mexican whose horse trading leads him to California and his destiny. With *Santa Fe Spirit* (1989), a musical for which Mares wrote both the script and the lyrics, he combines tragic and comic elements drawn from the history of New Mexico and its capital, Santa Fe. In *The Shepherd of Pan Duro* (also 1989) Mares incorporates two New Mexican yuletide traditions—the shepherds' play "Los Pastores," and "Las Posadas," or the search of the Holy Family for a resting place—into a powerful modern parable about the plight of the homeless in the contemporary United States.

With the exception of his initial comedy and his most recent work, historical drama has been a significant part of Mares's career as a playwright. Cultural resistance is the central theme of Mares's one-act play *Padre Antonio José Martínez de Taos* (1983), a dramatic monologue. The much-maligned Taos priest's prophetic role as cultural hero has been recently revealed by Chicano historians, particularly by Mares himself in the bilingual published version of the play, retitled *I Returned and Saw Under the Sun* (1989), and in *Padre Martínez: New Perspectives from Taos* (1988), edited by Mares, the only collection of historical and literary essays ever published on this key historical figure of the Southwest. Mares, who is Martínez's fifth great-nephew, has performed his dramatic monologue in communities across the state as part of the Chautauqua Series of the New Mexico Endowment for the Humanities.

Criticism and commentary on Mares concentrate on his dramatic work, the most visible part of his career. His popular monologue on Martínez has received much publicity and has created a wave of interest in Martínez and the defiant but humane values he represents. Other articles attest to "the pivotal position Mares now occupies in New Mexico letters," in the words of Stanley Noyes, who states: "Almost symbolically, it seems, E. A. Mares possesses the ability to create in his own poetry a cultural harmony and synthesis." More recently Bruce-Novoa has commented on the epic qualities of Mares's poetry,

which avoids the sometimes simplistic populism of other Chicano poets who deal with themes of myth and history.

E. A. Mares is a poet and historian caught between Hispanic and Anglo-American cultures and, like a "picaro coyote," plays the role of both trickster and mediator. With his essays, plays, poems, and translations, he has written a chapter in the intellectual history of the Hispanic Southwest. The themes of *mestizaje* (cultural synthesis), cultural resistance, and intellectual independence from ideologies motivate his work, which he in his own words sees "not as a parochial, ethnic or regional undertaking, but rather an international one. I hope it is one very small part of many efforts that will eventually make this planet a much more humane, a much more habitable planet than it is now for human beings."

References:

Juan Bruce-Novoa, "New Mexican Chicano Poetry: The Contemporary Tradition," in *Pasó Por Aquí: Critical Essays on the New Mexican Literary Tradition*, edited by Erlinda Gonzales-Berry (Albuquerque: University of New Mexico Press, 1989), pp. 267-296;

Howard Bryan, "Book Attests that New Mexico Also Has a Las Vegas," *Albuquerque Tribune*, 12 April 1984, p. A-3;

Geary Hobson, "The Unicorn Poem," *New Mexico Humanities Review*, 4 (Fall 1981): 86-87;

Mary Montaño Army, "New Life for an Old Myth," *Impact*, supplement to the *Albuquerque Journal*, 14 May 1985, pp. 5-14;

Stanley Noyes, "Notes on E. A. Mares; Poetry in New Mexico," *New Mexico Magazine*, 61 (March 1983): 19;

Leigh O'Rourke, "E. A. Mares; Write from the Height of Experience," *Artlines*, 4 (July 1983): 28-29.

Papers:

Mares's papers are in the Special Collections, Zimmerman Library, University of New Mexico, Albuquerque.

Eliud Martínez

(21 January 1935 -   )

Roberto Cantú
California State University, Los Angeles

BOOKS: *The Art of Mariano Azuela: Modernism in La malhora, El desquite, La Luciérnaga* (Pittsburgh: Latin American Literary Review Press, 1980); translated into Spanish by Manuel A. Serna-Maytorena as *Mariano Azuela y la altura de los tiempos* (Guadalajara, Mexico: Gobierno de Jalisco, Secretaria General, 1981);

Voice-Haunted Journey (Tempe, Ariz.: Bilingual Press, 1990).

OTHER: "Personal Vision in the Short Stories of Estela Portillo-Trambley," in *Beyond Stereotypes: The Critical Analysis of Chicana Literature*, edited by M. Herrera-Sobek (New York: Bilingual Press, 1985), pp. 71-90;

"Rodolfo 'Corky' Gonzales," in *Chicano Literature: A Reference Guide*, edited by Julio Martínez and Francisco Lomelí (Westport, Conn.: Greenwood, 1985), pp. 221-228;

"Tomás Rivera: Witness and Storyteller," in *International Studies in Honor of Tomás Rivera*, edited by Julián Olivares (Houston: Arte Público, 1986), pp. 39-52;

"Ron Arias' *The Road to Tamazunchale*: Cultural Inheritance and Literary Expression," in *The Road to Tamazunchale*, Chicano Classics, 3 (Tempe, Ariz.: Bilingual Review, 1987).

SELECTED PERIODICAL PUBLICATIONS—
UNCOLLECTED: "La visión alcohólica de Dionisio en *La luciérnaga* de Mariano Azuela," *Revista Universidad de Sonora*, 3 (December 1972): 14-22;

"Mariano Azuela and the Height of the Times: A Study of *La luciérnaga*," *Latin American Literary Review*, 3 (Fall-Winter 1974-1975): 113-130;

"*La malhora*: From the Novel of the Mexican Revolution to the Modern Novel," *Latin American Literary Review*, 4 (Spring-Summer 1976): 23-24;

"Ron Arias' *The Road to Tamazunchale*: A Chicano Novel of the New Reality," *Latin American*

Eliud Martínez (photograph by Marilyn Odello, Riverside *[California]* Press-Enterprise*)*

Literary Review, 5 (Spring-Summer 1977): 51-63;

"*I Am Joaquín* as Poem and Film: Two Modes of Chicano Expression," *Journal of Popular Culture*, 13 (Winter 1979): 505-515;

"Point of View in Mariano Azuela's *El desquite*," *Hispanófila*, 72 (May 1981): 51-67;

"Carlos Fuentes' Mexico: A Thousand Countries with a Single Name," *UCR Magazine* (June 1989): 52-59.

Eliud Martínez, an important critic and novelist, was the first of six children born to Estroberto and María Martínez in Pflugerville, Texas. In 1939, when he was four years old, the family moved to Austin and settled in its Mexican eastside barrio; Martínez's father worked as a construction laborer. Although having little formal education, the parents, according to Martínez, encouraged learning and professional advancement in their five sons and one daughter in spite of the widespread class and ethnic segregation which gave local Mexicans few hopes of upward economic mobility. In 1941 Martínez entered Bickler Elementary School where the children were mostly Mexican. He remembers being, at four years old, a daydreamer, hypersensitive, and anxious to begin his schooling. As is usually the case, he did not speak English when first attending elementary school; yet Martínez must have learned quickly for three years later—after displaying signs of an aesthetic sensibility and a marked academic inclination—he was transferred, upon the recommendation of his teachers, to what was considered a better school, Palm Elementary School, just ten blocks away. Thus began the journey that would take Martínez away from home and around the world (through his readings and actual travels) and, ultimately, home again.

Between 1946 and 1949 Martínez attended John T. Allan Junior High School where he recalls the high rate of student attrition among Mexican youth, who went on to the work force, military service, early marriage, or, occasionally, reform school. In a different area of Austin lived Anglo and German-American middle-class youth, who attended a different institution: University Junior High School. Black youth had their own school in a segregated part of the city. In 1949 Martínez entered Stephen F. Austin High School, the only one in Austin at the time, consequently the point of convergence for the few Mexican students who at that point had survived the Texas school system, and the majority of graduates from the University Junior High School who, upon enrollment in high school, must have felt assured of their future social and economic identity in the region. Martínez graduated from high

school in 1952 and went on to college with the intention of majoring in commercial art. His sister, Belia, also graduated from high school, but the other four brothers did not. In high school Martínez learned French (a language fomented by Austin's French Legation); later he developed a strong command of Italian, thus becoming a young polyglot in the Mexican eastside barrio.

Their achievements in school separated Martínez and his sister, Belia, from their brothers, who were continuously compared negatively in the light of the successes of the academically driven siblings. For example, Teodoro, a younger brother, did not have a comparable record in school (he was held back in first grade, thus suffering a personal humiliation) in spite of having a keen intelligence; the parental preference for some children over the others introduced more sibling rivalry. Memories of this troubled relation surfaced years later in *Voice-Haunted Journey* (1990) through metaphors of melancholia. In his detailed "Working Description of 'The Notebooks of Miguel Velásquez,' "—this being the title of Martínez's planned narrative trilogy of which *Voice-Haunted Journey* is the first volume—Martínez describes his main character as follows: "Miguel is troubled by thoughts of remorse and by a sense of guilt, which have beset him for many years, about not having been a good husband or a good father, son, brother or friend to others."

Martínez's fascination with art began at his grandfather's side during family visits to San Antonio. A heavy drinker, a man with literary interests, and a former *maderista* cavalry soldier (he fought for Francisco I. Madero against Porfirio Díaz during the Mexican revolution), Don Eusebio Martínez-Ortiz would always ask Martínez affectionately to draw soldiers for an aging grandfather ("píntame un mochito"). These repeated requests developed into an artistic flair that would eventually distinguish Martínez at school and pull him toward higher education. From 1963 to 1980 Martínez—a writer of various profiles and many talents—had nine art exhibitions, three of them one-man shows, winning a first prize in 1965 at the Juilliard School of Music, New York, and a second prize in 1969 at the Allentown Art Festival, Buffalo, New York. In 1980 Martínez made the decision to devote most of his artistic energies to writing what he calls autobiographical fiction. In retrospect, the grandfather's influence was decisive on Martínez's life as an artist. The fact that he is "the eldest son of the eldest son" adds a sense of destiny to *Voice-Haunted Journey,* a narrative constituted by the thematic threads made up of art, ancestry, and fate. His grandfather died in 1957 at the age of eighty-one, just two years before Martínez graduated from the University of Texas at Austin with a bachelor of fine arts in painting, the result of all those attempts, in his early youth, at drawing Mexican soldiers.

This early biographical account corresponds, in a striking manner, to a motif in Chicano literature: namely, the recurrent figure of a precocious male child—either firstborn, only son, or youngest of siblings—who, having either illiterate or Spanish monolingual parents, eventually feels different from them, resulting in the questioning of his ancestry and in the frequent adoption of a mentor figure. Since these mentors are by definition none other than idealized parent surrogates (powerful, wise, caring), some form of spiritual bond is immediately established between the hero and the mentor. In *Voice-Haunted Journey* this relation is predetermined between the main character, Miguel Velásquez—a middle-aged Chicano professor and artist who considers himself a failed scholar—and his grandfather, whose name is the same, who looks identical, and who also writes notebooks, but who fights in the Mexican Revolution of 1910 (therefore his mythical greatness in the grandson's eyes). But since the adoption of a surrogate parent implies a prior or simultaneous symbolical act of patri(matri)cide, most of these fictional characters, when incorporated to a reading of Freud's analysis of the family romance, will manifest a cluster of fixations associated with melancholia, remorse, and a feeling of "not being good enough," as expressed in the often-quoted "Poem for the Young White Man . . . " (1981), by Lorna Dee Cervantes.

In 1953, at eighteen and after one year at the University of Texas at Austin, where he majored in studio arts, Martínez left school and joined the Marine Corps, where he served until 1956. He was stationed in Japan and in Hawaii for almost two years and, as with other Mexicans in the U.S. military, returned a different man after being away from home. He enrolled at the University of Texas and graduated in 1959 with a B.F.A. and a minor in art history and criticism.

At the university he met Dr. Donald L. Weisman, who changed Martínez's mind regarding commercial art and who would become a mentor and a close friend, meeting frequently with him to discuss art, criticism, literature, and the life of an artist. Martínez admits that, thanks to

Martínez in 1952, when he graduated from Stephen F. Austin High School in Austin, Texas

Dr. Weisman's encouragement, he began for the first time in his life to reflect on the possibility of studying toward a Ph.D., a degree that was considered out of range for most Mexican-Americans. According to Martínez, "his faith in me has borne fruit." The friendship and correspondence between Martínez and Dr. Weisman continues to this day. When Martínez's planned trilogy, "The Notebooks of Miguel Velásquez," is completed, it will be dedicated to Dr. Weisman.

Just before graduating from the University of Texas, Martínez was involved as a key figure in a dramatic protest over the attempt by Texas legislators, in their opposition to alleged atheism in the college classroom, to put university faculty under oath regarding their belief in a supreme being. Martínez and a group of friends (students who participated in conversations almost daily at a tavern near campus) planned to stage a protest with Martínez as a Christ figure wearing, according to an article appearing in the Fort Worth *Star Telegram* (26 February 1959), "skimpy white cloth strips that covered his midsection and wearing a crude mesquite-thorn crown." Martínez's class-mates did not show up as agreed; nonetheless he went ahead with the plans on his own. Just before the one-man demonstration, the dean of student life warned Martínez, under threat of expulsion, not to protest; Martínez is quoted in the newspaper article as having declared, "I'm doing this in protest against legislative control of values," responding to the dean's warning with a firm "I've got to." The newspaper photographs reveal an ironic, self-assured, twenty-four-year-old Mexican Christ with a generous crop of curly black hair, a full beard and hairy chest—more of a Dionysus than a Christ—surrounded by hundreds of Anglo faces—students, faculty, and puzzled local police—betraying their amazement and disbelief. In Martínez's memory, this episode is "one of the beautiful things that happened in my life.'"

Martínez was not expelled from the university, even though the newspaper article declared a link between the local political demonstration and enthusiasm for Fidel Castro and the recent Cuban revolution, proof and vital evidence being Martínez's exuberant beard. This was followed by an intense period of national attention for Martínez ('I felt like a god," he recalls), who received thousands of letters of support and attended meetings with state legislators. Then came another qualitative leap in Martínez's destiny: at the tavern Martínez frequented, months after the protest, he met Dr. Eastin Nelson, director of the Latin American Studies Institute at the university. After recognizing Martínez as the cross-carrying Mexican student, Nelson encouraged him to apply for an E. D. Farmer International Scholarship. Martínez applied, was granted the scholarship, and found himself suddenly swept south to Mexico City for two years of intellectual turmoil and self-discovery: he was going back to the emotional center of his grandfather's memories.

Martínez studied at the Universidad Nacional Autónoma de México, where he remained for two consecutive scholarship terms in 1960 and 1961. At this institution Martínez studied history and criticism of Mexican art under distinguished Mexican professors, such as Dr. Francisco de la Maza and Dr. Justino Fernández; in addition, he audited classes given by Dr. Edmundo O'Gorman, one of Mexico's leading (and polemically brilliant) intellectual historians. Martínez then turned to extensive studies of Nahuatl culture in courses taught by Dr. Miguel León-Portilla, Mexico's foremost Nahuatl scholar. Like Carlos Fuentes before him, in this trip to Mexico, Martínez became Mexican by the power of his will, imagination, and his extensive studies.

In 1962 Martínez accepted a teaching assistantship in art history at the University of Illinois at Champaign-Urbana, where he became disillusioned with the academic emphasis on narrow specialization. With Dr. Weisman—painter, poet, novelist, filmmaker, art historian, and critic—as a model, Martínez sought after a different pedagogical future; even his two-year sojourn in Mexico had exposed him to professors whose broad scope in intellectual vision had deeply impressed him. As a result, Martínez's residence at the University of Illinois was brief. He recalls making an irreverent comment during the final examination in January 1963, confessing openly to the teacher, "I would rather go back to waiting on tables or washing dishes, rather than take classes with people like you." At twenty-eight, Martínez became a college dropout; he remembers having lived an intensely dissolute and bohemian life in Chicago (this life-style appears to have been only part-time, for he worked first in a bank, then as assistant director of an art gallery). From Chicago Martínez moved to New York, where he met Elisse Weintraub. They married on 25 December 1965.

Throughout these years of "counterculture," Martínez read widely and wrote extensively long letters to Dr. Weisman (at times three per week). Those letters evolved into the writing of his "notebooks" which, over the years, would turn into *Voice-Haunted Journey*. What followed was a progressive return to semiabandoned goals: travels and a professional vocation. In September 1966 Martínez and Elisse embarked on a long journey to Europe, traveling in a Volkswagen throughout most of the Continent. They returned to the United States the following summer with Martínez making preparations to fulfill his university goals. He enrolled at Ohio University at Athens in 1969, receiving his doctorate in 1975 in English and comparative literature. His dissertation reveals his interdisciplinary interests: art, criticism, literature, and history. As testimony of his cultural ancestry, his dissertation focused on the work of a Mexican writer known as the founder of the novel of the Mexican Revolution: Mariano Azuelo.

By the time Martínez completed his career objectives, he was already the father of two daughters, Laura, born 1968, and Tanya, born 1970;

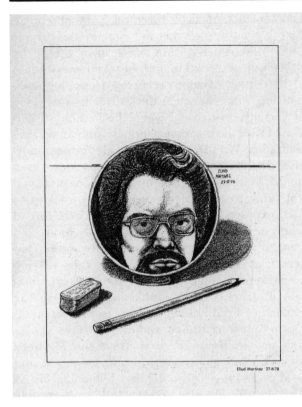

Eliud Martinez 27-8-78

Invitation—with a 1978 self-portrait of Martínez—to an exhibition of his artwork

suddenly the passing of time seemed swift to the Chicano polyglot from the eastside barrio who now had turned into a middle-aged paterfamilias, a university professor, but with no chosen pathway regarding his own artistic expression. With lingering voices of his grandfather—who wrote notebooks about his own haunted past in the revolution—Martínez began to think seriously of being a novelist himself.

In 1972 Martínez started his full-time teaching career at the University of California, Riverside, with a joint appointment—in Chicano studies, where he served as chair (1983-1985), and in comparative literature, where he was coordinator (1975-1977, and in 1987). When he arrived at Riverside, he had just lost a brother: on 23 November 1971 Teodoro died at the age of 35, a loss that had a lasting impact on Martínez, represented in the first paragraph of *Voice-Haunted Journey*. After Teodoro's funeral, and while visiting the Mexican cemetery in Pflugerville, the idea of writing a novel gathered momentum in Martínez's life. From beginning to completion, writing his novel and notebooks became an all-consuming activity. Martínez's problem was not the conventional "writer's block" but instead writing too much; yet, he was unable to find a beginning.

In 1979, during a troublesome tenure decision at the University of California, Riverside, Martínez returned to Pflugerville's Mexican cemetery to visit his brother's grave: "The beauty of childhood," he recalls, "came back to console me." This episode forms the conclusion in *Voice-Haunted Journey*, where one reads that Miguel Velásquez has the sudden revelation of how to begin his novel: with a brother's imaginary resurrection. A few months later, on 1 July 1979, Martínez was granted tenure. In the novel Martínez's masterful handling of narrative techniques, sophisticated characterization, and interdisciplinary breadth—with its numerous references, allusions and extended meditations on painting, film, and literature—is intellectually gratifying and a veritable quarry for literary critics who enjoy hermetic narratives.

A retrospective consideration of Martínez's scholarly work—such as his publications on Rodolfo "Corky" Gonzales, Carlos Fuentes, and, more specifically, on Mariano Azuela—sketches a well-planned theoretical exploration that evolves from the selected scholarly research represented by these essays to the full-blown aesthetic creativity represented by the novel. An example of the strategic importance that Martínez's studies in Mexico have had in his novelistic maturation is his own appropriation of José Ortega y Gasset's concept of "la altura de los tiempos" (the height of the times), paraphrased by Martínez in *The Art of Mariano Azuela* (1980) as "the intellectual and spiritual potentialities which prevail during any given historical period." His analysis of three modernist novels by Azuela is driven by the intent to question the judgment of Mexican literary critics that the first "modern" Mexican novelist is Agustín Yáñez, best known for his novel *Al filo del agua* (The Edge of the Storm, 1947); the premises of Martínez's argument are fully presented through an examination of Azuela's narrative techniques, particularly in his handling of the narrative vision which, according to Martínez, marks in Azuela's novelistic production "his main contribution to the twentieth century novel of consciousness."

The oppositional force of Martínez's scholarly work appears also in *Voice-Haunted Journey*, questioning, for instance, the political privileging in Chicano cultural discourse of only one ancestral past, be it Indian or Spanish, over and against the reality of modern Mexico, which is multiracial and multicultural, a nation which is, in Martínez's words (alluding to Carlos Fuentes's prior evaluation) "a thousand countries with a single name." Shortly before this phrase, one reads:

> Everywhere the living history of Mexico, the past alive in the present, surrounded him, confirmed in him once more a deep and abiding love of ancestry, travel, books and history. The names of streets, the ancient and colonial monuments, conjured up layer upon layer of the Mexican past, layer upon layer of Mexican thought and consciousness. The faces of the people, dark and fair, Indian, mestizo, Mediterranean, Arabic and Jewish, all spoke to him of a living past reaching far back in time.

Voice-Haunted Journey is a novel about a Chicano university professor who travels from southern California to the Bay Area, with plans to resume research at the University of California, Berkeley, library on formerly abandoned scholarly projects dealing with Edgar Allan Poe, Federico Fellini, Luis Buñuel, and Ingmar Bergman. The novel turns into an intricate account of the remembrances and self-introspection that take place in Miguel Velásquez's guilt-ridden mind during a forty-eight-

Eliud Martínez

minute flight to the Oakland Airport. Martínez has chosen the metaphor of travel to be the all-governing principle in his first novel, with the mythical Odysseus as a foregrounding figure.

Towering above the various discourses that crisscross the narrative, the lucid Miguel Velásquez has the existential obsession of expressing himself through a novel that he hopes will be filmed. This thematic dimension foregrounds a psychological polarity that thrusts him into moments of creativity (painting, writing notebooks, teaching) or, on the contrary, on to long periods of boredom, governed by the requirements of academic bureaucratic life with its innumerable committee meetings, petty power struggles (and the memos), alongside the futility of purposeless scholarly research.

The forty-eight-minute flight of Miguel Velásquez, covering 255 pages of narrative, takes off on different mental directions as the traveler tries to think of a way to begin his novel. The narrative tempo is lingering and reiterative, with the first 30 pages narrating the preparations for take-off; then, ten minutes pass between pages 30 to 133, followed by a faster temporal movement between pages 133 to 253, with thirty-eight minutes elapsing in the course of 120 pages. This journey takes place at different temporal and narrative levels, with the most obvious being in the present (a flight towards the Oakland Airport), driven by an obsession of a future project (the writing of a novel); secondly, the narration recollects remote memories of a trip to Europe with Miguel's wife; and thirdly, it is set in a recent past with lamenting memories of a brother's funeral ("his brother's death was announced in a dream"), with which the novel begins, returns to intermittently throughout the narration, and ends. The journey, consequently, reconciles the ambitions and self-doubts of the artist-professor with a family network that gives an extended meaning to his life. The telescoping of time in the narration serves only as a structural feature that hints at the psychological and intellectual depths of the novel.

When completed, the trilogy planned as "The Notebooks of Miguel Velásquez" will include two other novels, namely: "The Obstinate Blood" and "The Joint Appointment." This trilogy, Martínez reveals, "is a mixture of memories and lived experiences, fact and fantasy, fiction and dream, reflection and social commentary, historical and artistic interpretation." Much like other Chicano writers before him, Martínez's first novel was rejected by major eastern publishers, yet he did not give up; he rewrote parts of the novel, sent the manuscript to Bilingual Press, and got it published in 1990. In that same year, Martínez received a UC-MEXUS Creative Activities Grant that allowed him to work in the writing of "The Obstinate Blood." Martínez has written a novel in Spanish, entitled "La sangre hace su deber" (Blood Fulfills Its Duty); according to Martínez, it is a Spanish version of "The Obstinate Blood." This novel will be published by the Universidad Nacional Autónoma de México as part of its Chicano literature series entitled "Colección Rayuela." These are heightened times for Eliud Martínez: after twenty years of writing notebooks and an "unmanageable" novel, he has found the beginning that evaded him for so long, transforming it into an impressive literary debut.

José Montoya

(28 May 1932 -   )

Luis Leal
University of California, Santa Barbara

BOOKS: *El sol y los de abajo and Other R.C.A.F. Poems* (San Francisco: Pocho-Che, 1972);
Pachuco Art: A Historical Update (Sacramento, Cal.: Royal Chicano Air Force, 1977);
Thoughts on la Cultura, the Media, Con Safos and Survival (San Francisco: Galería de la Raza/Studio 24, 1979).

RECORDING: *Casindio-Chicano Music All Day*, Sacramento, Cal., Nonantzin, 1985.

OTHER: "Pobre viejo Walt Whitman," "El vendido," "Sunstruck While Chopping Cotton," "Lazy Skin," "In a Pink Bubble Gum World," "Los vatos," "La jefita," "Resonant Valley," and "La cantinera de Stockton," in *El Espejo / The Mirror*, edited by Octavio I. Romano and Herminio Ríos (Berkeley, Cal.: Quinto Sol, 1969), pp. 180-192;
"Forgive," in *A Mark in Time*, edited by Nick Harvey (San Francisco: Glide, 1971), p. 81;
"El Louie," in *Literatura chicana, texto y contexto / Chicano Literature, Text and Context*, edited by Antonia Castañeda-Schular, Tomás Ybarra-Frausto, and Joseph Sommers (Englewood Cliffs, N.J.: Prentice-Hall, 1972), pp. 173-176;
"Don't Ever Lose Your Driver's License," in *Giant Talk: An Anthology of Third World Writings*, edited by Quincy Troupe and Rainer Schulte (New York: Vintage, 1975), pp. 168-169;
"The People's Representative (A Song to People Afraid of Success)," "El veterano," "They Sent Men to Match Mountains," and "Until They Leave Us a Loan . . . As Related to Me by Elías, alias Eelye," in *Flor y Canto IV & V, An Anthology of Chicano Literature from the Festivals Held in Albuquerque, New Mexico, 1977 and Tempe, Arizona, 1978* (Albuquerque: Pajarito/Flor y Canto V Committee, 1980), pp. 102-108;
"Se fue Ricardo," "El barrio en enero," "Faltan quince pa las cuatro," and "Soledad," in *Antología histórica y literaria*, edited by Tino Villanueva (Mexico City: Fondo de Cultura Económica, 1980), pp. 322-325;
"Chicano Art: Resistance in Isolation: Aquí estamos y no nos vamos," in *Missions in Conflict: Essays on U.S.-Mexican Relations and Chicano Culture*, edited by Renate von Bardeleben, Dietrich Briesemeister, and Juan Bruce-Novoa (Tübingen, Germany: Narr, 1986), pp. 25-30;
"Pobre viejo Walt Whitman," "Sunstroke While Chopping Cotton," "El Louie," "Los vatos," "La jefita," and "The Trilogy Poems, I," in *Contemporary Chicano Poetry*, edited by Wolfgang Binder (Erlangen, Germany: Palm & Enke, 1986), pp. 106-118.

SELECTED PERIODICAL PUBLICATIONS—UNCOLLECTED: "Portfolio 5," *El Grito*, 2 (Spring 1969): 48-57;
"Rupert García and the San Francisco Museum of Modern Art," *Rayas*, 2 (March-April 1979): 5, 11.

The well-known poet and artist José Montoya, a third-generation New Mexican, was born on 28 May 1932 on El Gallego ranch, and his birth was registered in the town of Escoboza, in the Manzano mountains south of Albuquerque. His paternal ancestors had come to New Mexico during the nineteenth century from Parral, in the state of Chihuahua in northern Mexico. His mother's family, the Saezes (Saez being a contraction of Sáenz, according to Montoya), had come from Chihuahua about the same time. His grandfather, also named José Montoya, and the poet's father were born in Tierra Amarilla, New Mexico, the town made famous in Chicano literature by Sabine R. Ulibarrí. The young Montoya's maternal grandfather, Santiago Saez, had a farm in the same region.

In 1937, when Montoya was five years old, he moved with his family to Martíneztown, in the

El Sol Y Los De Abajo
and other R.C.A.F. poems
por JOSE MONTOYA

Cover for José Montoya's first book (1972), which includes poems based on his experiences with the Rebel Chicano Art Front, a group he helped found in Sacramento in 1970

central part of Albuquerque, and there he attended elementary school. In 1941 the family moved again, this time to California, where they lived at the Sierra Vista Ranches, near Delano. About the change from New Mexico to California, Montoya has said (in his interview with Wolfgang Binder), "To me it was a very exciting thing; . . . it was first of all, a land far, far away from where we had come from, where I was born; it was a long ways from the kind of landscape and environment that I was used to in New Mexico. For the first time . . . [I saw] the landscape shrouded in fog every morning." The Montoyas' stay at Sierra Vista was a short one: "in '42, when my younger sister was born, we were already in Delano, the town. And . . . I started going to school. I had already started school in Albuquerque in the first grade, so I re-

membered my first experiences in terms of going to a school."

Because of World War II Montoya's father decided to move to Oakland, where members of the immediate family and relatives began to work in the defense plants. For José living in a big city was a new and exciting experience: "in Oakland suddenly I was in a big city and had not even seen San Francisco. . . . I wanted to find what everything was all about." From Oakland he was sent to New Mexico to finish school, and his family joined him there in 1945: "We remained in New Mexico for at least a year and then [went] back to California. . . . After '46 we stayed in the San Joaquín Valley." Soon after his parents separated and his father went back to New Mexico, José's mother insisted that they settle down, in order for the children to obtain an education.

They settled in Fowler, California, and Montoya went to high school for three years, graduating in 1951. There he was encouraged to write, especially by one of his teachers, Adrian Sanford. Upon graduating, he joined the navy and served on a minesweeper in Korea.

After the Korean War, Montoya married and then worked in a San Diego window company for a few years. His interest in art led him to attend San Diego City College, where he received an associate of arts degree in 1956. Three years later he was awarded an art scholarship to the California College of Arts and Crafts in Oakland, where he received a B.A. in art education in 1962. That same year he began to teach at Wheatland High School (Wheatland, California). In 1970 he moved to Sacramento, where he helped found the Rebel Chicano Art Front (RCAF), humorously called, because of the acronym, the Royal Chicano Air Force. He continued to teach art and train art teachers at California State University, Sacramento, the institution from which he received his M.F.A. in 1971, and where he has been teaching in the Department of Art Education since 1970, as an assistant professor until 1974, as an associate professor until 1981, and as a full professor since that year. In 1970, in Sacramento, he began the successful program "Art in the Barrio." He taught art education during the summer of 1974 at Universidad Anáhuac in Mexico City, and in 1976 at Deguanawidah Quetzalcóatl, the Chicano-Indian University that was established near Davis, California, but which did not survive. He continued to write and paint, and became interested in popular music. He has excelled in several creative endeavors; as a painter and graphic artist he has had exhibits in New York, Mexico, Cuba, and Paris. His interest in music led him to organize, in September of 1983, his own musical group, the Trío Casindio. He is the father of six children. His wife, Mary, has been active as a community liaison for the barrio school of Sacramento.

Although he had been writing poetry for several years, it was not until 1969 that he began to publish poems. At a Chicano art exhibit in San Francisco in 1968 he had met Octavio Romano, who had heard about his poetry and asked him for some to be published in *El Grito*, one of the first contemporary Chicano journals. According to Montoya (in his interview with Juan Bruce-Novoa), Romano liked the poetry "and decided to hold it for *El Espejo*, the anthology. That's how I first got into print. *Espejo* came out [in 1969]

and I started to be known, give readings and all that. But I had been writing for a long time before then."

The anthology included nine of his poems, among them "La jefita" (The Dear Mother), one of his best-known compositions. In 1977 his work was recognized with a grant from the California Arts Council; in 1979 with a Writer's Fellowship from California State University, Sacramento; and in 1981 with a National Endowment for the Arts Writing Fellowship. Since 1980 he has been affiliated with the Crocker Art Museum Association and the Sacramento Metropolitan Arts Commission; during the period from 1980 to 1984 he served as a board member of the Washington Neighborhood Center in San Francisco.

Montoya has said that his writing has been influenced mostly by American authors. When he was in the navy he read John Steinbeck's *Tortilla Flat* (1935), a novel he rejected. But at San Diego City College he discovered and appreciated some of the other works of Steinbeck; Montoya told Bruce-Novoa that Steinbeck "couldn't write anything on Chicanos; but he could write." At Berkeley, Montoya read the poetry of Walt Whitman and William Carlos Williams, two poets whose works he enjoyed: "The one I could relate to most was William Carlos Williams. I liked the way he wrote, so I made an effort to find his work." Among Montoya's first published poems there is one dedicated to Whitman, "Pobre viejo Walt Whitman" (Poor Old Walt Whitman). Montoya also read, and heard recited, the poetry of the Beat poets, with whom he sympathized. However, he says, "They were so far out that it took the works of [T. S.] Eliot and [Ezra] Pound as well as Whitman and Williams to get me to accept their stuff early on. Now I consider them to have been an influence, especially [Gary] Snyder and [Allen] Ginsberg." At that time he also read French authors, among them Paul Verlaine, Arthur Rimbaud—who greatly impressed him—Jean-Paul Sartre, and Albert Camus, as well as some European philosophers (Søren Kierkegaard, Martin Heidegger, and Karl Jaspers).

In Montoya's first published poems, in *El Espejo*, he was mostly writing under the influence of Whitman. As Montoya has said (in the Binder interview), Whitman was the first poet to show him "that you did not have to rhyme and [use] meter, and I really, really liked him. When I was in Berkeley, I read the entire *Leaves of Grass* [1855]." After the first poem in Montoya's series, about Whitman, the other poems deal with the

Chicano experience. In the second poem, "El vendido" (The Sellout), he laments the preoccupation of some Chicanos with the good life:

From the pain
That hurts my Raza
Concerned now
With boats in the
Driveway, The Boy Scouts
    And the World Series.

About the poem "Sunstruck While Chopping Cotton," written in the early 1960s, Montoya has said (to Binder) that it deals with an experience he had at an early age in Hanford, California: "I had suffered sunstroke. I was on a water wagon that was all metal, and it was hot, and I was handing water to the workers. And the last thing I knew, I toppled. There were some very, very interesting hallucinations that went through my delirium." In 1963, during his second year teaching high school, he was able to structure those early images, and the poem was created. It is based principally on two motifs, the desert and the sea:

It was at first a single image.
A mirage-like illusional dance
. . . .
Not one but three Bothisattvas
Suspended in a cloud of yellow dust
Just above the rows of cotton
Galloping comically on skeletal mounts
Across the arid, sponge-like lust
Of a desiccated desert.
. . . .
They ride . . .
To the distant sea.
The cool sea.

In "La jefita," one of Montoya's most anthologized poems, he creates the image of a Chicana mother as being the backbone of the family, tirelessly working to keep the household going. The image of the *jefita* is vividly rendered by the use of onomatopoeic verses reflecting the never-ending activities of the hardworking *jefita* (literally, "little boss"). The use of English and Spanish, a technique at which Montoya is a master, is quite effective in this poem:

When I remember the campos
    y las noches [and the nights] and the sounds
of those nights en carpas [tents] o
vagones [freight cars] I remember my jefita's
    Palote [rolling pin]
    Clik-clok; clik-clak-clok

Y su tosecita [And her tiny cough]
(I swear, she never slept!)
. . . .
That woman—she only complains
in her sleep.

Two of the other poems, "Resonant Valley" and "La cantinera de Stockton" (Stockton's Barmaid), are also based on personal experiences in the fields and the barrio. In "Los vatos" (The Dudes) Montoya for the first time introduces a pachuco, a popular character in Chicano society during the 1940s and 1950s; later a pachuco was to be the subject of Montoya's best-known poem, "El Louie" (1972). The most striking formal characteristics of "Los vatos" are the long verse form; the prose introduction ("Back in the early fifties el Chonito and I were on the way to the bote [jail] when we heard the following dialogue"); and the dramatic narrative structure ("I sing of an unfortunate act of that epoch.") When questioned about this poem, Montoya told Binder that he had known pachucos in Albuquerque when he was a boy, and therefore he could write about them and paint them: "I have probably done more on the pachuco in the art than I have in the writing. . . . I think [of] *El Louie* and *Los vatos*, and maybe some of the language that I use in the poetry. But I think those are the only two times that I used the pachuco."

"El Louie" was an immediate success and has been widely anthologized and analyzed, especially by Bruce-Novoa and Ignacio Orlando Trujillo. Montoya writes about what he has experienced. He had known the model for Louie: a *vato* from Fowler, California, named Louie Rodríguez. According to Bruce-Novoa, "El Louie" is not only the most popular short Chicano poem but also the best:

"El Louie" is an interlingual elegy to Louie Rodríguez. . . . Louie, the epitome of the positive pachuco, rejects opportunities to ingress into the majority society and finally dies, a drug addict alone in a rented room. [The poem's] essential theme, the threat of disappearance, and its deep structure . . . are those of Chicano literature itself, and "El Louie" is thus an excellent paradigm of that literature.

In the late 1960s Montoya, as a poet, underwent a change. He decided to abandon Whitman and other learned poets and write in a popular vein, more like the Beat poets, making a more extensive use of Spanish and the language of the Chicano people and giving more importance to social issues. The result was the poetry included in his first published book, *El sol y los de Abajo* (The Sun and the Underdogs, 1972), a collection of twenty-four poems (three of them entirely in Spanish) published together with *Oración a la mano poderosa* (Oration to the Powerful Hand), by Alejandro Murguía, in a back-to-back edition illustrated by Armando Cide. Montoya's title poem, in seven parts, re-creates a Chicano world from the perspective of an underdog, from the time he is born until the moment he realizes that there is a way out of his miserable condition. Although the way out is not shown, at the end of the poem a note of hope is expressed. Like other Chicano writers of the period, Montoya derives inspiration from the philosophy of the ancient Mayan people:

But Chilam Balam's prophetic
Chant has been realized—and the
Dust that darkened the air begins
To clear y se empieza a ver el Sol [and the sun
  begins to show]
          I AM LEARNING TO SEE THE SUN.

The change that takes place, from despair to optimism, is symbolized by the sun.

The rest of the compositions in Montoya's 1972 collection contain the elements that, according to Bruce-Novoa, distinguish Montoya's poetry from that of other Chicano poets:

What is conveyed in Montoya's poetry, besides the balanced sense of healthy objectivity, is the natural, down-to-earth tone of a sincere, candid man. Everything in Montoya rings natural. His poetry flows like spontaneous speech. And . . . Montoya is the master, utilizing the two languages as smoothly as if they were one.

As a graphic artist, Montoya has been influenced by the Mexican engraver José Guadalupe Posada, as well as the muralists Diego Rivera, José Clemente Orozco, and David Alfaro Siqueiros. In 1975, with the collaboration of John M. Carrillo, Montoya wrote an unpublished paper about Posada, in which he includes a comparative analysis of his work and that of the Chicano art movement, as well as some notes about the influence of Posada's works on Chicano art.

In Montoya's paintings, as in his poetry, his subject matter is drawn from life in the barrio, and from the experiences of the Chicano people in their struggle for a better life. His close association with the community has inspired him to express on canvas not only the sufferings but also the aspirations of the people he knows and loves to the point of sacrificing himself to help them. As he says in his essay *Thoughts on la Cultura* (1979), "whatever training we may have or will acquire in the future has to be directed towards supporting and contributing to the struggle of our people rather than for our own interests."

The reception of Montoya's poetry and art by the public and critics alike has been quite favorable. He has been able to impress the critics with his rich depiction of life in the barrio and, especially, with his vindication of the pachuco and his culture, a theme later adapted for other media (film, theater, and the novel) by Luis Valdez and others. As Charles M. Tatum says in his reference to *El sol y los de abajo*, Montoya's heroes are "the *vatos locos* [crazy dudes] who are rejected by many of their own people and harassed by Anglos who do not understand their rebelliousness." Tatum also points out Montoya's use of humor and satire: "The poet takes a humorously irreverent swipe at different aspects of what he considers to be a society that alienates the individual."

Montoya's "El Louie" has been highly praised by most critics, since they find in it the essence of the personality of the pachuco. Carl R. Shirley considers it "one of the most famous poems about the zoot-suiter." Trujillo, in his extensive study of the linguistic aspects of this poem, observes that "El Louie," along with other poetic works of the 1960s, "is a key composition in the revival of mass interest in Chicano poetry and the resurgence of its writers. Not only has it been anthologized in various collections, but it has also been recited and dramatized because of its popular oral and visual quality." "El Louie" is not, of course, the only poem by Montoya worthy of study; that it has attracted the attention of the critics is perhaps due to its subject matter, the life of a pachuco, as well as the masterfully integrated use of English and Spanish.

"El Louie" and the rest of the poetic and artistic works of José Montoya are representative of the nature of Chicano literature and art that emerged during the first decade of the Chicano renaissance (1965-1975). Montoya, like other writers and artists of that period, is both a man of letters and an activist. His main interest is to place art and literature at the service of the people. For him, the function of art is social, and therefore it should be used to help the people and to vindicate their history and their cultural values. In this sense it is like the art and literature that appeared in Mexico as an aftermath of the revolution. Montoya, along with Rodolfo "Corky" Gonzales, Sergio Elizondo, Ricardo Sánchez, Luis Omar Salinas, and others, formed part of a group of writers that pioneered the renaissance of Chicano poetry. Their contributions to Chicano culture constitute a high point in the development of Chicano intellectual and artistic life during that most important decade.

Interviews:

Francisco A. Lomelí, *Voces Chicanas: José Montoya* [videocassette], Santa Barbara, Cal., Center for Chicano Studies, 1979;

Juan Bruce-Novoa, "José Montoya," in his *Chicano Authors: Inquiry by Interview* (Austin: University of Texas Press, 1980), pp. 114-136;

Wolfgang Binder, "José Montoya," in *Partial Autobiographies: Interviews with Twenty Chicano Poets*, edited by Binder (Erlangen, Germany: Palm & Enke, 1985), pp. 117-135.

Bibliography:

Arte Chicano: A Comprehensive Annotated Bibliography of Chicano Art, 1965-1981, compiled by Shifra M. Goldman and Tomás Ybarra-Frausto (Berkeley: University of California, Chicano Studies Library Publications, 1985), pp. 478-480.

References:

Juan Bruce-Novoa, "José Montoya's El Louie," in his *Chicano Poetry, A Response to Chaos* (Austin: University of Texas Press, 1982), pp. 14-25;

Katheryn M. Fong, "*Pachuco Art* Records Era of Zootsuits and Anti-Mexican Riots," *San Francisco Journal*, 1 March 1978, p. 6;

Alfred Frankenstein, "Montoya's Artistic Update on Chicano Zoot Suiters," *San Francisco Chronicle*, 18 February 1978, p. 36;

Robert G. Lint, "Art in Montoya's Resonant Valley," *Luz*, 4 (March-April 1975): 40;

Sharon MacLatchie, "Art in the Barrio: One Man's Commitment," *Luz*, 3 (December 1974): 17-18;

"R.C.A.F., Artistas precursores del arte chicano," *Hispano*, 8 (17 February 1976): 1;

Carl R. Shirley and Paula W. Shirley, *Understanding Chicano Literature* (Columbia: University of South Carolina Press, 1988), pp. 22, 48;

Ignacio Orlando Trujillo, "Linguistic Structures in José Montoya's *El Louie*," *Atisbos*, 3 (Summer-Fall 1978): 20-24; abridged in *Modern Chicano Writers*, edited by Joseph Sommers and Tomás Ybarra-Frausto (Englewood Cliffs, N.J.: Prentice-Hall, 1979), pp. 150-159.

Dorinda Moreno
(8 August 1939 -   )

María Teresa Márquez
University of New Mexico

BOOKS: *Las cucarachas* (N.p., n.d.);
The Image of the Chicana, and the La Raza Woman (Stanford: Moreno, 1975);
La mujer es la tierra: La tierra da vida (San Francisco: Casa Editorial, 1975).

RECORDING: *Chicano Art: A Renaissance*, includes poems read by Moreno, North Hollywood, Cal., Center for Cassette Studies, 1974.

OTHER: *La mujer: En pie de lucha, y la hora es ya*, edited, with contributions, by Moreno (Mexico City: Espina del Norte, 1973).

SELECTED PERIODICAL PUBLICATIONS—
UNCOLLECTED: "Canto a una Rosa," *Café Solo*, 8 (Spring 1974): 27;
"Eres la tierra" and "Viva Mexico: 'Canta y no llores,'" *Horizontes* (October 1985): 10-12.

Dorinda Moreno is a natural organizer and leader endowed with boundless energy and caring for people; she is also a poet and writer. Born on 8 August 1939 in Half Moon Bay, California, and raised in San Francisco and Mountain View, Moreno is still connected to strong Indo-Mexican roots in New Mexico. The mother of two daughters and a son, she now has three grandchildren. The third oldest in a family of eight brothers and sisters, Moreno grew up with an extended family of over two hundred members that included Garays, Martínezes, Espinozas, Bustillos, and Navarros. Early on, Moreno shouldered the responsibility of helping her mother and father in raising her younger brothers and sisters. Her parents were migrant farm workers up until the time Moreno was twelve; afterward her father worked as a gardener in San Francisco for twenty-eight years. His work experiences were the basis for some of Moreno's short stories, including "Zorbe el Tree," which she collected in her 1973 anthology, *La mujer: En pie de lucha, y la*

hora es ya (The Woman: On a Footing of Struggle, and the Hour Is Now).

Moreno's early childhood dream, as she moved from school to school, was to become a writer. Her later interests in history, social activism, and human development were stimulated by one of her aunts who had a tubercular lung removed, without anesthesia, at age thirteen. Aunt Lupe, bedridden, would read and talk to Moreno about Babe Zaharias Didrikson, Amelia Earhart, Helen Gahagan Douglass, and other heroes. Because Moreno regarded her high-school education as less than satisfactory, she enrolled in the American Correspondence School, the John Adams Adult School, and Los Angeles City College. A term in Don's Beauty School came two years after she attended Mission High School. Afterward, at age twenty-nine and with three children to raise, Moreno became a student at San Francisco State University, where she earned a B.A. in women's studies. Subsequently Moreno entered the M.A. program in journalism and communications for social change at Stanford University in 1974 but did not complete the degree. From 1972 to 1977, besides teaching courses in philosophy, history, journalism, theater writing, and Chicana studies at Napa College, Ohlone College, and San Francisco State University, Moreno founded or directed cultural groups such as Las Cucarachas-Mexcla Teatral and Concilio Mujeres. Las Cucarachas gained a reputation as a performing arts group that provided emerging Chicano actors, writers, and poets a forum for their work. Concilio Mujeres served as an important and influential center of information for Chicanas and Latinas.

Moreno's poetry is a social action. Her work is centered on ethnic and cultural consciousness, and her poetry frequently expresses concern for the plight of women who find themselves in unjust and oppressive circumstances. *La mujer*, which includes representative works by various authors (including Moreno) denouncing the injustices committed against people of color, is a

Dorinda Moreno's Fiftieth Birthday
'Roast/Toast' Celebration

Cover for an invitation to a 1989 birthday party for Dorinda Moreno

prime example. The social and political character of Moreno and her work is apparent. She indicates in the introduction that she understands the struggle of "mujeres del movimiento" (women of the movement) and the importance of maintaining a cultural history. Further, her poetry strives to awaken a social consciousness in Chicana women. In her poems in the book Moreno reminds readers that women have endured repression for centuries, and Moreno raises her voice against the oppression of indigenous women by European Christians. Moreno easily shifts from ancient religions and goddesses to contemporary social and political issues in "Glide, Sway, Sleek Black Cat ... Angela!," "Calley OOPS!," and "Ché—On Wings of Youth," in which she focuses on themes of injustice, pacifism, and discrimination. While Moreno draws the readers' attention to the injustices suffered by people of color, she remains optimistic for a posi-

tive future, and Moreno is willing to work toward that future.

La mujer es la tierra: La tierra da vida (The Woman Is the Land: The Land Gives Life, 1975) is partially autobiographical, and it reflects another aspect of Moreno's writing; this collection of prose and poetry expresses love for her children, especially for her son, Andre, who is called "Blaxican" (mixed race). Dedicated to activists Frida Kahlo and Rosaura Revueltas, the collection affirms a strong liberation ideology and reflects recurring themes: the suppression of women, family, and love, and the call to activism by women. Often delving into her own experiences, Moreno urges women to take action to bring about change. Struggle is necessary because the Chicana's condition is marked by discrimination and injustices.

"La mujer y el arte" (The Woman and Art) is Moreno's homage to Kahlo and Revueltas, who were instrumental in creating changes—Kahlo through her artistic, social, and political activities that challenged barriers imposed on women, and Revueltas through her literary portrayal of a woman fighting for economic dignity. "Rostro" (Countenance), a poem dedicated to Kahlo and Revueltas, is Moreno's appeal to artists to depict women in positive images. Moreno deplores art that perpetuates certain negative images of women. In another poem, "Mujer la Raza," she calls on women to take action:

> Mujeres SHOUT OUT!!!
> the anger in our souls
> Renunciating all the wrongs endured
> Retaliating the unequivocable pain
> that cannot be justified
> Nor our thirst for righteousness be
> satisfied with unfulfilled promises
> by the oppressive society
> aided with the false pride of our men
> who wrongfully feel our place is
> only in the home. . . .

Throughout her poetry Moreno insists that women should not accept existing conditions but challenge them. Moreno's poems are predominantly in free-verse form; for example, "Stations of the Cross Roads / Never-Forgotten Paths" incorporates excerpts from popular Mexican songs and popular phrases. This poem expresses the bittersweetness of having a "Blaxican" son.

Moreno's poetry is rooted in self-identification and positive self-image. The code-switching in *La mujer: En pie de lucha, y la hora es ya* and *La mujer es la tierra* manifests her ties to Indo-Mexican heritage: "Today I speak their languages, both English and Spanish, but still I am neither, nor do I want to be. . . . I am Chicana." Moreno writes poetry in Spanish, English, and what she terms Pocho. However, her other writings, including her short stories, are predominantly in English.

Refusing silence, Moreno has claimed a right to speak and to offer her own evidence on the condition of the Chicana. She has articulated her opposition to social and political conditions that deny women the legitimate evidence of their experience and stereotype their stories and self-definitions. Moreno takes risks in shaping the cultural awareness of the Chicana experience and voice, struggling to remedy the lack of cultural support. Emerging Chicana writers who have read her work or listened to Moreno publicly read her poetry see her as a role model. Her influence is still seen in the work of Chicana writers. Although she does not write poetry anymore, Moreno's place in the development of Chicano literature is secured. She now devotes her time to writing film scripts and novels. Her commitment to the Chicana struggle remains undiminished.

Bibliography:

Julio Martínez, *Chicano Scholars and Writers: A Bio-Bibliographic Directory* (Metuchen, N.J.: Scarecrow, 1979), pp. 334-335.

References:

G. Dávila, "Entrevistando a Dorinda Moreno," *Horizontes* (March-April 1984): 5;

Francisco A. Lomelí and Donaldo W. Urioste, *Chicano Perspectives in Literature* (Albuquerque: Pajarito, 1976), p. 29;

"Sounds of Sadness, Sounds of Sorrow, Sounds of Strength," in *Festival de flor y canto*, edited by Alurista and others (Los Angeles: University of Southern California Press, El Centro Chicano, 1976), p. 125;

"Speaker: Chicanas Must Join 'Sisters, Brothers,'" *Fresno Bee*, 10 March 1982, p. B5;

"Those Who Live by the Word," *Caminos*, 2 (February 1981): 37-39.

Carlos Morton
(15 October 1942 -   )

M. Alicia Arrizón
Stanford University

BOOK: *The Many Deaths of Danny Rosales and Other Plays* (Houston: Arte Público, 1983).

PLAY PRODUCTIONS: *El Jardín*, Iowa City, University of Iowa, 1975;
Las Many Muertes de Danny Rosales, San Diego, University of California, 1976;
El Garden, San Diego, University of California, 1977;
Las Many Muertes de Richard Morales, San Diego, Teatro Mil Caras, 1977;
Los Dorados, San Diego, California-Pacific Theatre, 1978;
Rancho Hollywood, San Francisco, Teatro Gusto, 1980;
Johnny Tenorio, San Antonio, Tex., Centro Cultural de Aztlán, 1983;
Pancho Diablo, Los Angeles, University of California, 1984;
La Malinche, Austin, University of Texas, 1984;
The Savior, Seattle, Group Theatre, 1988.

SELECTED PERIODICAL PUBLICATION—
UNCOLLECTED: "El Cuento de Pancho Diablo," *Grito del Sol*, 1 (1976): 39-85.

photograph by Larry García

Carlos Morton is one of the main contributors to the development of Chicano drama. He is the recipient of several drama prizes, such as the one he received in 1986 at the Second National Latino Playwriting Contest. In 1989 he became a Fulbright lecturer at the Universidad Nacionale Autónoma de México for a year.

Born in Chicago, Illinois, on 15 October 1942, Morton is the son of Ciro and Helen López Morton. Because his father served in the U.S. Army, he traveled with his family all over the United States and Latin America. He has lived for extended periods of time in Chicago, New York, San Diego, San Francisco, Los Angeles, El Paso, and Mexico. He also lived a few years in Panama and Ecuador, where his father was stationed. His travels and his bicultural background are important forces in Morton's creative process of becoming a playwright. Being bicultural has made him search for a firm identity.

Morton received his B.A. in English from the University of Texas at El Paso in 1975 and an M.F.A. in 1979 from the University of California, San Diego. He married Azalea Marín in 1981, and they have three children: Miguel Angel, Carlos Xunchu, and Seth. From 1979 to 1981 Morton worked as a playwright with the San Francisco Mime Troupe and taught courses in Chicano drama and creative writing at the University

186

of California, Berkeley. In 1981 he entered the Ph.D. program in drama at the University of Texas at Austin, where he was employed as an assistant instructor until 1985. Morton became an important force in the Latino artistic community of Austin while working on his doctorate. He completed it in 1987 with a dissertation titled "Three Plays on the Latin Experience in America: Johnny Tenorio, Malinche, and The Savior." He taught drama for three years at Laredo Junior College in Texas. Currently he is an associate professor in the Department of Theatre at the University of California, Riverside.

When Morton received a scholarship in the mid 1970s to study drama at the University of California, San Diego, he dropped everything to become a full-time writer. Previously he had experimented with prose and poetry, but he settled on playwriting as an avocation after several of his plays were produced and published. He considers Chicano drama as the literature of the Mexican-American people, characterized by a spirit that reflects their hopes and aspirations. He deals with the questions of the identity, origin, and future of the different generations of Mexican immigrants. Myth, history, and religion, combined with a sardonic and humorous theatricality, characterize Morton's symbolic system of writing and the aesthetics of his theater. The elements of myth, history, and religion are essential to the sociocultural context, the most valuable aspect of his playwriting.

Two of Morton's early plays are theological comedies: *El Jardín* (The Garden, 1975), printed in *The Many Deaths of Danny Rosales and Other Plays* (1983); and *Pancho Diablo* (Frankie Devil, 1984—written in 1976). In the first one, the historical conquest of America parallels the loss of Paradise in the biblical story of Adam and Eve to show that humankind (and, in particular, Chicanos) has been oppressed since the creation of the universe. In *Pancho Diablo*, Morton represents good versus evil with God as a Texas Ranger and the Devil as a *vato loco* (crazy dude). The Devil appears with a mustache, sunglasses, huaraches, and a Mexican poncho. He has long, thick, black hair, which he wears with a headband across his forehead. He quits his job in hell in order to live the life of a common man. God is described as benevolent except when he takes on the role of a ranger—in popular culture the oppressor of Chicanos. God is described as a hip and unfathomable man with a Zapata mustache who smokes

Cuban cigars. He is able to assume many disguises.

In order to give a Mexican flavor to *Pancho Diablo*, Morton creates prototypes reminiscent of real characters. In this play, as in *El Jardín*, the dramatic action is developed by means of the absurdity and humorous scenes—presented in terms of concrete stage images. However, the various themes manifest different levels of the Chicano experience, both cultural and political. In both plays, oppression is dramatized in a totally illogical world:

PANCHO DIABLO: The masses no comprenden porque hemos secuestrado a Lee Treviño, ni comprenden porque estamos destruyendo los Taco Bells; no comprenden porque [do not comprehend because we have kidnapped Lee Trevino, nor do they comprehend because] they themselves are too tied up in the pinche [damn] sistema that each day enslaves them más [more].

ALL: Yaaaaaaaaaaaaaa.

PANCHO DIABLO: While Gringolandia is engaged in a bloody class and race war, movimientos de liberación [movements of liberation] throughout el mundo (the world) will rise up to attack the tentacles of the octopus. Nosotros que estamos aquí en la panza de la bestia [We who are here in the belly of the beast] must strike the first blow para La Libertad!

ALL: Yaaaaaaaaaaaaaa.

PANCHO DIABLO: Y ahora, quiero presentarles al Vato [And now, I want to introduce you to the Dude] who's going to make all this possible; mi amigo and yours, La Muerte [Death]!

ALL: Yaaaaaaaaaaaaaa.

LA MUERTE APPEARS IN CALAVERA [skeleton] COSTUME[.]

Morton's symbolic system breaks from what he perceives to be the dead ritual of Christianity in Chicano culture. He uses theater to reawaken the audience to the human ritual, acclaiming the desire for freedom and justice. Essential ingredients in Morton's plays are humor and satire. The purpose of these is to make one feel concerned for whomever they may represent in real life: oppressors and oppressed. Whether he treats mythical, religious, and social themes or presents human beings in search of liberation, there is always a sense of humor in the character, situations, and language, as in *El Jardín*:

> **SERPIENTE**: My little quesadilla, once you discover the wheel, you'll have the mechanics to build a marvelous civilization.
>
> **EVA**: Will my people acknowledge this? Will women be appreciated? (Thunder and lightening build in intensity)
>
> **SERPIENTE**: My little jalapeño, you will be worshiped, idolized, put on pedestals! Take a bite!

The code-switching from English to Spanish makes the humor even funnier. Most of the time the plot is a collage of suggested issues such as exploitation, liberation, assimilation, and racism that never get well developed in the dramatic trajectory. Nevertheless, what is important is the form of theater taking place: a comedy, where the theme of oppression becomes a sardonic metaphor for the represented universe. In the situation above, Eve is being convinced to eat the forbidden fruit by the Devil, the serpent. She eats it, and then she and her beloved man are expelled from Eden. The next scene transports the spectator to Chicago, Illinois, where Adam and Eve are living in middle-class comfort. The abrupt presentation of different situations makes the dramatic experience be the action of time, which is constant change: from one era to another, from one generation to the next one, from the old world to the new. While in these pieces the intention is to present anti-Christianity, with a satirical interpretation of Latin-American culture and its dogmatic doctrine, the entangled politics are just a reflection of the street-level sense of humor.

The Many Deaths of Danny Rosales and Other Plays comprises four plays: the title play, *Rancho Hollywood*, *Los Dorados* (The Golden Ones), and *El Jardín*. The title work (performed in 1976) is based on the true story of the 1975 killing of a man named Richard Morales by a police chief near a small Texas community. This event took place five miles outside Castroville, Texas. In the play the twenty-six-year-old victim's name has been changed to Danny Rosales. The story is about injustice. The play was originally born as *Las Many Muertes de Richard Morales*, written by Morton with the collaboration of his fellow graduate students at the University of California, San Diego. This first script was performed and published in 1977.

Cover for the 1983 collection that includes, along with the title play, El Jardín, Los Dorados, *and* Rancho Hollywood

Los Dorados (performed in 1978) looks at American history from the point of view of the conquered mestizos. The setting is the lower California coast during the first three centuries of colonization. At the beginning of the play, Sinmuhow, a Native American woman, introduces the story:

> Damas y Caballeros, Ladies and Gentlemen, the play you are about to see, *Los Dorados*, is a mixture of facts and fiction about the clash between Native Americans and Spanish conquistadores in Southern California. *Los Dorados* means the golden ones en español; golden, because all have come to these shores in search of what is precious . . . be it gold, converts, fame or simply work. (Enter a native woman, Tupipe, who kneels before a campfire cooking. From the opposite side enters Capitán wandering aimlessly, lost and hungry. He reaches for a fruit from a tree and breaks the branch as she hears the sound and

looks up. He trys to eat the fruit without peeling it and tosses it away with disgust as she rises and walks cautiously toward the sound. He crashes in the underbrush towards her as she draws her bow and arrow. He trips and falls and she draws back the arrow and is about to shoot. He sees her, rises, draws his sword and totters, nearly exhausted. She notes his sad condition and lowers her guard. He backs away from her and puts his sword down on the ground as she lays her bow and arrow on the ground. They walk tentatively towards each other. She picks a fruit from the same tree he did and peels it for him. He devours it ravenously. He pulls out some coins and gives one to her and she takes it, bites it, spits it out and returns it with disgust. He takes a small mirror out of his pocket and gives it to her and she stares at it in astonishment.)

The play develops as an account of the submission of the Native Americans to the domain and power of the Spanish missionaries.

Rancho Hollywood (performed in 1980) is an attack on Hollywood's stereotyping of Latinos. It is a sardonic, extended metaphor for the false image of Latinos created by the movie and television industries. This play, like *Los Dorados*, is structured as theater within theater, where all the characters are seen as theatricalized. The games the characters play in *Rancho Hollywood*, moving in and out of the different roles they play, add to the interest. The production of a movie as a part of the action, setting the theatrical experience within the context of a film (*Ye Olde California Days*), accomplishes the richness of metatheater:

DIRECTOR: We could get O. J. Simpson to play the slave. Now we need a big name star for the, uh, Captain of the clipper ship. Someone with charisma, poise, good looks . . . I got it! I got it!

CAMERAMAN: Got what?

DIRECTOR: I'll play the part (The cameraman groans). You play my slave. Where are we? Where are we? (The other actors disperse, leaving the Director and Cameraman to set up the next scene).

CAMERAMAN: On a boat. Out in the harbor.

DIRECTOR: Oh, I love this. It's so Brechtian. What am I doing?

While the director is assisted by his cameraman as they shoot a movie, the cast members, protesting against them, give their own interpretation to the performance. They refuse to perform the stereotypical version the director wants them to do about the history of California. They organize and direct their own movie. Later the director takes on the role of Jed, a goldminer-soldier who fights against Rico, the governor of California:

RICO: (Seen at another part of the stage writing at a desk) To the Honorable President of the republic of Mexico. I am writing to you with a heavy heart. . . .

JED: (Appearing at another writing desk) The conquest of California would be absolutely nothing. It would fall like a ripened fruit from its bough into the hands of the Anglo-Saxon race as the people here are incapable of defending it (Jed pulls out a pistol and slams it on the desk).

RICO: The uncertainty in which we find ourselves in this territory because of the excessive introduction of armed adventures from the United States of the North leaves us no doubt of the war we shall have with them (pulls out his own pistol and loads it).

JED: (Addressing himself to the audience) Therefore, I said, let us strike now and free this blessed country from Mexican tyranny.

RICO: (To the audience as well) The Treasury Department is exhausted. We have no standing garrison other than volunteers. Please, send money, men, and material at once. God and Liberty, Río Rico, Los Angeles, California. May 25, 1846.

Morton does not necessarily document the historic event, but uses it as a mode of reinventing the past, revising the fall of the last California governor and the loss of the territory. Morton's version of this historic event is based on the case of Don Pío Pico, the last Mexican governor of California.

In *Johnny Tenorio* (1983) Morton re-creates the Spanish tradition of Don Juan, adapting it to contemporary Chicano culture. He writes of a lumpen-proletarian Don Juan named Johnny and sets the dramatic action in an impoverished west-side barrio of San Antonio, Texas. This play was originally commissioned in 1983 at the Centro Cultural de Aztlán, a Chicano arts center in San Antonio. It was first written in a mixture of Spanish and English for a bilingual audience and then translated for a subsequent (1984) production at the University of Texas before a mostly English-speaking audience. The play was designed for the Day of the Death celebration of 1 and 2 November, which, in many Spanish-speaking countries, is marked by productions of José Zorrilla's *Don Juan Tenorio*.

In *La Malinche* (1984) Morton develops the story of a Mayan woman who served as a translator for Hernán Cortés, conqueror of Mexico. Malinche was one of the many native women taken as slaves/lovers when the Spanish landed in Yucatán. Thanks to her intelligence and facility for languages, she became Cortés's principal translator and one of his trusted advisers. They fell in love, and she had a son named Martín. The son of Malinche and Cortés was raised as a Spaniard, inheriting his father's lands and title: marquis of the Valley of Oaxaca.

Morton adapted *Medea*, by Euripides, to the tale of Malinche, since both title characters are seen as "barbarians" who fell in love with soldiers of fortune of a supposed "higher civilization." Both aided their lovers in subduing their people, and both were later abandoned by these men.

La Malinche is set in the mid sixteenth century, immediately following the Spanish conquest. The figure of La Llorona (the weeping woman) acts as the conscience of Malinche. Morton parallels La Llorona with the chorus in Euripides' tragedy. In *La Malinche* a Catholic bishop takes the place of the king who banishes Medea, and the bishop acts as a counter to the heathen priestess La Llorona. Malinche, betrayed by the Spaniard who promised that the new rule would benefit the natives, sacrifices her son rather than see him killed by his enemies or used as an instrument of oppression against her people.

The Savior (1988) is the story of the ministry of Oscar Arnulfo Romero, archbishop of San Sal-vador from 1977 to 1980. Morton writes of the death of Archbishop Romero, who was shot by an unknown sniper at the altar of a chapel where he was saying mass on 24 March 1980 in El Salvador. In this drama, as in *Las Many Muertes de Richard Morales*, Morton documents a real event. He explains in the introduction to his dissertation (which includes the original script) that he was inspired to write *The Savior* after talking with priests and laity in Central America who had worked with Romero. Morton feels that this play affirms the kinship between Chicanos and Salvadorans who are tied together by blood, language, religion, and history. He points out that, as American citizens, Chicanos are also morally responsible for the actions of the U.S. government. Romero, who died as a pacifist, represents another victim of injustice toward human beings.

Within the context of Chicano theater, Morton has been especially influenced by Luis Valdez and his El Teatro Campesino. But while Luis Valdez came from a large, farm-working migrant family, Morton was born into an urban life-style and grew up in diverse places. Nevertheless, Morton uses the same tools employed by Valdez and other playwrights in the repertoire of Chicano drama: the myths akin to the Mexican-American culture, a sardonic view of humanity, and a folkloric interpretation of classic patterns. Morton skillfully employs characteristics of the classical rites to construct a comedy or a tragedy that deals with rituals. He sees theater as a criticism and reconstruction of these rituals as he perceives them in a Chicano context. In this sense, Carlos Morton not only sees theater as a ritual but as a combination of rituals within a ritual, in order to present a new perspective.

Ernesto Chávez Padilla
(9 March 1944 -   )

Edwin John Barton
California State University, Bakersfield

BOOKS: *The Baby Chook and Other Remnants*, by Padilla and Reymundo Gamboa (Tempe, Ariz.: Other Voices, 1974);
Cigarro Lucky Strike (San Francisco: MidiammiX, 1986).

OTHER: "Tortuga: The Black Sun of Salomón's Wards," in *Rudolpho A. Anaya: Focus on Criticism*, edited by César A. González-T. (La Jolla, Cal.: Lalo, 1990), pp. 231-251;
"The Ohming Instick," in *Viajemos 2001*, edited by Evelyn F. Brod and Carol J. Brady (New York: Macmillan, 1990), pp. 339-341;
"Fina, I am Fina," in *What Yellow Is*, edited by Catherine Kohler (Bakersfield, Cal.: Chard, 1991), pp. 12-15.

SELECTED PERIODICAL PUBLICATIONS—UNCOLLECTED: "Only This and Nothing More," *Imagine*, 2 (Winter 1985): 72-75;
"El Lunar de Hester," *Officio*, 6 (September 1987): 25-27;
"The Emperor of Backwards," *Orpheus* (Bakersfield, Cal.), 17 (1989): 131-136.

An accomplished poet, a novelist of much promise, and an editor/publisher of energy and generosity, Ernesto Padilla is currently an assistant professor of English at California State University, Bakersfield. Born in Las Cruces, New Mexico, in 1944, Padilla was the sixth of seven children of Vidal Eduardo and Tomasa Padilla, migrant farm workers. While he was still very young, his family moved to the agriculturally rich San Joaquin Valley in central California. There they settled in the town of Tulare, from which they were able to travel up and down the valley, picking fruits, vegetables, and cotton. Life in the Tulare barrio with summers spent working in the fields near San Jose was not easy, but, as Padilla recalls, "somehow I didn't miss much school." Indeed, by the time he left Tulare High School, he had made his mark as a star athlete and a student gifted in the study of mathematics.

By 1968 he had finished his undergraduate work at Sacramento State College (now California State University, Sacramento), and it was literature that had captured his imagination.

Inspired by one of his professors at Sacramento, Molly Irwin, Padilla changed his major to English and, in his senior year, enrolled in a creative-writing class focusing on poetry. Later, while studying for his teaching credential, Padilla encountered another professor with "the same passion for learning and helping others that Molly Irwin had. Frank Voci said to us that for our final paper in our class on 'the education of the disadvantaged' we could write a formal term paper or a story or a poem, but it must show passion and commitment," Padilla recalled. "I had taken a poetry writing class, so I thought I would save myself a lot of work and write a short poem instead of the much longer term paper." What started as something of a dodge became an important new beginning for Padilla. The poem he wrote to fulfill a course requirement was later published in *Quinto Sol*, the first important Chicano literary journal of the 1960s.

Padilla explains that the poem is "about a Mexican boy who speaks only Spanish in an American school. The teacher is giving a lecture about homing pigeons, and although the boy does not understand everything, he knows enough English to follow along. More important, he has his own pigeon, which was once taken away from him. But he knew that it would return to where it had been nurtured and loved, to where it felt comfortable. All of a sudden, the teacher decides that the Mexican kids in the back of the room are not paying attention, and she asks Armando, the protagonist, what a homing pigeon is, and he stumbles around with English and gives an answer mostly in Spanish. He is sent to the vice-principal's office, and he swears that he will never return to school but, instead, that he will go and pick cotton with his father.... In the end, all we know is that the child is like the homing pigeon. So I thank Frank Voci for pushing

Ernesto Chávez Padilla

me to produce this poem, but I thank Octavio Romano and Herminio Ríos [editor/publishers of *Quinto Sol*] for making me a writer." This same poem, "The Ohming Instick" (the protagonist's pronunciation), has since been published in five different books, including *Viajemos 2001*, a college-level Spanish textbook edited by Evelyn F. Brod and Carol J. Brady (1990).

Padilla was awarded a Ford Foundation Fellowship to pursue his graduate education, and in 1986 he received his Ph.D. in English. He specialized in Victorian literature and wrote his dissertation on Henry James. Since then, the obligations and pressures of academia have often made it difficult for him to find time to write. But Padilla has nevertheless managed to finish many poems and stories in the past few years. Perhaps his best poem is "Darkness on the Delta," which describes a spiritual journey to New Orleans:

> A dingy square of light
> shines out to the pavement,

flowing out in even waves
of laughter.
Here is the PRESERVATION OF JAZZ,
Bourbon and St. Peter,
A magical corner on the timeless delta,
a spur of light
somewhere along a river of dark history.
This promising bright patch of rhythm
edges out enough darkness to coax hope.
One more night,
I stand outside the pilgrim worn door.

The darkness penetrates my sleeveless stare.
The notes confirm deferred apocalypse.
Deceptively,
the tiny spigot of optimism
turns to flow.
Vision pushes back reality.
Inside, tiny faces with broadest smiles
crowd small tables,
drinking the syrup of ever flattening joy.

The poem presents a modernist aesthetic and perspective. Insight and hope are imaged as shards of light that manage to penetrate an immense darkness. Vision and belief arrive in epiphanic moments: the "bright patch of rhythm" and the almost imperceptible opening of "the tiny spigot of optimism." That which is worth living for comes in fragments and is worth the pilgrimage: the faces in a crowded room, a visit with old friends, the preservation through performance of a musical tradition.

Padilla's recent efforts in prose fiction are more obviously the works of a man who recalls what it was like to be a Chicano in California in the 1950s and 1960s. In a series of pieces entitled "The Santiago Stories" (which he hopes to turn into a novel), he offers a semi-autobiographical account of life in the barrio and of the cross-cultural struggles that attend those who escape. As Padilla puts it, "Santiago's situations in many ways mirror my own, but, of course, they are fictional. I want to turn the screw one more twist." Above all, he wishes to express "the universal through the particular and the regional"; his stories are not intended to explore and define the unique properties of Chicano experience so much as to express the sense in which the Chicano's struggle is parallel to all struggles.

The stories completed so far are vivid and entertaining, although they suffer in some cases from technical problems in the narration. Padilla plans to rewrite them, especially now that he has achieved a kind of breakthrough in narrative technique in "Fina, I Am Fina", published in *What Yellow Is*, edited by Catherine Kohler (1991). In this story Padilla finds an authentic voice in the person of a retired letter carrier who feels compelled to tell a story of petty sin, guilt, and despair before he dies. He begins by describing the home of an aging "Spanish lady" to whom he delivers mail:

Before I got my inheritance, I used to deliver mail. My route was over in the Barrio from "O"

street all the way over to "T" street. There was this three-room shack on "Q" street. It had many fruit trees, a giant mulberry, fig, apricot and plum trees, elegant bushes, great varieties of flowers, grape tresses hanging from the dilapidated car port. It was a jungle garden, verdant, quiet, just luscious. Every time I walked up to the mail drop at the front door, I imagined that I heard melodies of the wild, running water, monkeys chattering, peacocks calling out to their mates and birds singing.

I never saw the lady who lived there until the end, at the time when I finally blackened my soul with greed. But I will tell you of that in good time. You must hear it all, from the very beginning.

The teller of the tale here is an attenuated version of the Ancient Mariner; the advantage is that he can speak of the small comedies as well as the minor tragedies of ordinary life.

Padilla's other contribution to Chicano literature has been his small but ambitious Lalo Press ("Lalo" was his father's nickname). Volumes from Lalo include Juan Felipe Herrera's *Exile of Desire* (1982), a collection of poems by César A. González-T entitled *Unwinding the Silence* (1987), and Tino Villanueva's *Crónica de mis años peores* (1987). Padilla's efforts on behalf of these writers reflect his commitment to furthering the cause of Chicano literature. As he noted in an interview, "True, we don't have a Pulitzer prize winner or a Nobel prize winner yet, but it's just a matter of critical mass, a matter of mathematical probability. Let us be patrons of rising Chicano artists. Let's give them an opportunity. Let's give them another fifty years. We'll have a Pulitzer prize winner. Give us eighty years, and we'll have a Nobel prize winner. After all, it wasn't but thirty years ago when the majority of Chicanos were migrant farm workers (as I was) or exploited factory workers in the cities. The talent is here; being a teacher of both English and Math, I see it each new quarter."

Raymundo "Tigre" Pérez

(15 March 1946 -   )

Arcadio Morales
Stanford University

BOOKS: *Free, Free at Last* (Denver: Barrio, 1970);
Los Cuatro, by Pérez, Abelardo Delgado, Ricardo Sanchez, and Juan Valdez (Magdaleno Avila) (Denver: Barrio, 1970);
Phases (Corpus Christi, Tex., 1971);
The Secret Meaning of Death (Lubbock, Tex.: Trucha, 1972).

OTHER: "Hasta La Victoria Siempre," in *We Are Chicanos*, edited by Philip D. Ortego (New York: Washington Square, 1973);
Autobiographical sketch, "Revolutionary," "Farewell Comrade," "Just Us Three," "The Transmitter," and "Wings of Protest," in *El Quetzal Emplumece* (San Antonio, Tex.: Mexican American Cultural Center, 1976);
"To a Foreign Service Racist Gringa," *Caracol*, 3 (June 1977): 23.

The poetry of Raymundo "Tigre" Pérez is both a reflection and outgrowth of the Chicano movement. Pérez, like his contemporaries, sought to capture and interpret the social, political, and cultural anxieties of Chicanos through verse. Like many movement poets, he saw the means for social change embodied in the Chicano movement. Inspired by the movement, he adopted the role of a political troubadour rallying his people around the cry of revolution as a means of obtaining social justice. During his peak years as a poet (1970-1972) Pérez advocated revolution and portrayed "the Chicano movement as a focal point for this process," according to critic Charles M. Tatum. Poetry and politics, then, fused together to provide Pérez with form and forum.

Born on 15 March 1946 in a garage in Laredo, Texas, Pérez is a poet very closely linked to the social realities he writes about. He grew up in the streets of Laredo and is the son of a former boxer turned stevedore and a mother from the Tarascan Indian region of Pátzcuaro, Michoacán, Mexico. His mother's devotion was to religion, and she never lost faith regardless of how bad things got. Pérez's work reflects something of his father's fighting attitude and his mother's spirit of endurance. Pérez's social rebellion and poetic defiance seem to have emerged at an early age in opposition to what he termed his parents' belief in the utopian political propaganda of the time. He chose a less accepting path and heeded a warning offered by his grandmother whom he says was a major influence on him. She once said to him, "The world is a fierce beast just waiting to devour you. Beware!" It seems that Pérez took this advice to heart and learned to defend himself with the rhetoric of politics and the language of poetry.

His interest in poetry began when he was in junior high school, though he was ridiculed and humiliated about his poems back then. He did not comply with the way established poets wrote. This characteristic is apparent in his work even today; it is evident in the prosaic, oratorical quality and the tone of defiance. The streak of nonconformity also got him kicked out of school his first year at Laredo Junior College. He was labeled a stubborn, rebellious dreamer and an outspoken fanatic. Such harsh criticism did not deter Pérez from continuing with his studies, however. He later attended Metro State College in Denver (with the aid of a migrant-student program), transferred to the University of Colorado, and finally graduated from Oberlin College in Ohio with a bachelor's degree in political science.

Free, Free at Last (1970), one of his earliest collections, distinguishes Pérez as "one of the earliest poets to speak out against the Vietnam War" (as Tatum says). Published approximately two years after Pérez's tour of duty as a gunner's mate in Hanoi, the collection is dedicated to all his "brothers in arms in the United States, the Americas, and the World." He proclaims himself the "Voice of the thunder of guns," and he draws parallels between the suffering endured by Chicanos in Vietnam, and the cruelty inflicted on Chicanos back home by farmers and owners of "labor camps." Pérez sees himself as a messianic spirit speaking out in defense of his people: "I am the

194

Cover for Pérez's 1972 collection, which includes poems about what he has called the "many little deaths" that one must experience

light of the living dead. / I am the heart of the revolution." He also sees himself as recorder of events, a guardian of history helping to link the present to the future. He wants to leave behind some poetic remnants of the Chicano movement because he is afraid future generations will forget why they are free. He states, "I write to you people of tomorrow," and he personifies the movement as everyone's child in the poem "Hasta la victoria siempre" (Until the Victory Always). Pérez affirms his own identity in the poem "A Mexican-American Walked," and he entertains the rhetorical question "What are you?" by telling who he is, in the same poem. The message conveyed by the poet in this collection is that a strong sense of self-awareness and identity is the key to individual freedom. He rejoices for his people: "we are free, free at last / For we know who we are."

Pérez's return to civilian life after time in Vietnam led him to work first as a community organizer for a Minority Mobilization Vista Program. An affiliate of the Mexican American Youth Organization (MAYO), the program was so effective "it turned Texas upside down," according to Pérez (in his autobiographical sketch in *El Quetzal Emplumece*, 1976). He later began to edit various Chicano underground newspapers. Their titles, *Los Muertos Hablan* (The Dead Speak), *Valley of the Damned*, and *Tierra Caliente* (Hot Earth), are metaphorical representations of Chicano social and political conditions at the time in Texas. The newspapers came under severe political and police harassment. Pérez's voice, however, would not be silenced, as he found the newspapers a perfect vehicle for voicing his opposition to what he thought of as the unfulfilled social and political promises of "El Partido Viejo [The Old Party], the only ruling party of Laredo." Political repression and harassment culminated in the death of one individual and the beatings of Pérez's associates. Forced to disband the community of underground-newspaper writers, Pérez turned his journalistic pen to poetry.

Los Cuatro (The Four, 1970) established Pérez as one of several movement poets in the Southwest. The collection places him in the company of other poets—Abelardo "Lalo" Delgado, Ricardo Sanchez, and Juan Valdez (Magdaleno Avila)—who collaborated on the book. *Los Cuatro* typifies the collective consciousness of Chicano poets during this time. Pérez's voice is filled with the collective emotions of his people. The Chicano people represent his protagonists, and he is the omniscient narrator. His mind, voice, and heart combine to give life to the essential act of social poetics. Sanchez, in his introduction to *Los Cuatro*, comments that Pérez writes about "a truth he slings so poetically primitive." His poetry is primitive in the sense that it is stylistically raw and unrefined, and also because Pérez's concern is less with fancy poetic devices: his primary focus is the message not the mode. His intention, then, is to awaken the reader with the sobering language of cold realities. He is a poet grasping for urgent answers to solve the suffering of his people.

The suffering of his people causes Pérez inner turmoil. His poetic voice in *Los Cuatro* goes from being melancholy to being angry to being bitter. The poem "La Flauta" (The Flute), for example, echoes a dejected tone. The poem conveys the notion that the flute is the voice of the soul, and there is the sense that this voice and soul is that of the movement. The melody is an unnerving one because it is filled with *odio* (hatred) and *rencor* (resentment) for American society—the oppressors. Pérez continually wrestles with his bitter emotions. In "Along the Way" he speaks of the existential anxieties of loneliness and hopelessness. He nevertheless encourages Chicanos to face the revolution, sad and ugly though it be. Pérez takes the lead in facing this revolution by hurling forth his fervent anger and hostility, as in the poem "What Have You Done?" The speaker threatens, "I have come to kill you / . . . Cry white man . . . cry blood." The condemnation of and threat to a personified American society is also evident in subsequent collections by Pérez.

His close contact with and awareness of farmworker issues is obvious in his next collection, *Phases* (1971). Readers are introduced to the issues of exploitation and injustice, and the workers' perseverance in coping with repression. Pérez's experience as a labor organizer for a program designed to provide social services to migrant families allowed him to witness dehumanizing conditions firsthand. In this collection Pérez wastes little time in striking out against farmers who hire and exploit workers, treating them like human machines. He laments that farm workers are treated like "Invisible people swallowing [their] misery and hardships in a sea of tears." In this collection a preoccupation with natural symbols and metaphors is evident. For instance, Pérez speaks of the workers as "Human Leaves." The image of a downtrodden people is never more clear than in the poem of that title. The farm worker is seen as a leaf, trodden upon and smashed into the furrow of the earth by the oppressor farm owner, until other, newer leaves inevitably fall and replace the dead ones. Other striking images are seen in the poem "Addicts." Pérez utilizes images of death in nature to symbolize decrepit addicts. He paints a bleak picture of them as being "dismembered," "leafless," "warped, dry," and "useless human litter." He strives to transcend ethnic barriers and convey a level of understanding for the larger human condition. In "Artificial Man" Pérez's notion of living unconsciously is conveyed. He perceives humankind swaying back and forth like a pendulum, aimlessly, unconsciously ticking to the time of someone else's clock, with little or no control over life.

Pérez then criticizes the infighting within La Causa (the Chicano movement). He seems to sense that people in the movement have resigned themselves to exist divided, and he expresses strong disappointment and outright criticism of Chicanos who once broke a fast that was planned as a protest. He accuses them of being Chicanos who "have been dead, living dead." Pérez juxtaposes this political resignation with the theme of political perseverance in such poems as "La Huelga" (The Idleness) and "La Nacion." The former praises striking farm workers who are "carrying the banner for justice." The latter is an affirmation that the "cry of revolution still exists." Pérez's voice is less idealistic than in his earlier collections. At the age of twenty-five, when *Phases* was published, Pérez showed better depth and discrimination in selecting his language and images, but his themes of social protest and enduring optimism—always ending his collections with a cry of revolution—have remained constants in his poetry.

The Secret Meaning of Death (1972) represents a symbolic death for Pérez as a poet. Included in this collection are poems proclaiming the many little symbolic deaths he has experienced in his personal life. The title poem was written at the advent of the "bury [ing] of MAYO," the Mexican American Youth Organization that he felt made such significant contributions to the plight of Chicanos in Texas. The collection as a whole is much better than any of his previous works. It is more refined, and Pérez's ideas are crisper. His images are clearer, more focused, and readers get a more powerful picture of what he was hinting at in *Phases*. Pérez is more economical with his language, and a deep sense of despair and anxiety surfaces. He seems possessed by a quiet restlessness. Pérez sees himself as an insignificant gust of air in "A Thin Gust of Air," while in "Meaningless Symbols" he "floats like a cloud of mist." Despair and isolation are apparent. In "Dust" the speaker sees himself buried in a layer of dust. In "Tale" Pérez describes his dark mood in this way: "sitting on a rock I contemplate myself . . . dead. . . ." *The Secret Meaning of Death* seemed to be symbolic of Pérez's final act as a poet, but he quietly emerged again in *El Quetzal Emplumece*. The significance of this anthology is that it contains autobiographical information that puts Pérez's life in perspective. The real meaning of *The Secret Meaning of Death* is revealed by Pérez in his brief autobiographical sketch in the 1976 anthology: "There is one final death, but in between there are so many little deaths."

Pérez wrote most of his poetry from 1970 to 1972. Little critical attention has been given his work since. Discussion of it tends to focus more on the political activism and less on the specific work. His early work, lyrical and oratorical, was generally written to be read aloud. Doing so infuses vibrancy into the already sobering poetics of social protest. Pérez is best when he is introspective—probing deep into his heart for answers to questions wrought by his troubled psyche. Poetry for Pérez represents a purge. It gives him an outlet into which his political anger, frustration, and anxieties can be hurled. It is the creative vehicle for his defiance.

Biography:

Francisco Lomelí and Donaldo Urioste, *Chicano Perspectives in Literature: A Critical and Annotated Bibliography* (Albuquerque: Pajarito, 1976).

Reference:

Ricardo Sanchez, Introduction to *Los Cuatros*, by Sanchez, Pérez, Abelardo Delgado, and Juan Valdez (Magdaleno Avila) (Denver: Barrio, 1970);

Mary Helen Ponce

(24 January 1938 -   )

Angelina F. Veyna
University of California, Los Angeles

BOOKS: *Recuerdo: Short Stories of the Barrio* (Tujunga, Cal.: Ponce/Adame, 1983);
Taking Control (Houston: Arte Público, 1987);
The Wedding (Houston: Arte Público, 1989).

OTHER: "Las ánimas," in *La Gente de Aztlán* (Los Angeles: UCLA, 1982);
"Los tísicos," in *Southwest Tales: In Memory of Tomás Rivera: A Contemporary Fiction Collection*, edited by Alurista and Xelina Rojas-Uriusta (Colorado Springs: Maize, 1986);
"Recuerdo: How I Changed the War and Won the Game," "Recuerdo: Los Piojos," and "La Doctora Barr," in *Woman of her Word: Hispanic Women Write*, edited by Evangelina Vigil (Houston: Arte Público, 1987), pp. 113-115, 116-117;
"Chochis and the Movies at Sanfer," in *California Childhood: Recollections and Stories of the Golden State*, edited by Gary Soto (Berkeley: Creative Arts, 1988);
"Los calzones de la piña," in *Las Mujeres Hablan:*

An Anthology of Nuevo Mexicana Writers, edited by Tey Diana Rebolledo, Erlinda Gonzales-Berry, and Teresa Márquez (Albuquerque: University of New Mexico Press, 1988), pp. 52-55.

SELECTED PERIODICAL PUBLICATIONS—
UNCOLLECTED: "El Pedo," *Chismearte* (February 1982): 17;
"Latinas and Breast Cancer," *Corazón de Aztlán*, 1 (March-April 1982): 32;
"Las güisas," *Maize*, 6 (Fall-Winter 1982-1983): 54;
"Los vatos," *Maize*, 6 (Fall-Winter 1982-1983): 55;
"La despedida," *Maize*, 6 (Fall-Winter 1982-1983): 56;
"Juan Gómez-Quiñones: Escolar y Poeta," *Caminos*, 4 (June 1983): 54-55, 67;
"The Funeral of Daniel Torres: Winner of the Medal of Honor," *Chismearte*, 9 (September 1983): 35-37;
"El jabón de Doña Chonita," *Nuestro*, 7 (December 1983): 44-45;

Mary Helen Ponce in Albuquerque, February 1991

"Cuando 'la Lía' got Engaged," *Third Woman*, 2, no. 1 (1984): 53-56;

"Profile of Dr. Shirlene Soto: Vice Provost: CSU Northridge," *Caminos*, 5 (June 1984): 30;

"Cuando íbamos a la nuez," *FEM*, 8 (June-July 1984): 15-18;

"Wedding in Loreto," *Caminos*, 5 (December 1984): 30, 45;

"El Frijolero," *Trabajos Monográficos*, 1, no. 1 (1985): 22-27;

"Holy Week," *Nuestro*, 9 (April 1985): 42-46;

"Good Friday," *Hispanic Link Weekly Report* (April 1985); republished as "El viernes santo," *FEM*, 8 (June-July 1985): 10-12;

"My Boyfriend, Lupe F.," *Nuestro*, 9 (June-July, 1985): 50;

"El color rojo," *FEM*, 10 (October-November 1986): 39; republished as "The Color Red," *Frontiers*, 11, no. 1 (1990): 25;

"Remendar," *FEM*, 10 (October-November 1986): 22; republished as "Mending," *Frontiers*, 11, no. 1 (1990): 24-25;

"Sandy," *Saguaro: A Literary Journal*, 1 (Winter 1988): 47-52;

"Rose," *Phoebe*, 1 (October 1989): 73-74;

"Las Aleluyas," *Hispanic Link Weekly Report*, 8 (7 May 1990).

Mary Helen Ponce (née Merrihelen) is at the forefront of Chicano literature as one of its most prolific narrative writers. In addition to three books, she has published numerous articles and short stories in English and Spanish. Born and raised in the San Fernando Valley, she grew up among first- and second-generation Mexicans who in the 1940s adopted Southern California as their home. It is this era she has decided particularly to document in the course of her writing. Ponce tends to present everyday experiences and rituals in a simple manner, and likewise allows her characters to reveal themselves without excessive detail. As she develops her stories, she explores such issues as bilingualism, biculturalism, and acculturation. Ponce shares her perception of life in the San Fernando Valley in the following excerpt taken from an unpublished story:

We feared few things in the barrio. We knew everyone; everyone knew us. We belonged. We had family: parents, sisters, brothers, tías, tíos, abuelitos and padrinos [aunts, uncles, grandparents, and godparents]. Our's was a secure world. We were free to play in the streets, climb trees, and snitch fruit off a neighbor's tree without fear. The poverty of our homes, lack of education, and jobs, was something our parents and older siblings worried over. For us, the younger generation, there was only the security of community: la iglesia [the church], la escuela [the school], la tienda de Don Jesús [Don Jesus's grocery store].

Ponce believes she could have developed anywhere as a writer; however, the experience of living in an ethnically sheltered community in Southern California has particularly provided the experiences she has chosen to record. Ponce is able to transform Mexican daily life into a universal experience. She particularly addresses the female experience of this era and the effects of socialization as dictated by family, church, and the educational system. Ponce has participated and continues to participate actively in all three of these spheres, and each has provided her with great content for her narratives.

Mary Helen Ponce considers her birth order, the youngest of seven daughters and three brothers, to have played a major role in her literary development. She identifies her sisters as her primary role models because they urged her to develop multiple skills, and because they urged her always to seek the best of everything. Ponce believes that women of her generation had to work harder for social acceptance, forcing them to excel in different arenas. It was also one of her sisters, through her subscription to the Book of the Month Club, who first exposed Ponce to the greater world of literature.

Ponce earned a B.A. and an M.A. in Mexican-American studies from California State University at Northridge, and a second master's degree in history from the University of California at Los Angeles; she has also minored in anthropology and women's studies. She continued her studies at UCLA, but subsequently left in 1984 because she found herself dedicating most of her time to her creative writing. She was also disappointed in her attempt to develop an interdisciplinary major that would combine history and literature. Ponce is presently pursuing a doctorate at the University of New Mexico in the field of American studies. She considers this program as the vehicle by which she can explore both of her great loves—writing and history. This temporary relocation has especially afforded her a much-needed opportunity to continue to develop her

writing. Previously Ponce spent a major portion of her life as a homemaker, always attempting to balance parenting and reading time while raising her four children: Joseph, Ana, Mark, and Ralph, who continue to reside in Southern California. Ponce feels that in many respects her daily endeavors often made her feel like a "supermom."

Over the years, she has presented her creative and scholarly work at such campuses as UCLA, the University of New Mexico, and El Colegio de México in Mexico City. She has addressed such topics as oral history, pioneering Spanish-Mexican women in California, and Chicana literature. In 1981 she was invited to read her work at the annual meeting of the Mexican American National Women's Association in Washington, D.C., an event which Ponce considers a turning point in her life since it was there that she first reconciled the notion that she was, indeed, "a writer." More recently she was one of four authors invited to read at the 1990 New Mexico Women's History Conference. In addition to her academic publishing, Ponce has also always made an effort to share her writing with her local community, through such newspapers as *La Opinión*, the largest Spanish-language newspaper in Southern California.

Two creative skills which particularly characterize Ponce's writing are her ability to verbalize unspoken questions and her ability to interject humor when least expected. The former is especially evident in Ponce's stories which refer to the Catholic Church and its rituals. Throughout much of her writing, Ponce has been able to capture the dominant role of the church in Mexican communities. In "Holy Week" (1985), Ponce often elaborates on the church's unspoken rule of unquestionable belief in theological doctrine:

> At times what Father Mueller preached about Jesus Christ confused me: He was already dead and in heaven but on Good Friday, he was to once more be put to death! Although he had only recently been born—during Christmas—and was barely three months old, he had grown quite fast (After all, He was God) and was now a grown man who was destined to die on the cross.

"Holy Week" holds a special place in Ponce's heart because it provided her first experience of having a story control her; she explains that without realizing it, the story "changed her" and then followed its own course.

A story which illustrates Ponce's sense of humor is "My Boyfriend, Lupe F." (1985), in

TAKING CONTROL

Mary Helen Ponce

AN ARTE PUBLICO PRESS BOOK

Cover for Ponce's 1987 collection of short stories, most of which focus on exploited people who gain the ability to control their own lives

which she addresses one of the great dilemmas of life: Where does the nose go when you attempt a kiss?

> One thing that bothered me was where did the nose go? What if we bumped noses or hit each other with our noses. I watched the movie stars whenever I went to the movies and their noses used to slip right into place. Either way, I had made up my mind that it would be Lupe F. who would give me my first kiss. . . . I grabbed him and smacked him on the lips. We smashed noses. That was it.

Having an event or situation narrated from a child's perspective is not uncommon for Ponce. She especially has a talent for capturing children's most intimate thoughts. In "Holy Week" she explores a child's curiosity as to what might happen if she drinks "Holy Water." In "Rose"

(1989), Ponce describes the dismay experienced by a young girl upon realizing that another participant in a first communion ceremony is wearing the same veiled headpiece; and to make it worse, it was her own godmother who had given it to her!

Ponce's earliest writing efforts were autobiographical; as a result, she developed first-person narratives that would allow her to share intimate details, not necessarily of her own personal life, but of collective experiences of Mexican women. In fact, the titles of some of her earliest narratives are prefaced with "Recuerdo," which can be translated as either "I recall" or as "memory." She has expressed that her first efforts at exploring autobiography were the result of observing others write about everything that surrounded them. For example, "Los tísicos" (The Tubercular Ones, originally published in *FEM*, February-March 1986) was one of her early efforts at writing collective history, while "My Boyfriend, Lupe F." served as an experiment in autobiography; it was not until later that she began to write third-person narratives. Ponce explains that she writes from memory and that her narratives are chiefly the result of her elaborating on situations or people with whom she has come in contact and mentally "archived." Much of her writing, she explains, tends to reflect her appreciation for people who are direct and honest. Since she tends to be a perfectionist, she writes numerous drafts of her *cuentos* (tales), writing each one at least six times. This pursuit of perfection also challenges her to become more innovative in themes and in concepts as her work progresses.

Ponce recognizes that in her earlier efforts she was strongly influenced by the lyricism and tone of European authors. In her continuing development, however, she subsequently found herself being influenced more by authors such as Juan Rulfo and Ana María Matute. Ponce also notes that she has been influenced by philosophical and psychological novels; as a result, she often attempts to write so that the themes and issues remain with the audience upon concluding the stories.

After completing her graduate degrees, Ponce experienced great difficulty finding teaching positions. As a result, she found herself taking employment which involved teaching, but not necessarily in an academic setting. One of these positions was as a community liaison for the White Memorial Medical Center Cancer Clinic in Los Angeles. This venture into health education led her to write "Latinas and Breast Cancer" (1982), in which she discusses some of the cultural variables which inhibit Latina women from conducting or receiving breast examinations.

Ponce also explored a different realm of writing by interviewing two leaders of the Chicano academic community; this effort resulted in: "Juan Gómez-Quiñones: Escolar y poeta" (1983) and "Profile of Dr. Shirlene Soto: Vice Provost: CSU Northridge" (1984). Ponce used these interviews as an opportunity to experiment with journalistic writing, a form she had long wanted to attempt as a result of her admiration for Orillana Fallaci, an Italian photo journalist, whom she describes as being "honest, direct, and not prone to lying."

Ponce's narratives historically document the collective Mexicano experience. For example, in "Recuerdo: Los Piojos" (Memory: The Lice, originally published in *Chismearte*, February 1982), Ponce describes one of the most humiliating situations she observed, that of children having their heads examined for lice, a common practice in schools of that era. Her cultural sensitivity is demonstrated by her addressing not just one type of Mexican experience, but by portraying the heterogeneity of this population. The life-style of the upwardly mobile, which Ponce also describes, particularly tends to be excluded in works by Chicano and Chicana authors. "Cuando íbamos a la nuez" (When We Used to Go to the Nut, 1984), for example, documents the immigrant experience. In this story, Ponce demonstrates her ability to detail the daily activities of the working class. Many of her characters and their experiences can also represent non-Mexicans. Her references to *contratistas* (contractors) in this story, for example, could equally be applicable to any individual in any country who is out to exploit the working masses. Ponce also details common, everyday activities of the blue-collar community through her selection of representative action. In "Los calzones de la piña" (The Pineapple Pants, originally published in *Nuestro*, March 1985), for example, she describes the common practice of making clothing out of flour sacks.

Taking Control (1987) is a collection of several short narratives. She originally selected a title for the book that suggested the exploitation of the characters she portrayed; however, in a discussion with her publisher, she came to realize that in spite of the negative circumstances surrounding each character, these individuals ended up *taking control* of their situations and continuing on with their lives. Each of the stories shares

a different facet of the Mexicano community. For example, in "The Playgoers," Ponce describes the interaction of women across different generations and explores different aspects of female and Chicana experiences. The story line focuses on a young Chicana who invites her mother and her mother's friend to an evening of theater. Upon arrival at their destination, they become separated and each woman creates her own theatrical experience. The young woman, Becky, enjoys the performance of *Don Quixote*, the piece they were all originally expected to see. Becky's mother and her friend end up viewing a "modern" performance which almost culminates in a heart attack for Becky's mother because of the "scandalous" scenes onstage. The mother's friend, in turn, creates her own scenario by initiating a conversation with a man she finds attractive who sits nearby. The manner in which Ponce develops each woman's experience demonstrates her ability to incorporate cultural and generational nuances that only an "insider" could describe.

In "The Campout," Ponce portrays an acculturating, Mexican middle-class family that encounters its cultural "roots." The story unfolds with two families, one Mexican American and the other Anglo, experiencing a vacation in Baja California. As the characters converse with each other and enjoy the countryside, Ponce explores a selection of dichotomies present in our society: the middle-class American life-style in contrast to the economically depressed "border" reality; the perception of American-born Mexicans toward their *paisanos* (countrymen) across the border; misconceptions by certain Anglos toward members of border communities and vice versa. Throughout the story, Ponce explores how adolescents perceive these issues in contrast to the adults. Ponce also examines the different levels of "cultural awareness" displayed by the Mexican-American wife and husband.

Another story in *Taking Control*, "La Josie," is considered by Ponce to be one of her best examples of presenting women as both victims and survivors. The story is narrated by a woman who recalls her past experience of living next door to another woman, Josie. Both women are trying to survive personal problems: one does so by depending on a husband who exploits and abuses her, while the other addresses her trials essentially alone, even though she does have a young child. As Ponce develops both female characters, she elaborates on the everyday conflicts women must

Cover for Ponce's 1989 novel, about a young woman growing up in the San Fernando Valley during the 1940s and 1950s

the side effects during menstruation. She also describes her fear at having the company doctor conduct a personal examination. Ponce, without doubt, is one of the first Chicana authors to address such topics in her writing. She is equally successful in addressing women's intimate feelings in "The Painkillers," in which she describes a woman who has just undergone a hysterectomy.

Ponce's novel, *The Wedding* (1989), describes all of the thoughts, hopes, dreams, and realities experienced by a young working-class woman, Blanca, in preparation for the climax in her life. Through Blanca, the reader is provided a personal glimpse of life in the San Fernando Valley throughout the 1940s and 1950s. The reader is exposed to the personal and family dynamics involved in a courtship and throughout the development of a wedding. In the story are universally representative figures such as "the dominant friend" (Blanca's madrina [godmother]) and the "self-centered boyfriend/groom" ("Cricket"). Ponce also portrays the reality of subgroups in the barrio; in fact, underlying much of the novel is the rivalry between two opposing groups, the "Tacanos," the group to which Blanca's fiancé belongs, and their rivals, the "Planchados." The last chapter of the novel details a series of conflicts among guests at the wedding reception; however, the greater conflict is left with the reader: What will become of Blanca in her new marriage? This lingering moment of unclosure is a technique often utilized by Ponce to involve her audience.

As the story line, narrated by Blanca develops, Ponce demonstrates her skill at capturing the nuances and realities of the socialization process of a Mexican woman. Ponce explores the inconsistencies in self-perception experienced by a woman, especially where men are concerned: "Sometimes I don't know how come he liked me. I ain't shapely like Lucy, and I can't even tell jokes like Sally. All I gots is a job pulling feathers off turkeys." In order to afford her bridal gown, Blanca found herself having to work every Saturday for three months: "It was getting to where the dead turkeys whose feathers she was hired to remove, were appearing in her dreams. In her dreams the turkeys all looked like *Cricket*, especially when he yelled at her."

The reality of family and community pressure placed upon women to uphold certain values can be summarized in the following statement: "Ever since she could remember, Blanca had envisioned her wedding veil. It had to be made of *azares*, orange blossoms made of wax,

confront and depicts the intimate thoughts of uncertainty often experienced by persons who find other individuals, or agencies, controlling their lives. In "El Marxista," Ponce again explores the contradictions of life. She describes a man, from Mexico, who is supposed to epitomize class struggle against capitalism. Instead, the woman in the story discovers that he is in reality quite the opposite—a man who indulges in American materialism. In "The New Affirmative Action Officer," Ponce addresses sexism and its various ramifications as they affect one woman, Mónica Rubio. After she refuses advances made by her boss, he accuses Mónica of being absent from work too frequently. In an ensuing investigation, the company affirmative action officer invites Rubio to explain her side of the story. To explain her behavior, Rubio finds herself having to discuss intimate details such as her being absent because of the traditional headpiece worn by most Mexican-American brides. It was a sign of purity." In *The Wedding*, Ponce creatively describes the significance of social and religious rituals which validate both women and men among their friends and family and affirm their membership in their home community. In essence, Blanca participates in a mythical reality without consideration of the subsequent consequences. Ponce also utilizes a combination of English and Spanish as well as *caló* (slang) to typify the language of the time and of the barrio. When she chooses to use Spanish, it is because she feels that this language best expresses the sentiment of the moment. Her characters' practice of referring back and forth to both languages alludes to the bilingualism and biculturalism found in the local community. Unfortunately, in the process of publishing *The Wedding*, some chapters submitted by Ponce as part of her novel were excluded and other alterations were also made throughout the text. In the near future, Ponce expects to publish Blanca and Cricket's story in its original form.

Continuing actively to pursue new projects, Ponce is presently involved in the development and production of a play entitled "Blanca's Wedding." This is her first formal attempt at play writing, and she states that the effort calls for the use of "a whole different set of muscles." Ponce is also presently completing her autobiography, "Hoyt Street: Autobiographical Narrative." She also plans to address again women's collective experiences in "Mujeres Solas" (Single Woman), a collection of vignettes depicting elderly women, as narrated from a ten-year-old's perspective. Her purpose for undertaking this project is to recognize the survival efforts of women who have persevered in their barrios, women who often go unrespected in their local communities.

Ponce's future efforts will include writing about female garment workers and a biography on Fabiola Cabeza de Baca, the New Mexican author of *The Good Life* (1949) and *We Fed Them Cactus* (1954). As a socio-historical writer, Ponce also hopes to continue fictionalizing the Mexican and Chicano experience. Though she does not presently consider herself a feminist writer, she continues to address the historical and personal experiences of Chicana and Latina women, and she anticipates exploring a feminist perspective in future works.

Juanita Ponce-Montoya

(1949 -   )

Wolfgang Binder
University of Erlangen-Nuremberg

BOOK: *Grief Work* (Hicksville, N.Y.: Exposition, 1978).

SELECTED PERIODICAL PUBLICATION—
UNCOLLECTED: "Jack O'Neill," *Del Sol New Mexico* (December 1982): 68-69.

While Juanita Ponce-Montoya is the author of only one book of poetry so far, it is strikingly unified in theme. To a large extent it is based on traumatic personal experiences, and it illustrates a difficult triumph over feelings of loss and despair.

Ponce-Montoya was born in 1949 in Raton, New Mexico, as one of five children. After completing high school, at age twenty-one she married Juan Lorenzo Montoya, a pipe fitter. In 1971 her daughter, Anita, died when only five weeks old, because of oxygen deprivation; it was the first death to mark Ponce-Montoya's personal life. The birth of her son Juan in January 1972 proved a source of joy and vitality to her. For seven years she worked in the U.S. Air Force, in the areas of research and development and procurement of special weapons. Her hardworking, independent attitude toward life characterizes Ponce-Montoya's existence. It served her well after her husband was fatally injured in 1974, leaving her with two-year-old Juan, and she was five months pregnant with her second son, José.

Ponce-Montoya's courage and relentless energy surface when one considers her multiple efforts to survive economically: because she had a limited education, she began attending the University of Albuquerque after José was born. She worked odd jobs for the duration of her schooling. After her graduation she took only half-time nursing positions at Children's Psychiatric Hospital until 1983 so that she could raise her children with care and consistency. She supplemented her income by working summers on a big farm. She also got involved in real estate, making small investments and eventually buying and fixing up

Juanita Ponce-Montoya (photograph by Stuart Mitchell)

homes. She and her sons currently live in Albuquerque.

Ponce-Montoya has voiced her belief in the great potential existing in Chicano youths: "At some point, our children must be able to safely feel an acculturation without the threat of assimilation, without the fear of losing themselves, rising above the label of mediocrity, realizing that racial hatred in time can be converted in attitude— through basic human respect. They must know that they can be proud, that they can achieve, moreover that they can choose ... and the choices are endless."

Grief Work initially grew out of a desperate need to structure harrowing experiences. Ponce-Montoya uses poetry as a form of self-therapy. Yet many of the poems transcend this expediency by their forcefulness, honesty, and power. The book draws from the terrible experience of the loss of a much-loved husband; it is dedicated to Juan Lorenzo Montoya. *Grief Work* must be viewed as an extended chronicle—almost all the poems are dated—recording feelings of extreme despondency, but moving toward a cathartic affirmation of self near the end of part 2, which is aptly titled "Recovery." The time span covered in the poems runs from 4 April 1974 to 24 December 1975.

Ponce-Montoya's range of emotions proves remarkably large, offering a highly varied reading of the human condition and thus reaching beyond the undeniably close, direct autobiographical link between author and text. In part 1 the reader witnesses the development of a strong death wish in the survivor; the refusal to believe the sad fact of the loved one's death; feelings of an existential void, of the meaninglessness of life; and the frail beginnings of the concept that the memory of a past love enables a person to walk on.

The second phase of development in part 1 consists of the recognition of a fragile new life; a rebellious attitude against the many daily demands and against real and so-called friends, family, and outsiders; expressions of low self-esteem, of loneliness; and temptations to engage in physical love. This second phase also contains elements that point to the speaker's salvation: the admission, hitherto concealed, of her love for her parents; the recognition of her son John-John (Juan) as a life force; and the realization of the importance of friendship. By the end of May 1975 the entries/poems show signs of a renewed vitality, coupled with the quintessential acceptance of the painful past. The last poem of part 1, dated 4 June 1975 and titled "To a Husband; Good-

Bye," states hesitantly the liberating move away from a stifling, vampirelike memory, but it does so in a supplicating apostrophe, an indication that the battle has not yet been won:

> I've been estranged from myself too long
> > so leave me be!
> your soul no longer drinks of mine
> > the quench of my lifeblood, you see,
> is wrong!—so stay away, sweet memory
> and possess me nevermore.

Part 2 is a clearer but by no means linear continuation of the road to survival and acceptance. In poems dated from summer to late November 1975, the reader is drawn into a sensuous love affair, which, because of its urgency, is rendered in religious terminology. Love becomes, in its newly felt ecstasy, almost unnameable; it means "unison with God." It ultimately will make a rebirth possible. However, after indications of bewilderment and estrangement, the separation of the two lovers occurs in late November. Despite the hurt and the chronicled "emotional emptiness," the speaker finds herself not destroyed by this new loss. It is accepted with sentiments of hard-won generosity:

> NOW ... I'm happy that
> your soul is
> free
> even if you're far
> > from me
> and constant in the
> dream that fills
> > my empty cup
> to overspill.

Most of the poems in *Grief Work* are inner-directed, and the book is an intimate yet strong account of life coming from a Chicana who in writing this book *became* a poet. The volume belongs to the subgenre called "confessional poetry," but what it may lack in sophistication and poetic techniques, it compensates for by its stark, relentless truthfulness and the presence of a woman's voice that the reader will not forget.

Anthony Quinn

(21 April 1915 -   )

Genaro M. Padilla
University of California, Berkeley

BOOK: *The Original Sin: A Self-Portrait* (Boston: Little, Brown, 1972).

Anthony Quinn, from unlikely beginnings in revolutionary Mexico, is today internationally recognized as a consummate actor with over one hundred films to his credit. After he made his debut at twenty-one in a film called *Parole* (1936), Quinn made his way through a spate of "B movies" and went on to star in such classics as *The Ox-Bow Incident* (1943), *La Strada* (1954), *Requiem for a Heavyweight* (1962), *Lawrence of Arabia* (1962), and *Zorba the Greek* (1965), as well as his Oscar-winning roles in *Viva Zapata* (1952) and *Lust for Life* (1956). During his years as an actor, Quinn has also maintained a working interest in sculpture, painting, and architecture, and has written screenplays. In 1972 he published *The Original Sin: A Self-Portrait*, which, as described in the *New York Times Book Review* (8 October 1972), is "a story that is by turns embarrassingly candid, boldly awkward, funny, tragic, moving and full of life."

The Original Sin is not the typical egoistic telling of fabulous success as a Hollywood star but, quite to the contrary, the narrative of Quinn's search for emotional health, self-understanding, and a sense of how the familial and cultural substance of his experience brought him to a crisis of personal faith that had him on the brink of despair. Unlike most Hollywood autobiographies the book is not an "as-told-to" story but Quinn's own experiment in an autobiographical form that reads something like a first-person, confessional screenplay, complete with a cast of characters from his past, including the "Boy"—an adolescent alter ego, an eleven-year-old double who is the voice of a culturally different, socially marginalized childhood that makes Quinn's movement into the upper strata of American society uncertain and painful. Quinn, rather than enjoying his success, was anguished by his early family life and guilt-ridden by his jealous mistreatment of various women who were kind toward him. As

the psychiatrist, introduced early into the autobiography, reflects, Quinn is like the classic character he played in the Federico Fellini film *La Strada*, a loveless, joyless man, who "felt the immensity of space" only after he had wantonly destroyed the love offered to him.

The narrative risks that Quinn takes in the book do not always work convincingly, but the decision to write psychoanalytic autobiography was a courageous one. Set in a psychiatrist's office where he is beginning therapy, the autobiography begins with the psychiatrist reading from news clippings that in characteristic Hollywood style embroider Quinn's cultural origins. The clippings brag that his father was an "Irish adventurer" and his mother an "Aztec princess," and romanticize their participation in the Mexican revolution of 1910. Quinn's response to this "Indian princess crap" is largely what directs the narrative tone. Quinn feels deep antipathy for those forces in American society that, first, limited his creative aspirations and then, when he did succeed, invented a story that, in erasing his Mexican, lower-class origins, conformed to Hollywood's—and America's—fantasy of itself.

Since the glittering Hollywood image is what he wishes to exorcise, he retrieves his real Mexican-Irish past. Quinn's narrative of his birth in Chihuahua on 21 April 1915 and his early life in Mexico takes place during a visit Quinn has with his mother after his first session with the psychiatrist. Rather than relate the story himself, Quinn dramatizes his mother's telling of the events of his early years: he was the son of Manuela Pallares ("Nellie") Quinn, a self-sufficient woman but an obedient wife of Francisco Quinn, whom she followed while he was a soldier in Pancho Villa's army.

Much in this part of the narrative is reminiscent of Ernesto Galarza's autobiography *Barrio Boy* (1971) and especially José Antonio Villarreal's autobiographical novel *Pocho* (1970). In fact, Quinn's early narrative is a paradigmatic literary description of the family's exodus into the

Anthony Quinn as depicted in a mural by Eloy Torrez on a building on North Broadway Street in Los Angeles

United States during the latter stages of the Mexican revolution.

The Quinn story, one common during the revolution, is one of privation and hunger, constant movement, and, given his father's restlessness and emotional detachment, tense family relations. As Quinn's mother tells him, while his father romanticized the revolution, "To me it was just the smell of gunpowder and the crying of the wounded. We were just poor people fighting for our stomachs." His mother describes her movement from the interior to Juárez, into El Paso to search for her husband, the gradual drawing together of the family, and their inexorable movement into the United States. The chapter ends with the family at the end of the rail line in Los Angeles, where Quinn grew up in a poor east-side barrio and gradually made his way toward the studios of Cecil B. deMille.

While the autobiography details the events of Quinn's childhood and adolescence in Los Angeles and describes his inchoate desire to be "number one," the narrative retrieval of the past is hardly celebrative. It is a journey, rather, into the emotive turmoil of the past. Most haunting is the trauma he experienced after the death of his father when Quinn was eleven. His father's death was the central familial crisis of his childhood, one that fractured his personality, creating a split that widened as the years continued, until, as a man, he felt deeply divided. His confusion and guilt, coupled with the poverty and familial disintegration he experienced, created a furious rage within the boy to succeed at something, anything, just so long as he pleased his father's ghost and lifted himself from anonymity.

The entire middle section of the autobiography provides a rich description of Quinn's various adolescent careers. One chapter is about his conversion to the Holy Rollers and his first taste for the stage as a child preacher with the well-known evangelist Aimee Semple McPherson. Another describes his promising but short boxing career as a sixteen-year-old fighting in smokers for five dollars. Later he and a friend visited local dance halls trying to make some fast money as tango contestants. Quinn describes his first sexual encounter at sixteen with a sophisticated older woman who invited him home after a dance contest and seduced him. As he laughingly remembers, although he had just become a "man," when he got home, his grandmother discovered he had been with a woman and beat him with a shoe.

All during this period he was also an occasional high-school student, who, while studying basic architectural design, presented himself to Frank Lloyd Wright one afternoon with his portfolio. This is significant since Quinn remembers that it was one of the first expressions of his desire for a more creative, imaginative life. Quinn hated the standardization in architecture that is a metaphor for the deadening reduction of human spirit to conformity and machinelike existence. As Quinn remembers, Wright liked his vision of a world in which people did not have to live in boxes.

About this time, when he was eighteen, he met Sylvia, his girlfriend's mother and the woman who represents the major creative influence in his early life. McPherson introduced him to the stage when he preached in her tabernacle, Wright encouraged his vision of a wider life, but Sylvia opened the door to knowledge and intellectual creativity through philosophy, literature, painting, and music. She introduced him to works by George Santayana, Arthur Schopenhauer, Friedrich Nietzche, Henry David Thoreau, Ralph Waldo Emerson, and others. The effect was profound: "I suddenly found myself avariciously devouring philosophy and literature. I was a boy who had been in a coma for eighteen years, fed intravenously. Now I awakened. I began reading books from morning to night, drunk with discovery. Sylvia made me put my thoughts, impressions, into notebooks. . . . I read [Henry] Fielding and [Tobias] Smollett, [Charles] Baudelaire and [Honoré de] Balzac, Dante and [Gabriele] D'Annunzio. I read Ford Maddox Ford, Sinclair Lewis, [F.] Scott Fitzgerald, [Thomas] Wolfe, [Ernest] Hemingway. . . ."

The new world Quinn discovered was indeed strange given his feeling that he was an outsider, a groping kid from the barrio who wanted something he could not name. His encounter with this new world was almost lost at the beginning when he was asked about his cultural background:

"Are you Spanish, Tony?"

Oh, Christ! Here it comes, I thought. Here comes the demand for my pedigree. . . . I knew very well that it was more fashionable to be Spanish than Mexican.

"Mexican," I said.

He was extremely self-conscious and sensed himself in a hostile environment of ideas, books, names, and cultural behaviors that were foreign to him, and, given the snide remarks he overheard, meant to remain beyond him.

This scene is emblematic of Quinn's desire for intellectual and creative force in the face of social snobbery and limitation. Quinn's consistent examination of this intercultural and class conflict sets the autobiography squarely within the Chicano literary tradition. Many of the experiences Quinn describes are similar to those in other Chicano texts in which a young protagonist must struggle not only against poverty but also against multiple forms of social containment that act to limit access to the world. Even when Quinn broke through Hollywood studio gates, he struggled against the forces that sought to typecast him as a "foreigner"—an Indian, a Mexican, a Latin lover, or a festive Mediterranean.

Quinn's story of his rise to fame is in some respects the standard tale of the struggling young actor perfecting his craft and fighting for his first roles. However, before describing his work in Hollywood, Quinn inscribes his familial, cultural, and class identities, with their various manifestations in his personality. He made this narrative decision precisely because, on the verge of crisis, it was the deeply embedded, pre-Hollywood behavior that caused most of his anguish. Quinn understands that autobiography is principally about the forces that exert themselves upon the "self" rather than about achievement. Hence it makes perfect narrative sense not to relate the story of his first role on the stage until two-thirds of the way through the autobiography.

That first role was in Noel Coward's *Hay Fever* (1935), for which Quinn got reviews that made him "secretly fired with the idea of being an actor." He auditioned for a play produced by Mae West, called *Clean Sheets*, and, although initially told that she wanted "Latin types to play gigolos," Quinn got one of the weightier roles, a takeoff on John Barrymore. Barrymore, as it turned out, happened to be in the audience on opening night, came to Quinn's dressing room after the performance, and commended him. Quinn was on his way to his first film roles in *Parole* (1936),

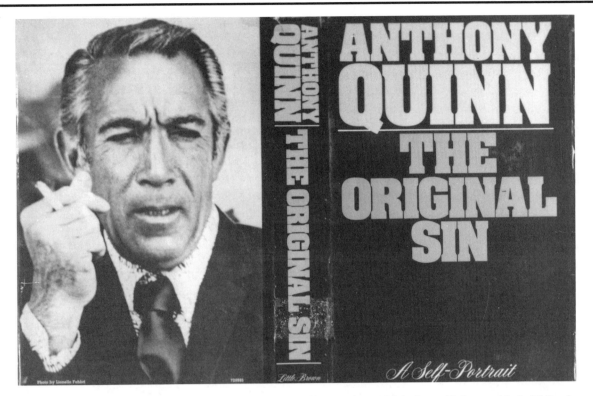

*Dust jacket for Quinn's autobiography, in which he writes of his Mexican-Irish heritage, his impoverished childhood,
and his Hollywood success*

The Plainsman (1937) with Gary Cooper, and *Swing High, Swing Low* (1937) with Carole Lombard.

Quinn's memories of notables such as Barrymore, West, Cooper, and Lombard are among the high points of the autobiography, because Quinn succeeds at describing himself in the course of relating his interaction with these members of the Hollywood elite. They had, he remembers, a "profound effect on my life," and his interaction with the elite became personal when he fell in love with and eventually married deMille's daughter, Katherine.

In large measure *The Original Sin* is an attempt to understand his long unreconciled behavior toward Katherine. For example, when he first entered the deMille estate, he was simultaneously enthralled and repulsed by the material opulence. As the "Boy" inside him says: " 'We didn't belong in that house. We had nothing in common with it. That's when you started to compete for *things*. . . . The boy turned around and made a dash for the door. I stayed." This material impulse, coupled with the trauma Quinn experienced upon discovering that Katherine was not a virgin on their wedding night, cut deeply into his spirit, filling him with social ambivalence and

nearly schizophrenic male anger, resentment, and cynicism.

The final chapters focus on his obsession with his wife's past, her background, and all the Hollywood people who were part of her universe. He became increasingly embittered about his relegation to certain roles, scapegoating Katherine: "I blamed her for all my failures. My career had been reduced to playing third-rate gangster parts, Mexican bandits and poor Indians who were always getting the shit kicked out of them by the big strong white man." Quinn knew he was being unfair to Katherine, especially since she repeatedly proved her trust and affection not only to him but to their four children.

As his psychiatrist tells him in the book, only when he has freed himself of the ghosts of the "Boy" and his father will he find peace and love. Quinn did not kill the "Boy," but in a long final chapter he confronts him in a strange, dreamlike scene. The "Man" chases the "Boy" in the old neighborhood, they struggle and accuse each other of betrayal, but somehow they move toward reconciliation. The autobiography concludes in perhaps too contrived an act of closure, but Quinn's strategy is to end in a symbolic act of self-acceptance, a rejoining of youthful ideals and adult realities. After a long and excruciating self-examination, Quinn can finally move on, because he accepts the contradictions inherent in experience.

What Quinn did move on to after *The Original Sin* was a final break with Katherine; a new marriage to an Italian woman, Yolanda; the making of another family; and acting in another group of films during the 1970s, in which he played strong, ethnic leads—Aristotle Onassis,

for instance, in *The Greek Tycoon* (1977) and the strong-willed patriarch in *The Children of Sánchez* (1978). In recent years he has toured the United States in *Zorba*, a successful stage production, and, between trips to New York and Europe, he lives in Beverly Hills, where he continues to write, paint, and sculpture.

Interview:

Tino Villanueva, "Autobiographical Disclosures," *Americas Review*, 16 (Fall-Winter 1988): 110-143.

Katherine Quintana Ranck

(4 October 1942 -   )

Diana González
Antelope Valley College

BOOK: *Portrait of Doña Elena* (Berkeley, Cal.: Tonatiuh-Quinto Sol, 1982).

SELECTED PERIODICAL PUBLICATION—
UNCOLLECTED: "Relics," *Grito del Sol* (Winter 1984): 31-36.

Narrative description is Katherine Quintana Ranck's greatest asset as a writer. Her works powerfully preserve a fast-disappearing traditional life-style once typical in the villages of rural New Mexico.

The last of eleven children, she was born Katherine Quintana on 4 October 1942 in Santa Fe to Ramón Trujillo Quintana and Lebradita Romero Quintana. Her maternal grandmother, Sofía Madrid Romero, was the inspiration for Ranck's first published work, *Portrait of Doña Elena* (1982). As a young girl, Ranck was an avid reader, pulling books at random from library shelves and thus discovering the classics by accident. Her years at Leah Harvey Junior High School in Santa Fe were vital in her formation as a writer, due to the influence and encouragement of eighth-grade teacher William Gill, who introduced Ranck to the formal study of literature and critiqued her first manuscript. Immediately

after graduating from high school at age seventeen, she married James Phillip Ranck in 1960. In 1968 they moved to the San Diego area and now reside in National City, California. In 1970 James Ranck suffered a massive coronary. Subsequent medical expenses and an uncertain financial future sent his wife job hunting, with bilingualism as her only marketable skill. Working at various medical-related clerical jobs, she was willing to accept the least popular nighttime schedules, because these allowed her to be home with her two children in the daytime, when she was needed the most. Ranck enrolled at Southwestern College in nearby Chula Vista, California, to upgrade her job skills, earning an associate degree in child development in 1978. She is currently director of child development programs for the National City Public Schools and is pursuing a graduate degree at National University in San Diego. The Rancks have two adult children, Kimberly and Lance, and a granddaughter, Kimberly Marie. Katherine Quintana Ranck's favorite pastimes include visiting small galleries that display the arts of the Southwest and reading literary works depicting the beauty of rural New Mexico and its peoples.

Katherine Quintana Ranck

Ranck's works are psychologically oriented whether narrated in the first or third person. Her fine descriptions are colored by the emotional involvement of the narrator and invite the sensory participation of the reader. Ranck's poetic prose tends to charm the reader into continuing with the work despite the lack of action, movement, or intricate story line.

Portrait of Doña Elena evolved from a creative-writing class Ranck took at Southwestern College under the guidance of instructor Joan Oppenheimer. When Ranck wrote a character sketch of her maternal grandmother, who had died in 1967 at the age of eighty-nine, the family would not let Ranck rest until the details were fleshed out into a complete work. In writing the short novel, Ranck reached back into her fond memories of childhood visits to her grandmother's rural New Mexican home in the village of Nambé, and she synthesized them into her first published literary work. Ranck recalled sensory impressions of her grandmother's wooden stove, water well, the homemade pies and freshly baked

bread in the old family home, as well as the warmth of an extended family living under the gentle protection of a revered matriarch. Ranck says of her novel, "Images were what I wrote, a portrait of the land and people I loved. The story line became a necessity, thin strands upon which to weave a tapestry." Protagonist-narrator Constance (Consuelo) Trujillo Sorensen is a Minnesota-raised artist who visits Nambé for the first time in search of her cultural roots. Persuading Doña Elena to sit for a portrait, Constance finds herself in a Hispanic environment that is initially uncomfortable, culturally and linguistically. Her emotional conflicts are resolved through the compassion of Doña Elena's family and the artistic and emotional support of grandson Roberto, a fellow artist and kindred spirit who leads her to a sense of artistic completion and personal well-being. The story is told through the eyes of an artist, thus conveying picturesque descriptions of the land itself and of the traditional types who sit for portraits, representing a bygone era. The book is mostly in English with a sprinkling of Spanish terms that are explained simply. It can be enjoyed on a variety of levels and is appropriate reading even for young adults.

The beauty of *Doña Elena* lies in its simplicity. It has a minimum of locales, few characters, and little dialogue to distract the reader from the feelings conveyed via narrative description, a typical example being Consuelo's first observation of Doña Elena in the village chapel:

> How old was she? I wondered as I gazed at the serene face with eyes set deep by age and thin lips that rhythmically parted over toothless gums. Wisps of white hair had strayed from beneath her shawl, and she lifted a small hand to brush them into their proper place. The skin of that hand was translucent. I was sure that it would feel like the skin of a newborn infant if I touched it, and I so wanted to touch it.

"Relics," published in 1984, evolved from a short-story contest at the Santa Barbara Writers' Conference in 1978. It is also an intensely sensorial work. Ranck explains, "In the short story 'Relics' I provide only the images; the reader is free to provide his own story. Perhaps that is why it took five years to find a publisher for it. No one wants to work harder than the author when reading a story." The theme again centers on internal conflict and a sense of incompleteness.

Much of Ranck's creative work is unpublished, most of it having been written for young children. On a regular basis she creates stories to be used in the instructional programs for the National City School District day-care and preschool centers. When still a classroom teacher, she often encouraged her students to create fiction orally, which she would then record and invite students to illustrate.

In her professional capacity as a child-development specialist, Ranck has written several articles for local newspapers, advising parents in matters related to their preschoolers. Her recent promotion to director of the program has added responsibilities, making her involvement in children's literature somewhat less frequent, although she can still manage at times to write stories for others to tell.

Katherine Quintana Ranck's publishing hiatus in recent years is due in part to her husband's heart condition, which has required two transplant surgeries, and partly to the demands a career in education has on her time and creative energies. She looks forward to the time when she can once again return to her literary endeavors and pursue the publication of several in-progress works.

John Rechy

(10 March 1934 -   )

Didier T. Jaén
University of California, Davis

See also the Rechy entry in *DLB Yearbook: 1982*.

BOOKS: *City of Night* (New York: Grove, 1963; London: MacGibbon & Kee, 1964); translated as *La Ciudad de la Noche* (Mexico City: Edivision, 1987);
Numbers (New York: Grove, 1967);
This Day's Death (New York: Grove, 1970; London: MacGibbon & Kee, 1970);
The Vampires (New York: Grove, 1971);
The Fourth Angel (New York: Viking, 1972; London: Allen, 1972);
The Sexual Outlaw: A Documentary (New York: Grove, 1977; London: Allen, 1978; enlarged, New York: Grove, 1984);
Rushes (New York: Grove, 1979);
Bodies and Souls (New York: Carroll & Graf, 1983; London: Allen, 1984);
Marilyn's Daughter (New York: Carroll & Graf, 1988);
The Miraculous Day of Amalia Gómez (New York: Arcade, 1991).

PLAY PRODUCTIONS: *Momma as She Became . . . But Not as She Was*, New York, 1978;

Tigers Wild, New York, 1986.

John Rechy has devoted some of his closely autobiographical writings to the exploration and presentation of derelict and homosexual life in the United States. His approach to the subject is explicit, anguished, intense, and sometimes sensationalistic. One critic, Terry Southern, has classified him with "the self-revelatory school of Romantic Agony" whose basic mandate is "Feel everything and leave nothing unsaid." But some of Rechy's works have a documentary quality that critics such as Lee T. Lemon relate to the social-reform novel and sociology. These views summarize the basic impact of Rechy's reports on the desperate agony of social outcasts in the midst of a repressive but "lost" society. In Rechy's work the plight of the outcast is only an extreme version of the essentially "lost" nature of the human condition.

Like the main character in his first novel (*City of Night*, 1963), Rechy grew up in El Paso, Texas, where he was born on 10 March 1934 to parents of Mexican and Scottish descent (Roberto Sixto Rechy and Guadalupe Flores Rechy). Span-

John Rechy (photograph by Tony Korody)

ish is his native language, and he did not learn to speak English until he went to school. The Chicano experience, however, has left only a very subtle imprint on Rechy's work, which deals mainly with a world and themes in which ethnic background is not paramount. Exceptions are *This Day's Death* (1970), *The Miraculous Day of Amalia Gómez* (1991), and some shorter pieces. At Texas Western College in El Paso, Rechy obtained his B.A.; then he attended the New School for Social Research in New York City. In 1961 he won the Longview Foundation Fiction Prize for "The Fabulous Wedding of Miss Destiny," a short story later incorporated into *City of Night* as one of its most outstanding passages.

The 1 February 1963 issue of *Library Journal* featured Rechy and several other first novelists for that year, with their photographs on the cover of the magazine and a few words by them about their work. Rechy wrote:

> I've lived briefly in New York, Los Angeles, San Francisco, New Orleans, and Chicago. Those cities provide the background for my first

novel. . . . The novel involved the journey of a narrator through those cities and "through" a series of other people's lives. The book was begun four years ago—but I didn't work consistently on it throughout that time. It was contracted for, unfinished, approximately two years ago. I work sporadically—sometimes not writing for weeks, other times working from eight in the morning until late at night, with only brief interruptions. I go through at least 12 complete versions, and some passages and pages through more than that. . . . The writers I admire most are [Fyodor] Dostoyevski and, among the Americans, [Nathaniel] Hawthorne, [Edgar Allan] Poe, and the earlier [William] Faulkner.

To the authors mentioned above one should add Tennessee Williams: "What I like about him is the giant dragon emotions; the raging emotions; the screaming about life"—Rechy said in a 1973 interview in the *Chicago Review*, and he added some comments that are revealing in relation to Rechy's own work: "I think his best play is *Suddenly Last Summer* [1958]. . . . It's the one that is fully realized, that moves relentlessly to violence and doesn't move back. [A] *Streetcar [Named Desire*, 1947] backs away from the building violence— it ends subdued, cowed. *Suddenly Last Summer* doesn't cop out; it moves to that hideous violence."

City of Night is a first-person narrative of a young male who gets paid for his sexual favors by other males. He drifts from New York to Los Angeles, Hollywood, San Francisco, and Chicago, all meccas of homosexual life, then to New Orleans for Mardi Gras. Through these adventures, a kaleidoscopic view of homosexual America—its seamy side, with all its little tragedies, black humor, and frenzied restlessness—is presented. It is a series of fragments held together by the point of view of the narrator, who is a participant and not simply an observer, afflicted with the same condition of the world he observes, and not just because of his sexual inclination but because of his relentless search for an elusive and mysterious satisfaction. His view of things is humorous, bitter, colorful, and yet sometimes obscure and indifferent. The novel is picaresque in terms of structure and the somber tone of its humor. This structure, perhaps more than anything else, has driven critics such as Peter Buitenhuis to question its claim to the title of novel, while at the same time, reluctantly, Buitenhuis acknowledges its impact: "*City of Night* is a remarkable book. Mr. Rechy can hardly be called a novelist. He lacks the art to shape experience into developing narrative; he has little of the craftsmanship, nothing of the detached lucidity which makes the true novelist" (*New York Times Book Review*, 30 June 1963). This criticism could be directed against many Spanish picaresque novels that have passed the test of centuries. However, *City of Night* is more unified and structured than many picaresque novels, and it has the redeeming qualities of an existentialist theme: it could be read as a parable of lost salvation.

The title and epigraph of the novel refer to a late-Romantic poem, "The City of Dreadful Night," published in 1874 by James Thompson. The city described in the poem, with images of night and darkness, of death, gloom, and desolation, is an allegorical dwelling for those who, having lost all hope or faith, encounter no solace in the world.

City of Night became an international bestseller, attaining a status that Rechy's following works have not, although *Numbers* (1967) and *The Sexual Outlaw* (1977) appeared on best-seller lists. In between the publications of his books, Rechy

has taught creative writing at Occidental College, the University of Southern California, and the University of California, Los Angeles, where he now teaches in the University Extension Program.

Rechy's second novel, *Numbers*, continues with the theme of the relentless search and, although less clearly, with the deep existential undertones of *City of Night*. In *Numbers*, Johnny Río (the main character), who had been a male hustler in Los Angeles, drives back to that city after a self-imposed exile of three years, during which he had saved money, been abstinent, exercised, and acquired a good tan. Now his purpose is to prove himself more handsome and desirable than ever, to conquer "the sex jungle," and then to leave. He has allotted himself ten days in California and also set an arbitrary figure of thirty conquests. After cruising around in various areas of Los Angeles, he selects Griffith Park as his main scene. It is here that he achieves his goal, each of the thirty acts being recounted for the reader ad nauseam. His goal achieved, Johnny is ready to leave, but, on the way, he turns his car once more into the park. . . . By the end of the book the count reaches thirty-seven. There would seem to be no aim to this novel, only the prurient excitement of sexual acts and the meaningless obsession of the addicted. However, as Rechy told William Leyland in a 1978 interview: "I think that Johnny Río in *Numbers* is a real existential creature trying to thwart the certain knowledge of doom by collecting and counting sex acts. *Numbers* is a very misunderstood book. . . . The reaction to it was outrage—but it's not a pornographic book. It's a book about a nightmare, about someone trying to avoid death. It's a beautifully structured book. (I am not modest, incidentally, about myself or my work.) Unfortunately, it is flawed; it is the one book of mine that I would like to rewrite some day, I hope. . . . I would like the thing to move relentlessly as a sexual horror story, an existential nightmare, and I think it slows down. . . ."

After the frantic and obsessive sex hunt of the main characters in Rechy's first two novels, *This Day's Death* has almost the quality of a slow-motion nightmare. In fact two intertwined nightmares, one in El Paso (the slow death of the protagonist's mother), the other in Los Angeles (an agonizingly long trial on sex-perversion charges), slowly grind down the main character, Jim Girard, and force him to grope with deeply hidden layers of his consciousness as he drives back and forth from one city to the other. Girard, drowning in his mother's obsessive love for him, begins to view her "death-in-life" as her ultimate weapon in the war to possess him. He must come to terms with his past and his love-hate attitudes, not only in relation to his mother but in all his relationships. In the other nightmare, although the alleged homosexual encounter (in Griffith Park) could have happened but never did, he is proclaimed guilty of the sex charges against him. The sentence forces him to accept his latent-homosexual inclination, as all his projects for a future heterosexual life as a lawyer are destroyed by the stroke of the pen of a particularly insensitive God-like judge.

The novel is thus an indictment of the whole judicial system including police, lawyers, and judges. This aspect of the work is the basis for Lemon's suggestion that "On one level, *This Day's Death* has to be read as a low-keyed but disturbing social reform novel. The targets are the police and the courts. . . . The question Rechy poses is: How does it feel to be an innocent man who comes to realize that his best hope is a guilty plea and a suspended sentence? What is the effect on family, business, friends, fiancée? *This Day's Death* is a powerful novel in part because Rechy has avoided the temptation to preach. Instead, he concentrates on one of the chief jobs of a novelist—that of communicating experience as he believes it to be."

During the battle between the mother's possessive love and her son's fight for liberation, Rechy's Chicano background comes to the surface in a way that is not as evident in most of his other works. That background may help explain the tormented love-hate battle that occurs perhaps more inside Girard's head than on the outside, and which sometimes reaches extraordinary proportions.

The two story lines in the novel could be separate, and in fact they are virtually maintained that way because of the necessity for Girard to keep secret his legal/sexual trouble. But it is the intertwining of the two and the need for a double life that give intensity to both. At the same time, this helps to underscore the indictment not only of the judicial system but of a society that criminalizes an otherwise harmless act and, therefore, provides the temptation for the system to corrupt itself into a travesty of justice. The troubles Girard encounters are not only those of an innocent, heterosexual man who accidentally is accused of a homosexual crime he did not commit but also, and at the same time, those of a la-

tent homosexual who could have committed, and later does commit, the act of which Girard is accused. This subtle fusion of two destinies in one is an interesting aspect of this novel. Thus the point of justice in question becomes not whether the act was committed or not, but whether in justice that act should be judged or not.

In many respects *The Vampires* (1971), Rechy's fourth novel, is unlike his other works. Although there are plenty of sexual encounters, sex itself is not the central preoccupation of the book. Evil is—presented through the topic of vampirism. Yet vampirism is mostly hinted at and represented mainly through sexual encounters, often bloody, always evil, and never "pure" in terms of sex, sensuality, or emotions. It is as if the theme of the book were the emasculation of purity as a definition of evil. But this point is not quite clear, and little else is either. The action takes place during a weekend on an island where a score of people have gathered as invited guests of the owner of the main house. They spend the weekend playing mysterious, symbolic, psychological games that lead to revelations of significant moments of their pasts and their psyches. Their names are exotic, perhaps symbolic, such as Savannah, the most beautiful woman in the world; Blue, a male prostitute; Topaze, a perfectly shaped midget; Malissa, the "queen of evil"; Joja and Bravo, actresses; La Duquesa, a drag queen in mourning; Tor, a bodybuilder; and the Mamaloi and the Papaloi, voodoo high priestess and high priest. There are also a Catholic priest, several former wives of the host, one of his sons, a hoodlum, and a couple of incestuous brother and sister twins who may have also been sired by the host. The games culminate in a murder that has been foreshadowed since the beginning of the book. Evil triumphs.

The purpose of the book is never quite clear. Is it an exorcism for the author? The reviewer for *Publishers' Weekly* called it "an adolescent fantasy novel with all the trappings of de Sade and none of the intelligence" (April 1971). It could easily be the basis for a weird, pornographic movie, its meaning densely buried beneath grave symbolism and a solemn tone. For Rechy it is a vision of hell. The novel is built around the concept of confession (as is the case in most of his books), in this instance a satanic confession of evil that reveals a search for purity.

The Fourth Angel (1972) departs in significant ways from Rechy's previous novels. A trio of adolescents, two boys and a girl who call them-

John Rechy
The Miraculous Day
of
Amalia Gómez

AZTLÁN ES UNA FÁBULA

A Novel
by the Author of
City of Night

Dust jacket for Rechy's 1991 book, his most "Chicano" novel

violence" (*Library Journal*, 1 September 1973). It is, in a sense, the world of *The Vampires*, or of vampire trainees.

In 1976 Rechy received a grant from the National Endowment for the Humanities, and during that time he wrote his next book. In *The Sexual Outlaw* Rechy does not attempt to write a novel but what he calls (in the full subtitle) "A Non-Fiction Account, with Commentaries, of Three Days and Nights in the Sexual Underground." The accounting of events, the obsessive search for promiscuous sexual encounters, is reminiscent of *Numbers*, and one of the motivating factors is that public homosexual encounters and behavior are forms of defiance and rebellion against repressive authorities in a society that makes a crime out of sexual acts between consenting adults, a point initially made in *This Day's Death*.

The form of the book constitutes the main departure for Rechy, as he describes it in the foreword for the 1984 edition:

> I conceived this book as a "prose documentary." The stark style I attempted—different from that of all my other books—and its "black-and-white" imagery are intended to suggest a documentary film. The "essays" function as "voice-overs" and speak at times in affirmation of Jim's [the protagonist's] actions, still others in argument, even opposition. The deliberate fluctuations and "contradictions" are essential to the meaning of this book.
>
> In writing *The Sexual Outlaw*, I attempted what I consider a new approach to the so-called non-fiction novel: I arranged random "real" experiences so that their structured sequence would stand for narrative development. Although there is a protagonist whom the book follows intimately, minute by recorded minute for a full weekend, there is no strict plot. . . .
>
> This book was composed in two main parts: the "experiential" passages in which the protagonist, Jim, sexhunts throughout Los Angeles for three days and nights; and various "essay-style" sections. The "experiential" chapters were written first, straight through, with only noted designations of where a certain "essay" would be inserted later. Then I wrote the individual "essay" sections.

The technique of concentrating action in a short but significant period of time that involves the lives of several "pastless" characters is used again in Rechy's novel *Rushes* (1979). The time is one long night at a "leather and Western" bar called Rushes on a cruising strip along the decay-

selves the Angels, are led by the girl, Shell, in a search for thrills in and around 1960s El Paso. They recruit a fourth Angel, Jerry, the character through whose point of view most of the story is told. Like the main character in *This Day's Death*, Jerry is obsessed with his mother. In this case she has died recently, and Jerry is looking for an escape or an adjustment to the reality of death. Although hardened on the outside, the four characters are essentially children at play, with all the fears and joys of childhood. Their experiments with hallucinogenic drugs reveal that charming and innocent side. Although Shell's method is to deny all softness and sentimentality, in the end, through Jerry's acceptance of his need for love or sympathy, the characters are confronted with their need for this basic "weakness" they have been trying to reject.

This story departs from the homosexual world but not entirely, and the world the novel presents is still that of "the social/sexual outsider" and of "the dark sensuality of barely contained

ing waterfront of an unnamed American city. Rechy explores the varying sexual needs, habits, fears, and concerns of his characters, but he is mainly interested in the exploration and evaluation of that aspect of the homosexual ethos that prizes macho types and attitudes above all. By internalizing society's predominant macho values, these homosexuals have moved to the opposite extreme from the drag queens and their female costumes. All the uniforms of the most outstanding macho stereotypes are paraded in a sexual charade of dominance and submission: the cowboy, the lumberjack, the military hero, the motorcycle cop, the Nazi officer, and an original uniform that does not belong to any real-life character but to the composite and synthesis of machismo in clothes: the leather man. Ironically the attitudes reflected in the uniforms also reflect society's contempt for homosexuals, stereotyped as sissies, but nonetheless a contempt extending to the macho types as well. Ironically, the book suggests, sexual freedom and gay liberation have led to the ghettoization of homosexuals, thus complying with society's repressive attitudes about them. They gather on the fringes of a society that rejects them and play games that society has imposed on them. The undercurrent of self-hatred that underlines these games overflows into contempt for all those who do not conform to the ideal of machismo, beauty, and youth, a contempt that gnaws at the self-assurance of even the most macho but yet uncertain demigods. Such a fringe world may seem a heavenly refuge— "No matter how cruel the Rushes may have been, it protected them from a vaster cruelty outside"— as a church would seem to the faithful.

On this level the novel can be read as a reenactment of a mystery play or sacramental rite. It is divided into two parts, each introduced with a traditional blessing in Latin from the Catholic Mass. Each chapter within the sections is also introduced with an epigraph taken from the Mass, in praise of or expressing gratitude to the Lord. Of the total of fifteen chapters, fourteen (the number of the Stations of the Cross) begin with a recurrent phrase, "As often as he comes to the Rushes," followed by a different name each time, underscoring the feeling of a recurrent ritual. Corresponding to the number of these chapters there is repeated reference to fourteen panels painted on the wall of the bar; these panels depict various scenes of a sexual nature with the theme of male dominance and submission. The main character, Endore, examines them toward the end of the book when, with the last call for drinks, the bright lights of the bar are turned on:

> It is the first time Endore has seen—remembers seeing—the panels in this damning light. Impressions—which may fade or become permanent this night of revelation—bombard him. There *is* a central figure which recurs from panel to panel, and—this astonished him—there is a definite sequence of events, like recorded stations, but they are scrambled, not in order. The "last" panel—the recurrent man now pinioned in ecstasy or pain against the trunk of a tree, the uniformed men assaulting his flesh or stripping the remnants of his clothes—depicts a final pornographic immolation, willing or forced. Now Endore is sure there are 14 panels, and one more, left blank. He looks at the vortex of scrawls entangling flushed organs; the vague, ghostly image there. The artist saw no meaning in the scattered procession of violence. He pulled back by leaving the summary panel undrawn, Endore knows—and now he too pulls back from the impact of the panels. Illumined, cracks in the walls slash the drawn figures like bolts of lightning.

In the novel, too, there is one more chapter, distinguished from the others in that it does not begin with the same sentence. In it the tensions built up throughout the novel climax in some final scenes of sadomasochism and violence.

Like Rechy's first book, *City of Night, Bodies and Souls* (1983) can be read as a parable of salvation. This concern, hinted at in the title, is stressed at several points throughout the work but is defined succinctly in the words of a charismatic television evangelist from Los Angeles called Sister Woman, who pays a central role in the story. In her words, "In the divine order of things all is perfect, and God's perfect design is called 'salvation.' There is no substitute." The human implications are possibly disastrous, since the concept renders all human things imperfect— all being failed attempts at substitution for that perfect fullness that only the divine can render. Seen from such a perspective, all human life and activity is lost, and humans are all "lost angels," including the "divinely" inspired evangelist, in search of a message that does not come. All offers of salvation become false. Substitution is the work of the deceiver.

These implications are obviously not intended by the character who spoke such words, but the basic theme is illustrated by the central story of the book: a rich and sinful old woman (readers do not know her sins), one of the many followers of Sister Woman, has died, leaving her fortune (millions) to Sister Woman's cause, but with one condition. Sister Woman must prove her claim that she can redeem condemned souls from the depths of hell, even after death, by offering proof that she has saved the sinful woman. The sinful woman's protégé, Orin, a particularly reticent but sincere youth, is the only one who knows the clue that will show proof of her salvation. He has come to Los Angeles to witness the proof and deliver, or withhold, the ransom inheritance. In a tense climax, Sister Woman, duly inspired, almost delivers the prescribed message but fails, thus showing herself a pawn of the deceiver: *"An evil God? A holy Satan?"*

Just as Sister Woman's offer of salvation is shown to fail, the stories of the other characters show them to be "substituting" various things for something they themselves do not know but can sense through their own wretched lives. The choice of characters and the generally ironic, often satirical, and even sarcastic style in which their stories are narrated give a clue. Through them, readers are also given a rich vision of the composition of the city from the lower depths to the top, the characters including Amber, a porn superstar; Manny Gomez, a Chicano from East L.A., who is exploring the punk rock scene; Hester Washington, a black maid from Watts who works in Bel Air for Mrs. Stephens, wife of a wealthy judge; Dave Clinton, an aging homosexual stripper who works in a fancy nightclub for women; a guest lecturer at a major university who lectures "On Nothing"; Mick Vale, a weight lifter competing for the title of "Mr. Universal"; Carla, a street tramp living on the edge of reality and in fear of young city muggers; Billy and Stud, street hustlers who fall in love with each other; Mandy Lang-Jones, a bitchy television reporter doing a series on "The Lower Depths," in which some of the other characters have appeared; and Officer Weston, a policeman with psychological problems and a secret lust for little girls. Although their lives at some points intersect, their stories are told in tightly wrought units, in separate chapters that could easily stand as independent works. The book could be seen as a collection of short stories tied together by their location in the city of Los Angeles and the accidental intersecting of some of the tales.

Further tying together of the stories is provided by the apparently aimless roaming of the main character, Orin, and his traveling companions, Lisa and Jessie; the three youths have recently arrived in the city and are acting as typical tourists in Los Angeles, but their travels provide biting visions of a shell of a city without a soul. Only Orin knows the purpose of his visit, but he is not talking; the other two live halfway between movie reality and childhood, escaping a vaguely cruel past and rushing toward nothing, perhaps living the moment but not its reality.

The lecturer lecturing "On Nothing," like Sister Woman, also announces the central theme: "There is no substitute for salvation," but he concludes that all the process of creation and history leads to nothing but an accident, that "either God is evil or destiny is chance" and that "The only liar greater than the artist [God being the artist] . . . is the critic, who interprets the artist's lie. . . . Critical interpretation is the greatest lie." Thus we see the lecturer as both a parallel and an antagonist to Sister Woman.

The association Terry Southern made between *City of Night* and a kind of romanticism is corroborated by Rechy's later works. The demonic or damned vision of the world is reminiscent of the works of some Romantics. *The Vampires* has many of the trappings of a Gothic novel and even recalls William Beckford's mystery celebrations in his great mansion at Fonthill (as described by Peter Quennell in *Romantic England*, 1970). But Rechy is also a twentieth-century writer: his view of the damned human condition is also the product of an existentialist and positivistic outlook, that of a humanity and a reality without God, or abandoned by God.

Rechy's works also weave a rich tapestry in which often-ignored segments of society, those relegated to the fringes, come to the center and are generously endowed with color (no matter how bleak) and life; his scathing sarcasm is endowed with compassion for the derelict. Rechy's works may lack illumination and revelation, but his central motivating factor is the suspicion that all illumination is deceptive, that certainty is unattainable. The only significant statement possible is *"I am here,"* the message Sister Woman fails to deliver in *Bodies and Souls*; that is all his characters can say.

Marilyn's Daughter (1988) introduces new themes in Rechy's work, yet follows familiar patterns. Like *City of Night* it traces the pilgrimage of a young character, this time a female, in search of an elusive personal essence or definition. The story opens with a posthumous note that throws open the question as to whether the main character, named Normalyn, is Marilyn Monroe's daughter. Her search for answers begins in Texas and takes her to California, to that "city of lost angels" (Los Angeles), which has become a leitmotiv in Rechy's work. Taking as a point of departure Hollywood's glamorous creation, Monroe—"a monument to the perfection of artifice," as characterized in the epigraph—the novel can be read as a parable of woman's search for identity in the post-Monroe era. Male characters, especially the Kennedys, appear as archetypal figures of masculine oppression of the female. In this context the Chicano presence is noted in one of the secondary characters, Ted Gonzalez, who, unsure of his own masculinity, initiates then averts an attempted rape of Normalyn.

Artifice and reality become inextricably intertwined and diffused in the novel. Rechy's style has changed, from the passionate expressiveness of *City of Night* to a terse, limpid, or translucent descriptive line (almost a parody of his former style), which somehow reminds one of Wayne Thiebaud's paintings, in the stark presentation of delineating contour and solid shapes of color without depth, constantly undermining realism by calling attention to artifice. Thus the novel calls attention to itself: it purports to deal with historical facts and characters—Monroe, the Kennedys, and their rumored relationship—yet all the "facts" are imaginings of fictional characters attempting to re-create an elusive reality.

In 1991 Rechy published *The Miraculous Day of Amalia Gómez*. The setting and characters make it his most clearly "Chicano" novel, as it is set in a Los Angeles barrio. The plot includes elements of magic realism.

Rechy is currently working on two new books: "In the Beginning," about a war in heaven; and "Autobiography: A Novel." Despite little acknowledgment as a Chicano writer, Rechy is one of the most successful. The scope of his writing overflows narrow classifications, and his is an unusual voice in contemporary American fiction.

Interviews:
James R. Giles and Wanda Giles, "An Interview with John Rechy," *Chicago Review*, 25 (Summer 1973): 19-31;

William Leyland, "John Rechy," in *Gay Sunshine Interviews*, volume 2, edited by Leyland (San Francisco: Gay Sunshine, 1978), pp. 251-268.

References:
Lee T. Lemon, "You May Have Missed These," *Prairie Schooner*, 45 (Fall 1971): 270-272;

Minority Voices, special Rechy issue, 3 (Fall 1979);

E. S. Nelson, "John Rechy, James Baldwin and the American Double Minority Literature," *Journal of American Culture*, 6 (Summer 1983): 70-74;

B. Satterfield, "John Rechy's Tormented World," *Southwest Review*, 67 (Winter 1982): 78-85;

Terry Southern, "Rechy and Gover," in *Contemporary American Novelists*, edited by Harry T. Moore (Carbondale & Edwardsville: Southern Illinois University Press, 1964), pp. 222-227;

T. Steuervogel, "Contemporary Homosexual Fiction and the Gay Rights Movement," *Journal of Popular Culture*, 20 (Winter 1986): 125-134.

Alberto Ríos
(18 September 1952 -   )

José David Saldívar
University of California, Santa Cruz

BOOKS: *Elk Heads on the Wall* (Berkeley: University of California, 1979);
Sleeping On Fists (Story, Wyo.: Dooryard, 1981);
Whispering to Fool the Wind (Riverdale-on-Hudson, N.Y.: Sheep Meadow, 1982);
The Iguana Killer: Twelve Stories of the Heart (Lewiston, Idaho: Blue Moon & Confluence, 1984);
Five Indiscretions (Riverdale-on-Hudson, N.Y.: Sheep Meadow, 1985);
The Lime Orchard Woman (Riverdale-on-Hudson, N.Y.: Sheep Meadow, 1988);
Teodor Luna's Two Kisses (New York: Norton, 1990).

Alberto Ríos circa 1985 (photograph by Karla Elling)

Since 1981, when he received the Academy of American Poets' Walt Whitman Award for *Whispering to Fool the Wind* (published in 1982), Alberto Ríos has been assured an important position in American literature. Ríos has been heralded as the major practitioner of the baroque in the Southwest, as the most articulate poetic voice of the American language in the 1980s, as the most technically sophisticated and complex poet from the borderlands, and even as the one on whose shoulders has fallen the mantle of genius previously worn by Lorna Dee Cervantes and Gary Soto. No matter how exaggerated these evaluations might seem, Ríos is surely one of the major vernacular voices in the postmodernist age. It is as a poet that he assumes his important position. However, Ríos also writes lyrically dazzling short stories.

Born on 18 September 1952 in Nogales, Arizona, Ríos is the son of a British mother, Agnes Fogg Ríos, and a Mexican father, Alberto Alvaro Ríos. Growing up on the Arizona-Mexico border, the young Ríos first learned Spanish. But when he entered grade school, like most Chicanos, he was forced to give up his first language. As Ríos recalls, "We got swats for speaking Spanish, even on the playground." By the time he was in junior high school, Ríos could no longer speak Spanish. As a result of his forced forgetting of that language, Ríos invented a third language—"one," he says, "that was all our own." Many of his most important early poems dramatize the essence of this uncanny third language.

In junior high Ríos began writing what he calls "mildly rebellious, abstract poems" in the back pages of his notebooks. He continued this practice in high school and college. Ríos attended the University of Arizona, and earned his B.A. with honors in 1974. Not satisfied with a double major in English and creative writing, Ríos earned another B.A. with honors in psychology

220

in 1975. Ríos then enrolled in law school at the same university but quit after a year to enroll in the M.F.A. program in creative writing, which he completed in 1979. Ríos is now an associate professor of English and director of the creative-writing program at Arizona State University.

Ríos became a technically brilliant poet at the University of Arizona, but, like many ethnic American writers, he had to spend much time in creative-writing workshops in arguments over the content of his work. His professors who were not from Arizona would want him to change the names of his characters because, according to Ríos, "they had never heard of a Sapito or a Graciela. These were the names of my relatives!"

In 1980 Ríos received a fellowship in creative writing from the National Endowment for the Arts. *Sleeping On Fists* (1981), a major chapbook, was completed during this period. Next came *Whispering to Fool the Wind*. The most striking quality about Ríos's early poems is that he draws from an oral culture that was passed on from his *nani* (grandmother), *abuelo* (grandfather), cousins, aunts, childhood friends, an Uncle Humberto, and a representative relative Ríos names Carlos. Because Ríos's poetic representation of his characters' stories hardly differs from their own speech and point of view, he is one of the great third-world American storytellers. Storytelling in verse, traditionally, is a difficult task because the details in prose fiction—a sense of being and time and of characters exchanging experiences—are seemingly at odds with the compactness of poetry. Nevertheless, Ríos is able to master this difficult procedure.

Extraordinary and magical things happen in *Whispering to Fool the Wind*. The character Pánfilo's head is deformed and "awkwardly" bent out of shape; a grandfather "who has served ants with the attitude of a waiter" is buried in his best suit; and poor, sad Uncle Humberto, a collector of butterflies, dies of excessive rage because one day Graciela, a "hard seamstress," refuses to give him pins. Ríos's "True Story of the Pins," like Gabriel García Márquez's children's stories, is an allegory of the storytelling process:

> Pins are always plentiful
> but one day they were not
> and your Uncle Humberto
> who collected butterflies
> you see here on the walls
> was crazy looking for some
> and he went to your cousin
> Graciela the hard seamstress

> who has pins it is rumored
> even in hard times, but when
> she found out why he wanted them
> . . . .
> . . . she firmly refused
> your poor Uncle Humberto.

Throughout *Whispering to Fool the Wind* magical-realist events are related with the greatest of accuracy without being forced on the reader. It is left up to readers to interpret things for themselves in a way that is most familiar to them.

Ríos's work reaches back to his own past and that of others. In "Madre Sofía," for example, he writes about his impressions of a local gypsy fortune-teller his mother once took him to see. His dramatization of the episode is through a child's point of view, syntax, and language:

> My mother took me because she couldn't
> wait the second ten years to know.
> This was the lady rumored to have been
> responsible for the box-wrapped baby
> among the presents at the wedding,
> but we went in anyway, through the curtains.

The child does not know how to feel about the lady with a "face mahogany" and "eyes half yellow half gray." But his description of the gypsy Sofía is one of the most fascinating and humorous pieces of writing in *Whispering to Fool the Wind*. For instance, the child sees "breasts as large as her / head, folded together, coming out of her dress / as if it didn't fit, not like my mother's." He is frightened by "those breasts swinging towards him," and he valiantly tries protecting "whatever it is that needs protection when a baseball is thrown." Later he metonymically associates the gypsy Sofía with Joaquín, the amputee with "quarter arms . . . who came back from the war to sit / in the park, always reaching for children."

In Ríos's verse, words, eyes, soul, and world are brought into bright connection. His poems in *Whispering to Fool the Wind* are in the vernacular rhythms of his ancestor's lives, as in "Carlos," for example, one of the most haunting poems in the collection:

> Carlos is the name
> by which loneliness
> knows each of us.
> Carlos the distant relative
> worse off than we are
> who drank medicines
> of poverty and died
> not in his sleep

but wide awake . . .
Carlos who lives inside
pain in each of us. . . .

Carlos appears, like a ghost, in several other poems in the book, as the representative border man.

The best poem in *Whispering to Fool the Wind*, and one of the most remarkable poems in Chicano literature, is "Nani," Ríos's sestina about his grandmother. "Nani" captures the reality of his invented third language:

Sitting at her table, she serves
the sopa de arroz [Spanish rice] to me
instinctively, and I watch her,
the absolute *mamá*, and eat words
I might have had to say more
out of embarrassment. To speak,
now-foreign words I used to speak,
too, dribble down her mouth as she serves
me albóndigas [meatballs]. No more
than a third are easy to me.
By the stove she does something with words
and looks at me only with her
back. I am full. I tell her
I taste the mint, and watch her speak
smiles at the stove. All my words
make her smile. Nani never serves
herself, she only watches me
with her skin, her hair. I ask for more.

Ríos's poetry is a kind of magical storytelling, and his stories are a kind of magical poetry. His collection of bucolic fables, *The Iguana Killer: Twelve Stories of the Heart* (1984), won the prestigious Western States Book Award for fiction, sponsored by the Western States Art Foundation in Santa Fe, New Mexico. Written for what Ríos calls a "young adult" audience, *The Iguana Killer* explores the luminous world of his childhood and border culture. In the title story young Sapito, like a mythical British knight, uses an American baseball bat his grandmother sends him to become the greatest iguana killer in tropical Mexico. "The Child," the most realistic story in the collection, tells the harrowing story of two Mexican widows, Mrs. Sandoval and Mrs. García, who on their bus trip from Guaymas to Nogales meet a mysterious man and a sick child who holds a devastating secret. At the end of the tale, Mrs. García reveals the lurid truth: "The child was dead. It had been dead for a long time. That is true. But it had also been operated on. The boy's insides had been cleaned out and replaced with bags of opium. . . . Then the boy was sewn

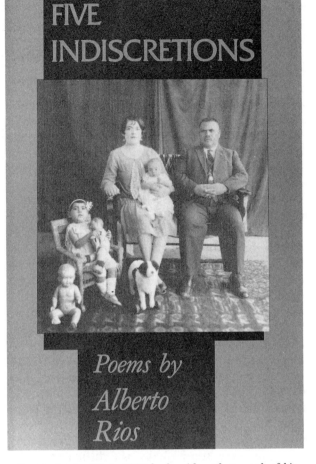

Dust jacket for Ríos's 1985 book, with a photograph of his sister, his parents, and himself as an infant (on his mother's lap)

up again, put into clothes." "A Friend, Brother Maybe" is about a young boy named Frankie who has behavioral problems. Mr. Johnson, a social worker, believes Frankie's illness can be cured instrumentally with a bizarre personality-modification machine.

While most of the young-adult stories in *The Iguana Killer* are straightforwardly narrated, "The Way Spaghetti Feels" and "The Birthday of Mrs. Piñeda," the best stories in the book, border on the metafictional and magical-realist impulse in postmodernist fiction. "The Birthday of Mrs. Piñeda," the most lyrical story in *The Iguana Killer*, is about a husband's desire to control his wife's discourse. At the end of the story, the husband finally allows Mrs. Piñeda to tell her own tale: "Mariquita Piñeda," Ríos writes, "began her story on her birthday, and it went on, and on, further, through the night and pushed a shoulder against lunch time of the next day."

Ríos's prize-winning collection of stories received highly favorable reviews. Jodi Daynard, in the *New York Times Book Review* (23 December 1984), favorably compared Ríos's *The Iguana Killer* with William Golding's *The Lord of the Flies* (1954), another book about children. E. J. Montini, in the *Arizona Republic* (23 October 1984), claimed, "It is the taking away of secrets, the cruel, sometimes crude manner in which they are exposed, that is at the heart of each story in *The Iguana Killer*." In brief, various reviewers were favorably impressed with Ríos's bicultural perspective, with his portrayal of young Chicanas (Daynard called "The Way Spaghetti Feels" "the best story in the collection"), and with the surreal language.

In Ríos's *Five Indiscretions* (1985) nearly every poem is about desire, sexuality, and religion, and nearly every poem deals with courtships between men and women. Most of the poems achieve a level of excellence not far below the peak moments in his earlier poetry. No Chicano poet writing today is a more exquisite—a more fastidiously deliberate—technician than Ríos. His poetry is always lavishly textured.

In part 1 the poems are written from a woman's perspective. Throughout this section Ríos juxtaposes poems about desire, religion, and violence. In "Prayers to the Dangerous," for example, he is able to bring into clear focus two of his central concerns, desire and religion:

Pretty girls go walking away to prayers.
What they pray for, C-shaped, is not so different:
homemade waffles, omelettes all filled with mush-
    rooms.
But in the omelettes
one girl thinks of fire: in his hands, and eyelids
as they drooped, that halfway excruciation
coming from a moment without a name yet,
pressing and pressing.

In the title poem Ríos gives readers the meandering, sad, tragic tale of a woman whose "power" is "never once making love to a man."

In part 2 Ríos shifts his focus from a feminine world to a masculine world, peopled with characters such as El Santo the Wrestler and Reies the Boxer. In Ríos's hyperbolic poem "On January 5, 1984, El Santo the Wrestler Died, Possibly," the wrestler is so fierce and tenacious that even in death, it is claimed, he would "get angry, get up, and come back after them. / That way for which he was famous." In another poem in this section, "The Famous Boxer Reies Madero

Lives," Ríos describes the fear, respect, and love the local villagers have for their aging pugilist,

who killed two men in the ring,
the old kind of ring that was dirty
with sweat and canvas and fingers.
So it is agreed: no one will come near him
even still, he has been too strong,
too loud and too admired.

In part 3 of *Five Indiscretions*, Ríos describes various courtships. All of the young lovers in this lyrical section are seen as "too beautiful," too "full of plums, of peacock feathers."

Finally, in part 4, Ríos concludes the book by giving the reader some powerful autobiographical poems. In his slightly exaggerated poem, "I Would Visit Him in the Corner," for example, Ríos tells of an uncle who, when he was young, had a spider crawl into his ear. Throughout his tortured life, the uncle suffered as his "ear grew bigger / because he kept hitting it, and when he was old / it became his habit, even when it bled." At the end of the poem Ríos startles the reader: "Finally in the red night scratching / with no one to see and nothing to hold / the spider carelessly left him." In "Seniors" Ríos nostalgically remembers the "French kiss" he got "in the catholic darkness." In "Dinner" he describes the sound his father from the Mexican jungles makes when he eats: "Tacaná [the volcano] erupt[ing] is the sound he makes / when he eats, with his mouth, with the way he breathes through his nose." In "Combing My Hair in the Hall," Ríos returns to his obsessive artistic theme, namely, the "third language" invented between an English-speaking grandson and a Spanish-speaking grandmother:

Then she spoke with her woman's hands
only, no words left, then only her smell
which had once been warm, *tortillas*,
or like sugar breads just made.
In the half-words of our other language,
in the language of the new world
of which she had had time to show me
only half, I tried to speak to her. . . .

Regrettably *Five Indiscretions*, Ríos's most ambitious book, has not received the acclaim and attention it deserves. The few book reviews, however, praised his ability to represent gender issues and his use of the American language. The writer for *Booklist* (1 May 1985), for example, claimed that "Ríos is especially impressive in conjuring the emerging sexuality of adolescent girls." Similarly *Library Journal* (1 May 1985) noted that Ríos "offers the insights into the lives of women seldom found in the work of a male writer." And Lawrence Joseph, in the *American Book Review* (May-June/July-August 1987) argued that "*Five Indiscretions* displays the breadth and richness of the *American* language—the American language of the 1980s, the language which will be ours in the 1990s, into the twenty-first century, a language which requires and will require complex techniques. In fifty years, when the revolutions of the American language are clearer to us, most of the poetry of the 1980s will pale beside Ríos's (in the same way that most of the poetry of the 1920s pales beside the poetry published in 1923 in *Harmonium* by one of Ríos's masters, Wallace Stevens)."

Alberto Ríos's works have been published in over one hundred magazines, and his poetry has often been anthologized. His poem "Chileño Boys," in *Five Indiscretions*, has been set to reggae music by David Broza for CBS records. In 1984 Ríos was the only Arizonan selected for the *Esquire* feature titled "The Best of the New Generation: Men and Women Under Forty Who Are Changing America."

References:

José David Saldívar, "The Real and the Marvelous in Nogales, Arizona," *Denver Quarterly*, 17, no. 2 (1982): 141-144;

Saldívar, "Towards a Chicano Poetics: The Making of the Chicano-Chicana Subject, 1969-1982," *Confluencia*, 1 (Spring 1985): 10-17.

Marina Rivera
(9 February 1942 -   )

Elaine Dorough Johnson
University of Wisconsin—Whitewater

BOOKS: *Mestiza* (Tucson: Grilled Flowers, 1977);
Sobra (San Francisco: Casa Editorial, 1977);
Fingers of Silence, by Rivera, Will Inman, Sheila Murphy, Burgess Needle, and David Chorlton (N.p.: Brushfire, 1981).

OTHER: *I Had Been Hungry All The Years: An Anthology of Women's Poetry*, edited by Glenna Luschei and Del Marie Rogers, includes poems by Rivera, as Silvia Ortiz (San Luis Obispo, Cal.: Solo, 1975), pp. 39-41;
Southwest: A Contemporary Anthology, edited by Karl and Jane Kopp, includes an essay and poems by Rivera (Albuquerque: Red Earth, 1977), pp. 261-265; 283-284;
"Mermaid and Knight, A Sculpture," in *Beyond Rice, A Broadside Series*, edited by Terrence Ames, Lorna Dee Cervantes, and Geraldine Kudaka (San Francisco: Mango & Noro, 1979).

SELECTED PERIODICAL PUBLICATIONS—
UNCOLLECTED: "Ritmo," *Caracol*, 4 (August 1978): 5;

"Villa" and "Esteban," *Revista Chicano-Riqueña*, 6 (Fall 1978): 2, 4;
"Glass/Bone" and "Lion Tamer's Wife," *Caracol*, 5 (May 1979): 5;
"The Man of O" and "Blow, Blow," *Revista Chicano-Riqueña*, 7 (Summer 1979): 22-24;
"Mulberry/Morera," *Palabra*, 2 (Fall 1980): 81-82;
"For Celia," *Denver Quarterly*, 16 (Fall 1981): 25-27;
"Why" and "Bees, Birds, Moths, Chickens," *Revista Chicano-Riqueña*, 9 (Winter 1981): 3-4.

Marina Rivera is a mature, highly skilled poet who writes not only of her experience as a Chicana—coping with poverty and surviving in an Anglo-American world—but of her universal human experience: of love, loss, anger, and of personal growth. Proud of her heritage, yet sternly individualistic, Rivera speaks to any audience appreciative of serious poetry.

Rivera was born on 9 February 1942 in Supe-

Marina Rivera (photograph by Jerry Glaser)

rior, Arizona, a small mining town approximately sixty miles east of Phoenix. Although she is a descendant of two large Mexican families, the ancestor who stands out most in her mind is her German maternal great-grandfather, a powerful shipper in what is now the southwestern United States. His parents were killed by Indians when he was very young, and he was adopted into a Mexican-American family. Rivera's mother, like Marina, was born in a small, rural community in eastern Arizona, where she remained throughout her childhood. Rivera's father was born in Mexico and is a naturalized citizen of the United States. His mother, fleeing the civil unrest of the Mexican revolution and harassed by Pancho Villa's troops, brought him across the border when he was a baby. Rebellious and strong as a youth, he was not afraid to challenge the local racial-segregation code, entering movie theaters and other public places marked as off-limits to Mexicans.

Rivera's family moved to Phoenix when she was a small child. There she was educated through her graduation from high school. As a World War II veteran, her father was entitled to a housing-project residence, although he had to fight to get his family in because white applicants were given preference. He was intent on his family's full participation in American society and refused to be tricked or bullied out of what he knew to be his due, color line or not. Since theirs was a predominantly Anglo-American neighborhood, Rivera and her brother grew up among English-speaking children, playing with them but always being made to feel different. Language was a complex and painful problem. Since the Rivera children had to use English among their playmates, and they were punished if caught speaking Spanish in school, they lost confidence in their ability to speak Spanish. Relatives, sensing their awkwardness, teased them. In spite of the frustration that language caused them, both Rivera and her brother excelled in all areas of academic experience. Still, because of their color, they were excluded from extracurricular social activities such as off-campus dances and private parties.

For her undergraduate education, facilitated by general academic and Vesta Club scholarships, Rivera went to Northern Arizona University in Flagstaff. Deeply grateful to the Vesta Club, a Phoenix-based group dedicated to helping Chicanos attend college, she pledged to them any profits that her poetry might subsequently bring her. Majoring in English and minoring in French, she graduated summa cum laude, receiving a B.A. in 1964. For her graduate work, Rivera went to the University of Arizona, earning an M.A. in public speaking in 1966 and an M.F.A. in poetry writing in 1981. While a graduate student, she became active in the Poetry Center, serving for a year as a member of the board of directors and participating in the various programs and readings. It was there that she met her husband, a fellow board member and an English department graduate student.

Describing her professional history, Rivera says, "I have been either a teacher or a student all my life." Her teaching career had its beginning at the University of Arizona, where she worked as a teaching assistant for two years. Since then she has taught in high schools in Phoenix, Flagstaff, and Tucson, Arizona; Hayward and Santa Ana, California; and Alpine, Texas. She has taught English, speech, and creative writing. Rivera's most recent teaching experience was in Arizona, where she taught for several years at Tucson High School. There her title was English Teacher for the Special Projects High School for Advanced Studies. In 1982 she left high-school teaching and moved to a rural community behind the Catalina Mountains, where she established a small upholstery business and began working as a language tutor for corporation families from Spain.

Rivera began publishing in 1972 in various little magazines in the Southwest. Her first poems, however, were written when she was a high-school student in Phoenix. Her two major publications, *Mestiza* and *Sobra* (both 1977), are collections of her most significant work during the 1972 to 1977 period. More recently, she has published in several journals, including *Revista Chicano-Riqueña*, *Palabra*, *Caracol*, and the *Denver Quarterly*. Her poems have also appeared in anthologies. Scattered throughout these journals and anthologies are many of the poems that form "The Celia Poems," a book awaiting publication. In 1981, with several others, she published the chapbook *Fingers of Silence*.

Many poems in *Mestiza* address the experience of living simultaneously in two cultures and coping with the tensions that this split produces in the psyche. When she talks about her formative years and the experiences and feelings out of which *Mestiza* flowed, Rivera states, "I came to know the best in both cultures and the worst in both. And I have never forgotten the worst. I feel a person apart. I have learned to look deeply into the eyes and judge others by their actions, by their love, by their lack, and have become somewhat deaf, dumb and blind about whom and what I am supposed to love. I tend to love who loves me, erratic as I am, but fiercely, loyally."

In some of the *Mestiza* poems the question of racial identity is explicit, although it is interwoven with intensely personal concerns and is rarely the primary theme. The speaker in "Even" admonishes an observer who would have her be "brown" through and through, saying she prefers a third direction, neither white nor brown but that of her own individual self. While color is mentioned in "Seek," whose title refers to the "hide and seek" game the poet used to play with her brother when they were children, the poem is really about the impact of his death—a blow so jarring that Rivera would never completely get over it. In "Chon" she speaks of her anger toward a vio-

lent uncle and the conflict that she feels as she sees him aging: "I know I ought to forgive you. / The hatred of the small, brown child / is the hardest kind of change, Chon." The poem "Coraje" (Courage) is an expression of the collective anger of Chicanos toward the prejudice they must face in society, yet the target of the anger is left unstated: "All day we taste its oil base, / . . . . / Not all our lives can make it thin." In "Cats," the animals' resistance, tenacity, and independent spirit in the face of intense abuse suggest the Chicanos' indomitability.

Natural elements are important in *Mestiza*, sometimes for their own sake and sometimes for their symbolic function. "Back Yard Birds" captures the lyrical frolicking of birds around a birdbath—their movement and the interplay of sun and water on their feathers. In another poem in this collection, "Mastic," readers see the same mulberry tree, bird feeder, and birdbath, yet these elements are present to express a human theme, the desire for love and attention: "Now you fill / the feeder, renew the water, come in." In "Hiker" two lovers are cast as snakes, one pursuing the other in an erotic aquatic ballet, acted out in an Edenic setting, "a place over-grown with trees, moss, grass." Nature is central to "Crib Death," which includes the reincarnation theme and the concept of the soul returning to the source. Readers also see the reliability of the natural order in contrast with the less dependable technological one: "They [souls] go rising like plumes of artichoke blossoms / safer than concords." The arid southwestern landscape serves as an important metaphoric reference in "Neighbor." The debris of old thoughts could explode in flames: "Your head an old meadow / of wood so dry and brittle / one warm thought / might set it aflame."

The title poem of the collection, "Mestiza," is a five-part piece that raises several issues concerned with Rivera's mixed cultural, racial background. In the first part, "Lo que quieren" (What They Want), the speaker expresses the same pique expressed in "Even"—at being lumped together with all Chicanos without respect for anyone's uniqueness. She is told to write poetry that is somehow the embodiment of all Chicano feeling, and she bristles at the assignment: "estoy invitada a leer / pero hay que escribir más poemas / hechos en forma tortillada / las líneas construyendo un serape, / las hebras sangrando caras color de café" (they invite me to read / but I have to write more poems / shaped like tortillas / the lines forming a serape, / the

Rivera in March 1985 (photograph copyright by La Verne H. Clark)

threads bleeding brown faces). The second part, "Papá," is a tribute to Rivera's father, who wanted her to achieve what he could not: success. Part 3 is a tribute to her mother, who managed to overcome poverty through her own hard work, "vendiendo huevos para comprar tela, / cosiendo en máquina de pie" (selling eggs to buy cloth, / sewing on a treadle machine). The fourth part, "Lo que quiero yo" (What I Want) is an assertion of Rivera's individuality, apart from any ethnic or gender identification: "no me llamen por la chicana, / ni por el chicano, / ni por las mujeres, / llámenme por mí misma / una mujer" (do not summon me for the Chicana / nor for the Chicano, / nor for women, / summon me for myself / one woman). In the final part, "Lo que sé" (What I Know), she speaks to her mother, who lost her only son and who reaches across the boundary of death, affirming their enduring communication in the face of an alien, uncomprehending world: "si todo el mundo me desconoce / tú me vas a entender, madre" (if everyone disavows me / you will understand me, mother).

Sobra, Rivera's second collection, is a much more private, personal, encoded work than *Mestiza*. Some of the same themes and images are

still present, however: navigating in the Anglo-American world—"How we wooed those / white school teachers" ("Denominator"); the effect of an adult's anger on children—"His anger / is a boot / in their lungs, / a glove / for the face" ("Cruising"); an older relative overcome by the brutal circumstances of his life—"He had the face of shorn down wood, / . . . / the pit he swallowed / death from in the mines" ("Uncle"); the fusion of human beings with nature—"you / who were like the unseen water in the creek" ("Way"); and the devastation of death—"Death rips you out, / the one the rest depends on" ("Mama Toña").

The reader of *Sobra* is confronted with an introspection so intense that it is more anguish than reflection. Similarly the examination of personal relationships is more probing, often revealing the total inability to communicate. In "Alarm" a pent-up scream is finally released, "loud as the floor tiles," and in "Stone" an unfathomable amount of anger is concentrated in a small stone. In the poem "Sobra" readers see the extreme alienation of the woman who spent hours staring "at the face that never / matched its voice." Lovers seem to be at cross purposes, their energies canceling each other out. In "Station," "Every window she opened / he would close. / Every switch she touched / he changed back." In "Looking at Your Hands" the lover withdraws, not giving of himself.

"Clouds" is the one poem in *Sobra* that deals directly with the issue of racism. In this poem a child greets a group of black children walking by, calling them "niggers," because it is the only name she knows, only to experience the same kind of labeling directed toward herself "a little further up that road." A teacher who encouraged Rivera and whom she thanked with a gift of paper roses is remembered in "For Rita Kohn." In "Album" her grandfather's house and her proud, happy mother on horseback are set in contrast to her broken, distraught mother after the death of Rivera's brother.

While such natural elements as stones, seashells, and water occur in *Sobra*, verdant images are rare. In fact in one poem, "Roots," the green, leafy part of the tree is declared to be false—"only a case, only a stand." What matters is the subterranean heart, lying in the roots. Nature seems out of place in the final poem, "Dream," which is clearly surrealistic in its depiction of an inside-out world where trees are bent ceilings and vegetables enter a person's system from the stomach's surface. This poem and others in *Sobra* are indicative of how different aesthetically this second collection is from *Mestiza*.

While the manuscript of "The Celia Poems" is yet to be published in book form, several individual poems have appeared in *Revista Chicano-Riqueña* and elsewhere. In "The Man of O," John, a materialistic, Anglo-American personnel manager, has a rigid attitude and insensitivity to the brown man's plight, and these are symbolized by the squares that fill John's world. With an abrupt, "No, next," he dismisses Juan, the job applicant "who has eaten circles all his life." Reminiscent of the rage expressed in the *Mestiza* poem "Tomás" is the anger of the woman in "The Lion Tamer's Wife." It progresses through the day in the form of claws that appear at breakfast, eyes that roar at lunch, and finally, by dinner, "a voice louder than cannon." The mulberry tree is a constant presence throughout Rivera's poetry. Unlike the verdant, bird-filled tree in "Back Yard Birds" and other *Mestiza* poems, the tree in "Mulberry/Morera" of "The Celia Poems" is a leafless winter tree, which represents the artist in a period of recovery, hibernation, and regeneration, accompanied by an intense concentration of creative energy. Humor is rare in Rivera's poetry. "Blow, Blow," however, a parody of a feverishly erotic tryst, offers an amusing glimpse into the bedroom activities of a couple who are both suffering from colds: "It is the call of bullfrogs in the ancient pond / the kind the really fat, slobby ones make." Sharing in their illness as they make love, "They give off smoke, camphor and mentholatum."

A sense of alienation combined with a defiant independence pervades many of "The Celia Poems." Rivera writes of parks, observing the children, the birds, the dogs, but, as in "For Celia," she knows she is not really part of the scene that she witnesses: "Let the voices lock over your head / in the laughter at the snapping swan. / Let the birds needle it all together. / It doesn't make you one. Get moving." The other elements are locked in, but she knows she is free to go, and go she must: "Trees line this park. / Traffic is the metal frame. / Clouds hold the top on. / But nothing holds you here. No one. / Walk. Walk away."

Rivera's work has not yet received the critical attention it deserves, a problem related in part to the lack of interest in Chicano literature on the part of mainstream journals. Furthermore, Chicano literature has been, until recently, a field dominated by male writers, as well as a literature defined by a political movement. Thus the work of a woman who writes primarily apolitical poetry and who is not affiliated with any writers' groups runs the risk of being overlooked, attention going instead to more "topical" writers, often male. The brief reviews that she has received in such publications as *Booklist* (15 April 1978), *Cafeteria* (December 1977), *Caracol* (September 1978), and *Carta Abierta* (February, July, and December 1977) have all been favorable. The most important published study of her work to date is Eliana Rivero's article on *Mestiza* (*Palabra*, Spring 1979). Rivero characterizes the artistic experience that Rivera affords her readers as one "con una vigorosa belleza de imágenes que se clavan en el ánimo, que nos bailan ante los ojos, que nos hablan de alguna época y alguna dimensión que nos son reconocibles a todos" (with vigorous beautiful images that penetrate the soul, that dance before our eyes, that speak to us of an epoch and a dimension that are recognizable to us all).

Currently Rivera, now divorced, is living in a setting of her choosing—as she describes it, "down a dirt road in a country setting back behind the Catalina Mountains." Having given up the security of steady employment that high-school teaching offered, as well as its accompanying frustrations and restrictions on her freedom, she supports herself primarily with the income that she earns from the Spaniards she tutors. She also continues her upholstery work: buying, restoring, and reselling antique chairs. In her own words, she has "chosen Catalina beauty over Tucson convenience." Enhancing her life in the country is Cas, a blue-eyed albino filly, whose training Rivera undertook alone, "a physical challenge," as she puts it, for someone who measures only five-feet-two-inches tall. She has also continued her writing, completing another collection in the winter of 1984: "Half a Caramel and a Cluster of Chile Pequín." Rivera describes this manuscript as "a reply, a calling and an acceptance, mentally true, emotionally false." She says, "*Half* is a message I wrenched out of myself for myself because I could not continue as I was and because I knew the making of that message, and only that, could heal me." Many of the poems reflect her new way of life and the landscape around her rural home. While not active in writers' circles she has taken advantage of several opportunities to read her work in public.

Marina Rivera is a very private person, and the hermetic intensity of her work reflects this. In the inner space of her artistic consciousness, personal experience is transformed into a poetry of unusual depth and honesty. Since her beginnings as a writer, Rivera's work has been a consistent expression of her desire to know the human heart, in all its profundity, regardless of ethnic or racial concerns: "If my work says anything it tries to say 'look deeply, choose the reflection of your own heart, no matter the color in those eyes.' "

Biography:

La Verne Harrell Clark, ed., *Focus 101* (Chico, Cal.: Heidelburg, 1979), pp. 97-99.

Reference:

Eliana Rivero, "Poesía en Arizona: Las voces de *Mestiza*," *Palabra*, 1 (Spring 1979): 26-33.

Octavio Romano
(1923 -)

George Mariscal
University of California, San Diego

SELECTED PERIODICAL PUBLICATIONS—
UNCOLLECTED: "Minorities, History, and the Cultural Mystique," *El Grito*, 1 (Fall 1967): 5-11;

Introduction to "Goodbye Revolution, Hello Slum," *El Grito*, special issue, 1 (Winter 1968): 8-14;

"The Anthropology and Sociology of the Mexican-Americans," *El Grito*, 2 (Fall 1968): 13-26;

"The History and Intellectual Presence of Mexican-Americans," *El Grito*, 2 (Winter 1969): 32-46;

Mugre de la canción, *El Grito*, 3 (Winter 1970): 50-55;

"Social Science, Objectivity and the Chicanos," *El Grito*, 4 (Fall 1970): 4-16;

"Selected Poems," *El Grito*, 4 (Winter 1971): 62-66;

"Notes on the Modern State," *El Grito*, 4 (Spring 1971): 78-88;

"Strings for a Holiday," *El Grito*, 5 (Fall 1971): 45-54;

"El mestizo," *El Grito*, 5 (Spring 1972): 39-41;

"The Scientist," *Grito del Sol*, 1, no. 1 (1976): 85-108;

"El llorón," *Grito del Sol*, 2, no. 2 (1977): 92-95;

"The Veil," *Grito del Sol*, 3, no. 4 (1978): 57-58;

"Jacinto en Tejas," *Grito del Sol*, 3, no. 4 (1978): 59-61;

"The Forest and the Tree," *Grito del Sol*, 3, no. 4 (1978): 63-68;

"The Pilgrimage," *Grito del Sol*, 5, no. 1 (1980): 61-64;

"Constitutional Issues and the Rise of the Professional Class in the United States," *Grito del Sol*, 5, no. 2 (1980): 9-24;

Introduction to *Grito del Sol Annual*, special issue, 9 (1984).

Besides being an important author of sociological and anthropological essays on the Chicano experience, Octavio Romano stands as one of the pioneers in the legitimization of Chicano studies. Founder of Quinto Sol Publications in 1967, he was instrumental in creating cultural organisms through which Chicano thought and artistic production would take its place within the international community.

He was born Octavio Ignacio Romano-Vizcarra in 1923 in Mexico City and raised in National City, California (where he was a high-school dropout). Romano obtained his B.A. and M.A. at the University of New Mexico and his Ph.D. in anthropology at the University of California, Berkeley, in 1962.

In 1967, while serving on both the California State Commission on Compensatory Education and the board of the Spanish Speaking People's Institute for Education, Romano, together with Nick C. Vaca, founded *El Grito*, a journal that was to have far-reaching consequences for Chicano studies and contemporary publishing ventures. In their first editorial they articulated a strategy intended to overcome the stereotypical representation of the Chicano, which informed all previous social-scientific discourse: "this great rhetorical structure is a grand hoax, a blatant lie—a lie that must be stripped of its esoteric and sanctified verbal garb and have its intellectually spurious and vicious character exposed to full view. Only Mexican-Americans themselves can accomplish the collapse of this and other rhetorical structures. . . . " Romano was at the time an assistant professor of behavioral sciences at the UC, Berkeley, School of Public Health. In his article for the first issue of *El Grito*—"Minorities, History, and the Cultural Mystique"—Romano called for cultural interdependence as well as a new cultural language that would "postulate that duplicity, complicity, coalitions, and social networks are much more fundamental to the historical process than are ethnicity, skin color, group history, tradition, and religious affiliation."

Throughout subsequent issues of *El Grito*, Romano figured as a major force. His lyrical introduction to "Goodbye Revolution, Hello Slum," a 1968 special issue of *El Grito*, set the stage for a reconstruction of Chicano history since 1910 and a

El Grito

winter 1970 $1.25

3-2

Cover for an issue of the influential journal founded in 1967 by Romano and Nick C. Vaca

renewed attack on Anglo-American academia. Although the word *Chicano* did not yet appear in Romano's vocabulary, the political subtext of his closing remarks was clear: "Someday, when all the rangers are totally disbanded and prostituted history no longer emits from the priesthood of the social scientists, the Mexican-Americans will be free." By the third issue of *El Grito* (Spring 1968), for which Romano served as principal editor, the highly charged issues of Vietnam and the assassination of Martin Luther King carried the journal far beyond exclusively Hispanic concerns.

In 1970 the Quinto Sol publishing house, of which Romano had been the principal founder, announced the first Premio Quinto Sol, a literary competition that in essence initiated the formation of a canon for Chicano literature. The first three winners continued to be the founding fathers of contemporary Chicano prose fiction well into the 1980s: Tomás Rivera, Rudolfo Anaya, and Rolando Hinojosa-Smith. Equally crucial to this enterprise was Romano's publication in 1969

of *El Espejo / The Mirror*, an anthology of "Mexican-American" literature, which includes texts by writers who would become increasingly influential in the coming years.

Romano's original fiction develops many of the concerns that inform his scholarly articles. His 1976 short story "The Scientist," for example, deals with Dr. Simón Bocanegra, an authority on mental health, who returns to a town called El Barrio to test a series of hypotheses he has theorized while at a university. The establishment of the Ajúa House, a psychiatric clinic, and the refinement of his theories lead to the blurring of the boundary between mental health and mental illness. Eventually five-sevenths of the townspeople are committed. After an unsuccessful rebellion by the community against Bocanegra's practices and a complete reversal of his original theory (he comes to believe that the abnormal are those who are rational and well-balanced), the psychiatrist finally becomes his only patient and "for days on end he could be heard in an encounter session with himself." After the doctor's death, his wife leaves with the local priest, and El Barrio returns to its former state.

This kind of satirical treatment of social scientists, and academia in general, forms the basis of other literary texts by Romano, such as the short story "Strings for a Holiday" (1971). Yet it is in his nonfiction writings that he has most effectively attacked the traditional Anglo-American representation of Chicano history, philosophy, and psychology. In his influential "The Historical and Intellectual Presence of Mexican-Americans" (1969) he analyzes the cultural diversity of Chicano reality and introduces innovative categories still being used today. This piece, together with the earlier "The Anthropology and Sociology of the Mexican-Americans" (1968), did much to change the stereotypical treatment of Chicanos in North American social sciences. In later years Romano explored the wider issues of institutional controls on minority populations, in studies such as "Notes on the Modern State" (1971).

Throughout the early 1970s Romano continued to promote Chicano artistic production through the *El Grito* book series with volumes devoted to poetry, drama, and other Chicano writings. In 1975 he founded the publishing firm of Tonatiuh International in Berkeley (of which Quinto Sol Publications became an affiliate) and renamed the quarterly journal *Grito del Sol*. Tonatiuh was to play a major role in the ongoing process of creating a Chicano canon, with its promotion and publication of "classic" texts such as Rudolfo Anaya's *Bless Me, Ultima* (1972), Estela Portillo Trambley's *Rain of Scorpions* (1975), and others. By 1980 Romano's own fiction had begun to show signs of change. In two short fictional pieces, "The Veil" (1978) and "The Pilgrimage" (1980), he abandons the academic environment for the more contemplative scene of individual characters' confrontations with their own past. In a theoretical study, "Constitutional Issues and the Rise of the Professional Class in the United States," originally read at the 1980 meeting of the American Association for the Advancement of Science, in San Francisco, he analyzes the broad issue of the function of professional elites in a democratic society.

In his introduction to the 1984 *Grito del Sol Annual*, Romano returned to topics that had concerned him throughout the previous eighteen years, as well as the accomplishments realized through the projects for which he himself was mainly responsible. He is especially proud of the fact that Tonatiuh Quinto Sol began as and continues to be a totally self-supporting enterprise: "As such, we are the only Chicano publishers in the nation who have never once depended on subsidies of any kind whatsoever." At the same time, in his attempt to distinguish the 1984 annual from similar collections of Chicano literature, Romano reiterates his principal intellectual preoccupations: "If, then, this anthology is not, (a) an example of literary lamentations by minorities, (b) pseudosociology, and/or, (c) a subliminal political tract, then what is it? Briefly, it is a sharing of human experience. . . . " For his unwavering dedication to the exploration, legitimization, and circulation of the Chicano experience in all of its forms, future writers and historians will owe Octavio Romano a debt of gratitude.

Reference:

Eugene Fraire-Aldava, "Octavio Romano's 'Goodbye Revolution, Hello Slum': A Study of Ironic Tone and Meaning," *Aztlán*, 3 (Spring 1972): 165-169.

Leo Romero
(25 September 1950 -   )

Enrique R. Lamadrid
University of New Mexico

BOOKS: *During the Growing Season* (Tucson: Maguey, 1978);

Celso (Berkeley: Tonatiuh-Quinto Sol International, 1980);

Agua Negra (Boise, Idaho: Ahsahta, 1981);

Celso (Houston: Arte Público, 1985);

Desert Nights (Santa Fe, N.Mex.: Fish Drum, 1989);

Going Home Away Indian (Boise, Idaho: Ahsahta, 1990).

PLAY PRODUCTIONS: *Celso, Voices of New Mexico*, Las Cruces, N.Mex., Readers theater, 1982;

I am Celso, by Romero, Jorge A. Huerta, and Rubén Sierra, Seattle, Wash., Group Theatre Company, Summer 1985.

OTHER: Philip D. Ortego, ed., *We Are Chicanos: An Anthology of Mexican-American Literature*, includes poetry by Romero (New York: Washington Square, 1973);

Walter Lowenfels, ed., *For Neruda, For Chile*, includes poetry by Romero (Boston: Beacon, 1975);

Reality in Conflict: Literature of Values in Opposition, includes poetry by Romero (Glenview, Ill.: Scott Foresman, 1976);

Sandscript: An Anthology of New Mexico Poetry, includes poetry by Romero (Las Cruces: New Mexico State Poetry Society, 1976);

Gene Frumpkin and Stanley Noyes, eds., *The Indian Río Grando: Recent Poems from 3 Cultures*, includes poetry by Romero (Cerrillos, N.Mex.: San Marcos, 1977);

Jane Kopp and Karl Kopp, eds., *Southwest: A Contemporary Anthology* (Albuquerque: Red Earth, 1977);

Francisco Jiménez and Gary D. Keller, eds., *Hispanics in the United States*, includes poetry by Romero (Ypsilanti, Mich.: Bilingual Review, 1980);

Rudolfo Anaya and Simon Ortiz, eds., *A Ceremony of Brotherhood: Tricentennial Anthology*, in-

cludes poetry by Romero (Santa Fe: Academia, 1981);

Nicolás Kanellos, ed., *A Decade of Hispanic Literature*, includes poetry by Romero (Houston: Revista Chicano-Riqueña, 1982);

Jiménez and Keller, eds., *Hispanics in the United States: An Anthology of Creative Literature*, volume 2, includes poetry by Romero (Ypsilanti, Mich.: Bilingual Review, 1982);

Bill Henderson, ed., *The Pushcart Prize VII: Best of the Small Presses*, includes poetry by Romero (Wainscott, N.Y.: Pushcart, 1982);

Ray Gonzales, ed., *Crossing the River*, includes poetry by Romero (Sag Harbor, N.Y.: Permanent Press, 1987);

Anaya, ed., *Voces: An Anthology of Nuevo Mexicano Writers*, includes poetry by Romero (Albuquerque: Norte/Academia, 1987);

Franca Minuzzo Bacchiega, *Sotto il Quinto Sole*, includes poetry by Romero (Florence, Italy: Passigli, 1989);

Jerome Beaty and J. Paul Hunter, eds., *New Worlds of Literature*, includes poetry by Romero (New York: Norton, 1989).

SELECTED PERIODICAL PUBLICATIONS—
UNCOLLECTED: "I Am Only a Weaver of Grass," "In the End It Will Be the Same As in the Beginning," and "For Pablo Neruda," *Café Solo*, 8 (1974): 33-34;

"This is the Way of the Falling Rain," "Her Name is Morning," and "Death in the Desert," *Spectrum*, 17 (1975): 30, 39, 54;

"Two Poems for Anne Sexton," *Southern Poetry Review*, 15 (1975): 34;

"When Maps Fail," "The Cacti Have Taken Steps," "Each Second Lengthens the Distance," "Datura," "During the Growing Season," and "For Lame Deer," *South Dakota Review*, 14 (Winter 1976-1977): 37-42;

"A Dark Shadow Which Could be Anything," *La Confluencia*, 1 (1977): 4;

"Drawing and Poem," *South Dakota Review*, 16 (1978): 50;

"The Dark Side of the Moon," "Fear of the Moon," "The Night is Overwhelmed," "The Moon is Lost," "The Ocean is Not Red," and "It Came to Earth," *Revista Chicano-Riqueña*, 7 (1979): 1-5;

"Too Many Years" and "Without Jesus, Mary, Joseph," *New America*, 3 (1979): 19, 72-73;

"Qué pendejos son los hombres viejos" and "A New Man," *Footprint Magazine* (Winter 1979-1980): 57-58;

"What Trees Dream About," *Berkeley Poetry Review*, 10 (1981): 27;

"Moonstruck" and "Earth, Texas," *Bilingual Review*, 9 (1982): 163-164;

"The Wind is Knocking" and "Between Yeso and Fort Sumner," *Puerto del Sol*, 18 (1983): 135-136;

"Agua y Flores" and "Hijita," *Tarasque I* (1983): 7-14;

"I Died and Found Myself in a Great Tree" and "In the Least Places," *Tyuonyi I* (1985): 109-111;

"What Was There To Do on the Plains" and "If There Had Been a Time After," *Fish Drum Magazine* (1988): 1-30;

"There Was Such Intense Anger in Him," "Desert Nights," "We Slept on the Porch," and "For Our Own Reasons," *Sonora Review*, 14-15 (1988): 59-66;

"Meet My Friend Thomas," *Floating Island*, 11 (1989): 114;

"Marilyn Monroe Indian," *South Dakota Review*, 27 (Winter 1989): 5-11;

"You Come Back Again," "Take My Picture, Says Pito," "I've Never Known a Dwarf Before," "I Bring Twins Over To Meet," "This Is Denise, I Say To Pito," "You See What Happens," "How Did I Land Up in this City," "Pito's Got Time," "Pito Had a Dream," "Diane's Knocking," and "When Pito Tried to Kill," *Americas Review*, 18 (Spring 1990): 37-53;

"Welcome, Says Skeleton" and "Well Look," *Northwest Review*, 28, no. 2 (1990): 74-76.

One of the most prolific of New Mexican poets, Leo Romero is best known for his fanciful portrayal of village characters in northern New Mexico, characters which critics have linked to the contemporary Latin-American currents of "magical realism." Central in his cast of characters is Celso, a classic picaro with roots that stretch from the mountains of New Mexico into the picaresque tradition of sixteenth-century Spain. Chicano critic Juan Bruce-Novoa has observed that "Romero's writing expands beyond the normal limits of poetry, invading both the realm of narrative fiction and drama. His poems are miniature stories garnered from the oral tradition; when read, especially if aloud, they may well evoke the mood of dramatic performance." A dramatic adaptation of the Celso poems by Jorge Huerta, well-known Chicano dramatist and critic, and Rubén Sierra, director of the Group Theatre Company in Seattle, has launched the regionally known poet into national prominence.

Leo Romero was born on 25 September 1950 in the house of his grandparents, Samuel and Adelaida Romero of Chacón, a remote northern New Mexican village at the upper end of the Mora Valley, seven miles north of Holman. Never to know his father, Leo was given his maternal family name and grew up experiencing a kind of half-orphanhood in a culture with both patriarchal and patrilineal values and traditions. At an early age he moved with his mother, Ortensia, two brothers, and a sister down the valley to Las Vegas, New Mexico, a city of sixteen thousand at the edge of the Great Plains. Although he grew up in the 1950s and 1960s, the era of the television generation, Leo Romero has memories of chopping wood and hauling blocks of ice home in his toy wagon for the family icebox. The family settled in Spanish-speaking west Las Vegas when he was about four, but they lived in a neigh-

*Romero speaking to a group of children as a representative of the Community and Public Affairs Office
at the Los Alamos National Laboratory during the 1980s*

borhood where English became the dominant language of the children. He remembers hurrying home from catechism class on Saturdays to listen to the comedy programs on the radio. Romero also remembers his fascination with the derelicts who haunted the streets of Las Vegas. His impressions of them figured strongly in his creative imagination. Romero attended South Public Elementary School and West Las Vegas Junior High and High Schools, where his first experiences with poetry were jaded by obligatory classroom recitations. By the ninth grade he was stitching together small collections of cartoons and captions satirizing classroom politics and personalities. After a confiscation, he was assigned to a young student teacher, Linda Estrada, who took a personal interest in his creativity and before long had him reading Robert Frost and T. S. Eliot.

In 1969 at the University of New Mexico, noted Native American poet Simon Ortiz was working as a counselor and encouraged some of Leo's early writing. His first published poem appeared in a 1971 publication called *New Mexico Magazine*, a landscape study of the vast stretch of high desert between Taos and southern Colorado. The student literary magazine, *Thunderbird*,

also printed many of his poems. At the university, he abandoned rhymed verse and punctuation as his own sparse but emotionally complex poetic style began to emerge. After graduating in 1973 with a B.A. in English, Romero had a brief seventeen-day career in the coast guard, which helped him overcome a childhood fear of deep water. In 1974 he began a master's program in creative writing at New Mexico State University, Las Cruces, where he twice served as poetry editor of the magazine *Puerto del Sol*. After the pressures of academe began stifling his creative energies, Romero escaped to northern New Mexico in 1975, returning briefly to Chacón. Six years later he returned to Las Cruces long enough to finish the M.A. he had begun. After several years working in eastern New Mexico, he made his way, via Albuquerque, back north where he currently lives in Santa Fe. After working for the Community and Public Affairs Office at the Los Alamos National Laboratory for several years, Romero opened Books, Books, and More Books, a thriving Santa Fe bookstore which he operates with painter Elizabeth Cook Romero, his wife. Over an eight-year period, Leo also conducted poetry workshops all over northern New Mexico for the

Poetry in the Schools program.

The breakaway summer of 1975 proved to be the most crucial formative experience in Romero's poetic career, later documented in the definitive *Agua Negra* collection (1981), now in its third printing. He returned to Chacón to the house he was born in and spent the season with his grandmother. In "Estafiate" he dramatizes her connection to the land and its mysteries:

> She walked slowly
> on her thin legs
> Her body bent forward
> by her humped back
> which she had gained
> with the years
> and made her look
> as if she were sinking back
> into the earth
> or shrinking back
> into a child[.]

Time passed in conversation with his grandmother and in simple activities like sitting on the portal and chopping wood. Among the belongings in his suitcase, there were three classic Spanish picaresque novels. Although he did no writing during this period, he tapped a wellspring of inspiration for his later poetry. What he discovered was his personal connection to what D. H. Lawrence termed "a spirit of place." Back in Chacón, Romero came to terms with his past: the uprooting from the rich village culture at such an early age, the deprivation of a paternal history, and the alienation from Spanish, his childhood tongue. His efforts to probe for his roots had previously been met with frustration and silence. His grandmother avoided discussing the past; it was too far away. Back in Chacón, he began to realize that the stories and oral traditions he had been deprived of were there all the time, in more subtle form than he had imagined. Many of his grandmother's anecdotes passed directly into later poems such as "In the Rincon":

> My grandmother would tell me
> of the cold
> sweet spring water
> in the Rincon
> She would go there
> when she was newly married
> And once she saw a bear
> who had come down
> from the mountains
> for chokeberries
> She fled and never returned
> to the Rincon[.]

Romero's poetic encounter with his past kindled an interest in history, but he soon realized it was a history he would have to invent, as expressed in "A Lying Moon and a Lonely Bird":

> I search for a history of this valley
> but no one wrote it down
> so I look for anything
> For a scrap of paper
> with a few words
> but I find nothing other
> than some names and dates
> written in family bibles
> I am left to construct a history
> where there are no written records[.]

Bruce-Novoa states that this theme is what links Romero to other Chicano poets: "A desire to document the life of one's community is characteristic of Chicano writing. It responds directly to the absence, or falsification, of that life in the written record presented by the dominant culture." The poet shares with the ethnohistorian the realization that history is a dynamic entity which resides alongside other kinds of belief and experience in the recollections of living people. What appear in Romero's poetry are the familiar themes, motifs, and voices from the oral traditions of New Mexican folklore, not reported in the manner of a folklorist, but lyrically recounted in new poetic creations.

One of the principal voices developed a persona of its own as it grew into Celso, the best known and most fully developed of Romero's village characters. As a social and literary type, Celso is part of a millennial tradition of tricksters, outcasts, and rogues that dates back to the picaresque animal fables of both Europe and America. His hybrid lineage includes the Spanish Lazarillo de Tormes, Coyote of the Native American tradition, and the mestizo Pito Pérez of revolutionary Mexico (from José Rubén Romero's novel *La vida inútil de Pito Pérez*, 1938). Not uncoincidentally, Romero's most recent unpublished manuscript is entitled "Pito." Romero contends, "To some people Celso would be just a drunk and a bum, but there's a little bit of Celso in everyone. We get in that mood when we don't take anything seriously. He's free of all the meaningless things we take so seriously. He jokes. He tells stories. He doesn't care about getting a car or getting a house. He doesn't care what people think of him. It takes great courage to live that way. It's a hard life. When he needs a bottle of

Cover for Romero's 1985 collection of poems about a New Mexican picaro

Celso avoided adults
like the plague

He never went into
his friends' houses
Their parents' first question
never varied[.]

The alienation and bitterness Celso experiences in his youth follow him into old age as seen in "As He Shuts the Door behind Him":

Celso dreads old age

The children will throw
rocks at me
and the dogs will
nip at my heels
he says to no one in particular[.]

But alienation from society is the most important prerequisite for unfettered criticism of it, for the picaresque genre has been the main vehicle for social criticism (in print) for centuries in the Hispanic world. For all the bitterness, there is an equal if not greater measure of magic and ecstasy. In "Dancing with Moonlight," Celso soars in a lyric fantasy:

When moonlight gets into your brain
it is called madness
but when it gets into your heart
it is called love, says Celso
His thoughts drifting away
to that one night he danced with moonlight[.]

Ecstasy also has a strong traditional association with the mysteries of Dionysius and his sacrament, alcohol. Celso's affair with the grape gives him divine (Dionysian) authority to seek out truth in the world (*in vino veritas*), even though the logical consequences may lead to blasphemy as easily as treason. Celso's alcoholism in this context is less like a disease and more like a gift, as shown in "The Sermon of the Grape":

Listen to Celso
preaching his gospel
The gospel of the Holy Grape

Drink of the blood
which is His blood
says Celso
holding a bottle
of red wine above his head

wine, he'll go to the church and pass out on the steps so that people will give him money, just so he'll go away."

In the mock-confessional first-person mode of classic picaros, Celso confides in the reader, seeking sympathy or expressing his defiance. A basic characteristic of picaros is their social alienation: some begin life as orphans. The poem "Celso's Father" (1980) expresses the bitterness of orphanhood in terms the poet is intimately familiar with:

When he was a child
Celso was always being asked
who his father was
. . . .
People never let up
They hounded him about the matter
The only solution was to run

. . . .

People pass by him
and they laugh at him
They know that he is not
to be taken seriously
. . . .
Celso has many disciples
The poor, the wretched
the misfits and outcasts
of Agua Negra
They gather about him
as long as the wine holds out[.]

Celso's delirium gives Romero access to lyrical moments of surrealism, and access to the folk realm of legend or supernatural belief. Celso thinks the moon is a woman, talks to animals and skeletons, runs from the devil, sees Jesus in double vision, sells holy water from the river, and listens to a ball of lightning that claims to be a lost soul. Picaro that he is, Celso puts the material, spiritual, and social world to the test.

In 1978 the Maguey Press of Tucson published a chapbook, Romero's first collection of poems, *During the Growing Season*. This small, finely crafted but errata-plagued edition is Celso's first appearance. This celebrated New Mexican picaro was presented to the world of Chicano publishing in 1980 when Tonatiuh-Quinto Sol International in Berkeley published a collection of poems entitled *Celso* as a special issue of the Grito del Sol series. It was this edition that later attracted the attention of Rubén Sierra, who sent the poems to Jorge Huerta with the idea of adapting the poems for dramatic presentation. In 1981, a time when very few Chicano writers were known or published outside the world of Chicano publishing houses, the nationally known Ahsahta Press poetry series of Boise State University published Romero's *Agua Negra* collection, which won the 1982 Pushcart Prize "Best of the Small Presses" competition. Agua Negra is the original Spanish name of Holman, New Mexico, a village near Chacón, famous in the mid-seventies for an apparition of the face of Christ on an adobe wall. In 1985 Arte Público Press in Houston published *Celso*, the definitive collection of Celso poems. Ahsahta also published Romero's latest book, *Going Home Away Indian*, in 1990.

Romero's steadily growing reputation has brought him many fellowships and honors, including the Wurlitzer Foundation Resident Artist Fellowship in 1979; the National Endowment for the Arts Creative Writing Fellowship in 1981; the National Hispanic Scholarship in 1981; the establishment in 1982 of a Leo Romero Archive in the

Special Collections Department, Zimmerman Library, University of New Mexico; and, in 1987, inclusion in the *New American Writing* exhibit of the National Education Association at the Frankfurt and Liber International Book Fairs in Europe, the first international exposure for the writer.

The critical reception of Romero's poetry has been consistently enthusiastic since the appearance of his first book. The poet affirms he has new work that will put Celso behind him, especially since the character seems to have taken on a career of his own. In his director's notes to the Group Theatre Company production, Jorge Huerta has some enlightening comments on the stage career of Celso:

we began to put Celso on his feet, moving him in his little house with natural characteristics while discovering the delightfully unnatural incidents in his rather eventful life. . . . Audiences loved Celso and their criticisms and comments helped us coalesce Leo Romero's wonderful character and language into what I feel is an important contribution to the American Theatre.

A memorable review of *Agua Negra* by Chicana playwright Denise Chávez that appeared in *Rio Grande Writers' Newsletter* (Winter 1981) is representative of the esteem in which Romero's poetic gifts are held:

The ongoing cyclical movements of Romero's poems are strong, blinding—as sharp knocks on the skull. He sobers, revealing the shadows of the mountains, and the creatures that inhabit that deep night, surrounding the small houses, where lone people sit inside: the spinster who did not see her husband in the well, Estefanita who danced in the fire, and her brother Manuel who would join her there. In the small villages of Romero's world the church bells are silent, and the terrible and quick beauty of life in its passing is recalled—and cherished.

In his poems Romero has successfully brought the magic of his regional culture to a national audience, not by merely describing its traditions, but rather by evoking the complex and lyrical orality which lies so close to its collective soul.

References:
Joe Adcock, "'I am Celso': Drunken Bum Keeps a Tight Grip on the Poet Who Created Him," *Seattle Post-Intelligence*, 31 May 1985;
Juan Bruce-Novoa, "New Mexican Chicano Poetry: The Contemporary Tradition," in *Pasó*

Por Aquí: Critical Essays on the New Mexican Literary Tradition, 1542-1988, edited by Erlinda Gonzales-Berry (Albuquerque: University of New Mexico Press, 1989), pp. 267-296;

Jim Kershner, " 'I am Celso': A Wine-Soaked Philosopher Comes Dramatically to Life . . . ," *Daily News Journal* (Kent, Wash.), 26 September 1986;

Meg Scherch, "Soaring With Celso at Taos . . . ," *Taos News*, 30 October 1986;

Papers:
Romero's papers are held in the Special Collections Department of the Zimmerman Library, University of New Mexico, Albuquerque.

Lin Romero
(15 October 1947 -   )

Miriam Daniel Fahey
Holy Names College

BOOK: *Happy Songs, Bleeding Hearts* (San Diego: Toltecas en Aztlán, 1974).

OTHER: Alurista, ed., *Festival de flor y canto*, includes poetry by Lin Romero (Los Angeles: University of Southern California, 1976), pp. 137-143;

"I Don't Sit High," "Untitled," and "Chicano Haiku," *Chismearte*, 1 (Fall-Winter 1977): 14-19;

Alurista, ed., *Literatura fronteriza*, includes poetry by Lin Romero (San Diego: Maize Press, 1982), pp. 47-52.

Lin Romero

Lin Romero's family originally lived in New York, but her father—believing Mexico would be a wholesome place to raise children—moved the family to Mexico City where the future Chicana poet was born on 15 October 1947. She received her early education at the bilingual American School Foundation. At seventeen she went to California and studied at San Francisco State University, the University of California, Los Angeles, and California State University, Los Angeles, where she graduated. At UCLA she wrote the poems included in Michael Victor Sedano's doctoral dissertation, "Chicanismo in Selected Poetry From the Chicano Movement, 1969-1972." In the epilogue of *Happy Songs, Bleeding Hearts* (1974), the reader learns Romero had experienced the "transient urban life of Mexico City" as well as that of Los Angeles. Roberto Sifuentes calls Romero's collection a "poetic chronicle" that presents "the last tear being dropped by a Chicano group for the indios lacandones," the Indians of the Yucatán peninsula of Mexico. Lin was a member of a group funded by the Centro de Estudios Xicanos de UCLA, and *Happy Songs, Bleeding Hearts* is her account of the group's trip into the land of the

> Lacandones, the ones who still live
> true and free con la tierra [with the earth]
> we thought, we hoped.

The brief book is a combination of poignant, revealing photos, and prose and verse that mingles English with Spanish and an occasional Mayan phrase.

Commenting on *Happy Songs, Bleeding Hearts* in *Chicano Literature* (1982), Charles M. Tatum declares that the "book title aptly catches the duality of the collective experience: beneath the happy sounds of song and dance reside both the memory and daily encounters with poverty and other forms of human suffering." Before visiting the jungle home of the Lacandones, the "last true people," Romero's group stopped at the town of San Cristóbal de las Casas in Chiapas, Mexico. At least seven tribes of Indians lived there, and Romero describes their circumstances as bleak: "Indios, people dying from hunger, disease, alcoholism, physical exhaustion and spiritual grief." Romero ridicules attempts of the Mexican government to help the Indians by incorporating them into a rapidly changing society:

> 1. Cut out your heart Indian
> we will give you a brand
> new shiny, reversible,
> washable, moldable, plastic
> one. Guaranteed for maybe five years with no
> money back.
>
> 2. Come to the city, pollute
> your soul and body. Forget
> your ways. Cut out your brain and if you like
> return to your land without
> your hands.
>
> 3. Depend on us for your food
> medicine, school and life.
> We will have more of you
> to clean our toilets and
> do not ask why.

The poet decries the fact that the Indians are being convinced to give up their old ways and dress in modern clothes, exchanging their talent for embroidery and weaving in order to work as maids, street sweepers, and construction workers, struggling just to get basic necessities.

The tone of *Happy Songs, Bleeding Hearts* changes when the group heads into the jungle lands of the Lacandones, the last remnant "of the once great Mayan empire." As their plane approaches, the poet anticipates that they "will hear cantos like never before / never again / cantos de sol y agua" [of the sun and water]. The group is welcomed by the leader of the Lacandones, tours their palm-tree houses, and shares a dinner with them of tortillas, chili, and fruit, but the poet is saddened when she sees the missionaries and anthropologists who "swallow the people alive / to return to Europe / burp them up / receive an applause." Despite this exploitation, the Lacandones were a jolly, generous people who shared what little they possessed with their guests.

Romero's journey, however, left her with a burden—"the burden of knowledge that our quest to gather truth and beauty found truth: dead bodies." This touching account of her visit to the dying people includes photographs of the pensive, stoic, questioning eyes and faces of young and old. These are pictures of musicians and leaders, women with plaited hair and children with unkempt tresses, all impassively awaiting their fate as they go about their daily rounds of marketing, gossiping, and praying.

Reflecting on her career during an interview, Romero revealed that she began writing poetry when she was in the sixth grade. Later she was influenced by several people connected with the Chicano movement—Alurista, Juan Felipe Herrera, and César González-T. of San Diego. Since the student uprisings at San Francisco State University in the late 1960s, Romero has been invited to participate in poetry readings. From San Francisco to San Diego, from Berkeley to Stanford, she has consistently contributed to Cinco de Mayo and other commemorative celebrations.

She admits that the bulk of her poems have not been published due to her own lack of organization. Nevertheless, some twenty have appeared in magazines and anthologies. A study of these poems reveals her desire for a new free world of Aztlán. She challenges her readers to return to their past and to recognize the value of the roots of la Raza (the Race) and challenges herself to be a means of peace.

References:

Michael Victor Sedano, "Chicanismo in Selected Poetry From the Chicano Movement 1969-1972: A Rhetorical Study," Ph.D. dissertation, University of Southern California, Los Angeles, June 1980;

Roberto Sifuentes, "Essay," in *A Decade of Chicano Literature (1970-1979)* (Santa Barbara: Causa, 1982), p. 61;

Rubén Sálaz-Márquez

(21 November 1935 -   )

Michael Amin
University of New Mexico

BOOKS: *La lectura cósmica del suroeste* (Albuquerque: Fine Line, 1976);
Heartland: Stories of the Southwest (Santa Fe, N.Mex.: Blue Feather, 1978);
I Am Tecumseh!: Book 1 (Albuquerque: Fine Line, 1980);
I Am Tecumseh!: Book 2 (Albuquerque: Cosmic House, 1985).

PLAY PRODUCTION: *Embassy Hostage: The Drama of Americans in Iran*, Albuquerque, Vortex Theatre, November 1983.

Rubén Sálaz-Márquez

Although considering himself a southwestern rather than a New Mexican writer, Rubén Sálaz-Márquez belongs to the tradition of the New Mexico writers who revere and lament the passing of time-honored ways of life, be they Indian or Hispanic. His poignant and often humorous descriptions of family life use the lessons of the past as guides to living in the ever-changing present.

Rubén Darío Sálaz-Márquez was born in Belen, New Mexico, on 21 November 1935 to Fernando Sálaz and the former Lucy Márquez. As a boy, passing through several Indian pueblos on the frequent trips between his hometown and that of his grandmother, Rubén·first became interested in Native Americans and their traditions. He was brought up in a traditional Hispanic setting, but, during his years as a college student at the University of New Mexico, from which he received his B.A. in history in 1958 and his M.A. in school administration in 1961, Sálaz-Márquez be- came aware of the negative stereotypes perpetuated about the Hispanic heritage in America. This prejudice piqued his desire to disseminate the truths of the Hispanic experience past and present.

Heartland (1978), Sálaz-Márquez's first foray into fiction, is a collection of ten short stories with contemporary and historical time frames. He intended that the stories be representational of the Southwest as a whole, but the geographical and psychological landscapes of the book are largely New Mexican. The stories with historical backgrounds, such as "Mistress of the Plains" and "Cibolero" (Buffalo Hunter), present Sálaz-Márquez's version of the life-styles and cultures of the long-defunct, pre-Anglo-American occupations by the mustangers and the *ciboleros* of what is now New Mexico. The Hispanics in these two stories are seen as sober and enterprising, with high morals. They are as one with their harsh environment. These people possess much freedom, but they are also bound together by a belief system that puts emphasis on family and communal life in harmony with nature. The outside world, particularly Anglo-Americans slowly encroaching on their homeland, spells disaster for the future of the traditional Hispanic culture.

This theme of the wise, native Hispanic or Indian contrasted with the aggressive righteousness of the conquering hordes is strongly reiterated in the stories "The Race" and "Liberation." In the former an Apache brave escapes the sadistic captivity of a cavalryman through sheer cunning and natural survival instinct, even in the face of great odds. In a more comedic mode, but no less serious in intent, "Liberation" details the bumbling, mock-heroic attempts of Anglo-Americans in California to force the independence/statehood question on perplexed but patient Hispanic leaders.

The strength of Sálaz-Márquez's collection lies in his treatment of contemporary Hispanic family life in New Mexico, explored in "Acculturation," "The Adobe Abode," and "The Last Penitente." In these stories the Hispanic protagonists are struggling to hold on to their cultural values and traditions in the face of overwhelming assimilation pressures. They face the ongoing changes with a mixture of humor and a sentimental longing for the pastoral way of life of their ancestors. "Acculturation" uses a simple breakfast conversation between a father and son to detail a subtle exploration of racial awareness and family togetherness. A Hispanic family's visit to the rural house of the father's elderly mother in "The Adobe Abode" becomes an elegiac look at traditional values and simple rural existence in contrast to the everyday stresses and assimilation

pressures that must be faced in modern city life. In "The Last Penitente" a young Hispanic scholar returns to his small New Mexico village and discovers through conversations with a village elder the reality and motivations behind the mysterious and much-maligned group called the Penitentes, of the northern New Mexican mountains. Again the contrasting worlds of two different generations of Hispanics is brought into focus.

Critical attention for the collection has been confined to newspaper reviewers in New Mexico. Yet the reviews have all been favorable if not incisive, an example being the one in the *Albuquerque Journal* of 24 December 1978, which noted that "the stories in *Heartland* are fascinatingly told. The author's background in history makes the reading of the tales interesting and compelling."

In 1980 Sálaz-Márquez released the first part of a proposed trilogy on the life of the Shawnee Indian chief Tecumseh. An exercise in historical narrative fiction, the novel was an attempt, in the words of Sálaz-Márquez in the *Albuquerque Journal* (5 October 1980), "to get a balance between the Indian point of view and that of the non-Indian historians." Moving away from the Southwest tableaus of *Heartland* and using as a setting the Ohio River valley in the American Revolution era, Sálaz-Márquez nevertheless returns to emphases on the virtue of family unity and on wistfulness for the days when it was possible to achieve communal bliss within an unthreatened monocultural environment. And again, invading Anglo-Americans are the disruptive and destructive forces.

I Am Tecumseh!: Book 1 describes Tecumseh's early years spent in rather idyllic circumstances, and then moves forward gradually to the destruction of and his separation from his immediate family, largely due to the onslaught from the eastern settlers. Tecumseh, whom Sálaz-Márquez considers one of the greatest Americans, is described in classic heroic-warrior terms. He represents all the accumulated wisdom, spirituality, and foresight of the Native American cultures. All of the acculturation he receives as a child from his immediate family and the elders of the tribe infuses within Tecumseh the requisites of sagacious leadership. Around the central focus on Tecumseh, the book introduces a varied cast of historical and fictional personalities both Indian and white, who provide the set of circumstances and the environment that Tecumseh must learn from and react to. Critically the book went unrecognized, possibly due to the shift from the southwestern locales of Sálaz-Márquez's earlier collection, thus foregoing the New Mexican critical attention largely focused on regional themes.

In November 1983 Sálaz-Márquez presented *Embassy Hostage*, a play that recounts the harrowing experiences of the protagonist Fernando Márquez, a captive Hispanic marine sergeant from New Mexico, in the early days of the Iranian hostage situation at the Tehran U.S. embassy. Through the rhetorical dialogue of the Iranian captors, in a series of interrogation scenes, and the internal dialogue of Márquez, in solitary flashbacks, Sálaz-Márquez ponders the plight and treatment of racial minorities worldwide at the hands of white Americans and their government. The bleak view of racism is contrasted with the promise shown in the companionship of Márquez's interracial group of acquaintances in the embassy. Sálaz-Márquez also explores the interesting and complex question of allegiance and patriotism to a country that has actively practiced prejudice against minorities.

Critical attention again remained local and was largely favorable. However, critics noted the need for extensive editing, particularly of an extended comedic scene containing a discourse on flatulence. Concerns about overdone polemics and problems of narrative focus were also evinced. K. C. Compton, writing in the *Albuquerque Journal* (17 November 1983), complained "many scenes seem tangential and others are awfully heavyhanded." The same reviewer also noted that "getting a clear sense of the playwright's message is no easy task."

The year 1985 saw the release of *I Am Tecumseh!: Book 2*, which picks up chronologically from the antecedent Tecumseh novel. In the post-American independence era in the late eighteenth and the early nineteenth centuries, Tecumseh comes into his seemingly predestined place as the leader of not only his people but also other tribes in a loose confederation. Tecumseh's people, with the other tribes of the region, face and attempt to resist the unchecked spread of white settlers into the West. This struggle for cultural survival in the midst of an onslaught represents a return to a popular theme in Sálaz-Márquez's fiction.

In the 1985 novel less emphasis is placed on familial aspects of Tecumseh's life; instead Sálaz-Márquez places him in a national, historical perspective. The novel introduces many actual historical luminaries and events, thus it often has more the feel of narrative history rather than fiction. This novel has received little critical attention, and thus it has languished in relative obscurity.

The vagaries of survival of cultural and individual identity in times of rapid change and forced assimilation, best brought to the fore in the short stories of *Heartland*, remain the major thematic concerns of Rubén Sálaz-Márquez. And, though firmly in the sentimental school of New Mexican writers, Sálaz-Márquez ranges far afield from the state in his attempts to document the effects of ongoing change in other cultures.

Philomeno "Phil" Sánchez

(20 November 1917-   )

Nasario García

New Mexico Highlands University

BOOK: *Don Phil-o-meno sí la mancha* (San Luis, Colo.: Sangre de Cristo, 1977).

Philomeno "Phil" Sánchez is one of countless Hispanic writers waiting to be discovered for their literary contributions. If not, he, like other unknown writers, will be pushed further into oblivion as more and more younger writers come to the forefront.

Philomeno Sánchez was born on 20 November 1917 on Amargura Street in San Luis, Colorado, in a region known locally as the Valle de Lágrimas (Valley of Tears). Sánchez has fond memories of his childhood, but he also recalls his family's modest existence: "Juimos muy pobrecitos y batallábamos mucho para vivir, pero pasamos una vida muy alegre" (We were very poor and we struggled a lot to survive, but we enjoyed a happy life). Because of the financial situation, he joined the Civilian Conservation Corps camps in 1935 and worked for the government until 1937 in order to help improve the family's economic lot.

Later his father summoned him back to San Luis to finish the twelfth grade. He graduated in 1938 from Mercy High School, a nun's school. For the next five years he was an amateur boxer, bringing many honors to San Luis, until he was drafted into the U.S. Army in 1943. Upon his discharge in 1946 he moved to Pueblo, Colorado, where he sold insurance until his father once again encouraged him to return to the valley to further his education. Sánchez then enrolled at Adams State College of Colorado in Alamosa, where he received his master's degree in teacher education in 1952. His teaching career spanned over twenty years in various public schools—from the first to the ninth grades—throughout the San Luis Valley. In 1975, at fifty-eight years of age, he had a heart attack, which forced him to retire. One year earlier his wife, Elsie Argüello-Sánchez, whom he had married circa 1947, succumbed to cancer. He continued to live in San Luis until 1979, when his house burned down.

Having lost all his possessions, he moved to Denver, where he lives alone, but quite content. Sánchez, like his father, believes that education is the key to success, and he questions the wisdom of working excessively just to accumulate material things.

A great deal of his philosophy of life is unveiled in his autobiographical novel, *Don Phil-o-meno sí la mancha* (Don Phil-o-meno on the Spot), self-published in 1977 and again in 1987. Sánchez's admiration for Miguel de Cervantes's *Don Quixote* is quite evident, and he confesses that he, too, like Quixote, has searched constantly for illusive dreams in his life. Writing about his experiences, or *aventuras*, as he calls them, because "se cree más lo escrito que lo platicao" (people believe the written word more than the spoken one), has enabled him to fulfill one of his dreams. Those who have read *Don Quixote* and appreciate Sancho Panza's repertoire of proverbs will also enjoy Sánchez's wit and wry humor.

While one must not dwell on the affinity between *Don Quixote* and *Don Phil-o-meno sí la mancha*, the thought is inevitable; Sánchez's title itself provides the reader with a clue to the humor that is contained in his book. The whimsical Panza seems to symbolize Quixote's alter ego, and Señor Bigotudo performs a similar function in *Don Phil-o-meno sí la mancha*. He is introduced as the sagacious old man (his mustache and beard symbolize his sagacity) who not only offers advice to Philomeno Sánchez but also serves as a balance between the outrageous and the rational, the frivolous and the prudent. Bigotudo's wisdom is reminiscent of the exempla that swept Europe and Spain during the Middle Ages. At one point he tells the protagonist,

> Mira Chiquillo, todas estas cosas que te estoy enseñando serán para ti una inmensidad de riquezas. Espero que las conserves en tu mente, y que sean útil [*sic*] para que puedas cosechar de ellas un fruto provechoso. Tú serás heredero de mi sabiduría, y acuérdate de esto: Los dicípulos [*sic*] salen mejores que los maestros. Pero sal de

Philomeno Sánchez

tu pueblo para donde no te conozcan, para que te den el crédito que se te merece, porque un profeta en su pueblo no es aceptado.

(Listen here young fellow, all of these things that I'm telling you about will be an immense richness to you. I hope that you keep them in mind, and that they're useful so that you're able to reap profitable fruit from them. You shall be an heir to my wisdom, and remember this: The disciples turn out better than their masters. But leave your town for places where they don't know you, so that they credit you with what you justly deserve, because a prophet is not accepted in his own town.)

Bigotudo at times is skeptical about getting his point across: "¿estás comprendiendo, o están las lecciones muy avanzadas?" (are you understanding, or are the lessons too advanced for you?). But he underestimates his student, who replies: "Oh, no, señor, . . . usted es un maestro de

gran categoría. Con usted hasta los burros que son burros aprenden a alzar la cola, aunque la tengan hecha bola" (Oh, no, sir, . . . you're a master of the first order. With you, even the donkeys that are jackasses learn to lift their tail, even if it's all rolled up). In the final analysis, the mentor learns as much from his disciple, if not more, because the sharing of experiences between "The Bearded Man" and "El Chiquillo" comprises moral underpinnings of sorts. Their encounters remind one also of a father-son relationship in the *disciplina clericales* literature also popular in medieval Spain.

Sánchez readily acknowledges his father's influence when he quotes him: "sí te dejo adagios; es todito lo que tengo. Tú verás cómo los usas porque de allí vendrá tu pago. Mi bendición que te acompañe en toditos tus quehaceres[;] . . . para mí serás un hijo que compliste tus deberes. Si quieres vivir contento, no engañes a las mujeres" (indeed I leave you adages; that's all I've got. You'll see how to use them because that's where you'll derive your profit from. May my blessings accompany you in all of your chores[;] . . . for me you'll always be a son who complied with his responsibilities. If you want to live happy, don't deceive women). Indelible as his father's advice may be, thanks to a multitude of *dichos*, or proverbs, throughout the novel, his father goes beyond merely giving advice on moral and ethical behavior.

A motif also popular in the Middle Ages in Spain comes into play in *Don Phil-o-meno sí la mancha*: the acknowledgment of fugacity coupled with a nostalgic desire for the past. As his father says: "Todito esto te digo, porque algún día tú lo verás. Los tiempos que ahora tenemos, nunca los veremos jamás" (I'm telling you all of this, because one of these days you're going to witness it. The times that we're now enjoying, we'll never see them again).

Sánchez's wife, Elsie, was the only person capable of neutralizing his mischievous nature. She clearly humbled him, as readers see in the following exchange between them in the book, as he reacts to seeing two beautiful girls:

"Nomás mira que pollas, y que piernitas de amoles. Esas no pueden mentir que no beben atole, y comen frijoles. Y fíjate en esas *headlights*, lo que tú les nombras limones, para mi parecen ser mejor coles. . . ."

(Just look at those chicks, and what dandy legs. Surely they can't lie that they do not drink blue corn gruel, or eat pinto beans. And look at those headlights, what you call lemons, as for me they're more like cabbages. . . .)

"¡Ah, qué mi Phil O'Menito sin venas! Por qué tan poquito te apenas . . . sabiendo que son hasta ajenas . . . de suerte no te condenas . . . y te cuelgan con unas cadenas . . . por querer traer las dos manos llenas. . . ."

(Ah, my poor little Philomeno without sense! Why do you worry so much . . . knowing full well that they're someone else's . . . you're lucky you're not doomed . . . and they hang you using chains . . . just because of trying to have both hands full. . . .)

Don Phil-o-meno sí la mancha also presents examples of folklore, such as *entriegas* (poetic renditions of marriage), *dichos* (sayings), *remedios* (remedies), *corridos* (ballads), *posadas* (ritualistic reen-

actments of Joseph and Mary seeking refuge), and other traditional customs that are fading further into the past and getting lost in the modern technological era. Sánchez's keen sensitivity and appreciation for his own culture and language in the San Luis Valley of Colorado are crystallized in his work. The ease with which he manipulates the Spanish language (his entire book, except for a smattering of English here and there, is written in his native tongue) is clearly an anachronism in the modern Southwest and is not only due to his cultural perspicacity but is a tribute to his poetics, reminiscent of the village *poeta* of yesteryear in New Mexico and southern Colorado.

Since his first and only book, Philomeno Sánchez has written little else, but he has begun to write, as a *recuerdo* (memoir) for his children, a long, comical poem titled "Las estaciones de esta cruz" (The Stations of This Cross). It is intended to be a parody on his own life following the structure of the Stations of the Cross, although he hastens to add that the poem is not meant to poke fun at the Stations themselves. Here is a sample taken from the "Prefacio e Introducción":

Quiero que usted se entere, de mis nobles situaciones,
No se vaya a confundir, y se llene de ilusiones.

Para que esté más claro, a Dios le pido licencia,
Que me ayude a concentrar, e ilumine mi conciencia.

Porque le quiero explicar, con mi poca inteligencia,
De lo que me ha pasado, que tengo por experiencia.
. . . .

Voy a escribir en poesía, creo que es mi imposición,
Para darle buen principio, esta es la introducción.

También será el prefacio, con todos sus ingredientes,
Y después sobre el autor, incluyendo a sus parientes.

Porque voy abrir la boca, pa' que se miren los dientes,
Como siempre ando obscuras, cuando no traigo mis lentes.

Le voy a decir un poco, de lo que ha sucedido,
Para que no esté en ayunas, de no haberme conocido.

(I want you to know, of my noble situations,
Do not go get confused, and end up full of illusions.

In order to be quite clear, I ask God permission,
May He help me concentrate, and thus illuminate my conscience.

Because I want to explain, with my limited intelligence,
What has happened to me, as part of my experience.
. . . .

I'm going to write in poetry, I believe it's my duty,
To start off right, this is the beginning.

It will also be the preface, with all its ingredients,
And later something about the author, including his relatives.

I'm going to open my mouth, so I can show off my teeth,
Since I am always in the dark, unable to see.

I'm going to tell you a little bit, of what has happened,
So you're not uninformed, of not having met me.)

If the use of the Spanish dialect that has typified northern New Mexico and southern Colorado for several centuries, so embedded in Sánchez's psyche, is as vibrant in this last work as in his first one, then he will have left a linguistic treasure.

Reference:
Nasario García, Prologue to Sánchez's *Don Phil-o-meno sí la mancha* (San Luis, Colo.: Sangre de Cristo, 1977).

Danny Santiago
(Daniel James)
(14 January 1911 - 18 May 1988)

Jonah Raskin
Sonoma State University

BOOK: *Famous All Over Town* (New York: Simon & Schuster, 1983).

PLAY PRODUCTIONS: *Winter Soldiers*, New York, Studio Theatre of the New School for Social Research, 29 November 1942;
Bloomer Girl, by Daniel and Lilith James, New York, Shubert Theatre, 5 October 1944.

OTHER: *Winter Soldiers*, as Dan James, in *The Best Plays of 1942-43*, edited by Burns Mantle (New York: Dodd, Mead, 1943), pp. 143-179;
"The Somebody," *Redbook* (February 1970): 68-69, 165, 168.

Danny Santiago occupies a curious place in Chicano literature. From 1970 when his first short story, "The Somebody," was published in *Redbook* (February) until 1983 when his novel, *Famous All Over Town*, was published by Simon and Schuster, Santiago maintained a low profile. He granted no interviews, answered no phones, and only corresponded with agents and editors through a post office box in Pacific Grove, California. Then in the summer of 1984 Santiago suddenly emerged from obscurity and into the limelight when his identity was revealed by novelist and screenwriter John Gregory Dunne.

"Danny Santiago is not his name," Dunne wrote in an explosive essay that appeared in the *New York Review of Books* (16 August 1984). "He is not a Chicano. Nor is he young. He is 73 years old. He is an Anglo. He is a graduate of Andover and Yale. His name is Daniel James." Dunne's article solved the Santiago mystery, but at the same time it opened the floodgates to cultural controversy. *Famous All Over Town* took on sig-

Daniel James, who wrote fiction under the pseudonym Danny Santiago (photograph by ABE)

nificance as a social document. It served as a springboard for heated debates about pen names and literary hoaxes, ethnic literature and literary ethics. It conferred visibility on the author after decades of anonymity, focusing attention on his membership in the American Communist party and his role in Hollywood during the era of the blacklist.

Danny Santiago's barrio in East Los Angeles—the setting of *Famous All Over Town*—is a long way from the middle-class neighborhood in Kansas City, Missouri, where Daniel Lewis James was born, the only child of D. L. James and Lillie Snider James. The James family was hardworking, prosperous, and respectable, though Dan James's paternal grandfather, a God-fearing Baptist, was a first cousin of Frank and Jesse James. The names of these nineteenth-century outlaws were forbidden at the dinner table; nevertheless, Dan grew up proud of his connection to the

legendary James brothers.

James's father managed the retail firm of T. M. James & Sons, purveyors of fine glass and china to the Kansas City elite. However, his father's true love was the theater, and in his spare time he wrote plays, some of which were produced by amateur and summer theater companies. In addition, the father belonged to the town's only literary society, where Dan James met Ernest Hemingway and the painter and muralist Thomas Hart Benton. The young James became an avid reader of H. L. Mencken's *American Mercury*, and was inspired by Sinclair Lewis and Clarence Darrow, whom he heard at the Unitarian Fellowship.

In 1927 Dan James graduated from Kansas City Country Day School, where he played football and wrote for the student newspaper. In 1928 he graduated from Andover Academy and in 1933 from Yale, where he majored in Greek. During his senior year he became involved in political causes and demonstrations, and wrote agit-prop sketches for the theater. A member of the New Haven branch of the John Reed Club (a radical organization of writers), James went on several hunger marches to the state capital, Topeka.

After graduation he returned to Kansas City and worked for T. M. James & Sons as a salesman in Oklahoma and southern Missouri. This was during the Depression and fine china was a luxury item that sold poorly, so James exchanged his white collar for blue. He took a job in the Oklahoma oil fields, and gained firsthand knowledge of proletarian life. In Carmel, California, where his family spent summers in an immense house on the coast, James met Lincoln Steffens, Ella Winter, and Langston Hughes, all of whom contributed to his growing knowledge of Marxism. In the mid 1930s James joined the Young Communist League and became an organizer for the Unemployed Council. Following a large, militant rally in Kansas City, he was arrested and jailed. His father provided bail and suggested that he write about, rather than participate in, the class struggle. Father and son collaborated on "Pier 17," a melodrama about the San Francisco General Strike of 1934. Dan James took the play to New York where it was rejected everywhere. In spite of this, he made New York his home for a year and a half, writing several one-act plays on political themes that were never produced, and acting in the Theatre Union production of John Howard Lawson's *Marching Song* (17 February 1937).

Returning to Carmel, James became involved in local theater groups and politics. He met Charlie Chaplin, who was beginning to work on *The Great Dictator* (1940), and was hired as his man Friday. In 1938 James moved to Hollywood and joined the Communist party, and in 1940 he married Lilith Stanward, a ballerina with a young daughter that James later adopted.

When the Nazis invaded the Soviet Union (June 1941), James wrote *Winter Soldiers*, a drama in two acts and eleven scenes, and nearly forty speaking roles. Produced by Erwin Piscator in New York at the Studio Theatre of the New School for Social Research, *Winter Soldiers* won the Sidney Howard Memorial Award, a fifteen-hundred-dollar grant given by the Playwright's Company to "the young American playwright showing the most promise." Lewis Nichols, the *New York Times* theater critic, called the play "exciting and moving . . . a perfect portrait of that

other column which also carries on the war for freedom," and Burns Mantle selected it as one of the ten best plays of the 1942-1943 season, commenting, "It embodies the will to win of freedom-loving peoples all over the world and is, I think, one of the truly significant dramas inspired by the global war." John Gregory Dunne called it "a curious relic." In hindsight, James described it as a "bad play that got good reviews. It was art as social weapon, but there was a lot more weapon than there was art." A celebration of the heroic partisan units engaged in guerrilla activity against the Nazi war machine, *Winter Soldiers* is melodramatic and sentimental, but it moves gracefully, and has a few well-drawn characters and several redeeming humorous moments.

In 1944 he collaborated with his wife Lilith on *Bloomer Girl*. Premiering on 5 October 1944 in the Shubert Theatre, New York, the musical comedy became a hit on Broadway for nearly two full seasons. The original idea was Lilith's and had emerged from a workshop on woman's rights. Professional Broadway writers were later brought in to develop the Jameses' play. The comedy is set in the mid nineteenth century and uses women's fashions to define fundamental social change. Though *Bloomer Girl* was a financial success, Dan James's life took a downward turn. At the end of World War II his dissatisfaction with the Communist party deepened, and he was increasingly uncomfortable with Marxist prescriptions for the arts. Finally, in 1948 he and Lilith left the Communist party—though without rancor or bitterness. At about the same time they became involved with the Los Angeles Mexican community. James told Dunne, "As many of the comrades took off for Europe and elsewhere, we moved into East Los Angeles and started making a new life for ourselves." The Mexican community was made up of three blocks in Lincoln Heights that would serve as the principal setting for *Famous All Over Town*. Dan and Lilith worked with teenage clubs, developed theater groups, and encouraged musical performances. They met young people and their families and participated in births, baptisms, marriages, and funerals, undergoing an initiation into another culture.

In 1947 the House Committee on Un-American Activities had begun its investigations of left-wing influence in the film industry. Former Communist party members, fellow travelers, and sympathizers informed on former friends and comrades. Dan and Lilith James were named on the morning of 19 September 1951. Later that day they appeared before the committee, and though James volunteered that he was "not a member of the Communist Party," he took the Fifth Amendment when asked whether or not he had ever been a member. James had prepared a speech and rehearsed his lines, carrying a copy of Voltaire's *Candide* in his pocket. "I had planned to say that Voltaire published that work under the pseudonym M. le Docteur Ralph, and that if the Committee was successful, American writers would have to follow in his footsteps and disguise their identities with pen names," James said. The committee did not give him the opportunity to make his statement.

From 1951 on James was blacklisted, persona non grata in the film and television industry, his name and Lilith's removed from the credits when *Bloomer Girl* was shown on NBC television in 1952. Convinced that his writing career as Daniel James was blocked, he decided to evade the blacklist by taking a pen name. As Daniel Hyatt he worked on the screenplays of two monster pictures—*The Giant Behemoth* in 1959 and *Gorgo* in 1961—and as Danny Santiago he wrote a series of short stories based on his experiences in East Los Angeles.

Taking the Danny Santiago persona enabled James to escape from writer's block and from old, inhibiting habits. "By writing as a Chicano I was able to get away from the cerebral and to feel strong passions," James said. "Living in the Mexican community I gradually stopped thinking about abstract ideas. I got rid of the 1930s Marxist insistence on art as a social weapon. I began to use my eyes and ears, to watch and to listen, and out of that process began to emerge the writing that finally was published as *Famous All Over Town*."

In the early 1960s James witnessed the destruction of the Chicano community in Lincoln Heights, an experience that significantly influenced his writing. "It was a village, a wonderful community and we saw it go," James said. "The Southern Pacific Railroad took it over. I was profoundly moved. From nowhere the figure of this kid Chato with his chalk came to me. Once he started to talk I knew him, what he was doing and what his attitudes were. That was the big flash—this young boy going out in his ruined street and making his mark on the walls with a piece of chalk." Through the 1950s and 1960s James continued to write stories about the Mexican world of East Los Angeles. Then in 1968 he approached John Gregory Dunne, took him into

Cover for the 1984 paperback edition of Santiago's novel about Chato Medina, a teenage boy growing up in the barrio

his confidence, and asked him to act as an intermediary and help find a publisher for his stories.

"I thought that they were very good—tough, funny, unsentimental, and undogmatic," Dunne said. "But I was not enthusiastic about his wish to send them out under the name 'Danny Santiago.' I had nothing against pseudonyms . . . but the idea of an Anglo presenting himself as a Chicano I found troubling." James was adamant about his pen name. Writing to Dunne about his identity as Danny Santiago, he explained, "He's so much freer than I am myself. He seems to know how he feels about everything and none of the ifs, ands, and buts that I'm plagued with. I don't plan to make a great cops and robbers bit out of him, but now at any rate I can't let him go. Maybe he'll prove to be a straight-jacket later on. We'll see. In any event, unless you feel too guilty about this mild little deception of mine, I'd like you to send on the stories." Uncomfortable though he was, Dunne agreed, and on 25 March

1968 he mailed several of Santiago's stories with a covering letter to Carl Brandt, his New York agent. There was almost immediate success, and in 1970 *Redbook* published "The Somebody," a short story which James considered his best piece of writing. Selected by Martha Foley for *Best American Short Stories* of 1971, "The Somebody" was widely anthologized in collections of ethnic literature and taught in Chicano literature classes. The praise is well deserved. Told in the first person by Chato Medina, "The Somebody" has a powerful, resonant voice, and captures the rhythms of Chicano speech and the energy of Chicano youth. In revised form it is a chapter in *Famous All Over Town*.

James was heartened by his literary success. He opened a savings account in the name of Danny Santiago, banking the proceeds from "The Somebody" and from two short stories published in *Playboy* that used Mexican characters: "A Message from Home," and "Goldilocks and the Three Beers." Encouraged by his agent, James began to shape the Santiago stories into a full-length novel. Then, in the early 1970s the book took an interesting turn. "I realized that the Chato character was me," James said. "Of course, he has none of the advantages that I had. He didn't go to college, and didn't study Marxism. He comes from a poor Mexican family and has little formal education and no ideology. But Chato and I are also very much alike. We're both writers. Like him I wanted to put my mark on the wall. His ruined street became all the constructs of my past, including the Communist Party, which had collapsed for me."

In 1976 he finished a version of *Famous All Over Town* and his agent Carl Brandt submitted it to New York publishers. James recalled that it was universally rejected, often on the grounds that it read like "the old ethnic novels of the 1930s." He withdrew the book from circulation for four years. Then, because of Brandt's insistence, James mailed his manuscript out again, and finally in 1981 Simon and Schuster accepted it for publication. James worked on it for another year, tightening the plot and fleshing out the characterization. In March 1983, thirty-one years after James first used the Danny Santiago pseudonym, *Famous All Over Town* made its debut.

From the start the novel attracted attention, in part because of the author's Chicano name, but also because it portrays the Chicano community, and one Chicano in particular: Rudy (Chato) Medina, a man-child of the barrio who comes of age in turbulent times. In *Famous All Over Town* James depicts a community in upheaval and transition. The old neighborhood is destroyed, the Medina family falls apart, and individuals go their own separate ways. Six chapters are set in Mexico when the California Medinas move briefly to the land of their ancestors. James shows us how they change in El Norte, and at the same time how they remain the same. Chato receives an education in Mexico and gains an appreciation of his origins and heritage, but he is unable to take up the rituals and traditions of village life after the bright lights of the big city. Returning to Los Angeles, Chato watches as bulldozers batter his home and the homes of his neighbors.

There are social messages about education, sex, family, violence, and police, but James does not lose sight of the fact that he must entertain readers in a television age. The thirty-three chapters are short and largely self-contained, a series of minidramas as contemporary as today's television situation comedies. Sadness and anger are strong emotional currents in the book, but the note of humor is never lost.

Reading *Famous All Over Town*, readers may or may not see the hand of a writer shaped by the 1930s, by Marxism, the contact with Charlie Chaplin, and experiences on Broadway and in Hollywood. James said that he accepted "much Marxist economic thinking," and there are some obvious legacies from his past. The Southern Pacific Railroad and the Los Angeles Police Department are the chief villains of the piece, and most of the characters are working class, albeit of Third World origin and identity. Still, James has not idealized or romanticized his proletarians, and he does not offer a social solution to the plight of the Chicanos. There is a strong sense of defiance and protest, but it is individual, almost anarchist, rather than collective and Marxist. Chato writes his name on walls all over East Los Angeles, a creative and political act. Arrested and incarcerated, Chato emerges from jail determined to become a writer and tell his own story. So *Famous All Over Town* is a novelist's novel, a story about the making of a writer. It offers yet another version of the portrait of the artist as a young man.

James's work was widely reviewed and warmly received when it was published in 1983. In the *New York Times* (24 April 1983), David Quammen called it "a classic" and pronounced Danny Santiago "a natural . . . a writer endowed as though genetically with the sure, pure sense of how to shape his material." In the *Los Angeles Times* (5 May 1983), Carolyn See called it "a touching book, well written—a dark mirror image of white, East Coast *Catcher in the Rye*—a sensitive story of more than justified adolescent depression." On the pop-culture front, reviewer and novelist David Guy concluded in *USA Today* (10 June 1983) that "Danny Santiago's apparent artlessness conceals a very intricate art," and that "the reader's final impression is of the enormous vitality of ghetto life and the injustice of any criticism from outsiders."

The novel sold modestly in hardback but slowly won respect and admiration in literary and intellectual circles. The American Academy and Institute of Arts and Letters selected it for the Rosenthal Award; "though not a commercial success," Dunne commented on the novel, it "is a considerable literary achievement." At the 16 May 1984 award ceremony, John Kenneth Galbraith declared,

> *Famous All Over Town* adds luster to the enlarging literary genre of immigrant experience, of social, cultural and psychological threshhold-crossing.... The durable young narrator spins across a multi-colored scene of crime, racial violence and extremes of dislocation, seeking and perhaps finding his own space. The exuberant mixes with the nerve-wracking; and throughout sly slippages of language enact a comedy on the theme of communication.

Then came the revelation that Danny Santiago was Dan James. A literary debate raged about the ethics of an Anglo taking a Latino pen name and writing about Chicano experience.

Yale professor R. M. B. Lewis, the chair of the seven-member American Academy Committee that picked *Famous All Over Town* for the Rosenthal Award, commented in the *New York Times* (22 July 1984), "I don't think when I was reading it I was too much concerned with whether the author was a Chicano or not, but now that I know I think I admire the novel all the more." Thomas Sanchez, the author of *Rabbit Boss* (1974) and *Zoot-Suit Murders* (1978), defended James and his novel in the *San Francisco Chronicle* (12 August 1984): "A work must be judged by the work itself, not the political or ethnic orientation of the author," Sanchez said. "A lot of professional Chicanos, professional blacks, professional Jews, professional Anglo-Saxons say no one else can cut into their territory. I don't believe in terms of the human race that there is any

such thing as territory. What creativity and art are all about are the absolute freedom to cross all those lines and go into any point of view in terms of the context of the work."

In the *Chronicle* (12 August 1984), Richard Rodríguez, the author of *Hunger of Memory* (1981), was sympathetic to James's need to take a pen name. It's "certainly understandable," he said, and went on to explain, "We've been working under an assumption for the past 25 years that only Hispanic writers can write about Hispanic experiences, that only black writers can write about black experiences, that only women can write about women. I think those are really dangerous assumptions." University of Texas professor, novelist, and critic Rolando Hinojosa-Smith said in an interview, "I can understand James taking a pen name after what he'd been through in the 1950s. I don't think it was intentionally deceptive or sinister, and I don't think that an injustice was done to the Chicano or the Mexican community. It's a funny novel and it's authentic."

However, there were also angry protests from both Anglos and Chicanos. In the *Chronicle* (12 August 1984), *Los Angeles Times* book editor Art Seidenbaum commented that he was enormously offended by James's appropriation of a Latino name. University of Southern California professor Félix Gutiérrez allowed that "You don't have to be a Latino to write on the Latino experience," but he suggested that "Dan James should write as Dan James, because a piece should stand on the merit of the writing, not the author's name." Philip Herrera, cofounder in 1977 with José M. Ferrer III of *Nuestro*, and the publisher of one of Santiago's stories, was offended. "We were deceived," he said. "We were trying to find Hispanic writers and we were led to believe that Danny Santiago was a Mexican-American.... We were trying to present the best image of Hispanics we could. We were not trying to publish Anglo writers with Spanish surnames." In Los Angeles, public schools had classroom discussions about the Santiago/James controversy. In San Francisco, Modern Times bookstore sponsored a panel discussion, "Danny Santiago: Art or Fraud?," with Rudolfo Anaya, Gary Soto, Myrta Chabrán, Tomás Ybarra-Frausto, and Juan Felipe Herrera. If nothing else, *Famous All Over Town* served as a platform that raised crucial issues about American literary and cultural life. No clear answers were provided, but the boundaries of the novel were redrawn, and the role of the art-

348

headlights had half-moons of dust. ~~Steam was coming from the~~ *The radiator was steaming* ~~radiator~~ and there was an evil smell of oil. *Oh-oh, I thought.* My father eased

himself out, ~~carefully~~ balancing his head like a melon which

might fall off and pop open on the ground.

"Flat tire," he mumbled.

No use mentioning the motor in his ~~present mood~~ *condition*. ~~I tried to tell him about Lena and how we should get her to the doctor but my father didn't listen.~~ He staggered off ~~to~~ *toward* the house.

At the door he aimed a giant belch at the sun, then stumbled in-

side. Aunts scattered. I steered him to my cot. He fell on it

and before I could ~~even~~ take off his shoes he was snoring. *My mother tapped me on the shoulder.* "Get his keys," ~~my mother ordered~~. I fished them from his

pocket. ~~There was a big wad of crumpled pesos in there too but I left them be, which I regretted it later.~~

"Open the ~~trunk~~ *Buick*," ~~my mother~~ *she* ordered. "Help ~~me unload~~."

"What about "~~Without~~ my father? He'~~ll~~ *gonna* be mad."

"My sisters can't wait for Santa Claus."

~~When I opened up I could see~~ My father's flat tire was no lie. *Everything in the trunk was trompled* ~~The sacks were all trompled around and some had grease on them. With my mother helping~~ I carried ~~them~~ *sacks* to the table where

we ate last night. More aunts ~~suddenly~~ had come*s* from where,

I couldn't guess, unless possibly they had been roosting in the *big* ~~big~~ tree ~~all night, like capilotes~~. They stood in a ~~hungry~~ *buzzardy* cir-

cle wearing their dusty blacks and brown. And how their eyes

Page from chapter 27 in the typescript for Famous All Over Town *(by permission of the Estate of Daniel James)*

ist was redefined. It appears that James played a pioneering role, albeit unintentionally, making it more acceptable for the Anglo writer to depict Third World experience.

In the midst of the debate about his book, Dan James stood his ground. He defended his decision to take a pen name and his right to describe the Chicano community. In *Time* (6 August 1984) he insisted that he "wasn't trying to jump on the ethnic bandwagon." Taking the pen name Danny Santiago, he explained, was a matter of his own survival as a creative writer. It had given him confidence and a sense of freedom. "The book. The book. That's the important thing," he announced in the *Washington Post* (23 July 1984). "Not the skin color or the ancestry of the author."

Controversy was no stranger to Dan James, and notoriety haunted him from the early 1950s to the mid 1980s. His own story reflects a significant portion of twentieth-century American history. However, he deserves to be remembered as a novelist and short-story writer, not as a sym-

bolic figure. *Famous All Over Town* is a work of integrity and imagination, a uniquely personal work that expresses a deep sense of anguish and dignity. The humor, the irony, and especially the tone of voice are very strong indeed. Long after the reader closes the book the narrator's language reverberates. The author died at seventy-seven on 18 May 1988, but *Famous All Over Town* assures Danny Santiago/Dan James an enduring place in literature.

References:

John Gregory Dunne, "The Secret of Danny Santiago," *New York Review of Books*, 16 August 1984, pp. 17-18, 20, 22, 24-27;

Gerald Haslam, "A Question of Authenticity, or Who Can Write What?," *Western American Literature* (Fall 1985): 246-250;

Jonah Raskin, "The Man Who Would Be Danny Santiago," *San Francisco Bay Guardian*, 28 November 1984, pp. 13-14, 19;

Anne C. Roark, "When Is a Pseudonym a Lie?," *San Francisco Chronicle, This World*, 12 August 1984, p. 17.

Nina Serrano
(1 September 1934 -)

Miriam Daniel Fahey
Holy Names College

BOOK: *Heart Songs: The Collected Poems of Nina Serrano (1969-1979)* (San Francisco: Pocho-Che, 1980).

SELECTED PERIODICAL PUBLICATION—
UNCOLLECTED: "Blessed Be," *Cambio*, 1 (August 1985).

Nina Serrano, an important poet and leader in the Chicano movement, was born on 1 September 1934 in the Bronx to an immigrant from Santander, Colombia, and his wife, whose parents were from Eastern Europe. Since Nina's parents had to work in restaurants and cafeterias in Manhattan, her early years were under the tutelage of a gentleman she called Uncle Paul—Augustín Polo Arroyo—who was born in Puerto Rico but lived in Cuba for many years. He loved the arts (performing, graphic, and visual) and was responsible for her love of them. Whether it was opera, ballet, theater, or vaudeville, he took Nina along. Her father also loved art—he was an artist—and so, like many working-class families in New York, they spent their Sundays in parks and museums where entry was free. Nina's interest in other peoples may have been spurred by the many languages heard as she passed through the city streets.

With regard to her formal education, Serrano recalls her early days at the San José day-care center where she was left in the morning on her parents' way to work and from which she was taken to attend classes in the New York public schools. Since Uncle Paul, with whom she spent a great deal of time, spoke mainly Spanish, the school authorities put her in speech-correction classes to eliminate her accent. As anything foreign was unpopular during World War II, she made an extreme effort to become proficient in English. When she was fourteen, a new public school called Performing Arts was opened; Serrano was in the first class. She continued improving her English and began training in theater. At sixteen she began taking classes in a the-

Nina Serrano

ater company and performing a classical repertoire.

Serrano spent the year after her high-school graduation doing low-paying jobs, studying theater, and looking for work on Broadway. The following year, 1953, she married and accompanied her husband to the University of Wisconsin, where she suffered culture shock. She continued her interest in drama, became involved in children's theater, and gained her first political experience as a staff person for the "Joe-Must-Go Club" (an anti-Joseph McCarthy group).

In 1955, after the birth of her son, Greg, she enrolled in the University of Wisconsin as a full-time speech-and-drama major. She became politically active in the peace and civil-rights movements and became president of the Student Peace Union. It was in this role that in 1957 she traveled by ship to England, where she left her infant son in the care of a baby-sitting service and continued on to Russia to attend the Moscow Youth Festival.

At the termination of the festival the young delegation was invited to go via the trans-Siberian railroad to China. Although the U.S. embassy warned the Americans of the consequences and required them to sign a document that they had been warned of the embargo being put on their trip, many of them, including Serrano, continued on. There were students from Indonesia, Australia, and Latin America, including future leaders of revolutions in Latin America. Serrano identified with that last group, who spoke Spanish and were fun-loving; this camaraderie helped her bear the separation from her husband and son.

While in China she studied the roles of women and children in theater, especially the Shanghai theater. She also studied Peking opera and inquired about education during her two-month stay. When she returned to the University of Wisconsin, she found a cold welcome and was discouraged from continuing. When she became pregnant with her second child, she was told she was too old to continue her studies. Nevertheless, she took her first video class shortly after her daughter, Valerie, was born in 1958. Serrano staged scenes from new British writers with a leftist orientation. She also became intensely interested in Bertolt Brecht's work.

In 1959 Serrano went with her husband and sister-in-law to Morelia, Mexico, to visit a Mexican family that had lived next to them in Madison. On this, her first visit to Latin America, she was shocked by the poverty. All the stories of Mexico she had heard were picturesque; no one had mentioned the dust, mud, flies, and naked children. For her the country was a tremendous shock in its contrast to Russia and China, where poverty was greater but cleanliness was given a high priority. The poverty of Mexico was disheartening and demoralizing to Serrano.

Back in Madison in 1960 she began working in an experimental school, team-teaching theater for children. She was excited about this educational principle, which she feels is still relevant.

With the money she earned, she subscribed to magazines that brought culture from areas far from Madison. A summer (1960) issue of the *Monthly Review* featured Cuba, which had just gone through its revolution. This article, plus the fact that her husband was in Cuba, as well as her imaginings of Cuba based on Uncle Paul's reminiscences, prompted her to take her children and join her husband in Havana, where she met revolutionary artists who had returned from exile or emerged from underground. She was excited about the education and culture that were blossoming in Cuba, and she took the opportunity to visit state schools to enlarge her vision of education beyond that in the United States.

Shortly after her return in 1961 she headed for California, having been attracted to San Francisco by a book of photography showing life in North Beach. She settled, with her children, on Dolores Street in the Mission District and become involved in a community radio station, KPFA, where she produced children's· programs—including plays about Gertrude Stein and Isadora Duncan—and a play by a New Left playwright. Because Serrano's children were of school age, she became active in the Alternative School and began teaching Spanish. The staff was complemented by people who were excited about teaching children and was supported by parents with a strong sense of participation. She evolved a method of teaching Spanish through songs, games, and plays.

With her interest in the theater as strong as ever, Serrano became director of a San Francisco mime group and also got involved in European repertory drama. In 1967 she and her husband went to Uruguay, Guatemala, and Mexico at a time of great political ferment. They traveled deep into the countries and were in touch with the protest movements; what she saw affected her greatly.

The following year, with her children, she accompanied her husband to Cuba, where he was to make a film on Fidel Castro. She had to play a large part in the production. For four months she traveled all over the island by jeep—the first woman to accompany the army—and filmed everything. It was on this trip that she met the Salvadoran Roque Dalton, who was the person who had the greatest influence on her literary career. While there she did her first writing—a play in collaboration with Dalton for Cuban video. Dalton inspired her and made her laugh.

It was an isolated time of extreme happiness for her.

After working with Dalton, Serrano became interested in the works of the poet Pablo Armando Fernández. She began writing poetry, and all the themes from the theater that had been inside her came out in verse. Writing plays had been liberating, but through poetry she could reach an audience more easily.

A key year in Serrano's involvement with the Chicano movement was 1972. While working in bilingual radio back in the United States, she met two men who wanted her to help cover the Raza Unida Conference in El Paso, Texas. There she met many active Chicanos, among them Reies López Tijerina of the Land Grant movement. She also met Lillian del Sol, a key community organizer in the Chicano moratoriums. Serrano built up an archive of television programs that are still used from time to time. She produced a Latin-American history program on KPSA in Berkeley, as well as a radio program called "Reflecciones de Raza" (Race Reflections) which was a model for bilingual radio programming.

In 1974 there was a break of a year in her active participation in Chicano activities in the Mission District. Her marriage had just broken up, and her daughter wanted a change from the inner-city high school she attended. So the two of them returned to Cuba, where Serrano took a job, and Valerie repeated tenth grade, developed good study habits, became interested in learning, and polished her Spanish.

On their return Serrano, who was a contributing editor to *Tin-Tan* (a quarterly published by Editorial Pocho-Che that lasted six issues), wrote a report on "The Second Congress of Women," which had been held in Cuba in November 1974. In the same publication she did a translation of Fernández's poem about Luis Talamántez and also commented on the latter's book *Life Within the Heart Imprisoned* (1976), judging it to be "a useful tool in La Raza [Chicano], ethnic and prison studies classes." (Talamántez was one of the San Quentin Six, a group of black and brown prisoners accused of five murders.)

In 1980 Serrano had her poems published in book form. The title, *Heart Songs*, aptly describes the contents. Fernando Alegría, in the introduction to the work, describes it as "poetry of hidden fire, [which] moves like a lens high and distant over the streets of San Francisco, the plains of Wisconsin, the toasted mesa of New Mexico

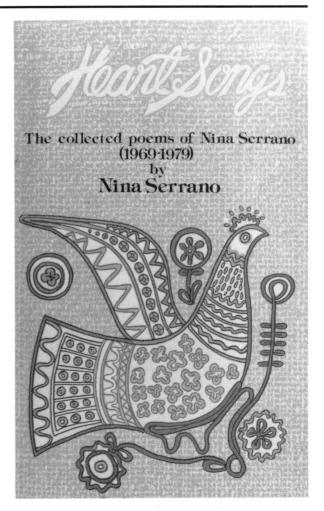

Cover for Serrano's 1980 book, her selection of the best poems from the first decade of her writing career

and the battle of buildings against bridges, windows against glass, in the multiple loneliness of New York."

The sixty poems are divided into five parts: "Early Songs," "Songs of Struggle," "Single Woman Songs," "Tropi-Cuba," and "End of the California Drought." Although the majority of Serrano's poems deal with the social problems of the 1960s and 1970s, there are several short lyric poems. One, accompanied by a whimsical drawing, is titled "Daughter Haiku":

Bright butterfly! Bringing joy.
How good it is
to watch your flight.

Another one, "For My Son . . . So Far Away," is dedicated to her son, Greg:

As the tree feels the flight of the leaf
and the rosebush the parting of her flower

and the grass thirsts for the dew
so I, my son, miss you.

There are poignant poems such as "In Memoriam," in which Serrano commemorates the death of Uncle Paul, and "Poetry in Action," in which she honors the Filipino worker, poet, and community organizer Serafin Syquia, also deceased. Many of Serrano's poems take up the cause of the underdogs, of those struggling for freedom. In the poems "San Francisco Chinatown Fair" and "New York City: March 9, 1970, to March 23, 1970," she focuses on explosive themes of the late 1960s and early 1970s: university uprisings and racial riots.

Having traveled extensively, Serrano was personally aware of conflicts in places such as Nicaragua, Cuba, Puerto Rico, Mexico, and Chile. The last lines of her "Elegy for Pablo Neruda" best sum up how she feels about innocent victims caught in the fray:

Because we're human
we cannot allow ourselves to be oppressed.
Because we're human
we cannot allow our sisters
and brothers to be oppressed.
Because we're human
we love.

Because we love,
we struggle.
Because we love,
because we're humans,
we write poems.
We sing with our insides.

Serrano has also written poems that eulogize women. One of these is "Lolita Lebrón," in which Serrano goes back to the 1950s in New York, where Lebrón worked for the benefit of Puerto Rican immigrants. Serrano recalls "the times of hate / the times of fear." There were witch-hunters pursuing communists, "naming names." There was wholesale banning of books. She comments on the execution of the Rosenbergs, the Taft-Hartley Act, and Elvis Presley howling, "I'm [sic] nothing but a hound dog." But the main focus of the poem is the activist and garment-factory worker Lebrón, who "looked at the moon / on hot nights / from her tenement roof," while "Her mind was on cutting the chains / tying her green island [Puerto Rico] / to the greedy mainland." Lebrón and three others "needed a gun / to shoot off the word / The word had to be heard...." The poet admires this woman who, "in her accented English," was willing to "take responsibility for all." Lebrón also "went on a hunger strike / to back up the prisoners' rebellion / at Attica." Lebrón personifies all those for whom "freedom is a constant struggle."

A tragic ending is painted in a poem about another woman, "Stone Cold Dead on Market Street": "the crazy beautiful black Carmen / dancing ... dancing, waving her delicate fan, / cooling the dancing bodies" is "murdered / by her junkie-lover with a gun." The poet condemns the remorseless killer to "loveless nights / because [he] killed / a life lover."

The poems in *Heart Songs* run the gamut from lyrical, familial themes and love songs to works about witches, pirates, nightmares, and revolutions. The tone that unifies the whole is Serrano's deep feeling of maternal love, compassion, and outrage at oppression and injustice.

Education had been an integral part of Serrano's development, so her involvement in New College of California for the San Francisco youths of the barrio is consonant with her previous contributions. In 1983 she began teaching a course called "Third World Voices," the history and literature of African and Asian Americans, Latinos, and Native Americans. Later she was hired to recruit Latino students for the developmental-studies program, and this job led to a position for her in the admissions office as community outreach coordinator. When the opportunity arose to teach oral communication, she accepted it; her theater background had prepared her.

A poem by Serrano was published in August 1985 in a new Oakland journal, *Cambio*. "Blessed Be" honors Ralph Madariaga, the founder and ongoing codirector of Galería de la Raza in San Francisco. "Blessed Be," which one might consider a modern beatitude, recalls this "Servant of art / Magician of film" who is an example to his students and who has filled many corners with color. Serrano fittingly conjures up a personified triptych of creativity, community, and tranquillity in the man who has given many years to local arts.

Nina Serrano continues to write poetry, and the titles of two unpublished poems speak for themselves: "Oration for a Candlelight Vigil and Rally for Peace and Non-intervention in Nicaragua ... Union Square, San Francisco, California"; and "An Eight Day Commemorative Poem for the Celebration of the Fortieth Anniversary of the Victory over Nazi Germany." A third poem, "Global Shadows," describes the invasion of Grenada by "young men" and epitomizes in the last lines Serrano's indignation and concern:

> Flying and jumping
> Floating and thumping
> Rip cord
> Grip life
> Rip life
> Life ripped away
>
> Hearts bleeding in the sun.

She summed up much of her life's work in a recent letter: "I believe the Chicano movement embodies in it the need for world peace, cultural exchange and understanding, as well as the burning desire for a more just and democratic society."

Bibliography:

La Mujer Chicana: An Annotated Bibliography (Austin, Tex.: Chicana Research and Learning Center, 1976), p. 78.

Reference:

Nick Harvey, ed., *Mark in Time, Portraits and Poetry/San Francisco* (San Francisco: Glide, 1971), p. 107;

Rubén Sierra
(6 December 1946 -   )

Arthur Ramírez
Sonoma State University

PLAY PRODUCTIONS: *La Raza Pura, or Racial, Racial*, San Antonio, St. Mary's University, 1968;

The Conquering Father, San Antonio, Downstage Theatre, 1972;

La capirotada de los espejos, Seattle, Teatro del Piojo, 1973;

Manolo, Seattle, Teatro Quetzalcóatl, 1975; revised, California State University, Northridge, 1982;

The Millionaire y el Pobrecito, Los Angeles, Public Theatre, 1979;

Articus and the Angel, Seattle, Group Theatre, 1983;

I Am Celso, adapted by Sierra and Jorge Huerta from Leo Romero's *Celso*, Los Angeles, University of California, 1985;

Say, Can You See, Seattle, Group Theatre, 28 April 1988.

VIDEOTAPE: *I Am Celso*, Seattle, KCTS Association, 1985.

OTHER: *La Raza Pura, or Racial, Racial*, in *Contemporary Chicano Theatre*, edited by Roberto J. Garza (Notre Dame, Ind.: University of Notre Dame Press, 1976), pp. 60-101;

Manolo, in *Nuevos Pasos: Chicano and Puerto Rican Drama*, edited by Nicolás Kanellos and Jorge A. Huerta (Gary, Ind.: Revista Chicano-Riqueña, 1979), pp. 67-109.

Rubén Sierra is one of the major figures of contemporary Chicano theater. He has distinguished himself as a playwright, actor, director, producer, and entrepreneur. Most of his plays are socially conscious dramas.

Sierra was born in San Antonio, Texas, on 6 December 1946. One of his great-grandfathers was a musician and writer in Mexico and Texas, and one of this ancestor's works was a *pastorela* (a pastoral Christmas play), *La caída de Luzbel* (The Fall of Luzbel). Sierra's paternal grandmother, herself a playwright and director, directed the play in 1927. As Sierra tells it (according to critic Bob Marvel), "My mother went to audition and was cast as Mary. My father was cast as Luzbel.

Rubén Sierra

That's how they met!" Sierra's mother continued as an actress and a singer. She was particularly well known as a *declamadora de poesía* (a reciter and performer of poetry).

Growing up in San Antonio was a decisive influence on Sierra because the city was full of ethnic and racial conflicts between Anglo-Americans and Chicanos. In his barrio Sierra became aware of the Chicano struggle against oppression. Because of his background Sierra developed an interest in drama with strong social relevance. Sierra noted that there was a lack of dramatic literature. An early goal of his was to provide material, training, and opportunities for Chicanos in theater.

After graduation from San Antonio College in 1967, Sierra attended St. Mary's University, where he graduated in 1970 with a B.A. in speech and drama as well as in sociology. Sierra served in the army between 1970 and 1972. Following his discharge, he was befriended by Tomás Ybarra-Frausto of the Teatro del Piojo (Theater of Lice), based at the University of Washington, Seattle. Sierra received his M.A. in directing from that university in 1974 and taught drama there until 1978, when he founded the Group, a multiethnic theater organization with a strong social consciousness. Since 1979 Sierra has also been director of the Ethnic Cultural Center

and the Theatre at the University of Washington, Seattle.

Sierra's first play, *La Raza Pura, or Racial, Racial*, premiered in 1968 at St. Mary's University. *La Raza Pura* includes twenty-five scenes, with slides, film, and music in a multimedia production. Various plot lines emerge: an interracial love affair between a Chicano and an Anglo girl; Scenes in the All-Purpose Racial Agency, involving "Rent a Race" for minority token appearances, the "buying" of jobs or races, and attempts to maintain racial purity; and other scenes and characters related to interracial conflict and the role of prejudice. The loosely constructed play at times seems like a revue, but it is a consistently biting satire. In the *San Antonio News* (28 October 1969) Tom Nickell referred to Sierra's "wit and toughness of mind," saying further that the play "goes from painfully funny to painfully melodramatic; yet even the near-maudlin moments succeed by dint of the irresistible force of a youthful sincerity." Nickell noted that the audience reaction was strong because of the controversial subject matter: "The reaction was—almost literally—explosive, several bomb scares threatened to halt the performances which played to packed—standing room only—multiracial audiences." *La Raza Pura* was clearly influenced by the Teatro

Campesino. Sierra's large production employed thirty-four actors to communicate the concept that racial purity is a myth. Jorge Huerta (in a review for *Revista Chicano-Riqueña*, Summer 1977) wrote: "The total integration of plot and character, which is the mainstay of an effective play, is, ironically, lacking in this play on racial integration. Nonetheless, *La Raza Pura* is important for its inventive use of multi media, and for the creativity of each of the scenes."

After returning from the service, Sierra offered his new play, *The Conquering Father* (1972), a meditation on time, God, and religion. This one-act play is an allegory, with characters such as Articus (the omnipotent being), Truthos (precocious spirit and conscience), Peter (keeper of time), Theman (a manifestation of humankind), and Mary (standing for the Catholic church). The setting is "Halls of Time in the Future." On the program there is a comment from the director, who was initially Sierra himself: "The audience should keep in mind that the questions posed in the play have no one answer or interpretation but rather a variety of both."

The central character in *The Conquering Father* is trying to discover why everything is out of balance. He meets figures out of history, religion, and politics. The church, embodied in Mary, has come to "help" humankind. A key role in the play is that of the seeker's conscience, Truthos, a raving maniac who is trying to be all things to everybody.

La capirotada de los espejos (The Mixture of Mirrors, 1973) was Sierra's first play produced in Seattle with the Teatro del Piojo. This series of *actos* (sketches), most of them by Sierra (the whole work was overseen by him), has a chronological arrangement. It deals with the history of the Chicanos, beginning with an Aztec myth about the making of the sun. Several stages in the evolution of Chicanos are covered, each showing Chicanos contending with the American system. "The audience was captured and moved throughout the program, which consisted of a fine mixture and balance of works by Los Piojos and Sierra," according to critics Frank S. Martínez and Blanca Estela Garza Martínez.

Sierra has been, throughout his career, closely associated with several theater companies: originally, in San Antonio, at St. Mary's University with the Shoestring Players. After being lured specifically for the purpose, Sierra worked closely with the Teatro del Piojo between 1972 and 1974. Later he was with Teatro Quetzalcóatl

(1974-1976). All during this time the operative concept was "teatro in action," which meant extensive touring all over the Northwest and beyond, in Utah, Colorado, Texas, California, Mexico City, and elsewhere, mostly Chicano areas within Washington itself, such as the Yakima Valley, where the theater groups went in support of strikes, for benefits, to give learning and teaching exercises, to be in antiwar marches, to increase awareness of certain problems—such as neglect, insensitivity, and the school dropout rate—or to warn against drug abuse. In spite of the serious theater work, there was still a great deal of humor. Sierra's motto, which continues to influence him, is: "We don't have to take ourselves seriously, but we can be serious about what we're doing." Since 1978 Sierra's home theater company has been the Group, with its strong social commitment.

Manolo, a three-act realistic drama, was developed with Teatro Quetzalcóatl in 1975. In 1982 a revised version, with significant differences from the original play, was performed at California State University, Northridge. *Manolo* focuses on the drug-addiction problem of a Vietnam veteran. After a treatment program to help him overcome his heroin addiction, Manolo is released from the service and returns to the barrio. His mother died while he was in Vietnam, so Manolo has less of a support system as he attempts to readjust. The addict's context, social setting, family and friends, and the oppressive barrio, as well as the drug pusher and his whole network, all contribute to Manolo's relapse and his struggles to rehabilitate himself.

The play is absorbing and grimly convincing. This hard-hitting cautionary work demonstrates how a morally good man can also fall prey to drug addiction. Another significant theme is the power of the individual, the freedom to choose, the acceptance of responsibility, and the importance of human bonds.

Manolo toured Texas and Colorado. In Pueblo, Colorado, the mayor proclaimed Drug Awareness Day to mark Teatro Quetzalcóatl's performance in September 1976. The theater troupe members were also made honorary citizens. As Huerta and Nicolás Kanellos point out, "Wherever the teatro toured the play, it received standing ovations from community audiences. A realistic production like *Manolo* is certainly new to most barrios and the appreciation of the community was the group's greatest reward" (*Nuevos Pasos*, 1979).

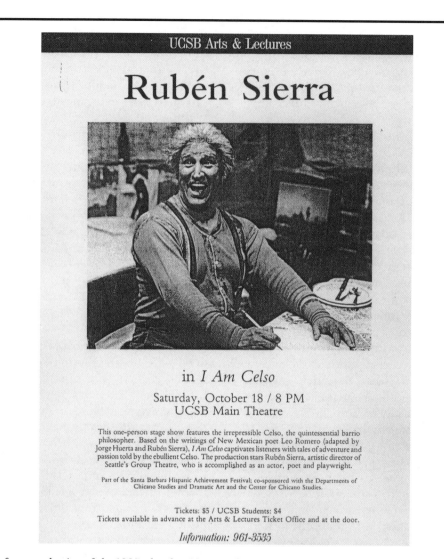

UCSB Arts & Lectures

Rubén Sierra

in *I Am Celso*

Saturday, October 18 / 8 PM
UCSB Main Theatre

This one-person stage show features the irrepressible Celso, the quintessential barrio
philosopher. Based on the writings of New Mexican poet Leo Romero (adapted by
Jorge Huerta and Rubén Sierra), *I Am Celso* captivates listeners with tales of adventure and
passion told by the ebullient Celso. The production stars Rubén Sierra, artistic director of
Seattle's Group Theatre, who is accomplished as an actor, poet and playwright.

Part of the Santa Barbara Hispanic Achievement Festival; co-sponsored with the Departments of
Chicano Studies and Dramatic Art and the Center for Chicano Studies.

Tickets: $5 / UCSB Students: $4
Tickets available in advance at the Arts & Lectures Ticket Office and at the door.

Information: 961-3535

Advertisement for a production of the 1985 play that Sierra and Jorge Huerta adapted from Celso *(1985) by Leo Romero*

Sierra had seen firsthand the problems of drug addiction in the barrio where he grew up. He had also served in the military in Vietnam and became aware of drug-abuse problems.

The Millionaire y el Pobrecito (and the Poor Little Boy, 1979) is a fifty-minute adaptation (for children) of Mark Twain's *The Prince and the Pauper* (1881). In Sierra's version the two boys who switch roles because of their remarkable physical likeness are the Anglo son of a millionaire and a poor Chicano youngster from the barrio. The charm, good cheer, and warmth in the play were particularly notable to critics. Jack Viertel in the *Los Angeles Herald Examiner* (31 March 1983) remarked that the play is "surprisingly fast-paced and breezy . . . pertinent and fun, [and] the cast is high-spirited."

Articus and the Angel, another allegory, pre-

miered in 1983. It was produced by the Group in Seattle and received good reviews.

In *I Am Celso* (1985) the title character is a picaresque barrio philosopher who is "between 50 and 100 years old" and is simultaneously the town drunk, a storyteller, and a poet. Celso, who lives in an adobe hut, tells of creating his own religion, "the Gospel of the Holy Grape." Celso is not just another drunk: "Everytime I get drunk," he says, "I become a poet." In recounting his adventures, he becomes many characters: a boy, a woman, a priest—and even a skeleton.

According to Sierra, "Celso speaks of the things we all think about: love, death, loneliness, women, desires." Sierra characterizes Celso as "a self-made man who has taken all of life's experiences and become a poet. He's gentle and funny and perceptive. He's the kind of guy you'd like to sit down and have a beer with.... When I look at Celso I see a Chicano character—the way he talks about things, the *ambiente* [feeling] about him. But Celso could also be a French peasant. He could be done in any language."

The drama critic for the *Seattle Times*, Wayne Johnson (7 June 1985), summed up his evaluation this way: "*I Am Celso* makes the playgoer more aware of the fascinating diversity of life—and grateful for that awareness. Not many evenings in the theatre accomplish that. *I Am Celso* and Rubén Sierra do."

Say, Can You See (1988), according to the advance publicity, is "a biting, satirical look at the melting pot concept which has made America what it is today." The production was presented in a multimedia cinematic style through the fast-paced use of music, sketches, and poetry.

Rubén Sierra remains one of the leading figures in Chicano theater. He has been called by *Seattle Post-Intelligencer* drama critic O. Casey Corr the "social conscience of Seattle theater, and possibly its single-most important figure" (quoted by Marvel). Sierra has high visibility in several areas, as director, actor, playwright, and producer. He has received many noteworthy awards, such as the Citizen Artist Award for 1985, presented by Allied Arts of Seattle. Sierra has also been on many boards and panels and is influencing the shape of theater and the arts. His broad-based theatrical activities, his lecturing and workshops, and his magnetic personality contribute to his significance as a major force in contemporary Chicano theater.

References:

Aurelia Betancourt, "Teatro Quetzalcóatl," *Metamorfosis*, 2 (1979): 16-19;

Jorge Huerta, *Chicano Theatre: Themes and Forms* (Ypsilanti, Mich.: Bilingual Press/Editorial Bilingüe, 1982), pp. 103-118;

Nicolás Kanellos, *Mexican American Theater: Legacy and Reality* (Pittsburgh: Latin American Literary Review Press, 1987);

Blanca Estela Garza Martínez and Frank S. Martínez, "Teatro del Piojo: Un recorrido histórico," *Metamorfosis*, 2, nos. 1-2 (1979): 8-15;

Bob Marvel, "Rubén Sierra," *Voz* (January-February, 1982): 10-13.

Beverly Silva

(12 May 1930 -   )

Judith Ginsberg
Modern Language Association

BOOKS: *The Second St. Poems* (Ypsilanti, Mich.: Bilingual Press/Editorial Bilingüe, 1983);
The Cat and Other Stories (Tempe, Ariz.: Bilingual Press/Editorial Bilingüe, 1986).

OTHER: *Nosotras: Latina Literature Today*, edited by Silva, Marí del Carmen Boza, and Carmen Valle (Tempe, Ariz.: Bilingual Press/ Editorial Bilingüe, 1986).

SELECTED PERIODICAL PUBLICATIONS— UNCOLLECTED: "Poet," *Reed* (1974): 26;
"Of Mice & Men," *Sow's Ear*, 2, no. 1 (1977);
"This Is No Poem: This Is a Woman," *Women Talking, Women Listening*, 3 (November 1977): 6-7;
"The Forgotten Student," *Mati*, 7 (Spring-Summer 1978): 16;
"Ms. Dickinson" and "To My Cunt," *Albatross* (Summer 1978): 36, 38;
"Tears," *Women Talking, Women Listening*, 4 (November 1978): 39;
"Afternoon Class," "Tan Triste," and "Commiserations upon Losing," *Caracol*, 5 (November 1978): 7, 19-20;
"The Man I Love," *Mango*, 2 (Winter 1979-1980): 61;
"I Have No Poem This Week," *Womankind*, 2, no. 14 (1980): 9;
"Memories of a San Jose Winter" and "Beautiful Bikers," *California in Rhyme and Rhythm*, 1 (May 1980): 68, 75-76;
"Untitled," "You See," and "Abstract," *Poet* (Autumn 1980): 109, 286, 334;
"Nunca Más," *New Voices*, 1 (Fall 1980): 33;
"The Real World" and "The Green Witch," *Wellspring*, 1, no. 2 (1980): 8, 9;
"To a Stepfather" and "I Have Locked My M.A. Degree in a Safety Deposit Box," *Crazy Ladies* (February 1981): 41-43;
"Easter Sunday," *Visions*, 6 (1981);
"To a Male Critic," *Snippets*, 2 (September-October 1981);
"Arithmetic," *Snippets*, 3 (January-February 1982);

Beverly Silva

"Graduation Night," *Berkeley Poets Cooperative*, 20 (1982): 74;
"Aeropuerto en Guadalajara," *Termino*, 1 (Fall 1983): 11;
"To the Committee," *Thirteen*, 2 (April 1984): 4;
"While You're Gone, Mi Amor," *Lucky Star*, 1, no. 5 (1984): 47;
"Sooper-Koo," *Berkeley Poets Cooperative*, 24 (1984): 24.

Beverly Silva's short stories and her confessional poetry give a touching and powerful vision of her struggle for self-expression and economic independence. Important themes of the Chicana and feminist perspectives make Silva's work a personal reflection of significant social movements of the past twenty years.

Silva was born in Los Angeles on 12 May 1930; her parents divorced when she was two. Because of the onslaught of the Depression, her maternal grandparents moved north to a ranch in Oregon, taking her with them. Her grandfather, a bricklayer with no formal education, spoke a smattering of six languages, and was a "born philosopher, storyteller and linguist." On weekends he would play the banjo and they would sing. In retrospect Silva finds her grandfather's gifts to her—his humor, courage, and ability to thrive in both North American and Mexican cultures—of the greatest importance in her own formation as an individual.

When Silva was six she left her grandparents to live with her newly married mother and stepfather in Portland, Oregon, the first of many family moves, since Silva's stepfather was a highway worker. She estimates that she had attended some twelve different schools by the time she entered high school. Despite the continual disruption in her education, she was always at the head of the class. Silva notes that she "wanted to be a writer for as long as I can remember, and the first real writing I remember was poems and skits I wrote for a geography class in fifth grade." Silva had also become an avid reader; her childhood favorites included fairy tales by the Brothers Grimm, Batman comics, Judy Bolton mysteries, and *Cosmopolitan* magazine.

Silva describes her teenage years as a nightmare. Her maternal grandparents had moved back to Mexico, and she sorely missed them. Her parents sent her back and forth between their homes in Southern California and Oregon, her stepfather was cruel, and she found herself in a home environment bereft of books and kindred spirits interested in intellectual pursuits. Her memories of this troubled period are of "principals' offices and bus depots." Although she made known her desire to attend college, study literature and languages, and become a writer, she was placed in a vocational-secretarial track and shut out of the kind of education she wanted. As she explains, "Poor girls from uneducated families did not talk about going to college or being a writer. They talked about marriage and babies. Even high school was not considered necessary for a girl." Unhappy at school, she frequently cut classes and read works by William Shakespeare; Lord Byron; John Keats; Alfred, Lord Tennyson; and the novels of John Galsworthy. From the age of fourteen she wrote stories, but she had to hide them because of ridicule from both family and friends.

During her senior year in high school in Oregon, Silva found an English teacher who helped her turn her anger into creative pursuits. Silva wrote, directed, and acted in school plays, and edited and wrote stories for the school newspaper. In addition, she edited the yearbook, wrote the class prophecy, and gave the senior speech at graduation. Yet, after earning her diploma from the small high school, there was no way for her to continue her studies. There were then no community colleges in the state, and no financial assistance was available from her family.

Silva's choices after high school were severely restricted: work in the fields, a department store, or a restaurant. She did a little of all three and then got married. Her husband, a logger, was killed by a falling tree five weeks after their marriage. Silva's story "A Small Western Town," in *The Cat and Other Stories* (1986), records the initiation of a young high-school graduate into the tedium of small-town, adult life. The protagonist lives a silent existence in the home of her dour aunt and dreams of being a writer. She saves money to escape to New York or California. Without resources to attend the nearby university, she is confined to work during the day as a waitress; loneliness and inertia lead her to spend long evenings at the local bar. Soon she is married, and her savings furnish the home she briefly shares with her husband. After her husband's sudden death just weeks after their marriage, however, she leaves the place where she has been so unhappy. At the end of the story the young narrator gets on a bus headed for California.

After her first husband's death, Silva went to live with her maternal grandparents, who had moved back to California. Six months later she went to Las Vegas, Nevada, where she married a man she had known only ten days. Together they hitchhiked around the western United States for six months. They then returned to Silva's grandparents' home in Los Gatos, where she gave birth to a son. Five happy years followed. During the day her husband worked with her grandfather as a hod carrier, and in the evenings after work she and her husband wrote stories and sent them—without luck—to magazines. A year after their second child was born, her husband had a mental breakdown and was committed to a state hospital. After nine months of treatment he was released, but he disappeared and Silva has never

Cover for Silva's first book (1983), which focuses on the chaotic life in a San Jose barrio

seen him again. Her second husband was the first real friend to take an interest in her writing, and his illness and subsequent disappearance were terrible blows.

A year later Silva married a man considerably older than she. They had two children and spent thirteen years together, the first five in Yellow Springs, Ohio. During her years in Ohio, the only part of her life spent away from the West Coast, she enjoyed the contact she had with educated people who shared her interest in literature. When she returned with her husband and children to California, she found herself on a prune ranch amid in-laws who disapproved of women's suffrage and most other activities away from the ranch.

Silva's third husband, like her family, found her desire to write both foolish and threatening. After one particularly unpleasant episode with him in 1964, she burned all her writings. Despite

this discouragement, in 1965, when her youngest child entered school, Silva began part-time classes at San Jose City College, transferring to San Jose State University four years later. She began her college career in her thirties, with all the advantages and liabilities of the self-taught. She had favorite authors—poets Robert Service and Edgar Allan Poe and novelists John Dos Passos and Ernest Hemingway—and higher education added new writers to her list. Silva discovered the intensity and directness of John Donne and Emily Dickinson, and developed a special appreciation for the street language of Langston Hughes, the humor and narrative skill of Geoffrey Chaucer, the beauty of Shakespeare's language, and the intense drama of Eugene O'Neill's works. Silva's admiration for Maya Angelou, whom she praises for "writing a novel that's like living," also reveals much about the aesthetic that informs Silva's own writing.

Silva started writing again in college, but she was timid about showing her work to anyone. When she did, she received mixed reactions. At this time Silva wrote mostly plays and short stories. In 1975, under the pressure of comprehensive examinations, she turned to writing poetry, which she found more satisfying because she could begin and end a piece quickly. "Also," she comments, "my emotional life at that time seemed to consist of bursts of intense feelings, and poetry was the best container for these feelings."

Although she did not participate in the student tumult of the late 1960s and early 1970s, she was a close observer and sympathizer. Her futuristic story "The Poster," included in *The Cat*, provides an ironic look at the student protesters fifty years after the uprisings of May 1970. The former students have become a conservative bunch, and the bankers are now the revolutionaries attempting to overthrow the university. They carry banners demanding: "Freedom, Equality, All Power for the People, Money for the People."

Another view of the 1960s is found in Silva's poem "Letter to an Old Friend," in *The Second St. Poems* (1983). A variation on the Dear John letter, the work gives a retrospective view of the bohemian style of that bygone era, pointing out its need of revision:

Now i haven't turned establishment
John,
but like i said
the hippies are dead

Silva in Hawaii, 1985

& your Goodwill clothes & love beads
just don't make it now.
Sure, i miss you, John,
but
the cockroaches in your pad
aren't funny anymore
a girl gets tired of sharing the sofa
with your dog
& somehow two master's degrees
don't make up for a night on the town.

The poem contrasts Silva then and now, her changing tastes and values. The appeal of the work lies in its straightforward yet rhythmic language and the succinct statement of its intention. Like many of Silva's poems, it is most effective when read aloud. María Inés Lagos-Pope has commented on Silva's use of *i* in lower case for the poetic *I*, even to start a sentence. Lagos-Pope interprets this usage as an indication that Silva "considers herself an equal of those who surround her and that the emphasis is on communication, on sharing, and not on the self." Other readers may find that this usage and the substitution of an ampersand for the word *and* has the effect of trivializing the poet's concerns.

Silva found her life greatly changed by the political events on campus of the late 1960s and early 1970s, and she was later unable to resume her unsatisfactory existence on the ranch. She subsequently divorced her third husband. Her story "Precious," also included in *The Cat*, records a woman's difficulties with a painful divorce in which every attempt she makes to support or improve herself is distorted into proof that she is crazy, unfit to be a mother, and unworthy of financial assistance. Society overwhelmingly favors the husband, who is able to deceive the judge about his financial situation. Ultimately the female narrator is alone, abandoned even by her children, with only her loyal cat, Precious, for company and solace.

The turbulence of Silva's personal life, however, did not deter her from achieving her goal, and she graduated from San Jose State in 1976 with an M.A. in English. She notes that at that time there were no classes in Chicano literature, and women's writing was only just beginning to penetrate the canon. Only after her comprehensive exams and her studying of the seventeenth and eighteenth centuries was she able to "discover" women's writings. She did not learn about Chicano writing until she was, as she puts it, "out of school and back starving in the barrio."

The year after her graduation she published "This Is No Poem: This Is a Woman" (November 1977), in which she addresses Walt Whitman, a symbol of the confident and accepted Anglo-Saxon American male writer, and asks for her place on the stage of literature: "i am the other half / & i, too, want to sing America. / . . . i am the other sex & for too long i was told to be / patient & perfect, Walt Whitman. While Ezra Pound / made a pact with you, my sisters had to wait." The speaker thinks she understands Hughes better than poets such as Whitman, Pound, and Allen Ginsberg because Hughes "dared to sing America even when he was sent to eat in / the kitchen when company came." He, too, was told to be "patient & perfect," but his response was to dream, boogie, and dare to sing "of the darker side of America." Silva's speaker invites Whitman to a reception of women poets and tells him that he can freely express his views on the "deliciousness of sex"—among Anne Sexton, Erica Jong, and Judy Grahn. He will be introduced to his female counterpart, "the common woman," who is no longer patient and perfect but who, with her sisters, welcomes Whitman and tells him in the poem's last line, "we, too, are America."

This work gives poetic form to Silva's view that "writing is supposed to be communication, and communication was an art long before people knew how to write. Literature too often becomes professors writing for professors, and thus when a woman or a Chicano writes something, it is not understood and thus judged to be inferior writing. i believe that the professors who deny the validity of our writing also deny the validity of our lives, and as a Chicana/feminist i can attest to this."

Despite her college degree, Silva still found economic survival to be a struggle. She was flexible and resourceful, though, and she found work as an apartment manager, a tutor, an English teacher with Poets in the Schools, and a ghostwriter for the welfare department. The late 1970s and early 1980s were the difficult years during which most of *The Second St. Poems* were written. Many of the poems depict the pain, violence, and uncertainty of life in this neighborhood (Second Street in San Jose) as they also describe Silva's loves, family, disappointments, and struggles. "Always close to death on Second St." records the all-night sirens, barroom knifings, prostitutes, poverty, drugs, and alcohol that define this environment: "Who could ever forget their mortality / living this close to death? / Still, who is prepared for the stranger / who breaks in late at night / leather jacket and fist in the face / all that can be remembered?" In this collection "Jose Luis," "Mi negro amor malcontento" (My Unhappy Black Love), and "He's Gone" portray Silva's lovers and her difficulties with them. The brief, touching poem "Pain," one of the best in the collection, conveys the psychic distress, which, coupled with the hazardous social conditions, made life on Second Street so difficult:

> Pain
> is a box.
> i'm in a box
> It is a house.
> Walls and a roof
> & a solid floor,
>
> but no door.

An economic system that humiliates the recipient of its aid and implicitly doubts her honesty is the backdrop of several of Silva's poems. For example, "General Assistance Is as Low as You Can Get" enumerates in telling detail the poet's material poverty and spiritual yearnings: "my total worth consisting of crates of books / & a heart filled with dreams. / i returned to my $60 a month room / looked at my $109 monthly grant / & said General Assistance really is as low as you can get. / Someday i'll write a poem about that." Here and in other poems the reader senses the immediacy of the experience that gave rise to the work of art; yet the self-consciousness of making poems about individuals and experiences at times detracts from the poem. The events and feelings of Silva's experiences could benefit from greater distillation. There is a tendency toward cliché, which detracts from the power of the experiences presented. With greater maturity, her vigor, vitality, and the point of view of an individual whose life refuses to be anonymous might be expressed with the forceful language it deserves.

Silva's dedication to her craft, despite the numerous and diverse hardships that she has encountered, evokes admiration. Aware of her difficult position outside the mainstream, she has persisted in writing. Although the work she does to earn her living leaves little time to pursue her writing, she has seized the little opportunities she has found. She has achieved a measure of recognition and critical attention, and she has completed her artistic apprenticeship. Her voice deserves to be heard, and one can only hope that she will continue to express the struggles she knows so well.

Reference:

María Inés Lagos-Pope, "A Space of Her Own: *The Second St. Poems* by Beverly Silva," introduction to *The Second St. Poems* (Ypsilanti, Mich.: Bilingual Press/Editorial Bilingüe, 1983).

Joseph V. Torres-Metzgar

(14 February 1933 -   )

LaVerne D. González
San Jose State University

BOOK: *Below the Summit* (Berkeley, Cal.: Tonatiuh, 1976).

Joseph V. Torres-Metzgar is first a history professor—his perspective is historical. His fiction, therefore, includes a larger look, a broader view. This is not to say that he writes historical fiction but that his 1976 novel has allegorical implications that lift it from the merely fictional to the profundity of parable, transcending time.

Born in Albuquerque, New Mexico, on Valentine's Day 1933 to David Metzgar and Josefita Torres-Metzgar, Joseph Torres-Metzgar is a direct descendant of the Sanchez, Barela, and Torres families. While "Metzgar" is a Pennsylvania-Dutch name, Grandfather Metzgar married a New Mexican Barela; thus Torres-Metzgar has roots embedded deeply in New Mexican history, and his first novel concerns, in part, cross-cultural conflicts and relationships. The Sanchez, Barela, and Torres families settled in what is now New Mexico during the 1700s, when the Spanish, led by Diego de Vargas Zapata, were reestablishing themselves there. During the late 1600s the Pueblo Indians had revolted, killing the Spaniards and driving them from the region. In 1841 forces of the Republic of Texas made a failed sortie into the area, but shortly afterward the Mexican War broke out. New Mexico became the forty-seventh state in 1912, and Torres-Metzgar's family had experienced all of this. New Mexico itself, in spite of the fact that Albuquerque has become a modern American city, remains a land of rugged and spacious beauty, combining Indian and Spanish heritages in spectacular fashion.

Ruins of early Indian civilizations, abandoned Spanish missions, crumbling military posts, and deserted mining towns remind inhabitants of the historical past that impinges on the present.

This background was the geographical and historical ambience for Torres-Metzgar's youth and maturation. He was an attentive, sensitive observer of the life about him, questioning, discovering, and searching. He attended Sacred Heart School and then St. Mary's High School in Albuquerque, both Catholic schools dedicated to instruction in religious values. Intrigued with learning, fascinated with language, and innately serious, he contemplated becoming a priest. Acting upon this idea, he attended Immaculate Heart of Mary Seminary in Santa Fe, New Mexico.

However, deciding that the monastical life did not wholly satisfy him, he joined the U.S. Air Force, serving from 1951 to 1955, stationed chiefly in Germany. The German landscape, in contrast to that of New Mexico, appeared inviting—very green, vibrant, and alive. The German experience provided him with ample opportunity for reflection and self-study. Enchanted with Germany, he returned after his military stint to the University of Munich, in the Bavarian area, and studied from 1957 to 1958, thus increasing both his knowledge and understanding of things German.

He completed his B.A. in 1960 at the University of New Mexico. Struggling through graduate school there, with his German wife and two children, he completed his M.A. in 1962 and his Ph.D. in history in 1965 at this same institution.

During the lean years of graduate school he became the Latin-American instructor for the Peace Corps Training Center at the University of New Mexico. He went on to become a history instructor and associate professor at Sul Ross State University in Alpine, Texas, where he became familiar with the Texan dialect that was to be important in his novel. In 1966 he accepted a position as a history professor at the University of Nevada at Reno, where he stayed until 1981, teaching U.S. intellectual and social history, the history of the Hispanic Southwest, and Latin-American history. He became involved there in Chicano studies and published several articles about the history of Albuquerque.

The accumulation of his heritages, observations, and experiences weighed heavily upon him, and in 1976 he published the result: *Below the Summit*. Superficially the novel is the account of Robby Lee Cross, or as his Texan counterparts say, "Robalee," a self-styled minister and cutlery salesman, married against the will of his father and the townspeople to a lovely and loving Mexican girl, María Dolores. Together with their young son, Danny, they live on a ranch outside Geneva Gap, a typical West Texas town: very religious, fiercely Texan, and anti-everything else. But at the outset, the ranch itself in its isolation appears idyllic—a Garden of Eden, the solution to cultural differences.

Marie (Robby Lee hates everything Mexican, so he has anglicized her name) spends most of her time on the ranch tending the vegetable garden and caring for her home, husband, and child. As the story begins, the reader sees her as a true child of nature—pregnant with her second child, rejoicing in the glory of her life in the valley beneath Sun Mountain:

> Marie loved the mountain. It towered over the snug valley and their ranch home with great authority, shielding them from the searing sand-laden winds of the desert stretches, and cast a long shadow over the valley through the early morning, protecting them from the singeing rays of the sun for a good portion of the long day. Living at the foot of Sun Mountain, Marie felt protected.

The mountain becomes a kind of primeval god, and the reader recognizes from the outset the warmth of this Chicana who lives intimately with nature about her and who loves passionately.

This oneness with nature and the land binds the Anglo and the Mexican in this mar-

riage, in addition to their great physical need for each other. But their passion is threatened by the pulls of their respective cultures, symbolized by the characters Brigette Obispo—the *bruja* (witch) of the Mexican community—and Cotton Zarler, the loudmouthed, redneck spokesperson and first citizen of Geneva Gap. The schism between Robby Lee and Marie broadens as he becomes increasingly plagued by his own prejudice and southern Baptist breeding, his misdirected religious exaggerations, and his unfounded jealousies. Marie, reacting to his animosity and sensing their incompatibility, resolves to return to her God and her people.

The early schism is broadened and deepened by the very force that should have united them, when the repressed, opposing religious beliefs surface as the relationship worsens. A further complication is introduced when Marie meets Dr. Tomas Serveto, a Chicano professor at the university, who is attempting to befriend Chicano students. Serveto, the embodiment of "the other way" (a nonprejudicial way of life), is eventually burned in effigy by the townspeople.

The appropriate use of the Texan dialect and the wealth of historical events give the novel authenticity, while the omniscient narrator allows the reader to enter the mind of Robby Lee and witness the internal war, as this minister of the Lord sinks further and further into decay. He suspects Marie of having an affair with Serveto, and at last, in a ritualistic act, Robby Lee stabs Marie, who lies trembling on the bed, having just been raped by his redneck friend Will Busbee. Rushing from the house, ignoring his screaming son who has witnessed the murder, Robby Lee is killed in a car accident. In the final chapter the reader learns that the Mexican community is attempting to bring the rapist to trial, and Danny, the Crosses' blond, blue-eyed son, is living in a Mexican town "Bein' raised lak a Mexican."

The allegorical intent of the work is immediately apparent in the epigraph:

> And they proceeded from Beer to Nahaliel, and from Nahaliel to Bamoth; then from Bamoth to the valley in the Moabitic country below the summit of Pesgah overlooking the desert.
> Numbers 21: 19-20, *The New English Bible*

West Texas serves as a microcosm of the larger American society. From the outset, the reader is struck with the protagonist's isolationist position—"he really did feel he was living on some last frontier." Initially Robby Lee is a tender man, treasuring the woods and their animal inhabitants, refusing even to run over a rabbit, and revering his home: "This was a good house Cross had built. It was a rock house. It was sturdy and strong and made from the stone of his bank. Cross believed it would stand forever. He often boasted to himself that not even a Texas tornado could hurt his home." Yet later, at the close of chapter 1, this sanctuary has been threatened by a huge black wolf that Robby Lee manages to fight off. Of course, the names Robby Lee Cross (symbolically and ironically the Christ figure) and María Dolores (suffering Mary) strengthen the allegorical implications. Their house is not built on rock and will self-destruct. The only chance for change lies with Serveto and his effort to work within the community, urging Chicanos to assert their rights. Torres-Metzgar in his novel has looked at the two ways of the Chicano—assimilation versus self-identification—and has created a parable to show his reader the larger truth.

Early critics of the novel, such as Charles M. Tatum (*Chicano Literature*, 1982) and Ricardo A. Valdez (*Latin American Review*, Spring-Summer 1977), denounced the character development as inadequate, overlooking the obvious genre—parable—in which the characters and plot contribute to meaning rather than remain separate entities. The book is intended to prick the balloon of myopic assimilationists, while depicting the vicissitudes of those who courageously pursue the only possible, long-term, successful stance for the Chicano to bring about change in contemporary society. The thesis certainly is not new. But what others have berated in strident voices, Torres-Metzgar has attacked more subtly. The novel's tone is ironic, relieved by soaring lyrical passages that reveal the ability of its author to combine the ironic and the lyrical successfully in a single work.

Presently divorced, Torres-Metzgar lives in San Francisco, after spending a three-year sojourn in El Salvador. He brings an unusual perspective, both professional and experiential, to the Hispanic scene, and he continues to write. His second novel (unpublished) is based on his Salvadoran experience.

Ernesto Trejo

(4 March 1950 - 1991)

Christopher Buckley
West Chester University

BOOKS: *The Day of Vendors* (Fresno: Calavera, 1977);

Instrucciones y señales (Mexico City: Máquina Eléctrica, 1977);

Los nombres propios (Mexico City: Latitudes, 1978);

El día entre las hojas (Mexico City: Fondo de Cultura Económica, 1984);

Entering a Life (Houston: Arte Público, 1990).

OTHER: Leonard Adame, ed., *Entrance: 4 Chicano Poets*, includes poetry by Trejo (Greenfield Center, N.Y.: Greenfield Review, 1975);

California Poetry Anthology, includes poetry by Trejo (San Francisco: Second Coming, 1976);

Gabriel Zaid, ed., *Asamblea de poetas*, includes poetry by Trejo (Mexico City: Siglo Veintiuno, 1980);

Sandro Cohen, ed., *Palabra nueva: Dos Décadas de poesía en México*, includes poetry by Trejo (Mexico City: Premia, 1981);

Antología de la poesía erótica, includes poetry by Trejo (Mexico City: Federacion Editorial Mexicana, 1982);

Parvada: Poetas jóvenes de Baja California, includes poetry by Trejo (Mexicali: Universidad Autonomas de Baja California, 1985);

Aurora Marya Saavedra, ed., *500 Años de poesía en el Valle de México*, includes poetry by Trejo (Mexico City: Extemporáneos Ediciones Especiales, 1986);

José Manuel DiBella, Sergio Gómez Montero, and Harry Polkinhorn, eds., *Mexico/Estados Unidos—Mexican/American Border Writing*, includes poetry by Trejo (San Diego: Dirección de Asuntos Culturales/Institute for Regional Studies of the Californias, 1987);

Trejo and Jon Veinberg, eds., *Piecework: 19 Fresno Poets*, includes poetry by Trejo (Albany, Cal.: Silver Skates, 1987).

Ernesto Trejo (photograph by María García)

TRANSLATIONS: Tristán Solarte, *The Rule of Three* (Iowa City: International Writing Program, University of Iowa, 1976);

Gary Soto, *Como arbustos de niebla* (Mexico City: Latitudes, 1980);

Tarumba: The Selected Poems of Jaime Sabines, edited and translated by Trejo and Philip Levine (San Francisco: Twin Peaks, 1987).

SELECTED PERIODICAL PUBLICATIONS—
UNCOLLECTED: "Five Valuable Instructions To Listen to Sibelius' 'Valse Triste,' " *Backwash*, 13 (Spring 1974): 19;

"Te dire, Alighieri," *Vuelta*, 1 (June 1977);

"Anillo de cristal" and "No hay más palabras,"
    Vida Literaria, 9 (April 1978);
"Furiosa Claridad," *Vuelta*, 2 (April 1978);
"Lo que sucedió," *Vuelta*, 3 (January 1979);
"Mujer y hombre," *D.F. Tips*, 2 (March 1979);
"El día," *Vuelta*, 6 (October 1982);
"2 AM," *Hojas*, no. 6 (October 1982).

A spare and considered surrealism resonates throughout the poems of Ernesto Trejo.
From his early work to his recent, whether in Spanish or in English, Trejo celebrates the imagination and its power to breathe a sense of expanded consciousness into the objects and events
of the world. He employs inventive language and
imagery, yet he is never overtaken by abstraction
or the temptations of style for its own sake. His
landscapes and scenarios are centered in the simple yet often unexpected situations of daily life.
Trejo manages to keep a clear narrative path moving through most of his work while at the same
time his phrasing emphasizes compression. This
technique makes the emotions and ideas of his
poems accessible to the reader even though Trejo
is working at the edge of the surreal image-
making process. With an understated magic resulting from both a powerful imagery and a great
sense of compassion, his work enlivens those por-
tions of life we often take for granted. His poems
make us take a second and third look at the
world around us and at ourselves.

Born on 4 March 1950 in Fresnillo—a small
mining town in central Mexico in the state of
Zacatecas—Ernesto was the fourth child of a prosperous family that was soon to experience economic hardships. As a result, his family moved to
Mexico City for two years and then to Mexicali
where most of his family still lives today. In a
1986 interview he said, "The first time that I saw
Dali's barren landscapes, I recognized them immediately, for they were all around me in Mexicali.
Looking back, I could say that I searched intuitively and found my sources as a poet; the truth
is that I was brought up on some good, but
mostly bad Modernistas, the Mexican post-
symbolists. I had no idea that the great López
Velarde—the first innovator and father-figure of
twentieth-century Mexican poetry—was born in a
town near Fresnillo." But poetry was not the
major concern of Ernesto's early life. In 1967,
drawn by the prospects of an education and a degree in engineering, Ernesto moved to Fresno,
California. He worked at his aunt's restaurant
and attended California State University, Fresno,

where his interests switched from engineering to
economics and then to poetry. He received a
B.A. and an M.A. in economics while studying poetry and poetry writing under the now-famous
group of Fresno poets and teachers, Philip Levine, Peter Everwine, Robert Mezey, and C. G.
Hanzlicek. Trejo's peers were the last of many
groups of good young poets to come out of
Fresno; among poets he befriended and worked
with were Gary Soto, Luis Omar Salinas, David
St. John, and Jón Veinberg. Around 1973, Trejo
began to publish some poems in literary magazines such as *Kayak*, *Partisan Review*, and *Backwash*. In 1975 Trejo's poetry appeared in *Entrance: 4 Chicano Poets*, which also included work
by Soto, Leonard Adame, and Salinas. After
Fresno, he was accepted into the prestigious Iowa
Writers' Workshop at the University of Iowa for
the M.F.A. program in poetry, and he received
his degree in 1976. While at Iowa, Trejo also
worked in the International Translation Program
and published *The Rule of Three* (1976), a book of
eleven poems translated from the Spanish of
Tristán Solarte, the contemporary Panamanian
poet and novelist.

Since that time Trejo has published poems
in both Spanish and English and has translated English poetry into Spanish and Spanish poetry into
English. Although he moved to Mexico City in
1976 to take a position as an economist with the
José López-Portillo government, he continued to
write poetry in both languages. In 1977 a small
press in Fresno, Calavera Press, published his
first book of English poems, a chapbook entitled
The Day of Vendors.

In these first groupings of poems Trejo established a voice and style which remain his hall-
mark today. Sharp turns of image and language
as well as narrative characterize the poems; his
work focuses on the individual imagination and
how it is tied to the deeper and more concrete
events in life, how the imagination can transform
the ordinary and make for an illuminated sense
of experience. Often he begins with a mundane occasion and then allows the imagination to take
over and change and amplify it. A good example
of this can be seen in the poem "This Is What Happened," in which Trejo explores the possible
meaning of an incident by letting the imagination
rewrite the plot of the first section of the poem
in which the speaker tells of his car crashing to
avoid hitting an animal. The second section of
the poem treats the incident in a more magical, sinister, and weighty manner:

Ernesto Trejo
EL DIA ENTRE
LAS HOJAS

letras mexicanas
FONDO DE CULTURA ECONOMICA

Cover for Trejo's 1984 collection of Spanish-language poems

You forgot the words and made some up. You
were confident. You knew
I would die that night yet you were confident.
You opened the door and swerved the car
at the curve. There were no animals.
There was only me on the shoulder of the road.
My body a still river, my head on a lagoon.
You thought you saw a swallow, a
black swallow, and still you didn't lose
control. The mountain to your left collapsed
and I leaped on you, where I have been ever since,
lodged somewhere between your neck and your
    shoulder.

Even when Trejo creates a poem which proceeds primarily on images, he anchors those images in a very personal tone, as in the opening of
"The Day of Vendors":

Before dawn I called for you,
my poem, but you didn't come.
I had woken up to the song

of the cardinal perched
on the fence. You weren't
at my desk in all the words
that I wrote down and crossed.
You weren't in my shoes nor in the letters
that had come and gone all month

nor in the space held by a window,
its fourteen trees, its seven stars
that always lag behind.

All of Trejo's work, whether in Spanish or
in English, demonstrates a fine balance between
imagination and startling imagery, and the personal and poignant tone of narrative. In 1977
Trejo published *Instrucciones y señales* (Instructions
and Signals), and in 1978 he published another
chapbook of poems in Spanish, *Los nombres
propios* (Proper Names). The poems of
Instrucciones y señales are more in the imagistic/
surreal vein, while *Los nombres propios* moves
more in a narrative mode. Both books show
Trejo's concern with writing poetry in Spanish
that is free of the rhetorical style of early modern Mexican poetry. This concern attracted Trejo
to the poems of Jaime Sabines and moved him to
his major work of translation (cotranslated with
Philip Levine), *Tarumba* (1987), a bilingual book
of the contemporary Mexican poet's work. Many
of the hallmarks of Sabines's work could well be
those of Trejo's; Sabines's vocabulary is collo-
quial, his themes are personal, and his strategies
are often imagistic. In the introduction, Trejo
and Levine state, "Sabines gives a human shape
to his images, so that the cumulative effect is to
give us a reflection of ourselves in the world, a
world transformed into our spirit." The poems
of Sabines filter the illogical and ungenerous details of life and offer a reality that, while not always desirable, is compassionate in its awareness.

Much the same can be said for Trejo's work
to date. In *El día entre las hojas* (The Day Among
the Leaves, 1984), his book-length collection of
poems in Spanish, Trejo is out to dissect appearance and reality and those fleeting moments
made accessible only through the power of memory. The book is divided into three sections: imagistic, narrative, and a third section that combines
aspects of both styles. There are "voices" in some
of these poems; we hear Sabines giving conflict-
ing answers to his conscience, Georg Trakl speaking of the "heavy song" as he listens to his sister
sobbing and sees her blue tears in the moonlight,
and Dante as he fights back his own arrogance
and greed. The short poem "Imaginaciones"

*Cover for Trejo's first full-length collection of poems
in English*

(Imaginations) echoes Ezra Pound's famous "In A Station of the Metro": the ducks in Chapultepec Park are white petals in the darkness, and black umbrellas under the rain have "black veins" trembling with every step. Do these images signify impending death? The answer, or a certain balance, may appear a few pages later in a poem dedicated to Luis Omar Salinas, "Cáscara de día" (The Day's Rind). A catalogue of everyday events—kids and dogs playing in the street, two drunk lovers making love on a creaky cot, people shopping on credit—is followed by nothing but the oncoming darkness.

　　Trejo's most recent publication is *Entering a Life* (1990). This is his first full-length collection of poems in English, and it brings together old work with new. Many of the new poems and the longer poems in this book show Trejo's skill with narrative and autobiographical material, for while the subject is personal and many poems often have "plot," Trejo is masterful at demonstrating the many dimensions one event might take on. The title poem is a fine example of the many takes on experience that Trejo's imagination and speculation can bring to an everyday domestic situation:

> I remember that when I was 12
> I heard about an uncle who twenty years before
> had gone away for good. But he hadn't died
> like his younger brother, whose life was taken
> 　　slowly
> by TB. My uncle who disappeared simply stopped
> writing home, stopped sending money & postcards
> from exotic places: Los Angeles, Pittsburgh,
> Des Moines. . .[.]

The poem goes on to explore the family story about Uncle Félix and the rumors about his whereabouts. The speaker makes up stories that show his compassion for his uncle's life; he imagines him alone running a motel in Missouri, doing time in El Paso for smuggling workers, or prospering as the owner of a jewelry store. Finally, he brings his imagination into the service of honor— he wants an honorable memory for his uncle and by extension an honorable life for himself:

> These stories went on for years, even after your
> 　　parents died
> & your brothers & sisters were scattered around
> 　　like bruised fruit.
> Uncle, after 20 years of stories I know so little.
> 　　I want
> to imagine you content, honoring your name. I
> 　　want you
> falling in love once with a girl whose love
> matched the intensity of yours. I see you
> 　　boisterous &
> the two of you drunk with love for a few years.
> Until one day she runs off with a lover & leaves
> 　　you
> with two daughters whom you raise. Years pass
> & you are left a little less happy & unsure
> of everything & ashamed at being shortchanged.

Trejo pulls out all the possibilities to get at the uncertainty of our lives, but always he shows in his speculation great compassion, for all of the outcomes are possible and real—all are earned by the true and human emotion which centers each poem. Even in the marvelous and somewhat surreal "E." poems in which Trejo creates a character who moves through life and is moved by it, we can tell that the poet's inventiveness is firmly anchored in the real world where often it is only imagination and song that lift us above our suffering and allow us to cherish our lives.

In 1983 Trejo returned to Fresno where he taught part-time for the Spanish and English departments at California State University. Trejo was on the English faculty at Fresno City College from 1985 to 1990, and he taught creative writing, basic writing, and an introduction-to-literature course that emphasized Latin-American writers. From the late 1970s to the present Trejo's poetry, translations, and critical expertise have been acknowledged and valued. As early as the late 1970s small literary magazines in America were paying attention to his work. In 1978 the *Chowder Review* ran a very favorable review of his first chapbook in English, *The Day of Vendors*, and in 1979 a review of *Entrance: 4 Chicano Poets* in *Abraxas* also praised Trejo's early work. In the early 1980s Trejo's poems drew critical praise in Mexico. Sandro Cohen, editor of the anthology *Palabra nueva* (1981), wrote that "Ernesto Trejo is a poet of measure, of contemplation. . . . Like those of Wordsworth's, Trejo's emotions are only valid when they are safely installed in the past, and this makes his poetry tranquil, meditative, with a power that is not perceived in action but in the recuperation of an ever slippery yesterday." Reviewing Trejo's *El día entre las hojas* for the journal *Vuelta* (5 October 1984), Cohen wrote, "There are in Trejo's poetry two aesthetic poles . . . there is the need to build elaborate metaphorical 'apparatuses': strange turns of language which owe their ethereal character to the fact that their metaphorical structure does not rest on specific properties of the immediate world. On the other hand . . . an opposite ethics . . . one which addresses objects directly to explore them more for what they are than for that which they could represent. 'One must sing the thing in itself,' could be the motto of his poetics."

Trejo was in demand for readings and conferences throughout the 1980s. In October 1985, along with Philip Levine, he was invited to give a reading of his own work and lecture on Sabines's at the New Latin American Poetry conference in Durango, Colorado. In 1987 he presented a paper on "Border Literature" in Mexicali sponsored by Dirreción de Asuntos Culturales and the Institute for the Regional Studies of the Californias of San Diego State University. He also gave poetry readings at the University of California, Santa Barbara, and at the University of Southern California, Los Angeles. In Fresno, Trejo often gave readings of his poetry; he read at the Metropolitan Museum in 1984 and 1989, at the Fresno Art Museum in 1990, and at the "Day of the Dead" reading in 1989 sponsored by the Arte Américas Foundation.

It is important too that Trejo's work is recognized by many well-known contemporary poets in the United States. Edward Hirsch, David St. John, and Gary Soto have all volunteered comment for Trejo's *Entering a Life*. Hirsch states, "Ernesto Trejo is a poet of mysteries and incarnations, of secret un-named presences, of the magical interior spaces of childhood and the luminous floating world that flares and throbs, that burns in time." St. John has written that "Ernesto Trejo's poetry is filled with an extra-ordinary exuberance and vitality. These are poems of enormous humor and wisdom. . . . These poems are like our fondest, wildest dreams—those which suddenly speak to us with the diamond-edged voice of true experience." And Gary Soto affirms, "He writes with great invention a long-lined, ambitious poem as well as a short refined lyric. In both instances, it's evident that he cares about his subjects, namely family, friends, childhood in Mexico and his adult years in the United States, the everyday life he carves for himself, and that often romantic but shadowy figure he calls 'E.'" All in all, the critical reception to the poetry of Ernesto Trejo is positive and enthusiastic. He will be read, spoken of, and written about favorably throughout the 1990s.

Gina Valdés
(6 June 1943 -   )

Rosaura Sánchez
University of California, San Diego

BOOKS: *There Are No Madmen Here* (San Diego: Maize, 1981);

Puentes y fronteras: Coplas chicanas (Los Angeles: Castle, 1982);

Comiendo lumbre; Eating Fire (Colorado Springs: Maize, 1986).

OTHER: "Este es un cuento; This Is a Story," M.A. thesis, University of California, San Diego, 1982.

Gina Valdés's prose and poetry, characterized by a tension between her social concerns and a strong metaphysical current, place her at an important crossroads within Chicano letters. She is fusing trends that have been central to Chicano literature.

Born in Los Angeles on 6 June 1943, Valdés spent her early childhood in Ensenada, Mexico, and her adolescence in Los Angeles. She graduated from George Washington High School in Los Angeles in 1961 and attended Palomar College in north San Diego County between 1976 and 1978 before transferring to the University of California, San Diego, where she received her B.A. in creative writing in 1981. Thereafter she began her graduate studies in the literature department and in 1982 received an M.A. in Spanish literature. Her M.A. thesis not only deals with the relationship between critical and creative writing but also includes a collection of Valdés's unpublished, original short stories, characterized by technical innovations and intergeneric experimentation.

Valdés married at an early age and resided for a short time in Japan, her husband Tadashi Hayakawa's country of origin. Her particular experience of a double migration, from Los Angeles to Mexico and then back to the United States, would serve as the basis for her novelette *María Portillo*, published as part of the *There Are No Madmen Here* collection (1981), which is strongly autobiographical in nature. Her frequent visits to Japan with her husband, on the other hand, af-

fected not only her physical bearing and life-style but also nurtured her interest in the occult and Asian traditions. Today Valdés resides primarily in San Diego, where she continues to write and teaches creative writing to children within the local school district, English as a second language for adults, and Spanish courses in the local universities and colleges. During the years 1987, 1988, and 1989 she traveled around California giving poetry readings and teaching for a short time in Chicano studies at the University of California, Davis. In fall 1990 she taught creative writing at Colorado College. Her daughter, Rosalía Hayakawa, an aspiring model and actress, resides in Los Angeles.

Valdés's work reveals an artistic commitment not only to aesthetics but to social change, evident in her literary themes: the feminist struggle, the plight of the undocumented worker, the border conflict, consumerism, and the alienation of the Chicano in the United States. One additional concern is bilingualism. Her fluency in English and Spanish has led not only to bilingual versions of most of her works but also to a consciousness of language itself, of its functions and meanings. Literary discourse is for Valdés an instrument for healing, a means to explore what is diseased and painful, while at the same time inducing a transformation, as much in the writer as in the reader or listener. Oral performances are an important part of her literary accomplishments; she has given many readings in Los Angeles, Davis, Tijuana, Laguna Beach, and San Diego. Her work can be viewed on the videotape *Rasgado en dos* (Ripped in Two), available through PBS.

María Portillo, written several years before its publication in 1981, deals with the plight of the title character, a Mexican woman with three daughters, all of whom are forced to return to Los Angeles from Ensenada after being abandoned by their bohemian father, who prefers a life of adventure to that of breadwinner. *María Portillo* focuses on the daily struggle of this Mexican woman to avoid starvation and support her family and also on the troubles of her young daughters, who grow up in an alien culture, and the problems of the extended family, including an alcoholic father.

The personal story of María is interwoven with a second narrative: the socioeconomic dilemma of Mexican immigrants in the United States. Unable to make ends meet with her wages as a garment worker, María joins her brother Ramón in selling tequila smuggled across the border. The plot is narrated against an extended-family backdrop; the reader is provided with insights into family relations, revealing what is ultimately an illusory support system, for the extended family provides more grief and despair than comfort.

The short stories published with *María Portillo* also deal with the Portillo family. These stories, written at a later time, reveal Valdés's more-developed skill and interest in experimentation and her greater concern with additional external forces that restrict and control the lives of the poor. The title story, "There Are No Madmen Here," incorporates ambiguity, as the main character, María, finds herself trapped in a mental institution while trying to deal with its bureaucratic system, which, far from providing assistance to those deemed different, deviant, or alcoholic, fosters policies that convert inmates into virtual vegetables. Those inmates protesting their treatment mysteriously disappear.

The tone of irony evident in this story is also present in "Nobody Listens," which provides a detailed study of the elderly Don Severino, María Portillo's father, who resides in a run-down hotel in downtown Los Angeles. The other story, "Rhythms," focuses on one of María's daughters, Yoli, as she and a friend sit in a U.S. classroom. Their alienation within the public school system provides the background for daydreaming and the consequent intersection of various spatial-time dimensions within the story: a mythic Indian past, summer in Ensenada, and a Los Angeles barrio dance. The narrative experimentation of these three stories reveals a decidedly new direction in Valdés's prose.

Her next work, *Puentes y fronteras* [Bridges and Borders]: *Coplas chicanas* (1982), offers a collection of *coplas* (four-line stanzas), written in the form and style of Mexican folk poetry. Valdés substitutes a female point of view for the traditional male perspective common to this poetic form. In reversing the traditional male/ female roles, she designates a male addressee, a male object of passion and desire, to whom she responds. Using various discourse strategies and codes, Valdés formulates her response at two levels: social and poetic.

The intertextuality allows for the intersection of popular and literary texts and of subjective and objective perspectives. At one level there is a clear response to the folk figure of La Llorona (the wailing woman), who is said to cry for her dead children. In several *coplas* this legendary figure is Mother Earth, wailing for her Mexican children who are forced to cross the border to work, even while facing beatings, death, and deportation at the hands of the *migra*, the Immigration and Naturalization officers. La Llorona is portrayed not only as a symbol of all exploited and degraded women but as a symbol of all who are oppressed and refuse to keep quiet. Her wail is thus, as Valdés suggests, a preamble to a more active struggle.

At another level the poetry recalls the *copla* form of the well-known "Llorona" folk song with its romantic themes. At this level Valdés effects a transformation in the typical interactional pattern, for the *moreno* (brown-skinned man) is no longer the male addresser who brags to La Llorona, his beloved, "Todos me dicen el negro, Llorona, negro pero cariñoso" (All call me dark, Llorona, dark but loving). Instead, the female voice—the Chicana *coplera*—addresses the *moreno*, turning the *copla* around, as in verse 57: "tápate con mis miradas para que no tengas frío" (cover yourself with my gaze so that you won't be cold). The female subject, protective and sensual, objectifies the male object and dares to verbalize her sexual arousal. But despite the explicitly erotic comments and sexual allusions, the female voice wavers between being dominant and assuming the subordinate role, as in *copla* 72, in which she sees herself as a musical instrument to be played.

The outstanding *coplas* in the book are those combining passionate and social themes. The female voice protests the exploitation of undocumented workers by capitalist interests and bemoans the establishment of legal barriers between people who share a common burden and toil together.

The same sociocritical stance is evident in Valdés's 1986 collection of poetry, *Comiendo lumbre; Eating Fire*. Using a heterogeneous voice, bilingual and bifunctional, she is conscious of love and suffering, of her own voice and that of others, of Latin America, of refugees, and of tor-

Where You From?

Soy de aquí
y soy de allá
from here
and from there
born in L.A.
del otro lado
y de éste
crecí en L.A.
y en Ensenada
my mouth
still tastes
of naranjas
con chile
soy del sur
y del norte
crecí zurda
y norteada
cruzando fron
teras crossing
San Andreas
tartamuda
y mareada
where you from?
soy de aquí
y soy de allá
I didn't build
this border
that halts me
the word fron
tera splits
on my tongue

Gina Valdés

*Fair copy of a poem by Valdés that shows her use of code-switching—the alternation of Spanish and English
(by permission of Gina Valdés)*

tured victims, and is conscious of the signs and symbols of the dominant class. She no longer sees words as immanently meaningful; she is aware of distortion and of the ideological nature of language. Words can be twisted and voices reduced to screeches. The worst is not mere silence: the progressive poet may be censured and her work edited; history can be rewritten; and reality can be reinterpreted.

In her 1986 collection Valdés departs from the *copla* form and writes in a freer style, offering poems with a great deal of code-switching (with English and Spanish mixed). The proximity of and distance between Mexico and the United States, economically and culturally; the continuing racism and economic exploitation of Chicanos; the social rejection of women who go against the norm; and the unending social and cultural contradictions—all these themes are explored as Valdés frames recollections of family life. Memories of lovemaking, on the other hand, inevitably lead to the poetic function, to her desire to write, to capture it all in written discourse and produce a revolution in literature.

The broader social context of these poems is evident in the poem "Working Women." The situation is typically Chicano, set in an urban area that brings together Chicanos, blacks, and whites. The poem provides fast takes of street nightlife: low riders, *cholos* (half-breeds), streetwalkers, pimps, cops, and the observant poet. What is striking is the use of this "working women's scene" as a metaphor for what many people do as workers: they peddle their wares; they sell labor power or else they do not eat; they do not pay the rent.

The underlying proposition of the poem is that contradictory standards exist. City lights, fancy cars, and fast-food restaurants are the fa-

cade. Behind the neon lights is degradation, as pushers and pimps look after the merchandise on display. Out on the streets the workers are plying their trade. Similarly the successful educator stands behind a facade, the facade of acceptability and social mobility. Within the sanctified halls of academia, one finds exploitation as well. This juxtaposition of unrelated domains such as "the red-light district," and the "school district" the view of work as hustling, and the code shifts from Spanish to English and from *caló* (Chicano slang) to popular speech produce an ironic tone. Again Valdés assumes a distance to focus both on her role and on her production. What is left ambiguous is whether writing, like teaching, is ultimately nothing more than a practice of "hustling verbs and other words."

Valdés's work is characterized by this intersection of social, erotic, and feminist elements. The voice is distinctive; it is soft yet critical; it is sensual yet social. The social criticism gives her poetry a dynamic quality, a cutting edge, a strength that puts it ahead of other poetic works that fail to go beyond sentimental trivialities or feminist harangues. Valdés's poetry ensures her a firm place in Chicano literature.

Valdés continues to write and is working on her third book-length manuscript of poetry in English. She has also begun some short pieces of fiction on the legendary theme of La Llorona. Within these short stories she plans to explore the function of tears as a means to effect transformation. Gina Valdés's works are those of a writer concerned with form, narrative technique, and language choice, while committed to the social function of literature.

Luis Miguel Valdez

(26 June 1940 -   )

Nicolás Kanellos
University of Houston

BOOKS: *Actos*, by Valdez and El Teatro Campesino (San Juan Bautista, Cal.: Cucaracha, 1971);

The Shrunken Head of Pancho Villa (San Juan Bautista, Cal.: Cucaracha, 1974);

Luis Valdez—Early Works: Actos, Bernabé and Pensamiento serpentino (Houston: Arte Público, 1990);

Zoot Suit and Other Plays (Houston: Arte Público, 1992).

PLAY PRODUCTIONS: *The Shrunken Head of Pancho Villa*, San Jose, San Jose State College Drama Department, 1963;

Las dos caras del patroncito, Delano, Cal., 1965;

La quinta temporada, Delano, Cal., Filipino Hall, 1966;

Los vendidos, Los Angeles, Elysian Park, 1967;

La Conquista de México, Del Rey, Cal., Centro Campesino Cultural, 1968;

No saco nada de la escuela, Fresno, Cal., St. John's Church, 1969;

The Militants, Fresno, Cal., 1969;

Bernabé, Fresno, Cal., 1970;

Huelguistas, Fresno, Cal., 1970;

Vietnam Campesino, Delano, Cal., Guadalupe Church, 1970;

Soldado Razo, Fresno, Cal., Chicano Moratorium on the War in Vietnam, 3 April 1971;

Dark Root of a Scream, Los Angeles, 1971;

La gran carpa de la Familia Rascuachi, 1971;

El fin del mundo, 1972;

El baile de los gigantes, Mexico City, Quinto Festival, 1974;

Zoot Suit, Los Angeles, Mark Taper Forum, April 1978;

Bandido, San Juan Bautista, Cal., 1981;

Corridos, San Juan Bautista, Cal., 1982;

I Don't Have to Show You No Stinking Badges, Los Angeles Theater Center, February 1986;

MOTION PICTURES: *I am Joaquín*, screenplay by Valdez, El Centro Campesino Cultural, 1969;

Los vendidos, screenplay by Valdez, 1972;

Zoot Suit, screenplay and direction by Valdez, Hollywood, Universal Pictures, 1982;

La Bamba, screenplay and direction by Valdez, Hollywood, Columbia Pictures, 1987.

TELEVISION: *Los vendidos*, Corporation for Public Broadcasting, 1972;

El Corrido, adaptation of his *La gran carpa de la Familia Rascuachi*, Corporation for Public Broadcasting, 1976, 1977;

Corridos! Tales of Passion and Revolution, Corporation for Public Broadcasting, 1987.

OTHER: *Aztlan: An Anthology of Mexican American Literature*, edited by Valdez and Stan Steiner (New York: Knopf, 1972);

Dark Root of a Scream, in *From the Barrio: A Chicano Anthology*, edited by Lillian Faderman and Luis Omar Salinas (San Francisco: Canfield, 1973), pp. 79-98;

La quinta temporada, in *Guerrilla Street Theater*, edited by Henry Lesnick (New York: Avon, 1973), pp. 197-212;

Los vendidos, in *People's Theater in Amerika*, edited by Karen Malpede Taylor (New York: Drama Book Specialists, 1973), pp. 300-308;

Bernabé, in *Contemporary Chicano Theater*, edited by Roberto J. Garza (Notre Dame: University of Notre Dame Press, 1976), pp. 30-58.

Luis Valdez is considered the father of Chicano theater. He has distinguished himself as an actor, director, playwright, and, most recently, a filmmaker. It was, however, his role as the founding director of El Teatro Campesino, a theater group of farmworkers in California, that inspired young Chicano activists across the country to use theater as a means of organizing students, communities, and labor unions through a format created by Valdez, the *acto* (skit). Valdez and El Teatro Campesino explored wide-ranging themes of Mexican-American life, including the rebirth of pre-Columbian art and thought in the Southwest. This exploration led to Valdez's creation of the *mito* (myth), inspired by Amerindian dance drama, as a Chicano theatrical genre. Unlike the *acto*, the *mito* was not successfully adopted by the politically active and progressively radical Chicano theaters in the Southwest. The *mito* and Valdez's mystical indigenism—as exemplified in the ending of one of his best plays, *La gran carpa de la Familia Rascuachi* (The Great Tent of the Rascuachi Family, 1971)—eventually led to a split with the Chicano theater movement in the mid 1970s.

After leaving the movement, Valdez and El Teatro Campesino became more involved in television and movie productions, as well as in the production of plays authored by Valdez alone, such as *Zoot Suit* (1978), *Corridos* (Ballads, 1982), and *I Don't Have to Show You No Stinking Badges* (1986). Of these, *Zoot Suit* was a resounding success in Los Angeles, drawing many Mexican Americans to mainstream theater houses for the first time in history. A docudrama with music, *Zoot Suit* is based on the famous Los Angeles Sleepy Lagoon murder case of 1942 and the "Zoot Suit Riots" of the following year. The play did not hold the same appeal for New York critics and audiences

and closed shortly after its opening at the Winter Garden Theatre on Broadway (March 1979). After his failure on Broadway, the indomitable Valdez went on to success as a movie director and screenwriter with his production of *La Bamba* (1987), the film biography of the ill-fated Chicano rock star Ritchie Valens. The title of the film is from Valens's hit recording of the same name. "La Bamba" was originally a folk song and dance from Veracruz. The film was simultaneously released in English and Spanish and earned millions of dollars in the United States and abroad. Valdez continues to develop his filmmaking, while his plays enjoy new productions on stages in Los Angeles, San Francisco, and San Diego, as well as in small Hispanic community theaters around the country. In the late 1980s and early 1990s Valdez has edited his most recent and most successful plays for publication, including *Zoot Suit, Corridos*, and *I Don't Have to Show You No Stinking Badges*, as well as his older, already-published plays, such as *Bernabé* (1976) and *The Shrunken Head of Pancho Villa* (1974).

As in the case of many other outstanding Chicano authors of Valdez's generation, such as Tomás Rivera, José Montoya, and Raymond Barrio, Luis Valdez was born into a family of migrant farmworkers (on 26 June 1940 in Delano, California). The second of the ten children of Armida and Francisco Valdez, Luis learned to place a premium on family values and unity that would last throughout his career; in founding El Teatro Campesino and developing theater as a career, he was assisted by at least one brother and one sister. Beginning to work the fields at the age of six, Valdez's education was constantly interrupted. He nevertheless finished high school and developed an incipient childhood interest in puppet theater. He went on to San Jose State College, where he majored in English but also pursued his interest in theater. While there he won a regional play-writing contest with his one-act *The Theft* (written circa 1961), and in 1963 the drama department produced his play *The Shrunken Head of Pancho Villa*, a work which includes many of the themes that would reappear throughout Valdez's writing career. After graduating from college in 1964, Valdez joined the San Francisco Mime Troupe at a stage in its evolution when it was engaged in "agitprop" (agitation and propaganda) theater, protesting American involvement in Vietnam, among other political themes. In its stage techniques the Mime Troupe was also experimenting with Italian commedia dell'arte, a form

Valdez during the Delano grape-pickers' strike, spring 1966. Valdez's theater group, El Teatro Campesino, accompanied and entertained the strikers.

In 1965 Valdez returned to Delano to assist in César Chávez's efforts to unionize farmhands. It was there that Valdez banded the workers together into a performing ensemble to dramatize the plight of workers and to gain support for their unionizing activities. He wed his formal dramatic training and his mime troupe experience with the farmworkers' practical experience, folklore, and memories of folk theater, at first employing such psychodramatic techniques as role reversal, and such elementary presentational and allegorical strategies as hanging signs with the characters' names around their necks. But soon El Teatro Campesino gave origin to a specific type of theater or genre, henceforth known as *teatro chicano* (Chicano theater), that followed a structure, the *acto*, and even an artistic and political canon delineated by Valdez. The *acto*, highly indebted in its structure and spirit to the commedia dell'arte and to agitprop theater, soon became a truly Mexican-American genre. The *acto* is basically a short, flexible, dramatic sketch that communicates directly through the language and culture of working-class Chicanos in order to present a clear and concise social or political message. Humor, often slapstick, is used as the opposition is satirized. According to Valdez in his preface to *Actos* (1971), the form is supposed to accomplish the following: "Inspire the audience to social action. Illuminate specific points about social problems. Satirize the opposition. Show or hint at solution. Express what people are feeling." The *acto* is usually improvised by the *teatro* collectively and then reworked into final form. It thus arises from the members' common experiences and reflects in an uncontrived fashion their participation in the culture and folklore of their communities.

In addition to this flexible, dynamic, dramatic genre created by Valdez and El Teatro Campesino out of raw experiences, Valdez articulated a canonizing ideology in his "Notes on Chicano Theater" (in *Luis Valdez—Early Works*, 1990): 1.) Chicanos must be seen as a nation with geographical, religious, cultural, and racial roots in Aztlán, the mythic homeland of the Aztecs (a geographic region roughly equivalent to the five Southwestern states of California, Colorado, Arizona, New Mexico, and Texas). *Teatros* must further the idea of nationalism and create a national theater based on identification with the Amerindian past. 2.) The organizational support of the national theater would be from within, because "the corazón de la Raza [heart of the Chicano peo-

very much related to and influencing Hispanic popular theater from the early Renaissance into Mexican vaudeville. In fact, the Mime Troupe even staged one of the sixteenth-century *pasos* (one-act comic pieces) of the Spanish playwright and director Lope de Rueda. These lessons in presentational (rather than representational) theater, as well as those in popular theater à la Lope de Rueda and the commedia dell'arte, served Valdez well in his next adventure, that of creating a grass-roots theater for Mexican farmworkers.

ple] cannot be revolutionized on a grant from Uncle Sam." 3.) Most important and valuable of all was that "The teatros must never get away from la Raza. . . . If the Raza will not come to the theater, then the theater must go to la Raza. This, in the long run, will determine the shape, style, content, spirit, and form of el teatro chicano."

The greatest contribution of Valdez and El Teatro Campesino was their inauguration of a true grass-roots theater movement. Following Valdez's directions, the university students and community people creating *teatro* held fast to the doctrine of never getting away from *la Raza*, the grass-roots Mexican American. In so doing they created the perfect vehicle for communing artistically within their culture and environment. At times they idealized and romanticized the language and culture of the *mexicano* in the United States. They discovered a way to mine history, folklore, and religion for those elements that could best solidify the heterogeneous community and satirize it as to class, cultural identity, and politics. The creation of art from the folk materials of a people, their music, humor, social configurations, and environment, represent Valdez's vision of a Chicano national theater.

Included in Valdez's 1971 collection are two of the finest *actos* from the farmworker period: *Las dos caras del patroncito* (The Two Faces of the Owner, 1965) and *La quinta temporada* (The Fifth Season, 1966). The former is a classic of agitation and propaganda, which, through the exchange of masks, allows for role reversals between the ranch owner and the campesino who works the fields. The comic, slapstick interplay has the effect of bringing the seemingly all-powerful ranch owner down to size so that the farmworker audience can see that the rancher is as vulnerable as the poor workers. The second *acto* is an allegory in which the seasons of the year are personified, as is the church, the unions, the *Raza*, and social justice. The fifth season, it turns out, is the season of social justice for the workers. In this *acto* a *pelado* (poor worker) is caught up in the cycle of feast and famine that typically entraps the campesino into a life of indentured servitude. With assistance from his people, the unions, and the church, he is able to break the cycle by forcing the *patrón* to pay him and treat him more equitably. Playing the role of the *pelado* in the original El Teatro Campesino cast was Felipe Cantú, who had experience, if not in acting, at least in seeing the *pelados* in Mexican tent theaters. Later in Valdez's career the *pelado* resurfaced, as did the tent theater or *carpa*.

In 1967 Valdez and El Teatro Campesino left the unionizing effort and Delano to relocate in Del Rey, California, and create their own Centro Campesino Cultural, where the work of expanding the *teatro* beyond farmworker concerns took place in a communelike environment. The first successful product of the new vision was *Los vendidos* (The Sellouts, 1967), which to this date is probably the Chicano play that has been staged most by all types of theaters. This somewhat allegorical *acto* (in the published *Actos*), which fixes various Chicano types within a political framework, also enjoyed a Corporation for Public Broadcasting national airing in 1972; it later won an Emmy. In 1968 Valdez's earlier black comedy exploring family relations and the Chicano historical imperative, *The Shrunken Head of Pancho Villa*, was produced by El Teatro Campesino. In 1970 the company produced Valdez's third play, *Bernabé*, which focuses on a visionary village idiot and his relationship with the earth from the perspective of pre-Columbian mythology. While both *The Shrunken Head of Pancho Villa* and *Bernabé* present typical Valdezian characters—such as the pachuco, the mother, and other family members—*Bernabé* opens the path for Valdez's subsequent exploration of pre-Columbian beliefs and art. Also, Valdez elaborates one of his favorite tropes here, life-as-death and death-as-life, which will reappear in many other works, including his long narrative poem *Pensamiento serpentino* (Serpentine Thought, in *Luis Valdez—Early Works*), which examines Chicano cultural development from within the framework of Mayan cosmology and philosophy.

Beginning in 1967 El Teatro Campesino began to tour nationally and to achieve a national reputation for expanding audiences for theater as well as for innovation and political comment. In 1968 El Teatro Campesino was awarded the Off-Broadway Obie award, and in 1969 and 1971 it received the Los Angeles Drama Critics Circle Award. During these and the next few years, through El Teatro Campesino, Valdez was to engage in a historical and thematic exploration of his peoples' culture, first dealing with contemporary issues, but then exploring theatrical forms that throughout history have appealed to grass-roots Mexican audiences. He dramatized the impact of the Vietnam War on Chicanos in *Vietnam Campesino* (1970) and *Soldado Razo* (Chicano Soldier, 1971). Both plays, also included in the pub-

Cover for Valdez's 1990 collection, which includes dramatic works performed during the early years of his theater group

lished *Actos*, highlight the excessive toll of the war on Chicano families and compare the oppression of Chicanos in the United States with American aggression against the Vietnamese. *Dark Root of a Scream* (1971) deals with the death of a soldier, only this time the perspective is broadened to include a parallelism with Aztec culture and Amerindian animal dualism. The soldier is seen as a sacrificial figure whose bleeding, pulsating heart is offered up to the gods at the end of the play.

The other plays from this fertile period that are included in the *Actos* are *La Conquista de México* (The Conquest of Mexico, 1968), *No saco nada de la escuela* (I Don't Get Anything Out of School, 1969), *The Militants* (1969), and *Huelguistas* (Strikers, 1970). *La Conquista de México* is a puppet show that in a mock-heroic, bilingual language reviews the history of the Spaniards' alliances with various Indian nations in conquering the Aztec federation; it points out the confusion and indecision of Montezuma II, while indicting the Spaniards' technological superiority and their spreading of smallpox. *The Militants* and *Huelguistas* are very short *actos* designed to promote unity among farmworkers and Chicano activists. The most enduring and universal of this group of *actos* is *No saco nada de la escuela*, a satirical analy-

sis of how the school systems miseducate and force minorities to give up their culture, drop out, or assimilate the values of the dominant society. *No saco nada de la escuela* is an eloquent but direct call for bilingual education and an education that includes Chicano and African-American history and culture. This *acto* was quickly adapted by scores of *teatros* across the country.

From this juncture on, Valdez was to research the types of theater that have historically engaged working-class Chicanos, first with his experiments in 1971 with the traditional religious drama of *Las cuatro apariciones de la Virgen de Guadalupe* (The Four Apparitions of Our Lady of Guadalupe)—which dramatizes the Mexican patron saint's revelations to Juan Diego—as well as the Christmas pageant of *Los posadas* (The Inns [where Mary and Joseph sought shelter]) and the folk play *Los pastores* (The Shepherds' Play), probably the oldest and most staged Spanish-language play in the United States and Mexico. The prominence of a masked devil and allegorical figures, especially in the latter, contributed to the roles of Death and other allegorical and narrative figures in several of Valdez's following plays, including *La gran carpa de la Familia Rascuachi, El fin del mundo* (The End of the World, 1972), and *Zoot Suit*. Passing through various greatly changed versions over the years, *El fin del mundo* takes the medieval theme of the end of the world and casts it into an Amerindian framework that explores the relationship of society to the natural environment. In addition to focusing on the central character of a pachuco, Valdez once again employs a series of allegorical figures and a whole cast of *calaveras* (masked and costumed Death figures similar to the ones in José Guadalupe Posada's engravings) as he makes a quasi-mystical path to his neo-Mayan or syncretic Catholic understanding of life. Writing in the *Los Angeles Times* in 1975, Lawrence Christon stated:

> the show is no Death Row shuffle. It's quite phantasmagoric, full of music and dancing and including a commedia routine in which the principals score each other like cons playing the dozens. . . . It doesn't go to the gut or groin as much as earlier works, but seems more intent on recapturing a higher plane.

In San Juan Bautista, California, El Teatro Campesino's home since the early 1970s, *Las cuatro apariciones de la Virgen de Guadalupe* has become an annual production, one that captures the spirituality and tradition of Chicanos. Ironically, Valdez's presentation of the Virgin of Guadalupe in another play led to that play's censure. *La gran carpa de la Familia Rascuachi* captures the epic spirit of the *corridos*, or folk ballads, as well as the comedy and pathos of the Mexican national archetype, the *pelado*, whose roots are in the Mexican circus and vaudeville. Obviously named for Mexican tent theaters, *carpas*, the play gradually evolved from 1971 to 1973, from an *acto* that dealt with the immigration of patriarch Jesús Pelado Rascuachi into a broader epic vision of the life of Chicanos in the United States, including birth, death, marriage, labor exploitation, unemployment, welfare, and assimilation. Sylvie Drake, in her *Los Angeles Times* review of the play (1 October 1973) stated, "Valdez seems to have condensed in 'La Carpa' all the forms he had adapted at various times along the way. . . . The fascinating aspect of this production is the degree to which it is both agitprop and mythological, literal and symbolic, primitive and unpolished but certainly far from unsophisticated."

The 1974 version of the play ends with the apotheosis of the Virgin of Guadalupe, alongside Jesús Cristo-Quetzalcóatl, a scene that inspired vociferous protest and criticism from radicalized and antireligious Latin-American and Chicano theater companies attending the play's showing at

Valdez and Richard Pryor in the 1977 film Which Way Is Up?

the Quinto Festival de los Teatros Chicanos Primer Encuentro Latinoamericano (Fifth Chicano Theater Festival First Latin-American Encounter) in Mexico City. Valdez was criticized so strongly that he never truly recovered from what he considered to be ingratitude and disloyalty from some of the very theater companies and actors that he had nurtured. This controversy quickly led to El Teatro Campesino's withdrawal from the official Chicano theater movement, as organized by TENAZ (Teatro Nacional de Aztlán, or National Theater of Aztlán), and a break in communications with the other groups for the ensuing years. In 1976 and 1977 Valdez and El Teatro Campesino adapted *La gran carpa de la Familia Rascuachi* for the Corporation for Public Broadcasting under the title of *El Corrido* (The Ballad). Also in 1976 El Teatro Campesino launched its first extended European tour with Valdez portraying Jesús Pelado Rascuachi in *La carpa*. The company performed in eight countries to critical success.

While Chicano theaters were generally becoming more and more radicalized along Marxist lines, El Teatro Campesino became more and more commercially oriented. Valdez's brother

Danny began to appear in Hollywood movies; Luis Valdez participated in the screenwriting and appeared, along with other members of El Teatro Campesino, in the Universal Studios movie *Which Way Is Up?* (1977), starring Richard Pryor. In the mid 1970s Hollywood and Broadway were about as far away from *la Raza* as one could get; nevertheless, having made his debut in Hollywood, Valdez began his march on Broadway in 1978 with a successful run of *Zoot Suit* at the Mark Taper Forum in Los Angeles, following his fellowship as a Rockefeller Foundation playwright in residence. Because of record, sold-out performances, the play was moved to the larger Aquarius Theater. The play eventually won the Los Angeles Critics Circle Award for "Distinguished Productions" and eight Drama-Logue Awards for "Outstanding Achievement in Theater." Based on its successful eleven-month run in Los Angeles, the play was given a Broadway production at the Winter Garden Theatre in March 1979. Whereas *Zoot Suit* had achieved critical success and had for the first time in history drawn large Mexican-American audiences to a mainstream theatrical venue, the play was rejected by critics and audiences alike in New York City, where to this date no theatrical work by Valdez has achieved great support from the Hispanic public, much less the general Broadway audiences.

Regarding the attitude that *Zoot Suit* faced in New York, Valdez stated the following in an interview with Roberta Oroña-Córdova:

This attitude I refer to is the white man's sense of arrogance and belief that the truth lies in Western European culture, and that whether you are talking about capitalism or communism, or about Protestantism or Catholicism, only *their* science, *their* religion, *their* politics and *their* arts are sophisticated enough to be valid. Naturally, the entire non-white world from Africa to Asia has been victimized and colonized by this incredibly arrogant attitude, but it is in America that this ignorance has come to roost. Here, a transplanted European culture is masquerading as American culture, and the way of life of the real natives has been distorted, stolen, ignored or forgotten.

Clayton Riley, writing in the *Los Angeles Times* (3 June 1979), had another explanation:

Modern colonialists expressed their resentment over his arrival on Broadway, confirming again the imperial assumption that poverty is a badge of honor for the masses—whether they want it or not. Once Valdez moved from the lettuce

fields and flatbed trucks, he'd become the noble savage ungracious enough to forget his place.... The importance of Luis Valdez and Henry Reyna [the protagonist of the play] coming here from the West has roots in a statement made several years ago by Karl Meninger, who said that Americans could never solve the nation's racial dilemma unless whites were willing to experience guilt. El Pachuco, the barrio bluesman [the narrator in *Zoot Suit*], specified the nature of risk for everyone who saw him, the chance at redemption through the dangerous waters of accepted culpability.

Despite its failure in New York and the Eurocentric attitudes that Valdez pointed out, *Zoot Suit* was made into a movie in 1981, and is widely available on videocassette. In 1982 the movie was nominated by the Hollywood Foreign Press Association for a Golden Globe Award, and it was subsequently shown at foreign film festivals; in 1982 it won first place at the Cartagena Film Festival in Colombia. Valdez wrote the screenplay, and, from that point on, his attention was captured by the movie industry.

Zoot Suit is a docudrama with music, articulated in typical Valdezian style—albeit without the usual campesino style because of Valdez's working with mainstream theater and equity actors—with El Pachuco as narrator and partial chorus, functioning much as Death does in the *actos*; the characters appearing from behind a backdrop (a superenlarged copy of the front page of the *Los Angeles Herald Examiner*); and with all of the Brechtian elements that serve to remind the audience that they are participating in theater, not life. In *Zoot Suit*, and in Henry Reyna, the main character, Valdez articulates all of his feelings about the prophetic rebelliousness of pachucos, their relationship with Amerindian culture, and the Anglo oppression of Mexican Americans during and after World War II, as he studies the famed Sleepy Lagoon murder case from East Los Angeles. What is new for Valdez in *Zoot Suit* is the necessary attention to historical fact, even down to adopting sections of courtroom transcriptions and quotes from press coverage of the events depicted in the play. Along with his attention to historical fact, Valdez also incorporates the music of the times, such as the mambo, and, of course, the style of dress. In the final analysis, *Zoot Suit* is a wonderful theatrical experiment, one that introduces to mainstream audiences the advances in stage technology and thought of one of the giants of modern drama.

Poster for the Broadway production of the play that spawned a revival of the zoot suit. Although the play had a run of eleven months in Los Angeles, it failed in New York.

The fact that it was unappreciated by the gatekeepers of the commercial stage in New York is of little import or relevance. The play was ahead of its time; in its historicity, its mining of the theatricality of American ethnic experience, its exploration of ethnic/minority archetypes, and its poetry, it can be compared favorably to the Pulitzer Prize-winning efforts of black playwright August Wilson.

Largely as a result of the impact of *Zoot Suit* on the Chicano communities of Southern California, something known as the "pachuco craze" appeared spontaneously, with youngsters and "low riders" reviving the zoot-suit attire and, to some extent, the ethos of the pachuco. Some Chicano intellectuals were taken aback by the craze and criticized Valdez's role in misrepresenting Chicano culture as having evolved from the rebelliousness of the pachuco. Valdez's artistic romanticism had

gone too far, they argued: first, his idealistic rendering of Amerindian culture had influenced too many students and artists adversely; now *Zoot Suit*, assisted by the power of mainstream theater and the media, was misleading mass audiences and elevating role models that really should be deplored instead of emulated. Historian Richard García wrote in 1982:

> Chicano intellectual thought still lies, for the most part, entangled in a web of myths, misinterpretations, and historical distortions. Within this realm lie the beliefs that the ideological consciousness of the Chicano movement was a product of Pachuquismo, Aztec thought, colonialism, or the peasant movements of Zapata and Villa during the Mexican Revolution.... Without a doubt Valdez's play is a tour de force of the Zoot Suitor experience, but the intellectual and philosophical underpinnings of the play ... are not. As a historian I must take exception with Luis Valdez's philosophy.... His premise is that the Pachucos were the prototype and the direct antecedents of the Chicano Movement activists as well as being the original carriers of "Chicano consciousness...." Unfortunately, this thesis while being romantic and self-serving is not historically true.

Despite the criticism, Valdez's career in film was under way, but the 1980s were also a very fruitful play-writing period for him. In 1981 El Teatro Campesino opened its first playhouse in San Juan Bautista, and that same year they staged the historical play written and directed by Valdez, *Bandido* (Bandit), based on the exploits of the infamous California outlaw Tiburcio Vásquez. El Teatro Campesino was now an equity house and principally a production company rather than a performing and touring ensemble. In 1982 it staged *Corridos*, a dramatization by Valdez of Mexican folk ballads. From the theater-lab production of San Juan Bautista, *Corridos* went on to become a hit at the San Francisco Marines Memorial Theater. In October 1984 *Corridos* reopened at the Old Globe Theater in San Diego. Both *Bandido* and *Corridos* are outgrowths of earlier preoccupations and styles developed with El Teatro Campesino. *Bandido* is an exploration of California myth and history, at times capturing the rebelliousness of the early Valdez, at other times attempting to set the record straight, as he did with the Sleepy Lagoon murder case in *Zoot Suit*. *Corridos*, while expanding on the combination of music, dance, and mime pioneered by El Teatro Campesino in a type of *acto* called a *corrido*, breaks new ground in exploring the poetic, symbolic, and psychosexual content of popular Mexican ballads. The play reignited one of the constant criticisms of Valdez's works over the years: the treatment of women and sex revealed an all too traditional, even macho attitude in Valdez. Reviewing the play for *Caminos* (December 1984), Katherine A. Díaz wrote:

> I had been overwhelmed by the talent and innovativeness of El Teatro Campesino. These feelings, however, were challenged by the discomforting thought that I had witnessed the portrayal of the usual stereotypical images of my community. Those of women were particularly disturbing. As one spectator observed, "Women are either whores or virgins, nothing in between." Why had these *corridos* been selected?. . . It is too easy for non-Latinos to leave the theater saying, "I told you Mexicans were like that. The men are drunks and lechers. And the women? Kept in their place."

Although *Corridos* dramatizes the heroic role of the *soldaderas* (soldier women) in the Mexican revolution (as represented in the *corrido* entitled "Adelita"), other parts of the play treat incest (as in "Delgadina") and macho bravura at the expense of women. While it may be argued that Valdez was keeping to the spirit of the grassroots folk songs, one is reminded that the few women forefronted in other Valdez plays are usually stereotypical, abnegated mothers, prostitutes, or the exalted Virgin of Guadalupe; males predominate in most of Valdez's works, as they did in the leadership of El Teatro Campesino. In studying *Los vendidos* and *Bernabé*, the anthropologist Margarita Melville has stated,

> One of the most discouraging roles for a woman is that of the Secretary, Miss Jímenez, in *Los vendidos* by Luis Valdez. . . . [The play] uses very effective stereotyping to illustrate the image of the Mexican American generally held by the majority population. Its ending is a wonderful surprise. Except that in the end, the ultimate sellout is the one female, the Secretary, the Chicana! In Luis Valdez's *Bernabé*, . . . women are absent from this beautiful play except as a guilt-inflicting, exploitative, and oppressive mother, a prostitute, and an allegory of land.

Aside from the treatment of women, *Corridos* is an entertaining and technically excellent pageant of the poetry, theater, and dynamism of working-class art. It takes Mexican songs that are dear to Mexican cultural identity and pre-

sents them in an instructive but delightful manner so that they are universally understood and enjoyed. Bernard Weiner, writing in the *San Francisco Chronicle* (21 April 1983) stated,

> On the surface, it's a revue of engaging folk songs from Mexican and Mexican-American history (1865-1925) that have been excitingly dramatized and choreographed. On a deeper level, however, these captivating ballads—representative of songs every society possesses, celebrating outlaws and heroes, or deriding certain traits and characters—reveal the culture, the times, the sexual and class politics. . . . The keys to enjoyment rest on the wonderfully inventive theatricalizations of Valdez: the creative use of simple props, the colorful costumes, the exciting choreography, the strong hypnotic arrangements by music director Frank González, and the outstanding performances by the triple-threat cast as they sing, dance and act their multiple roles.

So successful, in fact, was the staging of *Corridos* that it was accorded a video production in 1987 and aired nationally by the Corporation for Public Broadcasting. It, too, is still available on videocassette, and thus represents another incursion of Valdez and Mexican-American culture into mainstream and commercial venues never before open to Hispanics.

Valdez was becoming more sophisticated in his incursions into and manipulation of commercial theater and film and was continuing to explore the image of Mexicans in these media. These preoccupations became subjects for his 1986 play, *I Don't Have to Show You No Stinking Badges*. The play gets its name from the movie *The Treasure of the Sierra Madre* (1947), which itself is notable for the number of Mexican stereotypes it projects. Valdez's play, which opened in February at the Los Angeles Theater Center and ran for four and a half years, is once again about family dynamics, much like *The Shrunken Head of Pancho Villa* and *Dark Root of a Scream*. In *I Don't Have to Show You No Stinking Badges*, the family represents the Chicano middle class, and the play is the setting for the exploration of images and stereotypes of Mexicans and Chicanos. The protagonist, Sonny, resents his parents' work as Hollywood extras, exclusively playing maids and *bandidos*; Sonny drops out of college also to pursue a career in show business, but he is determined to be a star. Writing in the *Los Angeles Times* (2 February 1986), Elizabeth Venant noted that the title of the play "announces a refusal to

Valdez as the narrator for Corridos! Tales of Passion and Revolution, *which he also wrote and directed. The program was aired by the Corporation for Public Broadcasting in 1987 (photograph by Allen Nomura).*

show credentials—from passports to credit cards—as evidence of solid standing among the citizenry. . . . The story is a metaphor for a growing population of hybrid Americans that lives on society's fringes and that is now impatient to move into the Establishment."

I Don't Have to Show You No Stinking Badges seems to signify much the same thing in Valdez's career—an entry into the mainstream. When *Zoot Suit* closed on Broadway, Valdez declared, "I refuse to be left out of the mainstream of American theater" (quoted by Venant). As he told Venant, " 'Badges' hopefully is an American play. I've been trying to write a play that isn't thought of as a Chicano or a minority play. It's reaching out to the largest possible audience and it's going to use all the theatrical tricks. It's going to make itself as charming as it can."

Despite Valdez's attempts to make the play as entertaining and accessible as possible, Richard Stayton, writing in the *Los Angeles Herald Exam-*

iner (7 February 1986), contended that "Valdez has written a radical play for the 1980s in the style of our favorite genre, the prime-time TV family epic. (David Rabe's 'Sticks and Bones' was *the* American radical play of the 1970s, and it also used sitcoms for its model. . . .) The complex ironies and multiple-tiered realities attain a sophistication beyond our expectations. Using Brechtian distancing devices, Valdez forces us to examine the issues and the genre itself. Hollywood, argues Valdez, is a form of cultural imperialism more insinuating than any dogma."

Even while Valdez was rehearsing *I Don't Have to Show You No Stinking Badges*, he was writing and preparing the production of his hit movie *La Bamba*. Film critics have generally described the main characters as bland and flat and the script as limited to developing a known outcome, but the film succeeded in drawing millions to the theaters and became a box-office success in the United States and abroad. *La Bamba* also made history for its successful, simultaneous marketing in Spanish-language versions in American cities with high Hispanic populations. Typical of newspaper reviews was Peter Rainer's statement in the *Los Angeles Herald Examiner* (23 July 1987): "I wish that Valdez had gone with his theatrical instincts more, instead of opting for political 'correctness.' He might have located more of the passion in his story. Valens' life is immensely touching, but in 'La Bamba' you end up responding more to his story than to what Valdez did with it."

The response from the academic critics and the *teatro* movement people was almost all negative, with many concluding that Valdez's journey from political theater had ended up in producing pap and kitsch for the masses. Víctor Fuentes censured Valdez for depicting Valens's life without noting the racial and class discrimination and the oppression that surely surrounded the singer and Chicano society during his life. Instead, Valdez seems to promote the pursuit of the American dream in the film, following the line of a typical rags-to-riches story, only to create bathos before the protagonist fully achieves his goal.

The career of Luis Valdez has been multifaceted but consistent in its development of a national theater for Mexican Americans. As critic Jorge A. Huerta has stated in *Necessary Theater* (1989):

No other individual has made as important an impact on Chicano theater as Luis Valdez. Indeed, . . . it is impossible to discuss Chicano theater without talking about Valdez, for he initiated this vital movement. With Valdez's serious move into filmmaking in 1987, confirmed by the success of *La Bamba*, more has been written about this man than any other Chicano in the arts. But even before his name became a household word, Mr. Valdez's work as a playwright and director had placed him firmly in the history books of theater in the United States.

Starting with a commitment to provide a forum of expression for the farmworkers who were so important to his family and childhood experiences, Valdez used his love of theater to begin a trajectory of rediscovery and creation of the theatrical genres that have served Mexican peoples throughout history: allegorical plays, *carpas*, religious dramas, vaudeville, and dance dramas. His theatrical odyssey took him from the agricultural fields to Broadway and Hollywood, and he created a theatrical style, a successful genre (the *acto*), and a whole theatrical movement along the way. Valdez not only provided the basis and training for Chicano theaters but he also became a member of an exclusive group of modern theorists, including such other important figures as Augusto Boal, Enrique Buenaventura, and Joseph Chaikin. As a playwright Valdez has provided Mexican Americans and other Hispanics with a theatrical language and an example of how to dramatize their lives and cultures in the United States. As an entrepreneur Valdez has launched workshops, production companies, and theater and cinematic studios, and has provided opportunities for Hispanic artists from throughout the United States. In his career as a commercial filmmaker, he is providing the same kind of leadership: conquering new frontiers out of his desire to reform American culture and making it more representative of various cultures and peoples. While some critics have indicted Valdez's depiction of women and his overromanticizing of the pachuco, none can deny the importance of his role as an artistic leader, an innovator, and an energetic and tireless explorer of his people's art and culture; he is one of the very few artists who has been able to change the way his people are perceived.

Interviews:
Beth Bagby, "El Teatro Campesino: Interviews with Luis Valdez," *Tulane Drama Review*, 11 (Summer 1967): 71-80;
Roberta Oroña-Córdova, "*Zoot Suit* and the Pachuco Phenomenon: An Interview with Luis Valdez," in *Mexican American Theatre: Then and Now*, edited by Nicolás Kanellos (Houston: Arte Público, 1983), pp. 91-107.

References:
John Brokaw, "*Las Dos Caras del Patroncito, Los Vendidos* and *Soldado Razo*, by Luis Valdez," *Educational Theater Journal*, 26 (March 1974): 108-110;
Betty Diamond, "The Brown-Eyed Children of the Sun: The Cultural Politics of El Teatro Campesino," Ph.D. dissertation, University of Wisconsin-Madison, 1977;
Sylvie Drake, "El Teatro Campesino: Keeping the Revolution on the Stage," *Performing Arts* (September 1970): 56-62;
Arturo Flores, *El Teatro Campesino de Luis Valdez* (Madrid: Pliegos, 1990);
Víctor Fuentes, "Luis Valdez, Hollywood y Tezcatlipoca," *Chiricú*, 5, no. 2 (1988): 35-39;
Richard García, "Chicano Intellectual History: Myths and Realities," in *A Decade of Hispanic Literature: An Anniversary Anthology*, edited by Nicolás Kanellos (Houston: Arte Público, 1982), pp. 285-289;
Jorge A. Huerta, *Chicano Theater: Themes and Forms* (Ypsilanti, Mich.: Bilingual Press, 1982);
Huerta, ed., *Necessary Theater: Six Plays About the Chicano Experience* (Houston: Arte Público, 1989);
Francisco Jiménez, "Dramatic Principles of the Teatro Campesino," *Bilingual Review*, 2 (January-August 1975): 99-111;
Nicolás Kanellos, ed., *Hispanic Theatre in the United States* (Houston: Arte Público, 1984);
Kanellos, *Mexican American Theatre: Legacy and Reality* (Pittsburgh: Latin American Literary Review, 1987);
Kanellos, ed., *Mexican American Theatre: Then and Now* (Houston: Arte Público, 1983);
Francoise Kourilsky, "Approaching Quetzalcoatl: The Evolution of El Teatro Campesino," *Performance*, 2 (Fall 1973): 37-46;
Margarita Melville, "Female and Male in Chicano Theatre," in *Hispanic Theatre in the United States*, edited by Kanellos (Houston: Arte Público, 1984), pp. 71-79;
Manuel Pickett, "El Teatro Campesino: A Development of Art Through a Growth in Political Ideology," *Praxis*, 5 (March 1980);

Clayton Riley, " 'Zoot Suit' on the Great White Way," *Los Angeles Times*, 3 June 1979, "Calendar," p. 3;

David Savran, "Border Tactics: Luis Valdez Distills the Chicano Experience on Stage and Film," *American Theatre* (January 1988): 18;

Richard Stayton, " 'Badge' of Courage from Playwright Luis Valdez," *Los Angeles Herald Examiner*, 7 February 1986, p. 32;

El Teatro Campesino, *El Teatro Campesino: The First Twenty Years* (San Juan Bautista, Cal.: El Teatro Campesino, 1985);

Elizabeth Venant, "Valdez—A Life in the River of Humanity," *Los Angeles Times*, 2 February 1986, "Calendar," pp. 36-37, 42-43;

Bernard Weiner, "From Ballads to the Theater: Teatro Campesino's Revue of Mini-Operas," *San Francisco Chronicle*, 21 April 1983;

Yvonne Yarbro-Bejarano, "From 'Acto' to 'Mito': A Critical Appraisal of the Teatro Campesino," in *Modern Chicano Writers*, edited by Joseph Sommers and Tomás Ybarra-Frausto (Englewood Cliffs, N.J.: Prentice-Hall, 1979): 176-185.

Víctor Manuel Valle

(10 November 1950 -   )

Enrique R. Lamadrid
University of New Mexico

BOOK: *Illegal* (Los Angeles, 1977); republished in *Third Chicano Literary Prize Anthology, 1976-77* (Irvine: University of California, 1977), pp. 134-154.

OTHER: "Police Magazine," in *Calafia: The California Poetry*, edited by Ishmael Reed (Berkeley, Cal.: Y'Bird, 1979), p. 344;

"Comida" and "Food," in *Fiesta in Aztlán*, edited by Toni Empringham (Santa Barbara, Cal.: Capra, 1981), p. 17;

"Ciudad de Los Angeles," in *201: Homenaje a la ciudad de Los Angeles*, edited by Jesús Mena (Los Angeles, 1982), pp. 24, 26, 37;

"Chicano Art: An Emerging Generation" and "Chicano Writers: An Emerging Energy," in *Southern California's Latino Community* (Los Angeles: Los Angeles Times, 1983), pp. 92-102.

SELECTED PERIODICAL PUBLICATIONS—
UNCOLLECTED:
POETRY
"Retratos" and "Lagarto," *Tin Tan*, 4 (Summer-Fall 1976): 16;

"Windsor Woman," "Spin-off," and "Poem of John Valadez's Painting of El Che Entering Bolivia," *New* (October 1976): 36-37;

"Magazín de policía" and "Mode of Production," *Tin Tan*, 6 (Fall 1977): 24-25;

"To the Students of Hollenbeck Junior High" and "Remedio," *Rara Avis*, 4 (Fall 1979): 18-22;

"Gavilancillo" and "Penny # 20," *Rip Rap* (Spring 1980): 28, 31;

"Wedding," *Electrum*, 33 (Summer 1984): 35.
NONFICTION
"Ancient Art Survives in Whittier [California]," *Los Angeles Times*, 6 June 1982, XI: 5;

"The Aztecs Had a Cure," *Los Angeles Times*, 28 April 1983, II: 2-5;

"Veteran Latina Activist in a New Battle," *Los Angeles Times*, 19 July 1984, pp. 8-9.
TRANSLATIONS
José María Arguedas, "The Pongo's Dream," *Tin Tan*, 6 (Fall 1977): 8-9, 32;

Miguel Angel Asturias, "The Legend of El Cadejo," *Chismearte* (Summer 1978): 22-23;

José Gabriel Núñez, "The Long Road from Eden," *Chismearte* (Spring 1984): 2-7;

Víctor Manuel Valle in Whittier, California, with his grandmother Matilde Cobos and his daughters
Lucina (left) and Alejandra in 1987

Antonio Hernández Pérez, "Los árboles," *Chis-mearte* (Summer 1984): 19.

Víctor Manuel Valle is a poet, translator, editor, activist, and investigative journalist whose creative vision is rooted in the history of the valley of Los Angeles. Although Valle's poetry has motivated the rest of his work, his journalistic efforts have dominated his publications in recent years. Through his work as a translator, he has a thorough knowledge of contemporary Latin-American literature, which provides him with a hemispheric perspective. He is in the vanguard of Chicano literary and cultural affairs in Southern California.

Valle was born on 10 November 1950 and raised in Whittier, California; he was part of a family of dairy workers, former *villistas* (followers of

Pancho Villa), and other political exiles in the family's third generation of life in the United States. In his own words, Valle had "a rather mundane public life and education. However, privately, I learned to raise mockingbirds, *gorreones* [sparrows], pigeons, crows, lizards, deer, and about 13 dogs. . . . But the oral tradition of my grandparents and aunts provided me with insight and knowledge on Mexican history. Before my grandfather Alfredo died, my grandma Matilde wrote all his memoirs of *la Revolución* down. I'll be rewriting them some time in the future."

Valle's formative years and family background provided him with a rich, inspirational resource that fuels his literary and political endeavors. In 1974 he graduated cum laude with a B.A. in anthropology from California State University, Long Beach, where he also received an M.A. in comparative literature in 1978. His thesis project involved the translation of a collection of short stories by Peruvian writer José María Arguedas. In 1979 for his efforts Valle received the Translation Award from the Translation Center of Columbia University. His awareness of and personal identification with contemporary Latin-American literature was strongly reinforced by these efforts. In 1981 Valle graduated with an M.S.J. from the Medill School of Journalism of Northwestern University. He currently works as a staff writer at the Los Angeles Times and lives in South Whittier with his wife, María Lau, and daughter, Lucina.

Besides giving public poetry readings, Valle also brings his creative ear and eye to radio and videotape. In 1978 with John Valadez he produced a video program, "A Choice of Colors," a documentary of gangs and graffiti, which was exhibited at the San Francisco Museum of Modern Art in a show titled "The Aesthetics of Graffiti." In 1979 he produced a live radio special, "Nicaragua: Lucha de las Américas" (Nicaragua: Struggle of the Americas), which featured prominent Latin-American and Los Angeles poets and musical groups. Later Valle worked as associate editor for Somos magazine of San Bernardino and literary editor of Chismearte magazine, a quarterly publication of the Concilio de Arte Popular, a California consortium of Latino cultural workers. Valle has also worked under an artist-in-residence grant from the California Arts Council and conducted a writers' workshop for Latino writers of Los Angeles. The material from the workshop was compiled into an anthology, 201: Homenaje a la ciudad de Los Angeles (1982), which makes a definitive statement about the Latino experience in Los Angeles, ranging from short-story, poetry, script, and story-board writing to oral history, historical archives, photography, and graphic art.

Although poems by Valle have appeared in New magazine, Tin Tan, and Rara Avis, he is comparatively underpublished as a poet, considering the special qualities of his work. His reputation as a poet is largely based on his first book of poems, Illegal, which first appeared in 1977 in a limited underground edition but later that same year won the Third Irvine Chicano Prize for poetry. Valle's poems explore the links and contradictions between the deeply personal and the historical, opposite poles of experience that are usually alienated or dichotomized in most American poetry. In Valle's poetry they reach a powerful synthesis, as he is able to perceive the workings of his-

tory in the most insignificant everyday aspects of his life and in those of the people around him.

In "Carta" (Letter), an autobiographical poem about his childhood barrio, Valle understands in retrospect the forces that determined his consciousness. Simultaneously exploring the personal and the collective, the poem establishes Valle's link to the rest of humanity through his family and extended family: "esta red de ombligos y ojos, / este continente de barrios y / vecindades / ejes planetarias" (this net of umbilical cords and eyes, / this continent of barrios and / neighborhoods / planetary axis). The title of the collection, Illegal, derives from the fascination and respect he feels for the determination of his people to pursue their lives and destinies in their northern, mythic homeland of Aztlán. In "The Fence" Valle denounces the "American throwaway-life" and its economic dependence on cheap foreign labor. In Tijuana,

> At night the fence
> is torn and ripped by the desperate;
> has desperately torn and ripped their clothes;
> the inmates have made a path with their bodies
> leaving a trail of rags flapping in the wind.

"Mode of Production" (1977) is an ambitious and comprehensive overview of the clash of three civilizations: the Hispanic; the Anglo; and the Native American, a conflict from which emerges the contemporary Chicano. Rooted firmly in a dialectical vision, the poem traces the myths, religions, and ideologies of the West. Valle asks what Yahweh has to do with steel:

> God and Steel with Heavy Industry,
> Jesus and Mary with Capital Concentration,
> the Holy Spirit with Steam and Coal,
> Virginity and Purity with abstraction so absolute
> there could be the damnation
> of everlasting sin, everlasting life
> through the lamb of god and Kansas stockyards[.]

From contemporary myths of universal profit and progress is spawned the dominant Western mode of production: capitalism. Against this, Valle contrasts a tranquil, pre-Columbian way of life based on elemental absolutes on a more human scale. The myths produced by ancient modes of production are myths of cosmic harmony, which incorporate rather than oppose the forces of nature: "We were made in the image / of the corn we plant ... / gathered fist of seeds...."

Valle's view of poetry and the power of words is strongly manifested in "To the Students of Hollenbeck Junior High" (1979), drawn from his experiences in the National Endowment for the Humanities Poetry in the Schools Program. It conveys the joy and power he finds in words, not because they express things but because they do things: "We are all poets. / Say cebolla cilantro chile verde [onion coriander green chile] smell / in the air is the sound of a burning sun in your mouth." The accessibility and power of Valle's words remind readers that somewhere not too far beneath everything else, "We are all poets," a realization that creates freedom as well as responsibility:

> Poetry is a tool
> because it helps you take things apart;
> loosen people up.
> But it's also a telephone for sending
> secrets,
> or a radio blaring loud
> making everyone listen.
> Take this power into your life,
> free the words you speak.

Although Valle's concept of language as empowerment led into journalism, his social consciousness speaks through his poetry as well, with an easy fluidity in both English and Spanish, combined with a rare and exuberant enthusiasm.

Although his poetry has been anthologized and continues to appear in magazines with some regularity, critical attention to it is scant, compared to the following he has had as an essayist and journalist for *Somos, Chismearte,* and the *Los Angeles Times.* Valle reconciles the sometimes contradictory perspective of poetry and journalism: "Poetry, based on the emotions and the senses, is a reflective act; journalism is fast and reactive. But both require a sense of oral history, the skill to catch and interpret what people are saying." As a journalist, Valle expresses a sense of restlessness, using words to expose their sources, to question assumptions. That questioning is a part of Chicano reality: "Because our culture has been rejected, we harbor doubt within ourselves: 'What I'm seeing, is it real?' 'What my father is saying, is it true?' "

Valle's poetic and journalist gifts are well contrasted in a 1982 *Los Angeles Times* article, "Ancient Art Survives in Whittier," and an unpublished poem, "Teófilo," both about an octogenarian uncle of Valle's who cultivates the giant maguey in his Whittier backyard for the pulque, a wine fermented from its uncooked sap. In the article, Valle cites scientific and anthropological studies of the agave, its vitamin-laden juice, and its importance in agriculture. In both article and poem, Valle alludes to the mythology of pulque, the milk of the Aztec goddess Mayaguel, the mythical mother with her many breasts who led the Aztecs on their migration to the Valley of Mexico. In both works, he quotes his uncle Teófilo on the details of agave husbandry, but the poem is lyrical:

> "Cut only a few," he said, "to save aguamiel,"
> The sweet blood of Mayaguel,
> Mother of one hundred breasts.
> She gives sustenance
> To the people who walk in the desert,
> Suckles children who drown in rivers,
> Mothers that die in childbirth.
> Her Blood is burned on the pyre,
> Let upon the altar.

Such a pastoral sense of life in urban California shows the well-rooted vision of Víctor Manuel Valle, investigative poet/reporter.

Armando Vallejo

(31 October 1949 -   )

Víctor Fuentes
University of California, Santa Barbara

BOOKS: *Luna llena* (Santa Barbara, Cal.: Aztlán, 1979);

October: Memories of a Chicano (Santa Barbara, Cal.: Xalmán, 1986);

Copper Thunderbird / Pájarotrueno de cobre (Santa Barbara, Cal.: Xalmán, 1987);

Para morir en tus brazos y compromiso (Santa Barbara, Cal.: Xalmán, 1989);

Poemas de un emigrante / Poems of an Immigrant (Santa Barbara, Cal.: Xalmán, 1990).

OTHER: "Alicia," in *Pensamientos*, edited by Vallejo (Santa Barbara, Cal.: Santa Barbara City College, 1981);

"Un poemadibujo," "Salvador," "Tecolote II," "Para morir en tus brazos y compromiso," and "Los muchachos," in *Cenzontle: Chicano Writings of the 80's*, edited by María Herrera Sobek (Irvine: University of California, 1982), pp. 105-117;

"Palabras nuevas," "Mariposa chicana," and "Palabras nuevas II," in *Palabra nueva: Poesía chicana*, edited by Ricardo Aguilar, Armando Armengol, and Sergio Elizondo (El Paso, Tex.: Dos Pasos, 1985), pp. 139-145.

SELECTED PERIODICAL PUBLICATIONS—
UNCOLLECTED: "Trabajadores chicanos, mexicanos, Unanse," *Sí Se Puede*, 1 (March 1974): 4;

"Se mató la muerte" and "Chicana, 5 de mayo 74," *Xalmán* (1974); 12-13;

"Indochina tierra del vestido verde," *Sí Se Puede*, 1 (April 1975): 8;

"Silencio que pasa mi pueblo" and "Al pueblo de Vietnam," *Sí Se Puede*, 1 (May 1975): 5;

"Hermano, vamos a romper las ventanas de nuestro ser," *Sí Se Puede*, 2 (October 1975): 4;

"La despedida," "Hoy como siempre," and "Versos de un estudiante," *Sí Se Puede*, 3 (December 1976-April 1977): 4;

"A Short Story about Somebody's Short Life," *Xalmán* (Fall 1977): 20-21;

"Los perros del barrio," *Xalmán* (Spring 1979): 11;

"Doce lunas," *Xalmán* (Spring 1980): 11-12, 46;

"On Broadway," *Xalmán* (Spring/Fall 1981): 62-67;

"Víctor López, águila del cielo," *Xalmán* (1983-1984): 44-52;

"The Wall I," *Independent* (22-30 November 1989): 83.

From its first manifestations, Armando Vallejo's poetic voice has shown his love for life and political action. In spite of its technical or formal inexpertness, his early poetry was heard as an embodiment of an authentic new voice and not as a versified echo of ideological discourse, as is the case of much political poetry.

Born in Durango, Mexico, on 31 October 1949, Vallejo moved to the United States at an early age. With his mother and siblings he arrived in Santa Barbara, California, at the age of fourteen, and his schooling in his native language came to a quick halt. Although Vallejo completed his high-school and community-college studies in English, there remained alive in his sensitivity the memories of his birthplace (the streets of his childhood barrio and the essence and colors of his homeland) and of the Spanish language. Two factors brought about the poetic irruption of young Vallejo: the Chicano movement, linked to the national and world liberation movements of the 1960s, and his encounter, during his university studies, with great contemporary poets of the Spanish language.

Vallejo's arrival at the University of California, Santa Barbara, in the early 1970s allowed him firsthand experience of the social movements that had reached peaks of activity and participation from 1968 to 1971. In the midst of that vortex, Vallejo forged his poetic voice, later tempering it with the struggles that were to come in the fields and barrios of the United States, Chile, El Salvador, Nicaragua, Africa, and Indochina.

Armando Vallejo

During his university years Vallejo joined a group of Chicano students that saw the force and creativity of the incipient Chicano studies program in the integration of the university with the community. Vallejo collaborated in the university paper, *Sí Se Puede* (Yes, It Can Be Done), from 1973 to 1980. The principal goal of the paper was to encourage ties between university and community, and Vallejo also worked in the social and cultural center, the Casa de la Raza, born out of the combined efforts of the Chicano community of Santa Barbara and the university. Vallejo is now the executive director of this social and cultural center.

In *Sí Se Puede* Vallejo began to publish his poetry. The theme that gave rise to the title of the newspaper (inspired by the call to action of César Chávez's Farmworkers' Union) could also be applied to Vallejo's poetic task. From the time of his first poems, the voice of the people is the most important part of his poetry: "Tú eres el poeta / pueblo, gente, pueblo" (You are the poet / pueblo, people, pueblo), Vallejo writes, echoing, whether consciously or unconsciously, the great poet Miguel Hernández in his *Vientos del Pueblo* (Directions of the People, 1937).

His union with the people takes Vallejo to the oral origins of poetry. His is a spoken word before it is a written one; hence it matters little that in his written verse a *b* or *s* may slip through in place of a *v* or a *z*. Although his poetry only tends, on occasion, toward the rhyme of popular versification, in form it also has roots in popular poetry—in songs, proverbs, and sayings. One of his projects is the collection and publication of "Corridos y canciones de Aztlán" (Ballads and Songs of Aztlán). Vallejo's poetry and prose are rooted in popular culture. There is in his work much laughing, eating, and drinking, which celebrate life, work, and the struggles of the people

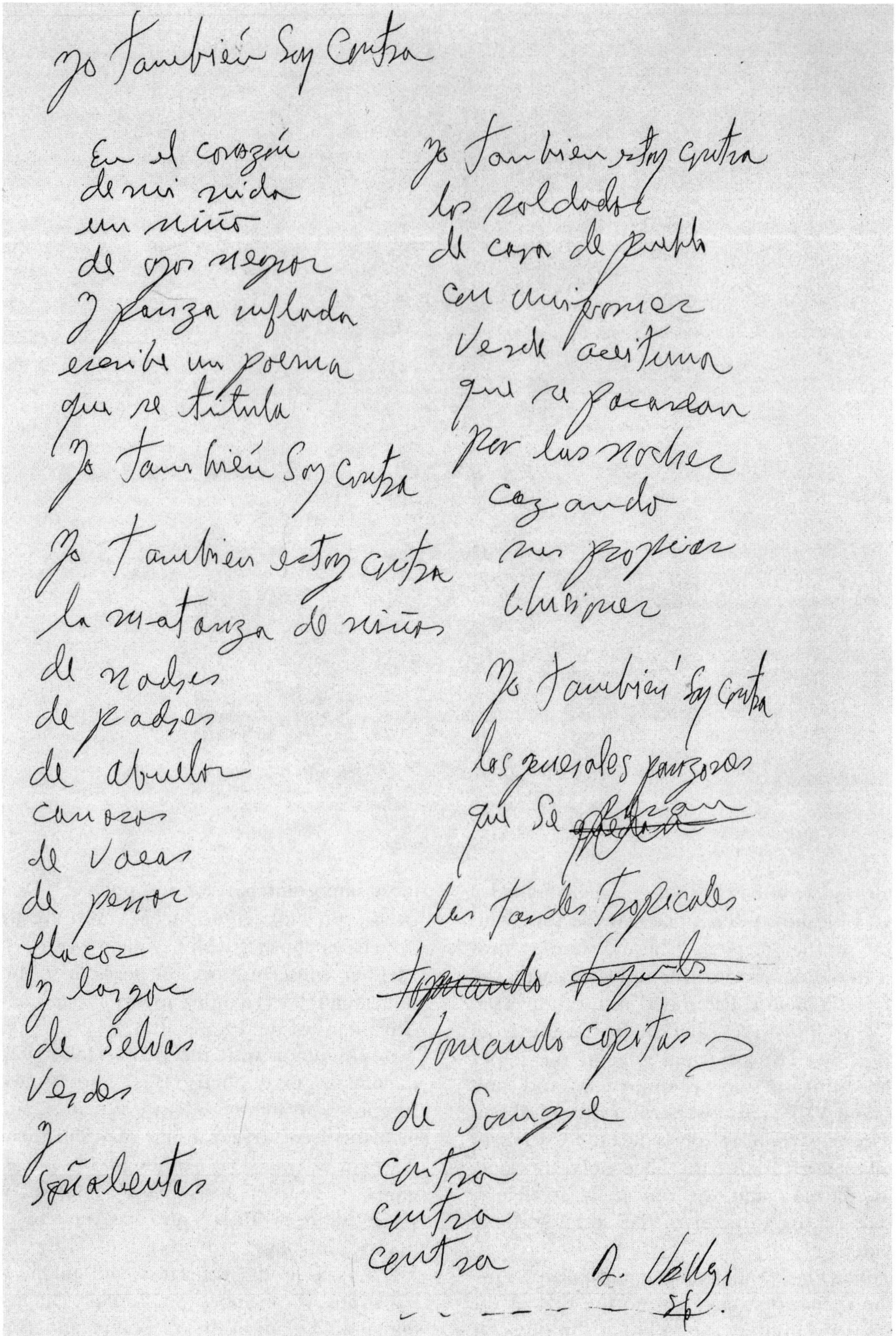

Yo también Soy Contra

En el corazón
de mi nido
un niño
de ojos negros
y panza inflada
escribe un poema
que se titula
Yo también Soy contra

Yo también estoy contra
la matanza de niños
de nodres
de padres
de abuelos
canosos
de vacas
de perros
flacos
y largos
de selvas
verdes
y
espeluznantes

Yo también estoy contra
los soldados
de cara de pueblo
con uniformes
verde aceituna
que se pasean
por las noches
cazando
sus propias
ilusiones

Yo también soy contra
los generales panzones
que se ~~pasean~~

las tardes tropicales
~~tomando~~ ~~copitas~~
tomando copitas
de sangre
contra
contra
contra

A. Vallejo
86

Draft for a poem (by permission of Armando Vallejo)

as they try to have a joyful encounter with the world.

Besides the inspiration that he found in popular culture and poetry, Vallejo also sought out the great contemporary poets in the Spanish language, especially those who have fused their original voices with the voice of the people: poets such as Antonio Machado, César Vallejo, Pablo Neruda, and Hernández. The tone of Vallejo's poetry reflects these influences.

Vallejo, together with Manuel Unzueta, Salvador Rodríguez del Pino, and Mireya Jaimes-Freyre, formed the group Xalmán (Alma Chicana de Aztlán) (Chicano Soul of Aztlán). Starting in 1977, *Xalmán* was the group's magazine, and it became a publication outlet for all Chicano and Latino literatures, though appearing irregularly. Vallejo was also involved in other cultural and creative activity during the late 1970s and early 1980s: he earned his M.A. in Spanish at the University of California, Santa Barbara, with a thesis on Chicano poetry; he taught courses on Mexican and Chicano literature and cinema at the university and junior-college level; and he directed a mural-painting project in Santa Barbara parks and schools, involving local artists, children, and teenagers. He also did illustrations for *Xalmán* and for the book *Fiesta in Aztlán: Anthology of Chicano Poetry* (1982), edited by Toni Empringham.

In 1979 Vallejo published *Luna llena* (Full Moon), a work that brings together a large part of his poetic journey. Many of his poems from newspapers and poetry readings are brought together in a harmonious whole. This collection of poetry is testimony to the changes and the growth of the poet. The evolving phases of his identity are also linked to the changes in the social and political struggles of Chicanos. These painful but hopeful changes are linked by Vallejo to the symbolism of the moon: the new moon and the full moon with all their mythical powers of creation and re-creation. In *Luna llena* Vallejo, through intuition, imagination, and a sense of magic, points to an exit from the "hell" of the oppression and injustice of the present-day world; he sides with "the forgotten ones" and "the poor of the earth."

Grace M. Bearse, in a review of *Luna llena* for *Revista Chicano-Riqueña* (Winter 1981), stressed that the themes of Vallejo's poems, like those of most Chicano literature, are chiefly protest and identification with "la Raza" (the Chicano people). She praises his expression of innermost grief in his poetry of social protest and the gentleness in his treatment of women, adding that "When he is in a fanciful mood he treats words as butterflies. They are colorful, lovely and elusive." The eminent critic Luis Leal, in his short introduction to *Luna llena*, praised the social vein of Vallejo's poetry, rooted in "the heart of humanity's sorrow." Leal noticed that there are two distinct visions in Vallejo: the painful one dealing with the toil of the farmworker; and the other one, of the barrio—nostalgic, imbedded in the symbolism of Aztlán, and also playful and joyful. As Vallejo writes in the poem "Message: Around the Corner with Chicano Words," "Aztlán barrio a la vuelta de la esquina de las esquinas redondas donde sentí mi primer beso donde sentí mi primer desencanto" (Aztlán barrio around the corner of the round corners where I felt my first kiss where I felt my first disenchantment). An example of the first vision is in the same poem, when even the grape cries and talks with pain, witnessing the suffering of the campesino:

Le pregunté que por qué lloraba
y me dijo no sé, pues siento
un no sé qué. Cuando veo
las caras de los campesinos
que me vienen a recoger.

(I asked her why she was crying
and she told me I don't know, I feel
and I don't know what. When I see
the faces of the campesinos
that come to harvest me.)

Vallejo categorically declares in this poem that he is neither a poet nor a writer and that he writes because "around the corner there are still barrios." Later in *Luna llena* he moves toward reconciliation—though still not free of tension—with his poetic side. Although the barrio and its people are the sustenance of the poetry in the book, a whole series of poems is centered on the theme of poetic creation and the poem itself: "Poetry of Our People (Raza)," "A Poem," "A Poet and His Poetry," and "A Poet and His Creation." The themes of Stéphane Mallarmé, regarding poetry as a matter of words and the poet confronting the blank page, are seen in *Luna llena*. A new aspect of Vallejo emerges—the self-reflexive poet, preoccupied with the criticism of language and the problem of creation, as in "Una poema chicano:

Moriré de poesía

Entre los seres
Agarrado de sus hombros

(I will die of poetry
Among the people
Clutched to their shoulders)[.]

In 1981 Vallejo published two booklets of poetry written by his students at Santa Barbara City College: *Pensamientos* (Thoughts) and *Reflexiones mezcladas* (Mixed Reflections). *Pensamientos* includes a poem of his, "Alicia," in which there is an evocation of his native city, which is rare in his poetry:

> Alicia
> Están lloviendo mariposas
> y en Durango
> siguen creciendo los recuerdos
>
> (Alicia
> It is raining butterflies
> and in Durango
> memories continue to grow)[.]

In 1982 a selection of Vallejo's poems was published in *Cenzontle: Chicano Writings of the 80's*, and in 1985 *Palabra nueva: Poesía chicana* (New Word: Chicano Poetry) included three of his poems. In 1989 he published *Para morir en tus brazos y compromiso* (To Die in Your Arms and Commitment).

In the title of the book are the two drives that constitute the thematic configuration of the poems therein: Eros and Thanatos—the Eros of personal love, sung about by the poet as lasting beyond death, but also the political Eros. Vallejo wishes to die in the arms of his beloved, but his embrace also includes the young Sandinistas in Nicaragua and the Chicano barrio activists. On the other hand, his poetical reflection about love and death (love beyond death), contains a strong denunciation of the death instinct, as seen in the Contra war or the killings in Chile and El Salvador.

This second book consolidates the expressive atmosphere of Vallejo's poetical world, the particular setting or ambience of his writing, namely the local *taquerías* (taco shops), streets, and parks of the barrio of Sal Si Puedes, suddenly transfigured by the fluttering of a dove or a butterfly or by the mysterious look of the *tecolote* (owl) in the poem of that name:

> Tecolote
> ¿Qué han visto tus ojos?
> ¿Qué escondes detrás de tu mirada?
> ¿Qué han escuchado tus oídos?
> ¿Qué han tocado tus plumas?
>
> (Owl
> What have your eyes seen?
> What do you hide behind your gaze?
> What have your ears heard?
> What have your feathers touched?)

In his brief but revealing introduction to *Para morir en tus brazos y compromiso*, Leal emphasized, as he had when writing about Vallejo's first book, the rich and profound imagery ("as profound as the daily occurrences of life"), and Leal called attention to some of the recurrent images: hot dogs, beer, and wine, associated with friendship and sharing; chromatic images; and images of transformation, as in this stanza from the title poem:

> Ahora paloma blanca
> Convertida en mariposa
> color turquesa
> te me escondes
> en el horizonte rojo
> de tus labios púrpuros
>
> (Now white dove
> Changed into turquoise-colored
> butterfly
> you hide from me
> on the red horizon
> of your purple lips)[.]

The friendship of Vallejo with the well-known Canadian-Indian painter Norval Morrisseau, who lived in Santa Barbara for a short while, seems to have had an influence on the evolution of Vallejo's poetry—an influence visible in *Para morir en tu brazos y compromiso*. There is a playing with the spatial arrangement of words, an intensification of color (Vallejo is also a painter), and, above all, a deliberate desire to use indigenous imagery and spirituality. The book includes a poem to Morrisseau, "Pájarotrueno de Cobre" (Copper Thunderbird—also in the chapbook of that name, published in 1987), in which the impact of the Indian painter and shaman is especially noticeable:

> Thunderbird
> la ternura de tu azul celeste
> y la inocencia de tus hijos
> pinturas
> de un antes de todo
> me dieron un correr

Vallejo painting a mural in Santa Barbara

hacia un nuevo nacer
entre el verdenieve de tus bosques
y el amarillocaliente de mis desiertos

(Thunderbird
the tenderness of your sky blue
and the innocence of your children
paintings
from a before everything
made me run
toward a new birth
among the snowgreen of your forests
and the hotyellow of my deserts)[.]

In the late 1970s and early 1980s Vallejo also published short stories and fragments of poetical prose, such as "Los perros del barrio" (The Barrio Dogs), "On Broadway," and "Víctor López, águila del cielo" (Víctor López, Eagle of the Sky). These works contain a mixture of popular-cultural, magic-realism, and biographical sketches. In 1986 Vallejo published a fragment of a novel, *October: Memories of a Chicano*, in which he experiments with writing only in English, and in 1990 he published a bilingual collection of poems, *Poemas de un emigrante / Poems of an Immigrant*. Both books are autobiographical, a mode favored by Chicano writers. In *Poemas de un*

emigrante, the images, metaphors, popular language, and rhythms characteristic of Vallejo's poetry exalt the human ancestral dignity of the Mexican and Latin-American immigrant. This immigrant also has an initiatory trip to the mythical-symbolic nucleus of the indigenous ancestors and a return to the mythical place of origin—Aztlán—be it in Ortega Park or in the dreams of the poet immigrant.

Moving to prose and to the use of more English, Vallejo has expanded his expressive repertoire. Nevertheless, using Spanish or English, writing poetry, fiction, or articles, Vallejo achieves the same result: an intensification of his particular expressive atmosphere, based on some key words and concepts and in recurrent and memorable images, which give the barrio and its people an aura of mythical plenitude. In the area of Santa Barbara that encompasses the Rose Café, Ortega Park, and streets such as Montecito, Sal Si Puedes, and Indio Muerto, and has its center in the Casa de la Raza, Vallejo continues attempting to forge—with his poetical words and his work as an activist—an inhabitable space where communication and expression of the Mexican or Chicano experience can be possible and lasting.

References:

Víctor Fuentes, "Armando Vallejo, Vientos del pueblo. . . ," Introduction to *Luna llena* (Santa Barbara, Cal.: Xalmán, 1979), pp. 1-2;

Fuentes, Introduction to Vallejo's *Poemas de un emigrante / Poems of an immigrant* (Santa Barbara, Cal., 1990), pp. 1-4;

Fuentes, Preface to Vallejo's *Para morir en tus brazos y compromiso* (Santa Barbara, Cal.: Xalmán, 1989), pp. 1-2;

Abd al-Hayy Moore, "Arts Festival Poetry Extrava-ganza," *Santa Barbara Arts Magazine* (April 1986): 21-23;

Luis Leal, Introduction to *Para morir en tus brazos y compromiso*, pp. iv-viii;

Leal, "La poesía de Armando Vallejo," Introduction to *Luna llena* (Santa Barbara, Cal.: Xalmán, 1979), pp. 3-4;

José Romero, "Guacha, ese poet," *Siempre* (19 November 1986): 52;

Perla Schwartz, "Poesía chicana reciente," *Excelsior Plural*, 15-18, (May 1986): 66-67.

Gloria Velásquez-Treviño

(21 December 1949 -)

Manuel de Jesús Hernández-G.
Arizona State University

SELECTED PERIODICAL PUBLICATIONS— UNCOLLECTED:

POETRY

"¿Quién soy?," *La Luz*, 6 (March 1977): 18;

"Llanto persiguiente," *Colorado North Review*, 13, no. 2 (1977): 30;

"Chicana," in "Mestizo: An Anthology of Chicano Literature," edited by José Armas, *De Colores*, special issue, 4, nos. 1-2 (1978): 176;

"Mi soledad," "La pobreza," "Gente del sol," "Social Security," and "Bella juventud," *Caracol*, 4 (June 1978): 4;

"Sa" and "Superwoman," *Grito del Sol*, 3 (July-September 1978): 111-112;

"Eres," "Recuerdos," "Dalin," "Déjenme morir," and "Rompecabezas," in "From Midwest to the West," edited by Marjorie Agosin and Patricia Montenegro, *Midwest-East, Midwest-West*, special issue, 1, no. 1 (1980): 12-16.

FICTION

"Fragment: 'Mercedes' from the novel *Soldaditos y muñecas*," *Tecolote*, 12 (March 1982): 5;

"La carta," in "El Gallo Ilustrado," supplement to *El Día* (Mexico City), 11 April 1982 pp.20-21;

"Fragment: 'El doctor Merry' from the novel *Soldaditos y muñecas*," *Tecolote*, 16 (December 1985): 7.

Gloria Velásquez-Treviño consciously began her career with the knowledge that her readers were chiefly her own people. She has developed a wide range of discourse, including images from pre-Columbian times to those of modern farm and urban workers, a discourse that features a clear, Chicana feminist voice. Her literary language exhibits influences from Mexican and Latin-American literatures, specifically, in her latest productions, magical realism.

Born in the small town of Loveland, Colorado, on 21 December 1949, Velásquez-Treviño claims heritage from a long-standing New Mexican family, with Navajo blood from her paternal grandfather. Her parents, Francisca Molinar-Velásquez and Juan Velásquez, earned a living until 1963 as migrant workers, traveling between Colorado and Texas, and they finally settled as factory and hospital workers in Johnstown, Colorado. Velásquez-Treviño experienced the migrant cycle of constant change as a child; she received her early education in Loveland, attended one school in Texas, and finished in Johnstown.

After graduating from Roosevelt High School in Johnstown, she worked as a secretary at the local Hewlett-Packard plant, attending college classes at night. After serving as a teacher's

Gloria Velásquez-Treviño

aide at local primary and secondary schools, she received a full-time fellowship to study at the University of Northern Colorado. Thus Velásquez-Treviño earned her B.A. in 1978, with a double major in Spanish and Chicano studies.

She participated in various "Canto al Pueblo" (Song of the People) festivals in Milwaukee, Wisconsin; Albuquerque, New Mexico; and Corpus Christi, Texas, between 1977 and 1979. These popular events had a profound effect on her writing, thus motivating her to pursue graduate studies in Latin-American literature at Stanford University. In her second year she won a literary prize from the Department of French and Italian.

She later delved into the subject of women in Chicano literature, concentrating on Chicana narrative production from the early 1900s to the 1970s. With the completion of her dissertation, "Cultural Ambivalence in Early Chicana Prose Fiction," Velásquez-Treviño received her Ph.D. in Spanish literature in 1985.

According to Arnold C. Vento in his "Contemporary Chicana Poetry: 1969-1977" (1978), Velásquez-Treviño's main themes include Chicana history and identity, the plight of the farm-worker, antiwar protests, male dominance, incest, the desertion of single mothers, the lack of medical care, and the problems of old age and alcoholism. To disseminate her message of resistance against marginality, economic denial, and male dominance, she relies on such techniques as satire, irony, and symbolism. Furthermore, one finds in her work magical realism, raw images of oppression, the narrator's direct link with the ill and abused, and her open repugnance for a sordid environment. She writes eulogies (to farmworkers, motherhood, and educational achievement), uses the image of the river as a symbol of regeneration, and makes use of historical similes grounded in poetic images of pre-Columbian society.

Her main concerns are the female experience and the plight of the farmworker. The poem "Chicana" (1978), a eulogy to the speaker's mother, is a synthesis of both concerns: "As I struggle to understand, / to seek answers to / fill the voids, / the needs / in my life, / I feel the strength of my mama / when she went to the field / and returned tired / at night / to some more work."

Page from a rough draft for a short story (by permission of Gloria Velásquez-Treviño)

Two of her other poems on the Chicana experience reveal her voice in its best form: "¿Quién soy?" (Who Am I?, 1977) and "Superwoman" (1978). "¿Quién soy?" establishes for Chicanas a feminist identity grounded in myth and history; "Superwoman," with its irony, demystifies all current female roles, such as the suffering mother, the dedicated wife, and the liberated woman. The second stanza in "Superwoman" presents self-criticism: "I am the super-liberated chicana / attending classes, / writing papers, / discussing psychology, / yet always silent."

In Velásquez-Treviño's story "La carta" (The Letter), published in the Mexican newspaper *El Día* (11 April 1982), the action unfolds as follows: the narrator/protagonist, Esperanza, fulfills her dead brother Antonio's last request, to deliver his letter from Vietnam to his fiancée, Alegría, but, due to her own mourning, Esperanza does not deliver the letter until a year after its arrival. During this time she suffers depression, drinks heavily, and consults unproductively with doctors. The hard fact of Antonio's death recalls the close bond she shared with her brother, as does the obligation to deliver his letter, especially since Esperanza originally saw Alegría as an intruder and edited all her brother's love letters to his fiancée.

In memorable detail "La carta" shows the pain of families whose relatives were killed in the Vietnam War. Very few Chicano writings of the 1970s examined this important issue.

The plight of women in a male-dominated society, as seen in Alegría's marriage of convenience—after hearing of Antonio's death—receives further development in "Fragment: 'Mercedes'" (1982) from the unpublished novel "Soldaditos y muñecas." The work first presents the protagonist as a victim of incest and then of desertion by the father of her children. "Mercedes" includes vivid, raw images of female oppression:

"How many times had she climbed those moldy stairs, breathed the smell of dirty diapers and recently cooked tortillas that turned her stomach, forcing her to cover her mouth and pause for a moment? . . . —Let me tell you [Mercedes says] last night a woman jumped from the sixth floor. Many onlookers showed up, firetrucks came and then Channel 7, you know, they always like to sensationalize things because we live in welfare housing. . . ."

On a positive note, the same short story introduces the image of the river as a symbol of regeneration. Beyond her own death wish, Mercedes sees in the river a form of escape from witnessing the oppressive situation faced by women: "How many times had she thought of committing suicide? Two, three, twenty. At age six she had wished to jump into the river, taste its water, allowing it to purify her, but something held her back." The narrator/protagonist directly links herself with the abused.

The short story "El doctor Merry" (1985; also from the unpublished novel) exposes the poor quality of medical care for Chicanos. The cause lies in insensitivity on the part of some Anglo doctors, such as the ironically named title character, who primarily pursue pleasure and wealth: "At nine o'clock he arrived and very sophisticatedly climbed off his Porsche, eaglelike nose, wearing his perfectly pressed shirt, holding his black briefcase with his long and cold fingers known by the whole town. Whistling a tune, he walked forward to the large doors on his office and disappeared."

Inversion, satire, irony, and humor, according to Gloria Velásquez-Treviño, serve to expose the passive image and subordinate position of Chicanas in a patriarchal society, which itself lives under domination. She continues to produce literary discourse with the specific intent of providing resistance to cultural domination.

Evangelina Vigil-Piñón

(29 November 1949 -   )

Elaine Dorough Johnson
University of Wisconsin—Whitewater

BOOKS: *Nade y Nade* (San Antonio: M & A Editions, 1978);
Thirty an' Seen a Lot (Houston: Arte Público, 1982);
The Computer Is Down (Houston: Arte Público, 1987).

VIDEOTAPE: *Night Vigil*, written and directed by Vigil-Piñón, Houston, De Colores Productions, 1984.

OTHER: "A platicar," "cool," "Desesperación," and "te avientas," in *Hembra: An Anthology of Writings by Chicanas*, edited by Inés Hernández-Tovar (Austin: Center for Mexican-American Studies, University of Texas, 1976);
"Como embrujada," "nomás uno sabe," and "simple time," in *Canto al Pueblo: An Anthology of Experiences*, edited by Leonard Carrillo, Antonio Martínez, Carol Molina, and Marie Wood (San Antonio: Penca, 1978);
"Downtown San Antonio in Front of the Majestic Theater," in *The Ethnic American Woman: Problems, Protests, Life-style*, edited by Edith Blicksilver (Dubuque, Iowa: Kendall/Hunt, 1978);
Angela de Hoyos, *Selections / Selecciones*, introduction by Vigil-Piñón (San Antonio: Descalzo, 1979);
"Los nombres," in *Ceremony of Brotherhood*, edited by Rudolfo A. Anaya and Simon J. Ortiz (Albuquerque: Academia, 1981);
Woman of Her Word: Hispanic Women Write, edited by Vigil-Piñón, includes three poems by her (Houston: Arte Público, 1983);
Trino Sánchez, *Father-Son Poems*, introduction by Vigil-Piñón (Lansing, Mich.: Lansing Press, 1984);
From the Inside, Out, edited by Vigil-Piñón (San Antonio: M & A Editions, 1984).

SELECTED PERIODICAL PUBLICATIONS—
UNCOLLECTED: "Communion," "you've just got to let it go," and "stature," *Imagine* (Summer 1984).

Evangelina Vigil-Piñón is one of the first writers from the Chicano community to capture the essence of the barrio—its sounds, its rituals, and its characters—from a perspective that transcends generational boundaries. She has accomplished this feat with a skillful, literary adaptation of oral language—whether Spanish or English or a blend of the two. Her work has always been characterized by a diversity of themes. Even as she was writing about the melancholy sound of the cicadas or the old-timers sitting around the plaza on a Sunday afternoon in their Stetsons, she was also writing bitingly satirical poems about the hypocrisy and macho posturing of some of her contemporaries. Her talent for putting sounds and images together won her early recognition. During a period when few Chicana authors were recognized, Vigil-Piñón was already seeing her poems printed in many periodical publications around the United States.

Vigil-Piñón, the second child in a family of ten children, was born in San Antonio, Texas, on 29 November 1949 and lived there until she went off to college in 1968. Her mother is a native of San Antonio, her family having emigrated from Parras, Mexico, in the early 1900s. Vigil-Piñón's father's family has roots in the area of Texas around the town of Seguin. During her later childhood years she lived with the extended family of her maternal grandmother and listened to her great-uncle tell stories about life in Mexico and the United States just after the turn of the century. Vigil-Piñón credits her mother, an avid reader, with giving her a love of books. Her father, a shoe repairman by trade, whose occasional avocation was playing the guitar and singing for friends and family, is the source of her interest in music and, according to family lore, of her tenacity. From her maternal grandmother she learned "to observe and listen for words of wis-

Evangelina Vigil-Piñón

dom which come only with experience." She attributes her sense of responsibility and discipline to her great-uncle, who was a father figure to her during her teenage years.

Even as a small child, Vigil-Piñón felt the urge to express herself creatively. She remembers wandering in a rose garden when she was five, taking in the fragrances, the sounds of music coming from neighbors' radios, and the sights of drifting cloud formations and migrating geese. She describes this "space" in which she explored her imagination as being "mysterious, solitary, even lonely. And intangible, like one's shadow." Vigil-Piñón's first artistic direction was toward the visual arts. Throughout elementary school she won prizes in poster and art contests, and in the sixth grade she was recommended by her principal to attend classes at a private art school in San Antonio, the Inman Christian Center. She and a classmate were the only grade-school students in attendance; most of the others were in their early twenties. Recalling her experience there, she says, "The art studio was a wonderful place—I loved the smell of paints and inks and art supplies all around, the students' canvasses on easels, situated in their particular nooks and corners of the rooms. . . . My teacher's name

was Mrs. Burk. She was the most inspiring teacher I've ever known." Throughout junior high school Vigil-Piñón continued her art studies and would probably have gone on to make a career in this field, had she not in high school been pushed in the direction of secretarial science.

Vigil-Piñón's second favorite hobby as a young girl was music. At home she would always sing along with the radio, and throughout school she participated in the choir. Music grew in importance in her life until, by the time she entered high school, it was her passion: "Music became central to my existence. But then music had really been in the center of my soul, nurtured by the culture of San Antonio, where people 'live' music."

Vigil-Piñón's first formal attempt at writing poetry dates back to her eighth year, when she wrote a four-line poem for a local poetry contest, winning third place. Describing what she felt when she mailed in her entry, she remembers "that same sense of seriousness, purpose and intent, which to this day I experience when I prepare my work for submission." Since her childhood days, when she would jot down lyrics to songs she heard on the radio, filling in the verses she missed with her own creations, music and poet-

Cover for Vigil-Piñón's 1982 collection of poems, mostly written between 1976 and 1980, while she was living in San Antonio

ry have been inseparable for her. Her poetic inspiration stems from life's rhythms, "the rhythm of time, the ticking of clocks, hearts beating. To me poetry is music. It is that song in our heart. Life is the dance to that music." During high school Vigil-Piñón combined music and poetry through her participation as a singer and lyricist, along with her cousins, in a neighborhood combo. She has continued songwriting and performing, adding classical guitar to her skills. Today she and her musician/artist husband, Mark Anthony Piñón, compose and play music together. (They were married on Valentine's Day 1983 and have a son, Marc Antony Piñón, born in 1984.)

In the fall of 1968, with a scholarship to study business administration, Vigil-Piñón enrolled in Prairie View A&M University, a predominantly black university in a small community west of Houston. Through the process of learning about black history, pride, music, and faith, she became very aware of her own cultural identity.

Since she was living so close to Houston, she visited the city frequently, becoming enamored of its cosmopolitanism and the academic opportunities afforded by the University of Houston, to which she ultimately transferred. Although in her junior year of business administration, Vigil-Piñón could not continue to ignore her artistic bent. Thus, after a year at the University of Houston she decided to major in English, taking a minor in political science. While her favorite area was American literature, primarily poetry, she enjoyed reading the works of a wide variety of writers, from Geoffrey Chaucer and William Shakespeare through William Wordsworth, Charles Dickens, Edgar Allan Poe, Ralph Waldo Emerson, and Walt Whitman, to Robert Frost, Stephen Crane, and Ernest Hemingway, and the more contemporary Denise Levertov, Sylvia Plath, Joyce Carol Oates, and Flannery O'Connor. Such contemporary counterculture poets as Amiri Baraka and Allen Ginsberg have also been important in Vigil-Piñón's formation as a writer. If, however, any single body of literature was the most influential in shaping her creative direction, it was that of American black writers—the essays of Frederick Douglass, James Baldwin's novels, and the poems of Nikki Giovanni and Ntozake Shange. Vigil-Piñón believes that "spirituality is central to Black culture, and rhythm and music are very much a manifestation and symbol of this in Black poetry—as is the ritual of song and dance in Native American works. Similarly, in the heart of Hispanic culture, one finds song, music and dance combined in an enduring ritual."

As a college student, Vigil-Piñón was involved in facilitating Mexican-American cultural activities—participating in budgeting, planning, coordinating, and publicity—for the Mexican-American Youth Organization. She also lobbied in Austin on behalf of Mexican-American studies programs. Such a program was finally established at Houston in her senior year, and she had the benefit of one course in Chicano politics.

Vigil-Piñón remained in Houston after her graduation in 1974, working in a variety of community-affairs-oriented jobs in counseling and television. During this period she wrote her first collection of poems, "Tanteadas y malas tanteadas" (Feeling the Way). Major themes in "Tanteadas" are barrio life, the transmission of Chicano cultural values, and the stupidity of macho behavior. While this collection was never published as a volume, some of the poems were published in Chicano literature journals, and six appear in *Thirty an' Seen a Lot* (1982). For example, "ay qué ritmo" (Oh What Rhythm), first published in *Caracol* (September 1976), received first prize in a national literary competition sponsored by the Coordinating Council of Literary Magazines before being included in *Thirty*. In "la canícula" (Dog Days) the poet captures the lazy summer days of her barrio childhood, spent dreaming of the future, listening to the drone of katydids, and watching barefoot, shirtless children playing in the street, rolling tires. "Mi abuelita y su hermano" (My Grandmother and Her Brother) is about the "conversaciones eternas" between Vigil-Piñón's grandmother and great-uncle, which they enjoyed whether in the cold of winter indoors or in the heat of summer, when they would sit outside fanning themselves, feeling the breeze, and listening to the sounds of the barrio. "Para El Machete Arturo Valdez" is a eulogy for a Chicano activist who urged his community to celebrate their cultural heritage and to never give up the struggle. In "ay qué ritmo" the poet denounces both the ridiculous, sexist behavior of the Latino macho man and the passivity of the young women who enjoy it and those who merely pretend to enjoy it, or wish that they did.

Vigil-Piñón moved back to San Antonio in 1976 and became involved in the arts and humanities, serving during various times with the Mexican-American Cultural Center, the Artists' Alliance of San Antonio, and the Texas Institute for Educational Development. Additionally, during the spring and fall of 1977, she taught freshman composition and American literature at the Universidad Jacinto Treviño; then, during the 1977-1978 academic year, she was writer in residence for the Harlandale Independent School District and the Texas Commission of the Arts. For the 1979-1980 period she received a National Endowment for the Arts Fellowship for Creative Writers, which enabled her to travel to the Caribbean and Central America, where she gained new perspectives on culture and politics.

During the late 1970s she also took graduate courses at Saint Mary's University and was exposed extensively to Mexican-American, Native American, and black American authors, deriving major inspiration for her own writing. During graduate school Vigil-Piñón continued to read and enjoy mainstream and counterculture American poets, especially Charles Bukowski, she says, "for his stark realism and boldness." The poetry of Giovanni was also of great importance to her during these years. Vigil-Piñón's participation in

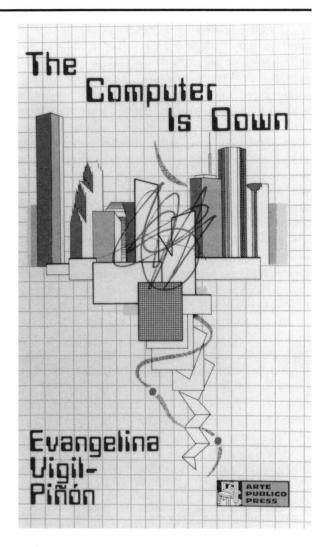

Cover for the 1987 collection that features some of Vigil-Piñón's poems about urban blight in Houston

public poetry readings enabled her to meet many writers, such as the poet Harryette Mullen.

In addition to her graduate studies in American literature, Vigil-Piñón maintained her own personal reading program. Between 1976 and 1979 she was reading many works written in Spanish, particularly Latin-American literature, discovering Gabriel García Márquez, Mariano Azuela, Juan Rulfo, Carlos Fuentes, Rubén Darío, and Pablo Neruda. During these years she began her research into *corridos* (old love ballads) and boleros.

In 1978 Vigil-Piñón decided to discontinue her studies to devote more time to her writing. Many of the poems in *Thirty* were written between 1976 and 1979, and her first book, *Nade y Nade* (Deeper and Deeper), was published in 1978.

Nade y Nade is a collection of thirty poems, most of them very brief; it is introduced by a one-page monologue, addressing various topics: sadness, the swift passage of time, the struggle for self-knowledge, and the need for communication with others. In spite of the weighty sound of these themes, the poems in this volume are neither ponderous nor bitter in tone. In fact many are characterized by gentleness and a contemplative spirit. Vigil-Piñón describes them as "introspective" and "esoteric." She says, "elemental to me then was focusing on the right questions . . . and viewing them keenly and from the 'best' perspectives." While working on the books "Tanteadas" and *Nade* she was reading the philosophies of Plato, Aristotle, and Friedrich Nietzsche, and she says her "concerns as a writer were existential." Using language that is intimate and conversational—a skillful blend of English and Spanish in many poems—Vigil-Piñón creates in *Nade* the illusion that one has entered the poet's head in midthought. The poem "original sin" is illustrative of this technique: "really frightens me to know / that I will die / as far as I can tell / never really recibiendo / comunión / con alguien más" (receiving / communion / with anyone else).

With just a few words of description combined with some brief dialogue, Vigil-Piñón is able to create the illusion of a real conversational exchange in an actual setting. For example, in "nomás uno sabe" (One Only Knows) readers hear the voice of a waitress who has taken a sympathetic interest in an old man standing at the bar, hunched wearily over his beer. She inquires about his health: "qué pasó pájaro / andas aplomao" (what's going on, old man / feeling a bit under?). He answers, "pues fíjate que sí / no me siento bien" (well, yes / just don't feel too good), and she interprets, "el malecito, eh" (a little cold, eh?). But he is unable to attribute how he feels to any specific cause: "no, no / nomás no me siento bien" (no, no / just don't feel good, that's all).

While the language of *Nade* is a very accurate, musical re-creation of Chicano speech, the poems themselves do not dwell on specifically Chicano subject matter. Vigil-Piñón's poems are about people, relationships, and living in the present moment. Although a melancholy air seems to pervade much of *Nade*, especially when she reflects on the passing of time—in "resbaladeras" (Slides), for example—the volume ends with the upbeat "dame una mordidita" (Give Me a Little Bite), a celebration of the senses. The speaker de-

scribes the pleasure she feels just sitting and listening to music as she eats "a nice crisp apple."

In 1981 Vigil-Piñón moved to Galveston, Texas, to work as poet in residence with the Galveston Cultural Arts Center and to complete work on *Thirty*. "Galveston," she says, "was very inspiring for me, as I love being by the sea. If there is one single element that has inspired me the most to write, it has to be the ocean, the sea, the surf, beaches and breezy umbrella skies." By the time she arrived in Galveston, she had completed several collections of poetry, most of them unpublished but including poems eventually collected in *Thirty*.

Thirty brings together poems written over a six-year period, when Vigil-Piñón was living in Houston, San Antonio, and Galveston, and reflects various stages in her development as a poet. Nevertheless, several themes are constant throughout the volume. Most numerous are the poems written between 1976 and 1980, when she was living in San Antonio. In these she speaks of enjoying such simple pleasures as music or good coffee; the wisdom of barrio elders; the transmission of knowledge from older relatives to children; nostalgia for a lost past; flirtatious women; courtship; and the artist's relationship with nature. "Los radios retumbando" (The Radios Resounding) brings together several of these themes. "Youthful brown-skinned drivers / bare-chested / adorned with crucitas y medallas" (crosses and medallions) are seen in their old cars, riding low, fine-tuning their radios, and flirting with the girls "clad in tight short-shorts / . . . / but minding the driving." One of several nostalgic poems of this group is "el mercado [the market] en San Antonio where the tourists trot," wherein the poet describes the stores, now abandoned, where she bought comic books as a child and where a ragged alcoholic now wanders, panhandling for nickels. The poem "sudden storm" shows her awe and delight in the presence of nature's power. In "cantina blues" she speaks of the *borrachedra* (drunken binge) that so often camouflages despair.

Vigil-Piñón's move to Galveston brought her to the shores of the Gulf of Mexico, and many of her poems of this period show the sea's influence. For example "night vigil" (produced as a videotape presentation in 1984) is a long recollection of Caribbean images, including the beauty of beaches and the sea's sensuality, which leads the poet to a heightened awareness of her own existence and of the sensuality of the life within her

Evangelina Vigil-Piñón (photograph copyright 1990 by George McInnis)

body. "Querida tierra" (Dear Earth) and "rapture," also written in Galveston, evoke the erotic sound of the sea—the rhythm of its waves on the shore and its "blue passion." "Evening news" and "el pésame" (Grief) reflect the impact of Vigil-Piñón's Latin-American travels on her artistic consciousness. The former is an outcry against the exploitation of the poor by the rich, whether those who suffer are in the Third World or in San Antonio. In the latter she incorporates chants and fragments of speeches to capture the Nicaraguan voices protesting the murder of six Salvadoran opposition leaders.

Completing *Thirty* in Galveston in 1981, Vigil-Piñón then moved to Houston in the spring of 1982 to become a guest lecturer in the University of Houston Department of English. In Houston she decided to embark on a new course professionally. As she explains, "realizing that I was getting nowhere financially through my usual employment as writer-in-residence and other temporary employment situations in the field of arts ad-

ministration, I decided to find a stable, full-time position. By chance I came upon a position in victim/witness assistance and management." She continues to be employed as a paralegal in this field, presently as a training-program administrator for the National College of District Attorneys. Naturally a major change in her personal life came about in 1983, when she and Piñón were married. While Vigil-Piñón has had less free time to write, she does not feel that her creative energies have been stifled. Instead, as she states, "I've learned to allow my creative energies to flow with surrounding energies. I snatch a poem here and there—that is, in addition to 'living it,' I write it down." Family life has been a positive experience for her: "Ensconced in a warm, loving relationship, I don't feel the solitude and sense of isolation which I experienced in my younger years. The transformation has been from the single, carefree writer, to the full-time professional, and mother and wife. . . . Yet, the creative process never remains the same, so I don't long for the inspirational elements of my past. The creative process is like an unwritten formula that a scientist tries compulsively to discover."

The year 1983 also saw the publication of the anthology *Woman of Her Word*, edited by Vigil-Piñón. A collection of literature and criticism by Hispanic women, the book is a major contribution to the field of contemporary minority literature. Vigil-Piñón's three poems included in the volume show a thematic continuity with her earlier work, while adding concerns not previously voiced. In "The Bridge People" she acknowledges the common humanity that links others with the homeless people in Houston, who must scavenge for resalable beer cans along the bayou's edge in order to support themselves; Vigil-Piñón also depicts the environmental degradation that the oil industry has brought to this once-beautiful city. In "Dumb Broad!" readers see a woman who primps in her rearview mirror while driving to work, accompanied by a man who sits beside her like a mannequin, tolerating the cigarette smoke that she carelessly puffs in his face. The omnipresent car radio appears, too, this time fine-tuned by the woman driver. Undocumented workers in "Telephone Line," anxious to maintain their lifeline to friends and family back in Mexico, tolerate slow service and trivial questions about phone color and cord length just to get that precious instrument that will put them in touch with home. These poems are longer and more thoroughly developed than most of those in *Thirty*, and they

311

are almost entirely in English. Whereas nostalgia, anger, and a sense of solitude are predominant emotions in Vigil-Piñón's earlier poems, these feelings seem to be lacking in her poems in *Woman*. The sensitivity to the fragility of the human being is still present, along with a heightened sense of the interconnectedness of all creatures. But also, in the latter two poems, readers encounter a much more fully developed sense of humor than in either *Nade* or *Thirty*. These three poems, plus "Houston, Texas," a poem extolling the dramatic, futuristic qualities of the big city, make up part of *The Computer Is Down*, published in 1987. Vigil-Piñón has worked on two other collections: "Hacia un Invierno" (Winter Nears) and "Twilight." Her poems in *Imagine* (Summer 1984)— "communion," "you've just got to let it go," and "stature"—are representative of these latter groups of poems, expressing more personal concerns: the nature of human knowledge and understanding, the passion of the artistic experience,

and determination in the face of predicted failure.

Vigil-Piñón's work has been recognized with various literary prizes, and it has received several favorable reviews, primarily those regarding *Thirty*. For instance, Julián Olivares has published a laudatory article about this work in *The Chicano Struggle: Analysis of Past and Present Efforts* (1984). Evangelina Vigil-Piñón's sharp eye for the details of daily life, combined with her excellent ear for the music of words, makes her poems perennially enjoyable and valuable.

Reference:

Julián Olivares, "Seeing and Becoming: Evangelina Vigil, *Thirty an' Seen a Lot*," in *The Chicano Struggle: Analysis of Past and Present Efforts*, edited by Juan A. García, Theresa Córdova, and Juan R. García (Binghamton, N.Y.: Bilingual Press/Editorial Bilingüe, 1984), pp. 152-165.

Alma Luz Villanueva

(4 October 1944 -   )

Santiago Daydí-Tolson
University of Wisconsin—Milwaukee

BOOKS: *Bloodroot* (Austin, Tex.: Place of Herons, 1977);

Mother, May I? (Pittsburgh: Motheroot, 1978);

Life Span (Austin, Tex.: Place of Herons, 1985);

The Ultraviolet Sky (Binghamton, N.Y.: Bilingual Press/Editorial Bilingüe, 1987).

OTHER: *Third Chicano Literary Prize*, includes twenty-two poems by Villanueva (Irvine: University of California, 1977);

"Golden Glass," in *Hispanics in the United States II*, edited by Francisco Jiménez and Gary D. Keller (Ypsilanti, Mich.: Bilingual Press/Editorial Bilingüe, 1982), pp. 70-72;

"La Chingada," in *Five Poets of Aztlán*, edited by Santiago Daydí-Tolson (Binghamton, N.Y.: Bilingual Press/Editorial Bilingüe, 1985), pp. 140-163.

Alma Villanueva has produced a richly varied and original body of work. Her poems, narratives, and plays maintain a highly personal tone and a unifying line of thought: the mysterious, ancient, and nature-bonded condition of womanhood and its stark contrast with an alienated modern world based on masculine principles, values, and objectives. Her passionate view of the world from the feminine perspective is her best contribution to Chicano literature. Although she deals with suffering, injustice, and human weaknesses, the final impression is always that of the joy of life and of confidence in a larger, almost sacred, scheme of things.

Villanueva was born in Lompoc, California, on 4 October 1944 to a German father she never knew and a Mexican mother. Her Mexican grandfather was a Baptist minister who had a college degree in philosophy, wrote poetry, and edited a newspaper in Hermosillo, Mexico. Her maternal grandmother, who raised her in the Mission District of San Francisco, was a Yaqui Indian from Sonora and the daughter of a healer and visionary. Through this grandmother, who had an extremely important influence on Villanueva's outlook on life, she learned Mexican traditions and learned of her German ancestry. When Villanueva was eleven years old, her grandmother died. At fifteen, after having experienced the lonely and difficult life of a child without a home, Villanueva had her first son. Married and a mother at such an early age, she never finished high school. While her husband was overseas with the U.S. Marines, she lived with her two children in precarious conditions in a poor neighborhood in San Francisco and had to take different jobs to maintain the family. Years later, after having divorced her husband, with whom she had a total of three children, she left the city to live on a farm. Searching always for a more direct contact with nature, she went to live for four years in the Sierra Nevada mountain range in central California, far from any population center. There she became more aware of nature's rhythms, and her writing acquired a stronger emphasis on nature and the processes of life and death. In her late thirties she finished her M.F.A. and had a fourth child. Married to a Chicano artist, Wilfredo Castaño, she currently lives with him and their child in a secluded corner of the California coast.

Womanhood is a central theme of Villanueva's poetry. She deals with it from different perspectives, stressing always in strong, emotional terms the affirmation of life and the love of everything alive. Passion, including sexual passion, is the essential motive of her work. Woman is individualized as a character, mostly Villanueva herself, living the turbulent experience of being lover, wife, and mother. At the same time, woman becomes an almost mythical universal force of procreation and love for all creatures. A clearly autobiographical perspective pervades her poems. From the narratives of personal experiences that include the presence of her loved ones, to the expression of philosophical and political points of view with respect to human existence and society, Villanueva's poems contain a warm feeling of concreteness and conviction. Her major themes, all

313

of them directly related to her view of womanhood, include the universal continuity of all life; the basically erroneous attitude of modern people toward nature and life; woman's special ability to understand this essential unity through time immemorial; a passion for life, natural love, the reproductive cycle, siblings, ancestors, and family ties; and the enjoyment of the material nature—blood and flesh—of oneself. All these themes are treated in her poems as personal, concrete experiences of life.

Although she had early experience with poetry and writing, both through her grandmother's traditional stories and poems and through the teachings and encouragement of one of the women who took care of her when she was a teenager, Villanueva did not write regularly until she was thirty years old. In 1977, three years after she began to write poetry in earnest, two collections of her first compositions appeared almost simultaneously: a selection of twenty-two poems that, having received the Third Chicano Literary Prize, were published in the 1977 anthology of that name; and *Bloodroot*, her first book, was also published in 1977.

In his 1980 analysis of her Chicano Literary Prize poems Alejandro Morales distinguishes three sections that deal respectively with early autobiography, the affirmation of feminine individualism over masculine dominance, and a recognition of woman's strengths and values. The whole grouping of poems is, in effect, an affirmation of woman, from the recognition of a lasting bond of love through generations of grandmothers, mothers, and daughters, to a superior understanding of the essence of life and the natural cycle of life

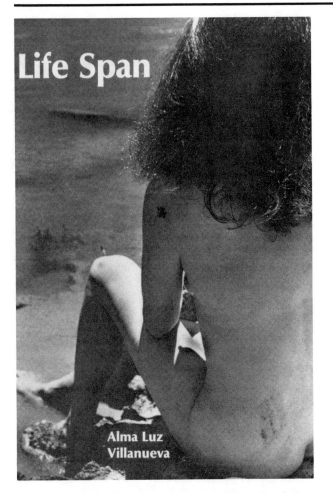

Cover for Villanueva's 1985 collection of twenty-six brief, lyrical poems, many of which center on the individual's communion with nature

and death. The image of the witch becomes a symbol of woman's superior powers to deal with existence—with material life and reality. Critics have insisted on the mythical quality of this poetry. The concrete images and topics preferred by Villanueva, the purposely eschatological and sexually explicit language she uses, and the symbols she selects to refer to concepts all create an immediate and physical image that counteracts any tendency to interpret her views on abstract terms. What matters to her is to demonstrate how woman has always had a special strength, an ability to generate life and make it survive against all odds in a violent, abusive, and destructive masculine society.

The closely knit thematic relationship of the poems selected for the Third Chicano Literary Prize is enriched and widened in the forty-seven poems that form *Bloodroot*. Of these, six are also included in the Irvine selection, indicating the continuity of themes and techniques. The word *blood*

is constant in Villanueva's vocabulary, and, as it appears in the title of her book, it is not the sign of death or violence, or of heroism and war, but the feminine element of life. As a woman Villanueva sees herself forming one universal body with all creation. But she is not so much interested in enjoying this sense of belonging to a greater form of existence. She wants to prove that everyone belongs to the same unity and that, although humans are all interrelated, many in the modern world—particularly men—are afraid of accepting this fact. According to Villanueva, women are the ones who maintain this ancient relationship with all life while men deny it. In this view of humankind and nature can be seen the influence of a Native American viewpoint, probably derived from her Yaqui grandmother.

Villanueva's second book, *Mother, May I?* (1978), is a long, autobiographical poem that represents an effort to deal in a more analytical way with her growing experiences as a woman in a masculine-oriented society. The poem is a condensed, highly emotive manifestation of the traditional narrative of youth, a literary form conceived as a means of analyzing and interpreting the process by which an individual becomes an adult and an active member of society. The poem recounts the basic experiences of childhood, adolescence, and early youth that have taken the poet from the magical and warm world of her grandmother and her Mexican ways, to the violent world of the city streets and parks—where children are sexually molested and grow used to acting defensively—and ultimately to Villanueva's difficult experiences as a young, single mother raising three children by herself in the worst sections of San Francisco. Each of these periods is represented vividly by realistic scenes corresponding to particularly shaking experiences: the beautiful childhood memory of cooking her first tortillas with her grandmother; the first shocking experience of being molested in the park; the sad moment of her grandmother's dying in an old people's home; the roughness of playing the tomboy in the streets of the barrio; and the bitter memory of being unable to utter a poetic word while working as fashion model and secretary in order to survive and raise her children. Beyond this anecdotal series of true personal experiences that gives a good idea of Villanueva's growing process as an individual, *Mother, May I?* offers an emotional portrait of a poet who has reached a personal understanding of herself and of the world through anger and love.

Following the same long structure, Villanueva wrote "La Chingada" (The Violated Woman, in *Five Poets of Aztlán*, 1985), again an effort to analyze her own condition as woman and Chicana. Less of an autobiography, this poem addresses the traditional view of womanhood in a world controlled by masculine values. To the mostly universalized view that dominates her analysis of woman in the present moment, this poem adds the ethnic factors affecting the Chicana experience. The autobiographical character of the previous poems is much less visible as Villanueva tries to create a more universal picture, with more symbolism and more emblematic characters. The mythical and historical figures of La Llorona (The Weeping Woman) and La Malinche (The Bad Woman)—taken from the Chicano context—are representatives not only of the Mexican tradition but of a wider situation affecting all women.

Life Span (1985) returns to brief compositions of a more lyrical character and represents a new stage in Villanueva's interpretation of the world and of herself. Written in the seclusion of the mountains, in close contact with nature, these poems seem to portray an inner world of an almost mystical character, based on the ancient wisdom she learned from her grandmother. A sense of structure and form brings to these poems a more contained tone and certain musical overtones not seen in her previous work. Passion is not absent in this book, but it has a maturity to it that brings a feeling of happiness and acceptance of life that was less evident in her earlier books.

With the twenty-six short poems of *Life Span*, Villanueva reaches a new level of awareness and poetic expression. The memories of a difficult childhood and youth are almost forgotten, as are the painful efforts to affirm the feminine principle, either in personal terms or in a wider, universal, symbolic representation. These are poems of maturity, the writings of a poet who has reached a sense of selfhood and has learned of her own standing in nature. The collection is a joyful song to life, love, and the passionate acceptance of one's own existence as part of a larger pattern of existence.

The individual's participation in life becomes a form of communion with all creation, a recognition of a fusion of all living and inert things in a mystical union of matter and spirit. The first poem of the collection, "Communion,"

Villanueva circa 1988 (photograph by Villanueva)

expresses this central conviction and the almost sacred joy of being alive and in love. Each new poem develops her basic confidence by pointing to a series of circumstantial personal experiences of this joy. As in her previous poems, the love for her husband, for sons and daughters, and for ancestral figures continues to be the most clearly present motif. The actual experience of giving birth is often present in the book. Eating and the need for nourishment form another leitmotiv in these poems. Another repeated image is that of herself as a winged woman, and the presence of eagles and owls and other birds as embodiments of life, love, and death. The sun and the moon, as well as the stars, the firmament, the mountains, and the oceans, are seen in terms of the minimal and most minute of things. But images of universal and cosmic forces are only an extension of the material world that surrounds the individual, making her an integral part of it.

Villanueva has also published several poems in periodicals and anthologies as well as a few short stories and a novel. The stories, like most of her poems, are closely related to her own experiences. "The Icicle," for example, with its autobiographical reminiscences of her childhood in San Francisco, tells a Christmas story of a girl who learns courage from direct experiences in the barrio. "Golden Glass" narrates, from the point of view of the mother—in loving and admiring terms—the first indications of a son's coming-of-age. Nature and boy are seen in perfect harmony, and the whole process of letting go is filled with happiness for the mother who sees her son become a man. Villanueva's novel, *The Ultraviolet Sky* (1987), deals, in her words, "with the integration of opposites."

For Villanueva writing represents another form of giving birth; since the time she wrote her first poems, when she generated through words her own individuality, all her writings have been part of a growing process toward reconciliation with the world and, in the end, toward reaching human wisdom. The strong inspiration generated by her own experience of life and her passion for all existence assure that she will continue writing about her encounters with nature and her inner self. Each new poem, each literary work, is a personal experience, an affirmation of her confidence. One can expect in the future a continuous literary production as this sensitive individual grows older and wiser.

Alma Villanueva's social concerns, centered in her opposition to a world of technological blindness and political stubbornness, fit within her general pattern of observation and probably will continue to be only a part of a richer, more engaging personal involvement with the world. In spite of the apparent absence of specific Chicano concerns and interests, Villanueva's poetry is an excellent example of a Chicano point of view. In essence her views on nature and woman stem from her traditional Chicano upbringing and point to an undercurrent of Native American spiritual and philosophical values that characterize an important part of Chicano literary production.

References:

Santiago Daydí-Tolson, Introduction to *Five Poets of Aztlán*, edited by Daydí-Tolson (Binghamton, N.Y.: Bilingual Press/Editorial Bilingüe, 1985), pp. 9-58;

Alejandro Morales, "Terra Mater and the Emergence of Myth in *Poems* by Alma Villanueva," *Bilingual Review / La Revista Bilingüe*, 7, no. 2 (1980): 123-142;

Marta Sánchez, "The Birthing of the Poetic 'I' in Alma Villanueva's *Mother, May I?*: The Search for a Female Identity," in *Contemporary Chicana Poetry: A Critical Approach to an Emerging Literature* (Berkeley: University of California Press, 1985), pp. 24-84.

Leonor Villegas de Magnón

(12 June 1876 - 17 April 1955)

Clara Lomas
Colorado College

BOOK: *The Rebel*, edited by Clara Lomas (Houston: Arte Público, forthcoming 1993).

SELECTED PERIODICAL PUBLICATIONS—
UNCOLLECTED: "Evolución mexicana," *Crónica* (Laredo, Tex.), September 1911, p. 1;
"Adelanto de los mexicanos de Texas," *Crónica* (Laredo, Tex.), 19 September 1911, p. 4;
"Cuentas de la Cruz Blanca Local," *Radical* (Laredo, Tex.), 5 March 1914;
"Justas aclaraciones," *Progreso* (Laredo, Tex.), 11 June 1915.

The recent unearthing of Leonor Villegas de Magnón's autobiographies marks still another retrieval effort which allows us a glimpse at women's historical struggles in appropriating a discursive voice to document their own stories. Official history nearly erased the memory of the nurses' involvement in the Mexican revolution of 1910, especially those from the Texas-Mexico border area. Leonor Villegas de Magnón made it her duty to leave a written record of that participation. She left two versions of her life story. The first 300-page Spanish text, entitled "La Rebelde" (The Rebel), was intended for a Mexican audience. After various unsuccessful attempts to have the Mexican government publish what they labeled "novelized memoirs," Villegas de Magnón wrote an English 483-page version entitled "The Lady Was a Rebel," aimed at a U.S. audience. She died on 17 April 1955, not having found a market for either version of her autobiography. Encouraged by historian Ruthe Winegarten, Clara Lomas located the Villegas de Magnón family in Houston. An old footlocker belonging to Leonor Villegas de Magnón, now owned by the family, was made available to Lomas. The scrapbook of newspaper clippings, photograph albums, correspondence, and drafts of the Spanish and English versions of Leonor Villegas de Magnón's autobiography contained in the footlocker have made it possible to begin reconstruct-

Villegas de Magnón and her secretary, Aracelito García, with the flag of La Cruz Blanca (The White Cross), the medical auxiliary that accompanied the Constitutionalist forces during the Mexican revolution of 1910 (Collection of the Villegas de Magnón family)

ing her life. Lomas will publish the English version of the autobiography as *The Rebel* in 1993.

Leonor Villegas was born on 12 June 1876 in Nuevo Laredo, Tamaulipas, Mexico, a few days after Porfirio Díaz, who was to be Mexico's dictator for the next thirty-four years, had triumphantly taken Mexico City. On that day her father affectionately called her "La Rebelde" (the

318

Rebel), after military men searching the area for insurgents suspected that the newborn child's cry was that of a hiding rebel. Later she would grow into the name when she opposed the Díaz dictatorship, rebelling against the ideals of her aristocratic class and against the traditional role of women in her society.

Villegas de Magnón's father, Joaquín Villegas, of Santander, Spain, had ventured to Cuba in the 1860s and then to Texas to look for his fortune in the ranching business. He married Valeriana Rubio, the daughter of one of the well-established families of Matamoros, who brought him a handsome dowry. Villegas's wealth later extended from ranching to mining, and import and export marketing. Leonor, along with her brothers, Leopoldo and Lorenzo, and her sister, Lina, were raised in the Mexico-Texas border area in an idyllic world created by their aristocratic parents. Leopoldo had been born in Corpus Christi, Texas, Lorenzo in Cuatro Ciénegas, Coahuila, and Lina in San Antonio, Texas. Bessie Lindheim noted that two of the Villegas children were born "under the American flag, two under the Mexican, but their mother declared: 'I shall wrap the flags together and they will be like one.'" The family's edenic world, however, came to an end when their mother died prematurely and their father remarried, a trauma Leonor Villegas would attempt to explore in her autobiographies. Their new stepmother, Heloise Monsalvatge, prompted the family to move to Laredo, Texas, and then sent the children off to boarding schools. From 1882 to 1885 Leonor attended the Ursuline Convent in San Antonio. In 1885 she transferred to the Academy of the Holy Cross in Austin where she stayed until 1889. Heloise then sent all of her husband's children to New York, instructing that "no one was to return without a diploma." Leonor entered Mount St. Ursula's Convent to study education. Although Leonor had contemplated the idea of becoming a nun, in 1895 after graduating with honors and teaching credentials, she returned to Laredo.

On 10 January 1901 Leonor Villegas married Adolfo Magnón, a United States citizen, and moved to Mexico City where her husband worked as an agent for several steamship companies. During the following nine years Villegas de Magnón lived in what she referred to in her English autobiography as "the zenith of glory and wealth" of the Porfiriato (Porfirio Díaz regime, 1876-1910). Given her upbringing in convents, Villegas de Magnón remembers that she "was en-

chanted by the lives of the wealthy, yet she could never accept it completely, seeing the sorrows and oppression of the poor."

After her three children, Leonor, Joaquín, and Adolfo, were born, Villegas de Magnón became involved with the sympathizers of Francisco Madero (opponent to Díaz and first president after his overthrow at the beginning of the Mexican revolution) and the anti-reelection campaign. Without her husband's knowledge of her actions, she would visit the Café Colón where Madero met with ideologues to plan the opposition campaign. Inspired by their talks, Villegas de Magnón began writing "fiery articles" against the dictatorship, signing with her family name. Shortly before the revolutionary movement broke out in 1910, she left for the border with her children to see her seriously ill father. On his deathbed, he expressed admiration for her courage, but told her that the majority of their Mexican properties had been confiscated due to her writings. Her previous political essays, however, were only the beginning of her collaboration with the revolutionary cause.

Separated from her husband during the first years of the revolution, Villegas de Magnón became actively involved in the political arena in the Laredo, Texas, area as a member of the Junta Revolucionaria (Revolutionary Council). She housed political exiles and contributed articles reporting on the latest developments of the revolutionary movement to the Idar family's *La Crónica* (The Chronicle) and to her brother's *El Progreso* (The Progress). After Madero took power in 1911, she opened one of the first bilingual schools in the area for young children. She became active in local sociocultural endeavors and founded the organization Unión, Progreso y Caridad (Union, Progress and Charity). Careful not to offend male egos and sensibilities nor to perturb the status quo too much, Villegas de Magnón used her organization to call for the extension of women's influence from the domestic to the public sphere: education of children, city beautification, charity work, and cultural and social events.

On 1 January 1914 when the revolutionary forces attacked Nuevo Laredo a second time, Villegas de Magnón founded and, with her inheritance, financed the Cruz Blanca (White Cross), a medical relief group for wounded soldiers. A few weeks later she recruited women and men from the border area to travel with the Constitutionalist forces from El Paso, Texas, to Mexico City.

Villegas de Magnón (second row, extreme right) and some of her students (Collection of the Villegas de Magnón family)

After the revolution, the group returned to Laredo to resume their normal lives. During this time Villegas de Magnón continued her work at her bilingual kindergarten in Laredo and worked for the State Democratic Executive Committee, Women's Division, of Texas. In 1940, in dire economic need, she returned to Mexico City to solicit employment with the Bloque de Veteranos Revolucionarios de Sindicato Unico de Trabajadores de la Secretaría de la Economía Nacional (Veteran's Administration). There she joined the Club Internacional de Mujeres (Women's International Club), and after years of lobbying, she and other women finally received official recognition as veterans of the revolution. Leaving a comfortable position at the National Department of Statistics in Mexico City, in 1946 she volunteered to work her own *parcela* (agricultural plot) in Rancherías Camargo, Tamaulipas, as part of the land redistribution program. After two unsuccessful years, having exhausted her credit and family's money and having experienced firsthand the failure of the program, she returned to Laredo. Her last duty, she noted in her autobiography, was to attempt "to do justice to those worthy nurses and brave women who so patriotically defended their country" by narrating their heroic deeds, lest they be relegated to oblivion.

In her attempt to assimilate the events of the Texas-Mexico border area from 1876 through 1920, Villegas de Magnón explores the themes of self and history. In the two versions of her autobiographical narrative, she provides an account from childhood to her most important heroic deed: the founding of the Cruz Blanca Constitucionalista (Constitutionalist White Cross) as part of the revolutionary effort. Narrated in the third person, the self-conscious texts are written in the style of revolutionary romanticism, too highflown and melodramatic for contemporary taste. Historical and personal events and incidents are intertwined to reflect a predestined lifeline: the date of her birth, her nickname, the burn on her right hand identical to that of Venustiano Carranza (president of Mexico, 1915-1920), and her mother's foresight. From a highly sensitive child and lonely orphan surfaces a brave woman with an altruistic sense of duty. Villegas de Magnón creates a persona who, among many other actors, lives out her role in a revolutionary theater.

The first quarters of both the Spanish and English manuscripts narrate the transition from a harmonious pastoral life-style at the hacienda—where proprietors and servants, shepherds and vaqueros dine, sing, and pray together—to a mercantile economy in which the family travels from northern Mexico and southern Texas to Europe.

Parallel to this socioeconomic shift is the transition suffered by La Rebelde from the secure world with her Mexican mother to becoming an orphan with an Americanized stepmother. The other three-quarters of the narrative center on the journey of the Cruz Blanca from El Paso to Mexico City with the Constitutionalists. The long trajectory is narrated in the form of diary entries delineating the medical relief group's daily chores and emphasizing its highly organized efficiency. Volunteers of Laredo and Nuevo Laredo carry out their roles not only as nurses and doctors, but as spies, informants, reporters, propagandists, printers, telegraph operators, and railroad engineers. Interwoven into the central narrative line are various stories of valiant women such as that of María de Jesús González, who volunteered as a messenger, became a spy, and later, dressed as a man, worked her way up the ranks to colonel. Many engaging anecdotes spring from La Rebelde's resourcefulness, whether due to her astute use of family finances and contacts or to her shrewdness and quick-thinking maneuvers.

Although the Spanish and English versions of the autobiography render the same story, comparison of the two reveals the implied readers Villegas de Magnón was addressing. In the Spanish version, the telling of events and the mentioning of names was most important. Expediency seemed imperative. The implied reader was familiar with the historical events being chronicled. In contrast, detail becomes important in the expanded English version; the reader requires explanatory remarks. Moreover, the deletions are telling. Deleted, for example, are narrator interruptions in the story line which boldly protest the calculated omissions of official history:

> la historia se ha encargado de relatar los hechos, pero se ha olvidado del importante papel de los pueblos de Laredo, Texas, Nuevo Laredo, Tamaulipas y otros fronterizos que en esos momentos se unieron en un fraternal acuerdo.

> (history has assumed responsibility for documenting the facts, but it has forgotten the important role played by the communities of Laredo, Texas, and Nuevo Laredo, Tamaulipas and other border cities which united themselves in a fraternal agreement.)

Although both versions include long lists of the *fronterizos*'s (border people's) names, the English version eliminates the following brief description:

> Estos son ejemplos de los llamados "Pochos" que tanto desprecian en la capital y que guardan en ambos puños fuertemente apretados el honor y el decoro internacional y de una psicología incomprensible y grandiosa. De ellos se servía la Rebelde y ellos fueron su inspiración.

> (These are examples of the so-called "Pochos" who are so despised in the capital [Mexico City] and who hold in both tight fists international honor and decorum as well as an incomprehensible and magnificent psychology. La Rebelde received assistance and inspiration from them.)

Although an attempt to rescue the "Pochos" from historical nonexistence, Villegas de Magnón's autobiography would come close to sharing their fate. In "Soy una triste peregrina" (I Am a Lonely Pilgrim), an unpublished poetic essay exploring her sentiments as a "wondering pilgrim," she queries,

> En las chozas, en los templos, en los palacios, en los campos de batalla, pides esa limosna [de amistad sincera] y nada encuentras? ¿y por qué? ¿Tan sólo por el delito de ser mujer?

> (In huts, in temples, in palaces, and in battlefields, you beg for that charity [of sincere friendship] and you find nothing. And, why? Is it only for the crime of being a woman?)

Neither Villegas de Magnón's aristocratic background nor her humanitarian or rebellious deeds have allowed her to overcome limitations imposed by gender. Restoration of autobiographical narratives such as hers will allow us better to understand links within our cultural heritage which take into account class, ethnic/national, gender, and spatial considerations.

References:

Bessie Lindheim, "Comments on 'The Lady Was a Rebel,'" presented at the Laredo Historical Society Meeting (Laredo, Tex.), 8 May 1970;

Clara Lomas, "Leonor Villegas de Magnon," in *Longman Anthology of World Literature by Women*, edited by Marian Arkin and Barbara Shollar (New York & London: Longman, 1989), pp. 181-184;

Ricardo Romero Aceves, "Leonor Villegas de Magnón," in *La mujer en la historia de México* (Mexico City: Costa-Amic Editores, 1982), p. 282;

J. B. Wilkinson, *Laredo and the Río Grande Frontier* (Austin: Jenkins, 1975), pp. 388-389.

Papers:
Leonor Villegas de Magnón's papers are cur-

rently held by the Villegas de Magnón family in Houston. Arrangements are being made to have the papers housed at the Center for United States Hispanic Literature at the University of Houston.

Helena María Viramontes
(26 February 1954 -   )

Sonia Saldívar-Hull
University of California, Los Angeles

BOOK: *The Moths and Other Stories* (Houston: Arte Público, 1985).

OTHER: "Miss Clairol," in *Chicana Creativity and Criticism: Charting New Frontiers in American Literature*, edited by Viramontes and María Herrera-Sobeck (Houston: Arte Público, 1987), pp. 101-105;
" 'Nopalitos': The Making of Fiction," in *Breaking Boundaries: Latina Writings and Critical Readings*, edited by Asunción Horno-Delgado, Eliana Ortega, Nina M. Scott, and Nancy Saporta Sternbach (Amherst: University of Massachusetts Press, 1989), pp. 33-38;
"Tears on My Pillow," in *New Chicana/Chicano Writing*, edited by Charles M. Tatum (Tucson: University of Arizona Press, 1992), pp. 110-115.

SELECTED PERIODICAL PUBLICATIONS—
UNCOLLECTED: "The Long Reconciliation Toward the Heartland," *XhismeArte*, 7 (January 1981): 16-19;
"My Sister Ruthie's Baby," *Hispanic Link* (3 February 1985);
"Spider's Face," *America's 2001*, 1 (March-April 1988);
"Dance Me Forever," *Pearl*, 6 (Spring-Summer 1988);
"Why Women Burn," *Blue Mesa Review*, 1 (Spring 1989): 177-186.

Helena María Viramontes, 1986 (photograph by George M. McInnis)

Helena María Viramontes's short stories about urban barrios and border towns relate previ-

ously unheard realities of Chicano life. Her relentlessly probing tales are typical of an emerging tendency in feminist Chicana authors to unveil the prejudices of the dominant society. Her art is always politically based, and the power of her words shows a Chicana subverting dominant patriarchal practices.

The daughter of working-class parents, Viramontes was born on 26 February 1954 and raised in East Los Angeles. Her father was a construction worker. Her mother was a traditional Chicana who not only raised six daughters and three sons but also found room in an already crowded house for friends and relatives who crossed the border from Mexico searching for the promises that "el otro lado" (the other side) offered. Viramontes vividly remembers "late night kitchen meetings where everyone talked and laughed in low voices"—voices aching with hopeful, optimistic plans for the future; voices spinning tales "of loves lost or won"; voices of men crying, and women laughing. These childhood memories served as her writing apprenticeship perhaps even more than the formal writers' school that she later attended.

Viramontes received her B.A. in English literature from Immaculate Heart College in 1975. In 1977 one of her first stories, "Requiem for the Poor," won first prize for fiction in a literary contest sponsored by *Statement Magazine* of California State University, Los Angeles. The following year she won first prize again with "The Broken Web." In 1979 she was awarded first prize for "Birthday" in the Chicano Literary Contest at the University of California, Irvine. She attended the creative writing program at this university in 1981 and now lives in Irvine, where she struggles to find time to write while being a mother.

Viramontes made the overall purpose of her writing evident in her 1985 collection, *The Moths and Other Stories*. Each one of her tales exhibits an acute sense of political and sociological awareness. "Growing" is a story in the literary tradition of the rite of passage. The story is told from the point of view of Naomi, a girl poised at the critical moment between childhood and adolescence. Naomi yearns to join a group of children playing baseball, but she is unable because of the strictures placed on the female as she approaches puberty. Not only does Naomi struggle with the transition from childhood to adolescence, she also struggles with the cultural transition that her family faces in a new country. She feels that her parents are unduly strict with her because they come from Mexico. They do not understand that "the United States is different. . . . Parents trust their daughters." To further add to Naomi's problems, her father has brought with him his patriarchal privileges. Viramontes, however, does not allow the assumption that his privilege as patriarch is a purely Latino prerogative. When he thunders "Tú eres mujer" (You are a woman) in order to control his daughter, the author links his voice with that of the Deity and to all men whose male rules transcend borders and cultures.

"Snapshots" examines a woman at the other end of the age spectrum. Olga is a postmenopausal woman who struggles to reconcile the woman she was raised to be—wife, mother, housewife—with the woman she now is, a divorcée on her own. What her grown daughter and ex-husband do not understand, however, is that her depression is not simply over the divorce, but over the wasted years spent perfecting a domestic career that now has no material value in modern society. In this scathing critique of the politics of housework, Olga emerges as an alienated laborer whose value has decreased. She has acquired the consciousness to ask, "How can people believe that I've fought against motes of dust for years or dirt attracting floors or perfected bleached white sheets when a few hours later the motes, the dirt, the stains return to remind me of the uselessness of it all?"

In "Neighbors," Viramontes goes even further in probing the specific problems of the aged. Heartrending scenes of a seventy-three-year-old woman whose body can no longer obey her strong mind's command mingle with Viramontes's sociological analysis of the urban landscape. The young men of the neighborhood cannot find jobs; urban renewal plans design skyscrapers and freeways but decimate barrio neighborhoods, replacing them with enclaves of the unemployed: "the neighborhood had slowly metamorphosed into a graveyard. . . . As a result, the children gathered near . . . in small groups to drink, to lose themselves in the abyss of defeat, to find temporary solace among each other."

In "The Broken Web," Viramontes gives voice to women who are linked through their oppression in patriarchal society. Martha learns the tragic history of how her mother killed her father, Tomás. The bullet that killed him also broke a statue of Jesus. With this double death blow, Viramontes irrevocably breaks the stereotype of the Chicana deferring to Father and Son.

Both "The Long Reconciliation" and "Birthday" deal with the issue of abortion. While "Birth-

Cover for Viramontes's collection of stories about the struggles of women in Chicano culture

day" is set in a contemporary setting where abortion is legal though never easy for any woman to undergo, "The Long Reconciliation" introduces the Western reader to the Chicanas' distinct historical past. Alice in "Birthday" undergoes an abortion without the support of her boyfriend. In "The Long Reconciliation," Amanda's historical context complicates the reasons for her self-induced abortion: "it would have been unbearable to watch a child slowly rot" given the material realities of life in prerevolutionary Mexico. The background of this story is the Mexican revolution, but like many revolutions, its ideals do not extend to the women left behind to tend the farms.

In "The Moths," Viramontes directly challenges the Chicano patriarchy. One strategy for resistance available to Chicanas is the formation of woman-to-woman bonds in a separate female sphere. "The Moths" illustrates the gender and therefore political ties between the fourteen-year-

old narrator and her *abuela* (grandmother). The grandmother's house is a sanctuary for the young woman as she attempts to escape her father's brutal domination. Viramontes exposes the complicity of other women in the patriarchal family structure who participate along with the father in physical abuse. The narrator of "The Moths" resists the socially constructed definition of "woman." A series of oppositions to what the culture sanctions as "female," "tradition," and "respect" opens the narrative. The father demands that his daughter attend church, but church for the young woman is just an empty building. God is dead for Viramontes's narrator; at best he is but an absentee landlord who allows the priests to trick the people into passivity.

In the final, powerful passage, the granddaughter holds her dead grandmother in a ritual bath. In the tradition of the magic realism of Third World American literature, moths emerge from the grandmother's "soul and out through her mouth fluttering to light," a warning about "moths that lay within the soul and slowly eat the spirit up."

While in "The Moths," Viramontes's antihegemonic strategy is a feminist one, in "The Cariboo Cafe," perhaps the most complex and successful story in the collection, the oppositional stance is against the political power of the U.S. government and its collaborators south of the border. Viramontes presents the reserve army of laborers that the United States creates and then designates as "other," the "illegal" immigrants. This story shows how to combine feminism with race and class consciousness. In this Chicana political discourse, Viramontes commits herself to a global solidarity with people who are immigrants to the United States. Here the author makes that final leap from filiation to affiliation, from ties to men and women of her own blood to political ties with the most recent wave of brown immigrants who have entered the United States in search of political freedom.

Viramontes gives the story of the murder of an undocumented female worker political significance in a version of life at the borders, the periphery of North American society. The Cariboo Cafe, a sleazy diner, attracts the outcasts of capitalism. Drug addicts, prostitutes, and undocumented workers frequent the place run by a petty-bourgeois man who ironically becomes the mouthpiece of the dominant society. While his dialect is that of the working class, he spouts dominant class ideology. Viramontes transforms this cynical short-order cook with a grease-stained apron into a grotesque Uncle Sam. He voices the dominant ideology not because of his class privilege but because of his privilege as a white man. It is here that Viramontes exposes how the hegemonic forces of race, class, and gender both intersect and collide.

The reader sees the urban landscape through the eyes of a child, Sonya. Both her father and mother work so that they may one day have, among other things, a toilet of their own. For feminists this turn of phrase resonates with Virginia Woolf's desire for financial independence for the woman writer, but it also emphasizes the vast difference between bourgeois feminism and Third World feminist concerns. When Sonya and her little brother get lost on their way home, they are drawn to the Cariboo Cafe, which Sonya thinks will be a sanctuary from the alleys and dead ends of the urban barrio. Viramontes tells the story of what happens to the children through the cafe owner, who gives his version as if he were on trial. Indeed, Viramontes puts U.S. immigration policies and ideology on trial in this story. The cafe owner relates how a Salvadoran refugee was killed by the police in his cafe, an incident tied to the fate of the children. When the cafe owner saw the *Salvadoreña* (female Salvadoran), he immediately labeled her as "other." The dominant race's rationale for excluding the brown races from integration into U.S. society is articulated through him: "Right off I know she's illegal, which explains why she looks like a weirdo." Sonya and her little brother, Macky, were taken by the *Salvadoreña*, who mistakes Macky for her missing son. This woman—a modern-day Llorona, the wailing woman of Chicano folklore—fled her country after her five-year-old son was murdered by the right-wing government with U.S. backing. The *Salvadoreña* cannot understand why the cafe owner calls the police to report a kidnapping. For her, the police here are no different from the police in the country she has fled; they will take her son away from her. She resists arrest and throws boiling coffee at the man pointing a gun at her. The final image is that of the bullet entering and shattering her forehead.

A personal journal entry reveals that "The Cariboo Cafe" was born out of Viramontes's sense of rage and anger over President Ronald Reagan's Central American policies. She wonders how "we can sit here peacefully when we know that our tax dollars are supporting the death squads in Central America. It is no secret. Just a matter of politics. . . . And our silence is our submission. Can you sleep at night?"

Viramontes is now at work on a novel and a second collection of stories, "Paris Rats in L.A." Her groundbreaking narrative strategies, combined with her sociopolitical focus, situate her at the forefront of an emerging Chicana literary tradition that redefines Chicano literature and feminist theory.

Appendix

A Forerunner of Chicano Literature:
Miguel de Quintana

A Forerunner of Chicano Literature: Miguel de Quintana

(1671 - April 1748)

Clark Colahan
Whitman College

New Mexico had no printing press until 1835. Folk literature preserved in a strong oral tradition has survived, along with a wealth of church and governmental records, reports, and letters, but apparently the only literary expression written in colonial New Mexico by a New Mexican and still available is the intense, terrified, yet protesting poetry and prose of Miguel de Quintana.

Although born in Mexico City in approximately 1671, Quintana arrived young in what is now New Mexico in the caravan of colonists brought by Diego de Vargas in 1693, following the Pueblo Indian revolt. According to historian Fray Angelico Chávez, the official description by the group's members says that Quintana was the "son of José, native of Mexico, twenty-two years old, able-bodied, round face, small forehead, large eyes, and a dimple in the chin." He lived the remaining years of his life in the Villa Nueva de Santa Cruz, an agricultural settlement some thirty miles north of Santa Fe; the settlement was founded in 1695 by Vargas for the new colonists.

For several years as a farmer Quintana supported his large family of his wife (the former Gertrudis de Trujillo) and six children. The hardships of this life-style are sketched in a letter he wrote in 1712 suing a neighbor for the theft of two horses by the neighbor's Apache servants. Quintana won the case, after describing his difficult living situation for the judge.

Quintana's early education in Mexico City, which can be inferred from the fact that he could read and could write in a clear, steady style, provided him increasingly with another source of income. His signature as a notary appears on several documents that he drew up in civil and criminal cases heard by the mayors of Santa Cruz. His neighbors also came to him for other services that could be performed by a liter-ate, intelligent individual having abilities not only in legal issues but in personal and literary matters as well. He skillfully combined multiple writing talents, such as those of the notary public/lawyer, the religious author who both composes prayers for individual cases and fills in as a playwright for local dramatic productions, and the public scribe who does not so much take down dictation from his illiterate customers as express their thought in his own, if conventional, words. As Chávez has described him, "Miguel had become a kind of poet laureate." Historian John Kessell's characterization is useful, too: "Miguel was a *santero* [sculptor] who worked in words." The comparison accurately suggests the similarities between Quintana's work as a writer and the religious images, usually made of carved and painted wood, crafted by New Mexican *santeros* for their neighbors in a style that can be described as baroque and naive.

Quintana, then, enjoyed considerable importance and recognition derived from his literary and legal activities. For example, people regularly asked him to write Christmas plays. A letter (in the Inquisition files) written to him in 1737 by a friend, Fray Juan Sánchez de la Cruz, characterizes Quintana as a man of importance in the town government. Even more convincing are the descriptive phrases used in a 1734 report by two priests whose relationship with him was more one of hostility than of friendship. Fray Manuel Sopeña stated that Quintana "siempre se ha ocupado en notario de los alcaldes mayores, actuando con todo juicio, y que sus escritos han tenido aceptación, y actualmente es notario en la judicatura eclesiástica" (has always worked as a notary of the mayors, acting with all good judgment, that his writings have had acceptance, and that currently he is a notary of the ecclesiastical jurisdiction). Fray Joseph Irigoyen declared that

329

Page from the poems by Miguel de Quintana that the Inquisition collected during its proceedings in the 1730s
(Archivo General de México, Ramo de la Inquisición, vol. 849, folio 465)

Quintana "pasa su vida con hacer escritos a los vecinos y que de él se valen para este fin, y que ésta es su vida y en esto se acostumbra . . . [;] que por el vulgo, muchos principales de este reino está tenido por hombre de entereza y de mucho juicio" (spends all his time writing things for his neighbors, that they make use of him for this purpose, and that this is his life and his usual activity . . . [;] not only the common men, but also many of the important people of this kingdom consider him a man of integrity and good judgment).

For reasons that are not entirely clear, Quintana's success elicited opposition from the two Franciscan priests quoted. In testimony given to the Inquisition they reported that he had stopped going to mass and was no longer participating in other religious activities, probably a reference to meetings of the Third Order of St. Francis. Irigoyen specifically accused Quintana of making excuses, such as pain in his spleen, to avoid religious duties, while he was allegedly always in good health when it came to having a good time. Stressing the gap between Quintana's conduct and his "Haciéndose tan santo en sus papeles" (pretending to be so holy in his writings), Irigoyen condemned him as a hypocrite and, with very little basis, a heretic.

The two denouncing priests, like many who brought charges to the attention of the Inquisition throughout its history, may have had more complex motives for their action than the unburdening of their consciences, a standard formula given as the reason for coming forward. Jealousy, either professional or simply personal, of Quintana's recognition in the community as a religious writer can reasonably be suspected to be one reason. Quintana himself suggests it when referring to Irigoyen as the *celoso* notary of the Inquisition, an adjective that can mean either "zealous" or "jealous."

A 1726 incident, described by Quintana in a personal note (filed by the Inquisition), supplies a more specific reason for his bad relationship with Sopeña. Quintana, when asked to write a Christmas play he very much wanted to do, felt tension resulting from a prohibition against such writing, apparently imposed by Sopeña. Under the pressure of this dilemma, which had been building for some time, something in Quintana's mind was triggered and broke through: a voice seemingly from heaven spoke to him, authorizing him to write, and removing any suspicion of hypocrisy and all need to obey Sopeña. From that

time on moments of fear and anxiety were relieved by encouraging and strengthening words spoken primarily by a voice Quintana characterizes as an irresistibly convincing spirit, and secondarily by the Virgin Mary and God the Father. These three voices dictated verses and prose, Quintana says, that he wrote down both as tokens of divine love and in obedience to their command.

While there is no reason to question Quintana's sincere belief in the authenticity of these heavenly voices, this new situation did offer practical advantages in his struggle for the freedom to write. He was now in possession of a higher and more traditional authorization allowing him to disregard the directives of the parish priest. The lives of Spanish mystics such as Saint Teresa and Saint John of the Cross, including investigations by the Inquisition in which they were vindicated and which did not prevent their later canonization, were well known in New Spain. The church at Santa Cruz, for example, constructed from 1733 to 1744 and contemporary with Quintana's writings, has had on its altar screen, very possibly since the eighteenth century, four Mexican paintings flanking the central crucifix; one of these shows Saint Teresa receiving inspiration from the dove of the Holy Spirit while she writes. The possibility of direct communion with God and the other heavenly personages was, and still is, a part of Hispanic Catholicism. New Mexico folklore records the frequent intervention of the saints in daily life in a visible and talkative manner. If one prefers a more clinical explanation, it can be observed that psychological studies of individuals receiving instructions and encouragement from voices heard within the mind suggest that the phenomenon is the result of paranoid schizophrenia, produced in part by personal conflicts of the kind distressing Quintana, but the nature of the voices always reflects beliefs within the person's culture.

The Inquisition collected and filed these "inspired" writings of Quintana and others as evidence, and for that reason they have survived. In quality the ones by Quintana are uneven and not as varied or polished as he must have been capable of at other times, although his command of language is unmistakable in places. Comparing the passages in prose and poetry, certain differences appear. He himself emphasizes that the voices who dictate to him do so in verse. The poetry is more insistent in its repetition of reassurances that he is on the right path, and an obsessive use of his own name seems to be a sign for him that he has been personally chosen for divine help. The limiting form of the four-line *redondilla* stanza predominant in New Mexico folk poetry combines with this restricted subject matter and style to produce repetitive poems, but they are nevertheless emotionally intense, as seen in these stanzas:

> *No temas inquisición,*
> *castigo daño ni afrenta.*
> *Es Dios, Miguel, quien te alienta*
> *con tan grande inspiración.*

> *De tu humilde corazón*
> *está Dios enamorado.*
> *Síguele, que no has errado;*
> *es grande tu locución.*

> (Don't Fear Inquisition,
> punishment, harm or disgrace,
> It is God, Miguel, who encourages you
> with such important inspiration.

> God is in love
> with your humble heart.
> Follow Him, for you have not erred;
> your words are great.)

In the prose the intellectual man of affairs comes out. He sometimes takes up a more reasoned, theological defense, as when insisting that God does not ask impossible things of his creatures. Quintana makes confident, even threatening assertions that he will be vindicated and his enemies dismayed. His vocabulary broadens and becomes more abstract; his are sentences filled with typical baroque intricacy and *retruécano*—contrast, antithesis, parallelism, plays on words, and, especially, accumulation building to a climax.

Though the Inquisition judge directing the investigation from Mexico City suspected it was a case of mental imbalance attributable to physical causes, Quintana's New Mexican accusers insisted he was perfectly sane and simply rebellious, so the file was officially closed by forcing the defiant writer to make a full recantation and promise of future obedience to the church, to be represented in the person of a confessor who would be understanding and consoling. Ludicrously the confessor turned out to be Irigoyen himself, and

in a few weeks Quintana was again taking down divine dictation that urged him to continue to fight. Though his new rebellious attitude was promptly discovered, there is no further documentation to indicate any further action in his case, leaving his story to be finished by the simple fact that he died eleven years later and was buried on 9 April 1748, leaving a few possessions to his daughter Lugarda.

Investigators are confronted by an open ending but Quintana's personality is compelling, and readers of his work and his story invariably want to arrange for themselves the pieces of the puzzle to make an image of a fitting ending. Whatever that image may be, Quintana's writings are valuable, first for their articulate documentation of a New Mexican writer's courage to differ with powerful and jealous authorities and of the terrifying fears his courage had to subdue. Second, they provide a literary record of an imaginative solution to a fundamental problem of freedom of expression—an extreme solution, certainly, but one based on traditional Hispanic beliefs very much alive in Quintana's community.

References:

Fray Angelico Chávez, "The Mad Poet of Santa Cruz," *New Mexico Folklore Record*, 3 (1948-49): 10-17;

Clark Colahan and Francisco Lomelí, "Miguel de Quintana: An Eighteenth-Century New Mexico Poet Laureate," in *Pasó por Aquí: Critical Essays on the New Mexico Literary Tradition, 1542-1988* (Albuquerque: University of New Mexico Press, 1989), pp. 65-78;

Colahan and Lomelí, "Miguel de Quintana, Poeta nuevomexicano ante la Inquisición, con muestras de su obra," Working Paper 102 (Albuquerque: Southwest Hispanic Research Institute, 1983);

Lomelí and Colahan, "Miguel de Quintana, Poeta Nuevomexicano ante la Inquisición," *Revista Chicano-Riqueña*, 12, (Summer 1984): 51-68.

Papers:
Unpublished poetry and prose of protest and exhortation by Quintana, letters, and other relevant documents are in the Archivo General de la Nación, Mexico City, Inquisición, vol. 849, folios 446-477.

Checklist of Further Readings

Acuña, Rodolfo. *Occupied America: The Chicano's Struggle Toward Liberation.* San Francisco: Canfield, 1972.

Alford, Harold J. *The Proud Peoples: The Heritage and Culture of Spanish-Speaking Peoples in the United States.* New York: McKay, 1972.

Baker, Houston A., Jr., ed. *Three American Literatures: Essays in Chicano, Native American, and Asian-American Literature for Teachers of American Literature.* New York: Modern Language Association, 1982.

Balassi, William, John F. Crawford, and Annie O. Eysturoy, eds. *This Is About Vision: Interviews with Southwestern Writers.* Albuquerque: University of New Mexico Press, 1990.

Binder, Wolfgang, ed. *Partial Autobiographies: Interviews with Twenty Chicano Poets.* Erlangen, West Germany: Palm & Enke, 1985.

Bornstein, Miriam. "The Voice of the Chicana in Poetry," *Denver Quarterly,* 16 (Fall 1981): 28-47.

Brokaw, John W. "A Mexican-American Acting Company, 1849-1924," *Educational Theatre Journal,* 27 (March 1975): 23-29.

Bruce-Novoa, Juan. "Canonical and Noncanonical Texts," *Américas Review,* 14 (Fall-Winter 1986): 119-135.

Bruce-Novoa. *Chicano Authors: Inquiry by Interview.* Austin: University of Texas Press, 1980.

Bruce-Novoa. *Chicano Poetry: A Response to Chaos.* Austin: University of Texas Press, 1982.

Candelaria, Cordelia. *Chicano Poetry: A Critical Introduction.* Westport, Conn.: Greenwood, 1986.

Chávez, John R. *The Lost Land: The Chicano Image of the Southwest.* Albuquerque: University of New Mexico Press, 1984.

Chicano Theatre One. San Juan Bautista, Cal.: Cucaracha, 1973.

Durán, Livie Isauro, and H. Russell Bernard, eds. *Introduction to Chicano Studies,* revised edition. New York: Macmillan, 1982.

Eger, Ernestina. *A Bibliography of Criticism of Chicano Literature.* Berkeley: Chicano Studies Library, 1982.

Englekirk, John E. "Notes on the Repertoire of the New Mexican Spanish Folk Theatre," *Southern Folklore Quarterly,* 4 (December 1940): 227-237.

Fisher, Dexter, ed. *Minority Language and Literature: Retrospective and Prospective.* New York: Modern Language Association, 1977.

García, Eugene E., Francisco A. Lomelí, and Isidro D. Ortíz, eds. *Chicano Studies: A Multidisciplinary Approach*. New York: Teachers College Press, 1984.

García, Richard A., ed. *The Chicanos in America, 1540-1974: A Chronology & Fact Book*. Dobbs Ferry, N.Y.: Oceana, 1977.

Hancock, Joel. "The Emergence of Chicano Poetry: A Survey of Sources, Themes and Techniques," *Arizona Quarterly*, 29 (Spring 1973): 57-73.

Heisley, Michael, ed. *An Annotated Bibliography of Chicano Folklore from the Southwestern United States*. Los Angeles: University of California Press, 1977.

Herrera-Sobek, María, ed. *Beyond Stereotypes: The Critical Analysis of Chicana Literature*. Binghamton, N.Y.: Bilingual/Editorial Bilingüe, 1985.

Huerta, Jorge A. "Chicano Agit-Prop: The Early *Actos* of El Teatro Campesino," *Latin American Theatre Review*, 10 (Spring 1977): 45-58.

Huerta. *Chicano Theatre: Themes and Forms*. Ypsilanti, Mich.: Bilingual/Editorial Bilingüe, 1982.

Jiménez, Francisco. "Dramatic Principles of the Teatro Campesino," *Bilingual Review/Revista Bilingüe*, 2 (January-August 1975): 99-111.

Jiménez, ed. *The Identification and Analysis of Chicano Literature*. Binghamton, N.Y.: Bilingual/Editorial Bilingüe, 1979.

Kanellos, Nicolás. "The Flourishing of Hispanic Theatre in the Southwest, 1920-30's," *Latin American Theatre Review*, 16 (Fall 1982): 29-40.

Kanellos. *Mexican American Theatre: Legacy and Reality*. Pittsburgh: Latin-American Literary Review, 1987.

Kanellos. "Mexican Community Theatre in a Midwestern City," *Latin American Theatre Review*, 7 (Fall 1973): 43-48.

Kanellos. *Two Centuries of Hispanic Theatre in the Southwest*. Houston: Revista Chicano-Riqueña, 1982.

Kanellos, ed. *Mexican American Theatre: Then and Now*. Houston: Arte Público, 1983.

Lattin, Vernon E., ed. *Contemporary Chicano Fiction: A Critical Survey*. Binghamton, N.Y.: Bilingual/Editorial Bilingüe, 1986.

Leal, Luis. *Aztlán y México: Perfiles literarios e históricos*. Binghamton, N.Y.: Bilingual/Editorial Bilingüe, 1985.

Leal, Fernando de Necochea, Francisco Lomelí, and Roberto G. Trujillo, eds. *A Decade of Chicano Literature (1970-1979): Critical Essays and Bibliography*. Santa Barbara: Editorial La Causa, 1982.

Lewis, Marvin A. *Introduction to the Chicano Novel*. Milwaukee: University of Wisconsin, Spanish Speaking Outreach Institute, 1982.

Lomelí, Francisco A., and Donaldo W. Urioste. *Chicano Perspectives in Literature: A Critical and Annotated Bibliography*. Albuquerque: Pajarito, 1976.

Márquez, Antonio. "The American Dream in the Chicano Novel," *Rocky Mountain Review*, 27 (1983): 4-19.

Martínez, Julio A., and Francisco A. Lomelí, eds. *Chicano Literature: A Reference Guide*. Westport, Conn.: Greenwood, 1985.

McWilliams, Carey. *North From Mexico: The Spanish-Speaking People of the United States*. Philadelphia: Lippincott, 1949.

Meier, Matt S., and Feliciano Rivera. *The Chicanos: A History of Mexican Americans*. New York: Hill & Wang, 1972.

Meyer, Doris L. "Anonymous Poetry in Spanish-Language New Mexico Newspapers, 1880-1900," *Bilingual Review/Revista Bilingüe*, 2 (September-December 1975): 259-275.

Moore, John W., and Alfredo Cuéllar. *Mexican Americans*. Englewood Cliffs, N.J.: Prentice-Hall, 1970.

Morgan, Thomas B. "The Latinization of America," *Esquire*, 99 (May 1983): 47-56.

Ordóñez, Elizabeth J. "Chicana Literature and Related Sources: A Selected and Annotated Bibliography," *Bilingual Review/Revista Bilingüe*, 7 (May-August 1980): 143-164.

Paredes, Américo. *"With His Pistol In His Hand": A Border Ballad and Its Hero*. Austin: University of Texas Press, 1958.

Paredes, Raymund A. "The Evolution of Chicano Literature," *MELUS*, 5 (Summer 1978): 71-110.

Paredes. "Mexican American Authors and the American Dream," *MELUS*, 8 (Winter 1981): 71-80.

Robinson, Cecil. *Mexico and the Hispanic Southwest in American Literature*. Tucson: University of Arizona Press, 1977.

Robinson. *With the Ears of Strangers: The Mexican in American Literature*. Tuscon: University of Arizona Press, 1963.

Rodriguez, Richard. "Mexico's Children," *American Scholar*, 55 (Spring 1986): 161-177.

Rodriguez del Pino, Salvador. *La Novela Chicana Escrita en Español: Cinco Auʋores Comprometidos*. Ypsilanti, Mich.: Bilingual/Editorial Bilingüe, 1982.

Rojas, Guillermo. "Toward a Chicano/Raza Bibliography," *El Grito*, 7 (December 1973): 1-85.

Saldivar, Ramón. "A Dialectic of Difference: Towards a Theory of the Chicano Novel," *MELUS*, 6 (Fall 1979): 73-92.

Sánchez, Marta Ester. *Contemporary Chicana Poetry: A Critical Approach to an Emerging Literature*. Berkeley: University of California Press, 1985.

Seator, Lynette. *"Emplumada*: Chicana Rites of Passage," *MELUS*, 11 (Summer 1984): 23-38.

Shirley, Carl R., and Paula W. Shirley. *Understanding Chicano Literature*. Columbia: University of South Carolina Press, 1988.

Sommers, Joseph, and Tomás Ybarra-Frausto, eds. *Modern Chicano Writers*. Englewood Cliffs, N.J.: Prentice-Hall, 1979.

Tatum, Charles M. *Chicano Literature*. Boston: Twayne, 1982.

Tatum. "Some Examples of Chicano Prose Fiction of the Nineteenth and Early Twentieth Centuries," *Revista Chicano-Riqueña*, 9 (Winter 1981): 58-67.

El Teatro Campesino. *El Teatro Campesino: The Evolution of America's First Chicano Theatre Company, 1965-1985*. San Juan Bautista, Cal.: El Teatro Campesino, 1985.

Trujillo, Robert G., and Andrés Rodríguez. *Literatura Chicana: Creative and Critical Writings Through 1984*. Oakland: Floricanto, 1985.

Valdez, Luis, and El Teatro Campesino. *Actos: El Teatro Campesino*. San Juan Bautista, Cal.: Cucaracha, 1971.

Vallejos, Tomás. "Ritual Process and the Family in the Chicano Novel," *MELUS*, 10 (Winter 1983): 5-16.

Vassallo, Paul. *The Magic of Words: Rudolfo A. Anaya and His Writings*. Albuquerque: University of New Mexico Press, 1982.

Ybarra-Frausto, Tomás. "The Chicano Movement and the Emergence of a Chicano Poetic Consciousness," *New Scholar*, 6 (1977): 81-109.

Ybarra-Frausto. "Punto de Partida," *Latin American Theatre Review*, 4 (Spring 1971): 51-52.

Zimmerman, Enid. "An Annotated Bibliography of Chicano Literature: Novels, Short Fiction, Poetry and Drama, 1970-1980," *Bilingual Review/Revista Bilingüe*, 9 (September-December 1982): 227-251.

Contributors

Michael Amin...*University of New Mexico*
M. Alicia Arrizón..*Stanford University*
Edwin John Barton ....*California State University, Bakersfield*
Wolfgang Binder...*University of Erlangen-Nuremberg*
Nuria Bustamante...*Los Angeles Harbor College*
Christopher Buckley...*West Chester University*
Cordelia Chávez Candelaria ....*Arizona State University*
Roberto Cantú...*California State University, Los Angeles*
Cida S. Chase...*Oklahoma State University*
Clark Colahan ....*Whitman College*
David Conde..*Metropolitan State College of Denver*
Santiago Daydí-Tolson...*University of Wisconsin—Milwaukee*
Patricia De La Fuente ....*University of Texas—Pan American*
Eduardo F. Elías ....*University of Utah*
Miriam Daniel Fahey ....*Holy Names College*
Lauro H. Flores ....*University of Washington*
Víctor Fuentes...*University of California, Santa Barbara*
Nasario García ....*New Mexico Highlands University*
Judith Ginsberg...*Modern Language Association*
Diana González...*Antelope Valley College*
LaVerne D. González ....*San Jose State University*
César A. González-T..*San Diego Mesa College*
Salvador Güereña ....*University of California, Santa Barbara*
Dina Gutiérrez-Castillo..*Santa Barbara City College*
Didier T. Jaén...*University of California, Davis*
Manuel de Jesús Hernández-G. ....*Arizona State University*
Elaine Dorough Johnson ....*University of Wisconsin—Whitewater*
Nicolás Kanellos..*University of Houston*
Enrique R. Lamadrid ....*University of New Mexico*
Luis Leal..*University of California, Santa Barbara*
Clara Lomas..*Colorado College*
Tiffany Ana López ....*University of California, Santa Barbara*
George Mariscal...*University of California, San Diego*
María Teresa Márquez...*University of New Mexico*
Manuel M. Martín-Rodríguez...*Yale University*
A. Gabriel Meléndez ....*University of New Mexico*
Arcadio Morales ....*Stanford University*
Genaro M. Padilla...*University of California, Berkeley*
Merrihelen Ponce ....*University of California, Santa Barbara*
Arthur Ramírez...*Sonoma State University*
Jonah Raskin ....*Sonoma State University*
Maria Montes de Oca Ricks ....*Washington State University*
Rowena A. Rivera..*Albuquerque, New Mexico*
Salvador Rodríguez del Pino..*University of Colorado*
Reynaldo Ruiz ....*Eastern Michigan University*
Carmen Salazar...*Los Angeles Valley College*

José David Saldívar ....*University of California, Santa Cruz*
Sonia Saldívar-Hull ....*University of California, Los Angeles*
Ramón Sánchez ....*University of Washington, Bothell*
Rosaura Sánchez...*University of California, San Diego*
Laura Gutiérrez Spencer ....*University of Nevada at Las Vegas*
Carmen Tafolla...*McAllen, Texas*
Héctor A. Torres ....*University of New Mexico*
Angelina F. Veyna ....*University of California, Los Angeles*

ISBN 0-8103-7599-0

90000

9 780810 375994

80: *Restoration and Eighteenth-Century Dramatists,* First Series, edited by Paula R. Backscheider (1989)

81: *Austrian Fiction Writers, 1875-1913,* edited by James Hardin and Donald G. Daviau (1989)

82: *Chicano Writers,* First Series, edited by Francisco A. Lomelí and Carl R. Shirley (1989)

83: *French Novelists Since 1960,* edited by Catharine Savage Brosman (1989)

84: *Restoration and Eighteenth-Century Dramatists,* Second Series, edited by Paula R. Backscheider (1989)

85: *Austrian Fiction Writers After 1914,* edited by James Hardin and Donald G. Daviau (1989)

86: *American Short-Story Writers, 1910-1945,* First Series, edited by Bobby Ellen Kimbel (1989)

87: *British Mystery and Thriller Writers Since 1940,* First Series, edited by Bernard Benstock and Thomas F. Staley (1989)

88: *Canadian Writers, 1920-1959,* Second Series, edited by W. H. New (1989)

89: *Restoration and Eighteenth-Century Dramatists,* Third Series, edited by Paula R. Backscheider (1989)

90: *German Writers in the Age of Goethe, 1789-1832,* edited by James Hardin and Christoph E. Schweitzer (1989)

91: *American Magazine Journalists, 1900-1960,* First Series, edited by Sam G. Riley (1990)

92: *Canadian Writers, 1890-1920,* edited by W. H. New (1990)

93: *British Romantic Poets, 1789-1832,* First Series, edited by John R. Greenfield (1990)

94: *German Writers in the Age of Goethe: Sturm und Drang to Classicism,* edited by James Hardin and Christoph E. Schweitzer (1990)

95: *Eighteenth-Century British Poets,* First Series, edited by John Sitter (1990)

96: *British Romantic Poets, 1789-1832,* Second Series, edited by John R. Greenfield (1990)

97: *German Writers from the Enlightenment to Sturm und Drang, 1720-1764,* edited by James Hardin and Christoph E. Schweitzer (1990)

98: *Modern British Essayists,* First Series, edited by Robert Beum (1990)

99: *Canadian Writers Before 1890,* edited by W. H. New (1990)

100: *Modern British Essayists,* Second Series, edited by Robert Beum (1990)

101: *British Prose Writers, 1660-1800,* First Series, edited by Donald T. Siebert (1991)

102: *American Short-Story Writers, 1910-1945,* Second Series, edited by Bobby Ellen Kimbel (1991)

103: *American Literary Biographers,* First Series, edited by Steven Serafin (1991)

104: *British Prose Writers, 1660-1800,* Second Series, edited by Donald T. Siebert (1991)

105: *American Poets Since World War II,* Second Series, edited by R. S. Gwynn (1991)

106: *British Literary Publishing Houses, 1820-1880,* edited by Patricia J. Anderson and Jonathan Rose (1991)

107: *British Romantic Prose Writers, 1789-1832,* First Series, edited by John R. Greenfield (1991)

108: *Twentieth-Century Spanish Poets,* First Series, edited by Michael L. Perna (1991)

109: *Eighteenth-Century British Poets,* Second Series, edited by John Sitter (1991)

110: *British Romantic Prose Writers, 1789-1832,* Second Series, edited by John R. Greenfield (1991)

111: *American Literary Biographers,* Second Series, edited by Steven Serafin (1991)

112: *British Literary Publishing Houses, 1881-1965,* edited by Jonathan Rose and Patricia J. Anderson (1991)

113: *Modern Latin-American Fiction Writers,* First Series, edited by William Luis (1992)

114: *Twentieth-Century Italian Poets,* First Series, edited by Giovanna Wedel De Stasio, Glauco Cambon, and Antonio Illiano (1992)

115: *Medieval Philosophers,* edited by Jeremiah Hackett (1992)

116: *British Romantic Novelists, 1789-1832,* edited by Bradford K. Mudge (1992)

117: *Twentieth-Century Caribbean and Black African Writers,* First Series, edited by Bernth Lindfors and Reinhard Sander (1992)

(Continued on back endsheets)